Instructor's Manual
with Full Solutions
to
For All Practical Purposes
Seventh Edition

Heidi A. Howard
Florida Community College at Jacksonville

W. H. Freeman and Company
New York

Printed in the United States of America

ISBN: 0-7167-6947-6
EAN: 9780716769477

First printing

W. H. Freeman and Company
41 Madison Avenue
New York, NY 10010
Houndmills, Basingstoke
RG21 6XS England

Instructor's Manual with Full Solutions
Table of Contents

PART I: Management Sciences

PART II: Statistics: The Science of Data

Part VI: On Size and Growth

Part VII: Your Money and Resources

Chapter 1
Urban Services

Chapter Outline

Introduction

Chapter Summary

Management science, or operations research, is a branch of mathematics that uses mathematical methods to find optimal solutions to management problems. Some of these problems involve finding efficient routes for services such as collecting coins from parking meters, collecting garbage, and delivering mail. The mathematical structure known as a *graph* is useful in analyzing routes.

A graph consists of a finite set of *vertices* together with edges connecting (some, all, or no) pairs of vertices. A path in a graph is a connected sequence of edges that begins and ends at a vertex. A path is called a *circuit* if it begins and ends at the same vertex. In many routing applications (e.g., mail delivery or garbage collection), the best solution would be a circuit that uses each edge (e.g., sidewalk or street) of an appropriate graph exactly once. Such circuits are called *Euler circuits*, in honor of the Swiss mathematician Leonhard Euler.

In order to have an Euler circuit, a graph must satisfy two conditions: it must be *connected* (i.e., it must have a path between any pair of its vertices); and, each of its vertices must have even *valences* (the number of edges meeting at that vertex). If the graph for a particular routing application does not have an Euler circuit, the best we can hope to do is find a circuit of minimum length. The problem of finding such a circuit is known as the *Chinese postman problem*. The solution process relies on "*eulerizing*" a graph, judiciously duplicating edges of the graph to produce a connected graph with even valences so that the total length of the duplicated edges (total number if all edges of the graph have the same length) is as small as possible. The Euler tour in the "new" graph can be traced on the original by interpreting the use of a duplicated edge as a reuse of the original edge it duplicates.

There are efficient procedures for finding good eulerizations and for solving the Chinese postman problem. The "*edge-walker*" method of the text is good for rectangular networks. More sophisticated procedures are needed in general.

Skill Objectives

1. Determine by observation if a graph is connected.

2. Identify vertices and edges of a given graph.

3. Construct the graph of a given street network.

4. Determine by observation the valence of each vertex of a graph.

5. Define an Euler circuit.

6. List the two conditions for the existence of an Euler circuit.

7. Determine whether a graph contains an Euler circuit.

8. If a graph contains an Euler circuit, list one such circuit by identifying the order in which the vertices are used by the circuit, or by identifying the order in which the edges are to be used.

9. If a graph does not contain an Euler circuit, add a minimum number of edges to "eulerize" the graph.

10. Find an Euler circuit in an eulerized graph and "squeeze" it onto the original graph. Be able to interpret, in terms of the original graph, the use of duplicated edges in the eulerization.

11. Identify management science problems whose solutions involve Euler circuits.

Teaching Tips

1. The concept of connectedness could be explored further by considering trees as opposed to circuits. This could begin to prepare the student for the work on trees in connectedness.

2. In preparation for assigning Exercise 6, you may want to explore in class discussion whether the placement of the vertices representing the cities affects the graph. In particular, consider three cities whose positions are collinear.

3. Figure 1.13 demonstrates the process of adding an edge in order to eulerize a graph. Students are sometimes confused by the fact that this added edge is curved rather than straight and attempt to attach unwarranted significance to this. A helpful explanation is that it is curved only so that it won't be confused with the original segment. In addition, you may want to emphasize that the curve could be drawn on either side of the original edge and that it indicates a retracing of that edge.

4. Some students want to eulerize graphs by connecting odd-valent vertices in a diagonal fashion. Emphasize the practical constraints that may prevent this approach. Note that in Exercises 35 and 36, the eulerization that minimizes the total length of the edges duplicated is not the eulerization that duplicates the fewest edges.

5. Ask students to construct a graph of a several-block area of their neighborhood and then look for an Euler circuit for the letter carrier to use. If an Euler circuit does not exist, ask students to produce optimal eulerizations.

6. An underlying principle of this chapter is the fact that a mathematical model, in this case a graph, is an abstraction of reality. The solution suggested by the model need not imply that streets would be added to an existing street network simply for the purpose of creating an Euler circuit.

Research Paper

Exercise 38 indicates that the problem situation resembles the one that inspired Euler. This refers to the historical Königsberg Bridge Problem (mentioned in Spotlight 1.1). You may choose to ask students to research the history of this town (once the capital of East Prussia) and this problem. Websites can be found that contain a map of the area, including the bridges. Also, you may choose to ask students to further investigate Euler's 1736 paper on the problem, which was divided into 21 paragraphs. Another historical figure that students could research is the life and contributions of the French mathematician Louis Poinsot (1777 – 1859). Other problems posed by Euler, such as the Thirty-Six Officers Problem, may be of interest to students.

Collaborative Learning

Euler Circuits

As an introduction to this chapter, duplicate the following exercise on Euler circuits and ask your students to answer the questions after discussing them in groups. (Do not introduce technical terms such as graph, edge, vertex, valence, or Euler circuit yet.)

You will find that most of the students are successful in answering questions a and b, but perhaps not question c. If in fact they do have difficulty answering part c, call their attention to the number of edges meeting at each of the vertices. (Resist using the word "valence.") Ask them to count these numbers for each of the graphs and then try again to answer part c, by looking for a pattern.

Eulerization

Duplicate the following eulerization exercises and have the students consider the problems in groups.

a. Which of the following diagrams can be drawn without lifting your pencil from the paper?

b. Which can be drawn as in part a, but with the additional requirement that you end the drawing at the starting point?

c. What do the diagrams that could be drawn in part a have in common? What about the diagrams that could be drawn in part b? In other words, try to determine simple conditions on a diagram that enables you to predict, in advance, whether or not it can be drawn according to the requirements in parts a or b.

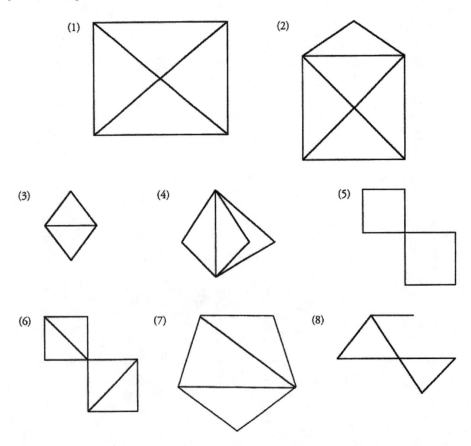

Eulerization

In each of the graphs below, an Euler circuit does not exist, since there are vertices with odd valences. It is possible to convert such graphs to ones having all vertices of even valence by duplicating one or more edges. For example, in the graph

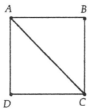

vertices *A* and *C* each have valence 3. Hence, if we duplicate edge *AC,* we obtain a modified graph in which each vertex has an even valence.

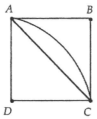

Do the same for each of the following graphs and then answer the questions that follow.

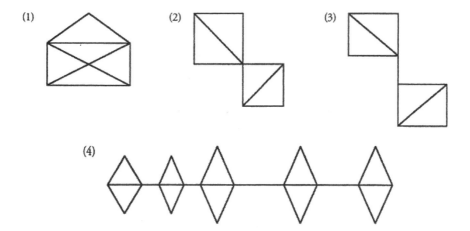

If a graph has 4 vertices with odd valences, what is the minimum number of duplications necessary to convert the graph to one in which all of the vertices are of even valence? Can this minimum number always be achieved?

Take a campus map (often found in the university catalog or directory), and pick out several key locations (library, dormitories, computer center, bookstore, etc.) and the streets or paths that connect them. Then ask the students whether an Euler circuit exists for this network. If not, how many edges have to be duplicated? By changing landmarks, you can obtain several new problems.

Solutions

Skills Check:

1. b   2. c   3. c   4. c   5. b   6. b   7. c   8. c   9. a   10. a

11. b   12. a   13. c   14. a   15. c   16. b   17. a   18. a   19. c   20. b

Cooperative Learning:
Euler Circuits:

a.   Diagrams (2), (3), (4), (5), (7), and (8) can be drawn without lifting the pencil from the paper.

b.   In (4) and (5) you can return to the starting point.

c.   In part a, there are at most 2 vertices with odd valences, while in part b there are no vertices with odd valences.

Eulerization:

(1)   Duplicate 1 edge.

(2)   Duplicate 2 edges.

(3)   Duplicate 4 edges.

(4)   Duplicate 9 edges.

If there are 4 vertices with odd valences, then there will be a *minimum* of two duplications. However, this minimum can't always be achieved, as we see from numbers (3) and (4).

Exercises:

1.   *E* has valence 0; *A* has valence 1; *H*, *D*, and *G* have valence 2; *B* and *F* have valence 3; *C* has valence 5. *E* is "isolated." *E* might have valence 0 because it is on an island with no road access.

2.   (a)   Yes.
     (b)   No. There is no way to get from *A* to *C*, *E*, or *H*.

3.   (a)   This diagram fails to be a graph because a line segment joins a single vertex to itself. The definition being used does not allow this.
     (b)   The edge *EC* crosses edges *AD* and *BD* at points which are not vertices; edge *AC* crosses *BD* at a point that is not a vertex.
     (c)   This graph has 5 vertices and 5 edges.

4.   (a)   6 stores.
     (b)   9 roads.
     (c)   *CBF*.
     (d)   *EDFB* or *EDCB*.

5.   (a)   *FDCBF*
     (b)   (i)   *BD*; *BCD*.
           (ii) *CBF*; *CDF*; *CDBF*.
     (c)   *CDFBC*

6.   *MLB*, *MRB*, *MNLB*; Jack is right.

7. (a) 4 vertices; 4 edges.

   (b) 7 vertices; 6 edges.

   (c) 10 vertices; 14 edges.

8. (a) $2 + 3 + 3 + 0 = 8$

   (b) $2 + 2 + 2 + 2 + 2 + 1 + 1 = 12$

   (c) 28

   (d) The number we obtain is twice the number of edges in the graph.

   (e) The fact that the sum of the valences of the vertices of a graph is always twice the number of edges in the graph follows from noticing that each vertex of an edge contributes a total of two to the sum because the edge has two endpoints.

9. Remove the edges dotted in the figure below and the remaining graph will be disconnected.

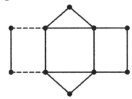

10. In any of these graphs, two edges can be removed and the graph will become disconnected. One of the disconnected pieces will be a single vertex.

11. (a)

   (b)

12. (a)

   (b) ☐ (

   (c) Yes. The sum of the valences of a graph with 6 vertices each of valence 2 is 12. Thus, all such graphs have 6 edges.

13. Yes, a disconnected graph can arise. One, possible example is shown below:

which gives rise to the disconnected graph:

14. (a)

(b) The edge might represent a bridge or tunnel. Recently, when a bridge collapsed because it was hit by a barge, there was a major disruption to the communities near the bridge on opposite sides of the river.

15. (a)    (b)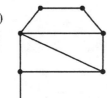

16. The street direction will matter for a problem involving how long it will take to get between two street intersections and for routing a street sweeper that follows traffic rules. The street direction may not matter for an inspector checking "manholes" located in the middle of streets or a service that involves walking along either side of the street such as inspecting sidewalks.

17. The supervisor is not satisfied because all of the edges are not traveled upon by the postal worker. The worker is unhappy because the end of the worker's route wasn't the same point as where the worker began. The original job description is unrealistic because there is no Euler circuit in the graph.

18.

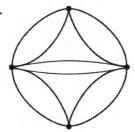

19. There is such an efficient route. The appropriate graph model has an additional edge joining the same pair of vertices for each of the edges shown in the graph of Exercise 17. Since this graph is connected and even-valent, it has an Euler circuit, any one of which will provide a route for the snowplow. Routes without 180-degree turns are better choices.

20. (a) Pothole inspection or inspecting the centerline for possible repainting because it had faded.

    (b) Street sweeping, snow removal, and curb inspections in urban areas.

21.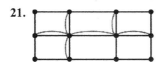

22. (a) The graph is a rectangular network with two rows and three columns No extra edges need to be added.

    (b)

23. (a) The largest number of such paths is 3. One set of such paths is *AF*, *ABEF*, and *ACF*.

    (b) This task is simplified by noticing there are many symmetries in this graph.

    (c) In a communication system such a graph offers redundant ways to get messages between pairs of points even when the failure of some of the communication links (edges removed) occurs.

24. Both are circuits; however, only graph (b) is an Euler circuit.

25. Do not choose edge 2, but edges 1 or 10 could be chosen.

26. Do not choose edge 3, but edges 9 or 10 could be chosen.

27.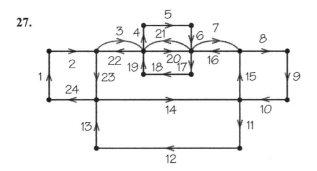

28. (a) The following diagram shows one of many solutions.

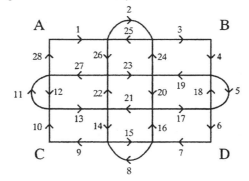

    (b) Answers will vary; there are many Euler circuits in the graph.

29. Two edges need to be dropped to produce a graph with an Euler circuit. Persons who parked along these stretches of sidewalk without putting coins in the meters would not need to fear that they would get tickets.

30. If one was outlining garden plots with a sprinkler hose, this tour would allow having the hoses as flat as possible because one hose would not have to cross another hose.

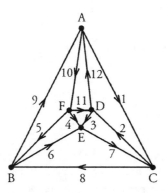

31. (a)   (b)

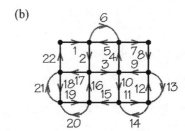

32. The curved edges on the first graph become double-traversals on the straight edges of the second graph.

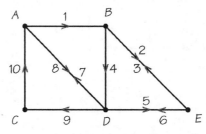

ABEBDEDADCA

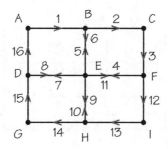

ABEBDEDADCA

33. (a) There are four 3-valent vertices. By properly removing two edges adjacent to these four vertices, (edge between left two 3-valent vertices and edge between right two 3-valent vertices) one can make the graph even-valent.

   (b) Yes, because the resulting graph is connected and even-valent.

   (c) It is possible to remove two edges and have the resulting graph be even-valent.

   (d) No, because the resulting graph is not connected, even though it is even-valent.

34. A minimum of three edges must be added: one edge along the horizontal segment in the first parallelogram and a segment along two opposite edges of the second parallelogram.

35. (a) 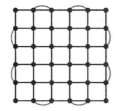   (c)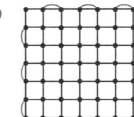

   (b)    (d)

   Nine is the best one can do.

36. (a) 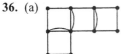   (b)    (c)

37.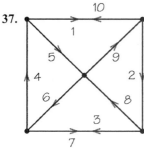

38. Represent each riverbank by a vertex and each island by a vertex. Represent each bridge by an edge. This produces the graph on the left. After eulerization we produce the graph on the right. An Euler circuit is shown on this graph. After squeezing this circuit into the original graph, we have a circuit with one repeated edge.

39. There are many different circuits which will involve three reuses of edges. These are the edges which join up the six 3-valent vertices in pairs.

40. The minimum length (36,000 feet) is obtained for any Euler circuit in the graph with edges duplicated as shown below. For minimizing total length it is better to repeat many shorter edges rather than a few long ones.

41. There are many circuits that achieve a length of 44,000 feet. The number of edges reused is eight because a shorter length tour can be found by repeating more shorter edges than fewer longer edges.

42. (a) The cheapest route has cost 49 and repeats edges *BC*, *CD*, and *DF*.

   (b) Three edges.

   (c) When there are different weights on the edges of a graph, the discussion about good eulerizations must be modified to take the size of the weights into account. It turns out there is an efficient, though complex, algorithm for finding minimum cost solutions to such problems.

   (d) The weight might represent time. Two blocks of the same physical length can take different times to traverse due to construction or other factors.

   (e) The weight might represent traversal time, traffic volume, number of potholes, number of stop signs, etc.

43. Both graphs (b) and (c) have Euler circuits. The valences of all of the vertices in (a) are odd, which makes it impossible to have an Euler circuit there.

(b) 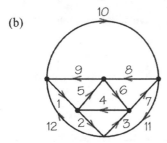   (c)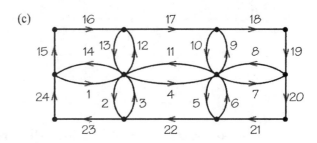

44. There are 5 different ways to eulerize this graph with 4 edges. One of them is shown below:

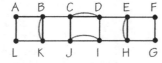

An Euler circuit in the original graph that repeats 4 edges is: *ABCDEHGFEHIJCDIJKBKLA*.

45. If the graph *G* is connected, the newly constructed graph will be even-valent and, thus, will have an Euler circuit. If *G* is not connected, the new graph will not have an Euler circuit because it, too, will not be connected.

46. A good eulerization duplicates the 5 "spokes" that go from the inner pentagon to the outer one. There are many Euler circuits in the eulerized graph.

47. (a)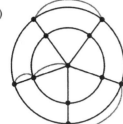

(b) The best eulerization for the four-circle, four-ray case adds two edges.

(c) Hint: Consider the cases where r is even and odd separately.

48. Pick any vertex and try to start an Euler circuit for the graph there. At some point the circuit traverses this special edge, crossing from the starting part of the graph to the other part. This special edge is the only connection between the parts, so we cannot return to the starting part and thus cannot have an Euler circuit. Since there is no Euler circuit, somewhere there must be a vertex with an odd valence.

49. A graph with six vertices where each vertex is joined to every other vertex will have valence 5 for each vertex.

50. Both graphs (a) and (c) have Euler circuits. In graph (b), there is no Euler circuit because some vertices have odd valences.

51. When you attach a new edge to an existing graph, it gets attached at two ends. At each of its ends, it makes the valence of the existing vertex go up by one. Thus the increase in the sum of the valences is two. Therefore, if the graph had an even sum of the valences before, it still does, and if its valence sum was odd before, it still is.

52. Dots without edges all have valence zero, and so the number of odd-valent vertices is zero, which is an even number. As edges are added, the number of odd-valent vertices will always increase by either 0 or 2. Thus, any graph has an even number of odd-valent vertices.

53.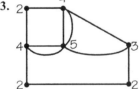

54. When $r = 1$, a formula for the number of repeated edges is $(s-1)$. If r and s are odd, where $r = 2a + 1$ and $s = 2b + 1$ (a and b positive integers which are at least 1) then a formula for the number of repeated edges is $2(a + b)$. Similar formulas hold for the cases where both r and s are even or one of them is even and the other odd. The exact form of the formula depends on the way one expresses these situations.

55. In chemistry when we say, for example, that hydrogen has valence 1, we mean that it forms one chemical bond with other elements. This usage has similarities with the graph theory concept of valence.

56. The thinking used to solve the Chinese postman problem does not apply directly for the situation described because the modeling assumptions for that problem are not met here.

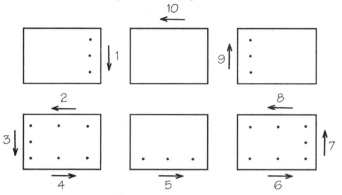

57. A tour that begins and ends at vertex *A* and which respects the traffic directions would be: *ABDEFBEBFEDBACDCA*. The cutting machine has to make "sharp turns" at some intersections.

Word Search Solution

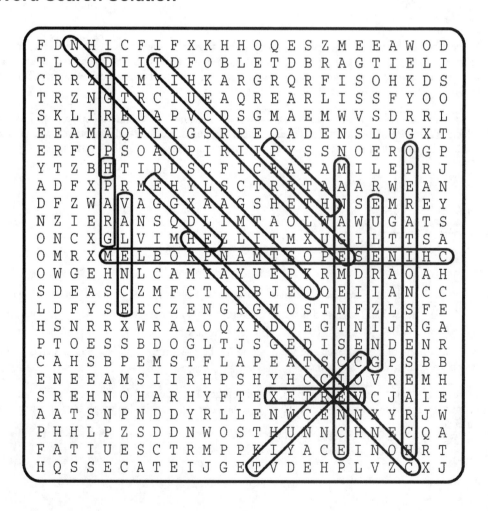

Chapter 2
Business Efficiency

Chapter Outline

Introduction

Chapter Summary

A *Hamiltonian circuit* in a graph is a simple circuit that contains every vertex of the graph. Unlike the situation with Euler circuits, there are no known conditions that guarantee that a graph has a Hamiltonian circuit. However, it is known that certain graphs have Hamiltonians (e.g., the complete graphs) and that others do not (e.g., the graph displayed in Fig. 2.2 in the text).

The *traveling salesman problem* (*TSP*) is to find in a given weighted graph a Hamiltonian circuit of least total weight. The problem is a generalization of the problem of finding the cheapest route for a salesman who must visit clients in several cities and then return home.

A naive solution to the problem is the brute force method (also known as exhaustive search). This method is computationally infeasible for relatively small values of n (e.g., $n = 20$). Unfortunately, there is no known algorithm that will generate optimal solutions more quickly. In fact, many experts believe that no such algorithm will ever be found.

Consequently, we use *heuristic algorithms* to solve this problem. Heuristics are fast algorithms but are not guaranteed to produce optimal solutions. Two such algorithms for the TSP are the *nearest-neighbor algorithm* and the *sorted-edges algorithm*. Both of these algorithms are greedy in the sense that each time a choice is made, they make the choice that seems best based on the objective of the problem. Unfortunately, these local best choices do not necessarily combine to give an optimal solution to the TSP.

A *tree* is a connected graph with no circuits. A *spanning tree* in a given graph is a tree built using all the vertices of the graph and just enough of its edges to obtain a tree. The *minimum-cost spanning tree* problem is to find a spanning tree of least total edge weight in a given weighted graph. A sorted-edges greedy approach can be used to get a solution to this problem. It is interesting that this algorithm, developed by *Kruskal*, always produces an optimal solution to this problem.

The final topic in this chapter is a lead-in to the next chapter. In a job composed of several tasks (e.g., assembling a bicycle), there is often an order in which the tasks must be performed. This ordering of tasks can be represented by using a *digraph* (short for directed graph). The vertices of the graph represent the tasks, and the edges are directed from one vertex to another. Directed edges are like one-way streets, represented by arrows pointing in the allowable direction of travel. A certain directed path in this graph, the *critical path*, corresponds to the sequence of tasks that will take the longest time to complete. Since our job is not complete until every possible sequence of tasks has been finished, the "length" of the critical path tells us the least amount of time it will take us to complete our job. It is possible for a digraph to have more than one critical path.

Skill Objectives

1. Give the definition of a Hamiltonian circuit.

2. Explain the difference between an Euler circuit and a Hamiltonian circuit.

3. Identify a given application as being an Euler circuit problem or a Hamiltonian circuit problem.

4. Calculate $n!$ for a given value of n.

5. Apply the formula $\dfrac{(n-1)!}{2}$ to calculate the number of Hamiltonian circuits in a graph with a given number of vertices.

6. Define algorithm.

7. Explain the term heuristic algorithm and list both an advantage and a disadvantage.

8. Discuss the difficulties inherent in the application of the brute force method for finding the minimum-cost Hamiltonian circuit.

9. Describe the steps in the nearest-neighbor algorithm.

10. Find an approximate solution to the traveling salesman problem by applying the nearest-neighbor algorithm.

11. Describe the steps in the sorted-edges algorithm.

12. Find an approximate solution to the traveling salesman problem by applying the sorted-edges algorithm.

13. Give the definition of a tree.

14. Given a graph with edge weights, determine a minimum-cost spanning tree.

15. Identify the critical path in an order-requirement digraph.

16. Find the earliest possible completion time for a collection of tasks by finding the critical path in an order-requirement digraph.

17. Explain the difference between a graph and a directed graph.

Teaching Tips

1. Perhaps the most important concept in this chapter (as well as in Chapters 3 and 4) is the notion of an algorithm. Stress that in most large-scale problems, algorithms are implemented on computers. Hence, detailed, step-by-step instructions must be provided, and the computer, having no judgment of its own, is incapable of determining cases in which it might be beneficial to deviate from these instructions.

2. It may be helpful to point out that the graph in Figure 2.3 is not drawn to scale, nor is it geographically accurate in terms of the positioning of the cities. Because a mathematical graph is a symbolic model, only the fact that there are four vertices in distinct locations needs to be constant. The positioning in this diagram makes the interpretation clear and easy to read.

3. When traveling by air, shortest distance doesn't necessarily correspond with least cost, as is normally the case with automobile travel. As a special project, students can check with an airline about fares between the cities demonstrated in the text example on page 41 and plan a least-cost version of the nearest-neighbor algorithm.

4. It might be helpful to define precisely what is meant by a heuristic algorithm, since students have probably never heard this term before.

5. Note that the nearest-neighbor algorithm starts at a specified vertex and that the route obtained may be different if the starting vertex is changed.

6. When discussing the sorted-edges algorithm, it may be helpful to indicate that a starting point is not critical. After the edges are linked, then the starting point may be selected and the route followed along the Hamiltonian circuit. You might consider discussing the minimum-cost spanning tree concept along with the sorted-edges algorithm to reinforce the concept. A discussion of the logic behind the two conditions below may help students who are having difficulty.

    a. Three edges cannot meet at a vertex; if this happened, it would mean that the city in question has been visited more than once. Two edges meeting at a vertex merely provide a way into the city and another way out of the city, whereas the third edge would then lead back to the same city, thus violating the premise of the Hamiltonian circuit.

    b. A circular tour cannot be created without all the cities; the creation of a circuit would end the tour, but the tour isn't over until all the vertices have been visited exactly once.

7. The concluding section on critical path analysis is a nice lead-in for Chapter 3; however, if you're running short of time, it can be delayed until then. One advantage of discussing it in this chapter is that students have an opportunity to explore the idea before coupling it with the scheduling concept in Chapter 3.

Research Paper

Have students research another method of finding an efficient way of traversing a graph such as Prim's method or Dijkstra's algorithm. Students should discuss this method (discovered and rediscovered) and its similarities and differences to those described in the text. Students should also research the lives of the people they are named after (Robert C. Prim and Edsger W. Dijkstra).

Collaborative Learning

Hamiltonian Circuits

Begin the lesson by defining Hamiltonian circuits. Either draw the following Hamiltonian circuit diagrams on the board or duplicate the page and distribute it to your students. Working in groups, ask them to find Hamiltonian circuits, if possible. After they decide which graphs have Hamiltonian circuits, ask them if they can find criteria for the existence of such a circuit, similar to those for an Euler circuit. (Of course, no such criteria are known to exist.) The difference between the two problems appears to be minimal, with the focus merely changed from edges to vertices. Many students find it striking that the Euler problem is easily solvable, while the Hamiltonian one is not.

Traveling Salesman Problem

To introduce the traveling salesman problem, ask the students to try to find the minimal Hamiltonian circuit in each of the complete graphs in the following TSP exercise.

Minimum-Cost Spanning Trees

After defining the notion of a minimum-cost spanning tree, but before introducing Kruskal's algorithm, have the students attempt to find the minimum-cost spanning tree for each of the graphs on the next page. Perhaps with some hints they can discover the algorithm themselves.

Hamiltonian Circuits

1. Find the Hamiltonian circuits in the following graphs, when possible.

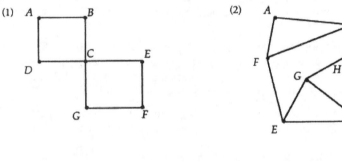

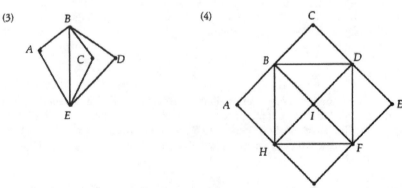

2. Use the campus map as in the exercise from Chapter 1, but now in the context of Hamiltonian circuits. If you wish, you can include distances and turn this into a Traveling Salesman's Problem.

Traveling Salesman Problem

In each of the following complete graphs, find the Hamiltonian circuit of shortest total length.

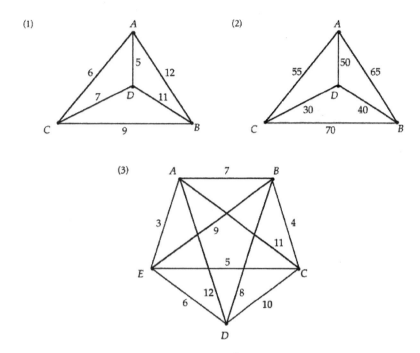

Minimum-Cost Spanning Trees

For each of the following graphs, find the minimum-cost spanning tree.

(1)

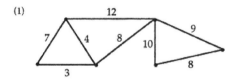

(2)

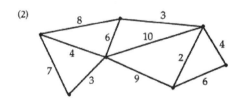

(3)

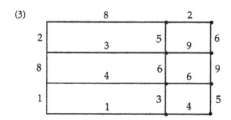

Solutions

Skills Check:

1. c   2. b   3. c   4. b   5. b   6. b   7. c   8. c   9. a   10. c

11. b   12. a   13. b   14. b   15. c   16. a   17. b   18. c   19. a   20. c

Cooperative Learning:
Hamiltonian Circuits:
In (1), (3), and (4) there are no Hamiltonian circuits. *ABCDHGEFA* is a Hamiltonian circuit for (2).

Traveling Salesman Problem:
(1) *ADCBA*—33

(2) *ABDCA*—190

(3) *ABCDEA*—30

Minimum-Cost Spanning Trees:

(1)

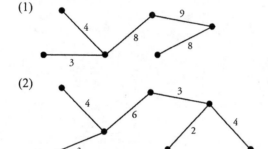

(2)

(3)

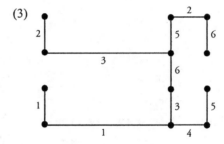

Exercises:

1. (a) $X_5X_6X_1X_3X_4X_2X_5$

    (b) $X_5X_4X_3X_2X_1X_6X_7X_8X_9X_{10}X_{11}X_{12}X_5$

    (c) $X_5X_4X_3X_1X_2X_7X_6X_9X_8X_5$

    (d) $X_5X_8X_3X_4X_7X_6X_1X_2X_5$

    (e) $X_5X_4X_3X_2X_8X_1X_{10}X_7X_6X_9X_5$

2. (a) Yes.

    (b) Yes.

    (c) Yes.

    (d) Yes

    (e) Yes.

    (f) Yes

3. (a) A Hamiltonian circuit will remain for (a) and (b), but there will be no Hamiltonian circuit for (c), (d), and (e),

    (b) The removal of a vertex might correspond to the failure of the equipment at that site.

4. Finding a Hamiltonian circuit in a graph would model running a collection of errands starting and ending at a dorm room, inspecting storm sewers after a storm, and a sequence of operations on individual cars that a robot on an automobile assembly line would need to carry out.

5. Other Hamiltonian circuits include *ABIGDCEFHA* and *ABDCEFGIHA*.

6. (a) 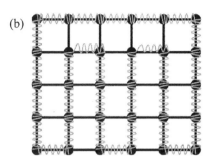 (b)

7. (a) a.   Add edge *AB*.

   b.   Add edge X_1X_3.

   (b)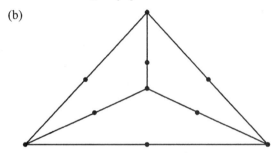

8. A Hamiltonian circuit must use edges *AD*, *DE*, *BE*, and *AB*. These edges already form a circuit making it impossible to visit *C* as part of the circuit.

9. The graph below has no Hamiltonian circuit and every vertex of the graph has valence 3.

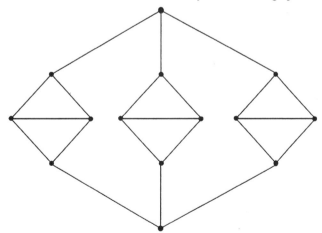

10. Any Hamiltonian circuit must use edge BC, but removal of this edge disconnects the graph into two components consisting of circuits. This precludes there being an edge in addition to BC to be part of a Hamiltonian circuit.

11. (a) Any Hamiltonian circuit would have to use both edges at the vertices X_5, X_4, and X_2. This would cause a problem in the way a Hamiltonian circuit could visit vertex X_1. Thus, no Hamiltonian circuit exists.

    (b) If there were a Hamiltonian circuit, it would have to use the edges X_4 and X_5 and X_6 and X_7. This would make it impossible for the Hamiltonian circuit to visit X_8 and X_9. Thus, no Hamiltonian circuit exists.

12. (a) $X_6 X_3 X_7 X_5 X_2 X_1 X_4 X_6$ is a Hamiltonian circuit.

    (b) There still is no Hamiltonian circuit.

13. (a) No Hamilton circuit.
    (b) No Hamilton circuit.
    (c) No Hamilton circuit.

14. (a) For any $m = 2$ and $n \geq 1$, the graph has a Hamiltonian circuit.
    (b) If either m or n is odd, the graph has a Hamiltonian circuit. If both m and n are even, the graph has no Hamiltonian circuit. A real-world application would be to design an efficient route to check that the traffic control equipment at each vertex was in proper working order. For grid graphs where there are an even number of blocks on each side, there is no Hamiltonian circuit. Yet, by repeating only one edge and vertex one can find a tour that visits all the other vertices in such a grid graph exactly once.

15. (a) There is a Hamiltonian path from X_3 to X_4.

    (b) No. There is a Hamiltonian path from X_1 to X_8 in graph (b).

    (c) Here are two examples. A worker who inspects sewers may start at one garage at the start of the work day but may have to report to a different garage for the afternoon shift. A school bus may start at a bus garage and then pick up students to take them to school, where the bus sits until the end of the school day.

16. (a)

    (b)

    (c)

17. (a) Hamiltonian circuit, yes. One example is: $X_1 X_3 X_7 X_5 X_6 X_8 X_2 X_4 X_1$; Euler circuit, no.
    (b) Hamiltonian circuit, yes. Euler circuit, yes.
    (c) Hamiltonian circuit, yes. Euler circuit, no.
    (d) Hamiltonian circuit, no. Euler circuit, yes. One example is as follows.
    $$U_1 U_2 U_5 U_6 U_{16} U_{15} U_{11} U_4 U_5 U_{12} U_{11} U_{10} U_{14} U_{13} U_7 U_3 U_8 U_{10} U_9 U_3 U_1.$$

18. The n-cube has 2^n vertices, and the number of edges of the n-cube is equal to twice the number of edges of an $(n-1)$-cube plus 2^{n-1}. A formula for this number is $n2^{n-1}$.

19. (a) Hamiltonian circuit, yes; Euler circuit, no.

   (b) Hamiltonian circuit, yes; Euler circuit, no.

   (c) Hamiltonian circuit, yes; Euler circuit, no.

   (d) Hamiltonian circuit, no; Euler circuit, no.

20.

21. (a) 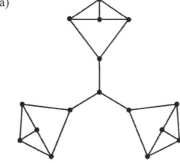   (b)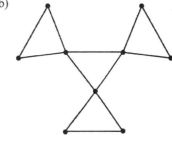

   (c) A graph has an Eulerian path if for two different vertices u and v of the graph there is a path from u to v that uses each edge of the graph once and only once.

22. $(12-2)\times(6-3)=10\times3 = 30$ weeks.

23. The new system is an improvement since it codes 676 locations compared with 504 for the old system. This is 172 more locations.

24. $52\times99\times98\times97\times96\times95$

25. (a) $9\cdot8\cdot7\cdot6\cdot5 = 15,120$

   (b) $(26)(26)(26) = 17,576$

26. (a) $3 \times 4 \times 4 \times 3 = 144$
   (b) $3 \times 1 \times 4 \times 3 = 36$

27. (a) $7\times6\times5\times4\times3 = 2520$

   (b) $7\times7\times7\times7\times7 = 16,807$

   (c) $7^5 - 7 = 16,800$

28. There are five ways to choose the position into which to put the note that is to be sharped, and seven ways to fill this position with a note. Since there is no repetition, the remaining four positions can be filled in $6\times5\times4\times3$ ways for a total of $5\times7\times6\times5\times4\times3 = 12,600$ ways to create the logo.

29. (a) $(26)(26)(26)(10)(10)(10)-(26)(26)(26) = 26^3\left(10^3-1\right)=17,558,424$

   (b) Answers will vary.

30. The number of different meal choices is $4(10)(8) = 320$. The number of choices avoiding pie as a dessert is $4(10)(5) = 200$.

31. With no other restrictions, $10^7 = 10,000,000$. With no other restrictions, $9\times10^2 = 900$.

32. (a) We can apply the fundamental principle of counting in the following way.

Step 1:   Pick one of the 4 positions to put the 0. This can be done in 4 ways.

Step 2.: Pick one of the remaining 9 digits to repeat. This can be done in 9 ways.

Step 3:   Pick two positions out of the remaining three to put the repeated digit into. This can be done in three ways.

Step 4.   Fill the fourth position with a digit different from 0 and the one used in Step 2. This can be done in 8 ways.

Hence, there are $4(9)(3)(8) = 864$.

(b) $10(10)(10)(10) = 10,000$.

33. These graphs have 6, 10, and 15 edges, respectively. The n-vertex complete graph has $\dfrac{n(n-1)}{2}$ edges. The number of TSP tours is 3, 12, and 60, respectively.

34. 5! = 120; 6! = 720; 7! = 5,040; 8! = 40,320; 9! = 362,880; 10! = 3,628,800. The number of TSP tours in a complete graph on 9 vertices is 20,160.

35. (a)

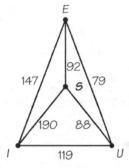

(b) (1) *UISEU;* mileage $= 119 + 190 + 92 + 79 = 480$
(2) *USIEU;* mileage $= 88 + 190 + 147 + 79 = 504$
(3) *UIESU;* mileage $= 119 + 147 + 92 + 88 = 446$

(c) *UIESU* (Tour 3)

(d) No.

(e) Starting from U, one gets *UESIU* Tour 1. From *S* one gets *SUEIS* Tour 2; from *E* one gets *EUSIE* Tour 2; and from *I* one gets *IUESI* Tour 1.

(f) *EUSIE* Tour 2. No.

36. *FMCRF* is quickest and takes 36 minutes.

37. *FMCRF* gets her home in 36 minutes.

38. *FMCR* is quickest and takes 30 minutes.

39. *MACBM* takes 344 minutes to traverse.

40. (a) The two methods give identical answers in this case: *BAEDCB.*

(b) If a complete graph has n vertices, then there are $\dfrac{(n-1)!}{2}$ Hamiltonian circuits. This graph would have $\dfrac{(5-1)!}{2} = \dfrac{4!}{2} = \dfrac{4 \times 3 \times 2 \times 1}{2} = \dfrac{24}{2} = 12$ Hamilton circuits to examine.

(c) Answers will vary.

41. A traveling salesman problem.

42. (a) *ACBDA* is both the nearest neighbor and sorted edges tour.

   (b) Nearest neighbor: *ABCDA* cost 1170; Sorted edge: *ABDCA* cost 1020

   (c) *ADBCEA* is the nearest neighbor tour; *ADEBCA* is the sorted edges tour.

43. A sewer drain inspection route at corners involves finding a Hamiltonian circuit, and there is such a circuit. If the drains are along the blocks, a route in this case involves solving a Chinese postman problem. Since there are 18 odd-valent vertices, an optimal route would require at least 9 reuses of edges. There are many such routes that achieve 9 reuses.

44. (a) *AFEDCBA* (from *A*); *BFACDEB* (from *B*)

   (b) Sorted edges: *AFEDBCA*

45. The complete graph shown has a different nearest-neighbor tour that starts at *A* (*AEDBCA*), a sorted-edges tour (*AEDCBA*), and a cheaper tour (*ADBECA*).

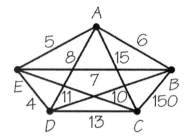

46. There would be $\frac{(20-1)!}{2} = 6.1 \times 10^{16}$ Hamiltonian circuits whose cost would have to be computed. This would take 1.9 years at a billion tours per second.

47. The optimal tour is the same but its cost is now $4200 + 10(30) = 4500$.

48. (a) The graph shown is not a tree because it contains a circuit.

   (b) The graph shown is a tree.

   (c) The graph shown is not a tree because it contains a circuit.

   (d) The graph shown is not a tree because it is not connected.

   (e) The graph shown is a tree.

   (f) The graph shown is not a tree because it is not connected.

   (g) The graph shown is a tree.

49. (a) a. Not a tree because there is a circuit. Also, the wiggled edges do not include all vertices of the graph.

   b. The circuit does not include all the vertices of the graph.

   (b) a. The tree does not include all vertices of the graph.

   b. Not a circuit.

   (c) a. Not a tree.

   b. Not a circuit.

   (d) a. Not a tree.

   b. Not a circuit.

50. (a)

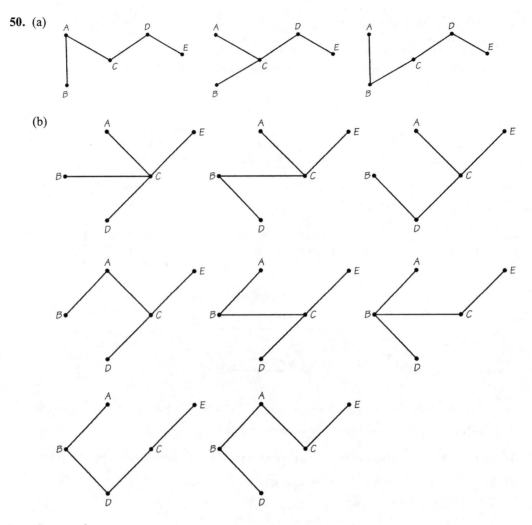

(b)

Continued on next page

50. continued

(c)

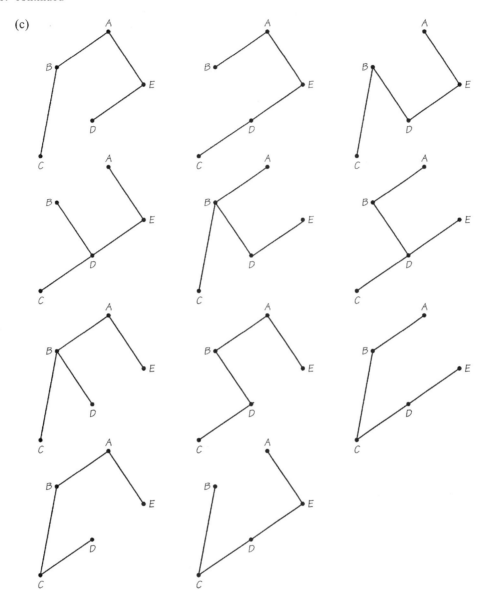

51. (a) 1, 2, 3, 4, 5, 8

(b) 1, 1, 1, 2, 2, 3, 3, 4, 5, 6, 6

(c) 1, 1, 1, 2, 2, 2, 2, 2, 3, 3, 3, 3, 4, 4, 4, 5, 5, 6, 7

(d) 1, 2, 2, 3, 3, 3, 4, 5, 5, 5, 6, 6

The cost is found by adding the numbers given.

52. (a) If G is connected and has 20 vertices, a spanning tree of G will have 19 edges.

(b) Any spanning tree of G will have 20 vertices.

(c) One can conclude that G must have at least 19 edges (when G itself is a tree), but nothing more. (If G cannot have two edges joining a single pair of vertices, then the largest number of edges G can have is 190.)

53. The spanning tree will have 26 vertices. H also will have 26 vertices. The exact number of edges in H cannot be determined, but H has at least 25 edges and no more edges than the complete graph having 26 vertices.

54. The wiggled edges in the figure constitute a spanning tree whose cost is minimal.

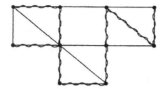

55. Yes.

56. Examples include the synthesis of the links to create a wireless communications network or a homeowner putting underground sprinkler pipes into a large garden.

57. Yes. Change all the weights to negative numbers and apply Kruskal's algorithm. The resulting tree works, and the maximum cost is the negative of the answer you get. If the numbers on the edges represent subsidies for using the edges, one might be interested in finding a maximum-cost spanning tree.

58. Air distances may yield a different solution.

59. A negative weight on an edge is conceivable, perhaps a subsidization payment. Kruskal's algorithm would still apply.

60. Kruskal's algorithm works by at each stage selecting the cheapest edge not already selected which does not form a circuit with the edges already chosen. If all the weights on the edges are different from each other then when a decision is made as to which edge to add next to those already selected, there will never be a tie. Thus, the choice at each stage is always unique, and, hence, there can only be one minimum cost spanning tree. If at some stage one cannot add an edge to those already chosen because a circuit would form, this makes no difference, because the next edge that can be added will never involve a choice among edges with the same weight.

61. Two different trees with the same cost are shown:

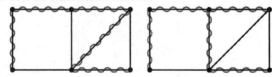

62. If one starts at vertex X_1, the edges are added in the order:

    (a) $X_1, X_6, X_2, X_5, X_2, X_2, X_7, X_2, X_3, X_8, X_8, X_9, X_9, X_4$

    (b) Starting at A, the edges are added in the order AB, BE, ED, DC.

63. (a) True

    (b) False (unless all the edges of the graph have the same weight)

    (c) True

    (d) False

    (e) False

64. (a) If the vertex costs are neglected, the solution has cost $2 + 4 + 8 = 14$. If the vertex costs are not neglected, using the vertex with weight 5 and the edges at it gives a cost of 24.

    (b) If the vertex costs are neglected, the solution has cost $2 + 4 + 7 = 13$.

65. (a) Answers will vary for each edge, but the reason it is possible to find such trees is that each edge is an edge of some circuit.

   (b) The number of edges in every spanning tree is five, one less than the number of vertices in the graph.

   (c) Every spanning tree must include the edge joining vertices C and D, since this edge does not belong to any (simple) circuit in the graph.

66. (a)

$$\overset{3}{\underset{A}{\bullet}}\overset{7}{\underset{B}{\bullet}}\overset{4}{\underset{C}{\bullet}}\underset{D}{\bullet}$$

   (b) The vertices in the graph might represent locations along a road, and the distances between the locations are given by the table shown. Distances along a road would naturally be represented by a graph which is a path. Alternatively, the vertices in the graph might represent manuscripts which were copied by hand from other manuscripts. The weights in the table in this case might represent numbers of key sentences where the manuscripts differ. The graph representing the table in this case being a path suggests that each manuscript was copied from a "prior" manuscript, rather than two manuscripts being copied from one common ancestor, say.

67.

	A	B	C	D
A	0	14	13	5
B	14	0	17	9
C	13	17	0	8
D	5	9	8	0

68. (a) The earliest completion time is 37 since the longest path, the unique critical path $T_1 T_4 T_7$ has length 37.

   (b) The earliest completion time is 38 since the longest path, the unique critical path $T_1 T_3 T_5 T_8$ has length 38.

69. (a) The earliest completion time is 22 since the longest path, the unique critical path $T_3 T_2 T_5$, has length 22.

   (b) The earliest completion time is 30 since the longest path, the unique critical path $T_3 T_5 T_7$, has length 30.

70.

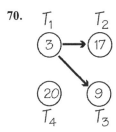

71. The only tasks which if shortened will reduce the earliest completion time are those on the critical path, so in this case, these are the tasks T_1, T_5, and T_7. If T_5 is shortened to 7, then the longest path will have length 28, and this becomes the earliest completion time. The tasks on this critical path are T_1, T_4, and T_7.

72. The critical path is T_1, T_5, T_7 with length 30. If T_5's time is reduced by 2, T_1, T_4, and T_7 will now also be a critical path, and the new lengths of both of these paths will be 28.

73. Different contractors will have different times and order-requirement digraphs. However, in any sensible order requirement digraph, the laying of the foundation will come before the erection of the side walls and the roof. The fastest time for completing all the tasks will be the length of the longest path in the order-requirement digraph.

74. One possibility is (times in minutes):

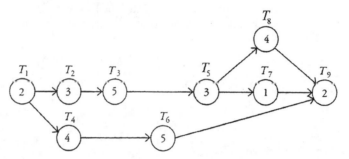

The earliest completion time is 19 minutes.

75. One example is given below.

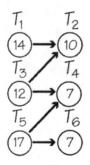

Word Search Solution

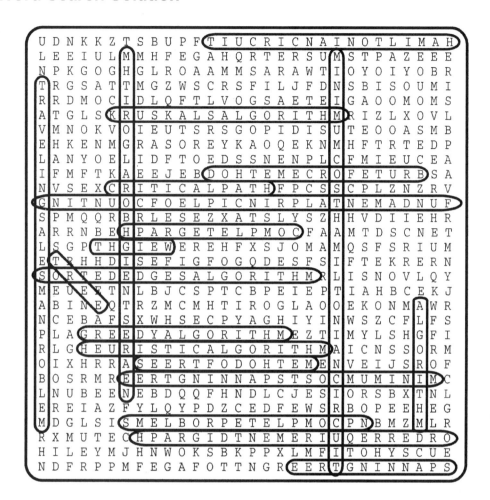

Chapter 3
Planning and Scheduling

Chapter Outline

Introduction

Chapter Summary

When scheduling tasks for processors (which can be either machines or people), we can consider two types of problems. In the first type, we have a fixed number of processors, each with unlimited time. In the second, we have an unlimited number of processors, each with the same fixed time to work.

The *list-processing algorithm* is an approach to solving the first type of problem. We assume we are given an *order-requirement digraph* for the tasks and a priority list for the tasks that can be independent of the order requirements. Additionally, we need two assumptions on the processors: (1) a processor works on an assigned task without interruption until the task is completed; and (2) no processor is ever voluntarily idle. Simply stated, the algorithm assigns the highest priority task currently ready to the lowest numbered processor currently idle. The schedule obtained by this algorithm will be optimal if its overall completion time equals the length of the critical path in the order-requirement digraph. The list-processing algorithm does not always produce an optimum schedule. Moreover, it is subject to several paradoxical quirks, which can occur when attempts are made to shorten the overall completion time.

Other scheduling methods can be used. *Critical-path scheduling* works first on those tasks that occur early in long paths of the order-requirement digraph. If the tasks being scheduled are independent (can be done in any order), the *decreasing-list algorithm* can be employed (schedule longer tasks first). Unfortunately, the scheduling problem is of the same character as the TSP. No computationally efficient method is known that will always produce an optimal schedule.

The second type of problem is a particular instance of the *bin-packing problem*: What is the least number of containers (of the same fixed capacity) needed to pack a given list of items (of various sizes, each less than the capacity of the bins). For this problem, we must again employ heuristic methods. *Next-fit* places items in a container until the next one won't fit and then moves on to a new container. *First-fit* keeps an ordered list of containers and places the next item in the first container in which it fits. *Worst-fit* is similar to first-fit, but places the next item in the container with the most leftover space.

There are many situations in which a schedule or a configuration must be produced that avoids conflicts. Examples include legislative bodies, in which representatives serve on several committees. If one or more members serve on two particular committees, then meetings of those committees must be scheduled at different times. Similarly, final examinations in a university are best arranged in a way that no student has a conflict between two exams scheduled at the same time. Since the number of slots for examinations is limited, this requirement produces a difficult scheduling problem. What is the minimum number of slots required to accommodate all of the examinations without conflicts?

Graph theory—in particular, *vertex coloring*—can be of use in solving such problems. Construct a graph in which vertices are joined by an edge if they are incompatible; e.g., two courses would be joined if there is at least one student in both of the classes. We then color the vertices in such a way that adjacent vertices (those joined by an edge) have different colors. The minimum number of colors required to accomplish this is called the *chromatic number* of the graph, and it yields the solution to the problem. Unfortunately, no algorithm for finding the chromatic number of graphs consisting of a large number of vertices is currently known.

Skill Objectives

1. State the assumptions for the scheduling model.

2. Compute the lower bound on the completion time for a list of independent tasks on a given number of processors.

3. Describe the list-processing algorithm.

4. Apply the list-processing algorithm to schedule independent tasks on identical processors.

5. For a given list of independent tasks, compare the total task time using the list-processing algorithm for both the non-sorted list and also a decreasing-time list.

6. When given an order-requirement digraph, apply the list-processing algorithm to schedule a list of tasks subject to the digraph.

7. Explain how a bin-packing problem differs from a scheduling problem.

8. Given an application, determine whether its solution is found by the list-processing algorithm or by one of the bin-packing algorithms.

9. Discuss advantages and disadvantages of the next-fit, bin-packing algorithm.

10. Solve a bin-packing problem by the non-sorted, next-fit algorithm.

11. Solve a bin-packing problem by the decreasing-time, next-fit algorithm.

12. Discuss advantages and disadvantages of the first-fit, bin-packing algorithm.

13. Apply the non-sorted, first-fit algorithm to a bin-packing problem.

14. Apply the decreasing-time, first-fit algorithm to a bin-packing problem.

15. Discuss advantages and disadvantages of the worst-fit, bin-packing algorithm.

16. Find the solution to a bin-packing problem by the non-sorted, best-fit algorithm.

17. Find the solution to a bin-packing problem by the decreasing-time, worst-fit algorithm.

18. List two examples of bin-packing problems.

19. Color the vertices of a graph so that adjacent vertices have different colors.

20. Determine the chromatic number of a graph.

21. Apply vertex coloring to produce schedules that avoid conflicts.

Teaching Tips

1. When applying the list-processing algorithm, some students find it helpful to construct a grid both above and below the rectangular diagram of processors so that task times can be diagrammed more accurately.

2. An emphasis on the fact that the list-processing algorithm requires a task to be placed on the lowest-numbered available processor at a given time can avoid a decision making problem some students face when more than one processor is available at the same time.

3. Working with an order-requirement digraph in conjunction with the list-processing algorithm poses a difficult process for some students. It may require a great deal of time and several examples. It's often helpful to work with students through at least one homework problem of this type. In addition, listing the task numbers in the rectangles on the scheduling diagram sometimes aids students in keeping on track.

4. Although the three bin-packing algorithms appear to be stated quite simply, many students have difficulty following their instructions. Careful and thorough explanation of these directions can be of help to students. Working through one example using all six versions of the bin-packing algorithms can pay learning dividends.

5. Students often question the need for the next-fit algorithm, since it often leaves bins only partially filled. This is most suitable when processors cannot be kept waiting, even if they are only partially full, as, for example, with delivery trucks being filled with perishable items.

6. It may be helpful to introduce the concept of bin-packing as simply a variant of the scheduling problem in which the processors are of fixed capacity with the number of processors variant. This offers the advantage of looking at the problem from a different perspective.

7. The problem of whether or not to introduce idle time on a processor when tasks are ordered according to a digraph creates difficulty for some students. It can be helpful to have them keep a list of tasks that are being put on hold temporarily because their predecessors have not yet been completed. Then, as a processor becomes ready for a task, the students should check the list before going on to new tasks, to see if any waiting task can now be scheduled. The only situation in which idle time can appear on the schedule before all of the tasks have been assigned is when no tasks were on hold and no new tasks can be scheduled.

Research Paper

Have students research the "knapsack problem". In this scenario you are given a set of items, each with a cost and a value. The task is to determine the number of each item to include in the knapsack so that the total cost is less than some given cost and one has the total value as large as possible. Students should compare this problem and its applications to the ones presented in this chapter.

Have students research the contributions of R. L. Brooks and what is known as Brooks' Theorem. This theorem pertains to an upper bound on the chromatic number of a graph.

Collaborative Learning

Scheduling

Two people are camping out and wish to cook a simple supper consisting of soup and hamburgers. In order to prepare the supper, several tasks must be performed.

T_1: Go to the store to buy matches – 10 minutes

T_2: Collect firewood– 8 minutes

T_3: Light the fire– 6 minutes

T_4: Get water from a well– 12 minutes

T_5: Cook soup (requires constant stirring)– 15 minutes

T_6: Make hamburger patties – 9 minutes

T_7: Cook hamburgers– 7 minutes

Each task requires only one of the campers and once a task is begun it cannot be interrupted.

Some of the tasks can be done simultaneously, but some cannot be done until others are completed. What is the shortest amount of time it will take for all of the tasks to be completed?

How should the work be divided between the two campers?

Vertex Coloring

Color the vertices of the following graphs in such a way that adjacent vertices have different colors. What is the minimum number of colors required for each graph?

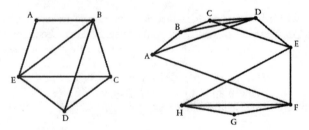

Conflict Resolution

A man wants to set up an aquarium in his home to contain five different types of fish—A, B, C, D, and E. However, some of these fish will eat other ones and thus cannot share a tank. The chart below displays the incompatibilities. (An X indicates that the two species cannot share a tank.)

What is the minimum number of tanks required, and which fish go into which tank?

	A	B	C	D	E
A		X		X	
B	X		X		X
C		X		X	
D	X		X		
E		X			

Solutions

Skills Check:

1. c   2. c   3. b   4. b   5. c   6. b   7. c   8. b   9. b   10. c

11. b   12. b   13. c   14. a   15. b   16. a   17. c   18. a   19. a   20. c

Cooperative Learning:
Conflict Resolution:
Set up the graph corresponding to the conflict matrix:

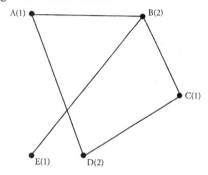

Exercises:

1. (a) Scheduling final examinations, the times for course being offered, cleaning of classrooms, etc.
   (b) Scheduling the buses, the selling of tickets, cleaning, etc.
   (c) Scheduling regular staff and supervisory staff, deliveries of items for sale, etc.
   (d) Scheduling meal times, shopping, etc.
   (e) Scheduling staff, maintenance of backup equipment, etc.
   (f) Scheduling nurses, doctors, operating rooms, medical imaging, etc.
   (g) Scheduling maintenance and repair of hoses and equipment, personnel to respond to alarms.
   (h) Scheduling store personnel, inventory work, shelving new books, and restoring books to proper order on the shelves.
   (i) Scheduling ground and squad car patrols around the clock, officers on surveillance assignments, general work involving nonemergency interaction with the public; arrangements must be made regarding who is on call for emergency duty.

2. Tasks include purchasing food, preparing the food for cooking, cooking the food, setting the table, cleaning the house, etc. The processors involved include the parents and three children, the stove (which cooks the turkey), etc. Since the human processors can work in parallel, some of these tasks can be done simultaneously. Some of the human processors can also work simultaneously with the stove.

3. Jocelyn must perhaps launder her clothes, arrange care for her cat, pack, arrange for a taxi to the airport, and get to the airport. Unless she can get a friend to help her with some of these tasks, she must do all the tasks herself. She can launder her clothes during the time she arranges for a taxi, but most of the tasks cannot be done simultaneously.

4. (a) The critical path has length 32.

   (b) (1) Processor 1: T_1, T_3, T_5, idle 30 to 44.

   Processor 2: T_2, T_4, T_6, T_7, idle 36 to 38.

   (2) Processor 1: T_2, T_5, T_6, T_7.

   Processor 2: T_1, T_3, T_4, idle 33 to 41.

   (c) No.

   (d) The sum of the task time divided by 2 is 37. Hence, no schedule can finish earlier than time 37.

5. (a) i. Processor 1: T_1 from 0 to 13, T_3 from 13 to 25, T_6 from 25 to 45.

   Processor 2: T_2 from 0 to 18, T_4 from 18 to 27, T_5 from 27 to 35, idle from 35 to 45.

   ii. Processor 1: T_1 from 0 to 13, T_3 from 13 to 25, T_4 from 25 to 34, T_5 from 34 to 42.

   Processor 2: T_2 from 0 to 18, T_6 from 18 to 38, idle from 38 to 42.

   (b) The schedule produced in (ii) is optimal, because the sum of the task times is 80 and no set of tasks can be arranged that will feasibly sum to 40 on each processor.

   (c) The critical path is T_2, T_6, and it has length 38. No schedule can be completed by time 38 on two processors because the sum of the task times divided by 2 is 40.

6. (a) i. Processor 1: T_1, T_3, T_6. Processor 2: T_2, T_4, T_5, idle 37 to 43.

   ii. Processor 1: T_1, T_3, T_4, T_5. Processor 2: T_2, T_6, idle 38 to 42. The second is optimal. The critical path is T_2, T_6 and has length 38. No schedule on two machines finishes by 38 because the total time for all the tasks is 80. Thus, on two machines no earlier time than $\frac{80}{2} = 40$ is possible.

   (b) The optimum completion time before and after the two task times are switched is the same.

7. (a) Processor 1: T_1, T_2, T_3, T_5, T_7.

   Processor 2: Idle 0 to 2, T_4, T_6, idle 4 to 5.

   (b) Processor 1: T_1, T_2, T_3, T_6, T_7.

   Processor 2: Idle 0 to 2, T_4, T_5, idle 4 to 5.

   (c) Yes.

   (d) No.

   (e) T_3 and T_5.

8. Hospital emergency room activities and police officer activities may have to be interrupted to start new tasks. For manufacturing machines in standard production runs, the assumption is reasonable.

9. (a) Processor 1: T_1, T_6, idle 15 to 21, T_7, idle 27 to 31.

   Processor 2: T_2, T_5, T_8.

   Processor 3: T_3, T_4, idle from 13 to 31.

   (b) Processor 1: T_1, T_6, idle 15 to 21, T_7, idle 27 to 31.

   Processor 2: T_3, T_4, idle from 13 to 21, T_8.

   Processor 3: T_2, T_5, idle from 21 to 31.

   (c) Processor 1: T_4, idle 10 to 11, T_6, idle 18 to 21, T_8.

   Processor 2: T_2, T_5, T_7, idle 27 to 31.

   Processor 3: T_1, T_3, idle 11 to 31.

10. (a) The order-requirement diagraph has only one task T_4 ready at time 0. Thus, no matter what list one starts with, one will skip over any tasks that are prior to T_4 in the list until one reaches T_4 because any other task would not be ready at time 0. Of course those lists that start with T_4 would assign T_4 to Machine 1 at time 0 because it is ready at this time.

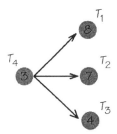

(b) So by part (a) we always assign T_4 to Machine 1 at time 0, which keeps that machine busy until time 3. Now, can we assign any task to machine 2 at any time between 0 and 3? No, because all of those tasks must wait until T_4 is done before they can begin. So Machine 2 stays idle from time 0 to time 3. Thus the same order-requirement digraph used for (a) works here.

11. Examples include inserting identical mirror systems on different models of cars and vaccinating different children against polio.

12. (a) Processor 1: T_1, T_2, T_4, T_6, T_7.
Processor 2: idle 0 to 1, T_3, T_5, idle 3 to 5.

(b) Processor 1: T_1, T_2, T_4, T_5.
Processor 2: idle 0 to 1, T_3, T_6, T_7.

(c) The schedule in (b) is optimal.

13. T_1, T_2, T_3, T_4, T_8, T_9, T_{10}, T_{11}, T_5, T_6, T_7, T_{12}.

14. (a) The critical path, which has length 17, is T_1, T_2, T_3.

(b) T_1, T_4, T_5, T_2, T_6, T_7, T_3 is the list to be used. The one processor would have the tasks scheduled on it: T_1, T_4, T_5, T_2, T_6, T_7, T_3.

(c) T_6, T_1, T_7, T_2, T_4, T_3, T_5 would be the list. The resulting schedule on one processor would be: T_1, T_7, T_4, T_2, T_5, T_6, T_3.

(d) No idle time. Their completion times are the same.

(e) Earlier completion of tasks giving rise to cash payments.

(f) The required schedule is Processor 1: T_1, T_6, T_3; Processor 2: T_4, T_5, T_2, T_7.

(g) The completion time does halve $(40 \rightarrow 20)$. As the number of processors goes up, the completion time may decrease, but at some point the length of the critical path will govern the completion time rather than the number of processors.

(h) (i) Completion time goes down by 7.
(ii) Completion time is 19 for two processors using the decreasing time list.

15. (a) No. Consider the tasks that begin after the stretch where all machines are idle. Pick one of these tasks T and say machine 1 was the machine that it was given to. This task was ready for machine 1 just prior to when it began T because no task was just being completed on any other machine at this time because they were all idle. Thus, T should have begun earlier on machine 1.

(b) This schedule cannot arise using the list-processing algorithm, because T_2 should have been scheduled at time 0.

(c) Use the digraph with no edges and the list: T_2, T_1, T_3, T_4, T_5.

16. (a) 55 minutes.

(b) Mike: T_1, T_2, T_3, T_8, T_9.
Mary: T_4, T_7, T_5, T_6, idle 22–33.

(c) Mike: T_1, T_2, T_3, idle 20–21.
Mary: T_4, T_5, T_6.
Jack: T_7, T_8, T_9, idle 14–21.

(d) Tasks that, when completed, result in hot food for eating should be completed as close to the end as possible.

17. (a) T_1, T_2, T_3, and T_6 are ready at time 0.

(b) No tasks require that T_1 and T_6 be done before these other tasks can begin.

(c) The critical path consists only of T_6 and has length 20.

(d) Processor 1: T_1, T_6: Processor 2: T_2, T_4, idle from 18 to 30: Processor 3: T_3, T_5, idle from 12 to 30.

(e) No.

(f) Processor 1: T_6, idle from 20 to 22: Processor 2: T_3, T_5, T_1: Processor 3: T_2, T_4, idle from 18 to 22.

(g) Yes.

(h) Another list leading to the same optimal schedule is T_6, T_3, T_2, T_4, T_5, T_1.

18. (a) T_6, T_2, T_4, T_3, T_1, T_5.

(b) Processor 1: T_6, idle 20–22;
Processor 2: T_2, T_4, T_5;
Processor 3: T_3, T_1, idle 18–22.
This schedule is optimal for 3 processors.

(c) It is no better than the best schedule found there.

19. (a) $5! = 120$

(b) No. Whatever list is used, T_1 must be assigned to the first machine at time 0 because it is the only task ready at time 0.

(c) No. First, while Processor 1 works on T_1. Processor 2 must be idle. Second, the task times are integers with sum 31. If there are two processors, one of the processors must have idle time since when 2 divides 31, there is a remainder of 1.

(d) No.

20. (a) $120 - 24 = 96$.

   (b) No, because Task 1 is a predecessor of all the other tasks.

   (c) Answers will vary.

   (d) Answers will vary.

   (e) The list T_1, T_3, T_2, T_5, T_4 will yield an optimal schedule.

21. Using the order-requirement digraph shown and any list with one or more processors yields the same schedule:

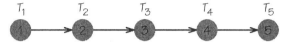

22. If one uses the digraph with no edges and schedules three tasks whose completion times are 6, 8, and 14 on one machine, each of the 6 possible scheduling lists will yield a different schedule.

23. (a) One reasonable possibility is (time in min):

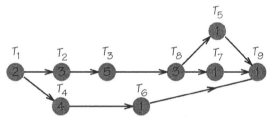

The earliest completion time is 15.

   (b) The decreasing-time list is T_3, T_4, T_2, T_8, T_1, T_5, T_6, T_7, T_9. The schedule is Processor 1: T_1, T_4, T_6, idle 7 to 10, T_8, T_5, T_9; Processor 2: idle 0 to 2, T_2, T_3, idle 10 to 13, T_7, idle 14 to 15.

24. Not if the number of processors is the same. If the number of processors is different, two schedules can end at the same time and have different amounts of idle time.

25. No. At time 11, T_4 should been assigned to Machine 1 because Machine 1 was free at this time and T_4 was ready.

26. No. If T_3 could be scheduled at time 12 on Robot 1, the order requirement digraph could not have required that this task await the completion of T_2. In this case, this task could have been started at time 8 on Robot 1.

27. (a) Task times: $T_1 = 3$, $T_2 = 3$, $T_3 = 2$, $T_4 = 3$, $T_5 = 3$, $T_6 = 4$, $T_7 = 5$, $T_8 = 3$, $T_9 = 2$, $T_{10} = 1$, $T_{11} = 1$, and $T_{12} = 3$. This schedule would be produced from the list: T_1, T_3, T_2, T_5, T_4, T_6, T_7, T_8, T_{11}, T_{12}, T_9, T_{10}.

   (b) Task times: $T_1 = 3$, $T_2 = 3$, $T_3 = 3$, $T_4 = 2$, $T_5 = 2$, $T_6 = 4$, $T_7 = 3$, $T_8 = 5$, $T_9 = 8$, $T_{10} = 4$, $T_{11} = 7$, $T_{12} = 9$, and $T_{13} = 3$. This schedule would be produced from the list: T_1, T_5, T_7, T_4, T_3, T_6, T_{11}, T_8, T_{12}, T_9, T_2, T_{10}, T_{13}.

28. Tasks could be rearranged in order of increasing time on each machine; tasks could be reordered so those that, when completed, resulted in a cash payment were completed as early as possible.

29. (a) (i) Processor 1: T_1, T_3, T_5, T_7, idle from 16 to 20; Processor 2: T_2, T_4, T_6, T_8.

(ii) Processor 1: T_8, T_5, T_4, T_1; Processor 2: T_7, T_6, T_3, T_2.

(b) The schedule in (ii) is optimal.

30. (a) (i) Processor 1: T_1, T_4, T_7, idle 12–15;   Processor 2: T_2, T_5, T_8;
Processor 3: T_3, T_6, idle 9–15.

(ii) Processor 1: T_8, T_3, T_2; Processor 2: T_7, T_4, T_1, idle 12–13;
Processor 3: T_6, T_5, idle 11–13.

(b) Neither of these schedules are optimal. An optimal schedule is achieved when the list T_8, T_7, T_2, T_3, T_6, T_5, T_4 is used. The idea for finding an optimal schedule is based on the fact that the total task time is 36.

31. Such criteria include decreasing length of the times of the tasks, order of size of financial gains when each task is finished, and increasing length of the times of the tasks.

32. Examples of scheduling projects with due dates include construction projects, military procurement projects, and plane departures from the gates at an airport. An example of a situation where there might be release times would be for planes to enter a runway holding area or for a construction project where materials are delivered to a site but cannot arrive too early lest this get in the way of current activities because there is little storage space at the site.

33. (a) Machine 1: T_1, T_6, T_{10}, idle from 8 to 9; Machine 2: T_3, T_4, T_{11}, T_{12}; Machine 3: T_2, T_7, idle from 8 to 9; Machine 4: T_5, T_8, T_9, idle from 8 to 9.

(b) Machine 1: T_1, T_8, T_{10}; Machine 2: T_5, T_6, T_2, T_{13}; Machine 3: T_7, T_{12}; Machine 4: T_4, T_{11}, idle from 9 to 12; Machine 5: T_3, T_9, idle from 11 to 12.

The schedule in part (a) had to have idle time because the total task time was 33, and 33 is not exactly divisible by 4. The schedule in part (b) had to have idle time because the total task time was 56, and 56 is not exactly divisible by 5.

34. (a) (i) Processor 1: T_1, T_2, T_5, T_6.
Processor 2: T_3, T_7, T_4, idle 30–56.

(ii) Processor 1: T_1, T_4, T_7, T_6.
Processor 2: T_3, T_2, T_5, idle 31–55.

The decreasing time list is: T_6, T_5, T_4, T_1, T_7, T_2, T_3, yielding the schedule:
Processor 1: T_1, T_4, T_7, T_6.
Processor 2: T_2, T_3, T_5, idle 31–55.

(b) These schedules are not optimal since the list T_3, T_2, T_1, T_7, T_5, T_4, T_6, yields the schedule:
Processor 1: T_3, T_1, T_5, T_6.
Processor 2: T_2, T_7, T_4, idle 32–54.
The completion time is 54.

(c) The critical path method gives rise to the list: T_1, T_2, T_3, T_5, T_4, T_7, T_6. This list gives rise to the schedule:
Processor 1: T_1, T_4, T_7, T_6.
Processor 2: T_2, T_3, T_5, idle 31–55.

35. (a) List for (i) yields (with items coded by task time): Machine 1: 12, 9, 15, idle from 36 to 50; Machine 2: 7, 10, 13, 20. List for (ii) yields: Machine 1: 12, 13, 20; Machine 2: 7, 9, 15, 10, idle from 41 to 45. List for (iii) yields: Machine 1: 20, 12, 9, idle from 41 to 45; Machine 2: 15, 13, 10, 7.

   (b) These schedules complete earlier than those where precedence constraints hold. An optimal schedule is possible, however: Machine 1: 20, 10, 13; Machine 2: 12, 15, 9, 7. The associated list is: T_6, T_1, T_5, T_7, T_2, T_4, T_3.

   (c) The critical path list is T_6, T_5, T_4, T_1, T_7, T_2, T_3 using the first processor. It finishes at time 41 and is idle until 45, when processor 2 finishes.

36. (a) With this list the order of the tasks on the processors is: Machine 1: 8, 17, 16, 5, 3, 7, 2, 1, idle 59 to 61; Machine 2: 11, 14, 9, 2, 1, 18, 6. The completion time is 61.

   (b) The list is: 18, 17, 16, 14, 11, 9, 8, 7, 6, 5, 3, 2, 2, 1, 1. On two processors we get the schedule: Machine 1: 18, 14, 11, 7, 6, 2, 2; Machine 2: 17, 16, 9, 8, 5, 3, 1, 1. The completion time is 60 on both machines.

   (c) The answer in (b) is one optimal schedule

   (d) Using the original list we get the schedule: Machine 1: 19, 20, 1, 2, 3, 5, 11, 17, 18, 2, 16; Machine 2: 19, 20, 1, 2, 3, 5, 11, 18, 17, 16, 2. Both machines finish at time 114. The decreasing list is: 20, 20, 19, 19, 18, 18, 17, 17, 16, 16, 11, 11, 5, 5, 3, 3, 2, 2, 2, 2, 1, 1. Machine 1: 20, 19, 18, 17, 16, 11, 5, 3, 2, 2, 1; Machine 2: 20, 19, 18, 17, 16, 11, 5, 3, 2, 2, 1. Both machines finish at time 114. Both lists lead to optimal schedules.

37. (a) The tasks are scheduled on the machines as follows: Processor 1: 12, 13, 45, 34, 63, 43, 16, idle 226 to 298; Processor 2: 23, 24, 23, 53, 25, 74, 76; Processor 3: 32, 23, 14, 21, 18, 47, 23, 43, 16, idle 237 to 298.

   (b) The tasks are scheduled on the machines as follows: Processor 1: 12, 24, 14, 34, 25, 23, 16, 16, 76; Processor 2: 23, 23, 21, 63, 43, idle 173 to 240; Processor 3: 32, 23, 53, 74, idle 182 to 240; Processor 4: 13, 45, 18, 47, 43, idle 166 to 240.

   (c) The decreasing-time list is 76, 74, 63, 53, 47, 45, 43, 43, 34, 32, 25, 24, 23, 23, 23, 23, 21, 18, 16, 16, 14, 13, 12. The tasks are scheduled on three machines as follows: Processor 1: 76, 45, 43, 24, 23, 18, 16, 13; Processor 2: 74, 47, 34, 32, 23, 21, 14, 12, idle 257 to 258; Processor 3: 63, 53, 43, 25, 23, 23, 16, idle 246 to 248. The tasks are scheduled on four machines as follows: Processor 1: 76, 43, 24, 23, 16, idle 182 to 194; Processor 2: 74, 43, 25, 23, 16, 13; Processor 3: 63, 45, 32, 23, 18, 12, idle 193 to 194; Processor 4: 53, 47, 34, 23, 21, 14, idle 192 to 194.

   (d) The new decreasing time list is 84, 82, 71, 61, 55, 45, 43, 43, 34, 32, 25, 24, 23, 23, 23, 23, 21, 18, 16, 16, 14, 13, 12. The tasks are scheduled as follows: Processor 1: 84, 45, 43, 25, 23, 23, 16, 12; Processor 2: 82, 55, 34, 32, 23, 18, 14, 13; Processor 3: 71, 61, 43, 24, 23, 21, 16, idle 259 to 271.

38. T_2, T_3, T_1, T_4, T_5; decreasing time list is T_4, T_5, T_3, T_2, T_1. Machine 1: T_4, T_2, T_1; Machine 2: T_5, T_3, idle 28 – 32. The completion time is 32.

39. Examples include jobs in a videotape copying shop, data entry tasks in a computer system, and scheduling nonemergency operations in an operating room. These situations may have tasks with different priorities, but there is no physical reason for the tasks not to be independent, as would be the case with putting on a roof before a house had walls erected.

40. An algorithm that will give an optimal answer every time is the list-processing algorithm using any list. The total time to complete all the tasks will be nk. When the number of machines is smaller than the number of tasks, the completion time will depend on whether the number of processors exactly divides n. An example where all the tasks times might be equal would be to fill a collection of identical boxes with identical objects.

41. Each task heads a path of length equal to the time to do that task.

42. Case I: Using 10-foot horizontal shelves and 6-foot vertical boards, the list of decreasing board lengths is 10, 10, 10, 10, 6, 6, 2, 2, 2, 2.

First-fit-decreasing:
BIN 1: 10;
BIN 2: 10;
BIN 3: 10;
BIN 4: 10;
BIN 5: 6, 2, 2;
BIN 6: 6, 2, 2.

Next-fit-decreasing:
BIN 1: 10;
BIN 2: 10;
BIN 3: 10;
BIN 4: 10;
BIN 5: 6;
BIN 6: 6;
BIN 7: 2, 2, 2, 2.

Worst-fit-decreasing:
BIN 1: 10;
BIN 2: 10;
BIN 3: 10;
BIN 4: 10;
BIN 5: 6, 2, 2;
BIN 6: 6, 2, 2.

Case II: Using boards that add up to 10- and 6-foot lengths, the list of decreasing board lengths is 7, 5, 5, 4, 4, 3, 3, 3, 3, 3, 2, 2, 2, 2, 2, 2, 2, 2, 2, 2.

First-fit-decreasing:
BIN 1: 7, 3;
BIN 2: 5, 5;
BIN 3: 4, 4, 2;
BIN 4: 3, 3, 3;
BIN 5: 3, 2, 2, 2;
BIN 6: 2, 2, 2, 2, 2;
BIN 7: 2.

Next-fit-decreasing:
BIN 1: 7;
BIN 2: 5, 5;
BIN 3: 4, 4;
BIN 4: 3, 3, 3;
BIN 5: 3, 3, 2, 2;
BIN 6: 2, 2, 2, 2, 2;
BIN 7: 2, 2, 2.

Worst-fit-decreasing:
BIN 1: 7, 3;
BIN 2: 5, 5;
BIN 3: 4, 4, 2;
BIN 4: 3, 3, 3;
BIN 5: 3, 2, 2, 2;
BIN 6: 2, 2, 2, 2, 2;
BIN 7: 2.

By using the 10- and 6-foot boards, you need to buy 1 less board. Also, the system will be easier to make structurally sound with single pieces of wood. You are encouraged to try other combinations of board lengths.

43. The times to photocopy the manuscripts, in decreasing order, are 120, 96, 96, 88, 80, 76, 64, 64, 60, 60, 56, 48, 40, 32. Packing these in bins of size 120 yields Bin 1: 120; Bin 2: 96; Bin 3: 96; Bin 4: 88, 32; Bin 5: 80, 40; Bin 6: 76; Bin 7: 64, 56; Bin 8: 64, 48; Bin 9: 60, 60. Nine photocopy machines are needed to finish within 2 minutes using FFD. The number of bins would not change, but the placement of the items in the bins would differ for worst-fit decreasing.

44. The bins have capacity 135.

First-fit uses 5 bins.

    Bin 1: 80, 50;

    Bin 2: 90, 20;

    Bin 3: 130;

    Bin 4: 60, 30, 30;

    Bin 5: 90, 40.

The decreasing list is: 130, 90, 90, 80, 60, 50, 40, 30, 30, 20.

First-fit decreasing uses 5 bins.

    Bin 1: 130;

    Bin 2: 90, 40;

    Bin 3: 90, 30;

    Bin 4: 80, 50;

    Bin 5: 60, 30, 20.

Either of these packings is optimal.

Using first-fit on the list: 60, 50, 40, 40, 60, 90, 90, 50, 20, 30, 30, 50 yields (bin capacity 135):

    Bin 1: 60, 50, 20;

    Bin 2: 40, 40, 50;

    Bin 3: 60, 30, 30;

    Bin 4: 90;

    Bin 5: 90;

    Bin 6: 50.

The decreasing list is: 90, 90, 60, 60, 50, 50, 50, 40, 40, 30, 30, 20.

Using first-fit on this list yields:

    Bin 1: 90, 40;

    Bin 2: 90, 40;

    Bin 3: 60, 60;

    Bin 4: 50, 50, 30;

    Bin 5: 50, 30, 20.

The decreasing time solution is optimal and uses one fewer bin than first-fit applied to the original list.

45. (a) Using the next-fit algorithm, the bins are filled as follows: Bin 1: 12, 15; Bin 2: 16, 12; Bin 3: 9, 11, 15; Bin 4: 17, 12; Bin 5: 14, 17; Bin 6: 18; Bin 7: 19; Bin 8: 21; Bin 9: 31; Bin 10: 7, 21; Bin 11: 9, 23; Bin 12: 24; Bin 13: 15, 16; Bin 14: 12, 9, 8; Bin 15: 27; Bin 16: 22; Bin 17: 18.

    (b) The decreasing list is 31, 27, 24, 23, 22, 21, 21, 19, 18, 18, 17, 17, 16, 16, 15, 15, 15, 14, 12, 12, 12, 12, 11, 9, 9, 9, 8, 7. The next-fit decreasing schedule is Bin 1: 31; Bin 2: 27; Bin 3: 24; Bin 4: 23; Bin 5: 22; Bin 6: 21; Bin 7: 21; Bin 8: 19; Bin 9: 18, 18; Bin 10: 17, 17; Bin 11: 16, 16; Bin 12: 15, 15; Bin 13: 15, 14; Bin 14: 12, 12, 12; Bin 15: 12, 11, 9; Bin 16: 9, 9, 8, 7.

    (c) The worst-fit schedule using the original list is Bin 1: 12, 15, 9; Bin 2: 16, 12; Bin 3: 11, 15; Bin 4: 17, 12; Bin 5: 14, 17; Bin 6: 18, 7; Bin 7: 19, 9; Bin 8: 21, 15; Bin 9: 31; Bin 10: 21, 9; Bin 11: 23, 8; Bin 12: 24; Bin 13: 16, 12; Bin 14: 27; Bin 15: 22; Bin 16: 18.

    (d) The worst-fit decreasing schedule would be Bin 1: 31; Bin 2: 27, 9; Bin 3: 24, 12; Bin 4: 23, 12; Bin 5: 22, 14; Bin 6: 21, 15; Bin 7: 21, 15; Bin 8: 19, 17; Bin 9: 18, 18; Bin 10: 17, 16; Bin 11: 16, 15; Bin 12: 12, 12, 11; Bin 13: 9, 9, 8, 7.

46. (a) (Next-fit):
   Bin 1: 100, 120, 60, 90, 110;
   Bin 2: 45, 30, 70, 60, 50, 40, 25, 65, 25, 55;
   Bin 3: 35, 45, 60, 75, 30, 120, 100;
   Bin 4: 60, 90 85.

   (b) The decreasing list is: 120, 120, 110, 100, 100, 90, 90, 85, 75, 70, 65, 60, 60, 60, 60, 55, 50, 45, 45, 40, 35, 30, 30, 25, 25.
   (Next-fit decreasing):
   Bin 1: 120, 120, 110, 100;
   Bin 2: 100, 90, 90, 85, 75;
   Bin 3: 70, 65, 60, 60, 60, 60, 55, 50;
   Bin 4: 45, 45, 40, 35, 30, 30, 25, 25.

   (c) (First-fit): same solution as next-fit.

   (d) (First-fit decreasing):
   Bin 1: 120, 120, 110, 100, 30;
   Bin 2: 100, 90, 90, 85, 75, 40;
   Bin 3: 70, 65, 60, 60, 60, 60, 55, 50;
   Bin 4: 45, 45, 35, 30, 25, 25.

47. The bins have a capacity of 120. (First fit): Bin 1: 63, 32, 11; Bin 2: 19, 24, 64; Bin 3: 87, 27; Bin 4: 36, 42; Bin 5: 63. This schedule would take five station breaks; however, the total time for the breaks is under 8 minutes. The decreasing list is 87, 64, 63, 63, 42, 36, 32, 27, 24, 19, 11. (First-fit decreasing): Bin 1: 87, 32; Bin 2: 64, 42, 11; Bin 3: 63, 36, 19; Bin 4: 63, 27, 24. This solution uses only four station breaks.

48. Bin 1: 8, 1;
   Bin 2: 7, 2;
   Bin 3: 9;
   Bin 4: 5;
   Bin 5: 7, 3;
   Bin 6: 6, 4.

49. (a) There are theoretical results that show that best fit "usually" performs better than worst fit.

   (b) Try 8, 7, 5, 3, 3, 2 in bins of capacity 14.

50. Bin 1: 6, 3, 1;
   Bin 2: 9, 1;
   Bin 3: 5, 2, 2, 1;
   Bin 4: 8, 2;
   Bin 5: 9;
   Bin 6: 7, 3;
   Bin 7: 5, 4;
   Bin 8: 7, 2;
   Bin 9: 6, 3;
   Bin 10: 8, 2;
   Bin 11: 7, 3;
   Bin 12: 6, 4;
   Bin 13: 5, 5;
   Bin 14: 7, 2;
   Bin 15: 2, 3, 5;
   Bin 16: 6, 2, 2;
   Bin 17: 7, 3;
   Bin 18: 4, 6.

Continued on next page

50. continued

The decreasing list is: 9, 9, 8, 8, 7, 7, 7, 7, 7, 6, 6, 6, 6, 6, 5, 5, 5, 5, 5, 4, 4, 4, 3, 3, 3, 3, 3, 3, 2, 2, 2, 2, 2, 2, 2, 2, 2, 1, 1, 1.

Bin 1: 9, 1;
Bin 2: 9, 1;
Bin 3: 8, 2;
Bin 4: 8, 2;
Bin 5: 7, 3;
Bin 6: 7, 3;
Bin 7: 7, 3;
Bin 8: 7, 3;
Bin 9: 7, 3;
Bin 10: 6, 4;
Bin 11: 6, 4;
Bin 12: 6, 4;
Bin 13: 6, 3, 1;
Bin 14: 6, 2, 2;
Bin 15: 5, 5;
Bin 16: 5, 5;
Bin 17: 5, 2, 2;
Bin 18: 2, 2, 2.

51. The total performance time exceeds what will fit on four disks. Using FFD, one can fit the music on five disks.

52. Consider the list 8, 8, 5, 3, 5, 5, 5 to be packed in bins of capacity 11. Using first-fit, we get:

Bin 1: 8, 3;
Bin 2: 8;
Bin 3: 5, 5;
Bin 4: 5, 5.

When worst-fit is used, we get:

Bin 1: 8;
Bin 2: 8;
Bin 3: 5, 3;
Bin 4: 5, 5;
Bin 5: 5.

The list 8, 8, 5, 3, 5, 5, 5, 8, 8, 5, 5, 2 yields 7 bins when first-fit is used, 8 bins when worst-fit is used, and 9 bins when next-fit is used.

53. For problems with few weights to be packed, small integer weights, and a small integer as bin capacity, this method can work well. However, when these special conditions are not met, it is very time-consuming to carry out this method. For example, imagine trying to use this method for 2000 random real numbers of the form $.xyz$, where x, y, and z are decimal digits and the bin capacity is 1.

54. The amount of time available to record on each side of a record can be thought of as a bin capacity. N records would mean that $2N$ bins would be available. However, since the movements should be configured consecutively, the algorithms we have developed might not yield acceptable solutions. Put somewhat differently, we are packing bins but with extra constraints on the packings. Tapes present similar problems to records since they involve taping in two directions on the same tape. In this sense (they do not have "two sides"), compact disks are closer to the model we have been using.

55. It makes sense to leave bins open as more items arrive to be packed if the cost of having many bins open at once is reasonable and there is room to have many partially-filled bins open without incurring great inconvenience or cost. One such example might be a company that has room for many identical trucks to park as they are loaded with goods to be delivered. There may be complex cost trade-offs between sending off fewer trucks because we wait to pack as much into each truck as possible and sending out more partially-filled trucks.

56. If one has to pack trucks of the same capacity using a single loading dock, it might be natural to send a truck on its way when the next item would not fit into the space left in the partially-filled truck. Any situation where keeping many bins up simultaneously is costly or storing an item temporarily is costly will encourage using an approach where when the next item will not fit into the currently open bin that bin is closed.

57. (a) The schedule with four secretaries is as follows: Processor 1: 25, 36, 15, 15, 19, 15, 27; Processor 2: 18, 32, 18, 31, 30, 18; Processor 3: 13, 30, 17, 12, 18, 16, 16, 16, 14; Processor 4: 19, 12, 25, 26, 18, 12, 24, 9.

The schedule with five secretaries is as follows: Processor 1: 25, 25, 31, 12, 16, 14; Processor 2: 18, 12, 17, 12, 15, 30, 9; Processor 3: 13, 32, 26, 16, 15, 18; Processor 4: 19, 36, 18, 19, 24; Processor 5: 30, 18, 15, 18, 16, 27.

(b) The decreasing time list is 36, 32, 31, 30, 30, 27, 26, 25, 25, 24, 19, 19, 18, 18, 18, 18, 18, 17, 16, 16, 16, 15, 15, 15, 14, 13, 12, 12, 12, 9.

The schedule using this list on four processors would be Processor 1: 36, 25, 19, 18, 17, 16, 13, 9; Processor 2: 32, 26, 25, 18, 16, 15, 12; Processor 3: 31, 27, 24, 18, 16, 15, 12, 12; Processor 4: 30, 30, 19, 18, 18, 15, 14.

The schedule using this list on five processors would be Processor 1: 36, 24, 18, 16, 14, 12; Processor 2: 32, 25, 18, 18, 15, 12; Processor 3: 31, 25, 19, 18, 15, 9; Processor 4: 30, 27, 18, 17, 15, 13; Processor 5: 30, 26, 19, 16, 16, 12.

(c) The five-processor decreasing-time schedule is optimal (time 120), but the four-processor decreasing-time schedule is not. One can see this, since when the task of length 17 scheduled on processor 1 and the task of length 18 on processor 3 are interchanged, the completion time is reduced to 154 from 155 for the four-processor, decreasing-time schedule.

(d) As a bin-packing problem, each bin will have a capacity of 60. Using the decreasing list, we obtain the following packings: (First-fit decreasing): Bin 1: 36, 24; Bin 2: 32, 27; Bin 3: 31, 26; Bin 4: 30, 30; Bin 5: 25, 25, 9; Bin 6: 19, 19, 18; Bin 7: 18, 18, 18; Bin 8: 18, 17, 16; Bin 9: 16, 16, 15, 13; Bin 10: 15, 15, 14, 12; Bin 11: 12, 12.

(e) NFD uses 13 bins. Bin 1: 36; Bin 2: 32; Bin 3: 31; Bin 4: 30, 30; Bin 5: 27, 26; Bin 6: 25, 25; Bin 7: 24, 19; Bin 8: 19, 18, 18; Bin 9: 18, 18, 18; Bin 10: 17, 16, 16; Bin 11: 16, 15, 15; Bin 12: 15, 14, 13, 12; Bin 13: 12, 12, 9. WFD uses 11 bins. Bin 1: 36, 24; Bin 2: 32, 26; Bin 3: 31, 27; Bin 4: 30, 30; Bin 5: 25, 25; Bin 6: 19, 19, 18; Bin 7: 18, 18, 18; Bin 8: 18, 17, 16; Bin 9: 16, 16, 15, 13; Bin 10: 15, 15, 14, 12; Bin 11: 12, 12, 9.

(f) An optimal packing with 10 bins exists. Bin 1: 36, 24; Bin 2: 32, 16, 12; Bin 3: 31, 17, 12; Bin 4: 30, 30; Bin 5: 27, 18, 15; Bin 6: 26, 18, 16; Bin 7: 25, 19, 16; Bin 8: 25, 19, 15; Bin 9: 18, 18, 12, 9; Bin 10: 18, 15, 14, 13.

58. <u>First-fit</u>

(a) First-fit, capacity 9:
  Bin 1: 8, 1;
  Bin 2: 5, 3, 1;
  Bin 3: 4, 3, 2;
  Bin 4: 7, 2;
  Bin 5: 8, 1;
  Bin 6: 8, 1;
  Bin 7: 6, 3;
  Bin 8: 5, 2, 2;
  Bin 9: 3, 5, 1;
  Bin 10: 4, 2, 3;
  Bin 11: 6, 2;
  Bin 12: 5, 4;
  Bin 13: 6, 2;
  Bin 14: 7;
  Bin 15: 7;
  Bin 16: 8;
  Bin 17: 6;
  Bin 18: 5, 4;
  Bin 19: 6;
  Bin 20: 4, 5;
  Bin 21: 7;
  Bin 22: 4.

(b) First-fit, capacity 10
  Bin 1: 8, 2;
  Bin 2: 5, 3, 1, 1;
  Bin 3: 4, 3, 3;
  Bin 4: 7, 2, 1;
  Bin 5: 8, 2;
  Bin 6: 8, 2;
  Bin 7: 6, 3, 1;
  Bin 8: 5, 5;
  Bin 9: 4, 2, 3, 1;
  Bin 10: 6, 4;
  Bin 11: 5, 2, 2;
  Bin 12: 6, 4;
  Bin 13: 7;
  Bin 14: 7;
  Bin 15: 8;
  Bin 16: 6, 4;
  Bin 17: 5, 5;
  Bin 18: 6, 4;
  Bin 19: 7.

(c) First-fit, capacity 11
  Bin 1: 8, 3;
  Bin 2: 5, 4, 2;
  Bin 3: 3, 6, 1, 1;
  Bin 4: 7, 3, 1;
  Bin 5: 8, 2, 1;
  Bin 6: 8, 2, 1;
  Bin 7: 5, 3, 2;
  Bin 8: 5, 4, 2;
  Bin 9: 6, 3, 2;
  Bin 10: 5, 4, 2;
  Bin 11: 6, 5;
  Bin 12: 7, 4;
  Bin 13: 7, 4;
  Bin 14: 8;
  Bin 15: 6, 5;
  Bin 16: 6, 4;
  Bin 17: 7.

(d) First-fit, capacity 12
  Bin 1: 8, 3, 1;
  Bin 2: 5, 4, 3;
  Bin 3: 7, 5;
  Bin 4: 8, 3, 1;
  Bin 5: 8, 2, 2;
  Bin 6: 6, 2, 1, 3;
  Bin 7: 5, 2, 4, 1;
  Bin 8: 2, 6, 3, 1;
  Bin 9: 5, 4, 2;
  Bin 10: 6, 6;
  Bin 11: 7, 5;
  Bin 12: 7, 4;
  Bin 13: 8, 4;
  Bin 14: 6, 5;
  Bin 15: 7, 2;
  Bin 16: 4.

Continued on next page

58. continued

<u>First-fit decreasing</u>
The decreasing list is: 8, 8, 8, 8, 7, 7, 7, 7, 6, 6, 6, 6, 6, 5, 5, 5, 5, 5, 5, 4, 4, 4, 4, 4, 4, 3, 3, 3, 3, 3, 2, 2, 2, 2, 2, 2, 2, 1, 1, 1, 1, 1.

(a) First-fit decreasing, capacity 9
   Bin 1: 8, 1;
   Bin 2: 8, 1;
   Bin 3: 8, 1:
   Bin 4: 8, 1;
   Bin 5: 7, 2;
   Bin 6: 7, 2;
   Bin 7: 7, 2;
   Bin 8: 7, 2;
   Bin 9: 6, 3;
   Bin 10: 6, 3;
   Bin 11: 6, 3;
   Bin 12: 6, 3;
   Bin 13: 6, 3;
   Bin 14: 5, 4;
   Bin 15: 5, 4;
   Bin 16: 5, 4;
   Bin 17: 5, 4;
   Bin 18: 5, 4;
   Bin 19: 5, 4;
   Bin 20: 2, 2, 2, 1.

(b) First-fit decreasing, capacity 10
   Bin 1: 8, 2;
   Bin 2: 8, 2;
   Bin 3: 8, 2;
   Bin 4: 8, 2;
   Bin 5: 7, 3;
   Bin 6: 7, 3;
   Bin 7: 7, 3;
   Bin 8: 7, 3;
   Bin 9: 6, 4;
   Bin 10: 6, 4;
   Bin 11: 6, 4;
   Bin 12: 6, 4;
   Bin 13: 6, 4;
   Bin 14: 5, 5;
   Bin 15: 5, 5;
   Bin 16: 5, 5;
   Bin 17: 4, 3, 2, 1;
   Bin 18: 2, 2, 1, 1, 1, 1.

(c) First-fit decreasing, capacity 11
   Bin 1: 8, 3;
   Bin 2: 8, 3;
   Bin 3: 8, 3;
   Bin 4: 8, 3;
   Bin 5: 7, 4;
   Bin 6: 7, 4;
   Bin 7: 7, 4;
   Bin 8: 7, 4;
   Bin 9: 6, 5;
   Bin 10: 6, 5;
   Bin 11: 6, 5;
   Bin 12: 6, 5;
   Bin 13: 6, 5;
   Bin 14: 5, 4, 2;
   Bin 15: 4, 3, 2, 2;
   Bin 16: 2, 2, 2, 2, 1, 1, 1;
   Bin 17: 1, 1.

(d) First-fit decreasing, capacity 12
   Bin 1: 8, 4;
   Bin 2: 8, 4;
   Bin 3: 8, 4;
   Bin 4: 8, 4;
   Bin 5: 7, 5;
   Bin 6: 7, 5;
   Bin 7: 7, 5;
   Bin 8: 7, 5;
   Bin 9: 6, 6;
   Bin 10: 6, 6;
   Bin 11: 6, 5, 1;
   Bin 12: 5, 4, 3;
   Bin 13: 4, 3, 3, 2;
   Bin 14: 3, 3, 2, 2, 2;
   Bin 15: 2, 2, 2, 1, 1, 1, 1.

All of the solutions using the decreasing list, with capacity 9–12 are optimal.

59. (a) Packing boxes of the same height into crates: packing want ads into a newspaper page.

   (b) We assume, without loss of generality, $p \geq q$. One heuristic, similar to first-fit, orders the rectangles $p \times q$ as in a dictionary (i.e., $p \times q$ listed prior to $r \times s$ if $p > r$ or $p = r$ and $q \geq s$). It then puts the rectangles in place in layers in a first-fit manner; that is, do not put a rectangle into a second layer until all positions on the first layer are filled. However, extra room in the first layer is "wasted."

   (c) The problem of packing rectangles of width 1 in an $m \times 1$ rectangle is a special case of the two-dimensional problem, equivalent to the bin-packing problem we have discussed.

   (d) Two 1×10 rectangles cannot be packed into a 5×4 rectangle, even though there would be an area of 20 in this rectangle.

60. One example would be scheduling advertisements in station breaks, where the breaks can have two different lengths. Variants of the algorithms for bins of one size can be developed; however, one must develop a way to address the fact that an item might fit in a bin of larger size, but not of smaller size.

61. There is an example of a bin-packing problem for which a given list takes a certain number of bins, and when an item is deleted from the list, more bins are required. In this example, the deleted item is not first in the list.

62. The answer to Exercise 54 mentions one such "paradoxical" situation. Another possible paradox would be: a given set of weights requires a certain number of bins; when these weights are all decreased by, say, 1, more bins are required. Still another possible paradox would be: a given set of weights requires, say, N bins of capacity W. When the capacity is increased to, say, $W + 1$, more than N bins are required. Problems such as these make nice research projects.

63. (a) Graphs (a), (d), (e), and (f) can be colored with three colors, but graphs (b) and (c) cannot.

   (b) Graphs (a), (b), (d), (e), and (f) can be colored with four colors, but graph (c) cannot.

   (c) The chromatic number for graphs (a) through (f) are, respectively, 3, 4, 5, 2, 3, and 2.

64. (a) The only graphs shown whose vertices can be colored with two colors are (b), (c), and (e).

   (b) The only graphs shown whose vertices can be colored with three colors are (b), (c), (e), and (h).

   (c) The chromatic number is 4 for (a), 2 for (b), 2 for (c), 4 for (d), 2 for (e), 6 for (f), 5 for (g), and 3 for (h).

65. (a) Construct the graph shown below:

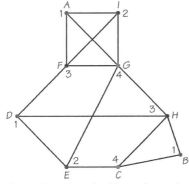

   The vertices of this graph can be colored with no fewer than four colors (1, 2, 3, 4 are used to denote the colors in the figure). Hence, four tanks can be used to display the fish.

   (b) The coloring in (a) shows that one can display two types of fish in three of the tanks, and three types of fish in one tank. Since 4 does not divide 9, one cannot do better.

66. (a) 5

(b) Yes, because 5 divides 10.

(c) Equalizing numbers in each enclosure may make observing this enclosure more interesting for the public. If the enclosures are not equal in size, equalization may mean that a small enclosure gets too many animals.

67. (a) The graph for this situation is shown below. The vertices can be labeled with the colors 1, 2, 3 as shown.

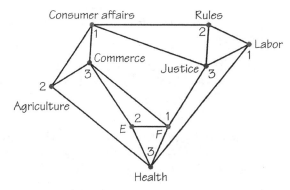

(b) Since the vertices can be colored with three colors (and no fewer), the minimum number of time slots for scheduling the committees is three.

(c) The committees can be scheduled in three rooms during each time slot. This might be significant if there were only three rooms that had microphone systems.

68. (a) The chromatic number is 4. There is a coloring using each color twice and one color three times. There is also a coloring using one color 4 times, two colors 2 times, and one color 1 time.

(b) There is a coloring with 5 colors, where each color is used twice.

(c) There is a coloring with 3 colors, where each color is used six times.

(d) There is a coloring with 4 colors, but the colors cannot be used equally often.

69. (a) Three time slots. To solve this problem, draw a graph by joining the vertices representing two committees if there is no x in the row and column of the table for these two committees.

(b) It is possible to three-color this graph so that each of the three colors is used three times. This means that one needs three rooms to arrange the scheduling of the nine committees.

70. (a) Three frequencies.

(b) Each frequency can be used twice.

71. Start at any vertex of the tree and label this vertex with color 1; color any vertex attached by an edge to this vertex with color 2. Continue to color the vertices in the tree in this manner, alternating the use of colors. If some vertex were attached to both a vertex colored 1 and another vertex colored 2, at some stage this would imply the graph had a circuit (of odd length), which is not possible, since trees have no circuits of any length.

72. Yes. The graph with the n vertices each joined to the others requires n colors.

73. The edge-coloring numbers for graphs (a) through (f) of Exercise 63 are, respectively, 6, 8, 6, 3, 3, and 4. The minimum edge-coloring number of any graph is either the maximal valence of any vertex in the graph or one more than the maximal valence. (This fact was discovered by the Russian mathematician Vizing.)

74. There are applications of edge colorings of graphs to designing timetables. Also, because one can find out information about vertex colorings for certain graphs by studying edge colorings, one can extend the applicability of the edge-coloring concept.

75. (a) Graph (a) four colors; graph (b) two colors; graph (c) four colors; graph (d) four colors; graph (e) two colors; graph (f) three colors.

(b) Coloring the maps of countries in an atlas would be one application of face colorings of graphs.

76. The minimum number of play groups is 3 because the chromatic number for this graph is 3. Since there are 7 children, the only number of play groups which could be set up which is conflict free would be if each child formed his/her own play group! With 3 play groups one can form two groups of size 2 and one group of size 3.

77. 3

78. Removing a single edge will not change the chromatic number of this graph.

Word Search Solution

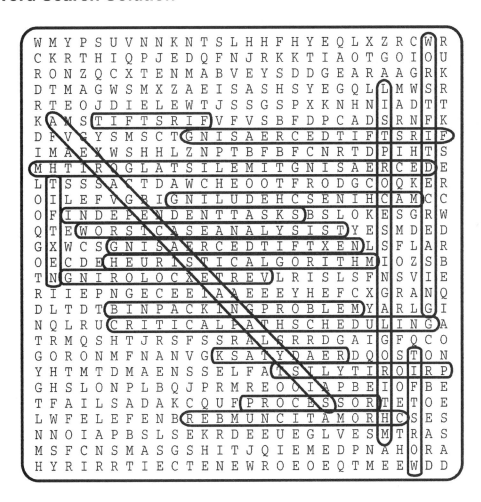

Chapter 4
Linear Programming

Chapter Outline

Introduction

Chapter Summary

A fundamental management problem that a company faces is determining how much of each of its products to produce in order to maximize profit. This problem is called a mixture problem, and linear programming is a powerful technique used to solve such problems. To get started, we must know certain information about the mixture problem:

- what products are to be made
- what resources will be needed
- how much of each resource is available
- how much of each resource is used by each product
- how much profit is generated by each unit of each product

The variables in the problem are the number of units of each product produced. They are assumed to be nonnegative (*minimum constraints*). A *production policy* is a specification of how many units of each product are to be made. To be achievable, a production policy has to satisfy the natural constraints of the problem, since no policy can use more of a resource than the company has available. Production policies satisfying all problem constraints are called *feasible solutions* to the problem, and the set of all feasible solutions is called the *feasible region*.

The profit function is an expression built from the variables and per-unit profits that tell us how much profit is produced by a given feasible solution. To solve our *mixture problem*, we need to find a feasible solution that produces the largest possible profit. *Linear programming* applies in the case when the problem constraints are linear inequalities and the profit function is linear in the variables. In this case, the feasible region is polygonal in 2-space and polyhedral in 3-space. It will have an analogous structure in higher dimensions.

The geometry of this situation is crucial to the solution. A fundamental result, the *corner point principle*, states that the optimal solution occurs at a corner of the feasible region. This result suggests a possible solution strategy.

- find all corners of the feasible region
- determine the profit at each corner point
- choose the production policy of any corner producing the maximum profit

Computationally, this procedure suffers from the same problem as the brute force method applied to the TSP; for large problems there are just too many corners to check quickly. Fortunately, faster algorithms exist to solve linear programming problems. The simplex method developed by George Dantzig starts at some corner of the feasible region and then moves from corner to neighboring corner, always going to a corner where profit is the same or larger, until it locates a corner producing maximum profit. An alternative to the simplex method is Karmarker's algorithm, which bores into the interior of the feasible region to decide which corner to examine next. The simplex method is fast in practice but can be shown no more efficient than the brute force method on certain cleverly constructed problems. Karmarker's algorithm provides a computationally efficient method for solving linear programming problems.

In the transportation problem, we are interested in meeting demands while minimizing cost. Information can be set up in a *tableau*. The tableau shows costs and *rim conditions* for the transporation problem. Using the *Northwest Corner Rule* (*NCR*), we can obtain a feasible solution. This solution, however, may not be optimal. By calculating and comparing the values of *indicator cells*, we can improve on the feasible solution. Using the *stepping stone method*, we look at indicator cells that have negative values and determine an optimal solution.

Skill Objectives

1. Create a chart to represent the given information in a linear programming problem with two variables.

2. From its associated chart, write the constraints of a linear programming problem as linear inequalities.

3. List two implied constraints in every linear programming problem.

4. Formulate a profit equation for a linear-programming problem when given the per-unit profits.

5. Describe the graphical implications of the implied constraints $x \geq 0$ and $y \geq 0$.

6. Draw the graph of a line in a coordinate-axis system.

7. Graph a linear inequality in a coordinate-axis system.

8. Determine by a substitution process whether a point with given coordinates is contained in the graph of a linear inequality.

9. Indicate the feasible region for a linear programming problem by shading the graphical intersection of its constraints.

10. Locate the corner points of a feasible region from its graph.

11. Evaluate the profit function at each corner point of a feasible region.

12. Apply the corner point theorem to determine the maximum profit for a linear programming problem.

13. Interpret the corner point producing the maximum profit as the solution to the corresponding linear programming problem.

14. List two methods for solving linear programming problems with many variables.

15. Given a tableau, apply the Northwest Corner Rule to find a feasible solution.

16. Calculate the cost of the system found by the Northwest Corner Rule.

17. Calculate the value of indicator cells.

18. Use the stepping stone method to find an optimal solution.

Teaching Tips

1.   The material differs significantly from that in other texts. The basic ideas are introduced one at a time; first, mixture problems having just one resource, then resource constraints are added, followed by minimum quantities for products and, finally, two products and two resources. Along the way, the students are introduced to the profit function, making mixture charts, the feasible region, and the corner principle.   Although this approach is nonstandard, the slow buildup of ideas enables students to comprehend the material more thoroughly.

2.   Because many of the students taking this course have only an algebra background, a review of coordinate graphing is often helpful. This is especially true when graphing linear inequalities. The concept of selecting a test point often requires additional explanation.

3.   A short review of the concept of set intersection may be helpful when indicating the feasible region on a linear programming graph.

4.   The instructor will need to decide whether to require the student to find the intersection point of two boundary lines by solving a system of linear equations, or to have the coordinates of that point provided to the student.   Requiring the solution will probably necessitate reviewing that procedure in class discussion.

5.   When setting up the chart for a linear programming problem, you may want to interchange the rows and columns in the text example.   If the variables name the columns and the resources the rows, then the inequalities can be written easily from the chart in a horizontal fashion. This may be easier for the student because of its visual simplicity.

6.   When graphing several linear inequalities, students find it helpful to have colored pens or pencils to indicate the different half-planes.   It is then easier to find the feasible region because the intersection is the region that contains all the colors.

7.   Text Exercises 30–41 offer a variety of settings for linear programming problems. These can be used to advantage in working through examples with students.

8.   You may choose to prepare in advance blank tableaux for students to use during lecture of applying the Northwest Corner Rule to find a feasible solution.

Research Paper

In this chapter, two methods for solving linear programming problems with many variables are briefly discussed.   These are the simplex method and Karmarkar's algorithm.   Prior to Karmarkar's algorithm (1984), Leonid Khaciyan presented a method guaranteeing to solve any linear programming problem in 1979.   Students can further investigate these methods and their origins, discuss their similarities and differences, or prepare a general discussion of the contributions of these two mathematicians.

Collaborative Learning

Linear Programming

You live on a farm and bake chocolate chip cookies and chocolate chip muffins in your home, and sell them to the public. One morning, you check your supplies and discover that you are low on flour and chocolate chips, but have plenty of the other ingredients. Your car is in the repair shop and there are 2 feet of snow on the ground, so there is no way to replenish your supplies until tomorrow.

Each batch of cookies requires 2 pounds of flour and 1 pound of chocolate chips; each batch of muffins uses 3 pounds of flour and 2 pounds of chocolate chips. You have 60 pounds of flour and 36 pounds of chocolate chips on hand.

Your profit on each batch of cookies is $8, and on muffins your profit is $13 per batch. How should you divide your baking between cookies and muffins in order to maximize your profit for the day?

Hints:

a. If no cookies are baked, how many batches of muffins can be baked? What will the profit be in this case?

b. Answer the same questions if no muffins are baked.

c. Which is more profitable: baking only cookies or only muffins?

d. Is there a mix of cookies and muffins that makes even more money than either only muffins or only cookies?

Solutions

Skills Check:

1. a   2. c   3. b   4. b   5. b   6. c   7. c   8. c   9. b   10. c

11. b   12. c   13. c   14. c   15. c   16. c   17. c   18. a   19. a   20. c

Exercises:

1. (a) $2x + 3y = 12$

   y-intercept: Substitute $x = 0$. x-intercept: Substitute $y = 0$.

   $2(0) + 3y = 12$ $2x + 3(0) = 12$

   $0 + 3y = 12$ $2x + 0 = 12$

   $3y = 12 \Rightarrow y = \frac{12}{3} = 4$ $2x = 12 \Rightarrow x = \frac{12}{2} = 6$

   y-intercept is $(0, 4)$. x-intercept is $(6, 0)$.

   Graph:

   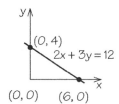

   (b) $3x + 5y = 30$

   y-intercept: Substitute $x = 0$. x-intercept: Substitute $y = 0$.

   $3(0) + 5y = 30$ $3x + 5(0) = 30$

   $0 + 5y = 30$ $3x + 0 = 30$

   $5y = 30 \Rightarrow y = \frac{30}{5} = 6$ $3x = 30 \Rightarrow x = \frac{30}{3} = 10$

   y-intercept is $(0, 6)$. x-intercept is $(10, 0)$.

   Graph:

   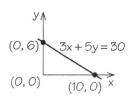

   (c) $4x + 3y = 24$

   y-intercept: Substitute $x = 0$. x-intercept: Substitute $y = 0$.

   $4(0) + 3y = 24$ $4x + 3(0) = 24$

   $0 + 3y = 24$ $4x + 0 = 24$

   $3y = 24 \Rightarrow y = \frac{24}{3} = 8$ $4x = 24 \Rightarrow x = \frac{24}{4} = 6$

   y-intercept is $(0, 8)$. x-intercept is $(6, 0)$.

   Graph:

   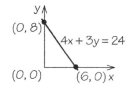

Continued on next page

1.   continued

(d) $7x + 4y = 42$

   y-intercept: Substitute $x = 0$.

   $7(0) + 4y = 42$

   $0 + 4y = 42$

   $4y = 42 \Rightarrow y = \frac{42}{4} = 10.5$

   y-intercept is $(0, 10.5)$.

   x-intercept: Substitute $y = 0$.

   $7x + 4(0) = 42$

   $7x + 0 = 42$

   $7x = 42 \Rightarrow x = \frac{42}{7} = 6$

   x-intercept is $(6, 0)$.

   Graph:

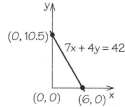

(e) $x = -3$

   This form represents a vertical line.

   y-intercept: None

   x-intercept: $(-3, 0)$.

   Graph:

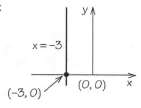

(f) $y = 6$

   This form represents a horizontal line.

   y-intercept is $(0, 6)$.

   x-intercept: None

   Graph:

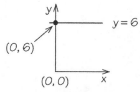

2.   (a) $4x + 3y = 18$ and $x = 0$

   Note: This situation is shown only for the first quadrant.

   The y-intercept of $4x + 3y = 18$ can be found by substituting $x = 0$.

   $4(0) + 3y = 18$

   $0 + 3y = 18 \Rightarrow 3y = 18 \Rightarrow y = \frac{18}{3} = 6$

   The y-intercept is $(0, 6)$.

   The x-intercept of $4x + 3y = 18$ can be found by substituting $y = 0$.

   $4x + 3(0) = 18$

   $4x + 0 = 18 \Rightarrow 4x = 18 \Rightarrow x = \frac{18}{4} = 4.5$

   The x-intercept is $(4.5, 0)$.

   $x = 0$ represents a vertical line, namely the y-axis.

   Continued on next page

2. **(a)** continued

To find the point of intersection, substitute $x = 0$ into $4x + 3y = 18$.

$$4(0) + 3y = 18$$
$$0 + 3y = 18$$
$$3y = 18 \Rightarrow y = \tfrac{18}{3} = 6$$

The point of intersection is therefore $(0, 6)$.

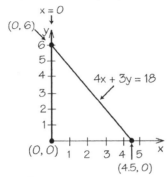

(b) $5x + 3y = 45$ and $y = -5$

Note: This situation is shown only for the first and fourth quadrants.

The y-intercept of $5x + 3y = 45$ can be found by substituting $x = 0$.

$$5(0) + 3y = 45$$
$$0 + 3y = 45$$
$$3y = 45 \Rightarrow y = \tfrac{45}{3} = 15$$

The y-intercept is $(0, 15)$.

The x-intercept of $5x + 3y = 45$ can be found by substituting $y = 0$.

$$5x + 3(0) = 45$$
$$5x + 0 = 45$$
$$5x = 45 \Rightarrow x = \tfrac{45}{5} = 9$$

The x-intercept is $(9, 0)$.

$y = -5$ represents a horizontal line, which lies below the x-axis.

To find the point of intersection, substitute $y = -5$ into $5x + 3y = 45$.

$$5x + 3(-5) = 45$$
$$5x + (-15) = 45$$
$$5x - 15 = 45$$
$$5x = 60 \Rightarrow x = \tfrac{60}{5} = 12$$

The point of intersection is therefore $(12, -5)$.

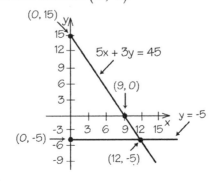

3.   Note: These situations are shown only for the first quadrant.

(a) $x + y = 10$ and $x + 2y = 14$

The y-intercept of $x + y = 10$ can be found by substituting $x = 0$.

$$0 + y = 10$$
$$y = 10$$

The y-intercept is $(0, 10)$.

The x-intercept of $x + y = 10$ can be found by substituting $y = 0$.

$$x + 0 = 10$$
$$x = 10$$

The x-intercept is $(10, 0)$.

The y-intercept of $x + 2y = 14$ can be found by substituting $x = 0$.

$$0 + 2y = 14$$
$$2y = 14$$
$$y = \tfrac{14}{2} = 7$$

The y-intercept is $(0, 7)$.

The x-intercept of $x + 2y = 14$ can be found by substituting $y = 0$.

$$x + 2(0) = 14$$
$$x + 0 = 14$$
$$x = 14$$

The x-intercept is $(14, 0)$.

To find the point of intersection, we can multiply both sides of $x + y = 10$ by -1, and add the result to $x + 2y = 14$.

$$-x - y = -10$$
$$\underline{x + 2y = 14}$$
$$y = 4$$

Substitute $y = 4$ into $x + y = 10$ to solve to x.

$$x + 4 = 10 \Rightarrow x = 6$$

The point of intersection is therefore $(6, 4)$.

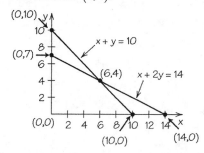

Continued on next page

3. continued

(b) $y - 2x = 0$ and $x = 4$

$x = 4$ represents a vertical line, which lies to the right of the y-axis.

By substituting either $x = 0$ or $y = 0$, we see that $y - 2x = 0$ passes through $(0,0)$, the origin. By substituting an arbitrary value (except 0) for one of the variables, we can find another point that lies on the graph of $y - 2x = 0$. Since we see the point of intersection with the graph of $x = 4$, we could use this value.

$$y - 2(4) = 0$$
$$y - 8 = 0$$
$$y = 8$$

Thus, a second point on the graph of $y - 2x = 0$ is $(4,8)$. This is also the point of intersection between the two lines.

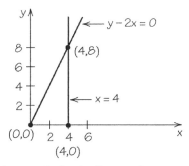

4. Note: These situations are shown only for the first quadrant.

(a) $x \geq 8$

The graph of $x = 8$ represents a vertical line with x-intercept $(8,0)$. Since any value of x to the right of this line is greater than 8, we shade the portion to the right of this vertical line.

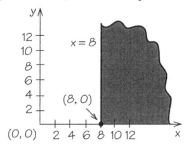

(b) $y \geq 5$

The graph of $y = 5$ represents a horizontal line with y-intercept $(0,5)$. Since any value of y above this line is greater than 5, we shade the portion above this horizontal line.

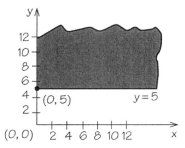

Continued on next page

4.   continued

(c) $5x + 3y \leq 15$

The y-intercept of $5x + 3y = 15$ can be found by substituting $x = 0$.

$$5(0) + 3y = 15 \Rightarrow 0 + 3y = 15 \Rightarrow 3y = 15 \Rightarrow y = \tfrac{15}{3} = 5$$

The y-intercept is $(0, 5)$.

The x-intercept of $5x + 3y = 15$ can be found by substituting $y = 0$.

$$5x + 3(0) = 15 \Rightarrow 5x + 0 = 15 \Rightarrow 5x = 15 \Rightarrow x = \tfrac{15}{5} = 3$$

The x-intercept is $(3, 0)$.

We draw a line connecting these points. Testing the point $(0, 0)$, we have the statement $5(0) + 3(0) \leq 15$ or $0 \leq 15$. This is a true statement, thus we shade the half-plane containing our test point, the down side of the line.

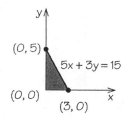

(d) $4x + 5y \leq 30$

The y-intercept of $4x + 5y = 30$ can be found by substituting $x = 0$.

$$4(0) + 5y = 30 \Rightarrow 0 + 5y = 30 \Rightarrow 5y = 30 \Rightarrow y = \tfrac{30}{5} = 6$$

The y-intercept is $(0, 6)$.

The x-intercept of $4x + 5y = 30$ can be found by substituting $y = 0$.

$$4x + 5(0) = 30 \Rightarrow 4x + 0 = 30 \Rightarrow 4x = 30 \Rightarrow x = \tfrac{30}{4} = 7.5$$

The x-intercept is $(7.5, 0)$.

We draw a line connecting these points. Testing the point $(0, 0)$, we have the statement $4(0) + 5(0) \leq 30$ or $0 \leq 30$. This is a true statement, thus we shade the half-plane containing our test point, the down side of the line.

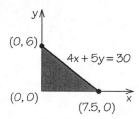

5.   Note: These situations are shown only for the first quadrant.

(a) $x \geq 4$

The graph of $x = 4$ represents a vertical line with x-intercept $(4,0)$. Since any value of x to the right of this line is greater than 4, we shade the portion to the right of this vertical line.

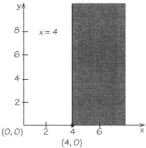

(b) $y \geq 9$

The graph of $y = 9$ represents a horizontal line with y-intercept $(0,9)$. Since any value of y above this line is greater than 9, we shade the portion above this horizontal line.

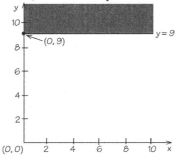

(c) $3x + 2y \leq 18$

The y-intercept of $3x + 2y = 18$ can be found by substituting $x = 0$.

$$3(0) + 2y = 18 \Rightarrow 0 + 2y = 18 \Rightarrow 2y = 18 \Rightarrow y = \tfrac{18}{2} = 9$$

The y-intercept is $(0,9)$.

The x-intercept of $3x + 2y = 18$ can be found by substituting $y = 0$.

$$3x + 2(0) = 18 \Rightarrow 3x + 0 = 18 \Rightarrow 3x = 18 \Rightarrow x = \tfrac{18}{3} = 6$$

The x-intercept is $(6,0)$.

We draw a line connecting these points. Testing the point $(0,0)$, we have the statement $3(0) + 2(0) \leq 18$ or $0 \leq 18$. This is a true statement, thus we shade the half-plane containing our test point, the down side of the line.

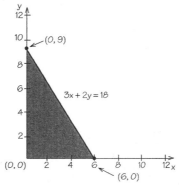

Continued on next page

5.   continued
   (d) $7x + 2y \leq 42$

   The y-intercept of $7x + 2y = 42$ can be found by substituting $x = 0$.

   $$7(0) + 2y = 42 \Rightarrow 0 + 2y = 42 \Rightarrow 2y = 42 \Rightarrow y = \tfrac{42}{2} = 21$$

   The y-intercept is $(0, 21)$.

   The x-intercept of $7x + 2y = 42$ can be found by substituting $y = 0$.

   $$7x + 2(0) = 42 \Rightarrow 7x + 0 = 42 \Rightarrow 7x = 42 \Rightarrow x = \tfrac{42}{7} = 6$$

   The x-intercept is $(6, 0)$.

   We draw a line connecting these points. Testing the point $(0,0)$, we have the statement $7(0) + 2(0) \leq 42$ or $0 \leq 42$. This is a true statement, thus we shade the half-plane containing our test point, the down side of the line.

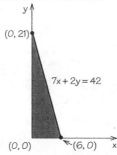

6.   (a) $2x + 4y \leq 28$

   (b) $2x + 0.5y \leq 40$ (pruning)

   $0.5x + 0.25y \leq 2$ (shredding)

7.   (a) $6x + 4y \leq 300$

   (b) $30x + 72y \leq 420$

8. $12x + 10y \leq 640$ (beef)

   $4x + 3y \leq 480$ (pork)

9. $x \geq 0;\ y \geq 0;\ x + 2y \leq 12$

   The constraints of $x \geq 0$ and $y \geq 0$ indicate that we are restricted to the upper right quadrant created by the x-axis and y-axis.

   The y-intercept of $x + 2y = 12$ can be found by substituting $x = 0$.

   $$0 + 2y = 12 \Rightarrow 2y = 12 \Rightarrow y = \tfrac{12}{2} = 6$$

   The y-intercept is $(0, 6)$.

   The x-intercept of $x + 2y = 12$ can be found by substituting $y = 0$.

   $$x + 2(0) = 12 \Rightarrow x + 0 = 12 \Rightarrow x = 12$$

   The x-intercept is $(12, 0)$.

   We draw a line connecting these points. Testing the point $(0,0)$, we have the statement $0 + 2(0) \leq 12$ or $0 \leq 12$. This is a true statement, thus we shade the half-plane containing our test point, the down side of the line, which is contained in the upper right quadrant.

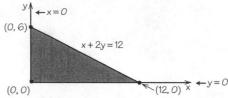

10. $x \geq 0;\ y \geq 0;\ 2x + y \leq 10$

The constraints of $x \geq 0$ and $y \geq 0$ indicate that we are restricted to the upper right quadrant created by the x-axis and y-axis.

The y-intercept of $2x + y = 10$ can be found by substituting $x = 0$.

$$2(0) + y = 10 \Rightarrow 0 + y = 10 \Rightarrow y = 10$$

The y-intercept is $(0, 10)$.

The x-intercept of $2x + y = 10$ can be found by substituting $y = 0$.

$$2x + 0 = 10 \Rightarrow 2x = 10 \Rightarrow x = \tfrac{10}{2} = 5$$

The x-intercept is $(5, 0)$.

We draw a line connecting these points. Testing the point $(0, 0)$, we have the statement $2(0) + 0 \leq 10$ or $0 \leq 10$. This is a true statement, thus we shade the half-plane containing our test point, the down side of the line, which is contained in the upper right quadrant.

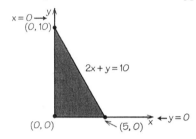

11. $x \geq 0;\ y \geq 0;\ 2x + 5y \leq 60$

The constraints of $x \geq 0$ and $y \geq 0$ indicate that we are restricted to the upper right quadrant created by the x-axis and y-axis.

The y-intercept of $2x + 5y = 60$ can be found by substituting $x = 0$.

$$2(0) + 5y = 60 \Rightarrow 0 + 5y = 60 \Rightarrow y = \tfrac{60}{5} = 12$$

The y-intercept is $(0, 12)$.

The x-intercept of $2x + 5y = 60$ can be found by substituting $y = 0$.

$$2x + 5(0) = 60 \Rightarrow 2x + 0 = 60 \Rightarrow 2x = 60 \Rightarrow x = \tfrac{60}{2} = 30$$

The x-intercept is $(30, 0)$.

We draw a line connecting these points. Testing the point $(0, 0)$, we have the statement $2(0) + 5(0) \leq 60$ or $0 \leq 60$. This is a true statement, thus we shade the half-plane containing our test point, the down side of the line, which is contained in the upper right quadrant.

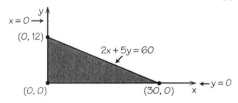

12. $x \geq 10;\ y \geq 0;\ 3x + 5y \leq 120$

The constraints of $x \geq 10$ and $y \geq 0$ indicate that we are restricted to the upper right quadrant, to the right of the vertical line $x = 10$.

The point of intersection between $x = 10$ and $3x + 5y = 120$ can be found by substituting $x = 10$ into $3x + 5y = 120$.

$$3(10) + 5y = 120 \Rightarrow 30 + 5y = 120 \Rightarrow 5y = 90 \Rightarrow y = \tfrac{90}{5} = 18$$

Thus, the point of intersection is $(10, 18)$.

The y-intercept of $3x + 5y = 120$ can be found by substituting $x = 0$.

$$3(0) + 5y = 120 \Rightarrow 0 + 5y = 120 \Rightarrow y = \tfrac{120}{5} = 24$$

The y-intercept is $(0, 24)$.

The x-intercept of $3x + 5y = 120$ can be found by substituting $y = 0$.

$$3x + 5(0) = 120 \Rightarrow 3x + 0 = 120 \Rightarrow 3x = 120 \Rightarrow x = \tfrac{120}{3} = 40$$

The x-intercept is $(40, 0)$.

We draw a line connecting these points. Testing the point $(0, 0)$, we have the statement $2(0) + 5(0) \leq 120$ or $0 \leq 120$. This is a true statement, thus we shade the half-plane containing our test point, the down side of the line, which is contained in the upper right quadrant to the right of the vertical line $x = 10$.

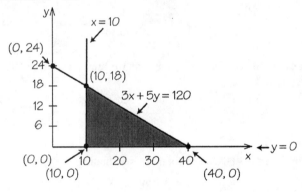

13. $x \geq 0; \; y \geq 4; \; x + y \leq 20$

The constraints of $x \geq 0$ and $y \geq 4$ indicate that we are restricted to the upper right quadrant, above the horizontal line $y = 4$.

The point of intersection between $y = 4$ and $x + y = 20$ can be found by substituting $y = 4$ into $x + y = 20$.

$$x + 4 = 20 \Rightarrow x = 16$$

Thus, the point of intersection is $(16, 4)$.

The y-intercept of $x + y = 20$ can be found by substituting $x = 0$.

$$0 + y = 20 \Rightarrow y = 20$$

The y-intercept is $(0, 20)$.

The x-intercept of $x + y = 20$ can be found by substituting $y = 0$.

$$x + 0 = 20 \Rightarrow x = 20$$

The x-intercept is $(20, 0)$.

We draw a line connecting these points. Testing the point $(0,0)$, we have the statement $0 + 0 \leq 20$ or $0 \leq 20$. This is a true statement, thus we shade the half-plane containing our test point, the down side of the line, which is contained in the upper right quadrant above the horizontal line $y = 4$.

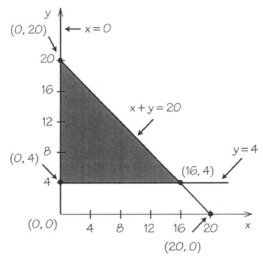

14. $x \geq 2; \, y \geq 6; \, 3x + 2y \leq 30$

The constraints of $x \geq 2$ and $y \geq 6$ indicate that we are restricted to the upper right quadrant, to the right of the vertical line $x = 2$ and above the horizontal line $y = 6$.

The point of intersection between $x = 2$ and $y = 6$ is $(2,6)$.

The point of intersection between $x = 2$ and $3x + 2y = 30$ can be found by substituting $x = 2$ into $3x + 2y = 30$.

$$3(2) + 2y = 30 \Rightarrow 6 + 2y = 30 \Rightarrow 2y = 24 \Rightarrow y = \tfrac{24}{2} = 12$$

Thus, the point of intersection is $(2,12)$.

The point of intersection between $y = 6$ and $3x + 2y = 30$ can be found by substituting $y = 6$ into $3x + 2y = 30$.

$$3x + 2(6) = 30 \Rightarrow 3x + 12 = 30 \Rightarrow 3x = 18 \Rightarrow x = \tfrac{18}{3} = 6$$

Thus, the point of intersection is $(6,6)$.

The y-intercept of $3x + 2y = 30$ can be found by substituting $x = 0$.

$$3(0) + 2y = 30 \Rightarrow 0 + 2y = 30 \Rightarrow 2y = 30 \Rightarrow y = \tfrac{30}{2} = 15$$

The y-intercept is $(0,15)$.

The x-intercept of $3x + 2y = 30$ can be found by substituting $y = 0$.

$$3x + 2(0) = 30 \Rightarrow 3x + 0 = 30 \Rightarrow 3x = 30 \Rightarrow x = \tfrac{30}{3} = 10$$

The x-intercept is $(10,0)$.

We draw a line connecting these points. Testing the point $(0,0)$, we have the statement $3(0) + 2(0) \leq 30$ or $0 \leq 30$. This is a true statement, thus we shade the half-plane containing our test point, the down side of the line, which is contained in the upper right quadrant to the right of the vertical line $x = 2$ and above the horizontal line $y = 6$.

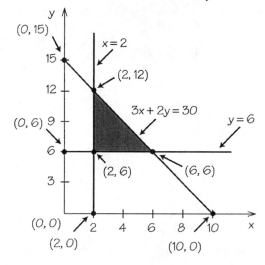

15. For Exercise 9: $x \geq 0$; $y \geq 0$; $x + 2y \leq 12$

$(2,4)$: Since $2 \geq 0$, the constraint $x \geq 0$ is satisfied.

Since $4 \geq 0$, the constraint $y \geq 0$ is satisfied.

Since $2 + 2(4) = 2 + 8 = 10 \leq 12$, the condition $x + 2y \leq 12$ is satisfied.

Thus, $(2,4)$ is feasible.

$(10,6)$: Since $10 \geq 0$, the constraint $x \geq 0$ is satisfied.

Since $6 \geq 0$, the constraint $y \geq 0$ is satisfied.

Since $10 + 2(6) = 10 + 12 = 22 > 12$, the condition $x + 2y \leq 12$ is not satisfied.

Thus, $(10,6)$ is not feasible.

For Exercise 11: $x \geq 0$; $y \geq 0$; $2x + 5y \leq 60$

$(2,4)$: Since $2 \geq 0$, the constraint $x \geq 0$ is satisfied.

Since $4 \geq 0$, the constraint $y \geq 0$ is satisfied.

Since $2(2) + 5(4) = 4 + 20 = 24 \leq 60$, the condition $x + 2y \leq 12$ is satisfied.

Thus, $(2,4)$ is feasible.

$(10,6)$: Since $10 \geq 0$, the constraint $x \geq 0$ is satisfied.

Since $6 \geq 0$, the constraint $y \geq 0$ is satisfied.

Since $2(10) + 5(6) = 20 + 30 = 50 \leq 60$, the condition $x + 2y \leq 12$ is satisfied.

Thus, $(10,6)$ is feasible.

For Exercise 13: $x \geq 0$; $y \geq 4$; $x + y \leq 20$

$(2,4)$: Since $2 \geq 0$, the constraint $x \geq 0$ is satisfied.

Since $4 \geq 4$, the constraint $y \geq 4$ is satisfied.

Since $2 + 4 = 6 \leq 20$, the condition $x + y \leq 20$ is satisfied.

Thus, $(2,4)$ is feasible. Note: It is on the boundary.

$(10,6)$: Since $10 \geq 0$, the constraint $x \geq 0$ is satisfied.

Since $6 \geq 4$, the constraint $y \geq 4$ is satisfied.

Since $10 + 6 = 16 \leq 20$, the condition $x + y \leq 20$ is satisfied.

Thus, $(10,6)$ is feasible.

16. For Exercise 10: $x \geq 0$; $y \geq 0$; $2x + y \leq 10$

$(2,4)$: Since $2 \geq 0$, the constraint $x \geq 0$ is satisfied.

Since $4 \geq 0$, the constraint $y \geq 0$ is satisfied.

Since $2(2) + 4 = 4 + 4 = 8 \leq 10$, the condition $2x + y \leq 10$ is satisfied.

Thus, $(2,4)$ is feasible.

$(10,6)$: Since $10 \geq 0$, the constraint $x \geq 0$ is satisfied.

Since $6 \geq 0$, the constraint $y \geq 0$ is satisfied.

Since $2(10) + 6 = 20 + 6 = 26 > 10$, the condition $2x + y \leq 10$ is not satisfied.

Thus, $(10,6)$ is not feasible.

Continued on next page

16. continued

For Exercise 12: $x \geq 10; y \geq 0; 3x + 5y \leq 120$

$(2,4):$ Since $2 < 10,$ the constraint $x \geq 10$ is not satisfied.

Thus, $(2,4)$ is not feasible. Note: There is no need to check the other constraints.

$(10,6):$ Since $10 \geq 10,$ the constraint $x \geq 10$ is satisfied.

Since $6 \geq 0,$ the constraint $y \geq 0$ is satisfied.

Since $3(10) + 5(6) = 30 + 30 = 60 \leq 120,$ the condition $3x + 5y \leq 120$ is satisfied.

Thus, $(10,6)$ is feasible. Note: It is on the boundary.

For Exercise 14: $x \geq 2; y \geq 6; 3x + 2y \leq 30$

$(2,4):$ Since $2 \geq 2,$ the constraint $x \geq 2$ is satisfied.

Since $4 < 6,$ the constraint $y \geq 6$ is not satisfied.

Thus, $(2,4)$ is not feasible. Note: There is no need to check the other constraint.

$(10,6):$ Since $10 \geq 2,$ the constraint $x \geq 2$ is satisfied.

Since $6 \geq 6,$ the constraint $y \geq 6$ is satisfied.

Since $3(10) + 2(6) = 30 + 12 = 42 > 30,$ the condition $3x + 2y \leq 30$ is not satisfied.

Thus, $(10,6)$ is not feasible.

17. We wish to maximize $\$2.30x + \$3.70y.$

Corner Point	Value of the Profit Formula: $\$2.30x + \$3.70y$								
$(0,0)$	$\$2.30(0)$	+	$\$3.70(0)$	=	$\$0.00$	+	$\$0.00$	=	$\$0.00$
$(0,30)$	$\$2.30(0)$	+	$\$3.70(30)$	=	$\$0.00$	+	$\$111.00$	=	$\$111.00*$
$(12,0)$	$\$2.30(12)$	+	$\$3.70(0)$	=	$\$27.60$	+	$\$0.00$	=	$\$27.60$

Optimal production policy: Make 0 skateboards and 30 dolls for a profit of $111.

18. We wish to maximize $\$5.50x + \$1.80y.$

Corner Point	Value of the Profit Formula: $\$5.50x + \$1.80y$								
$(0,0)$	$\$5.50(0)$	+	$\$1.80(0)$	=	$\$0.00$	+	$\$0.00$	=	$\$0.00$
$(0,30)$	$\$5.50(0)$	+	$\$1.80(30)$	=	$\$0.00$	+	$\$54.00$	=	$\$54.00$
$(12,0)$	$\$5.50(12)$	+	$\$1.80(0)$	=	$\$66.00$	+	$\$0.00$	=	$\$66.00*$

Optimal production policy: Make 12 skateboards and 0 dolls for a profit of $66.

19. Note: These situations are shown only for the first quadrant.

(a) $5x + 4y = 22$ and $5x + 10y = 40$

The y-intercept of $5x + 4y = 22$ can be found by substituting $x = 0$.

$$5(0) + 4y = 22$$
$$0 + 4y = 22$$
$$4y = 22$$
$$y = \tfrac{22}{4} = 5.5$$

The y-intercept is $(0, 5.5)$.

The x-intercept of $5x + 4y = 22$ can be found by substituting $y = 0$.

$$5x + 4(0) = 22$$
$$5x + 0 = 22$$
$$5x = 22$$
$$x = \tfrac{22}{5} = 4.4$$

The x-intercept is $(4.4, 0)$.

The y-intercept of $5x + 10y = 40$ can be found by substituting $x = 0$.

$$5(0) + 10y = 40$$
$$0 + 10y = 40$$
$$y = \tfrac{40}{10} = 4$$

The y-intercept is $(0, 4)$.

The x-intercept of $5x + 10y = 40$ can be found by substituting $y = 0$.

$$5x + 10(0) = 40$$
$$5x + 0 = 40$$
$$5x = 40$$
$$x = \tfrac{40}{4} = 8$$

The x-intercept is $(8, 0)$.

To find the point of intersection, we can multiply both sides of $5x + 4y = 22$ by -1, and adding the result to $5x + 10y = 40$.

$$-5x - 4y = -22$$
$$\underline{5x + 10y = 40}$$
$$6y = 18 \Rightarrow y = \tfrac{18}{6} = 3$$

Substitute $y = 3$ into $5x + 10y = 40$ and solve for x.

$$5x + 10(3) = 40 \Rightarrow 5x + 30 = 40 \Rightarrow 5x = 10 \Rightarrow x = \tfrac{10}{5} = 2$$

The point of intersection is therefore $(2, 3)$.

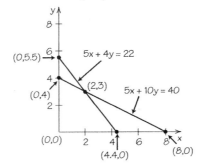

Continued on next page

19. continued

(b) $x + y = 7$ and $3x + 4y = 24$

The y-intercept of $x + y = 7$ can be found by substituting $x = 0$.

$$0 + y = 7$$
$$y = 7$$

The y-intercept is $(0, 7)$.

The x-intercept of $x + y = 7$ can be found by substituting $y = 0$.

$$x + 0 = 7$$
$$x = 7$$

The x-intercept is $(7, 0)$.

The y-intercept of $3x + 4y = 24$ can be found by substituting $x = 0$.

$$3(0) + 4y = 24$$
$$0 + 4y = 24$$
$$y = \tfrac{24}{4} = 6$$

The y-intercept is $(0, 6)$.

The x-intercept of $3x + 4y = 24$ can be found by substituting $y = 0$.

$$3x + 4(0) = 24$$
$$3x + 0 = 24$$
$$3x = 24$$
$$x = \tfrac{24}{3} = 8$$

The x-intercept is $(8, 0)$.

To find the point of intersection, we can multiply both sides of $x + y = 7$ by -3, and adding the result to $3x + 4y = 24$

$$-3x - 3y = -21$$
$$\underline{3x + 4y = 24}$$
$$y = 3$$

Substitute $y = 3$ into $3x + 4y = 24$ and solve for x.

$$3x + 4(3) = 24 \Rightarrow 3x + 12 = 24 \Rightarrow 3x = 12 \Rightarrow x = \tfrac{12}{3} = 4$$

The point of intersection is therefore $(4, 3)$.

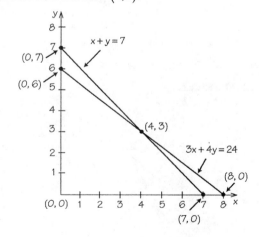

20. $x \geq 0; \; y \geq 0; \; 3x + y \leq 9; \; x + 2y \leq 8$

The constraints of $x \geq 0$ and $y \geq 0$ indicate that we are restricted to the upper right quadrant created by the x-axis and y-axis.

The y-intercept of $3x + y = 9$ can be found by substituting $x = 0$.

$$3(0) + y = 9 \Rightarrow 0 + y = 9 \Rightarrow y = 9$$

The y-intercept is $(0, 9)$.

The x-intercept of $3x + y = 9$ can be found by substituting $y = 0$.

$$3x + 0 = 9 \Rightarrow 3x = 9 \Rightarrow x = \tfrac{9}{3} = 3$$

The x-intercept is $(3, 0)$.

We draw a line connecting these points. Testing the point $(0, 0)$, we have the statement $3(0) + 0 \leq 9$ or $0 \leq 9$. This is a true statement.

The y-intercept of $x + 2y = 8$ can be found by substituting $x = 0$.

$$0 + 2y = 8 \Rightarrow 2y = 8 \Rightarrow y = \tfrac{8}{2} = 4$$

The y-intercept is $(0, 4)$.

The x-intercept of $x + 2y = 8$ can be found by substituting $y = 0$.

$$x + 2(0) = 8 \Rightarrow x + 0 = 8 \Rightarrow x = 8$$

The x-intercept is $(8, 0)$.

We draw a line connecting these points. Testing the point $(0, 0)$, we have the statement $0 + 2(0) \leq 8$ or $0 \leq 8$. This is a true statement.

Thus, we shade the part of the plane in the upper right quadrant which is on the down side of both the lines $3x + y = 9$ and $x + 2y = 8$.

Three of the corner points, $(0, 0)$, $(0, 4)$, and $(3, 0)$ lie on the coordinate axes. The fourth corner point is the point of intersection between the lines $3x + y = 9$ and $x + 2y = 8$. We can find this by multiplying both sides of $3x + y = 9$ by -2, and adding the result to $x + 2y = 8$.

$$-6x - 2y = -18$$
$$\underline{x + 2y = 8}$$
$$-5x = -10 \Rightarrow x = \tfrac{-10}{-5} = 2$$

Substitute $x = 2$ into $x + 2y = 8$ and solve for y.

$$2 + 2y = 8 \Rightarrow 2y = 6 \Rightarrow y = \tfrac{6}{2} = 3$$

The point of intersection is therefore $(2, 3)$.

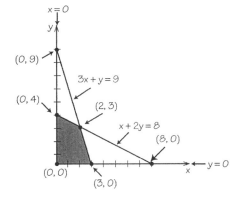

21. $x \geq 0; \ y \geq 0; \ 2x + y \leq 4; \ 4x + 4y \leq 12$

The constraints of $x \geq 0$ and $y \geq 0$ indicate that we are restricted to the upper right quadrant created by the x-axis and y-axis.

The y-intercept of $2x + y = 4$ can be found by substituting $x = 0$.

$$2(0) + y = 4 \Rightarrow 0 + y = 4 \Rightarrow y = 4$$

The y-intercept is $(0, 4)$.

The x-intercept of $2x + y = 4$ can be found by substituting $y = 0$.

$$2x + 0 = 4 \Rightarrow 2x = 4 \Rightarrow x = \tfrac{4}{2} = 2$$

The x-intercept is $(2, 0)$.

We draw a line connecting these points. Testing the point $(0, 0)$, we have the statement $2(0) + 0 \leq 4$ or $0 \leq 4$. This is a true statement.

The y-intercept of $4x + 4y = 12$ can be found by substituting $x = 0$.

$$4(0) + 4y = 12 \Rightarrow 0 + 4y = 12 \Rightarrow y = \tfrac{12}{4} = 3$$

The y-intercept is $(0, 3)$.

The x-intercept of $4x + 4y = 12$ can be found by substituting $y = 0$.

$$4x + 4(0) = 12 \Rightarrow 4x + 0 = 12 \Rightarrow 4x = 12 \Rightarrow x = \tfrac{12}{4} = 3$$

The x-intercept is $(3, 0)$.

We draw a line connecting these points. Testing the point $(0, 0)$, we have the statement $4(0) + 4(0) \leq 12$ or $0 \leq 12$. This is a true statement.

Thus, we shade the part of the plane in the upper right quadrant which is on the down side of both the lines $2x + y = 4$ and $4x + 4y = 12$.

Three of the corner points, $(0, 0)$, $(0, 3)$, and $(2, 0)$ lie on the coordinate axes. The fourth corner point is the point of intersection between the lines $2x + y = 4$ and $4x + 4y = 12$. We can find this by multiplying both sides of $2x + y = 4$ by -4, and adding the result to $4x + 4y = 12$.

$$-8x - 4y = -16$$
$$\underline{4x + 4y = 12}$$
$$-4x \qquad = -4 \Rightarrow x = \tfrac{-4}{-4} = 1$$

Substitute $x = 1$ into $2x + y = 4$ and solve for y.

$$2(1) + y = 4 \Rightarrow 2 + y = 4 \Rightarrow y = 2$$

The point of intersection is therefore $(1, 2)$.

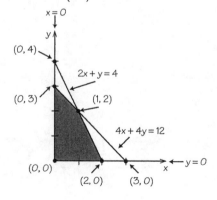

22. $x \geq 0;\ y \geq 2;\ 5x + y \leq 14;\ x + 2y \leq 10$

The constraints of $x \geq 0$ and $y \geq 2$ indicate that we are restricted to the upper right quadrant, above the horizontal line $y = 2$.

The y-intercept of $5x + y = 14$ can be found by substituting $x = 0$.

$$5(0) + y = 14 \Rightarrow 0 + y = 14 \Rightarrow y = 14$$

The y-intercept is $(0, 14)$.

The x-intercept of $5x + y = 14$ can be found by substituting $y = 0$.

$$5x + 0 = 14 \Rightarrow 5x = 14 \Rightarrow x = \tfrac{14}{5} = 2.8$$

The x-intercept is $(2.8, 0)$.

We draw a line connecting these points. Testing the point $(0, 0)$, we have the statement $5(0) + 0 \leq 14$ or $0 \leq 14$. This is a true statement.

The y-intercept of $x + 2y = 10$ can be found by substituting $x = 0$.

$$0 + 2y = 10 \Rightarrow 2y = 10 \Rightarrow y = \tfrac{10}{2} = 5$$

The y-intercept is $(0, 5)$.

The x-intercept of $x + 2y = 10$ can be found by substituting $y = 0$.

$$x + 2(0) = 10 \Rightarrow x + 0 = 10 \Rightarrow x = 10$$

The x-intercept is $(10, 0)$.

We draw a line connecting these points. Testing the point $(0, 0)$, we have the statement $0 + 2(0) \leq 10$ or $0 \leq 10$. This is a true statement.

Thus, we shade the part of the plane in the upper right quadrant which is on the down side of both the lines $5x + y = 14$ and $x + 2y = 10$, which is also above the horizontal line $y = 2$.

Two of the corner points, $(0, 2)$ and $(0, 5)$, lie on the coordinate axes. The third corner point is the point of intersection between the lines $5x + y = 14$ and $y = 2$. We can find this by substituting $y = 2$ into $5x + y = 14$ to solve for y. We have $5x + 2 = 14 \Rightarrow 5x = 12 \Rightarrow x = \tfrac{12}{5} = 2.4$.

The point of intersection is therefore $(2.4, 2)$.

The fourth corner point is the point of intersection between the lines $5x + y = 14$ and $x + 2y = 10$. We can find this by multiplying both sides of $5x + y = 14$ by -2, and adding the result to $x + 2y = 10$.

$$-10x - 2y = -28$$
$$\underline{\quad x + 2y = 10 \quad}$$
$$-9x \qquad = -18 \Rightarrow x = \tfrac{-18}{-9} = 2$$

Substitute $x = 2$ into $x + 2y = 10$ and solve for y. We have $2 + 2y = 10 \Rightarrow 2y = 8 \Rightarrow y = \tfrac{8}{2} = 4$.

The point of intersection is therefore $(2, 4)$.

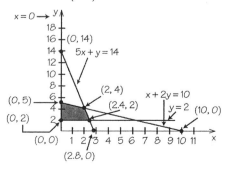

23. $x \geq 4$; $y \geq 0$; $5x + 4y \leq 60$; $x + y \leq 13$

The constraints of $x \geq 4$ and $y \geq 0$ indicate that we are restricted to the upper right quadrant, to the right of the vertical line $x = 4$.

The y-intercept of $5x + 4y = 60$ can be found by substituting $x = 0$.
$$5(0) + 4y = 60 \Rightarrow 0 + 4y = 60 \Rightarrow y = \tfrac{60}{4} = 15$$
The y-intercept is $(0, 15)$.

The x-intercept of $5x + 4y = 60$ can be found by substituting $y = 0$.
$$5x + 4(0) = 60 \Rightarrow 5x + 0 = 60 \Rightarrow 5x = 60 \Rightarrow x = \tfrac{60}{5} = 12$$
The x-intercept is $(12, 0)$.

We draw a line connecting these points. Testing the point $(0, 0)$, we have the statement $5(0) + 4(0) \leq 60$ or $0 \leq 60$. This is a true statement.

The y-intercept of $x + y = 13$ can be found by substituting $x = 0$.
$$0 + y = 13 \Rightarrow y = 13$$
The y-intercept is $(0, 13)$.

The x-intercept of $x + y = 13$ can be found by substituting $y = 0$.
$$x + 0 = 13 \Rightarrow x = 13$$
The x-intercept is $(13, 0)$.

We draw a line connecting these points. Testing the point $(0, 0)$, we have the statement $0 + 0 \leq 13$ or $0 \leq 13$. This is a true statement.

Thus, we shade the part of the plane in the upper right quadrant which is on the down side of both the lines $5x + 4y = 60$ and $x + y = 13$, which is also to the right of the vertical line $x = 4$.

Two of the corner points, $(4, 0)$ and $(12, 0)$, lie on the coordinate axes. The third corner point is the point of intersection between the lines $x + y = 13$ and $x = 4$. We can find this by substituting $x = 4$ into $x + y = 13$ to solve to y. We have, $4 + y = 13 \Rightarrow y = 9$. The point of intersection is therefore $(4, 9)$.

The fourth corner point is the point of intersection between the lines $5x + 4y = 60$ and $x + y = 13$. We can find this by multiplying both sides of $x + y = 13$ by -4, and adding the result to $5x + 4y = 60$.

$$\begin{aligned} -4x - 4y &= -52 \\ 5x + 4y &= 60 \\ \hline x &= 8 \end{aligned}$$

Substitute $x = 8$ into $x + y = 13$ and solve for y. We have $8 + y = 13 \Rightarrow y = 5$. The point of intersection is therefore $(8, 5)$.

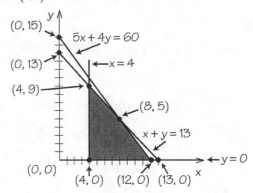

24. For Exercise 21: $x \geq 0$; $y \geq 0$; $2x + y \leq 4$; $4x + 4y \leq 12$

$(4, 2)$: Since $4 \geq 0$, the constraint $x \geq 0$ is satisfied.

Since $2 \geq 0$, the constraint $y \geq 0$ is satisfied.

Since $2(4) + 2 = 8 + 2 = 10 > 4$, the condition $2x + y \leq 4$ is not satisfied.

There is no need to check the fourth constraint.

Thus, $(4, 2)$ is not feasible.

$(1, 3)$: Since $1 \geq 0$, the constraint $x \geq 0$ is satisfied.

Since $3 \geq 0$, the constraint $y \geq 0$ is satisfied.

Since $2(1) + 3 = 2 + 3 = 5 > 4$, the condition $2x + y \leq 4$ is not satisfied.

There is no need to check the fourth constraint.

Thus, $(1, 3)$ is not feasible.

For Exercise 23: $x \geq 4$; $y \geq 0$; $5x + 4y \leq 60$; $x + y \leq 13$

$(4, 2)$: Since $4 \geq 4$, the constraint $x \geq 4$ is satisfied.

Since $2 \geq 0$, the constraint $y \geq 0$ is satisfied.

Since $5(4) + 4(2) = 20 + 8 = 28 \leq 60$, the condition $5x + 4y \leq 60$ is satisfied.

Since $4 + 2 = 6 \leq 13$, the condition $x + y \leq 13$ is satisfied.

Thus, $(4, 2)$ is feasible.

$(1, 3)$: Since $1 < 4$, the constraint $x \geq 4$ is not satisfied.

There is no need to check the other three constraints.

Thus, $(1, 3)$ is not feasible.

25. Maximize $P = 3x + 2y$ subject to $x \geq 3$; $y \geq 2$; $x + y \leq 10$; $2x + 3y \leq 24$

We need to first graph the feasible region while finding the corner points.

The constraints of $x \geq 3$ and $y \geq 2$ indicate that we are restricted to the upper right quadrant, to the right of the vertical line $x = 3$ and above the horizontal line $y = 2$.

The point of intersection between $x = 3$ and $y = 2$ is $(3, 2)$.

The y-intercept of $x + y = 10$ can be found by substituting $x = 0$.

$$0 + y = 10 \Rightarrow y = 10$$

The y-intercept is $(0, 10)$.

The x-intercept of $x + y = 10$ can be found by substituting $y = 0$.

$$x + 0 = 10 \Rightarrow x = 10$$

The x-intercept is $(10, 0)$.

The y-intercept of $2x + 3y = 24$ can be found by substituting $x = 0$.

$$2(0) + 3y = 24 \Rightarrow 0 + 3y = 24 \Rightarrow 3y = 24 \Rightarrow y = \tfrac{24}{3} = 8$$

The y-intercept is $(0, 8)$.

The x-intercept of $2x + 3y = 24$ can be found by substituting $y = 0$.

$$2x + 3(0) = 24 \Rightarrow 2x + 0 = 24 \Rightarrow 2x = 24 \Rightarrow x = \tfrac{24}{2} = 12$$

The x-intercept is $(12, 0)$.

Continued on next page

25. continued

Testing the point $(0,0)$ in both $x+y \le 10$ and $2x+3y \le 24$, we have the following.

$$0+0 = 0 \le 10 \text{ and } 2(0)+3(0) = 0 \le 24$$

Since these are both true statements, we shade the down side of the line of both lines which is contained in the upper right quadrant to the right of the vertical line $x=3$ and above the horizontal line $y=2$.

The point of intersection between $x=3$ and $2x+3y=24$ can be found by substituting $x=3$ into $2x+3y=24$. We have $2(3)+3y=24 \Rightarrow 6+3y=24 \Rightarrow 3y=18 \Rightarrow y=\frac{18}{3}=6$. Thus, the point of intersection is $(3,6)$.

The point of intersection between $y=2$ and $x+y=10$ can be found by substituting $y=2$ into $x+y=10$. We have, $x+2=10 \Rightarrow x=8$. Thus, the point of intersection is $(8,2)$.

The final corner point is the point of intersection between $x+y=10$ and $2x+3y=24$. We can find this by multiplying both sides of $x+y=10$ by -2, and adding the result to $2x+3y=24$.

$$-2x-2y = -20$$
$$\underline{2x+3y = 24}$$
$$y = 4$$

Substitute $y=4$ into $x+y=10$ and solve for x. We have, $x+4=10 \Rightarrow x=6$. The point of intersection is therefore $(6,4)$.

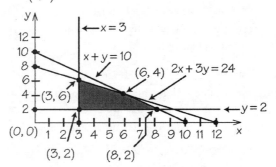

We wish to maximize $P = 3x+2y$.

Corner Point	Value of the Profit Formula: $3x+2y$
$(3,6)$	$3(3) + 2(6) = 9 + 12 = 21$
$(3,2)$	$3(3) + 2(2) = 9 + 4 = 13$
$(8,2)$	$3(8) + 2(2) = 24 + 4 = 28*$
$(6,4)$	$3(6) + 2(4) = 18 + 8 = 26$

The maximum value occurs at the corner point $(8,2)$, where P is equal to 28.

26. Maximize $P = 3x - 2y$ subject to $x \geq 2; y \geq 3; 3x + y \leq 18; 6x + 4y \leq 48$

We need to first graph the feasible region while finding the corner points.

The constraints of $x \geq 2$ and $y \geq 3$ indicate that we are restricted to the upper right quadrant, to the right of the vertical line $x = 2$ and above the horizontal line $y = 3$.

The point of intersection between $x = 2$ and $y = 3$ is $(2,3)$.

The y-intercept of $3x + y = 18$ can be found by substituting $x = 0$.

$$3(0) + y = 18 \Rightarrow 0 + y = 18 \Rightarrow y = 18$$

The y-intercept is $(0,18)$.

The x-intercept of $3x + y = 18$ can be found by substituting $y = 0$.

$$3x + 0 = 18 \Rightarrow 3x = 18 \Rightarrow x = \tfrac{18}{3} = 6$$

The x-intercept is $(6,0)$.

The y-intercept of $6x + 4y = 48$ can be found by substituting $x = 0$.

$$6(0) + 4y = 48 \Rightarrow 0 + 4y = 48 \Rightarrow 4y = 48 \Rightarrow y = \tfrac{48}{4} = 12$$

The y-intercept is $(0,12)$.

The x-intercept of $6x + 4y = 48$ can be found by substituting $y = 0$.

$$6x + 4(0) = 48 \Rightarrow 6x + 0 = 48 \Rightarrow 6x = 48 \Rightarrow x = \tfrac{48}{6} = 8$$

The x-intercept is $(8,0)$.

Testing the point $(0,0)$ in both $3x + y \leq 18$ and $6x + 4y \leq 48$, we have the following.

$$3(0) + 0 = 0 \leq 18 \text{ and } 6(0) + 4(0) = 0 \leq 48$$

Since these are both true statements, we shade the down side of the line of both lines which is contained in the upper right quadrant to the right of the vertical line $x = 2$ and above the horizontal line $y = 3$.

The point of intersection between $x = 2$ and $6x + 4y = 48$ can be found by substituting $x = 2$ into $6x + 4y = 48$. We have, $6(2) + 4y = 48 \Rightarrow 12 + 4y = 48 \Rightarrow 4y = 36 \Rightarrow y = \tfrac{36}{4} = 9$. Thus, the point of intersection is $(2,9)$.

The point of intersection between $y = 3$ and $3x + y = 18$ can be found by substituting $y = 3$ into $3x + y = 18$. We have $3x + 3 = 18 \Rightarrow 3x = 15 \Rightarrow x = \tfrac{15}{3} = 5$. Thus, the point of intersection is $(5,3)$.

The final corner point is the point of intersection between $3x + y = 18$ and $6x + 4y = 48$. We can find this by multiplying both sides of $3x + y = 18$ by -4, and adding the result to $6x + 4y = 48$.

$$
\begin{array}{r}
-12x - 4y = -72 \\
6x + 4y = 48 \\
\hline
-6x = -24 \Rightarrow x = \tfrac{-24}{-6} = 4
\end{array}
$$

Substitute $x = 4$ into $3x + y = 18$ and solve for y. We have, $3(4) + y = 18 \Rightarrow 12 + y = 18 \Rightarrow y = 6$.

The point of intersection is therefore $(4,6)$.

Continued on next page

26. continued

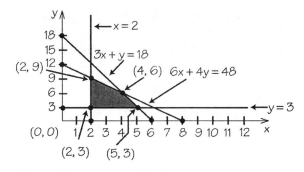

We wish to maximize $P = 3x - 2y$.

Corner Point	Value of the Profit Formula: $3x - 2y$
$(2,3)$	$3(2) - 2(3) = 6 - 6 = 0$
$(5,3)$	$3(5) - 2(3) = 15 - 6 = 9*$
$(4,6)$	$3(4) - 2(6) = 12 - 12 = 0$
$(2,9)$	$3(2) - 2(9) = 6 - 18 = -12$

The maximum value occurs at the corner point $(5,3)$, where P is equal to 9.

27. Maximize $P = 5x + 2y$ subject to $x \geq 2;\ y \geq 4;\ x + y \leq 10$

We need to first graph the feasible region while finding the corner points.

The constraints of $x \geq 2$ and $y \geq 4$ indicate that we are restricted to the upper right quadrant, to the right of the vertical line $x = 2$ and above the horizontal line $y = 4$.

The point of intersection between $x = 2$ and $y = 4$ is $(2,4)$.

The y-intercept of $x + y = 10$ can be found by substituting $x = 0$.

$$0 + y = 10 \Rightarrow y = 10$$

The y-intercept is $(0,10)$.

The x-intercept of $x + y = 10$ can be found by substituting $y = 0$.

$$x + 0 = 10 \Rightarrow x = 10$$

The x-intercept is $(10,0)$.

Testing the point $(0,0)$ in $x + y \leq 10$, we have the following.

$$0 + 0 = 0 \leq 10$$

Since this is a true statement, we shade the down side of this line which is contained in the upper right quadrant to the right of the vertical line $x = 2$ and above the horizontal line $y = 4$.

The point of intersection between $x = 2$ and $x + y = 10$ can be found by substituting $x = 2$ into $x + y = 10$. We have $2 + y = 10 \Rightarrow y = 8$. Thus, the point of intersection is $(2,8)$.

The point of intersection between $y = 4$ and $x + y = 10$ can be found by substituting $y = 4$ into $x + y = 10$. We have $x + 4 = 10 \Rightarrow x = 6$. Thus, the point of intersection is $(6,4)$.

Continued on next page

27. continued

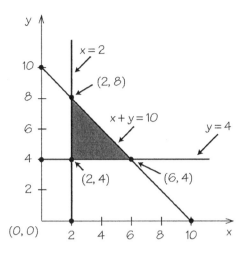

We wish to maximize $P = 5x + 2y$.

Corner Point	Value of the Profit Formula: $5x + 2y$
$(2,4)$	$5(2) + 2(4) = 10 + 8 = 18$
$(2,8)$	$5(2) + 2(8) = 10 + 16 = 26$
$(6,4)$	$5(6) + 2(4) = 30 + 8 = 38*$

The maximum value occurs at the corner point $(6,4)$, where P is equal to 38.

28. (a) $x \geq 0; y \geq 0; 7x + 4y \leq 13$

The constraints of $x \geq 0$ and $y \geq 0$ indicate that we are restricted to the upper right quadrant created by the x-axis and y-axis.

The y-intercept of $7x + 4y = 13$ can be found by substituting $x = 0$.

$$7(0) + 4y = 13 \Rightarrow 0 + 4y = 13 \Rightarrow 4y = 13 \Rightarrow y = \tfrac{13}{4}$$

The y-intercept is $\left(0, \tfrac{13}{4}\right)$. For graphing purposes, treat $\tfrac{13}{4}$ as $3\tfrac{1}{4}$.

The x-intercept of $7x + 4y = 13$ can be found by substituting $y = 0$.

$$7x + 4(0) = 13 \Rightarrow 7x + 0 = 13 \Rightarrow 7x = 13 \Rightarrow x = \tfrac{13}{7}$$

The x-intercept is $\left(\tfrac{13}{7}, 0\right)$. For graphing purposes, treat $\tfrac{13}{7}$ as $1\tfrac{6}{7}$.

We draw a line connecting these points. Testing the point $(0,0)$, we have the statement $7(0) + 4(0) \leq 13$ or $0 \leq 13$. This is a true statement, thus we shade the half-plane containing our test point, the down side of the line, which is contained in the upper right quadrant.

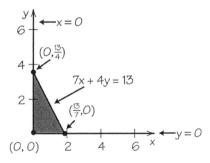

Continued on next page

28. continued

(b) According to the optimal production policy, we are looking for the maximum of $P = 21x + 11y$, given our constraints.

Corner Point	Value of the Profit Formula: $21x + 11y$
$(0,0)$	$21(0)\ +\ 11(0)\ =\ 0\ +\ 0\ =\ 0$
$\left(0,\frac{13}{4}\right)$	$21(0)\ +\ 11\left(\frac{13}{4}\right)\ =\ 0\ +\ \frac{143}{4}\ =\ 35\frac{3}{4}$
$\left(\frac{13}{7},0\right)$	$21\left(\frac{13}{7}\right)\ +\ 11(0)\ =\ 39\ +\ 0\ =\ 39*$

The maximum value occurs at the corner point $\left(\frac{13}{7},0\right)$.

29. (a) The optimal corner point for Exercise 28 being $\left(\frac{13}{7},0\right)$, the coordinates of $Q = (2,0)$.

(b) $(2,0)$ is not a feasible point.

(c) The profit at $(2,0)$ is greater than the profit at $\left(\frac{13}{7},0\right)$.

(d) Since $0 \geq 0$ and $3 \geq 0$ the constraints $x \geq 0$ and $y \geq 0$ are satisfied, respectively. Also, since $7(0) + 4(3) = 0 + 12 = 12 \leq 13$, the constraint $7x + 4y \leq 13$ is satisfied. Thus, $R = (0,3)$ is feasible. The profit at R is $21(0) + 11(3) = 33$. This is less than the profit at Q.

(e) Solving maximization problems involving linear constraints but where the variables are required to take on integer values cannot be solved by first solving the associated linear programming problem and rounding the answer to the nearest integers. This example shows the rounded value used to obtain an integer solution may not be feasible. Even if the rounded value is feasible it may not be optimal. "Integer programming" is unfortunately a much harder problem to solve than linear programming.

For Exercises 30 – 41, part (e) (using a simplex algorithm program) will not be addressed in the solutions.

30. (a) Let x be the number of shirts and y be the number of vests.

	Cloth (600 yds)	Minimums	Profit
Shirts, x items	3	100	$5
Vests, y items	2	30	$2

(b) Profit formula: $P = \$5x + \$2y$

Constraints: $x \geq 100$ and $y \geq 30$ (minimums); $3x + 2y \leq 600$ (cloth)

(c) Feasible region:

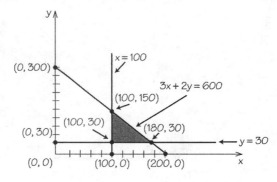

Continued on next page

30. continued

Corner points: One corner point is the point of intersection between $x = 100$ and $y = 30$, namely $(100, 30)$. Another is the point of intersection between $x = 100$ and $3x + 2y = 600$. Substituting $x = 100$ into $3x + 2y = 600$, we have the following.

$$3(100) + 2y = 600 \Rightarrow 300 + 2y = 600 \Rightarrow 2y = 300 \Rightarrow y = 150$$

Thus, $(100, 150)$ is the second corner point. The third corner point is the point of intersection between $y = 30$ and $3x + 2y = 600$. Substituting $y = 30$ into $3x + 2y = 600$, we have the following.

$$3x + 2(30) = 600 \Rightarrow 3x + 60 = 600 \Rightarrow 3x = 540 \Rightarrow x = 180$$

Thus, $(180, 30)$ is the third corner point.

(d) We wish to maximize $\$5x + \$2y$.

Corner Point	Value of the Profit Formula: $\$5x + \$2y$						
$(100, 30)$	$\$5(100)$	$+$	$\$2(30)$	$=$	$\$500 +$	$\$60$	$= \$560$
$(100, 150)$	$\$5(100)$	$+$	$\$2(150)$	$=$	$\$500 +$	$\$300$	$= \$800$
$(180, 30)$	$\$5(180)$	$+$	$\$2(30)$	$=$	$\$900 +$	$\$60$	$= \$960*$

Optimal production policy: Make 180 shirts and 30 vests.

With zero minimums, the feasible region looks like the following.

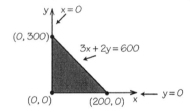

We wish to maximize $\$5x + \$2y$.

Corner Point	Value of the Profit Formula: $\$5x + \$2y$						
$(0, 0)$	$\$5(0)$	$+$	$\$2(0)$	$=$	$\$0 +$	$\$0$	$= \$0$
$(0, 300)$	$\$5(0)$	$+$	$\$2(300)$	$=$	$\$0 +$	$\$600$	$= \$600$
$(200, 0)$	$\$5(200)$	$+$	$\$2(0)$	$=$	$\$1000 +$	$\$0$	$= \$1000*$

The production policy changes to make 200 shirts and no vests.

31. (a) Let x be the number of oil changes and y be the number tune-ups.

	Time (8,000 min)	Minimums	Profit
Oil changes, x	20	0	$15
Tune-ups, y	100	0	$65

(b) Profit formula: $P = \$15x + \$65y$

Constraints: $x \geq 0$ and $y \geq 0$ (minimums); $20x + 100y \leq 8,000$ (time)

(c) Feasible region:

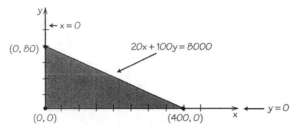

Corner points: The corner points are intercepts on the axes. These are $(0,0)$, $(0,80)$, and $(400,0)$.

(d) We wish to maximize $\$15x + \$65y$.

Corner Point	Value of the Profit Formula: $\$15x + \$65y$						
$(0,0)$	$\$15(0)$	+	$\$65(0)$	=	$\$0$ +	$\$0$ =	$\$0$
$(0,80)$	$\$15(0)$	+	$\$65(80)$	=	$\$0$ +	$\$5200$ =	$\$5200$
$(400,0)$	$\$15(400)$	+	$\$65(0)$	=	$\$6000$ +	$\$0$ =	$\$6000*$

Optimal production policy: Schedule 400 oil changes and no tune-ups.

With non-zero minimums, the constraints are as follows.

$$x \geq 50 \text{ and } y \geq 20 \text{ (minimums)}; 20x + 100y \leq 8,000 \text{ (time)}$$

The feasible region looks like the following.

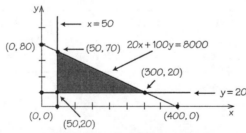

Corner points: One corner point is the point of intersection between $x = 50$ and $y = 20$, namely $(50,20)$. Another is the point of intersection between $x = 50$ and $20x + 100y = 8000$. Substituting $x = 50$ into $20x + 100y = 8000$, we have the following.

$$20(50) + 100y = 8000 \Rightarrow 1000 + 100y = 8000 \Rightarrow 100y = 7000 \Rightarrow y = 70$$

Thus, $(50,70)$ is the second corner point. The third corner point is the point of intersection between $y = 20$ and $20x + 100y = 8000$. Substituting $y = 20$ into $20x + 100y = 8000$, we have the following.

$$20x + 100(20) = 8000 \Rightarrow 20x + 2000 = 8000 \Rightarrow 20x = 6000 \Rightarrow x = 300$$

Thus, $(300,20)$ is the third corner point.

Continued on next page

31. continued

We wish to maximize $\$15x + \$65y$.

Corner Point	Value of the Profit Formula: $\$15x + \$65y$
$(50, 20)$	$\$15(50)$ + $\$65(20)$ = $\$750$ + $\$1300$ = $\$2050$
$(50, 70)$	$\$15(50)$ + $\$65(70)$ = $\$750$ + $\$4550$ = $\$5300$
$(300, 20)$	$\$15(300)$ + $\$65(20)$ = $\$4500$ + $\$1300$ = $\$5800*$

Optimal production policy: Schedule 300 oil changes and 20 tune-ups.

32. (a) Let x be the number of minutes processing mail orders and y be the number of minutes processing voice-mail orders.

	Time (90 min)	Minimums	Profit
Mail order, x minutes	10	0	$\$30$
Voice-mail order, y minutes	15	0	$\$40$

(b) Profit formula: $P = \$30x + \$40y$

Constraints: $x \geq 0$ and $y \geq 0$ (minimums); $10x + 15y \leq 90$ (time)

(c) Feasible region:

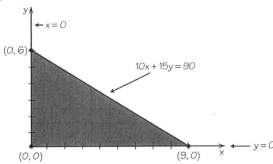

Corner points: The corner points are intercepts on the axes. These are $(0,0)$, $(0,6)$, and $(9,0)$.

(d) We wish to maximize $\$30x + \$40y$.

Corner Point	Value of the Profit Formula: $\$30x + \$40y$
$(0, 0)$	$\$30(0)$ + $\$40(0)$ = $\$0$ + $\$0$ = $\$0$
$(0, 6)$	$\$30(0)$ + $\$40(6)$ = $\$0$ + $\$240$ = $\$240$
$(9, 0)$	$\$30(9)$ + $\$40(0)$ = $\$270$ + $\$0$ = $\$270*$

Optimal production policy: Process 9 mail orders and no voice-mail orders.

Continued on next page

32. continued

With non-zero minimums, the constraints are $x \geq 3$ and $y \geq 2$ (minimums); $10x + 15y \leq 90$ (time). The feasible region looks like the following.

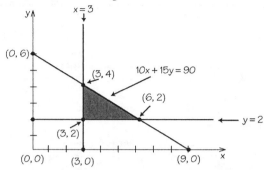

Corner points: One corner point is the point of intersection between $x = 3$ and $y = 2$, namely $(3, 2)$. Another is the point of intersection between $x = 3$ and $10x + 15y = 90$. Substituting $x = 3$ into $10x + 15y = 90$ we have the following.

$$10(3) + 15y = 90 \Rightarrow 30 + 15y = 90 \Rightarrow 15y = 60 \Rightarrow y = 4$$

Thus, $(3, 4)$ is the second corner point. The third corner point is the point of intersection between $y = 2$ and $10x + 15y = 90$. Substituting $y = 2$ into $10x + 15y = 90$ we have the following.

$$10x + 15(2) = 90 \Rightarrow 10x + 30 = 90 \Rightarrow 10x = 60 \Rightarrow x = 6$$

Thus, $(6, 2)$ is the third corner point.

We wish to maximize $\$30x + \$40y$.

Corner Point	Value of the Profit Formula: $\$30x + \$40y$
$(3, 2)$	$\$30(3) \; + \; \$40(2) \; = \; \$90 \; + \; \$80 \; = \; \$170$
$(3, 4)$	$\$30(3) \; + \; \$40(4) \; = \; \$90 \; + \; \$160 \; = \; \$250$
$(6, 2)$	$\$30(6) \; + \; \$40(2) \; = \; \$180 \; + \; \$80 \; = \; \$260*$

Optimal production policy: Process 6 mail orders and 2 voice-mail orders.

33. (a) Let x be the number of routine visits and y be the number of comprehensive visits.

	Doctor Time (1800 min)	Minimums	Profit
Routine, x visits	5	0	$\$30$
Comprehensive, y visits	25	0	$\$50$

(b) Profit formula: $P = \$30x + \$50y$

Constraints: $x \geq 0$ and $y \geq 0$ (minimums); $5x + 25y \leq 1800$ (time)

(c) Feasible region:

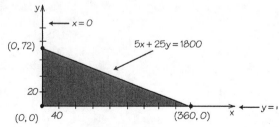

Continued on next page

33. (c) continued

Corner points: The corner points are intercepts on the axes. These are $(0,0)$, $(0,72)$, and $(360,0)$.

(d) We wish to maximize $\$30x + \$50y$.

Corner Point	Value of the Profit Formula: $\$30x + \$50y$							
$(0,0)$	$\$30(0)$	+	$\$50(0)$	=	$\$0$	+	$\$0$	=	$\$0$
$(0,72)$	$\$30(0)$	+	$\$50(72)$	=	$\$0$	+	$\$3600$	=	$\$3600$
$(360,0)$	$\$30(360)$	+	$\$50(0)$	=	$\$10,800$	+	$\$0$	=	$\$10,800*$

Optimal production policy: Schedule 360 routine visits and no comprehensive visits. With non-zero minimums, the constraints are as follows.

$$x \geq 20 \text{ and } y \geq 30 \text{ (minimums)}; 5x + 25y \leq 1800 \text{ (time)}$$

The feasible region looks like the following.

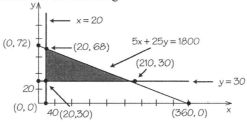

Corner points: One corner point is the point of intersection between $x = 20$ and $y = 30$, namely $(20,30)$. Another is the point of intersection between $x = 20$ and $5x + 25y = 1800$. Substituting $x = 20$ into $5x + 25y = 1800$, we have the following.

$$5(20) + 25y = 1800 \Rightarrow 100 + 25y = 1800 \Rightarrow 25y = 1700 \Rightarrow y = 68$$

Thus, $(20,68)$ is the second corner point. The third corner point is the point of intersection between $y = 30$ and $5x + 25y = 1800$. Substituting $y = 30$ into $5x + 25y = 1800$, we have the following.

$$5x + 25(30) = 1800 \Rightarrow 5x + 750 = 1800 \Rightarrow 5x = 1050 \Rightarrow x = 210$$

Thus, $(210,30)$ is the third corner point.

We wish to maximize $\$30x + \$50y$.

Corner Point	Value of the Profit Formula: $\$30x + \$50y$							
$(20,30)$	$\$30(20)$	+	$\$50(30)$	=	$\$600$	+	$\$1500$	=	$\$2100$
$(20,68)$	$\$30(20)$	+	$\$50(68)$	=	$\$600$	+	$\$3400$	=	$\$4000$
$(210,30)$	$\$30(210)$	+	$\$50(30)$	=	$\$6300$	+	$\$1500$	=	$\$7800*$

Optimal production policy: Schedule 210 routine visits and 30 comprehensive visits.

34. (a) Let x be the number of loaves of multigrain bread and y be the number of loaves of herb bread.

	Breads (600 loaves)	Minimums	Profit
Multigrain, x loaves	1	100	$\$8$
Herb, y loaves	1	200	$\$10$

(b) Profit formula: $P = \$8x + \$10y$

Constraints: $x \geq 100$ and $y \geq 200$ (minimums); $x + y \leq 600$ (breads)

Continued on next page

34. continued

(c) Feasible region:

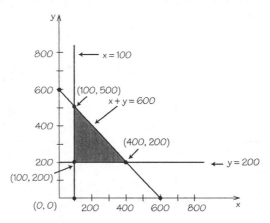

Corner points: One corner point is the point of intersection between $x = 100$ and $y = 200$, namely $(100, 200)$. Another is the point of intersection between $x = 100$ and $x + y = 600$. Substituting $x = 100$ into $x + y = 600$, we have the following.

$$100 + y = 600 \Rightarrow y = 500$$

Thus, $(100, 500)$ is the second corner point. The third corner point is the point of intersection between $y = 200$ and $x + y = 600$. Substituting $y = 200$ into $x + y = 600$, we have the following.

$$x + 200 = 600 \Rightarrow x = 400$$

Thus, $(400, 200)$ is the third corner point.

(d) We wish to maximize $\$8x + \$10y$.

Corner Point	Value of the Profit Formula: $\$8x + \$10y$
$(100, 200)$	$\$8(100)$ + $\$10(200)$ = $\$800$ + $\$2000$ = $\$2800$
$(100, 500)$	$\$8(100)$ + $\$10(500)$ = $\$800$ + $\$5000$ = $\$5800^*$
$(400, 200)$	$\$8(400)$ + $\$10(200)$ = $\$3200$ + $\$2000$ = $\$5200$

Optimal production policy: Make 100 multigrain and 500 herb loaves. With zero minimums, the feasible region looks like the following.

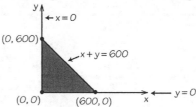

We wish to maximize $\$8x + \$10y$.

Corner Point	Value of the Profit Formula: $\$8x + \$10y$
$(0, 0)$	$\$8(0)$ + $\$10(0)$ = $\$0$ + $\$0$ = $\$0$
$(0, 600)$	$\$8(0)$ + $\$10(600)$ = $\$0$ + $\$6000$ = $\$6000^*$
$(600, 0)$	$\$8(600)$ + $\$10(0)$ = $\$4800$ + $\$0$ = $\$4800$

Optimal production policy: Make no multigrain and 600 herb loaves.

35. (a) Let x be the number of hours spent on math courses and y be the number of hours spent on other courses.

	Time (48 hr)	Minimums	Value Points
Math, x courses	12	0	2
Other, y courses	8	0	1

(b) Value Point formula: $V = 2x + y$

Constraints: $x \geq 0$ and $y \geq 0$ (minimums); $12x + 8y \leq 48$ (time)

(c) Feasible region:

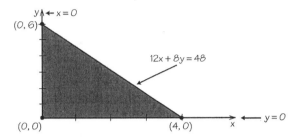

Corner points: The corner points are intercepts on the axes. These are $(0,0)$, $(0,6)$, and $(4,0)$.

(d) We wish to maximize $2x + y$.

Corner Point	Value of the Value Point Formula: $2x + y$
$(0,0)$	$2(0) + 0 = 0 + 0 = 0$
$(0,6)$	$2(0) + 6 = 0 + 6 = 6$
$(4,0)$	$2(4) + 0 = 8 + 0 = 8*$

Optimal production policy: Take four math courses and no other courses.

With non-zero minimums, the constraints are $x \geq 2$ and $y \geq 2$ (minimums); $12x + 8y \leq 48$ (time). The feasible region looks like the following.

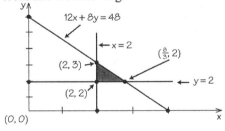

Corner points: One corner point is the point of intersection between $x = 2$ and $y = 2$, namely $(2,2)$. Another is the point of intersection between $x = 2$ and $12x + 8y = 48$. Substituting $x = 2$ into $12x + 8y = 48$, we have the following.

$$12(2) + 8y = 48 \Rightarrow 24 + 8y = 48 \Rightarrow 8y = 24 \Rightarrow y = 3$$

Thus, $(2,3)$ is the second corner point.

Continued on next page

35. continued

The third corner point is the point of intersection between $y = 2$ and $12x + 8y = 48$.
Substituting $y = 2$ into $12x + 8y = 48$, we have the following.

$$12x + 8(2) = 48 \Rightarrow 12x + 16 = 48 \Rightarrow 12x = 32 \Rightarrow x = \frac{32}{12} = \frac{8}{3} = 2\frac{2}{3}$$

Thus, $\left(\frac{8}{3}, 2\right)$ is the third corner point.

We wish to maximize $2x + y$.

Corner Point	Value of the Profit Formula: $2x + y$
$(2,2)$	$2(2)$ + 2 = 4 + 2 = 6
$(2,3)$	$2(2)$ + 3 = 4 + 3 = 7
$\left(\frac{8}{3}, 2\right)$	$2\left(\frac{8}{3}\right)$ + 2 = $5\frac{1}{3}$ + 2 = $7\frac{1}{3}$*

Optimal production policy: Take $2\frac{2}{3}$ math courses and 2 other courses. However, one cannot take a fractional part of a course. So given the constraint on study time, the student should take two math courses and 2 other courses.

36. (a) Let x be the number of "Hot" sites maintained and y be the number of "Cool" sites maintained.

	Layout (12 hr)	Content (16 hr)	Minimums	Profit
"Hot", x sites	1.5	1	0	$50
"Cool", y sites	1	2	0	$250

(b) Profit formula: $P = \$50x + \$250y$

Constraints: $x \geq 0$ and $y \geq 0$ (minimums); $1.5x + y \leq 12$ (layout); $x + 2y \leq 16$ (content)

(c) Feasible region:

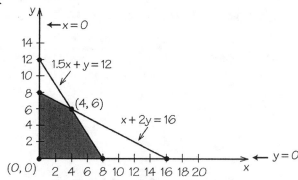

Corner points: Three of the corner points are intercepts on the axes. These are $(0,0)$, $(0,8)$, and $(8,0)$. The final corner point is the point of intersection between $1.5x + y = 12$ and $x + 2y = 16$. We can find this by multiplying both sides of $1.5x + y = 12$ by -2, and adding the result to $x + 2y = 16$.

$$-3x - 2y = -24$$
$$\underline{x + 2y = 16}$$
$$-2x \qquad = -8 \Rightarrow x = \frac{-8}{-2} = 4$$

Substitute $x = 4$ into $x + 2y = 16$ and solve for y. We have $4 + 2y = 16 \Rightarrow 2y = 12 \Rightarrow y = 6$.
The point of intersection is therefore $(4,6)$.

Continued on next page

36. continued

(d) We wish to maximize $\$50x + \$250y$.

Corner Point	Value of the Profit Formula: $\$50x + \$250y$							
$(0,0)$	$\$50(0)$	+	$\$250(0)$	=	$\$0$	+	$\$0$	=	$\$0$
$(0,8)$	$\$50(0)$	+	$\$250(8)$	=	$\$0$	+	$\$2000$	=	$\$2000*$
$(8,0)$	$\$50(8)$	+	$\$250(0)$	=	$\$400$	+	$\$0$	=	$\$400$
$(4,6)$	$\$50(4)$	+	$\$250(6)$	=	$\$200$	+	$\$1500$	=	$\$1700$

Optimal production policy: Maintain no "hot" and 8 "cool" sites.

With non-zero minimums, the constraints are as follows.

$$x \geq 2 \text{ and } y \geq 3 \text{ (minimums)}; 1.5x + y \leq 12 \text{ (layout)}; x + 2y \leq 16 \text{ (content)}$$

The feasible region looks like the following.

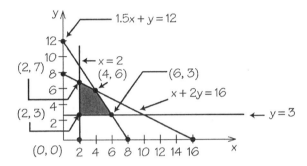

Corner points: One corner point is the point of intersection between $x = 2$ and $y = 3$, namely $(2,3)$. Another is the point of intersection between $x = 2$ and $x + 2y = 16$. Substituting $x = 2$ into $x + 2y = 16$, we have the following.

$$2 + 2y = 16 \Rightarrow 2y = 14 \Rightarrow y = 7$$

Thus, $(2,7)$ is the second corner point. The third corner point is the point of intersection between $y = 3$ and $1.5x + y = 12$. Substituting $y = 3$ into $1.5x + y = 12$, we have the following.

$$1.5x + 3 = 12 \Rightarrow 1.5x = 9 \Rightarrow x = 6$$

Thus, $(6,3)$ is the third corner point. The fourth corner point is the point of intersection between $1.5x + y = 12$ and $x + 2y = 16$. In part (a) this was found to be $(4,6)$.

We wish to maximize $\$50x + \$250y$.

Corner Point	Value of the Profit Formula: $\$50x + \$250y$							
$(2,3)$	$\$50(2)$	+	$\$250(3)$	=	$\$100$	+	$\$750$	=	$\$850$
$(2,7)$	$\$50(2)$	+	$\$250(7)$	=	$\$100$	+	$\$1750$	=	$\$1850*$
$(6,3)$	$\$50(6)$	+	$\$250(3)$	=	$\$300$	+	$\$750$	=	$\$1050$
$(4,6)$	$\$50(4)$	+	$\$250(6)$	=	$\$200$	+	$\$1500$	=	$\$1700$

Optimal production policy: Maintain 2 "hot" and 7 "cool" sites.

37. (a) Let x be the number of Grade A batches and y be the number of Grade B batches.

	Scrap cloth (100 lb)	Scrap Paper (120 lb)	Minimums	Profit
Grade A, x batches	25	10	0	$500
Grade B, y batches	10	20	0	$250

(b) Profit formula: $P = \$500x + \$250y$

Constraints: $x \geq 0$ and $y \geq 0$ (minimums); $25x + 10y \leq 100$ (cloth); $10x + 20y \leq 120$ (paper)

(c) Feasible region:

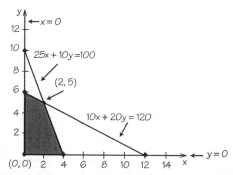

Corner points: Three of the corner points are intercepts on the axes. These are $(0,0)$, $(0,6)$, and $(4,0)$. The final corner point is the point of intersection between $25x + 10y = 100$ and $10x + 20y = 120$. We can find this by multiplying both sides of $25x + 10y = 100$ by -2, and adding the result to $10x + 20y = 120$.

$$-50x - 20y = -200$$
$$\underline{10x + 20y = 120}$$
$$-40x \qquad = -80 \Rightarrow x = \tfrac{-80}{-40} = 2$$

Substitute $x = 2$ into $25x + 10y = 100$ and solve for y. We have the following.

$$25(2) + 10y = 100 \Rightarrow 50 + 10y = 100 \Rightarrow 10y = 50 \Rightarrow y = 5$$

The point of intersection is therefore $(2,5)$.

(d) We wish to maximize $\$500x + \$250y$.

Corner Point	Value of the Profit Formula: $\$500x + \$250y$						
$(0,0)$	$\$500(0)$	+	$\$250(0)$	=	$\$0$ +	$\$0$ =	$\$0$
$(0,6)$	$\$500(0)$	+	$\$250(6)$	=	$\$0$ +	$\$1500$ =	$\$1500$
$(4,0)$	$\$500(4)$	+	$\$250(0)$	=	$\$2000$ +	$\$0$ =	$\$2000$
$(2,5)$	$\$500(2)$	+	$\$250(5)$	=	$\$1000$ +	$\$1250$ =	$\$2250*$

Optimal production policy: Make 2 grade A and 5 grade B batches.

With non-zero minimums $x \geq 1$ and $y \geq 1$, there will be no change because the optimal production policy already obeys these non-zero minimums.

38. (a) Let x be the number of modest houses and y be the number of deluxe houses.

	Space (100 acres)	Money in thousands ($2600)	Minimums	Profit in thousands
Modest, x houses	1	$20	0	$25
Deluxe, y houses	1	$40	0	$60

(b) Profit formula: $P = \$25x + \$60y$

Constraints: $x \geq 0$ and $y \geq 0$ (minimums)

$x + y \leq 100$ (space)

$20x + 40y \leq 2600$ (available funds)

(c) Feasible region:

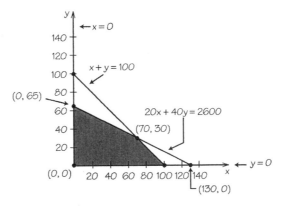

Corner points: Three of the corner points are intercepts on the axes. These are $(0,0)$, $(0,65)$, and $(130,0)$. The final corner point is the point of intersection between $x + y = 100$ and $20x + 40y = 2600$. We can find this by multiplying both sides of $x + y = 100$ by -20, and add the result to $20x + 40y = 2600$.

$$-20x - 20y = -2000$$
$$\underline{20x + 40y = 2600}$$
$$20y = 600 \Rightarrow y = 30$$

Substitute $y = 30$ into $x + y = 100$ and solve for y. We have $x + 30 = 100 \Rightarrow x = 70$. The point of intersection is therefore $(70,30)$.

(d) We wish to maximize $\$25x + \$60y$.

Corner Point	Value of the Profit Formula: $\$25x + \$60y$ (in thousands)						
$(0,0)$	$\$25(0)$	+	$\$60(0)$	=	$\$0$ +	$\$0$ =	$\$0$
$(0,65)$	$\$25(0)$	+	$\$60(65)$	=	$\$0$ +	$\$3900$ =	$\$3900*$
$(100,0)$	$\$25(100)$	+	$\$60(0)$	=	$\$2500$ +	$\$0$ =	$\$2500$
$(70,30)$	$\$25(70)$	+	$\$60(30)$	=	$\$1750$ +	$\$1800$ =	$\$3550$

Optimal production policy: Build no modest and 65 deluxe houses.
Continued on next page

38. continued

With non-zero minimums, the constraints are as follows.

$x \geq 20$ and $y \geq 20$ (minimums); $x+y \leq 100$ (space); $20x+40y \leq 2600$ (available funds)

The feasible region looks like the following.

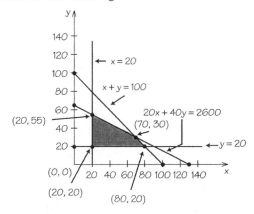

Corner points: One corner point is the point of intersection between $x = 20$ and $y = 20$, namely $(20,20)$. Another is the point of intersection between $y = 20$ and $x+y = 100$. Substituting $y = 20$ into $x+y = 100$, we have $x+20 = 100 \Rightarrow x = 80$. Thus, $(80,20)$ is the second corner point. The third corner point is the point of intersection between $x = 20$ and $20x+40y = 2600$. Substituting $x = 20$ into $20x+40y = 2600$, we have the following.

$$20(20)+40y = 2600 \Rightarrow 400+40y = 2600 \Rightarrow 40y = 2200 \Rightarrow y = 55$$

Thus, $(20,55)$ is the third corner point. The fourth corner point is the point of intersection between $x+y = 100$ and $20x+40y = 2600$. In part (a) this was found to be $(70,30)$.

We wish to maximize $\$25x+\$60y$.

Corner Point	Value of the Profit Formula: $\$25x+\$60y$ (in thousands)						
$(20,20)$	$\$25(20)$	+	$\$60(20)$	=	$\$500$ + $\$1200$	=	$\$1700$
$(20,55)$	$\$25(20)$	+	$\$60(55)$	=	$\$500$ + $\$3300$	=	$\$3800*$
$(80,20)$	$\$25(80)$	+	$\$60(20)$	=	$\$2000$ + $\$1200$	=	$\$3200$
$(70,30)$	$\$25(70)$	+	$\$60(30)$	=	$\$1750$ + $\$1800$	=	$\$3550$

Optimal production policy: Make 20 modest and 55 deluxe houses.

39. (a) Let x be the number of cartons of regular soda and y be the number of cartons of diet soda.

	Cartons (5000)	Money ($5400)	Minimums	Profit
Regular, x cartons	1	$1.00	600	$0.10
Diet, y cartons	1	$1.20	1000	$0.11

(b) Profit formula: $P = \$0.10x + \$0.11y$

Constraints: $x \ge 600$ and $y \ge 1000$ (minimums)

$$x + y \le 5000 \text{ (cartons)}; 1.00x + 1.20y \le 5400 \text{ (money)}$$

(c) Feasible region:

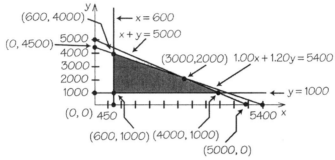

Corner points: One corner point is the point of intersection between $x = 600$ and $y = 1000$, namely $(600,1000)$. Another is the point of intersection between $y = 1000$ and $x + y = 5000$. Substituting $y = 1000$ into $x + y = 5000$, we have $x + 1000 = 5000 \Rightarrow x = 4000$. Thus, $(4000,1000)$ is the second corner point. The third corner point is the point of intersection between $x = 600$ and $1.00x + 1.20y = 5400$. Substituting $x = 600$ into $1.00x + 1.20y = 5400$, we have the following.

$$1.00(600) + 1.20y = 5400 \Rightarrow 600 + 1.20y = 5400 \Rightarrow 1.20y = 4800 \Rightarrow y = 4000$$

Thus, $(600,4000)$ is the third corner point. The fourth corner point is the point of intersection between $x + y = 5000$ and $1.00x + 1.20y = 5400$. We can find this by multiplying both sides of $x + y = 5000$ by -1, and adding the result to $1.00x + 1.20y = 5400$.

$$\begin{array}{r} -x - \quad y = -5000 \\ 1.00x + 1.20y = 5400 \\ \hline 0.20y = 400 \Rightarrow y = 2000 \end{array}$$

Substitute $y = 2000$ into $x + y = 5000$ and solve for y. We have $x + 2000 = 5000$ or $x = 3000$. The point of intersection is therefore $(3000,2000)$.

(d) We wish to maximize $\$0.10x + \$0.11y$.

Corner Point	Value of the Profit Formula: $\$0.10x + \$0.11y$
$(600,1000)$	$\$0.10(600)$ + $\$0.11(1000)$ = $\$60$ + $\$110$ = $\$170$
$(4000,1000)$	$\$0.10(4000)$ + $\$0.11(1000)$ = $\$400$ + $\$110$ = $\$510$
$(600,4000)$	$\$0.10(600)$ + $\$0.11(4000)$ = $\$60$ + $\$440$ = $\$500$
$(3000,2000)$	$\$0.10(3000)$ + $\$0.11(2000)$ = $\$300$ + $\$220$ = $\$520*$

Optimal production policy: Make 3000 cartons of regular and 2000 cartons of diet.

With zero minimums there is no change in the optimal production policy because the corresponding corner point does not touch either line from a minimum constraint.

40. (a) Let x be the number of pheasants and y be the number of partridges.

	Bird count (100)	Cost ($2400)	Minimums	Profit
Pheasants, x	1	$20	0	$14
Partridges, y	1	$30	0	$16

(b) Profit formula: $P = \$14x + \$16y$

Constraints: $x \geq 0$ and $y \geq 0$ (minimums); $x + y \leq 100$ (bird count); $20x + 30y \leq 2400$ (money)

(c) Feasible region:

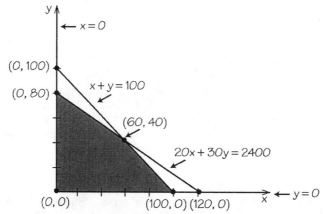

Corner points: Three of the corner points are intercepts on the axes. These are $(0,0)$, $(0,80)$, and $(100,0)$. The final corner point is the point of intersection between $x + y = 100$ and $20x + 30y = 2400$. We can find this by multiplying both sides of $x + y = 100$ by -20, and adding the result to $20x + 30y = 2400$.

$$-20x - 20y = -2000$$
$$\underline{20x + 30y = 2400}$$
$$10y = 400 \Rightarrow y = 40$$

Substitute $y = 40$ into $x + y = 100$ and solve for y. We have $x + 40 = 100 \Rightarrow x = 60$. The point of intersection is therefore $(60, 40)$.

(d) We wish to maximize $\$14x + \$16y$.

Corner Point	Value of the Profit Formula: $\$14x + \$16y$						
$(0,0)$	$\$14(0)$	+	$\$16(0)$	=	$0 +	$0 =	$0
$(0,80)$	$\$14(0)$	+	$\$16(80)$	=	$0 +	$1280 =	$1280
$(100,0)$	$\$14(100)$	+	$\$16(0)$	=	$1400 +	$0 =	$1400
$(60,40)$	$\$14(60)$	+	$\$16(40)$	=	$840 +	$640 =	$1480*

Optimal production policy: Raise 60 pheasants and 40 partridges.

With nonzero minimum of $x \geq 20$ and $y \geq 10$, there is no change because the optimal production policy obeys these minimums.

41. (a) Let x be the number of desk lamps and y be the number of floor lamps.

	Labor (1200 hr)	Money ($4200)	Minimums	Profit
Desk, x lamps	0.8	$4	0	$2.65
Floor, y lamps	1.0	$3	0	$4.67

(b) Profit formula: $P = \$2.65x + \$4.67y$

Constraints: $x \geq 0$ and $y \geq 0$ (minimums)

$$0.8x + 1.0y \leq 1200 \,(\text{labor})$$

$$4x + 3y \leq 4200 \,(\text{money})$$

(c) Feasible region:

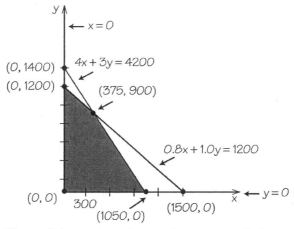

Corner points: Three of the corner points are intercepts on the axes. These are $(0,0)$, $(0,1200)$, and $(1050,0)$. The final corner point is the point of intersection between $0.8x + 1.0y = 1200$ and $4x + 3y = 4200$. We can find this by multiplying both sides of $0.8x + 1.0y = 1200$ by -3, and adding the result to $4x + 3y = 4200$.

$$-2.4x - 3y = -3600$$
$$\underline{4x + 3y = 4200}$$
$$1.6x \qquad = 600 \Rightarrow x = 375$$

Substitute $x = 375$ into $0.8x + 1.0y = 1200$ and solve for y. We have the following.

$$0.8(375) + y = 1200 \Rightarrow 300 + y = 1200 \Rightarrow y = 900$$

The point of intersection is therefore $(375, 900)$.

(d) We wish to maximize $\$2.65x + \$4.67y$.

Corner Point	Value of the Profit Formula: $\$2.65x + \$4.67y$					
$(0,0)$	$\$2.65(0)$ +	$\$4.67(0)$ =	$\$0.00$ +	$\$0.00$ =	$\$0.00$
$(0,1200)$	$\$2.65(0)$ +	$\$4.67(1200)$ =	$\$0.00$ +	$\$5604.00$ =	$\$5604.00*$
$(1050,0)$	$\$2.65(1050)$ +	$\$4.67(0)$ =	$\$2782.50$ +	$\$0.00$ =	$\$2782.50$
$(375,900)$	$\$2.65(375)$ +	$\$4.67(900)$ =	$\$993.75$ +	$\$4203.00$ =	$\$5196.75$

Optimal production policy: Make no desk lamps and 1200 floor lamps.

Continued on next page

41. continued

With non-zero minimums, the constraints are as follows.

$x \geq 150$ and $y \geq 200$ (minimums); $0.8x + 1.0y \leq 1200$ (labor); $4x + 3y \leq 4200$ (money)

The feasible region looks like the following.

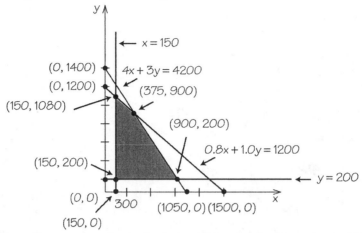

Corner points: One corner point is the point of intersection between $x = 150$ and $y = 200$, namely $(150, 200)$. Another is the point of intersection between $y = 200$ and $4x + 3y = 4200$. Substituting $y = 200$ into $4x + 3y = 4200$, we have the following.

$$4x + 3(200) = 4200 \Rightarrow 4x + 600 = 4200 \Rightarrow 4x = 3600 \Rightarrow x = 900$$

Thus, $(900, 200)$ is the second corner point. The third corner point is the point of intersection between $x = 150$ and $0.8x + 1.0y = 1200$. Substituting $x = 150$ into $0.8x + 1.0y = 1200$, we have the following.

$$0.8(150) + y = 1200 \Rightarrow 120 + y = 1200 \Rightarrow y = 1080$$

Thus, $(150, 1080)$ is the third corner point. The fourth corner point is the point of intersection between $0.8x + 1.0y = 1200$ and $4x + 3y = 4200$. In part (a) this was found to be $(375, 900)$.

We wish to maximize $\$2.65x + \$4.67y$.

Corner Point	Value of the Profit Formula: $\$2.65x + \$4.67y$ (in thousands)						
$(150, 200)$	$\$2.65(150)$	$+$	$\$4.67(200)$	$=$	$\$397.50 +$	$\$934.00$	$= \$1331.50$
$(150, 1080)$	$\$2.65(150)$	$+$	$\$4.67(1080)$	$=$	$\$397.50 +$	$\$5043.60$	$= \$5441.10*$
$(375, 900)$	$\$2.65(375)$	$+$	$\$4.67(900)$	$=$	$\$993.75 +$	$\$4203.00$	$= \$5196.75$
$(900, 200)$	$\$2.65(900)$	$+$	$\$4.67(200)$	$=$	$\$2385.00 +$	$\$934.00$	$= \$3319.00$

Optimal production policy: Make 150 desk lamps and 1080 floor lamps.

For Exercises 42 – 45, part (c) (using a simplex algorithm program) will not be addressed in the solutions.

42. (a) Let x be the number of toy A, y be the number of toy B, and z be the number of toy C.

	Shaper (50)	Smoother (40)	Painter (60)	Minimums	Profit
Toy A, x	1	2	1	0	$4
Toy B, y	2	1	3	0	$5
Toy C, z	3	2	1	0	$9

(b) Profit formula: $P = \$4x + \$5y + \$9z$

Constraints: $x \geq 0$, $y \geq 0$, and $z \geq 0$ (minimums)

$x + 2y + 3z \leq 50$ (shaper)

$2x + y + 2z \leq 40$ (smoother)

$x + 3y + z \leq 60$ (painter)

(c) Optimal product policy: Make 5 toy A, no toy B, 15 toy C for a profit of $155.

43. (a) Let x be the number of chairs, y be the number of tables, and z be the number of beds.

	Chis (80 hr)	Sue (200 hr)	Juan (200)	Minimums	Profit
Chairs, x	1	3	2	0	$100
Tables, y	3	5	4	0	$250
Beds, z	5	4	8	0	$350

(b) Profit formula: $P = \$100x + \$250y + \$350z$

Constraints: $x \geq 0$, $y \geq 0$, and $z \geq 0$ (minimums)

$x + 3y + 5z \leq 80$ (Chris); $3x + 5y + 4z \leq 200$ (Sue); $2x + 4y + 8z \leq 200$ (Juan)

(c) Optimal product policy: Make 50 chairs, 10 tables, and no beds each month for a profit of 7500 in one month.

44. (a) Let x be the number of boxes of Special Mix, y be the number of boxes of Regular Mix, and z be the number of boxes of Purist Mix.

	Chocolate (1000 lb)	Nuts (200 lb)	Fruit (100 lb)	Minimums	Profit
Special, x boxes	3	1	1	0	$10
Regular, y boxes	4	0.5	0	0	$6
Purist, z boxes	5	0	0	0	$4

(b) Profit formula: $P = \$10x + \$6y + \$4z$

Constraints: $x \geq 0$, $y \geq 0$, and $z \geq 0$ (minimums)

$3x + 4y + 5z \leq 1000$ (chocolate)

$x + 0.5y + 0z \leq 200$ (nuts)

$x + 0y + 0z \leq 100$ (fruit)

(c) Optimal product policy: Make 100 boxes of Special, 175 boxes of Regular, and 0 boxes of Purist for a profit of $2050.

45. (a) Let w be the number of pounds of Excellent coffee, x be the number of pounds of Southern coffee, y be the number of pounds of World coffee, and z be the number of pounds of Special coffee.

	African (17,600 oz)	Brazilian (21,120 oz)	Columbian (12,320 oz)	Minimums	Profit
Excellent, w pounds	0	0	16	0	$1.80
Southern, x pounds	0	12	4	0	$1.40
World, y pounds	6	8	2	0	$1.20
Special, z pounds	10	6	0	0	$1.00

(b) Profit formula: $P = \$1.80w + \$1.40x + \$1.20y + \$1.00z$

Constraints: $w \geq 0,\, x \geq 0,\, y \geq 0,$ and $z \geq 0$ (minimums)

$$0w + 0x + 6y + 10z \leq 17,600 \,(\text{African})$$

$$0w + 12x + 8y + 6z \leq 12,120 \,(\text{Brazilian})$$

$$16w + 4x + 2y + 6z \leq 12,320 \,(\text{Columbian})$$

(c) Optimal product policy: Make 470 pounds of Excellent, none of Southern, 2400 pounds of World, and 320 pounds for a profit of $4046.

46. Minimize $C = 4x + 7y$ subject to $x \geq 3;\, y \geq 2;\, x + y \leq 10;\, 2x + 3y \leq 24$

The corner points are $(3,6), (3,2), (8,2),$ and $(6,4)$.

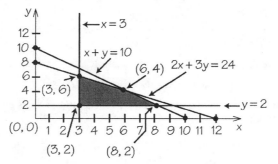

We wish to minimize $C = 4x + 7y$.

Corner Point	Value of the cost: $4x + 7y$
$(3,6)$	$4(3)\ +\ 7(6)\ =\ 12\ +\ 42\ =\ 54$
$(3,2)$	$4(3)\ +\ 7(2)\ =\ 12\ +\ 14\ =\ 26*$
$(8,2)$	$4(8)\ +\ 7(2)\ =\ 32\ +\ 14\ =\ 46$
$(6,4)$	$4(6)\ +\ 7(4)\ =\ 24\ +\ 28\ =\ 52$

The minimum value occurs at the corner point $(3,2)$, where C is equal to 26.

47. Minimize $C = 3x + 11y$ subject to $x \ge 2; \; y \ge 3; \; 3x + y \le 18; \; 6x + 4y \le 48$

The corner points are $(2,3),(5,3),(4,6)$, and $(2,9)$.

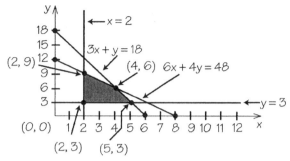

We wish to minimize $C = 3x + 11y$.

Corner Point	Value of the Profit Formula: $3x + 11y$						
$(2,3)$	$3(2)$	$+$	$11(3)$	$=$	$6 +$	$33 =$	$39*$
$(5,3)$	$3(5)$	$+$	$11(3)$	$=$	$15 +$	$33 =$	48
$(4,6)$	$3(4)$	$+$	$11(6)$	$=$	$12 +$	$66 =$	78
$(2,9)$	$3(2)$	$+$	$11(9)$	$=$	$6 +$	$99 =$	105

The minimum value occurs at the corner point $(2,3)$, where C is equal to 39.

48. The only feasible point with integer coordinates for the collection of inequalities $x \ge 0, \; y \ge 0$ and $x + y = 0.5$ is $(0,0)$.

49. (a) Let x be the number of business calls and y be the charity calls.

	Time (240 min)	Minimums	Profit
Business, x calls	4	0	$0.50
Charity, y calls	6	0	$0.40

(b) Profit formula: $P = \$0.50x + \$0.40y$

Constraints: $x \ge 0$ and $y \ge 0$ (minimums); $4x + 6y \le 240$ (time)

(c) Feasible region:

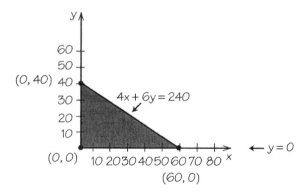

Corner points: The corner points are intercepts on the axes. These are $(0,0)$, $(0,40)$, and $(60,0)$.

Continued on next page

49. continued

(d) We wish to maximize $\$0.50x + \$0.40y$.

Corner Point	Value of the Profit Formula: $\$0.50x + \$0.40y$							
$(0,0)$	$\$0.50(0)$	$+$	$\$0.40(0)$	$=$	$\$0.00$	$+$	$\$0.00$	$=$ $\$0.00$
$(0,40)$	$\$0.50(0)$	$+$	$\$0.40(40)$	$=$	$\$0.00$	$+$	$\$16.00$	$=$ $\$16.00$
$(60,0)$	$\$0.50(60)$	$+$	$\$0.40(0)$	$=$	$\$30.00$	$+$	$\$0.00$	$=$ $\$30.00*$

Optimal production policy: Make 60 business and no charity calls.

With non-zero minimums, the constraints are as follows.

$$x \geq 12 \text{ and } y \geq 10 \text{ (minimums)}; 4x + 6y \leq 240 \text{ (time)}$$

The feasible region looks like the following.

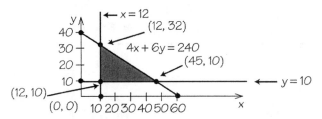

Corner points: One corner point is the point of intersection between $x = 12$ and $y = 10$, namely $(12,10)$. Another is the point of intersection between $x = 12$ and $4x + 6y = 240$. Substituting $x = 12$ into $4x + 6y = 240$, we have the following.

$$4(12) + 6y = 240 \Rightarrow 48 + 6y = 240 \Rightarrow 6y = 192 \Rightarrow y = 32$$

Thus, $(12,32)$ is the second corner point. The third corner point is the point of intersection between $y = 10$ and $4x + 6y = 240$. Substituting $y = 10$ into $4x + 6y = 240$ we have the following.

$$4x + 6(10) = 240 \Rightarrow 4x + 60 = 240 \Rightarrow 4x = 180 \Rightarrow x = 45$$

Thus, $(45,10)$ is the third corner point.

We wish to maximize $\$0.50x + \$0.40y$.

Corner Point	Value of the Profit Formula: $\$0.50x + \$0.40y$							
$(12,10)$	$\$0.50(12)$	$+$	$\$0.40(10)$	$=$	$\$6.00$	$+$	$\$4.00$	$=$ $\$10.00$
$(12,32)$	$\$0.50(12)$	$+$	$\$0.40(32)$	$=$	$\$6.00$	$+$	$\$12.80$	$=$ $\$18.80$
$(45,10)$	$\$0.50(45)$	$+$	$\$0.40(10)$	$=$	$\$22.50$	$+$	$\$4.00$	$=$ $\$26.50*$

Optimal production policy: Make 45 business and 10 charity calls.

50. (a) Let x be the number of gallons of premium and y be the number of gallons of regular.

	High Octane (500 gal.)	Low Octane (600 gal.)	Minimums	Profit
Premium, x gallons	0.5	0.5	0	$0.40
Regular, y gallons	0.25	0.75	0	$0.30

(b) Profit formula: $P = \$0.40x + \$0.30y$

Constraints: $x \geq 0$ and $y \geq 0$ $\left(\text{minimums}\right)$

$$0.5x + 0.25y \leq 500 \left(\text{high octane}\right)$$

$$0.5x + 0.75y \leq 600 \left(\text{low octane}\right)$$

(c) Feasible region:

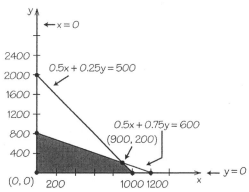

Corner points: Three of the corner points are intercepts on the axes. These are $\left(0,0\right)$, $\left(0,800\right)$, and $\left(1000,0\right)$. The final corner point is the point of intersection between $0.5x + 0.25y = 500$ and $0.5x + 0.75y = 600$. We can find this by multiplying both sides of $0.5x + 0.25y = 500$ by -1, and adding the result to $0.5x + 0.75y = 600$.

$$-0.5x - 0.25y = -500$$

$$\underline{0.5x + 0.75y = 600}$$

$$0.50y = 100 \Rightarrow y = 200$$

Substitute $y = 200$ into $0.5x + 0.25y = 500$ and solve for x. We have the following.

$$0.5x + 0.25\left(200\right) = 500 \Rightarrow 0.5x + 50 = 500 \Rightarrow 0.5x = 450 \Rightarrow x = 900$$

The point of intersection is therefore $\left(900, 200\right)$.

(d) We wish to maximize $\$0.40x + \$0.30y$.

Corner Point	Value of the Profit Formula: $\$0.40x + \$0.30y$						
$\left(0,0\right)$	$\$0.40\left(0\right)$	+	$\$0.30\left(0\right)$	=	$\$0$ +	$\$0$ =	$\$0$
$\left(0,800\right)$	$\$0.40\left(0\right)$	+	$\$0.30\left(800\right)$	=	$\$0$ +	$\$240$ =	$\$240$
$\left(1000,0\right)$	$\$0.40\left(1000\right)$	+	$\$0.30\left(0\right)$	=	$\$400$ +	$\$0$ =	$\$400$
$\left(900,200\right)$	$\$0.40\left(900\right)$	+	$\$0.30\left(200\right)$	=	$\$360$ +	$\$60$ =	$\$420*$

Optimal production policy: Make 900 gallons of premium and 200 gallons of regular.

With non-zero minimums $x \geq 100$ and $y \geq 100$, there will be no change because the optimal production policy already obeys these non-zero minimums.

51. (a) Let x be the number of bikes and y be the number of wagons.

	Machine (12 hr)	Paint(16 hr.)	Minimums	Profit
Bikes, x	2	4	0	\$12
Wagons, y	3	2	0	\$10

(b) Profit formula: $P = \$12x + \$10y$

Constraints: $x \geq 0$ and $y \geq 0$ (minimums); $2x + 3y \leq 12$ (machine); $4x + 2y \leq 16$ (paint)

(c) Feasible region:

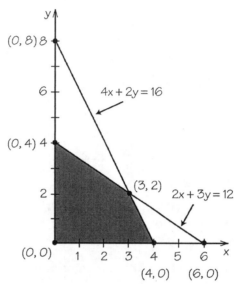

Corner points: Three of the corner points are intercepts on the axes. These are $(0,0)$, $(0,4)$, and $(4,0)$. The final corner point is the point of intersection between $2x + 3y = 12$ and $4x + 2y = 16$. We can find this by multiplying both sides of $2x + 3y = 12$ by -2, and adding the result to $4x + 2y = 16$.

$$-4x - 6y = -24$$
$$\underline{4x + 2y = 16}$$
$$-4y = -8 \Rightarrow y = 2$$

Substitute $y = 2$ into $4x + 2y = 16$ and solve for x. We have the following.

$$4x + 2(2) = 16 \Rightarrow 4x + 4 = 16 \Rightarrow 4x = 12 \Rightarrow x = 3$$

The point of intersection is therefore $(3,2)$.

(d) We wish to maximize $\$12x + \$10y$.

Corner Point	Value of the Profit Formula: $\$12x + \$10y$
$(0,0)$	$\$12(0) + \$10(0) = \quad \$0 + \quad \$0 = \quad \$0$
$(0,4)$	$\$12(0) + \$10(4) = \quad \$0 + \$40 = \$40$
$(4,0)$	$\$12(4) + \$10(0) = \$48 + \quad \$0 = \$48$
$(3,2)$	$\$12(3) + \$10(2) = \$36 + \$20 = \$56^{*}$

Optimal production policy: Make 3 bikes and 2 wagons.

With non-zero minimums $x \geq 2$ and $y \geq 2$, there will be no change because the optimal production policy already obeys these non-zero minimums.

52. (a)

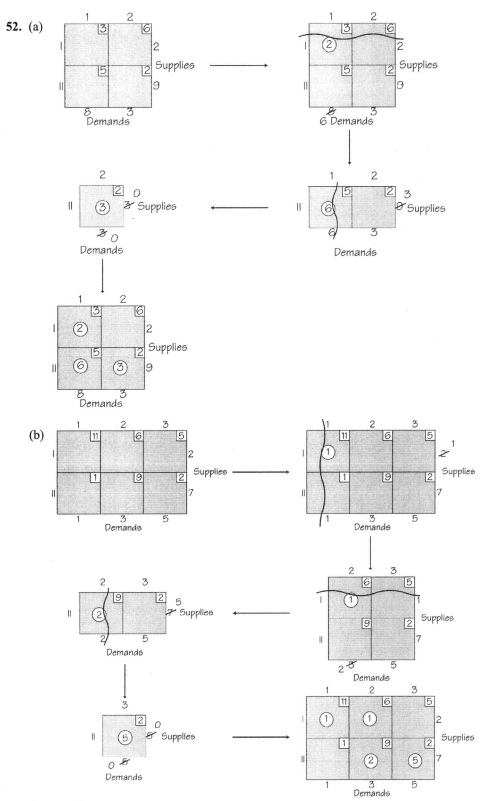

Continued on next page

52. continued

(c)

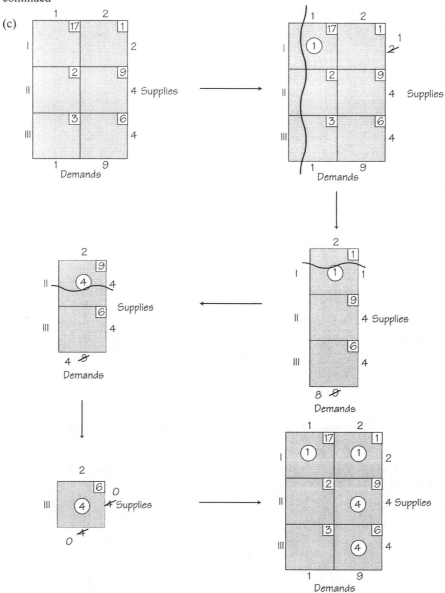

(d) Answers will vary.

For (a) we might have two companies that supply a total of 11 units of lemon ices, and two stores that require 11 units of lemon ices. For (b) we have two coal mines which can supply a total of 9 units of coal, and three coal burning power plants which require 9 units of coal. For (c) we have three orchards which can supply 10 units of apples and two supermarket chains which require 10 units of apples.

(e) For (a) the cost is $2(3)+6(5)+3(2)=6+30+6=42.$

For (b) the cost is $1(11)+1(6)+2(9)+5(2)=11+6+18+10=45.$

For (c) the cost is $1(17)+1(1)+4(9)+4(6)=17+1+36+24=78.$

53. (a)

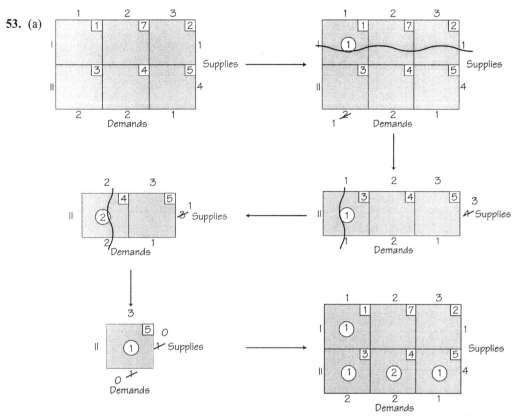

(b) The cost for this solution is $1(1) + 1(3) + 2(4) + 1(5) = 1 + 3 + 8 + 5 = 17$.

(c) The indicator value for cell $(I, 2)$ is $7 - 1 + 3 - 4 = 5$.

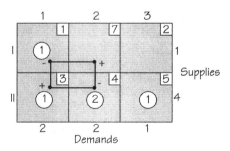

The indicator value for cell $(I, 3)$ is $2 - 1 + 3 - 5 = -1$.

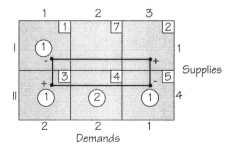

54. (a)

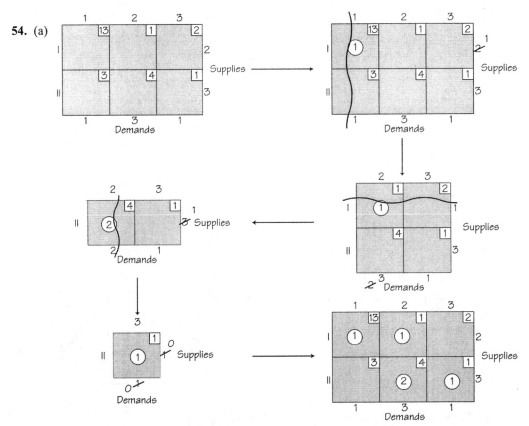

(b) The indicator value for cell $(\text{II},1)$ is $3-13+1-4=-13$.

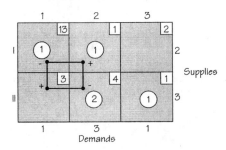

The indicator value for cell $(\text{I},3)$ is $2-1+4-1=4$.

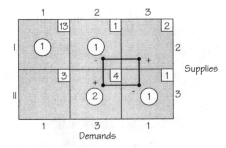

Continued on next page

54. continued

(c) The cost for this solution is $1(13)+1(1)+2(4)+1(1)=13+1+8+1=23$.

We get a cheaper solution, as shown below, by shipping using cell $(\text{II},1)$.

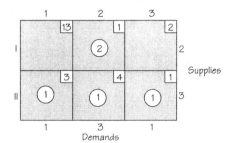

The new solution has cost $2(1)+1(3)+1(4)+1(1)=2+3+4+1=10$. This saves 13 units of cost over the previous solution, as would be expected because the indicator value is -13, and we shipped one more unit via cell $(\text{II},1)$.

55. (a) The graph is a tree because it is connected and has no circuit.

(b) If we add the edge joining Vertex I to Vertex 2 we get the circuit 2, I, 1, II, 2.

If we add the edge from Vertex I to Vertex 3 we get the circuit 3, I, 1, II, 3.

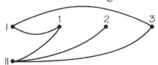

(c) For the circuit 2, I, 1, II, 2 it corresponds to the following circuit of cells.

$$(\text{I},2),(\text{I},1),(\text{II},1),(\text{II},2),(\text{I},2)$$

For the circuit 3, I, 1, II, 3 it corresponds to the following circuit of cells.

$$(\text{I},3),(\text{I},1),(\text{II},1),(\text{II},3),(\text{I},3)$$

56. (a)

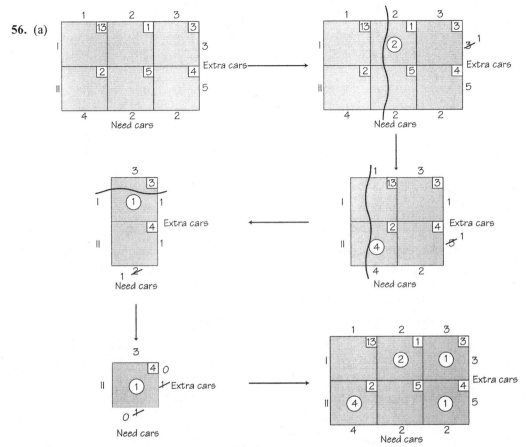

In row I the minimum cost is 1 $\left(\text{cell}\,(\text{I},2)\right)$ and for row II the minimum cost is 2 $\left(\text{cell}\,(\text{II},1)\right)$. Thus, the row with the minimum value is row 1. Since this minimum cost occurs in column 2, we try shipping as much as we can via this cell. This means we can ship 2 units in cell $(\text{I},2)$. So we cross out column 2, and reduce the rim condition for row I to a 1. We now have a 2×2 tableau.

We find the minimum cost for row I is 3 (there is a tie for two different cells) and the minimum cost for row II is 2, in cell $(\text{II},1)$. So the row with minimum value is row II; so in this row we ship as much as we can via cell $(\text{II},1)$. We can ship 4 via this cell, so now we cross out column 1. The rim value for this row is reduced from 5 to 1. We now have a tableau with one column (column 3) and two rows; row I has a minimum of 3 and row II a minimum of 4; so we ship first via the minimum row cost (row I whose cost is 3) in cell $(\text{I},3)$ (1 unit) and cross out row I, and finally, in cell $(\text{II},3)$, 1 unit (cost 4).

So the cells with circled numbers are: $(\text{I},2)$ with a 2; $(\text{I},3)$ with a 1; $(\text{II},1)$ with a 4; and $(\text{II},3)$ with a 1.

(b) The cost of the solution above is $2(1)+1(3)+4(2)+1(4)=2+3+8+4=17.$

Continued on next page

56. continued

(c)

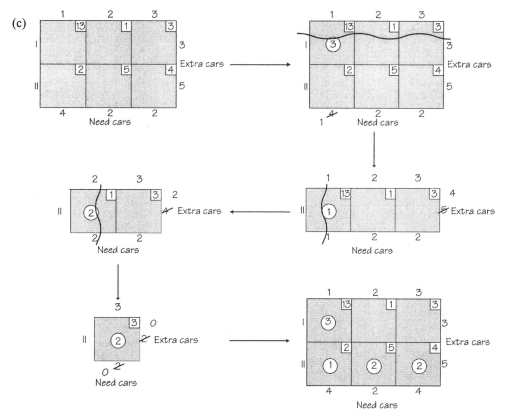

The cost of this solution is $3(13)+1(2)+2(5)+2(4)=39+2+10+8=59,$ which is 42 units more expensive than the solution we found in (b). It is often worth using a more complex method to find a better initial solution to a problem than using a simple method, which finds a poor initial solution, as the Northwest Corner Rule does for this problem.

57. (a) (i)

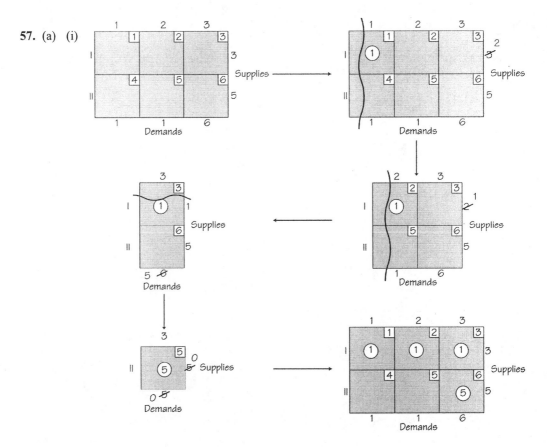

(ii) Since the rim values are the same, the end result will be the same (relative to the new table)

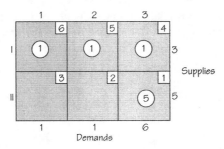

Continued on next page

57. (a) continued

(iii)

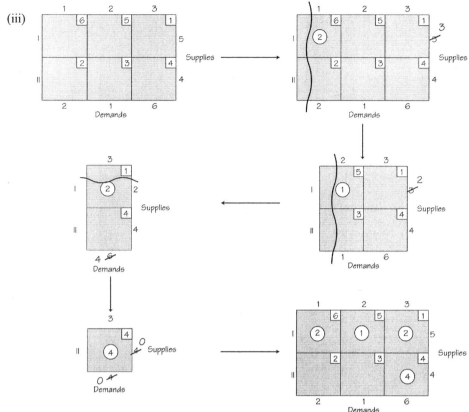

(b) For (i) the indicator value for each non-circled cell is calculated as follows.

cell $(\text{II},1): 4-6+3-1=0$

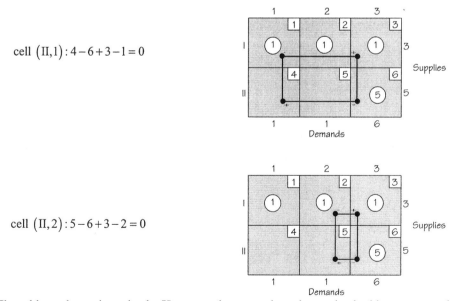

cell $(\text{II},2): 5-6+3-2=0$

The tableau shown is optimal. However, there are also other optimal tableaux, as can be seen from the fact that the indicator values for each of the cells that have no circled entries are 0.

Continued on next page

57. (b) continued

For (ii) the indicator value for each non-circled cell is calculated as follows.

cell $(\text{II},1): 3 - 1 + 4 - 6 = 0$

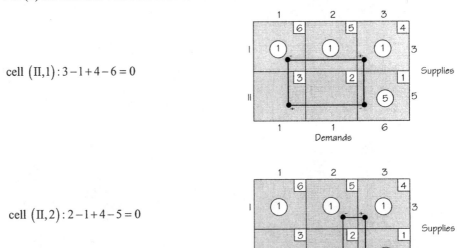

cell $(\text{II},2): 2 - 1 + 4 - 5 = 0$

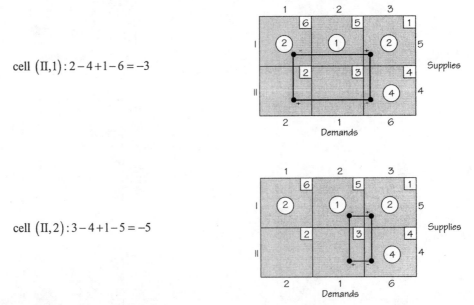

The tableau shown is optimal, although there are also other optimal tableaux.

For (iii) the indicator value for each non-circled cell is calculated as follows.

cell $(\text{II},1): 2 - 4 + 1 - 6 = -3$

cell $(\text{II},2): 3 - 4 + 1 - 5 = -5$

The tableau shown is not optimal. The current cost is as follows.

$$2(6) + 1(5) + 2(1) + 4(4) = 12 + 5 + 2 + 16 = 35$$

Continued on next page

57. (b) continued

Since cell $(\text{II},1)$ has a more negative indicator value, we can reduce the cost more by using that cell. Increasing by 2, we obtain the following tableau.

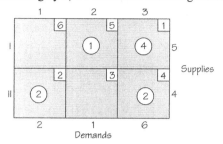

The cost is now $1(5)+4(1)+2(4)+2(2)=5+4+8+4=21$. We can reduce the cost more by using cell $(\text{II},2)$. Increasing by 1, we obtain the following tableau.

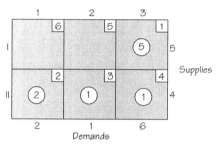

The cost is now $2(2)+1(3)+1(4)+5(1)=4+3+4+5=16$.

58. (a)

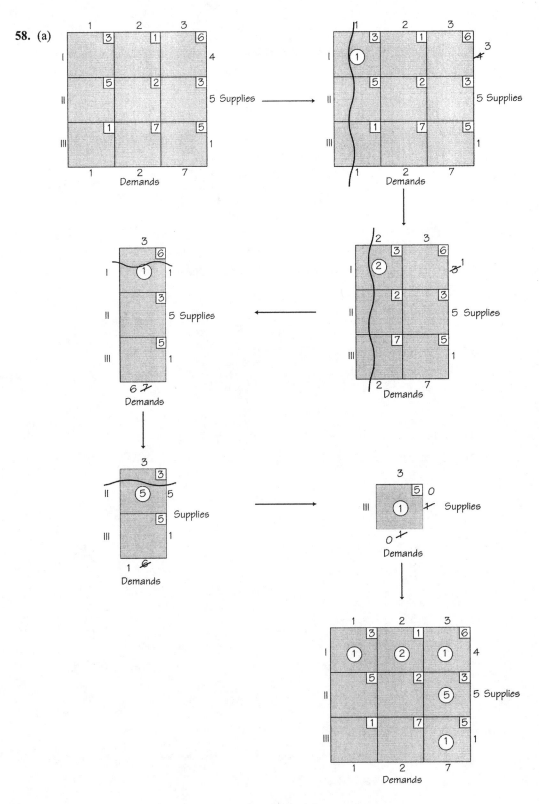

(b) The cost is given by $1(3)+2(1)+1(6)+5(3)+1(5)=3+2+6+15+5=31.$

Continued on next page

58. continued

(c) The indicator value for cell $(II,1)$ is $5-3+6-3=5$.

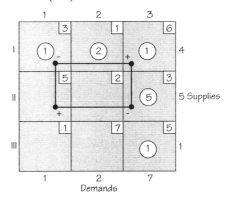

The indicator value for cell $(II,2)$ is $2-3+6-1=4$.

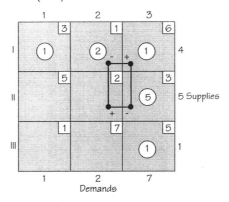

The indicator value for cell $(III,1)$ is $1-5+6-3=-1$.

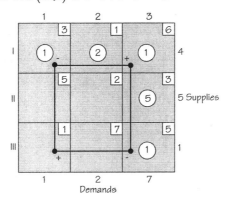

Continued on next page

58. (c) continued

The indicator value for cell $(\text{III}, 2)$ is $7 - 5 + 6 - 1 = 7$.

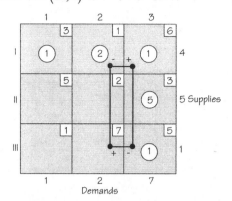

Since one of these cells has an indicator value, which is negative, the initial solution we found is not optimal.

Word Search Solution

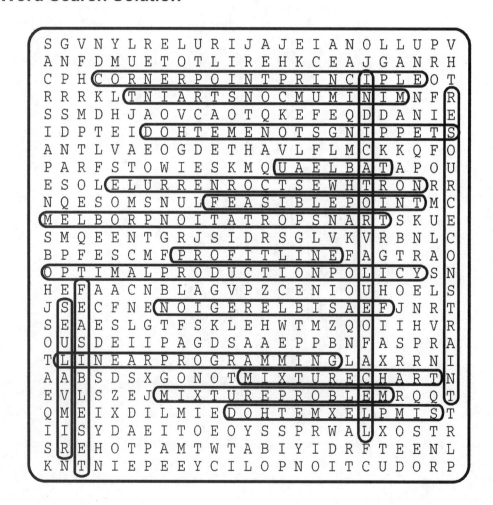

Chapter 5
Exploring Data: Distributions

Chapter Outline

Chapter Summary

The description of data is an important link between its collection and its interpretation. Exploratory data analysis combines numerical summary with graphical display in an attempt to discern patterns in data. *Data* are often values of a numeric variable. The pattern of these values is called a distribution. In general, one expects chance deviation from a smooth distribution. Important deviations are called outliers.

In analyzing data, it is wise to proceed from the simple to the complex, to analyze variables one at a time and then to seek relations between variables. Visual displays are useful tools in data analysis because of the eye's uncanny ability to see pattern as well as deviation from pattern. *Histograms* and *stemplots* can be extremely suggestive. *Boxplots* provide both a visual and numeric summary of data and can be useful in comparing distributions for several variables.

Numerical summary of data should give a measure of *center* and of spread for the data. Typically used measures of center are the *mean* (arithmetic average) and *median* (midpoint of the data set). Measures of spread or *variability* include the range of the data set (difference between the high and low values), quartiles (the values that have 25% and 75% of the data lying below them), standard deviation, and *variance*. The *five-number summary* of a set of data provides the median, the upper and lower quartiles, and the high and low values for the data set. A boxplot is a visual display of the five-number summary.

Another and very important visual display is given by normal distributions. All *normal curves* are symmetric and bell-shaped. These are the main characteristics of a normal distribution. A particular normal curve is completely specified by its mean μ (center point) and standard deviation s (spread). Any normal distribution satisfies the *68–95–99.7 rule*. Also, the first and third quartiles of any normal distribution can be easily calculated given its mean and standard deviation.

Skill Objectives

1. Construct a histogram for a small data set.

2. List and describe two types of distribution for a histogram.

3. Identify from a histogram possible outliers of a data set.

4. Construct a stemplot for a small data set.

5. Calculate the mean of a set of data.

6. Sort a set of data from smallest to largest and then determine its median.

7. Determine the upper and lower quartiles for a data set.

8. Calculate the five-number summary for a data set.

9. Construct the diagram of a boxplot from the data set's five-number summary.

10. Calculate the standard deviation of a small data set.

11. Describe a normal curve.

12. Given the mean and standard deviation of a normally distributed data set, compute the first and third quartiles.

13. Explain the 68–95–99.7 rule.

14. Sketch the graph of a normal curve given its mean and standard deviation.

15. Given the mean and standard deviation of a normally distributed data set, compute the intervals in which the data set fall into a given percentage by applying the 68–95–99.7 rule.

Teaching Tips

1. You may wish to give handouts that include a few different data sets when the chapter is introduced for students to become familiar with. These data sets can be used for exploring the different types of statistical analysis in the chapter. By having these data sets already prepared, you can forgo having to write them on the board and having students copy them during the lecture.

2. Students can easily get the terms skewed right and skewed left confused. Emphasize that the location of the "tail" indicates the direction.

3. When constructing a histogram, students often need help in determining appropriate classes for data of a given range. When listing intervals for a histogram, students are often confused about how to handle data points that occur at the endpoints of the interval. It may be helpful to explain that these are normally done in an arbitrary fashion. If, for example, an interval goes from 5.10 to 5.20, one approach is to end that interval at 5.19 (assuming measurements are done to the nearest hundredth) and start the next at 5.20. An equally desirable approach would be to end the first interval at 5.20 and then begin the next at 5.21. Without attempting to apply sophisticated statistical guidelines, you may want to examine different data sets and discuss appropriate classes.

4. Be clear to your students as to your expectations regarding the use of calculators/spreadsheets in their work. If technology is emphasized, let students know what is required regarding intermediate calculations.

5. A helpful approach to determining both the median and lower and upper quartiles is to work out examples when the number of data points is even and a multiple of 4, when it is even but not a multiple of 4, and when it is odd. Subdividing the set of an odd number of data points results in eliminating the median from the set when analyzing the lower and upper halves, whereas subdividing for an even number places each one of the two middle points in a different half.

6. Using the formula $\frac{n+1}{2}$ to determine the location of the median within a sorted data set sometimes creates confusion, because students don't understand the difference between a cardinal and an ordinal number. Reporting the answer to this calculation as the "nth" location within the set helps the student understand this distinction.

7. Although sorting the data points in a set can be done either from lowest to highest or from highest to lowest, the natural progression for the sort, when written in a vertical fashion, is to go from low to high. Then the concepts of lower and upper quartiles flow naturally. In a hierarchical order, "lower" comes before "higher."

8. An example that emphasizes to students that mean and median are measures of describing center and that the mean is sensitive to outliers is the following.

   A town advertises that its average salary is $100,000. Would you want to move there?

   As it turns out, there are 11 people in that town. One makes $1,000,000 and the rest make $10,000.

   You may also choose to briefly mention *mode* at this point to simply emphasize that the term "average" depends on the form of measurement.

9. Exercise 12 has an outcome of the gap between the median and the mean being cut about in half when removing the high outlier. This data set can also be used in discussing standard deviation. In this data set, the standard deviation drops from 13.2 to 9.9.

10. When introducing the concept of the normal curve, you may wish to concentrate first on the base line because of its similarity to the number line. The mean plays the role of the origin, and the standard deviation markings, the units. Inserting a specific mean and standard deviation then becomes an exercise in relabeling the mean and calculating the units, which are three standard deviations from the mean. Some students will need a lot of practice in labeling normal curves with given means and standard deviations.

Research Paper

Exercise 18 deals with the popular vote by the successful candidate in the presidential elections from 1948 to 2004. Students can write a paper using this data to determine the winning candidates in each election. Students can indicate which parties were involved and determine if any other statistical data may be of interest (such as if a candidate was incumbent). You may also ask students to further research presidential statistical data such as age when taking office, age when leaving office, or number of days in office.

Collaborative Learning

Data Analysis

Suppose you are the president of CBS, and you are preparing to submit a bid on televising the World Series. You have to decide on how much to bid, depending on how much advertising revenue you expect to receive. However, there is a good deal of uncertainty in this matter, since the length of the World Series is not known in advance. The series is played on a best 4-out-of-7 basis, so that the series can last anywhere from 4 to 7 games. To assist you in your calculations, you decide to look to the past. The following table tells you the length of the series in each of the years from 1905 on. (1903, 1919, 1920, and 1921 are left out because those series were played on a best 5-out-of-9 basis. Also, the series was not played in 1904 and 1994.)

Using the data, do the following.

1. Construct a frequency chart of the number of games in a World Series.

2. Draw a histogram of the number of games in a World Series.

3. Find the mean number of games in a World Series.

4. Find the standard deviation of the number of games in a World Series.

1905 5	1924 7	1940 7	1956 7	1972 7	1988 5
1906 6	1925 7	1941 5	1957 7	1973 7	1989 4
1907 4	1926 7	1942 5	1958 7	1974 5	1990 4
1908 5	1927 4	1943 5	1959 6	1975 7	1991 7
1909 7	1928 4	1944 6	1960 7	1976 4	1992 6
1910 5	1929 5	1945 7	1961 5	1977 6	1993 6
1911 6	1930 6	1946 7	1962 7	1978 6	1995 6
1912 7	1931 7	1947 7	1963 4	1979 7	1996 6
1913 5	1932 4	1948 6	1964 7	1980 6	1997 7
1914 4	1933 5	1949 5	1965 7	1981 6	1998 4
1915 5	1934 7	1950 4	1966 4	1982 7	1999 4
1916 5	1935 6	1951 6	1967 7	1983 5	2000 5
1917 6	1936 6	1952 7	1968 7	1984 5	2001 7
1918 6	1937 5	1953 6	1969 5	1985 7	2002 7
1922 4	1938 4	1954 4	1970 5	1986 7	2003 6
1923 6	1939 4	1955 7	1971 7	1987 7	2004 4

Solutions

Skills Check:

1. a   2. a   3. b   4. b   5. c   6. a   7. b   8. c   9. b   10. b

11. c   12. c   13. b   14. a   15. b   16. a   17. a   18. a   19. b   20. c

Exercises:

1. (a) The individuals in the data set are the make and model of 2004 motor vehicles.

    (b) The variables are vehicle type, transmission type, number of cylinders, city MPG, and highway MPG. Histograms would be helpful for cylinders (maybe), and the two MPGs (certainly).

2. The distribution is skewed to the right. Shakespeare uses many words of two, three, and four letters and a few long words (10, 11, and 12 letters). Most English prose will show a similarly shaped distribution of word lengths because so many common words (I, you, him, her, and, or, not,…) are short.

3. Draw a histogram with a peak at the right and lower bars trailing out to the left of the peak.

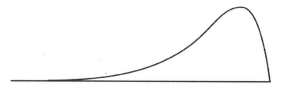

Most coins were minted in recent years, producing a peak at the right (highest-numbered years, like 2004 and 2005). There are few coins from 1990 and even fewer from 1980.

4. Here is a histogram that includes the outlier. The histogram shows the shape (roughly symmetric, plus the outlier) better than the stemplot.

Class	Count
6 – 10	0
11 – 15	2
16 – 20	5
21 – 25	7
26 – 30	5
31 – 35	1
36 – 40	0
41 – 45	0
46 – 50	0
51 – 55	0
56 – 60	0
61 – 65	0
66 – 70	1

5. (a) Otherwise, big countries would top the list even if they had low emissions for their size.

   (b) Using class widths of 2 metric tons per person, we have the following.

Class	Count
0.0 – 1.9	20
2.0 – 3.9	9
4.0 – 5.9	3
6.0 – 7.9	4
8.0 – 9.9	6
10.0 – 11.9	3
12.0 – 13.9	0
14.0 – 15.9	0
16.0 – 17.9	2
18.0 – 19.9	1

   The distribution is skewed to the right.   There appear to be three high outliers: Canada, Australia, and the United States.

6. From top left, (a) is study time: right-skewed; (b) is handedness: most people are right-handed; (c) is gender: majority female but more balanced than handedness; (d) is height, single-peaked and roughly symmetric.

7. (a) Alaska is 5.7% and Florida is 17.6%.

   (b) The distribution is single-peaked and roughly symmetric. The center is near 12.7% (12.7% and 12.8% are the 24th and 25th in order out of 48, ignoring Alaska and Florida). The spread is from 8.5% to 15.6%.

8. Rounding the data to the nearest 10, we have the following.

   140   160   110   150   130   100   100   **0**80   150

   170   200   270   100   170   360   150   150   260

   Truncating the zero as described, we have the following.

   14   16   11   15   13   10   10   08   15

   17   20   27   10   17   36   15   15   26

   There is one high outlier (359) which we omit from the stemplot. The distribution is single-peaked and slightly right-skewed. Control of glucose is poor: all but five are above 130. Here is the stemplot:

   ```
   0 | 8
   1 | 000134
   1 | 5555677
   2 | 0
   2 | 67
   ```

9. Here is the stemplot.

$$
\begin{array}{r|l}
10 & 139 \\
11 & 5 \\
12 & 669 \\
13 & 77 \\
14 & 08 \\
15 & 244 \\
16 & 55 \\
17 & 8 \\
18 & \\
19 & \\
20 & 0 \\
\end{array}
$$

There is one high outlier, 200. The center of the 17 observations other than the outlier is 137 (9th of 17). The spread is 101 to 178.

10. Here is the stemplot.

$$
\begin{array}{r|l}
48 & 8 \\
49 & \\
50 & 7 \\
51 & 0 \\
52 & 6799 \\
53 & 04469 \\
54 & 2467 \\
55 & 03578 \\
56 & 12358 \\
57 & 59 \\
58 & 5 \\
\end{array}
$$

The distribution is roughly symmetric and single-peaked except for one low observation, which may be an outlier.

11. (a) $\overline{x} = \frac{154+109+137+115+152+140+154+178+101+103+126+126+137+165+165+129+200+148}{18} = \frac{2539}{18} \approx 141.1$.

    (b) Without the outlier, $\overline{x} = \frac{154+109+137+115+152+140+154+178+101+103+126+126+137+165+165+129+148}{17} = \frac{2339}{17} \approx 137.6$. The high outlier pulls the mean up.

12. (a) Here is the stemplot, with the outlier.

$$
\begin{array}{r|l}
1 & 69 \\
2 & 455 \\
3 & 334477 \\
4 & 025669 \\
5 & \\
6 & \\
7 & 3 \\
\end{array}
$$

    (b) For all 18 years, $\overline{x} = \frac{16+25+24+19+33+25+34+46+37+33+42+40+37+34+49+73+46+45}{18} = \frac{658}{18} \approx 36.56$. To determine the median, we must put the data in order from smallest to largest.

    16 19 24 25 25 33 33 34 **34 37** 37 40 42 45 46 46 49 73

    Since there are 18 pieces of data, the median is the mean of the 9th and 10th pieces of data. $M = \frac{34+37}{2} = \frac{71}{2} = 35.5$.

    For the 17 years other than 2001, $\overline{x} = \frac{16+25+24+19+33+25+34+46+37+33+42+40+37+34+49+46+45}{17} = \frac{585}{17} \approx 34.41$. Taking out 73 as a piece of data, we have now 17 pieces of data.

    16 19 24 25 25 33 33 34 **34** 37 37 40 42 45 46 46 49

    The median is the $\frac{17+1}{2} = \frac{18}{2} = 9$th piece of data, namely $M = 34$. Removing the high outlier cuts the gap between the median and the mean about in half.

13. The distribution of incomes is strongly right-skewed, so the mean is much higher than the median. Thus, $57,852 is the mean.

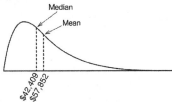

14. The distribution of household assets is very right-skewed. Most young households have few assets, but a few wealthy households have large assets. The strong skewness pulls the mean up.

15. Examples will vary.
One high outlier will do it. For example, 1, 2, 3, 3, 4, 17. These data have third quartile 4 and mean, $\bar{x} = \frac{1+2+3+3+4+17}{6} = \frac{30}{6} = 5$.

16. Examples will vary.
We want 10 to be the 3rd (in increasing order) of the 5 observations. To get mean 7, the sum must be 35. So, for example, 1, 1, 10, 10, 13 will do.

17. The five-number summary is Minimum, Q_1, M, Q_3, Maximum.
The minimum is 5.7 and maximum is 17.6. The median is the mean of the 25th and 26th pieces of data, namely $\frac{12.7+12.8}{2} = \frac{25.5}{2} = 12.75$. There are 25 pieces of data below the median, thus Q_1 is the 13th piece of data, 11.7. There are 25 pieces of data above the median, thus Q_3 is the 38th piece of data, namely 13.5. Thus, the five-number summary for these 50 observations is 5.7, 11.7, 12.75, 13.5, 17.6.

18. (a) Round to full percents.

Year	1948	1952	1956	1960	1964	1968	1972	1976
Percent	50	55	75	50	61	43	61	50

Year	1980	1984	1988	1992	1996	2000	2004
Percent	51	59	54	43	49	48	51

All percents are on stems 4, 5, and 6. The stemplot is

```
4 | 3389
5 | 000114579
6 | 11
```

b) To determine the median, we must put the data in order from smallest to largest.

43.2 43.4 47.9 49.2 49.6 49.7 50.1 **50.7** 51.2 53.9 55.1 57.4 58.8 60.7 61.1

Since there are 15 pieces of data, the 8th piece of data is the median, namely 50.7%.

c) Since there are 7 pieces of data above the median, the third quartile is the 12th piece of data, namely 57.4%. So, the 1956, 1964, 1972, and 1984 elections were landslides.

19. To determine the minimum, maximum, and median, we must put the 21 pieces of data in order from smallest to largest.

13 15 16 16 17 19 20 22 23 23 **23** 24 25 25 26 28 28 28 29 32 66

The minimum is 13 and the maximum is 66. The median is the $\frac{21+1}{2} = \frac{22}{2} = 11$th piece of data, namely 23. Since there are 10 observations to the left of the median, Q_1 is the mean of the 5th and 6th pieces of data, namely $\frac{17+19}{2} = \frac{36}{2} = 18$. Since there are 10 observations to the right of the median, Q_3 is the mean of the 16th and 17th pieces of data, namely $\frac{28+28}{2} = \frac{56}{2} = 28$.

Thus, the five-number summary is 13, 18, 23, 28, 66.

20. To determine the minimum, maximum, and median, we must put the 21 pieces of data in order from smallest to largest.

4.88 5.07 5.10 5.26 5.27 5.29 5.29 5.30 5.34 5.34 5.36 5.39 5.42 5.44 5.46

5.47 5.50 5.53 5.55 5.57 5.58 5.61 5.62 5.63 5.65 5.68 5.75 5.79 5.85

The minimum is 4.88 and the maximum is 5.85. The median is the $\frac{29+1}{2} = \frac{30}{2} = 15^{th}$ piece of data, namely 5.46. Since there are 14 observations to the left of the median, Q_1 is the mean of the 7th and 8th pieces of data, namely $\frac{5.29+5.30}{2} = \frac{10.59}{2} = 5.295$. Since there are 14 observations to the right of the median, Q_3 is the mean of the 22th and 23th pieces of data, namely $\frac{5.61+5.62}{2} = \frac{11.23}{2} = 5.615$.

Thus, the five-number summary is 4.88, 5.295, 5.46, 5.615, 5.85. The quartiles are roughly equidistant from the median (symmetry). The minimum (a possible outlier) is farther from the median than is the maximum.

21. To determine the minimum, maximum, and median, we should put the 48 pieces of data in order from smallest to largest. It may be easier, however, to create a stemplot.

```
 0 | 001122223357899
 1 | 02478
 2 | 3558
 3 | 67899
 4 | 68
 5 | 1
 6 | 18
 7 | 36
 8 | 018
 9 | 017
10 | 02
11 | 0
12 |
13 |
14 |
15 |
16 | 0
17 | 0
18 |
19 | 9
```

The minimum is 0.0 and the maximum is 19.9. Since there are 48 pieces of data, the median is the mean of the 24th and 25th pieces of data, namely $\frac{2.8+3.6}{2} = \frac{6.4}{2} = 3.2$. Since there are 24 observations to the left of the median, Q_1 is the mean of the 12th and 13th piece, of data, namely $\frac{0.7+0.8}{2} = \frac{1.5}{2} = 0.75$. Since there are 24 observations to the right of the median, Q_3 is the mean of the 36th and 37th pieces of data, namely $\frac{7.6+8.0}{2} = \frac{15.6}{2} = 7.8$.

Thus, the five-number summary is 0.0, 0.75, 3.2, 7.8, 19.9. The third quartile and maximum are much farther from the median that the first quartile and minimum, showing that the right side of the distribution is more spread out than the left side.

22. The minimum is 4123 and the maximum is 29,875. Since there are 56 pieces of data, the median is the mean of the 28th and 29th pieces of data, namely $\frac{19,910+20,234}{2} = \frac{40,144}{2} = 20,072$. Since there are 28 observations to the left of the median, Q_1 is the mean of the 14th and 15th pieces of data, namely $\frac{15,500+15,934}{2} = \frac{31,434}{2} = 15,717$. Since there are 28 observations to the right of the median, Q_3 is the mean of the 42nd and 43rd pieces of data, namely $\frac{27,904+28,011}{2} = \frac{55,915}{2} = 27,957.5$.

Thus, the five-number summary is 4123, 15717, 20072, 27957.5, 29875. The boxplot displays these five numbers.

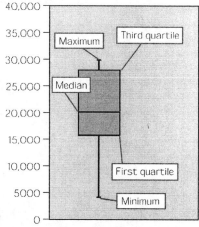

It cannot, however, show the clusters in the data.

23. The income distribution for bachelor's degree holders is generally higher than for high school graduates: the median for bachelor's is greater than the third quartile for high school. The bachelor's distribution is very much more spread out, especially at the high-income end but also between the quartiles.

24. (a) The median is at the $\frac{n+1}{2} = \frac{14,959+1}{2} = \frac{14,960}{2} = 7480$th position in the list. The value of the median is (from the data file) $46,000.

(b) Q_1 is the median of the 7479 observations to the left of the median, position 3740. Similarly, Q_3 has position $7480 + 3740 = 11,220$. Although student answers may vary slightly, the values of the quartiles are $Q_1 = \$31,000$ and $Q_3 = \$65,000$.

25. (a) Placing the data in order from smallest to largest, we have the following.

2.0	2.5	3.0	7.1	10.1	10.3	12.0	12.1
12.9	14.7	14.8	17.6	18.0	18.5	20.1	21.3
21.7	24.9	26.9	28.3	29.1	30.5	31.4	32.5
32.9	33.7	34.6	34.6	35.1	36.6	37.0	37.7
37.9	38.6	42.7	43.4	44.5	44.9	46.4	47.6
49.4	50.4	51.9	53.2	54.2	56.4	57.4	58.8
61.4	63.1	64.9	65.6	69.5	69.8	79.5	81.1
82.2	92.2	97.7	103.1	118.2	156.5	196.0	204.9

Continued on next page

25. (a) continued

Either a histogram or a stemplot will do. By rounding to the nearest whole number and using the ones digit as leaves, we have the following stemplot, with three high outliers (156.5, 196.0, 204.9) omitted.

```
 0 | 2337
 1 | 0022355889
 2 | 0125789
 3 | 1133455577889
 4 | 3355689
 5 | 0234679
 6 | 1356
 7 | 00
 8 | 012
 9 | 28
10 | 3
11 | 8
```

Here is the histogram using class widths of 20 (thousand) barrels of oil.

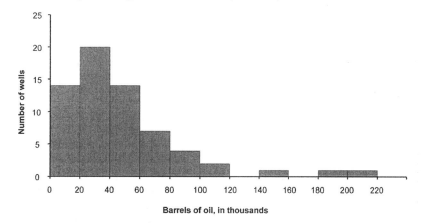

The distribution is right-skewed with high outliers.

(b) $\bar{x} = \frac{3087.9}{64} \approx 48.25$ and since there are 64 pieces of data, the median is the mean of the 32nd and 33rd pieces of data, namely $M = \frac{37.7+37.9}{2} = \frac{75.6}{2} = 37.8$. The long right tail pulls the mean up.

(c) The minimum is 2.0 and the maximum is 204.9. As found in part b, the median is 37.8. Since there are 32 observations to the left of the median, Q_1 is the mean of the 16th and 17th piece of data, namely $\frac{21.3+21.7}{2} = \frac{43}{2} = 21.5$. Since there are 32 observations to the right of the median, Q_3 is the mean of the 48th and 49th piece of data, namely $\frac{58.8+61.4}{2} = \frac{120.2}{2} = 60.1$.

Thus, the five-number summary is 2.0, 21.5, 37.8, 60.1, 204.9. The third quartile and maximum are much farther above the median that the first quartile and minimum are below it, showing that the right side of the distribution is much more spread out than the left side.

26. Each bar represents a single word length. The bar heights appear to be roughly 5%, 17%, 22%, 24%, 12%, 7%, 6%, 3%, and four shorter bars at the right. Q_1 is the 25% point, which is in the 3rd bar, so $Q_1 = 3$. M is the 50% point, so $M = 4$, and similarly $Q_3 = 5$. The five-number summary is 1, 3, 4, 5, 12.

27. For the data in Table 5.1, $M = 4.7\%$, $Q_1 = 2.1\%$, and $Q_3 = 8.7\%$. So $IQR = 8.7 - 2.1 = 6.6$ and $1.5 IQR = 1.5(6.6) = 9.9$. Values less than $2.1 - 9.9 = -7.8$ or greater than $8.7 + 9.9 = 18.6$ are suspected outliers. By this criterion, there are 5 high outliers: Arizona, California, Nevada, New Mexico, and Texas.

28. From Exercise 21, the five-number summary is 0.0, 0.75, 3.2, 7.8, 19.9. So $IQR = 7.8 - 0.75 = 7.05$ and $1.5 IQR = 1.5(7.05) = 10.575$. Observations above $7.8 + 10.575 = 18.375$ are suspected outliers. Only the United States meets this criterion. The histogram in Exercise 5 suggests that there are three clear outliers, not just one.

29. (a) Placing the data in order (not required, but helpful), we have the following hand calculations.

Observations x_i	Deviations $x_i - \bar{x}$	Squared deviations $\left(x_i - \bar{x}\right)^2$
4.88	−0.57	0.3226
5.07	−0.38	0.1429
5.10	−0.35	0.1211
5.26	−0.19	0.0353
5.27	−0.18	0.0317
5.29	−0.16	0.0250
5.29	−0.16	0.0250
5.30	−0.15	0.0219
5.34	−0.11	0.0117
5.34	−0.11	0.0117
5.36	−0.09	0.0077
5.39	−0.06	0.0034
5.42	−0.03	0.0008
5.44	−0.01	0.0001
5.46	0.01	0.0001
5.47	0.02	0.0005
5.50	0.05	0.0027
5.53	0.08	0.0067
5.55	0.10	0.0104
5.57	0.12	0.0149
5.58	0.13	0.0174
5.61	0.16	0.0262
5.62	0.17	0.0296
5.63	0.18	0.0331
5.65	0.20	0.0408
5.68	0.23	0.0538
5.75	0.30	0.0912
5.79	0.34	0.1170
5.85	0.40	0.1616
sum = **157.99**	sum = **0.00**	sum = **1.3669**

$\bar{x} = \frac{157.99}{29} \approx 5.448$ and $s^2 = \frac{1.3669}{29-1} = \frac{1.3669}{28} \approx 0.0488$ which implies $s \approx \sqrt{0.0488} \approx 0.221$.

(b) The median is the $\frac{29+1}{2} = \frac{30}{2} = 15^{\text{th}}$ piece of data, namely 5.46 (From Exercise 10). The mean and median are close, but the one low observation pulls $\bar{x}$ slightly below M.

30. (a) $\bar{x} = \frac{5.6+5.2+4.6+4.9+5.7+6.4}{6} = \frac{32.4}{6} = 5.4$.

(b) Placing the data in order (not required, but helpful), we have the following hand calculations.

Observations x_i	Deviations $x_i - \bar{x}$	Squared deviations $\left(x_i - \bar{x}\right)^2$
4.6	-0.8	0.64
4.9	-0.5	0.25
5.2	-0.2	0.04
5.6	0.2	0.04
5.7	0.3	0.09
6.4	1.0	1.00
sum = 157.99	sum = 0.00	sum = 2.06

Thus, $s^2 = \frac{2.06}{6-1} = \frac{2.06}{5} = 0.412$ and $s = \sqrt{0.412} \approx 0.642$.

31. Since the standard deviation, s, is 15 we have the variance $s^2 = 15^2 = 225$.

32. (a), (b), (d) are in the units of the original observations, years for (a) and (d) and seconds for (b). The correlation (c) has no units.

33. For both data, $\bar{x} = 7.50$ and $s = 2.03$ (to two decimal places). Data A has two low outliers:

```
3 | 1
4 | 7
5 |
6 | 1
7 | 3
8 | 1178
9 | 113
```

and Data B has one high outlier:

```
 5 | 368
 6 | 69
 7 | 079
 8 | 58
 9 |
10 |
11 |
12 | 5
```

Additional comments may vary.

34. (a) Strong skewness and high outliers, so prefer the five-number summary.

(b) Symmetric (and close to normal, as we will see), so use $\bar{x}$ and s.

(c) Irregular with clusters, so no numerical summary does well.

35. With most non-graphing calculators, this goes quickly. Some calculators, e.g., the Sharp EL-509S, already give a wrong answer for three central zeros. The TI-30Xa handles four zeros but is wrong for five central zeros. In both cases, the calculators report $s = 0$, so an alert user knows the result is wrong. With a spreadsheet program such as Excel, we have the following results.

Observations x_i	Deviations $x_i - \overline{x}$	Squared deviations $\left(x_i - \overline{x}\right)^2$		
1001	-1	1	$s^2 = \frac{2}{2}$	1
1002	0	0	$s = \sqrt{s^2}$	1
1003	1	1		
sum = **3006** **sum =** **0**		**sum =** **2**		
$\frac{3006}{3} =$ 1002				

Altering the data as described be have the following.

Observations x_i	Deviations $x_i - \overline{x}$	Squared deviations $\left(x_i - \overline{x}\right)^2$		
10001	-1	1	$s^2 = \frac{2}{2}$	1
10002	0	0	$s = \sqrt{s^2}$	1
10003	1	1		
sum = **30006** **sum =** **0**		**sum =** **2**		
$\frac{30006}{3} =$ 10002				

Continuing this process we have the following.

Observations x_i	Deviations $x_i - \overline{x}$	Squared deviations $\left(x_i - \overline{x}\right)^2$		
100000000000001	-1	1	$s^2 = \frac{2}{2}$	1
100000000000002	0	0	$s = \sqrt{s^2}$	1
100000000000003	1	1		
sum = **300000000000006** **sum =** **0**		**sum =** **2**		
$\frac{300,000,000,000,006}{3} =$ 100000000000002				

At the next stage, we have the following. Note that the observations are as recorded from Excel.

Observations x_i	Deviations $x_i - \overline{x}$	Squared deviations $\left(x_i - \overline{x}\right)^2$		
1000000000000000	0	0	$s^2 = \frac{0}{2}$	0
1000000000000000	0	0	$s = \sqrt{s^2}$	0
1000000000000000	0	0		
sum = **3000000000000000** **sum =** **0**		**sum =** **0**		
$\frac{3,000,000,000,000,000}{3} =$ 1000000000000000				

36. The samples are small, so graphs mainly protect against outliers and other deviations. The stemplots are as follows.

Group 1		Group 2		Group 3	
0		0	29	0	4
1	699	1	224457789	1	225889
2	01247789	2	0	2	22
3	3	3		3	

Here is the histogram using class widths of 10 trees per 0.1 hectare in area.

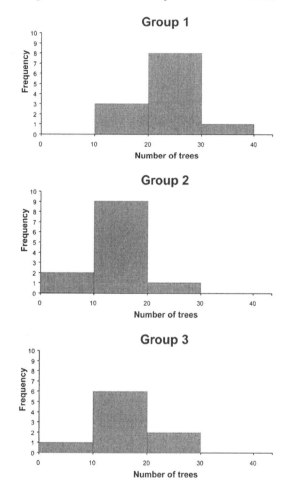

All three samples are at least roughly single-peaked and symmetric, so that use of $\bar{x}$ and s is justified.

Continued on next page

36. continued

Group 1:

Observations x_i	Deviations $x_i - \bar{x}$	Squared deviations $\left(x_i - \bar{x}\right)^2$
16	-7.75	60.0625
19	-4.75	22.5625
19	-4.75	22.5625
20	-3.75	14.0625
21	-2.75	7.5625
22	-1.75	3.0625
24	0.25	0.0625
27	3.25	10.5625
27	3.25	10.5625
28	4.25	18.0625
29	5.25	27.5625
33	9.25	85.5625
sum = 285	**sum = 0**	**sum = 282.25**

$\bar{x} = \frac{285}{12} = 23.75$ and $s^2 = \frac{282.25}{12-1} = \frac{282.25}{11} \approx 25.6591$ which implies $s \approx \sqrt{25.6591} \approx 5.065$.

Group 2:

Observations x_i	Deviations $x_i - \bar{x}$	Squared deviations $\left(x_i - \bar{x}\right)^2$
2	-12.083333	146.00694
9	-5.083333	25.84027
12	-2.083333	4.34028
12	-2.083333	4.34028
14	-0.083333	0.00694
14	-0.083333	0.00694
15	0.916667	0.84028
17	2.916667	8.50695
17	2.916667	8.50695
18	3.916667	15.34028
19	4.916667	24.17361
20	5.916667	35.00695
sum = 169	**sum = 0.000004**	**sum = 272.91667**

$\bar{x} = \frac{169}{12} \approx 14.08$ (we used $\bar{x} \approx 14.083333$ in the deviations calculations for better accuracy and rounded to five decimal places in the calculation of squared deviations) and $s^2 \approx \frac{272.91667}{12-1} = \frac{272.91667}{11} \approx 24.8106$ which implies $s \approx \sqrt{24.8106} \approx 4.981$.

Continued on next page

36. continued

Group 3:

Observations x_i	Deviations $x_i - \overline{x}$	Squared deviations $\left(x_i - \overline{x}\right)^2$
4	-11.777778	138.71605
12	-3.777778	14.27161
12	-3.777778	14.27161
15	-0.777778	0.60494
18	2.222222	4.93827
18	2.222222	4.93827
19	3.222222	10.38271
22	6.222222	38.71605
22	6.222222	38.71605
sum = 142	sum = -0.000002	sum = 265.55556

$\overline{x} = \frac{142}{9} \approx 15.78$ (we used $\overline{x} \approx 15.777778$ in the deviations calculations for better accuracy and rounded to five decimal places in the calculation of squared deviations) and $s^2 \approx \frac{265.55556}{9-1} = \frac{265.55556}{8} \approx 33.1944$ which implies $s \approx \sqrt{33.1944} \approx 5.761$.

In summary, we have the following calculations.

Group 1	Group 2	Group 3
$\overline{x} = 23.75$	$\overline{x} = 14.08$	$\overline{x} = 15.78$
$s = 5.065$	$s = 4.981$	$s = 5.761$

The effect of logging is clear: Group 1 (never logged) has many more species than Groups 2 and 3. Waiting 8 years (Group 3) has little effect on species richness. All three groups have similar standard deviations, so that comparisons of means are straightforward.

37. (a) $s = 0$ is smallest possible: 1, 1, 1, 1

 (b) Largest possible spread: 0, 0, 10, 10.

 (c) In part (a), the answer is not unique. Any other set of four identical numbers will yield a standard deviation of 0, i.e. the values do not deviate from the mean, which is that repeated number. In part b, the answer is unique. The data are spread out as much as possible, given the constraints.

38. Sketch a normal curve, mark the axis with 266 at the center of the curve and 250 and 282 at the change-of-curvature points. These three points set the proper scale.

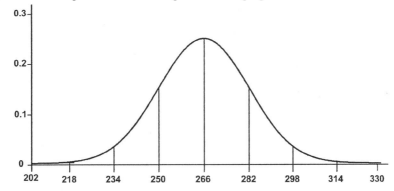

39. Left-skewed, so the mean is pulled toward the long left tail: A = mean and B = median.

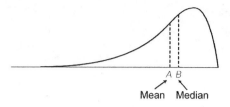

40. Think of the letter M.

41. (a) $\mu \pm 3\sigma = 336 \pm 3(3) = 336 \pm 9$, or 327 to 345 days.

(b) Make a sketch: 339 days is one σ above μ; 68% are with σ of μ.

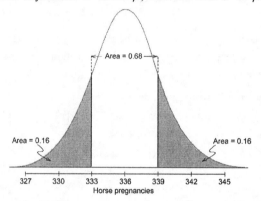

32% lie farther from μ. Thus, half of these, or 16%, lie above 339.

42.

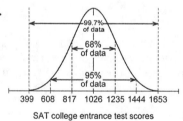

(a) $\mu \pm \sigma = 1026 \pm 209$, or 817 to 1235.

(b) 95% of scores lie within 2 standard deviations from the mean. Thus, the top 2.5% is 2 standard deviations above the mean. Given the following:

$$\sigma + 2\sigma = 1026 + 2(209)$$
$$= 1026 + 418 = 1444,$$

we have 2.5% lie above 1444.

43. The quartiles are $\mu \pm 0.67\sigma = 1026 \pm 0.67(209) \approx 1026 \pm 140$, or $Q_1 = 886$ and $Q_3 = 1166$.

44.

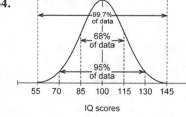

Since $\sigma - 2\sigma = 100 - 2(15) = 100 - 30 = 70$, 70 is 2σ below μ; because 95% of values lie within 2σ of μ, 2.5% of people have IQ scores below 70.

45.

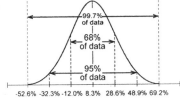

Yearly stock return

(a) $\mu \pm 2\sigma = 8.3 \pm 2(20.3) = 8.3 \pm 40.6$, or -32.3% to 48.9%.

(b) A loss of 32.3% or greater.

46. The quartiles mark the middle 50% of the distribution. They are located at $\mu \pm 0.67\sigma = 8.3 \pm 13.6$, or -5.3% to 21.9%.

47. (a) Normal curves are symmetric, so median = mean = 10%.

(b) Because 95% of values lie within 2σ of μ, $\mu \pm 2\sigma = 10 \pm 2(0.2) = 10 \pm 0.4$ implies 9.6% to 10.4% is the range of concentrations the cover the middle 95% of all the capsules.

(c) The range between the two quartiles covers the middle half of all capsules. Thus, $\mu \pm 0.67\sigma = 10 \pm 0.67(0.2) = 10 \pm 0.134$ implies 9.866% to 10.134% is the desired range.

48.

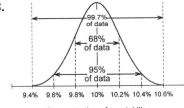

Concentration of a painkiller

(a) 10.4% is 2σ above μ, so 2.5% of capsules lie above there.

(b) 10.6% is 3σ above μ. Because 99.7% of capsules lie within 3σ of μ, 0.3% lie outside and half of these, 0.15% (0.0015) lie above.

49.

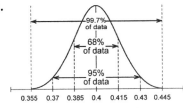

Portion of people who stay home for fear of crime

(a) 50% above 0.4, because of the symmetry of normal curves; 0.43 is 2σ above μ, so 2.5%.

(b) $\mu \pm 2\sigma = 0.4 \pm 2(0.015) = 0.4 \pm 0.03$, or 0.37 to 0.43.

50. (a) Jermaine's standard score is $\frac{27-20.8}{4.8} = 1.29$.

(b) Tonya's standard score is $\frac{1318-1026}{209} = 1.40$.

(c) Tonya stands higher in the distribution of scores, at 1.4 standard deviations above the mean.

51. Lengths of red flowers are somewhat right-skewed, with no outliers:

37	489
38	00112289
39	268
40	67
41	5799
42	02
43	1

Lengths of yellow flowers are quite symmetric, with no outliers:

34	66
35	247
36	0015788
37	01
38	1

52. For the red variety, the $n = 23$ ordered lengths are

37.40	37.78	37.87	37.97	38.01	38.07	38.10	38.20	38.23
38.79	38.87	39.16	39.63	39.78	40.57	40.66	41.47	41.69
41.90	41.93	42.01	42.18	43.09				

The minimum is 37.40, and the maximum is 43.09. Since there are 23 pieces of data, the median is the $\frac{23+1}{2} = \frac{24}{2} = 12^{\text{th}}$ piece of data, namely 39.16. Since there are 11 observations to the left of the median, Q_1 is the $\frac{11+1}{2} = \frac{12}{2} = 6^{\text{th}}$ piece of data, namely 38.07. Since there are 11 observations to the right of the median, Q_3 is the $12 + 6 = 18^{\text{th}}$ piece of data, namely 41.69.

Thus, the five-number summary is 37.40, 38.07, 39.16, 41.69, 43.09.

The $n = 15$ yellow lengths in order are

34.57	34.63	35.17	35.45	35.68	36.03	36.03	36.11	36.52
36.66	36.78	36.82	37.02	37.10	38.13			

The minimum is 34.57, and the maximum is 38.13. Since there are 15 pieces of data, the median is the $\frac{15+1}{2} = \frac{16}{2} = 8^{\text{th}}$ piece of data, namely 36.11. Since there are 7 observations to the left of the median, Q_1 is the $\frac{7+1}{2} = \frac{8}{2} = 4^{\text{th}}$ piece of data, namely 35.45. Since there are 7 observations to the right of the median, Q_3 is the $8 + 4 = 12^{\text{th}}$ piece of data, namely 36.82.

Thus, the five-number summary is 34.57, 35.45, 36.11, 36.82, 38.13.

From these numbers, draw the boxplots.

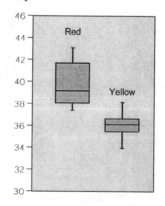

Most of the red flowers are longer than all the yellow flowers. The greater variability and the right skewness of the red distribution are also visible.

53. Red:

Observations x_i	Deviations $x_i - \bar{x}$	Squared deviations $(x_i - \bar{x})^2$
37.40	−2.311304	5.34213
37.78	−1.931304	3.72994
37.87	−1.841304	3.39040
37.97	−1.741304	3.03214
38.01	−1.701304	2.89444
38.07	−1.641304	2.69388
38.10	−1.611304	2.59630
38.20	−1.511304	2.28404
38.23	−1.481304	2.19426
38.79	−0.921304	0.84880
38.87	−0.841304	0.70779
39.16	−0.551304	0.30394
39.63	−0.081304	0.00661
39.78	0.068696	0.00472
40.57	0.858696	0.73736
40.66	0.948696	0.90002
41.47	1.758696	3.09301
41.69	1.978696	3.91524
41.90	2.188696	4.79039
41.93	2.218696	4.92261
42.01	2.298696	5.28400
42.18	2.468696	6.09446
43.09	3.378696	11.41559
sum = 913.36	**sum = 0.000008**	**sum = 71.18206**

$\bar{x} = \frac{913.36}{23} \approx 39.71$ (we used $\bar{x} \approx 39.711304$ in the deviations calculations for better accuracy and rounded to five decimal places in the calculation of squared deviations). We therefore have $s^2 \approx \frac{71.18206}{23-1} = \frac{71.18206}{22} \approx 3.2355$ which implies $s \approx \sqrt{3.2355} \approx 1.799$.

Yellow:

Observations x_i	Deviations $x_i - \bar{x}$	Squared deviations $(x_i - \bar{x})^2$
34.57	−1.61	2.5921
34.63	−1.55	2.4025
35.17	−1.01	1.0201
35.45	−0.73	0.5329
35.68	−0.50	0.2500
36.03	−0.15	0.0225
36.03	−0.15	0.0225
36.11	−0.07	0.0049
36.52	0.34	0.1156
36.66	0.48	0.2304
36.78	0.60	0.3600
36.82	0.64	0.4096
37.02	0.84	0.7056
37.10	0.92	0.8464
38.13	1.95	3.8025
sum = 542.70	**sum = 0.00**	**sum = 13.3176**

$\bar{x} = \frac{542.70}{15} = 36.18$ and $s^2 = \frac{13.31766}{15-1} = \frac{13.31766}{14} \approx 0.9513$ which implies $s \approx \sqrt{0.9513} \approx 0.975$.

The mean and standard deviation are better suited to the symmetrical yellow distribution.

54. Take $\mu = 36.18$ and $\sigma = 0.975$ millimeters.

(a) The middle 50% is spanned by the quartiles, which are 0.67σ on either side of the mean. So the range is from

$36.18 - 0.67(0.975) = 35.53$ millimeters to $36.18 + 0.67(0.975) = 36.83$ millimeters

(b) The 95 part of 68-95-99.7 rule says that the middle 95% of the distribution lies within 2σ of μ. So the range is from

$36.18 - 2(0.975) = 34.23$ millimeters to $36.18 + 2(0.975) = 38.13$ millimeters.

55. The top 2.5% of the distribution lies above
$$36.18 + 2(0.975) = 38.13 \text{ millimeters.}$$
The top 16% of the distribution lies above
$$36.18 + 1(0.975) = 37.155 \text{ millimeters.}$$
The top 25% of the distribution lies above
$$36.18 + 0.67(0.975) = 36.83 \text{ millimeters.}$$
The value 37.4 is between 37.155 and 38.13, so between 2.5% and 16% of yellow flowers are longer that 37.4 millimeters.

Word Search Solution

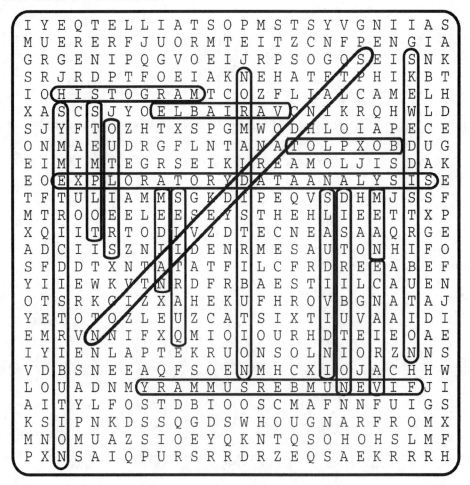

Chapter 6
Exploring Data: Relationships

Chapter Outline

Chapter Summary

A useful device for examining the relationship between two variables is the scatterplot, consisting of points in the plane. These points represent pairs of values for the variables in question, one variable being plotted along the x-axis and the other along the y-axis. Often, a scatterplot suggests a linear relation between the two variables; i.e., the points look as though they may be scattered about a line in the plane. Such a line is called a regression line, which is often used to predict the value of y for a given value of x. There are several ways of producing regression lines, depending on the method used to measure the discrepancy between the line and the data. The most common of these lines is the *least-squares regression line*, which minimizes the sum of the squares of the vertical distances between the data and the line.

However, the least-squares regression line exists for any set of data, even one that does not follow a linear pattern. Hence, there are situations in which it is not appropriate to compute this line nor to use it in predicting values of y. One way to determine whether the relationship between x and y is linear is through *correlation,* denoted by r, which measures the direction and strength of the linear relationship between two variables. r is always a number between -1 and 1. Values of r close to 0 indicate a very weak linear relationship; but if $| r |$ is close to 1, then the linear relationship is strong, with the slope of the line determined by the sign of r.

Skill Objectives

1. Draw a scatterplot for a small data set consisting of pairs of numbers.

2. From a scatterplot, draw an estimated regression line.

3. Compute the correlation for a small data set consisting of pairs of numbers and understand the significance of the correlation between two variables.

4. Describe how the concept of distance is used in determining the least-squares regression line.

5. Compute the equation of the least-squares regression line for a small data set.

6. Understand correlation and regression describe relationships that need further interpretation because association does not imply causation and outliers have an effect on these relationships.

Teaching Tips

1. When discussing the rationale for the least-squares regression line, some students notice that the concept of distance used is not the ordinary geometric distance from a point to a line, but rather vertical distance.   Demonstrating the difference between the complexity of the algebraic expressions for the two makes the choice obvious.   In addition, commenting on the reason for squaring the distance provides a nice review of the subtraction of signed numbers.

2. As students attempt to draw a scatterplot of data given from observations, they have a good opportunity to review the concepts of independent and dependent variable and functional notation.

3. When trying to draw a regression line by hand, it should be observed that a rule of thumb is that about half of the data points should lie above the line and half should lie below.

4. Depending on which forms of technology you choose to implement in the discussion of these topics, you may choose to remind students to be very careful when they input data. If one piece of data is not correctly placed in the calculator or spreadsheet, all calculations and displays will be inaccurate.

Research Paper

In the early 1800's, Karl Friedrich Gauss (1777–1855) introduced the procedure for obtaining least-squares estimates. This German born mathematician, who is also sometimes called the "prince of mathematics," has played a very important role in mathematics and statistics. Students can research the life of Gauss and his contributions to mathematics and statistics. Also, the life and contributions of the Scottish born George Undy Yule (1871–1951) can be suggested as a topic for a paper.

Spreadsheet Project

To do this project, go to http://www.whfreeman.com/fapp7e.

Spreadsheets are used in this project to analyze mean, standard deviation (Chapter 5) and the least –squares line. You will need two dice. If dice are not available, a calculator such as a TI-83 can simulate a toss of a die. The following screens will guide you to simulating the toss of a die.

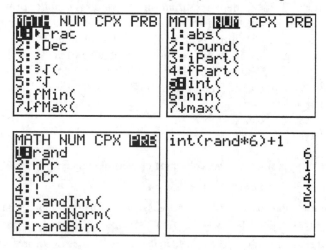

Collaborative Learning

Correlation Calculation

Professor Amanda Nunley gives a pop quiz before each exam in her algebra course. She has collected the following data regarding the average of the quizzes and the average of the exams for her ten students.

	Dean M.	John S.	Nadia A.	Denis P.	Scott H.	Dan D.	Joanne P.	Kevin L.	Adam A.	Phil P.
Quiz Average	52	86	72	35	90	92	85	62	54	77
Exam Average	63	91	83	60	89	95	87	65	77	80

1. Draw a scatterplot by treating the quiz average as the explanatory variable and the exam average as the response variable. The regression line has already been drawn in.

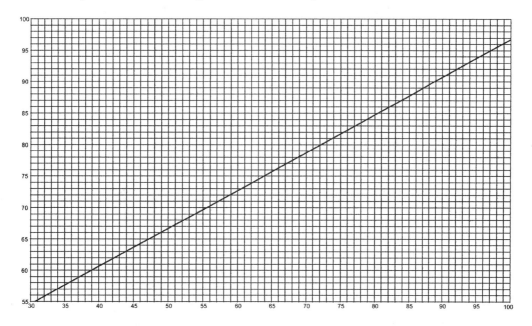

2. Determine how many units are between each point and the regression line. This distance should be determined by counting the number of units (points) above or below the line to each point. If a point is above the line, consider the distance has a sign of positive. If the point is below the line, consider the distance as a sign of negative.

3. Find the sum of all 10 "distances" you found in Part 2. What observation do you make about the sum? What observations can you make about the number of points above or below the line?

4. Determine the slope of the regression line. Give an interpretation of the meaning of the slope of the regression line for average quiz scores verses average exam scores

5. Determine the y-intercept of this line. Give an interpretation of the meaning of the y-intercept of the regression line for average quiz scores verses average exam scores.

6. Fill in the following table of values.

	x	y	x^2	y^2	xy
	52	63			
	86	91			
	72	83			
	35	60			
	90	89			
	92	95			
	85	87			
	62	65			
	54	77			
	77	80			
Sum	$\sum x =$	$\sum y =$	$\sum x^2 =$	$\sum y^2 =$	$\sum xy =$

7. Another way to calculate correlation is to use the following formula.

$$r = \frac{n\sum xy - \left(\sum x\right)\left(\sum y\right)}{\sqrt{n\left(\sum x^2\right) - \left(\sum x\right)^2}\sqrt{n\left(\sum y^2\right) - \left(\sum y\right)^2}}$$

Using the calculations from Part 6 (where $n = 10$), determine the correlation.

8. Interpret the meaning of the correlation in terms of average quiz scores verses average exam scores

Solutions

Skills Check:

1. a   2. a   3. c   4. b   5. c   6. c   7. a   8. b   9. c   10. b

11. c   12. b   13. b   14. b   15. a   16. a   17. a   18. c   19. a   20. b

Exercises:

1. (a) It is more reasonable to explore study time as an explanatory variable and the exam grade as the response variable.

    (b) It is more reasonable to explore the relationship only.

    (c) It is more reasonable to explore rainfall as an explanatory variable and the corn yield as the response variable.

    (d) It is more reasonable to explore the relationship only.

2. There is a moderately strong positive linear pattern, but the two clusters and the outlier marked A are at least as important. Brand A is much lower in both calories and sodium than any other brand. (In fact, it is the only brand made from veal and also weighs less than others.) The regression line has been drawn based on the data points.

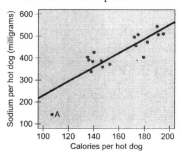

3. (a) Life expectancy increases with GDP in a curved pattern. The increase is very rapid at first, but levels off for GDP above roughly $5000 per person.

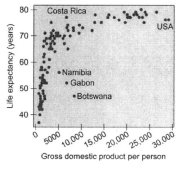

    (b) Richer nations have better diets, clean water, and better health care, so we expect life expectancy to increase with wealth. But once food, clean water, and basic medical care are in place, greater wealth has only a small effect on lifespan.

4. (a) Here is the scatterplot, with time as the explanatory variable:

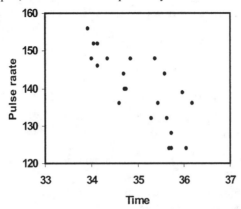

Using a TI-83, we get the following.

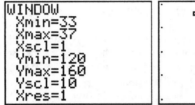 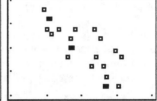

(b) Negative: We expect faster times (fewer minutes) to lead to higher pulse rates.

(c) Moderately strong negative linear relationship. (The correlation is $r = -0.746$.)

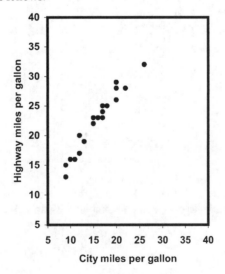

5. (a) The scatterplot is as follows.

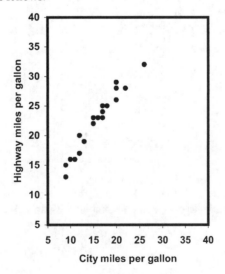

Continued on next page

5. (a) continued
Using a TI-83, we get the following.

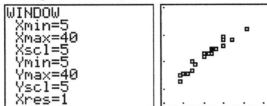

Purists should notice that because the variables measure similar quantities the plot is square with the same scales on both axes.

(b) There is a strong positive straight-line relationship.

6. The scatterplot, with time as the explanatory variable, is

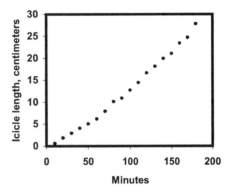

Using a TI-83, we get the following.

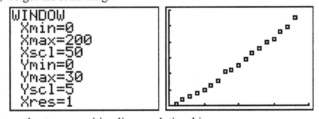

There is an extremely strong positive linear relationship.

7. (a) Here is the scatterplot, with speed as the explanatory variable:

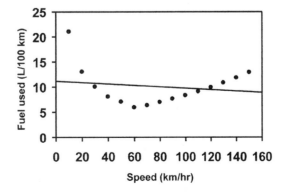

Continued on next page

7. (a) continued
    Using a TI-83, we get the following.

       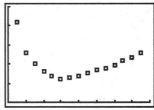

    (b) The relationship is curved; fuel usage first decreases as speed increases (higher gears cover more distance per motor revolution) then increases as speed is further increased (air resistance builds at higher speeds).

    (c) There is no overall direction.

    (d) The relationship is quite strong. There is little scatter about the overall curved pattern.

8. Answers will vary.
    Positive: years of schooling and income (for adults).
    Negative: age and speed to walk or run a mile (for adults).

9. The estimated slope would be $\dfrac{506-386}{191-139} = \dfrac{120}{52} \approx 2.31$.

10. (a) Slope $= -9.695$. For each additional minute, pulse rate decreases by about 9.7 beats per minute on average.

    (b) Since pulse $= 479.9 - (9.695 \times 34.30) = 479.9 - 332.5385 = 147.3615$, the prediction of approximately 147.4 beats per minute is low by $152 - 147.4 = 4.6$ beats per minute.

11. (a) Choose two values of weeks, preferably near 1 and 150. Find pH from the equation given, plot the two points (weeks horizontal) and draw the line through them.

    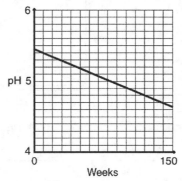

Continued on next page

11. (a) continued

Using a TI-83, we get the following.

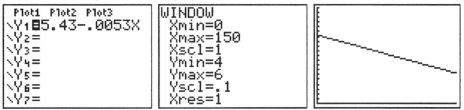

(b) Week 1: predicted pH $= 5.43 - (0.0053 \times 1) = 5.43 - 0.0053 = 5.4247 \approx 5.42$

Week 150: predicted pH $= 5.43 - (0.0053 \times 150) = 5.43 - 0.795 = 4.635 \approx 4.64$

(c) The slope -0.0053 says that on average pH declined by 0.0053 per week during the study period.

12. (a) Slope $= -2.02$. This indicates as the percent taking increases, predicted SAT score decreases.

(b) Since predicted SAT score $= 1150 - (2.02 \times 82) = 1150 - 165.64 = 984.36$, the predicted score is 984.

13. Some sample ages would be as follows.

Age of Woman	Age of Man
18	20
20	22
27	29
32	34
41	43

Using a TI-83, we get the following.

L1	L2	▇ 3
18	20	------
20	22	
27	29	
32	34	
41	43	
------	------	
L3 =		

```
WINDOW
 Xmin=0
 Xmax=50
 Xscl=5
 Ymin=0
 Ymax=50
 Yscl=5
 Xres=1
```

Using the linear regression feature, we obtain the following.

```
LinReg
 y=a+bx
 a=2
 b=1
```

The line is $y = x + 2$, and the slope would be 1.

14. Since $b = 1.1$ kilograms per additional centimeter of height, we have $b = 1.1 \times 1000 = 1100$ grams per additional centimeter of height.

15. With a correlation of 0.9757, the indication is a very strong straight-line pattern.

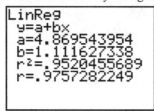

16. (a) With a correlation of −0.746, the indication is a moderately strong negative linear relationship.

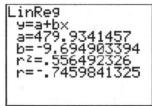

(b) The correlation, r, would not change.

17. The correlation is 0.9934. The correlation is stronger when the Insight is added, because that point extends (strengthens) the straight-line pattern.

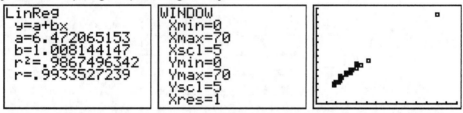

18. The correlation is 0.9958. This matches the close-to-perfect straight-line pattern of the scatterplot.

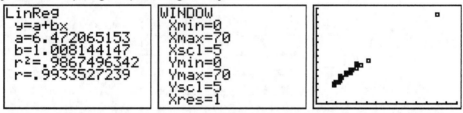

19. See the answer to Exercise 7 for the scatterplot. The correlation is −0.1700. Correlation measures the strength of only linear (straight-line) relationship. This relationship is strong but curved.

20. Correlation does not change when units of measurement change.

21. The correlation would be 1 because there is a perfect straight-line relationship, $y = x + 2$. This is verified by using the sample data from Exercise 13.

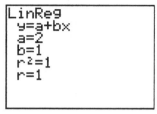

22. Think about which relationships are stronger and determine accordingly.

(a) $r = 0.5$, heredity partly determines height of son;

(b) $r = 0.2$, weaker relationship than (a) and (c);

(c) $r = 0.8$, height of same person.

23. (a) Negative: older cars will in general sell for lower prices.

(b) Negative: heavier cars will (other things being equal) get fewer miles per gallon.

(c) Positive: taller people are on average heavier than shorter people.

(d) Small: there is no reason to expect that height and IQ are related.

24. (a) Correlation does not make sense for gender, which does not have meaningful numerical values.

(b) r is always between -1 and 1, so r = 1.09 is impossible.

(c) r has no units.

25. Ask how similar the market sector of each fund is to large U.S. stocks and arrange in order.

(a) Dividend Growth, $r = 0.98$; Small Cap Stock, $r = 0.81$; Emerging Markets, $r = 0.35$.

(b) No: it just says that they tend to move in the same direction, whether up or down.

26. (a) The plot shows a strong linear pattern, so we think all come from one species.

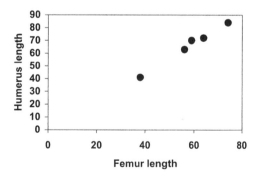

Using a TI-83, we get the following.

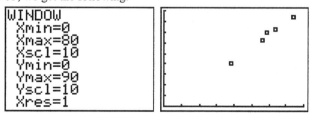

Continued on next page

26. continued

(b) *Step 1*: We have for the femur $\bar{x} = 58.2$, $s_x = 13.20$ and for humerus $\bar{y} = 66$, $s_y = 15.89$.

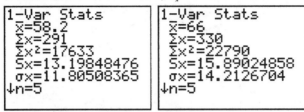

Step 2: The terms in the sum for r are as follows.

$$\frac{38-58.2}{13.20}\times\frac{41-66}{15.89}, \quad \frac{56-58.2}{13.20}\times\frac{63-66}{15.89}, \quad \frac{59-58.2}{13.20}\times\frac{70-66}{15.89},$$

$$\frac{64-58.2}{13.20}\times\frac{72-66}{15.89}, \text{ and } \frac{74-58.2}{13.20}\times\frac{84-66}{15.89}$$

Step 3: Substituting into the formula for r we have the following.

$$r=\frac{1}{5-1}\left[\frac{38-58.2}{13.20}\times\frac{41-66}{15.89}+\frac{56-58.2}{13.20}\times\frac{63-66}{15.89}+\frac{59-58.2}{13.20}\times\frac{70-66}{15.89}\right.$$

$$\left.+\frac{64-58.2}{13.20}\times\frac{72-66}{15.89}+\frac{74-58.2}{13.20}\times\frac{84-66}{15.89}\right]$$

$$=\frac{1}{4}\left[\frac{-20.2}{13.20}\times\frac{-25}{15.89}+\frac{-2.2}{13.20}\times\frac{-3}{15.89}+\frac{0.8}{13.20}\times\frac{4}{15.89}\right.$$

$$\left.+\frac{5.8}{13.20}\times\frac{6}{15.89}+\frac{15.8}{13.20}\times\frac{18}{15.89}\right]$$

$$=\frac{1}{4}\left[\frac{505}{209.748}+\frac{6.6}{209.748}+\frac{3.2}{209.748}+\frac{34.8}{209.748}+\frac{284.4}{209.748}\right]$$

$$=\frac{1}{4}\left[\frac{834}{209.748}\right]=\frac{834}{838.992}\approx 0.994$$

(c) The two approximations, 0.994, match to three decimal places.

```
LinReg
y=a+bx
a=-3.659586682
b=1.196900115
r²=.9883313819
r=.9941485714
```

27. (a) Predicted MPG $= 4.87 + 1.11x$.

```
LinReg
y=a+bx
a=4.869543954
b=1.111627338
r²=.9520455689
r=.9757282249
```

(b) Predicted MPG $= 4.87 + 1.11(18) = 4.87 + 19.98 = 24.85$ MPG.

(c) We assess accuracy from how closely the points in the plot follow a straight line. Looking at the plot in Exercise 5, we expect quite accurate predictions.

28. (a) Predicted length $= -2.395 + 0.158x$.

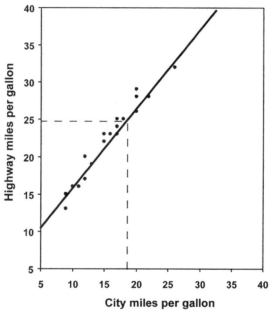

```
LinReg
y=a+bx
a=-2.394771242
b=.1584829721
r²=.9915332415
r=.9957576219
```

(b) Predicted length $= -2.395 + 0.158(75) = -2.395 + 11.85 = 9.455 \approx 9.46$ cm.

29. Choose two city MPG values, such as $x = 10$ and $x = 30$, and use the equation of the line to find each value of y. Plot the two points and draw the line between them. Here is the plot.

$x = 10$: Predicted MPG $= 4.87 + 1.11(10) = 4.87 + 11.1 = 15.97$ MPG.

$x = 30$: Predicted MPG $= 4.87 + 1.11(30) = 4.87 + 33.3 = 38.17$ MPG.

Predicted highway mileage of a car that gets 18 mpg in the city is approximately 25 mpg (24.85 mph) from exercise 27.

Using a TI-83, we get the following.

30. Choose two times, such as $x = 50$ and $x = 150$, use the equation of the line to find each value of y. Plot the two points and draw the line between them. Here is the plot.

$x = 50$: Predicted length $= -2.395 + 0.158(50) = -2.395 + 7.9 = 5.505$ cm.

$x = 150$: Predicted length $= -2.395 + 0.158(150) = -2.395 + 23.7 = 21.305$ cm.

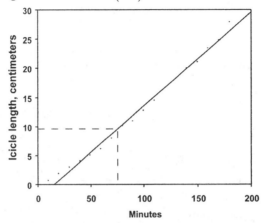

Predicted length of icicle is approximately 9.5 cm (9.46 cm) from exercise 28.

Using a TI-83, we get the following.

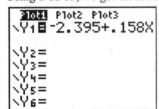 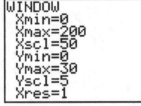 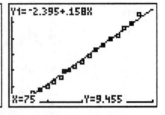

31. Since predicted fuel $= 11.058 - 0.0147 \times$ speed, we have the following.

Speed = 10 kph: predicted fuel $= 11.058 - 0.0147 \times 10 = 11.058 - 0.147 = 10.911$ kpg

Speed = 70 kph: predicted fuel $= 11.058 - 0.0147 \times 70 = 11.058 - 1.029 = 10.029$ kpg

Speed = 150 kph: predicted fuel $= 11.058 - 0.0147 \times 150 = 11.058 - 2.205 = 8.853$ kpg

The predicted values from the equation given are approximately 10.9, 10.0, and 8.85, respectively. The observed values are 21.00, 6.30, and 12.88, respectively. The least-squares line gives the best straight-line fit, which is of little value here.

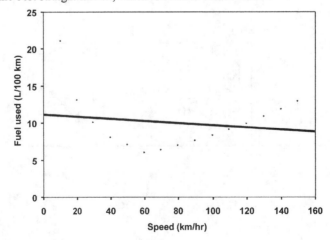

Continued on next page

31. continued

Using a TI-83, we get the following.

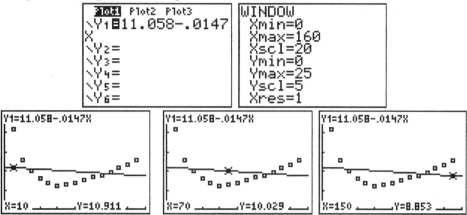

32. Slope $b = 0.158$ centimeter per additional minute of water flow.   This is the same as $\dfrac{0.158}{2.54} \approx 0.062$ inch per minute.

33. The slope of the least-squares line is $b = r\dfrac{s_y}{s_x} = 0.5\left(\dfrac{2.7}{2.5}\right) = 0.54$.   The intercept is as follows.

$$a = \overline{y} - b\overline{x} = 68.5 - (0.54)(64.5) = 68.5 - 34.83 = 33.67$$

For $x = 67$, we predict $33.67 + (0.54)(67) = 33.67 + 36.18 = 69.85$ inches.

34. (a) Slope is $b = r\dfrac{s_y}{s_x} = 0.6\left(\dfrac{8}{30}\right) = 0.16$.   The intercept is as follows.

$$a = \overline{y} - b\overline{x} = 75 - (0.16)(280) = 75 - 44.8 = 30.2$$

(b) For $x = 300$, we predict $30.2 + (0.16)(300) = 30.2 + 48 = 78.2$, or 78 was Julie's exam score.

35. The predicted y for $x = \overline{x}$ is as follows.

$$\text{predicted } y = a + b\overline{x} = \left(\overline{y} - b\overline{x}\right) + \left(r\dfrac{s_y}{s_x}\right)\overline{x} = \overline{y} - \left(r\dfrac{s_y}{s_x}\right)\overline{x} + \left(r\dfrac{s_y}{s_x}\right)\overline{x} = \overline{y}$$

36. (a) For $x = $ time and $y = $ length, $x = 95$, $s_x = 53.3854$, $\overline{y} = 12.6611$, $s_y = 8.4967$ and $r = 0.9958$.   The regression line has slope $b = r\dfrac{s_y}{s_x} = 0.9958\left(\dfrac{8.4967}{53.3854}\right) \approx 0.1585$ and intercept $a = \overline{y} - b\overline{x} = 12.6611 - (0.1585)(95) = 12.6611 - 15.0575 = 2.3964$.   These results agree up to roundoff error with those in Exercise 28.   Carrying fewer places in intermediate steps will increase the roundoff error.

(b) Reverse the roles of x and y.   The slope is now $b = r\dfrac{s_y}{s_x} = 0.9958\left(\dfrac{53.3854}{8.4967}\right) \approx 6.2567$, and the intercept is as follows.

$$a = \overline{y} - b\overline{x} = 95 - (6.2567)(12.6611) = 95 - 79.21670437 = 15.78329563 \approx 15.78$$

If length $x = 15$, we predict time to be as follows.

$$15.78 + (6.2567)(15) = 15.78 + 93.8505 = 109.6305 \approx 109.6 \text{ minutes}$$

Look at the plot in Exercise 6 to see that this is reasonable.

37. First compare the distributions for the two years. To make the boxplots, we need the five-number summary for each data set.

Putting the 2002 data in order, we have the following.

$$-50.5, -49.5, -47.8, -42, -37.8, -26.9, -23.4, -21.1, -18.9, -17.2, -17.1,$$
$$-12.8, -11.7, -11.5, -11.4, -9.6, -7.7, -6.7, -5.6, -2.3, -0.7, -0.7, 64.3$$

The minimum is -50.5 and the maximum is 64.3. The median is the $\frac{23+1}{2} = \frac{24}{2} = 12^{th}$ piece of data, namely -12.8. Since there are 11 observations to the left of the median, Q_1 is the $\frac{11+1}{2} = \frac{12}{2} = 6^{th}$ piece of data, namely -26.9. Since there are 11 observations to the right of the median, Q_3 is the $12 + 6 = 18^{th}$ piece of data, namely -6.7.

Thus, the five - number summary is $-50.5, -26.9, -12.8, -6.7, 64.3$.

Putting the 2003 data in order, we have the following.

$$14.1, 19.1, 22.9, 23.9, 26.1, 27.5, 28.7, 29.5, 30.6, 31.1, 32.1,$$
$$32.3, 35.0, 36.5, 36.9, 36.9, 41.8, 43.9, 57.0, 59.4, 62.7, 68.1, 71.9$$

The minimum is 14.1 and the maximum is 71.9. The median is the $\frac{23+1}{2} = \frac{24}{2} = 12^{th}$ piece of data, namely 32.3. Since there are 11 observations to the left of the median, Q_1 is the $\frac{11+1}{2} = \frac{12}{2} = 6^{th}$ piece of data, namely 27.5. Since there are 11 observations to the right of the median, Q_3 is the $12 + 6 = 18^{th}$ piece of data, namely 43.9.

Thus, the five - number summary is 14.1, 27.5, 32.3, 43.9, 71.9.

Here are boxplots.

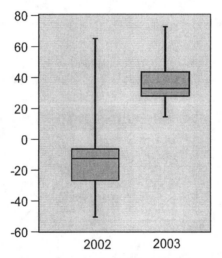

Using a TI-83, we get the following. The top boxplot is for 2002 and the bottom one is for 2003.

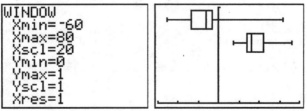

Continued on next page

37. continued

Histograms (or stemplots) show that the 2003 returns are roughly single-peaked and symmetric, and that the 2002 returns are left-skewed with an extreme high outlier. Below are the histograms.

Class	Count
$-60 - (-40.1)$	4
$-40 - (-20.1)$	4
$-20 - (-0.1)$	14
$0 - 19.9$	0
$20 - 39.9$	0
$40 - 59.9$	0
$60 - 79.9$	1

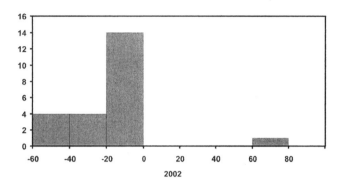

Class	Count
$0 - 19.9$	2
$20 - 39.9$	14
$40 - 59.9$	4
$60 - 79.9$	3

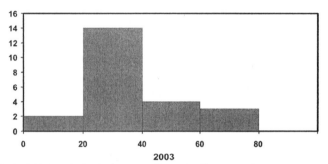

The median returns are -12.8% in 2002 and 32.1% in 2003 (from the five - number summary). The correlation is $r = -0.616$; because of the influence of outliers on correlation, it is better to report the correlation without the outlier, $r = -0.838$.

With Outlier

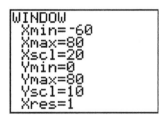 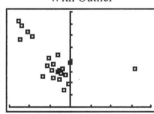 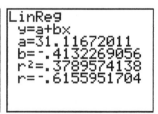

Without Outlier (64.3, 32.1)

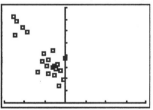 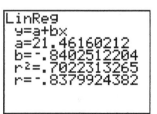

Continued on next page

37. continued
That is, the funds that went down most in 2002 tended to go up most in 2003. The scatterplot confirms this:

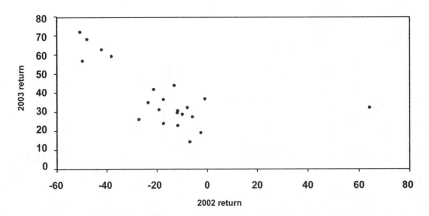

38. We have $r = 0.481$. The scatterplot shows that five points lie close to a line, but the point $(10,1)$ lies far from the line at the lower right. This outlier reduces r.

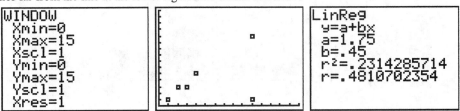

39. (a) All four sets of data have $r = 0.816$ and regression line $y = 3.0 + 0.5x$ to a close approximation.

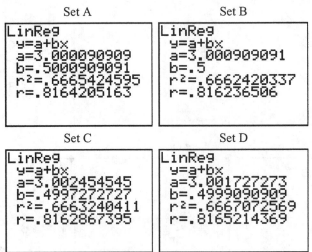

Continued on next page

39. continued

(b) Here are the plots:

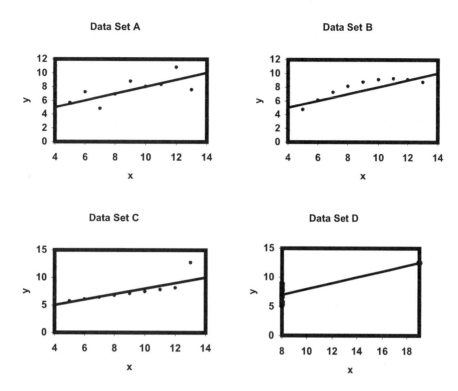

Using a TI-83, we get the following.

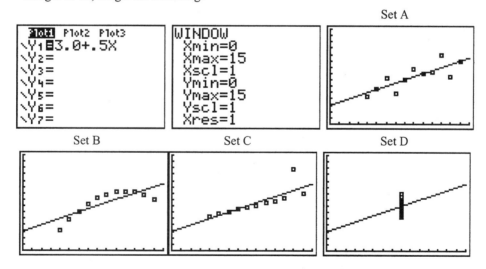

(c) Only A is a normal" regression setting in which the line is useful for prediction. Plot B is curved, C has an extreme outlier in y, and D has all but one x identical. The lesson: Plot your data before calculating.

In Exercises 40 – 44, answers will vary.

40. Children who watch lots of TV may lack parental supervision. Such children would study less and read less and take part in fewer outside activities.

41. Heavier people who are concerned about their weight may be more likely than lighter people to choose artificial sweeteners in place of sugar.

42. Companies with many employees tend to pay their CEOs more than smaller companies. If they lay off (say) 5% of their employees, the number laid off is greater than 5% for smaller companies. So CEO pay and numbers laid off both tend to go up with company size.

43. Higher income generally means better water and sewage utilities, better diet, and better medical care, which will produce better health. But better health means more children can go to school and more workers are able to work and can stay on the job, which raises national income. For example, AIDS is having a direct negative effect on the economies of African nations.

44. Suppose that SAT scores roughly measure some combination of ability plus knowledge. Students in general are learning more in school, so SAT scores in general go up. But grade inflation means that A students are weaker on the average than they once were, so SAT scores for A students go down.

45. Explanatory: parents' income. Response: amount of college debt.
We expect a negative association: children of richer parents do not need to borrow as much to pay for college.

46. (a) IQ is supposed to measure "general problem-solving ability" and understanding written material is one kind of problem solving. The scatterplot does show a general lower-left to upper-right pattern, that is, a positive association.

(b) There are four children with IQs roughly 108 to 125 who have much lower reading scores than other children with similar IQs.

(c) The lower-left to upper-right pattern is roughly a straight line, but the association is weak because there is a great deal of scatter above and below a line that would describe the overall pattern.

47. (a) There is a positive association, so *r* will be positive. The pattern is a bit irregular, so *r* won't be close to 1.

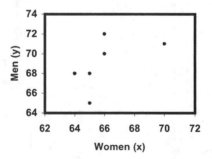

Using a TI-83, we get the following.

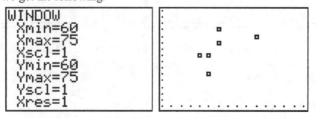

Continued on next page

47. continued

(b) $r = 0.5653$.

```
LinReg
y=a+bx
a=24
b=.6818181818
r²=.3196022727
r=.5653337711
```

48. Correlation is not affected by changing the scale of one or both variables. Subtracting 3 inches from all male heights and changing from inches to centimeters are both changes of scale. So r is unchanged.

49. (a) The slope is $b = 0.68$. For each additional inch of women's height, the height of the next man dated goes up by 0.68 inch on average.

(b) The prediction is as follows.

predicted male height = $24 + 0.68 \times$ female height
$$= 24 + (0.68)(67) = 24 + 45.56 = 69.56 \text{ inches}$$

Word Search Solution

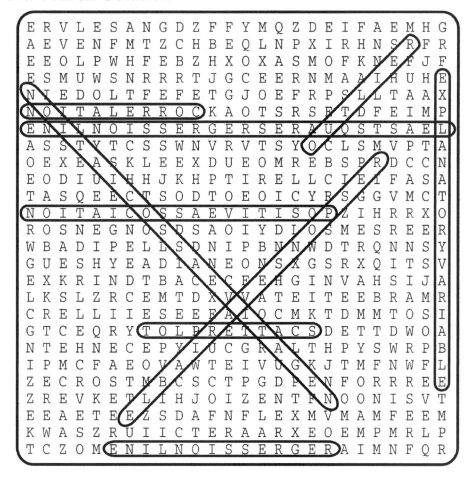

Chapter 7
Data for Decisions

Chapter Outline

Introduction

Chapter Summary

Statistics is the science of data. Designs for producing data that will convincingly answer specific questions are indispensable in statistics. Generally, data are generated by sampling or by conducting experiments.

A *sample* is a part of a large population. Hopefully, information obtained from the sample will allow us to draw conclusions about the *population* as a whole. In order for this to be possible, the sample must be representative of the population. Typically, samples are chosen at random, perhaps by assigning a number to each member of the population and then by using a table of random digits to select the individuals to be included in the sample. Random sampling avoids the *bias* that can result when an investigator chooses convenient subjects or allows subjects to choose themselves (as in a phone-in poll). Sometimes, more complex samples may be needed; for example, we may require that the age distribution of the sample subjects be the same as that of the population as a whole. Even in these situations, random sampling is used within the specified subcategories of the sample.

Experiments aim to show that certain treatments produce certain effects. Responses to treatment can be *confounded* with other variables in the environment so that no clear conclusions can be drawn. Good experimental design attempts to minimize confounding by comparing subjects who receive treatment, to a *control group* that receives none. Subjects are randomly assigned to the two groups; randomization is used to produce two groups that are essentially similar prior to treatment. The groups are observed again after treatment. Random sampling eliminates bias but not variability. Different samples will usually yield different outcomes. However, this variability can be minimized by choosing a large enough sample. Differences unlikely to occur by chance provide evidence that the differences can be attributed to the effects of the treatment. Such differences are called *statistically significant*.

Statistical inference draws conclusions from data. Generally, these conclusions concern the estimation of a population parameter based on a statistic provided by a sample. Statistical inference is based on the idea that one needs to see how trustworthy a procedure is if it is repeated many times. An important method of inference is determining confidence intervals. With confidence intervals, we take as our basic estimate of an unknown population parameter the appropriate sample statistic. A confidence interval adds a margin of error so we obtain a range of values "statistic ± margin of error" that tells us the accuracy of our estimate. By revisiting the 68-95-99.7 rule, the 95% confidence interval is discussed. We can be sure that the true population parameter for 95% of all samples will be within this interval. Confidence intervals are easy to obtain if the sampling distribution of our statistic is normal or approximately normal. Fortunately, this is the case with sample proportion and sample mean.

Skill Objectives

1. Identify the population in a given sampling or experimental situation.

2. Identify the sample in a given sampling or experimental situation.

3. Explain the difference between a population and a sample.

4. Analyze a sampling example to detect sources of bias.

5. Identify several examples of sampling that occur in our society.

6. Use a table of random digits to select a random sample from a small population.

7. Select a numbering scheme for a population from which a random sample will be selected from a table of random digits.

8. Explain the difference between an observational study and an experiment.

9. Recognize the confounding on the effects of two variables in an experiment.

10. Explain the difference between the experimental group and the control group in an experiment.

11. Design a randomized comparative experiment and display it in graphical form.

12. Explain what is meant by statistically significant.

13. Describe the placebo effect.

14. Discuss why double blindness is desirable in an experiment.

15. Define statistical inference.

16. Explain the difference between a parameter and a statistic.

17. Identify both the parameter and the statistic in a simple inferential setting.

18. Compute the sample proportion when both the sample size and number of favorable responses are given.

19. Using an appropriate formula, calculate the standard deviation of a given statistic.

20. Explain the difference between the population mean and the sample mean.

21. Given a sample proportion and sample size, list the range for a 95% confidence interval for the population proportion.

22. Calculate differing margins of error for increasing sample sizes.

23. Discuss the effect of an increased sample size on the statistic's margin of error.

Teaching Tips

1. Spending time explaining carefully the structure of the table of random digits found in the text might save time and student error when working the exercises. Students sometimes think that the space between each block of five digits somehow separates them so that you must move on to the next block after selecting a number from one block. Explaining that the space serves the same purpose as a comma when writing ordinary numbers (for ease of reading) helps their understanding.

2. A second question often raised is about the numbering of lines in the table of random digits. Students who have done programming on personal computers are aware that to avoid having the computer always return to the start of the list, it may be necessary to insert a programming code to seed the random number generator. In a sense, then, by specifying which row to use in the table, we are avoiding the predictability of always returning to the beginning of the list.

3. Some students have trouble understanding that the maximum number needed to name items in a population determines the number of digits to be used in all the numbers. If there are 100 items in a population and the numbering scheme begins with zero, then the largest number needed is 99, which has two digits. Consequently, the numbering will progress: 00, 01, 02, 03, . . ., 99. On the other hand, if the numbering scheme begins with one, then the largest number needed is 100, requiring three digits. The numbering would then proceed: 001, 002, . . . 010, 011, 012, . . ., 099, 100.

4. One way to explain that each of the ten digits, 0 through 9, has equal likelihood of being in a particular spot in a table of random digits is to imagine that a jar is filled with ten Ping-Pong balls, each painted with a single digit, and that all ten digits are used. Then the jar is shaken up to mix the balls and a blindfolded person reaches in the jar and selects a Ping-Pong ball. That number is written down, the ball is returned to the jar, and the jar is shaken once again. The process is then repeated many times to construct the table.

5. Stress that randomization has radically different purposes in the two types of statistical problems discussed in this chapter. When selecting a sample for, say, a political poll, the purpose is to obtain a group of people that closely mirrors the entire population politically, ethnically, economically, and so forth. On the other hand, in medical experimentation, where the subjects are always volunteers, there is no possibility of such a mirroring of the general population. Here, the random allocation of subjects to the treatment and control groups is to try to assure that these two groups are as alike as possible, so that any difference in the outcome of the experiment can be attributed only to the treatment.

6. Students need to know the level of precision expected in the answer. It may be a good idea to develop a standard for this chapter for ease in comparing responses.

7. To introduce the idea of confidence intervals informally, ask the students the following question: "Suppose that a sample produces a value of $\hat{p}$ = 45%. How confident are you that the actual value of p is exactly 45%?" Most of them will admit they have very little confidence in this as an exact value. Then ask, "How confident are you that p lies between 44% and 46%? Or between 43% and 47%?" As you expand the interval surrounding 45%, the students will see clearly that our confidence increases as the interval grows.

8. A review of the normal curve and the 68–95–99.7 rule can help lay the foundation for the 95% confidence interval. Drawing a normal curve with appropriate labeling of mean and standard deviation markings for each confidence-interval problem may help reinforce the relationship between the 95% confidence interval and the two-standard deviation range on either side of the mean.

9. Point out that the margin of error determines the *length* of the confidence interval. For example, if the margin of error is 3%, then the confidence interval has length 6%.

10. Students often need extra practice on how changing the sample size affects the error margin. Giving them lots of examples with samples whose sizes are perfect squares makes the arithmetic easier; however, it's important for them to see that not all problems in real world settings have easy answers. After they feel comfortable with the ideas involved, you may want to extend their practice to include irrational numbers and determine an appropriate precision level for the answers.

Research Paper

In 1937, Jerzy Neyman invented the measure of uncertainty called the confidence interval. Neyman (1894–1981) was born in Bendery, Moldavia. Students can further research the life of Neyman and his contributions to mathematics and statistics. Also, the life and contributions of the British born Egon Pearson (1895–1980) can be suggested as a topic for a paper.

Collaborative Learning

Sampling

You can give your students the experience of sampling within the classroom. Hand out index cards and ask each student to write down on the card the number of siblings in his or her family. Collect the cards and then have several (10 or more) students randomly choose different samples of 5 cards each. Ask them to calculate the mean number of siblings in their sample. When all the sample means have been announced, have the students construct a histogram of the results. Then calculate the mean for the entire class, and compare it with the results of the sampling.

Solutions

Skills Check:

1. b   2. a   3. c   4. b   5. a   6. c   7. a   8. b   9. a   10. a

11. c   12. b   13. b   14. b   15. c   16. b   17. b   18. c   19. a   20. a

Exercises:

1. Population: U.S. residents aged 18 and older. Sample: The 1,002 who responded.

2. All households in the United States.

3. Students passing the student center may not fairly represent all students. For example, they may underrepresent commuters or students whose classes are far from the center. In addition, a woman student may be reluctant to stop men, thus underrepresenting male students.

4. Population: "constituents," probably adults living in her district. Sample: the 361 who wrote letters. Those who wrote probably feel strongly about gun control, and may not represent all constituents (voluntary response).

5. (a) This isn't clear: possibly its readers, possibly all adults in its circulation area.

   (b) Larger; People with strong opinions, especially negative opinions, are more likely to respond. This is bias due to voluntary response.

6. Answers will vary.

   (a) Print a coupon in the campus newspaper asking students to check their opinion, cut out the coupon, and mail it in.

   (b) Ask all the students in a large sociology course to record their opinion as part of an exam in the course. (This is a convenience sample.)

7. If we assign labels 01 to 33 to the complexes in alphabetical order and start at line 117 in Table 7.1, our sample is 16 = Fairington, 32 = Waterford Court, and 18 = Fowler.

8. If we assign labels 01 to 32 in alphabetical order and start at line 105 in Table 7.1, our sample is 29 = Shen, 07 = Delluci, 19 = Molina, 14 = Glauser, 17 = Johnson, 13 = Garcia. (Don't forget to skip the second 29.)

9. (a) 001 to 371.

   (b) Area codes labeled 214, 235, 119, 033, 199.

10. (a) 00001 to 14959.

    (b) People labeled 12609, 14592, 06928. (Look at groups of 5 digits.)

11. If you always start at the same point in the table, your sample is predictable in advance. Repeated samples of the same size from the same population will always be the same - that's not random.

12. (a) False: The number of 0's in a row is random.

    (b) True.

    (c) False: All strings of four digits have the same chance to occur, one in 10,000.

13. (a) Because $\frac{200}{5} = 40$ we divide the list into 5 groups of 40. (By the way, if the list has 204 rooms, we divide it into 5 groups of 40 and final group of 4. A sample contains a room from the final group only when the first room chosen is among the first 4 in the list.) Label the first 40 rooms 01 to 40. Line 120 chooses room 35. The sample is rooms 35, 75, 115, 155, and 195.

   (b) Each of the first 40 rooms has chance 1 in 40 to be chosen. Each later room is chosen exactly when the corresponding room in the first 40 is chosen. So every room has equal chance, 1 in 40. The only possible samples consist of 5 rooms spaced 40 apart in the list. An SRS gives *all* samples of 5 rooms an equal chance to be chosen.

14. Students over 21 have chance $\frac{3}{30}$ and students under 21 have chance $\frac{2}{20}$, so each student has chance 1 in 10. The sample always contains exactly 3 students over 21 and 2 students under 21. An SRS would allow any sample of 5 of the 50 students.

15. (a) All people aged 18 and over living in the United States.

   (b) Of the 1800 called, 669 did not respond. The rate is $\frac{669}{1800} \approx 0.37 = 37\%$.

   (c) It is hard to remember exactly how many movies you saw in exactly the past 12 months.

16. Answers will vary.
   Fewer people are home to answer in the summer vacation months. This is particularly true in Italy, where most people vacation in August. High nonresponse increases the risk that those who do respond are not typical of the entire population.

17. Answers will vary.
   People are more reluctant to "change" the Constitution than to "add to" it. So the wording "adding to" will produce a higher percent in favor.

18. Yes. The study gives one of two treatments (animation or textbook) to each subject. Imposing treatments is the mark of an experiment. The explanatory variable is method of instruction (text or animation). The response variable is increase in understanding, probably measured by testing before and after instruction.

19. No treatment was imposed on the subjects. This observational study collected unusually detailed information about the subjects, but made no attempt to influence them.

20. Answers will vary.
   (a) The study gathered information from interviews and records, but did not impose any treatment on the subjects. The explanatory variable is a measure (not spelled out in detail) of time spent watching TV as a child. The response variables are measures of aggressive behavior, from police records and perhaps also from the interviews.

   (b) Children who watch large amounts of TV may have relatively little parental supervision. Their parents may be less likely to read to them, supervise their school work or even see that they always go to school, and discipline them. Undisciplined children who skip school may show more frequent aggressive behavior. We can't say that this is directly due to watching TV. A group of children who watched the same amount of TV but had more parental supervision in other areas might show different behavior.

21. Answers will vary.
   (a) It is an observational study that gathers information (e.g., through interviews) without imposing any treatment.

   (b) "Significant" means "unlikely to be due simply to chance."

   (c) Nondrinkers might be more elderly or in poorer health than moderate drinkers.

22. The design resembles Figure 7.3. Be sure to show randomization, the groups sizes and the treatments, and the response variable.

23. The design resembles Figure 7.3. Be sure to show randomization, two groups and their treatments, and the response variable (change in obesity).

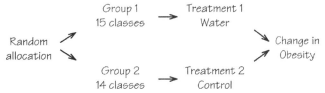

If we label the 29 classes 01 to 29 and choose 15 for the treatment group, this group contains classes 17, 09, 22, 13, 07, 02, 27, 01, 18, 25, 29, 19, 14, 15, 08. We used lines 103 to 106 of Table 7.1, skipping many duplicate pairs of digits. The remaining 14 classes make up the control group.

24. (a) Students choose the instruction method they prefer. The two groups of students may differ in many ways. For example, self-paced instruction may attract more older students who live off-campus or more students who work many hours each week.

   (b) The design resembles Figures 7.3:

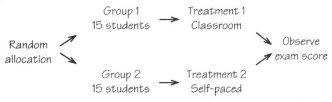

If we label the subjects 01 to 30, Group 1 contains subjects numbered 07, 20, 24, 17, 09, 06, 15, 23, 16, 19, 18, 08, 30, 27, and 12. The remaining 15 subjects make up Group 2.

25. This is a randomized comparative experiment with four branches, similar to Figure 7.4 with one more branch. The "flow chart" outline must show random assignment of subjects to groups, the four treatments, and the response variable (health care spending).

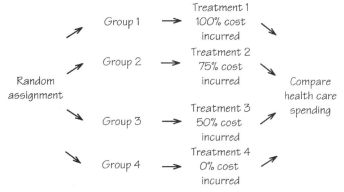

We can't show the group sizes because we don't know how many people or households are available to participate.

26. This is a randomized comparative experiment with four branches, similar to Figure 7.4 with one more branch. The "flow chart" outline must show random assignment of subjects to groups, the group sizes and treatments, and the response variables (number and severity of headaches). It is best to use groups of equal size, with 9 of the 36 subjects in each group. If we label the subjects 01 to 36 in alphabetical order, the first group contains subjects labeled 05 = Chen, 16 = Imrani, 17 = James, 20 = Maldonado, 19 = Liang, 32 = Vaughn, 04 = Bikalis, 25 = Padilla, and 29 = Trujillo. We used lines 130 to 132 of Table 7.1 and skipped many duplicate pairs of digits.

27. (a) There are 6 treatments, each combination of a level of discount and fraction on sale. In table form, the treatments are

	Discount level		
	20%	40%	60%
50% on sale	1	2	3
100% on sale	4	5	6

(b) The outline randomly assigns 10 students to each of the 6 treatment groups, then compares the attractiveness ratings. It resembles Figure 7.4, but with 6 branches.

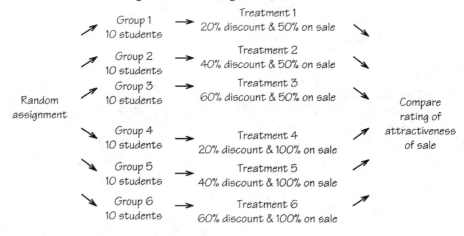

Label the subjects 01 to 60 and read line 123 of Table 7.1. The first group contains subjects labeled 54, 58, 08, 15, 07, 27, 10, 25, 60, 55.

28. *Randomized* means that chance was used to assign subjects to the treatments. *Double-blind* means that people working with the subjects did not know which treatment a subject received. *Comparative* means that controlled release (CR) was compared with at least one other treatment.

29. The design resembles Figure 7.3:

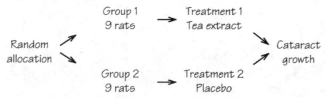

(b) Label the rats 01 to 18. The tea group contains 15, 06, 13, 09, 18, 03, 05, 16, 17.

30. The assignment in the previous exercise put 3 of the 7 genetically defective rats in the tea group. Continue from the point in line 130 at which that assignment ended: the tea group for the second random assignment contains rats 17, 05, 04, 16, 18, 07, 13, 02, 08, with again 3 of the 7 defective rats. On average, in the long run, half the defective rats (3) will be assigned to each group.

31. (a) This is a randomized comparative experiment with four branches, similar to Figure 7.4 with one more branch. The "flow chart" outline must show random assignment of subjects to groups, the group sizes and treatments, and the response variable (colon cancer). It is best to use groups of equal size, 216 people in each group.

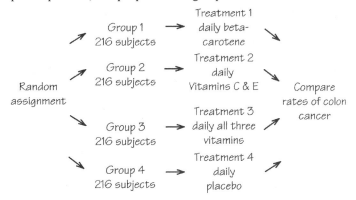

(b) With labels 001 to 864, the first five chosen are 731, 253, 304, 470, and 296.

(c) Those working with the subjects did not know the contents of the pill each subject took daily.

(d) The differences in colon cancer cases in the four groups were so small that they could easily be due to the chance assignment of subjects to groups.

(e) People who eats lots of fruits and vegetables may eat less meat or more cereals than other people. They may drink less alcohol or exercise more.

32. The average earnings of men exceeded those of women by so much that it is very unlikely that the chance selection of a sample would produce so large a difference if there were not a difference in the entire student population. But the black-white difference was small enough that it might be due to the accident of which students were chosen for the sample.

33. During the experiment, only the experimental cars had center brake lights, so they attracted attention. Once most cars had them, they were less noticed and so did a poorer job of preventing collisions. This is an example of an experiment that could not be completely realistic.

34. Any differences in disclosure between black and white subjects were so small that they could just be chance variation. Females disclosed more than males, and the difference between the genders was so large that it would rarely happen just by chance.

35. (a) What percent of college students say that being very wealthy is one of their goals in life? Consider themselves conservatives? Have had five drinks in one sitting in the past week?

(b) Will offering nightly tutoring sessions improve performance in a math course? Will showing videos of drunken students reduce binge drinking?

36. 621 is a statistic (describes this sample); 35% is a parameter (describes the population of residential telephone numbers).

37. Both are statistics because both describe the sample (the subjects who took part in the study).

38. (a) The mean is $p = 0.5$; the standard deviation is as follows.

$$\sqrt{\frac{p(1-p)}{n}} = \sqrt{\frac{0.5(1-0.5)}{14,941}} = \sqrt{\frac{0.5(0.5)}{14,941}} \approx 0.0041$$

(b) $0.5 \pm (2)(0.0041) = 0.5 \pm 0.0082$

$$0.5 - 0.0082 = 0.4918 \text{ to } 0.5 + 0.0082 = 0.5082$$

(c) $0.5 \pm (3)(0.0041) = 0.5 \pm 0.0123$

$$0.5 - 0.0123 = 0.4877 \text{ to } 0.5 + 0.0123 = 0.5123$$

39. (a) The mean is $p = 0.14$; the standard deviation is as follows.

$$\sqrt{\frac{p(1-p)}{n}} = \sqrt{\frac{0.14(1-0.14)}{500}} = \sqrt{\frac{0.14(0.86)}{500}} \approx 0.0155$$

(b) $0.14 \pm (2)(0.0155) = 0.14 \pm 0.031$

$$0.14 - 0.031 = \underline{0.109} \text{ to } 0.14 + 0.031 = \underline{0.171}$$

40. The mean remains $p = 0.5$. The standard deviation is $\sqrt{\dfrac{p(1-p)}{n}} = \sqrt{\dfrac{0.5(1-0.5)}{n}} = \sqrt{\dfrac{0.5(0.5)}{n}}$.

For $n = 1000$: standard deviation is $\sqrt{\dfrac{0.5(0.5)}{1000}} \approx 0.0158$

For $n = 4000$: standard deviation is $\sqrt{\dfrac{0.5(0.5)}{4000}} \approx 0.0079$

For $n = 16,000$: standard deviation is $\sqrt{\dfrac{0.5(0.5)}{4000}} \approx 0.00395$

The 95% ranges are as follows.

For $n = 1000$: $0.5 \pm (2)(0.0158) = 0.5 \pm 0.0316$

$$0.5 - 0.0316 = 0.4684 \text{ to } 0.5 + 0.0316 = 0.5316$$

For $n = 4000$: $0.5 \pm (2)(0.0079) = 0.5 \pm 0.0158$

$$0.5 - 0.0158 = 0.4842 \text{ to } 0.5 + 0.0158 = 0.5158$$

For $n = 16,000$: $0.5 \pm (2)(0.00395) = 0.5 \pm 0.0079$

$$0.5 - 0.0079 = 0.4921 \text{ to } 0.5 + 0.0079 = 0.5079$$

We see that $\hat{p}$ becomes more likely to take values very close to the true p as the sample size n increases.

41. (a) Each digit in the table has one chance in 10 to be any of the ten possible digits 0, 1, 2, 3, 4, 5, 6, 7, 8, 9. So in the long run, 60% of the digits we encounter will be 0, 1, 2, 3, 4, or 5 and 40% will be 6, 7, 8, or 9.

(b) Line 101 contains 29 digits 0 to 5. This stands for a sample with $\frac{29}{40} = 0.725 = 72.5\%$ "yes" responses. If we use lines 101 to 110 to simulate ten samples, the counts of "yes" responses are 29, 24, 23, 23, 20, 24, 23, 19, 24, and 18. Thus, three samples are exactly correct $\left(\frac{24}{40} = 0.60 = 60\%\right)$, one overestimates, and six underestimate.

42. The sample size is $n = 3160$. The sample proportion of coaching is $\hat{p} = \frac{427}{3160} \approx 0.135$. The approximate 95% confidence interval is calculated as follows.

$$\hat{p} \pm 2\sqrt{\frac{\hat{p}(1-\hat{p})}{n}} = 0.135 \pm 2\sqrt{\frac{0.135(1-0.135)}{3160}} = 0.135 \pm 2\sqrt{\frac{0.135(0.865)}{3160}} \approx 0.135 \pm 0.012$$

$$0.135 - 0.012 = 0.123 \text{ to } 0.135 + 0.012 = 0.147$$

43. The sample proportion who claim to have attended is $\hat{p} = \frac{750}{1785} \approx 0.420$. The approximate 95% confidence interval is calculated as follows.

$$\hat{p} \pm 2\sqrt{\frac{\hat{p}(1-\hat{p})}{n}} = 0.420 \pm 2\sqrt{\frac{0.420(1-0.420)}{1785}} = 0.420 \pm 2\sqrt{\frac{0.420(0.580)}{1785}} \approx 0.420 \pm 0.023$$

$$0.420 - 0.023 = 0.397 \text{ to } 0.420 + 0.023 = 0.443$$

44. (a) The sample proportion with a TV is $\hat{p} = \frac{692}{1048} \approx 0.660$. The approximate 95% confidence interval is calculated as follows.

$$\hat{p} \pm 2\sqrt{\frac{\hat{p}(1-\hat{p})}{n}} = 0.660 \pm 2\sqrt{\frac{0.660(1-0.660)}{1048}} = 0.660 \pm 2\sqrt{\frac{0.660(0.340)}{1048}} \approx 0.660 \pm 0.029$$

$$0.660 - 0.029 = 0.631 \text{ to } 0.660 + 0.029 = 0.689$$

    (b) The article claims a margin of error for 95% confidence of ±3%. Calculation gave margin of error ±2.9%, which agrees with the article when rounded.

45. (a) The sample proportion who admit running a red light is $\hat{p} = \frac{171}{880} \approx 0.194$. The approximate 95% confidence interval is calculated as follows.

$$\hat{p} \pm 2\sqrt{\frac{\hat{p}(1-\hat{p})}{n}} = 0.194 \pm 2\sqrt{\frac{0.194(1-0.194)}{880}} = 0.194 \pm 2\sqrt{\frac{0.194(0.806)}{880}} \approx 0.194 \pm 0.027$$

$$0.194 - 0.027 = 0.167 \text{ to } 0.194 + 0.027 = 0.221$$

    (b) It is likely that more than 171 ran a red light, because some people are reluctant to admit illegal or antisocial acts.

46. (a) $0.70(1009) \approx 706$

    (b) In many samples taken by Harris's methods, the sample result will be within ±3 points of the truth about the population 95% of the time.

    (c) The sample proportion is $\hat{p} = 0.7$. The approximate 95% confidence interval is calculated as follows.

$$\hat{p} \pm 2\sqrt{\frac{\hat{p}(1-\hat{p})}{n}} = 0.7 \pm 2\sqrt{\frac{0.7(1-0.7)}{1009}} = 0.7 \pm 2\sqrt{\frac{0.7(0.3)}{1009}} \approx 0.7 \pm 0.029$$

$$0.7 - 0.029 = 0.671 \text{ to } 0.7 + 0.029 = 0.729$$

    The calculated margin of error ±2.9% agrees closely with the announced 3%.

47. If Harris takes a very large number of poll samples using the same methods, the poll result will be within ±3% percentage points of the truth about the population in 95% of the samples. The usual language for this is "95% confidence."

48. No. We are only 95% confident, not certain, that the truth is captured within the margin of error.

49. (a) $\frac{1468}{13,000} \approx 0.113 = 11.3\%$.

   (b) The response rate is so low that it is likely that those who responded differ from the population as a whole. That is, there is a bias that the margin of error does not include.

50. Undercoverage: Gallup polls are conducted by telephone, so the sample excludes people without fixed-line telephones, that is, poor people and also people who have only cell phones. Nonresponse: it is common for half the people called to never answer or refuse to participate.

51. (a) No. The number of e-filed returns in all states is much larger than the sample size. When this is true, the margin of error depends only on the size of the sample, not on the size of the population.

   (b) The sample sizes vary from 970 to 49,000, so the margins of error will also vary.

52. To halve the margin of error, we require four times as many subjects. This is justified as follows. Let E be the margin of error.

$$E = 2\sqrt{\frac{\hat{p}(1-\hat{p})}{n}} \Rightarrow \frac{E}{2} = \frac{2\sqrt{\frac{\hat{p}(1-\hat{p})}{n}}}{2} \Rightarrow \frac{E}{2} = \frac{2\sqrt{\frac{\hat{p}(1-\hat{p})}{n}}}{\sqrt{4}} \Rightarrow \frac{E}{2} = 2\sqrt{\frac{\hat{p}(1-\hat{p})}{4n}}$$

Thus, we would need $4 \times 1009 = 4036$ subjects.

53. The margin of error for 90% confidence comes from the central 90% of a normal sampling distribution. We need not go as far out to cover 90% of the distribution as to cover 95%. So the margin of error for 90% confidence is smaller than for 95% confidence.

54. (a) We impose a treatment (full light or shade) on the seedlings, rather than just observing seedlings in nature.

   (b) The individuals are the 200 seedlings. The treatments are the two levels of light (full or 5%). The response variable is dry weight of young trees at the end of the experiment. (Strictly speaking, the average weights for the two treatment groups will be compared.)

   (c) The design is like that in Figure 7.3, substituting the details from (b) and 100 seedlings in each group.

55. The sample proportion of successes is $\hat{p} = \frac{7}{97} \approx 0.072$. That is, there were 7.2% successes in the sample. The approximate 95% confidence interval is calculated as follows.

$$\hat{p} \pm 2\sqrt{\frac{\hat{p}(1-\hat{p})}{n}} = 0.072 \pm 2\sqrt{\frac{0.072(1-0.072)}{97}} = 0.072 \pm 2\sqrt{\frac{0.072(0.928)}{97}} \approx 0.072 \pm 0.052$$

$$0.072 - 0.052 = 0.020 \text{ to } 0.072 + 0.052 = 0.124$$

We are 95% confident that the true proportion of articles that discuss the success of blinding is between 0.020 and 0.124 (that is, 2.0% to 12.4%).

56. (a) 0001 to 2654 (0000 to 2653 is also correct; just be sure to use four digits in all labels).

    (b) Read four-digit groups from line 103. The first three that are labels are 0977, 0095, and 2269.

    (c) Nonresponse. Many students will probably ignore an email from someone they don't know.

57. The distribution of the sample proportion $\hat{p}$ is approximately normal with mean $p = 0.1$ (that is, 10%) and standard deviation

$$\sqrt{\frac{p(1-p)}{n}} = \sqrt{\frac{0.1(1-0.1)}{97}} = \sqrt{\frac{0.1(0.9)}{97}} \approx 0.030$$

or 3%. Notice that 7% is one standard deviation below the mean. By the 68 part of the 68-95-99.7 rule, 68% of all samples will have between 7% and 13% that discuss blinding. Half the remaining 32% lie on either side. So 16% of samples will have fewer than 7% articles that discuss blinding. That is, the probability is about 0.16.

Word Search Solution

Chapter 8
Probability: The Mathematics of Chance

Chapter Outline

Chapter Summary

Probability is the mathematics of random phenomena. For such phenomena, individual outcomes are uncertain but, in the long run, a regular pattern describes how frequently each outcome occurs.

A probability model for a random phenomenon consists of a sample space, which is the set of all possible outcomes, and a way of assigning probabilities to events (sets of outcomes). There are two important ways of assigning probabilities. First, assign a probability to each outcome and then determine the probability of an event by adding the probabilities of the outcomes that comprise the event. This method is particularly appropriate for finite sample spaces. Often counting methods (*combinatorics*) is used to determine how many elements are in the sample space or in a subset of the same space. Secondly, and this method is useful if the outcomes are numbers, we can assign probabilities directly to intervals of numbers as areas under a curve.

In either case, the probability of an event must be a number between 0 and 1, and the probabilities of all outcomes must add up to 1 (interpreted in the second case as: the total area under the curve is exactly 1). Moreover, if two events A and B are disjoint (meaning that they have no outcomes in common), then $P(A \text{ or } B) = P(A) + P(B)$. In the particular case of a sample space having k outcomes that are equally likely, these conditions imply that each outcome must be assigned probability $\frac{1}{k}$. A *probability histogram* gives a visual representation of a probability model. The height of each bar gives the probability of the outcome at its base, and the sum of the heights is 1.

For a random phenomenon with numerical outcomes, the average outcome to expect in the long run is called its mean, denoted μ. The mean is a weighted average of the outcomes, each outcome weighted by its probability. The law of large numbers tells us that the mean, $\bar{x}$, of actually observed outcomes will approach μ as the number of observations increases.

Probability density curves (or just density curves) are important in assigning probabilities. *Continuous probability models* such as the *uniform distribution* or the *normal distribution* assign probabilities as area under the curves. Since any normal distribution is symmetric about its mean and satisfies the 68–95–99.7 rule, this distribution is used in a variety of applications.

Sampling distributions are important in statistical inference. Random sampling ensures that each sample is equally likely to be chosen. Any number computed from a sample is called a statistic, and the term *sampling distribution* is applied to the distribution of any statistic. In particular, a statistic is a random phenomenon. An important statistic is the sample mean, $\bar{x}$. The central limit theorem tells us that the sampling distribution of this statistic is approximately normal if the sample size is large enough.

Skill Objectives

1. Explain what is meant by random phenomenon.

2. Describe the sample space for a given random phenomenon.

3. Explain what is meant by the probability of an outcome.

4. Describe a given probability model by its two parts.

5. List and apply the four rules of probability and be able to determine the validity/invalidity of a probability model by identifying which rule(s) is (are) not satisfied.

6. Compute the probability of an event when the probability model of the experiment is given.

7. Apply the addition rule to calculate the probability of a combination of several disjoint events.

8. Draw the probability histogram of a probability model, and use it to determine probabilities of events.

9. Explain the difference between a discrete and a continuous probability model.

10. Determine probabilities with equally likely outcomes.

11. Use the fundamental principal of counting to determine the number of possible outcomes involved in an event and/or the sample space.

12. List two properties of a density curve.

13. Construct basic density curves that involve geometric shapes (rectangles and triangles) and utilize them in determining probabilities.

14. State the mean and calculate the standard deviation of a sample statistic $\left(\hat{p}\right)$ taken from a normally distributed population.

15. Explain and apply the 68–95–99.7 rule to compute probabilities for the value of $\hat{p}$ from a single simple random sample (SRS).

16. Compute the mean (μ) and standard deviation (σ) of an outcome when the associated probability model is defined.

17. Explain the significance of the law of large numbers.

18. Explain the significance of the central limit theorem.

Teaching Tips

1. Probability experiments (binomial) such as tossing coins, answering questions on a true/false test, or recording the sex of each child born to a family provide an easy-to-understand approach to probability. Tree diagrams can be useful in such examples, but you may want to use the columnar-list approach.

Coin #1	Coin #2	Coin #3
H	H	H
H	H	T
H	T	H
H	T	T
T	H	H
T	H	T
T	T	H
T	T	T

   Using this diagram to count the number of times a specific event occurs in the sample space helps some students set up numerical values for the probability model. It's then interesting to note that other experiments that have only two outcomes behave the same way structurally.

2. The concept of the mean of a probability model (expected value) seems to be more easily understood by some when it is placed in a monetary context. The example of betting $1 on red in a roulette game generates student interest, and the resulting mean has meaning. Initially applying the same concept to an event that is not associated with money, however, tends not to be as interesting and therefore can be confusing. Giving an explanation of mean as a kind of average and then discussing average winnings may help put it in perspective.

3. Students will need to apply the 68-95-99.7 rule throughout this chapter. Although the rule and applications were given in Chapter 5, you may choose to have them concentrate on the following diagram by inserting a specific mean and labeling the values that are one, two, and three standard deviations from the mean. Also, you may mention that in the *Student Study Guide* a page of "blank" normal distributions such as the one below appear after the Homework Help feature.

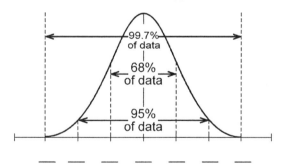

4. The first two text exercises provide nice hands-on activities that can pay dividends in terms of student understanding. Some students need this tactile approach to reinforce the concepts.

5. Another readily accessible source of a distribution of digits is a phone book. You may choose to tear pages out and ask students to collect information such as how many numbers end in an even or an odd digit. You may consider including or not the first three digits of the telephone number in other data collection activities.

6. For students who enjoy gambling, analyzing the game of craps with respect to the probability of winning on the first roll or losing on the first roll is a fairly simple example. Students seem to enjoy problems involving the rolling of dice.

Research Paper

A famous equation in fluid dynamics is the Bernoulli equation. It was derived by the Dutch-born mathematician, Daniel Bernoulli (1700–1782). The family name Bernoulli is also a prominent part of probability theory. Daniel Bernoulli's uncle Jakob Bernoulli (1654–1705) wrote *Ars Conjectandi* (the Art of Conjecturing). This work was groundbreaking in probability theory. In the binomial distribution, in which experiments yield a success or failure, the terms Bernoulli experiment or Bernoulli trial are used. These terms are a result Jakob's body of work which was published after his death. Students can further research the life of Bernoulli family members. To focus on probability theory, direct students to research only Jakob Bernoulli.

Note: Jakob Bernoulli's first name can also appear as Jacob, James, or Jacque.

Collaborative Learning

Estimating Probability

This exercise, involves tossing a fair coin and an unmarked (no H's or T's) version of the diagram below. An unmarked copy of the diagram below along with a table to organize the experimental results appear on the next page. Break students into groups in which they start at the top of the triangle. A student should toss the coin. If the coin lands tails, students should follow the path down and to the right. If the coin lands heads, students should follow the path down and to the left. It will take three tosses in order to land at a point (A, B, C, or D).

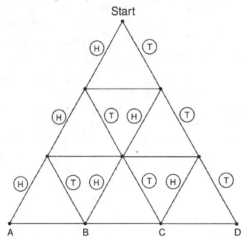

Have students in a group perform this experiment (tossing the coin three times and recording the terminal point) 40 times. Combine the results of each group on the board. Have the class find the experimental probability of terminating at one of the four points for the collective results.

Bear in mind before you perform this experiment that many students will assume the probability of landing at any of the four terminal points must be 0.25, "because there are only four possibilities, A, B, C or D."

After the results are combined, ask students to determine the possible ways of obtaining each terminal point by first examining the sample space of tossing a coin three times. After the pattern of exactly 3 heads for A, 2 heads for B, 1 head for C, 0 heads for D (or similar phrasing), ask students to construct the actual *probability model* and the *probability histogram*.

Follow this up by asking students to construct the probability model and the probability histogram based on an expanded version of the experiment. They do not need to actually perform the experiment.

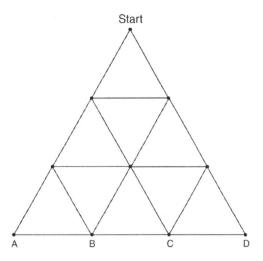

	A	B	C	D
Tally				

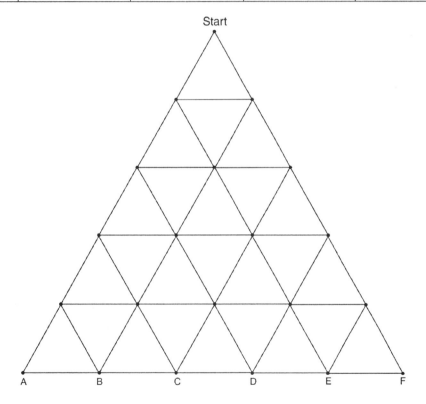

Solutions

Skills Check:

1. a   2. b   3. b   4. c   5. a   6. b   7. b   8. c   9. b   10. a

11. b   12. c   13. a   14. c   15. c   16. b   17. a   18. a   19. c   20. c

Exercises:

1. Results will vary, but the probability of a head is usually greater than 0.5 when spinning pennies. One possible explanation is the "bottle cap effect." The rim on a penny is slightly wider on the head side, so just as spinning bottle caps almost always fall with the open side up, pennies fall more often with the head side up.

2. Results will vary.

3. The first five lines contain 200 digits, of which 21 are zeros. The proportion of zeros is $\frac{21}{200} = 0.105$.

TABLE 7.1   Random   Digits

101	19223	95034	05756	28713	96409	12531	42544	82853
102	73676	47150	99400	01927	27754	42648	82425	36290
103	45467	71709	77558	00095	32863	29485	82226	90056
104	52711	38889	93074	60227	40011	85848	48767	52573
105	95592	94007	69971	91481	60779	53791	17297	59335
106	68417	35013	15529	72765	85089	57067	50211	47487

4. (a) Probability 0.
   (b) Probability 1.
   (c) Probability 0.01, once per 100 trials on the average in the long run.
   (d) Probability 0.6.

5. (a) $S = \{0, 1, 2, 3, 4, 5, 6, 7, 8, 9, 10\}$.
   (b) $S = \{0, 10, 20, 30, 40, 50, 60, 70, 80, 90, 100\}$.
   (c) $S = \{\text{Yes, No}\}$.

6. (a) $S = \{\text{Female, Male}\}$.
   (b) $S = \{6, 7, 8, 9, 10, 11, 12, 13, 14, 15, 16, 17, 18, 19, 20\}$.
   (c) S = whole numbers from 50 to 180 (use judgment for lower and upper limits).

7. (a) $S = \{$HHHH, HHHM, HHMH, HMHH, MHHH, HHMM, HMMH, MMHH, HMHM, MHHM, MHMH, HMMM, MMMH, MHMM, MMHM, MMMM$\}$.
   (b) $S = \{0, 1, 2, 3, 4\}$.

8. (a) $S = \{\text{Right; Left}\}$.
   (b) S = whole numbers from 48 to 84 (use judgment for lower and upper limits).
   (c) S = whole numbers from 0 to 360 (use judgment for lower and upper limits).

9. (a) The given probabilities have sum 0.81, so the probability of any other topic is $1 - 0.81 = 0.19$.
   (b) The probability of adult or scam is $0.145 + 0.142 = 0.287$.

10. (a) $1 - 0.71 = 0.28$, because the probabilities of all education levels must sum to 1.

(b) $1 - 0.12 = 0.88$, or $0.31 + 0.28 + 0.29 = 0.88$.

11. Answers will vary. Any two events that can occur together will do.

A = a student is female and B = a student is taking a mathematics course.

12. (a) The probability of choosing one of the most popular colors is as follows.
$$0.201 + 0.184 + 0.116 + 0.115 + 0.088 + 0.085 = 0.789$$

Thus, the probability of choosing any other color than the six listed is $1 - 0.789 = 0.211$.

(b) $0.201 + 0.184 = 0.385$.

13. (a) Here is the probability histogram:

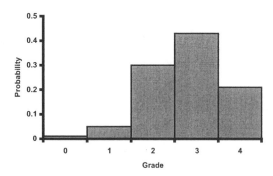

(b) $0.43 + 0.21 = 0.64$.

14. The probability histograms show that owner-occupied housing units tend to have more rooms than rented units. The center is around 6 rooms, as opposed to around 4 rooms for rented housing. Presumably more of the owner-occupied units are houses, while more rented units are apartments. The distribution for rented units is also more strongly peaked.

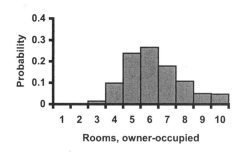

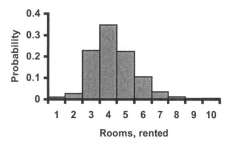

15. (a) Yes: the probabilities are between 0 and 1, inclusively, and have sum 1.
$$0 + \tfrac{1}{6} + \tfrac{1}{3} + \tfrac{1}{3} + \tfrac{1}{6} + 0 = \tfrac{1}{6} + \tfrac{2}{6} + \tfrac{2}{6} + \tfrac{1}{6} = \tfrac{6}{6} = 1$$

(Think of a die with no 1 or 6 face and two 3 and 4 faces.)

(b) No: the probabilities are between 0 and 1, but the sum is greater than 1.
$$0.56 + 0.24 + 0.44 + 0.17 = 1.41$$

(c) Yes: the probabilities are between 0 and 1, inclusively, and have sum 1.
$$\tfrac{12}{52} + \tfrac{12}{52} + \tfrac{12}{52} + \tfrac{16}{52} = \tfrac{52}{52} = 1$$

16. For owner-occupied units, we have the following probability.

$$P(5,6,7,8,9,10) = 0.238 + 0.266 + 0.178 + 0.107 + 0.050 + 0.047 = 0.866$$

For rented units, we have the following probability.

$$P(5,6,7,8,9,10) = 0.224 + 0.105 + 0.035 + 0.012 + 0.004 + 0.005 = 0.385$$

17. Each count between 1 and 12 occurs 3 times in the 36 possible outcomes. For example, 1 and 7 can only occur when the first die shows a 1.

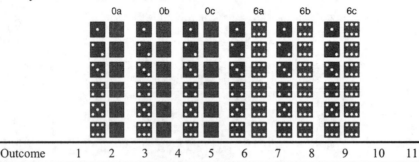

Outcome	1	2	3	4	5	6	7	8	9	10	11	12
Probability	$\frac{1}{12}$	$\frac{1}{12}$	$\frac{1}{12}$	$\frac{1}{12}$	$\frac{1}{12}$	$\frac{1}{12}$	$\frac{1}{12}$	$\frac{1}{12}$	$\frac{1}{12}$	$\frac{1}{12}$	$\frac{1}{12}$	$\frac{1}{12}$

18. There are 16 possible outcomes for the two dice, all equally likely $\left(\text{probability } \frac{1}{16}\right)$. Counting outcomes and adding 1 to the sum gives the model

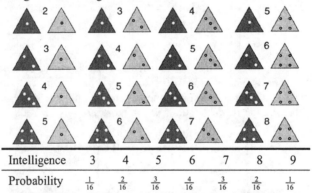

Intelligence	3	4	5	6	7	8	9
Probability	$\frac{1}{16}$	$\frac{2}{16}$	$\frac{3}{16}$	$\frac{4}{16}$	$\frac{3}{16}$	$\frac{2}{16}$	$\frac{1}{16}$

The probability of intelligence 7 or higher is $\frac{3}{16} + \frac{2}{16} + \frac{1}{16} = \frac{6}{16} = \frac{3}{8}$.

19. All 90 guests are equally likely to get the prize, so $P(\text{woman}) = \frac{42}{90} = \frac{7}{15}$.

20. (a) Using first letters to stand for names, the possible choices are: AD, AJ, AS, AR, DJ, DS, DR, JS, JR, SR.

(b) There are 10 choices, so each has probability $\frac{1}{10} = 0.1$.

(c) Four choices include Julie, so the probability is $\frac{4}{10} = 0.4$.

(d) Three choices qualify, so the probability is $\frac{3}{10} = 0.3$.

21. (a) $2 \times 2 \times 2 \times 2 \times 2 \times 2 \times 2 \times 2 \times 2 \times 2 = 2^{10} = 1024.$

   (b) $\dfrac{2}{1024} = \dfrac{1}{512}.$

22. (a) $24 \times 24 \times 24 = 24^3 = 13,824.$

   (b) $\dfrac{14 \times 14 \times 14}{13,824} = \dfrac{2744}{13,824} \doteq \dfrac{343}{1728} \approx 0.1985.$

23. There are $36 \times 36 \times 36 = 36^3 = 46,656$ different codes. The probability of no x is as follows.

$$\frac{35 \times 35 \times 35}{46,656} = \frac{42,875}{46,656} \approx 0.919$$

The probability of no digits is $\dfrac{26 \times 26 \times 26}{46,656} = \dfrac{17,576}{46,656} = \dfrac{2197}{5832} \approx 0.377.$

24. $\dfrac{14 \times 10 \times 14}{24 \times 24 \times 24} = \dfrac{1960}{13,824} = \dfrac{245}{1728} \approx 0.1418.$

25. The possibilities are *ags, asg, gas, gsa, sag, sga*, of which "*gas*" and "*sag*" are English words. The probability is $\frac{2}{6} = \frac{1}{3} \approx 0.333.$

26. The number of IDs is the sum of the numbers of 3-, 4-, and 5-character IDs, or the following.

$$26^3 + 26^4 + 26^5 = 17,576 + 456,976 + 11,881,376 = 12,355,928$$

The number of IDs with no repeats, again adding over the three ID lengths, is as follows.

$$(26)(25)(24) + (26)(25)(24)(23) + (26)(25)(24)(23)(22) = 8,268,000$$

The probability of no repeats is $\dfrac{8,268,000}{12,355,928} \approx 0.669.$

27. There are $26 \times 36^2 + 26 \times 36^3 + 26 \times 36^4 = 44,916,768$ possible IDs. The number of IDs with no numbers is the sum of the numbers of 3-, 4-, and 5-character IDs, or the following.

$$26^3 + 26^4 + 26^5 = 15,576 + 456,976 + 11,881,376 = 12,355,928.$$

The probability is therefore $\dfrac{12,355,928}{44,916,768} \approx 0.275.$

28. (a) The probability for each square face is $\frac{0.72}{6} = 0.12$ because the 6 square faces are equally likely. The probability of a triangle is $1 - 0.72 = 0.28$, so the probability for each triangle face is $\frac{0.28}{8} = 0.035.$

   (b) Answers will vary.
   Start with a different probability for squares. If each square face has probability 0.1, the 6 square faces have combined probability 0.6, the 8 triangle faces have combined probability 0.4, and each triangle face has probability 0.05.

29. (a)   The area is $\frac{1}{2} \times$ base $\times$ height $= \frac{1}{2}(2)(1) = 1$.

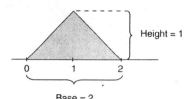

(b)   Probability $\frac{1}{2}$ by symmetry or finding the area, $\frac{1}{2} \times$ base $\times$ height $= \frac{1}{2}(1)(1) = \frac{1}{2}$. .

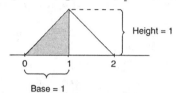

(c)   The area representing this event is $\left(\frac{1}{2}\right)(0.5)(0.5) = 0.125$.

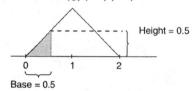

30. (a)   Height 0.5 between 0 and 2, height 0 elsewhere.

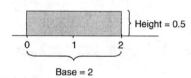

(b)   Probability $\frac{1}{2}$ by symmetry or finding the area, base $\times$ height $= (1)(0.5) = 0.5$.

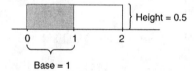

(c)   Probability $=$ Area $=$ base $\times$ height $= (0.8)(0.5) = 0.4$.

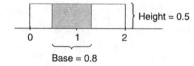

31. The area is the half of the square below the $y = x$ line.   The probability is the area, $\left(\frac{1}{2}\right)(1)(1) = \frac{1}{2}$.

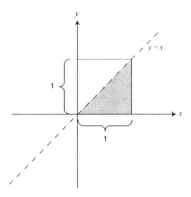

The area is half the square.

32. Because earnings are \$400 times sales, the probability model is as follows.

Earnings	\$0	\$400	\$800	\$1200
Probability	0.3	0.4	0.2	0.1

The mean for this model is as follows.

$$(0)(0.3) + (400)(0.4) + (800)(0.2) + (1200)(0.1) = 0 + 160 + 160 + 120 = \$440$$

33. The mean is as follows.

$$\mu = (0)(0.01) + (1)(0.05) + (2)(0.30) + (3)(0.43) + (4)(0.21)$$
$$= 0 + 0.05 + 0.60 + 1.29 + 0.84 = 2.78$$

The variance is as follows.

$$\sigma^2 = (0 - 2.78)^2 (0.01) + (1 - 2.78)^2 (0.05) + (2 - 2.78)^2 (0.30) + (3 - 2.78)^2 (0.43) + (4 - 2.78)^2 (0.21)$$
$$= (-2.78)^2 (0.01) + (-1.78)^2 (0.05) + (-0.78)^2 (0.30) + (0.22)^2 (0.43) + (1.22)^2 (0.21)$$
$$= (7.7284)(0.01) + (3.1684)(0.05) + (0.6084)(0.30) + (0.0484)(0.43) + (1.4884)(0.21)$$
$$= 0.077284 + 0.15842 + 0.18252 + 0.020812 + 0.312564$$
$$= 0.7516$$

Thus, the standard deviation is $\sigma = \sqrt{0.7516} \approx 0.8669$.

34. The mean intelligence is

$$\mu = (3)\left(\frac{1}{16}\right) + (4)\left(\frac{2}{16}\right) + (5)\left(\frac{3}{16}\right) + (6)\left(\frac{4}{16}\right) + (7)\left(\frac{3}{16}\right) + (8)\left(\frac{2}{16}\right) + (9)\left(\frac{1}{16}\right)$$
$$= \frac{3}{16} + \frac{8}{16} + \frac{15}{16} + \frac{24}{16} + \frac{21}{16} + \frac{16}{16} + \frac{9}{16} = \frac{96}{16} = 6,$$

as the symmetry of the model demands.

35. The mean for owner-occupied units is $\mu = (1)(0.000) + (2)(0.001) + ... + (10)(0.047) = 6.248$.

For rented units, $\mu = (1)(0.011) + (2)(0.027) + ... + (10)(0.005) = 4.321$.

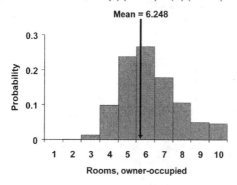
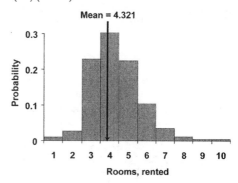

36. For nonword errors, we have the following.

$$\mu = (0)(0.1) + (1)(0.2) + (2)(0.3) + (3)(0.3) + (4)(0.1)$$
$$= 0 + 0.2 + 0.6 + 0.9 + 0.4 = 2.1$$

For word errors, we have the following.

$$\mu = (0)(0.4) + (1)(0.3) + (2)(0.2) + (3)(0.1) = 0 + 0.3 + 0.4 + 0.3 = 1$$

The models show that there are likely to be fewer word errors than nonword errors, and the smaller mean number of word errors describes this fact.

37. Both models have mean 1, because both density curves are symmetric about 1.

38. Answers will vary.

Selling 12 policies collects just $3000 plus costs and profit. One loss, though unlikely, would be catastrophic. If the company sells thousands of policies, the law of large numbers says that its mean payout per policy will be very close to the average loss of $250. It gets to keep its costs and profit.

39. (a) $\mu = (1)\left(\frac{1}{6}\right) + (2)\left(\frac{1}{6}\right) + (3)\left(\frac{1}{6}\right) + (4)\left(\frac{1}{6}\right) + (5)\left(\frac{1}{6}\right) + (6)\left(\frac{1}{6}\right) = \frac{1}{6} + \frac{2}{6} + \frac{3}{6} + \frac{4}{6} + \frac{5}{6} + \frac{6}{6} = \frac{21}{6} = 3.5$.

(b)

Outcome	2	3	4	5	6	7	8	9	10	11	12
Probability	$\frac{1}{36}$	$\frac{2}{36}$	$\frac{3}{36}$	$\frac{4}{36}$	$\frac{5}{36}$	$\frac{6}{12}$	$\frac{5}{36}$	$\frac{4}{36}$	$\frac{3}{36}$	$\frac{2}{36}$	$\frac{1}{36}$

The mean is as follows.

$$\mu = (2)\left(\frac{1}{36}\right) + (3)\left(\frac{2}{36}\right) + (4)\left(\frac{3}{36}\right) + (5)\left(\frac{4}{36}\right) + (6)\left(\frac{5}{36}\right) + (7)\left(\frac{6}{36}\right)$$
$$+ (8)\left(\frac{5}{36}\right) + (9)\left(\frac{4}{36}\right) + (10)\left(\frac{3}{36}\right) + (11)\left(\frac{2}{36}\right) + (12)\left(\frac{1}{36}\right)$$
$$= \frac{2}{36} + \frac{6}{36} + \frac{12}{36} + \frac{20}{36} + \frac{30}{36} + \frac{42}{36} + \frac{40}{36} + \frac{36}{36} + \frac{30}{36} + \frac{22}{36} + \frac{12}{36} = \frac{252}{36} = 7$$

(c) Answers will vary.

We could roll two dice separately and add the spots later. We expect the average outcome for two dice to be twice the average for one die. Remember that expected values are averages, so they behave like averages.

40. (a) Twelve of the 38 slots win, so the probability of winning is $\frac{12}{38}$. The probability model is as follows.

Outcome	Win \$2	Lose \$1
Probability	$\frac{12}{38}$	$\frac{26}{38}$

(b) Joe gains \$2 if he wins and otherwise loses \$1. So, the mean is the following.

$$\mu = (2)\left(\tfrac{12}{38}\right) + (-1)\left(\tfrac{26}{38}\right) = \tfrac{24}{38} + \left(-\tfrac{26}{38}\right) = -\tfrac{2}{38} \approx -\$0.053 \text{ (a loss of 5.3 cents)}$$

This is the same as the mean for bets on red or black in Example 13. The variance is as follows.

$$\left[2-(-0.053)\right]^2 \left(\tfrac{12}{38}\right) + \left[-1-(-0.053)\right]^2 \left(\tfrac{26}{38}\right) = (2.053)^2 \left(\tfrac{12}{38}\right) + (-0.947)^2 \left(\tfrac{26}{38}\right)$$
$$= (4.214809)\left(\tfrac{12}{38}\right) + (0.896809)\left(\tfrac{26}{38}\right)$$
$$= \tfrac{50.577708}{38} + \tfrac{23.317034}{38} = \tfrac{73.894742}{38} \approx 1.9446$$

The standard deviation is $\sqrt{1.9446} \approx 1.394$.

(c) The law of large numbers says that in the very long run Joe will lose an average of close to 5.3 cents per bet.

41. (a) $\mu = (1)\left(\tfrac{1}{6}\right) + (3)\left(\tfrac{1}{6}\right) + (4)\left(\tfrac{1}{6}\right) + (5)\left(\tfrac{1}{6}\right) + (6)\left(\tfrac{1}{6}\right) + (8)\left(\tfrac{1}{6}\right) = \tfrac{1}{6} + \tfrac{3}{6} + \tfrac{4}{6} + \tfrac{5}{6} + \tfrac{6}{6} + \tfrac{8}{6} = \tfrac{27}{6} = 4.5.$

(b) $\mu = (1)\left(\tfrac{1}{6}\right) + (2)\left(\tfrac{2}{6}\right) + (3)\left(\tfrac{2}{6}\right) + (4)\left(\tfrac{1}{6}\right) = \tfrac{1}{6} + \tfrac{4}{6} + \tfrac{6}{6} + \tfrac{4}{6} = \tfrac{15}{6} = 2.5.$

(c) The mean count for the two dice is 7. This is the same as for rolling two standard dice, with mean 3.5 for each. See the answer to Exercise 39.

42. Your digits can appear in six orders, so six of 1000 three-digit numbers win. So the mean is $\mu = (81.33)(0.006) + (-1)(0.994) = 0.48798 + (-0.994) = -0.50602$, or essentially an average loss per ticket of 51 cents.

43. (a) Since $0.00039 + 0.00044 + 0.00051 + 0.00057 + 0.00060 = 0.00251$, the probability is therefore $1 - 0.00251 = 0.99749$.

(b) The probability model for the company's cash intake is as follows.

Probability	Outcome
0.00039	$175 - 100,000 = -99,825$
0.00044	$2(175) - 100,000 = -99,650$
0.00051	$3(175) - 100,000 = -99,475$
0.00057	$4(175) - 100,000 = -99,300$
0.00060	$5(175) - 100,000 = -99,125$
0.99749	875

From this table, the mean is as follows.

$$(-99,825)(0.00039) + (-99,650)(0.00044) + (-99,475)(0.00051)$$
$$+ (-99,300)(0.00057) + (-99,125)(0.00060) + (875)(0.99749)$$
$$= (-38.93175) + (-43.846) + (-50.73225) + (-56.601) + (-59.475) + 872.80375$$
$$= 623.21775 \approx 623.218$$

44. The mean is $(\mu - \sigma)(0.5) + (\mu + \sigma)(0.5) = 0.5\mu - 0.5\sigma + 0.5\mu + 0.5\sigma = \mu$

The variance is as follows.

$$\left[(\mu - \sigma) - \mu\right]^2 (0.5) + \left[(\mu + \sigma) - \mu\right]^2 (0.5) = (\mu - \sigma - \mu)^2 (0.5) + (\mu + \sigma - \mu)^2 (0.5)$$
$$= \sigma^2 (0.5) + \sigma^2 (0.5) = \sigma^2$$

45. Sample means $\bar{x}$ have a sampling distribution close to normal with mean $\mu = 0.15$ and standard deviation $\dfrac{\sigma}{\sqrt{n}} = \dfrac{0.4}{\sqrt{400}} = \dfrac{0.4}{20} = 0.02$. Therefore, 95% of all samples have an $\bar{x}$ between $0.15 - 2(0.02) = 0.15 - 0.04 = 0.11$ and $0.15 + 2(0.02) = 0.15 + 0.04 = 0.19$.

46. (a) The mean is 300, so the probability of a higher score is about 0.5. A score of 335 is one standard deviation above the mean, so by the 68 part of the 68-95-99.7 rule the probability of a higher score is half of 0.32, or 0.16.

(b) The average score of $n = 4$ students has mean 300 and standard deviation. $\dfrac{\sigma}{\sqrt{n}} = \dfrac{35}{\sqrt{4}} = \dfrac{35}{2} = 17.5$. The probability of an average score higher than 300 is still 0.5 Because 335 is now two standard deviations above the mean, the 95 part of the 68-95-99.7 rule says that the probability of a higher average score is 0.025.

47. (a) The standard deviation of the average measurement is $\dfrac{\sigma}{\sqrt{n}} = \dfrac{10}{\sqrt{3}} \approx 5.77$ mg.

(b) To cut the standard deviation in half (from 10 mg to 5 mg), we need $n = 4$ measurements because $\dfrac{\sigma}{\sqrt{n}}$ is then $\dfrac{\sigma}{\sqrt{4}} = \dfrac{\sigma}{2}$. Averages of several measurements are less variable than individual measurements, so an average is more likely to give about the same result each time.

48. The average winnings per bet has mean $\mu = -0.053$ for any number of bets. The standard deviation of the average winnings is $\dfrac{1.394}{\sqrt{n}}$.

(a) After 100 bets, $\dfrac{1.394}{\sqrt{100}} = \dfrac{1.394}{10} = 0.1394$. Thus, the spread of average winnings is as follows.

$$-0.053 - 3(0.1394) = -0.053 - 0.4182 = -0.4712$$
$$\text{to}$$
$$-0.053 + 3(0.1394) = -0.053 + 0.4182 = 0.3652$$

(b) After 1000 bets, $\dfrac{1.394}{\sqrt{1000}} \approx 0.0441$. Thus, the spread of average winnings is as follows.

$$-0.053 - 3(0.0441) = -0.053 - 0.1323 = -0.1853$$
$$\text{to}$$
$$-0.053 + 3(0.0441) = -0.053 + 0.1323 = 0.0793$$

49. (a) Sketch a normal curve and mark the center at 4600 and the change-of-curvature points at 4590 and 4610. The curve will extend from about 4570 to 4630. This is the curve for one measurement. The mean of $n = 3$ measurements has mean $\mu = 4600$ mg and standard deviation 5.77 mg. Mark points about 5.77 above and below 4600 and sketch a second curve.

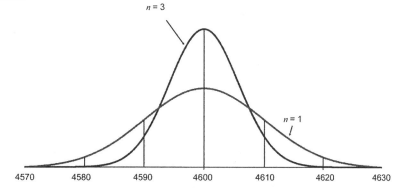

n = 3

n = 1

| 4570 | 4580 | 4590 | 4600 | 4610 | 4620 | 4630 |

(b) Use the 95 part of the 68-95-99.7 rule with $\sigma = 10$.

$$4600 - 2(10) = 4600 - 20 = 4580 \text{ to } 4600 + 2(5.77) = 4600 + 20 = 4620$$

(c) Now the standard deviation is 5.77, so we have the following.

$$4600 - 2(5.77) = 4600 - 11.54 = 4588.46 \text{ to } 4600 + 2(10) = 4600 + 11.54 = 4611.54$$

50. The mean intelligence (from Exercise 34) is $\mu = 6$. The variance is as follows.

$$\sigma^2 = (3-6)^2\left(\tfrac{1}{16}\right) + (4-6)^2\left(\tfrac{2}{16}\right) + (5-6)^2\left(\tfrac{3}{16}\right) + (6-6)^2\left(\tfrac{4}{16}\right) + (7-6)^2\left(\tfrac{3}{16}\right) + (8-6)^2\left(\tfrac{2}{16}\right) + (9-6)^2\left(\tfrac{1}{16}\right)$$

$$= (-3)^2\left(\tfrac{1}{16}\right) + (-2)^2\left(\tfrac{2}{16}\right) + (-1)^2\left(\tfrac{3}{16}\right) + (0)^2\left(\tfrac{4}{16}\right) + (1)^2\left(\tfrac{3}{16}\right) + (2)^2\left(\tfrac{2}{16}\right) + (3)^2\left(\tfrac{1}{16}\right)$$

$$= (9)\left(\tfrac{1}{16}\right) + (4)\left(\tfrac{2}{16}\right) + (1)\left(\tfrac{3}{16}\right) + (0)\left(\tfrac{4}{16}\right) + (1)\left(\tfrac{3}{16}\right) + (4)\left(\tfrac{2}{16}\right) + (9)\left(\tfrac{1}{16}\right)$$

$$= \tfrac{9}{16} + \tfrac{8}{16} + \tfrac{3}{16} + \tfrac{0}{16} + \tfrac{3}{16} + \tfrac{8}{16} + \tfrac{9}{16} = \tfrac{40}{16} = 2.5$$

Thus, $\sigma = \sqrt{2.5} \approx 1.58$. By the central limit theorem, the average score in 100 games is approximately normal with mean 6 and standard deviation $\dfrac{1.58}{\sqrt{100}} = \dfrac{1.58}{10} = 0.158$. Therefore, the middle 68% of average scores lie within one standard deviation of the mean as follows.

$$6 + 0.158 = 5.842 \text{ to } 6 + 0.158 = 6.158$$

51.

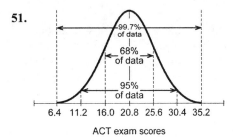

ACT exam scores

(a) Because 25.6 is one standard deviation above the mean, the probability is about 0.16.

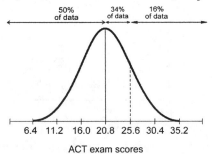

ACT exam scores

(b) The mean remains $\mu = 20.8$. The standard deviation is $\dfrac{\sigma}{\sqrt{9}} = \dfrac{4.8}{3} = 1.6$.

(c) Because $25.6 = 20.8 + 4.8 = 20.8 + 3(1.6)$ is three standard deviations above the mean, the probability is about 0.0015. (This is half of the 0.003 probability for outcomes more than three standard deviations from the mean, using the 99.7 part of the 68-95-99.7 rule.)

52. (a) The population proportion of single-occupant vehicles is $p = 0.7$. The sample proportion, $\hat{p}$, of single-occupant vehicles in a random sample of $n = 84$ has mean $p = 0.7$ and standard deviation $\sqrt{\dfrac{p(1-p)}{n}} = \sqrt{\dfrac{0.7(1-0.7)}{84}} \sqrt{\dfrac{0.7(0.3)}{84}} = \sqrt{\dfrac{0.21}{84}} = \sqrt{0.0025} = 0.05$.

(b) Because $0.6 = 0.7 - 0.1 = 0.7 - 2(0.05)$ is two standard deviations below the mean, the probability is 0.975.

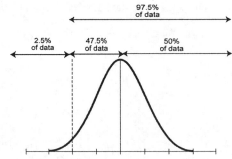

53. (a) There are $26 \times 10 \times 10 \times 26 \times 26 \times 26 = 45,697,600$ different license plates of this form.

(b) There are $26 \times 10 \times 10 = 2600$ plates ending in AAA, because that leaves only the first three characters free.

(c) The probability is $\dfrac{2600}{45,697,600} \approx 0.0000569$.

54. (a) There are only 100 plates like this, because Jerry has specified all four letters exactly. The probability is $\dfrac{100}{45,697,600} \approx 0.0000022$.

(b) The number of possible plates that meet Jerry's new specification is as follows.
$$4 \times 10 \times 10 \times 4 \times 4 \times 4 = 25,600$$
The probability that he will get such a plate is $\dfrac{25,600}{45,697,600} \approx 0.00056$.

55. (a) The probability is $0.07 + 0.08 = 0.15$.

(b) The complement to the event of working out at least one day is working out no days. Thus, using the complement rule, the desired probability is $1 - 0.68 = 0.32$.

56. The mean is as follows.
$$\mu = (0)(0.68) + (1)(0.05) + (2)(0.07) + (3)(0.08)$$
$$+ (4)(0.05) + (5)(0.04) + (6)(0.01) + (7)(0.02)$$
$$= 0 + 0.05 + 0.14 + 0.24 + 0.20 + 0.20 + 0.06 + 0.14 = 1.03 \text{ days}$$

As you interview more and more people, the average number of days, $\overline{x}$, that these people work out will always get closer and closer to 1.03.

57. (a) The variance is as follows.
$$\sigma^2 = (0-1.03)^2(0.68) + (1-1.03)^2(0.05) + (2-1.03)^2(0.07) + (3-1.03)^2(0.08)$$
$$+ (4-1.03)^2(0.05) + (5-1.03)^2(0.04) + (6-1.03)^2(0.01) + (7-1.03)^2(0.02)$$
$$= (-1.03)^2(0.68) + (-0.03)^2(0.05) + (0.97)^2(0.07) + (1.97)^2(0.08)$$
$$+ (2.97)^2(0.05) + (3.97)^2(0.04) + (4.97)^2(0.01) + (5.97)^2(0.02)$$
$$= (1.0609)(0.68) + (0.0009)(0.05) + (0.9409)(0.07) + (3.8809)(0.08)$$
$$+ (8.8209)(0.05) + (15.7609)(0.04) + (24.7009)(0.01) + (35.6409)(0.02)$$
$$= 0.721412 + 0.000045 + 0.065863 + 0.310472 + 0.441045 + 0.630436 + 0.247009 + 0.712818$$
$$= 3.1291$$

Thus, the standard deviation is $\sigma = \sqrt{3.1291} \approx 1.7689$ days.

(b) The mean, $\overline{x}$, of $n = 100$ observations has mean $\mu = 1.03$ and standard deviation
$$\frac{\sigma}{\sqrt{n}} = \frac{1.7689}{\sqrt{100}} = \frac{1.7689}{10} \approx 0.177.$$

The central limit theorem says that $\overline{x}$ is approximately normal with this mean and standard deviation. The 95 part of the 68-95-99.7 rule says that with probability 0.95, values of $\overline{x}$ lie between $1.03 - 2(0.177) = 1.03 - 0.354 = 0.676$ days and $1.03 + 2(0.177) = 1.03 + 0.354 = 1.384$ days.

Word Search Solution

```
A D R T I M R O E D N D E M R V E H M Z E A E G U
J O C M X T G G N J X C I E L A X F A R S A E R O
C O M B I N A T O R I C S A E E T L G B H T L P V
B S M N C I H T E S G O L N Z O A M X Y T O W F C
N C I D V P O I W R A N D O M P H E N O M E N O N
P O E D L E Y Z S N P P S F Z W E R E U O S T A D
R M Q H H A H W A Z P R M A W R H O J P J O Y R O
F P F P X W J C M N R O H P N T R E R W R V A V G
A L R R S F S O P E O B J R P E E H O L E F N A N
Z E K O J Y T I L I B A B O R P E T E R C S I D G
E M R B I M N Z I E A B S B E R I T A I A L E D S
F E P B N R E S N E B I E A H A Y I A D P B E I J
P N I B G E V R G I I L M B E F D M O E S V D T Q
X T I I D S E S D J L I X I G I P I E E L K I E D
P R G L E G T K I T I T F L N D A L P N L E P O D
F U S I E H N M S R T Y E I Z T A L T I P N I J J
E L J T D E I I T Q Y H E T C O A A S W M E J J B
O E F Z I S O A R S M I F Y N C J R E M A I T U B
I D O N S I J X I O S M M M T G T E A S Q A L E O
L P V X U N S P B G D T T O E Q N N K A A F A E N
I O H S E E I M U T E O M D I O T E H G J L U R S
S B F T Z E D Q T Z L G F E V R U C Y T I S N E D
P E Y M A G E P I E H R X L T G E T S Q E I J M R
D E A G N L A W O F L A R G E N U M B E R S D T M
P M I E V E U E N E O M O H X N H R R R T H N E F
```

Chapter 9
Social Choice: The Impossible Dream

Chapter Outline

Introduction
Section 9.1   Majority Rule and Condorcet's Method
Section 9.2   Other Voting Systems for Three of More Candidates
Section 9.3   Insurmountable Difficulties: Arrow's Impossibility Theorem
Section 9.4   A Better Approach? Approval Voting

Chapter Summary

Social-choice theory developed from the attempt to explain voting and other group decision-making processes. Groups face the problem of turning individual preferences for different outcomes into a single choice for the group as a whole. How groups can best solve this problem is one of the basic questions in social choice.

Majority rule is perhaps the simplest voting method. The candidate receiving a majority (over 50%) of the votes cast is elected. This method works fine if there are only two candidates. However, as the number of candidates grows, it becomes increasingly unlikely that any candidate will obtain a majority of the votes cast. If it is desired that the winner should have an absolute majority, there could be a provision for a runoff election. This could be between the top two vote-getters, as in French presidential elections. Runoffs are just one example of *sequential voting* schemes. Another option, more common in American elections, would be to dispense with majority rule and adopt the *plurality method* in which the candidate with the highest vote total, majority or not, wins.

Voters generally have a most-preferred candidate in an election, and it is these top choices alone that influence the outcome in majority rule or the plurality method. If other methods are used, say a sequential method, then each voter's ranking of the entire list of candidates is important because the voter's top choice may not be in the running at a particular point in the election. These rankings are called preference list ballots.

Borda count, the method used in sports polls, asks the voter to rank the candidates in order from most preferred to least preferred and then assigns a point value to each position. The points are totaled for each candidate, and the candidate with the most points wins.

The *Hare system* also asks the voter to rank the candidates in order from most preferred to least preferred. In this system a winner is determined by repeatedly deleting the "least preferred" candidate. In this system, the winner will proportionally be the choice of the majority of the voters.

Condorcet's method requires that each candidate go head-to-head with each of the other candidates in a plurality election. To be a winner, a candidate must defeat each of his/her opponents. An interesting observation regarding Condorcet's method is that group preferences need not be transitive; that is, the group can prefer *A* to *B*, *B* to *C*, and yet prefer *C* to *A*. This phenomenon is referred to as the Condorcet paradox.

Kenneth Arrow's impossibility theorem established that if the vote is between three or more candidates, then any voting method will occasionally yield paradoxical results. Furthermore, any voting method is subject to manipulation through insincere, or strategic, voting (Chapter 10). These facts paint a gloomy picture, but voting is such an integral part of democratic society that it is important to recognize the shortcomings as well as the vulnerabilities of voting methods.

Voting turns out to be a complex activity. Several things can influence the outcome of an election: the voting method, individual preference list ballots, strategic voting, and, for sequential methods, the order of the various votes.

Skill Objectives

1. Analyze and interpret preference list ballots.

2. Rearrange preference list ballots to accommodate the elimination of one or more candidates.

3. Explain the difference between majority rule and the plurality method.

4. Discuss why the majority method may not be appropriate for an election in which there are more than two candidates.

5. Apply the plurality voting method to determine the winner in an election whose preference list ballots are given.

6. Apply the Borda count method to determine the winner from preference list ballots.

7. Apply the sequential pairwise voting method to determine the winner from preference list ballots.

8. Apply the Hare system method to determine the winner from preference list ballots.

9. Apply the plurality runoff method to determine the winner from preference list ballots.

10. Apply the approval voting method to determine the winner from a vote.

11. Determine whether a Condorcet winner exists and explain the Condorcet winner criterion (CWC).

12. Explain independence of irrelevant alternatives (IIA).

13. Explain Pareto condition.

14. Explain monotonicity.

15. Explain the Condorcet paradox.

16. Explain Arrow's impossibility theorem.

Teaching Tips

1. Surprisingly, some students have difficulty reading a preference schedule and understanding the order involved. It could be helpful later to take the time in the beginning to discuss this thoroughly. You may want to poll the class on some item of common interest and then use their responses to set up preference list ballots. For example, you might ask them to rank three television programs that are being aired at the same time. This preference schedule could then serve as the basis for discussion when investigating various voting schemes.

2. The Hare system is easy for most students to understand conceptually; however, they often experience frustration when trying to reorder the preference schedule after an elimination. It helps considerably to have several copies of blank preference list ballots with elimination preference list ballot(s) following, so that the progression can be followed with ease in the classroom. Convey to students that there are such resources available to assist them with the text exercises. These resources are available in the Student Study Guide.

3. The concept of the Condorcet winner may be more understandable if the student first writes out all possible two-candidate contests. This will bring about an elimination process for which the preference list ballots will need to be altered so that only two candidates remain. Erase all other candidates from the chart first and then move the two remaining candidates vertically upward into blank spaces. It seems like a time-consuming process, but it pays dividends in terms of student learning.

4. In the Borda count method, it is useful to have the students first calculate the total number of points to be distributed. For instance, if there are 25 voters and each ballot ranks 4 candidates, with the distribution of 6 points (3-2-1-0), the total number of points is 150. The students should check their totals against this number after calculating the number of points for each candidate.

5. In the Borda count method, the text uses 0 points for the last-place candidate up to $n-1$ for the first-place candidate where n represents the number of candidates on a ballot. If we let v be the number of voters, then the total number of points is $\frac{n(n-1)}{2} \cdot v$. Ask students to determine if other formulas exist for other point distributions. Start with 25 voters and each ballot ranks 4 candidates, with the distribution of 10 points (4-3-2-1). After that, allow for other less standard scenarios like 7-3-2-0. Also, discuss whether or not the method shown in the text on page 350 (replacing candidates on ballots by boxes and counting) is valid for other point distributions discussed here.

6. In Example 1 of the text, it was shown that AG is the winner using Condorcet's method. Explain to students that when one is determining who the winner is using Condorcet's method, one should consider all the possible one-on-one competitions. For n candidates, there will be $\frac{n!}{2 \cdot (n-2)!}$ pairings to consider.

7. The plurality runoff method is a one-time runoff, even if there are three candidates in the runoff (ties for first- or second- place). If the runoff is between two candidates, you are looking for the candidate with the majority of the votes. Otherwise, as the name of the method indicates, one would look for the candidate with a plurality of votes. Ask students to determine if it would be possible to have a tie for first-place with this method. You may choose to remind students at this point that in this chapter it is assumed that there are an odd number of voters. Follow up this discussion with determining possible scenarios with an even number of voters.

8. Approval voting is an important concept because of increased public interest in this method. It may be helpful to work an example by conducting an in-class survey of campus issues of interest.

9. Spreadsheets such as Excel are very helpful in performing the tedious calculations. We have made available Excel spreadsheets for 3 as well as 4 candidates. These spreadsheets will calculate Borda scores, one-on-one competition results, and the number of first-place votes for all possible ballots. They allow the flexibility of changing the points assigned to each place in the Borda method. They are initially set up with 1 voter per ballot (even though that yields an even number of voters). If a ballot is not needed, then one can simply hide that column.

Points for Borda method

You should find these spreadsheets helpful in quickly generating examples, showing that the Borda method fails the Condorcet winner criterion, examining outcomes with an even number of voters, etc. The spreadsheet for 4 candidates contains all of the twenty-four possible ballots. You will find these spreadsheets at http://www.whfreeman.com/fapp7. Since a complete spreadsheet for 5 candidates requires 120 possible ballots, we have not included additional spreadsheets.

Research Paper

1. Have students investigate the life and contributions of Marquis of Condorcet (1743–1794), the eighteenth century French mathematician and philosopher. Other figures mentioned in this chapter to consider include Kenneth O. May (1915–1977) and Chevalier de Borda (1733–1799) aka Jean-Charles de Borda.

2. Have students investigate conditions other than those described in the text, such as the Condorcet loser criterion, and consistency criterion.

Spreadsheet Project

To do this project, go to http://www.whfreeman.com/fapp7e.

Spreadsheets are used in this project to analyze Borda counts and approval voting. Using the automatic recalculation feature of spreadsheets, these activities allow the investigation of insincere voting strategies and their impact on the voting results. This activity can provide an introduction to a topic that will be further address in Chapter 10: Manipulability.

Collaborative Learning

Group Ranking

As an ice-breaker, duplicate the following exercise and have your students discuss the problem in groups.

A small New England town is faced with the following problem:

Five capital projects have been proposed for the next year:

1. Repave the main road.

2. Plant 100 new trees.

3. Build a cabana at the town swimming pool.

4. Replace the floor of the school gym.

5. Build a bandstand in the town's central square.

The problem is that the town's income for the next year is uncertain, so there may not be enough money for all of the projects. All issues are dealt with at town meetings in which each citizen casts a vote. The citizens decide to *rank* the projects in order of importance, and to start funding from the top of the ranks. Each citizen will submit his or her rankings that will be used to determine the group ranking. Devise a method (or methods) for determining the *group* ranking from the individual rankings.

Solutions

Skills Check:

1. b   2. c   3. b   4. b   5. c   6. d   7. b   8. b   9. c   10. a

11. a   12. c   13. a   14. b   15. c   16. a   17. b   18. b   19. c   20. c

Exercises:

1. Minority Rule satisfies condition (1): An exchange of marked ballots between two voters leaves the number of votes for each candidate unchanged, so whichever candidate won on the basis of having fewer votes before the exchange still has fewer votes after the exchange. Minority rule also satisfies condition (2): Suppose candidate X receives n votes and candidate Y receives m votes, and candidate X wins because $n < m$. Now suppose that a new election is held, and every voter reverses his or her vote. Then candidate X has m votes and candidate Y has n votes, and so candidate Y is the winner. Minority rule, however, fails condition (3): Suppose, for example, that there are 3 voters and that candidate X wins 1 out of the 3 votes. Now suppose that one of the 2 voters who voted for candidate Y reverses his or her vote. Then candidate X would have 2 votes, and candidate Y would have 1 vote, thus resulting in a win for candidate Y.

2. Suppose that candidate X is the winner regardless of who votes for whom (imposed rule). Conditions (1) and (3) are satisfied: The outcome of an election is not affected by anything in particular, not by an exchange of ballots, as in condition (1), or by a change in a single ballot, as in condition (3). Condition (2), however, fails: If every voter reversed his or her vote, candidate X still wins, so the outcome of the election is not reversed.

3. A dictatorship satisfies condition (2): If a new election is held and every voter (in particular, the dictator) reverses his or her ballot, then certainly the outcome of the election is reversed. A dictatorship also satisfies condition (3): If a single voter changes his or her ballot from being a vote for the loser of the previous election to a vote for the winner of the previous election, then the single voter could not have been a dictator (since the dictator's ballot was not a vote for the loser of the previous election). Thus, the outcome of the new election is the same as the outcome of the previous election. A dictatorship, however, fails to satisfy condition (1): If the dictator exchanges his/her marked ballot with any voter whose marked ballot differs from that of the dictator, then the outcome of the election is certainly reversed.

4. For each of the following, assume that there are 4 voters (one of whom is named Nadia) and 2 candidates (named A and B).

    (a) A voting system satisfying condition (1), but neither conditions (2) nor (3): A wins if and only if he or she receives 1, 2, or 4 votes.

    (b) A voting system satisfying condition (2), but neither conditions (1) nor (3): A wins if and only Nadia votes for B. (Nadia is the antidictator)

    (c) A voting system satisfying condition (3), but neither conditions (1) nor (2): Nadia gets 2 votes; the other three voters get 1 vote; and A wins if and only if he gets a total of 4 or 5 votes.

5. With an odd number of voters, each one-on-one score will have a winner because there cannot be a tie. If one of the candidates, say A, is the winner by Condorcet's method, then A would have beaten every other candidate in a one-on-one competition. It would be impossible for another candidate, say B, to have beaten A. Hence, B could not also be a winner.

6. Answers will vary.

7.

22%	23%	15%	29%	7%	4%
D	D	H	H	J	J
H	J	D	J	H	D
J	H	J	D	D	H

(a) We must check the one-on-one scores of D versus H, D versus J, and H versus J.

D versus H: D is over H on $22\% + 23\% + 4\% = 49\%$ of the ballots, while the reverse is true on $15\% + 29\% + 7\% = 51\%$. Thus, H defeats D, 51% to 49%.

D versus J: D is over J on $22\% + 23\% + 15\% = 60\%$ of the ballots, while the reverse is true on $29\% + 7\% + 4\% = 40\%$. Thus, D defeats J, 60% to 40%.

H versus J: H is over J on $22\% + 15\% + 29\% = 66\%$ of the ballots, while the reverse is true on $23\% + 7\% + 4\% = 34\%$. Thus, H defeats J, 66% to 34%.

Yes, there is a Condorcet winner. Since H can defeat both D and J in a one-to one competition, Elizabeth Holtzman (H) is the winner by Condorcet's method.

(b) D has $22\% + 23\% = 45\%$ of the first-place votes. H has $15\% + 29\% = 44\%$ of the first-place votes. J has $7\% + 4\% = 11\%$ of the first-place votes. Since D has the most first-place votes, Alfonse D'Amato (D) is the winner by plurality voting.

8.

Rank	Number of voters (9)						
	3	1	1	1	1	1	1
First	A	A	B	B	C	C	D
Second	D	B	C	C	B	D	C
Third	B	C	D	A	D	B	B
Fourth	C	D	A	D	A	A	A

(a) A has $3 + 1 = 4$ first-place votes. B has $1 + 1 = 2$ first-place votes. C has $1 + 1 = 2$ first-place votes. D has 1 first-place vote. Since A has the most first-place votes, A is the winner by plurality voting.

(b)

Preference	1st place votes × 3	2nd place votes × 2	3rd place votes × 1	4th place votes × 0	Borda score
A	4×3	0×2	1×1	4×0	13
B	2×3	2×2	5×1	0×0	15
C	2×3	3×2	1×1	3×0	13
D	1×3	4×2	2×1	2×0	13

Thus, B has the highest Borda score and is declared the winner.

Note, the Borda score for each candidate could also have been determined firstly by individually replacing the candidates below the one you are determining the score for by a box.

For A:

Rank	Number of voters (9)						
	3	1	1	1	1	1	1
First	A	A	B	B	C	C	D
Second	☐	☐	C	C	B	D	C
Third	☐	☐	D	A	D	B	B
Fourth	☐	☐	A	☐	A	A	A

To show that the Borda score for candidate A is 13, it needs to be noted that each box below A counts 3 times in the first column. The Borda score for A is $(3 \times 3) + (4 \times 1) = 9 + 4 = 13$.

Continued on next page

8. (b) continued

For B:

Rank				Number of voters (9)			
	3	1	1	1	1	1	1
First	A	A	B	B	C	C	D
Second	D	B	☐	☐	B	D	C
Third	B	☐	☐	☐	☐	B	B
Fourth	☐	☐	☐	☐	☐	☐	☐

To show that the Borda score for candidate B is 15, it needs to be noted that each box below B counts 3 times in the first column. The Borda score for B is $(3 \times 1) + (12 \times 1) = 3 + 12 = 15$.

For C:

Rank				Number of voters (9)			
	3	1	1	1	1	1	1
First	A	A	B	B	C	C	D
Second	D	B	C	C	☐	☐	C
Third	B	C	☐	☐	☐	☐	☐
Fourth	C	☐	☐	☐	☐	☐	☐

There are 13 boxes below C, each with a value of 1. The Borda score for C is 13.

For D:

Rank				Number of voters (9)			
	3	1	1	1	1	1	1
First	A	A	B	B	C	C	D
Second	D	B	C	C	B	D	☐
Third	☐	C	D	A	D	☐	☐
Fourth	☐	D	☐	D	☐	☐	☐

To show that the Borda score for candidate D is 13, it needs to be noted that each box below D counts 3 times in the first column. The Borda score for D is $(2 \times 3) + (7 \times 1) = 6 + 7 = 13$.

(c) Since D has the least number of first-place votes (see Part a), D is eliminated.

Rank				Number of voters (9)			
	3	1	1	1	1	1	1
First	A	A	B	B	C	C	C
Second	B	B	C	C	B	B	B
Third	C	C	A	A	A	A	A

A now has $3 + 1 = 4$ first-place votes. B now has $1 + 1 = 2$ first-place votes. C now has $1 + 1 + 1 = 3$ first-place votes. Since B has the least number of first-place votes, B is eliminated.

Rank				Number of voters (9)			
	3	1	1	1	1	1	1
First	A	A	C	C	C	C	C
Second	C	C	A	A	A	A	A

A now has $3 + 1 = 4$ first-place votes. C now has $1 + 1 + 1 + 1 + 1 = 5$ first-place votes. Thus, C is the winner by the Hare system.

(d) In sequential pairwise voting with the agenda A, B, C, D, we first pit A against B. There are 4 voters that prefer A to B and 5 prefer B to A. Thus, B wins by a score of 5 to 4. A is therefore eliminated, and B moves on to confront C.

There are 6 voters who prefer B to C and 3 prefer C to B. Thus, B wins by a score of 6 to 3. C is therefore eliminated, and B moves on to confront D.

There are 4 voters who prefer B to D and 5 prefer D to B. Thus, D wins by a score of 5 to 4.

Thus, D is the winner by sequential pairwise voting with the agenda A, B, C, D.

9.

	Number of voters (7)				
Rank	**2**	**2**	**1**	**1**	**1**
First	C	D	C	B	A
Second	A	A	D	D	D
Third	B	C	A	A	B
Fourth	D	B	B	C	C

(a) A has 1 first-place vote. B has 1 first-place vote. C has $2 + 1 = 3$ first-place votes. D has 2 first-place votes. Since C has the most first-place votes, C is the winner by plurality voting.

(b)

Preference	1st place votes $\times$ 3	2nd place votes $\times$ 2	3rd place votes $\times$ 1	4th place votes $\times$ 0	Borda score
A	1×3	4×2	2×1	0×0	13
B	1×3	0×2	3×1	3×0	6
C	3×3	0×2	2×1	2×0	11
D	2×3	3×2	0×1	2×0	12

Thus, A has the highest Borda score and is declared the winner.

Note, the Borda score for each candidate could also have been determined firstly by individually replacing the candidates below the one you are determining the score for by a box.

For A:

	Number of voters (7)				
Rank	**2**	**2**	**1**	**1**	**1**
First	C	D	C	B	A
Second	A	A	D	D	□
Third	□	□	A	A	□
Fourth	□	□	□	□	□

To show that the Borda score for candidate A is 13, it needs to be noted that each box below A counts 2 times in the first and second columns. The Borda score for A is therefore $(4 \times 2) + (5 \times 1) = 8 + 5 = 13$.

For B:

	Number of voters (7)				
Rank	**2**	**2**	**1**	**1**	**1**
First	C	D	C	B	A
Second	A	A	D	□	D
Third	B	C	A	□	B
Fourth	□	B	B	□	□

To show that the Borda score for candidate B is 6, it needs to be noted that each box below B counts 2 times in the first column. The Borda score for B is $(1 \times 2) + (4 \times 1) = 2 + 4 = 6$.

For C:

	Number of voters (7)				
Rank	**2**	**2**	**1**	**1**	**1**
First	C	D	C	B	A
Second	□	A	□	D	D
Third	□	C	□	A	B
Fourth	□	□	□	C	C

To show that the Borda score for candidate C is 11, it needs to be noted that each box below C counts 2 times in the first and second columns. The Borda score for C is therefore $(4 \times 2) + (3 \times 1) = 8 + 3 = 11$.

Continued on next page

9. **(b)** continued

For D:

Rank	Number of voters (7)				
	2	2	1	1	1
First	C	D	C	B	A
Second	A	☐	D	D	D
Third	B	☐	☐	☐	☐
Fourth	D	☐	☐	☐	☐

To show that the Borda score for candidate D is 12, it needs to be noted that each box below D counts 2 times in the second column. The Borda score for D is $(3 \times 2) + (6 \times 1) = 6 + 6 = 12$.

(c) Since A and B have the least number of first-place votes (see Part a), both are eliminated.

Rank	Number of voters (7)				
	2	2	1	1	1
First	C	D	C	D	D
Second	D	C	D	C	C

C now has $2 + 1 = 3$ first-place votes. D now has $2 + 1 + 1 = 4$ first-place votes. Thus, D is the winner by the Hare system.

(d) In sequential pairwise voting with the agenda B, D, C, A, we first pit B against D. There are 3 voters who prefer B to D and 4 prefer D to B. Thus, D wins by a score of 4 to 3. B is therefore eliminated, and D moves on to confront C.

There are 4 voters who prefer D to C and 3 prefer C to D. Thus, D wins by a score of 4 to 3. C is therefore eliminated, and D moves on to confront A.

There are 4 voters who prefer D to A and 3 prefer A to D. Thus, D wins by a score of 4 to 3.

Thus, D is the winner by sequential pairwise voting with the agenda B, D, C, A.

10.

Rank	Number of voters (8)					
	2	2	1	1	1	1
First	A	E	A	B	C	D
Second	B	B	D	E	E	E
Third	C	D	C	C	D	A
Fourth	D	C	B	D	A	B
Fifth	E	A	E	A	B	C

(a) A has $2 + 1 = 3$ first-place votes. B has 1 first-place vote. C has 1 first-place vote. D has 1 first-place vote. E has 2 first-place votes. Since A has the most first-place votes, A is the winner by plurality voting.

(b)

Preference	1st place votes × 4	2nd place votes × 3	3rd place votes × 2	4th place votes × 1	5th place votes × 0	Borda score
A	3×4	0×3	1×2	1×1	3×0	15
B	1×4	4×3	0×2	2×1	1×0	18
C	1×4	0×3	4×2	2×1	1×0	14
D	1×4	1×3	3×2	3×1	0×0	16
E	2×4	3×3	0×2	0×1	3×0	17

Thus, B has the highest Borda score and is declared the winner.

Continued on next page

10. (b) continued

Note, the Borda score for each candidate could also have been determined firstly by individually replacing the candidates below the one you are determining the score for by a box.

For A:

	Number of voters (8)					
Rank	**2**	**2**	**1**	**1**	**1**	**1**
First	A	E	A	B	C	D
Second	☐	B	☐	E	E	E
Third	☐	D	☐	C	D	A
Fourth	☐	C	☐	D	A	☐
Fifth	☐	A	☐	A	☐	☐

To show that the Borda score for candidate A is 15, it needs to be noted that each box below A counts 2 times in the first column. The Borda score for A is $(4\times2)+(7\times1)=8+7=15$.

For B:

	Number of voters (8)					
Rank	**2**	**2**	**1**	**1**	**1**	**1**
First	A	E	A	B	C	D
Second	B	B	D	☐	E	E
Third	☐	☐	C	☐	D	A
Fourth	☐	☐	B	☐	A	B
Fifth	☐	☐	☐	☐	B	☐

To show that the Borda score for candidate B is 18, it needs to be noted that each box below B counts 2 times in the first and second columns. The Borda score for B is therefore $(6\times2)+(6\times1)=12+6=18$.

For C:

	Number of voters (8)					
Rank	**2**	**2**	**1**	**1**	**1**	**1**
First	A	E	A	B	C	D
Second	B	B	D	E	☐	E
Third	C	D	C	C	☐	A
Fourth	☐	C	☐	☐	☐	B
Fifth	☐	☐	☐	☐	☐	C

To show that the Borda score for candidate C is 14, it needs to be noted that each box below C counts 2 times in the first and second columns. The Borda score for C is therefore $(3\times2)+(8\times1)=6+8=14$.

For D:

	Number of voters (8)					
Rank	**2**	**2**	**1**	**1**	**1**	**1**
First	A	E	A	B	C	D
Second	B	B	D	E	E	☐
Third	C	D	☐	C	D	☐
Fourth	D	☐	☐	D	☐	☐
Fifth	☐	☐	☐	☐	☐	☐

To show that the Borda score for candidate D is 16, it needs to be noted that each box below D counts 2 times in the first and second columns. The Borda score for D is $(3\times2)+(10\times1)=6+10=16$.

Continued on next page

10. (b) continued

For E:

Rank	Number of voters (8)					
	2	**2**	**1**	**1**	**1**	**1**
First	A	E	A	B	C	D
Second	B	□	D	E	E	E
Third	C	□	C	□	□	□
Fourth	D	□	B	□	□	□
Fifth	E	□	E	□	□	□

To show that the Borda score for candidate E is 17, it needs to be noted that each box below E counts 2 times in the second column. The Borda score for E is $(4 \times 2) + (9 \times 1) = 8 + 9 = 17$.

(c) Since B, C, and D have the least number of first-place votes (see Part a), they are all eliminated.

Rank	Number of voters (8)					
	2	**2**	**1**	**1**	**1**	**1**
First	A	E	A	E	E	E
Second	E	A	E	A	A	A

A now has $2 + 1 = 3$ first-place votes. E now has $2 + 1 + 1 + 1 = 5$ first-place votes. Thus, E is the winner by the Hare system.

(d) In sequential pairwise voting with the agenda B, D, C, A, E, we first pit B against D. There are 5 voters who prefer B to D and 3 prefer D to B. Thus, B wins by a score of 5 to 3. D is therefore eliminated, and B moves on to confront C.

There are 6 voters who prefer B to C and 2 prefer C to B. Thus, B wins by a score of 6 to 2. C is therefore eliminated, and B moves on to confront A.

There are 3 voters who prefer B to A and 5 prefer A to B. Thus, A wins by a score of 5 to 3. B is therefore eliminated, and A moves on to confront E.

There are 3 voters that prefer A to E and 5 prefer E to A. Thus, E wins by a score of 5 to 3.

Thus, E is the winner by sequential pairwise voting with the agenda B, D, C, A, E.

11.

Rank	Number of voters (5)				
	1	**1**	**1**	**1**	**1**
First	A	B	C	D	E
Second	B	C	B	C	D
Third	E	A	E	A	C
Fourth	D	D	D	E	A
Fifth	C	E	A	B	B

(a) A has 1 first-place vote. B has 1 first-place vote. C has 1 first-place vote. D has 1 first-place vote. E has 1 first-place vote. Since all candidates have the same number of first-place votes, they tie.

(b)

Preference	1st place votes × 4	2nd place votes × 3	3rd place votes × 2	4th place votes × 1	5th place votes × 0	Borda score
A	1×4	0×3	2×2	1×1	1×0	9
B	1×4	2×3	0×2	0×1	2×0	10
C	1×4	2×3	1×2	0×1	1×0	12
D	1×4	1×3	0×2	3×1	0×0	10
E	1×4	0×3	2×2	1×1	1×0	9

Thus, C has the highest Borda score and is declared the winner.

Continued on next page

11. (b) continued

Note, the Borda score for each candidate could also have been determined firstly by individually replacing the candidates below the one you are determining the score for by a box.

For *A*:

	Number of voters (5)				
Rank	**1**	**1**	**1**	**1**	**1**
First	A	B	C	D	E
Second	☐	C	B	C	D
Third	☐	A	E	A	C
Fourth	☐	☐	D	☐	A
Fifth	☐	☐	A	☐	☐

The Borda score for candidate *A* is 9 since there are 9 boxes.

For *B*:

	Number of voters (5)				
Rank	**1**	**1**	**1**	**1**	**1**
First	A	B	C	D	E
Second	B	☐	B	C	D
Third	☐	☐	☐	A	C
Fourth	☐	☐	☐	E	A
Fifth	☐	☐	☐	B	B

The Borda score for candidate *B* is 10 since there are 10 boxes.

For *C*:

	Number of voters (5)				
Rank	**1**	**1**	**1**	**1**	**1**
First	A	B	C	D	E
Second	B	C	☐	C	D
Third	E	☐	☐	☐	C
Fourth	D	☐	☐	☐	☐
Fifth	C	☐	☐	☐	☐

The Borda score for candidate *C* is 12.

For *D*:

	Number of voters (5)				
Rank	**1**	**1**	**1**	**1**	**1**
First	A	B	C	D	E
Second	B	C	B	☐	D
Third	E	A	E	☐	☐
Fourth	D	D	D	☐	☐
Fifth	☐	☐	☐	☐	☐

The Borda score for candidate *D* is 10 since there are 10 boxes.

For *E*:

	Number of voters (5)				
Rank	**1**	**1**	**1**	**1**	**1**
First	A	B	C	D	E
Second	B	C	B	C	☐
Third	E	A	E	A	☐
Fourth	☐	D	☐	E	☐
Fifth	☐	E	☐	☐	☐

The Borda score for candidate *E* is 9 since there are 9 boxes.

Continued on next page

11. continued

(c) Since all candidates have the same least number of first-place votes (see Part a), they all tie.

(d) In sequential pairwise voting with the agenda A, B, C, D, E, we first pit A against B. There are 3 voters who prefer A to B and 2 prefer B to A. Thus, A wins by a score of 3 to 2. B is therefore eliminated, and A moves on to confront C.

There is 1 voter who prefers A to C and 4 prefer C to A. Thus, C wins by a score of 4 to 1. A is therefore eliminated, and C moves on to confront D.

There are 2 voters who prefer C to D and 3 prefer D to C. Thus, D wins by a score of 3 to 2. C is therefore eliminated, and D moves on to confront E.

There are 2 voters who prefer D to E and 3 prefer E to D. Thus, E wins by a score of 3 to 2.

Thus, E is the winner by sequential pairwise voting with the agenda A, B, C, D, E.

12.

	Number of voters (7)				
Rank	**2**	**2**	**1**	**1**	**1**
First	A	B	A	C	D
Second	D	D	B	B	B
Third	C	A	D	D	A
Fourth	B	C	C	A	C

(a) A has $2 + 1 = 3$ first-place votes. B has 2 first-place votes. C has 1 first-place vote. D has 1 first-place vote. Since A has the most number of the first-place votes, A is the winner by plurality voting.

(b)

Preference	1st place votes × 3	2nd place votes × 2	3rd place votes × 1	4th place votes × 0	Borda score
A	3×3	0×2	3×1	1×0	12
B	2×3	3×2	0×1	2×0	12
C	1×3	0×2	2×1	4×0	5
D	1×3	4×2	2×1	0×0	13

Thus, D has the highest Borda score and is declared the winner.

Note, the Borda score for each candidate could also have been determined firstly by individually replacing the candidates below the one you are determining the score for by a box.

For A:

	Number of voters (7)				
Rank	**2**	**2**	**1**	**1**	**1**
First	A	B	A	C	D
Second	☐	D	☐	B	B
Third	☐	A	☐	D	A
Fourth	☐	☐	☐	A	☐

To show that the Borda score for candidate A is 12, it needs to be noted that each box below A counts 2 times in the first and second columns. The Borda score for A is therefore $(4 \times 2) + (4 \times 1) = 8 + 4 = 12$.

continued on next page

12. (b) continued

For *B*:

Rank	2	2	1	1	1
		Number of voters (7)			
First	*A*	*B*	*A*	*C*	*D*
Second	*D*	☐	*B*	*B*	*B*
Third	*C*	☐	☐	☐	☐
Fourth	*B*	☐	☐	☐	☐

To show that the Borda score for candidate *B* is 12, it needs to be noted that each box below *B* counts 2 times in the second column. The Borda score for *B* is $(3\times2)+(6\times1)=6+6=12$.

For *C*:

Rank	2	2	1	1	1
		Number of voters (7)			
First	*A*	*B*	*A*	*C*	*D*
Second	*D*	*D*	*B*	☐	*B*
Third	*C*	*A*	*D*	☐	*A*
Fourth	☐	*C*	*C*	☐	*C*

To show that the Borda score for candidate *C* is 5, it needs to be noted that each box below *C* counts 2 times in the first column. The Borda score for *C* is $(1\times2)+(3\times1)=2+3=5$.

For *D*:

Rank	2	2	1	1	1
		Number of voters (7)			
First	*A*	*B*	*A*	*C*	*D*
Second	*D*	*D*	*B*	*B*	☐
Third	☐	☐	*D*	*D*	☐
Fourth	☐	☐	☐	☐	☐

To show that the Borda score for candidate *D* is 13, it needs to be noted that each box below *D* counts 2 times in first and second columns. The Borda score for *D* is $(4\times2)+(5\times1)=8+5=13$.

(c) Since *C* and *D* have the least number of first-place votes (see Part a), both are eliminated.

Rank	2	2	1	1	1
		Number of voters (7)			
First	*A*	*B*	*A*	*B*	*B*
Second	*B*	*A*	*B*	*A*	*A*

A now has 2 + 1 = 3 first-place votes. *B* now has 2 + 1 + 1 = 4 first-place votes. Thus, *B* is the winner by the Hare system.

(d) In sequential pairwise voting with the agenda *B, D, C, A,* we first pit *B* against *D*. There are 4 voters who *B* to *D* and 3 prefer *D* to *B*. Thus, *B* wins by a score of 4 to 3. *D* is therefore eliminated, and *B* moves on to confront *C*.

There are 4 voters who prefer *B* to *C* and 3 prefer *C* to *B*. Thus, *B* wins by a score of 4 to 3. *C* is therefore eliminated, and *B* moves on to confront *A*.

There are 4 voters who prefer *B* to *A* and 3 prefer *A* to *B*. Thus, *B* wins by a score of 4 to 3.

Thus, *B* is the winner by sequential pairwise voting with the agenda *B, D, C, A.*

13.

Rank	Number of voters (7)				
	2	**2**	**1**	**1**	**1**
First	C	E	C	D	A
Second	E	B	A	E	E
Third	D	D	D	A	C
Fourth	A	C	E	C	D
Fifth	B	A	B	B	B

(a) A has 1 first-place vote. B has 0 first-place votes. C has $2 + 1 = 3$ first-place votes. D has 1 first-place vote. E has 2 first-place votes. Since C has the most first-place votes, C is the winner by plurality voting.

(b)

Preference	1st place votes × 4	2nd place votes × 3	3rd place votes × 2	4th place votes × 1	5th place votes × 0	Borda score
A	1×4	1×3	1×2	2×1	2×0	11
B	0×4	2×3	0×2	0×1	5×0	6
C	3×4	0×3	1×2	3×1	0×0	17
D	1×4	0×3	5×2	1×1	0×0	15
E	2×4	4×3	0×2	1×1	0×0	21

Thus, E has the highest Borda score and is declared the winner.

Note, the Borda score for each candidate could also have been determined firstly by individually replacing the candidates below the one you are determining the score for by a box.

For A:

Rank	Number of voters (7)				
	2	**2**	**1**	**1**	**1**
First	C	E	C	D	A
Second	E	B	A	E	☐
Third	D	D	☐	A	☐
Fourth	A	C	☐	☐	☐
Fifth	☐	A	☐	☐	☐

To show that the Borda score for candidate A is 11, it needs to be noted that each box below A counts 2 times in the first column. The Borda score for A is $(1 \times 2) + (9 \times 1) = 2 + 9 = 11$.

For B:

Rank	Number of voters (7)				
	2	**2**	**1**	**1**	**1**
First	C	E	C	D	A
Second	E	B	A	E	E
Third	D	☐	D	A	C
Fourth	A	☐	E	C	D
Fifth	B	☐	B	B	B

To show that the Borda score for candidate B is 6, it needs to be noted that each box below B counts 2 times in the second column. The Borda score for B is $3 \times 2 = 6$.

Continued on next page

13. (b) continued

For *C*:

	Number of voters (7)				
Rank	**2**	**2**	**1**	**1**	**1**
First	*C*	*E*	*C*	*D*	*A*
Second	☐	*B*	☐	*E*	*E*
Third	☐	*D*	☐	*A*	*C*
Fourth	☐	*C*	☐	*C*	☐
Fifth	☐	☐	☐	☐	☐

To show that the Borda score for candidate *C* is 17, it needs to be noted that each box below *C* counts 2 times in the first and second columns. The Borda score for *C* is therefore $(5 \times 2) + (7 \times 1) = 10 + 7 = 17$.

For *D*:

	Number of voters (7)				
Rank	**2**	**2**	**1**	**1**	**1**
First	*C*	*E*	*C*	*D*	*A*
Second	*E*	*B*	*A*	☐	*E*
Third	*D*	*D*	*D*	☐	*C*
Fourth	☐	☐	☐	☐	*D*
Fifth	☐	☐	☐	☐	☐

To show that the Borda score for candidate *D* is 15, it needs to be noted that each box below *D* counts 2 times in the first and second columns. The Borda score for *D* is therefore $(4 \times 2) + (7 \times 1) = 8 + 7 = 15$.

For *E*:

	Number of voters (7)				
Rank	**2**	**2**	**1**	**1**	**1**
First	*C*	*E*	*C*	*D*	*A*
Second	*E*	☐	*A*	*E*	*E*
Third	☐	☐	*D*	☐	☐
Fourth	☐	☐	*E*	☐	☐
Fifth	☐	☐	☐	☐	☐

To show that the Borda score for candidate *E* is 21, it needs to be noted that each box below *E* counts 2 times in the first and second columns. The Borda score for *E* is $(7 \times 2) + (7 \times 1) = 14 + 7 = 21$.

(c) Since *B* has the least number of first-place votes (see Part a), *B* is eliminated.

	Number of voters (7)				
Rank	**2**	**2**	**1**	**1**	**1**
First	*C*	*E*	*C*	*D*	*A*
Second	*E*	*D*	*A*	*E*	*E*
Third	*D*	*C*	*D*	*A*	*C*
Fourth	*A*	*A*	*E*	*C*	*D*

A now has 1 first-place vote. *C* now has 2 + 1 = 3 first-place votes. *D* now has 1 first-place vote. *E* has 2 first-place votes. Since *A* and *D* have the least number of first-place votes, they are both eliminated.

Continued on next page

13. (c) continued

	Number of voters (7)				
Rank	2	2	1	1	1
First	C	E	C	E	E
Second	E	C	E	C	C

C now has $2 + 1 = 3$ first-place votes. E now has $2 + 1 + 1 = 4$ first-place votes. Thus, E is the winner by the Hare system.

(d) In sequential pairwise voting with the agenda A, B, C, D, E, we first pit A against B. There are 5 voters who prefer A to B and 2 prefer B to A. Thus, A wins by a score of 5 to 2. B is therefore eliminated, and A moves on to confront C.

There are 2 voters who prefer A to C and 5 prefer C to A. Thus, C wins by a score of 5 to 2. A is therefore eliminated, and C moves on to confront D.

There are 4 voters who prefer C to D and 3 prefer D to C. Thus, C wins by a score of 4 to 3. D is therefore eliminated, and C moves on to confront E.

There are 3 voters who prefer C to E and 4 prefer E to C. Thus, E wins by a score of 4 to 3.

Thus, E is the winner by sequential pairwise voting with the agenda A, B, C, D, E.

14.

	Number of voters (7)						
Rank	1	1	1	1	1	1	1
First	C	D	C	B	E	D	C
Second	A	A	E	D	D	E	A
Third	E	E	D	A	A	A	E
Fourth	B	C	A	E	C	B	B
Fifth	D	B	B	C	B	C	D

(a) A has 0 first-place votes. B has 1 first-place vote. C has 3 first-place votes. D has 2 first-place vote. E has 1 first-place votes. Since C has the most first-place votes, C is the winner by plurality voting.

(b)

Preference	1st place votes $\times$ 4	2nd place votes $\times$ 3	3rd place votes $\times$ 2	4th place votes $\times$ 1	5th place votes $\times$ 0	Borda score
A	0×4	3×3	3×2	1×1	0×0	16
B	1×4	0×3	0×2	3×1	3×0	7
C	3×4	0×3	0×2	2×1	2×0	14
D	2×4	2×3	1×2	0×1	2×0	16
E	1×4	2×3	3×2	1×1	0×0	17

Thus, E has the highest Borda score and is declared the winner.

Note, the Borda score for each candidate could also have been determined firstly by individually replacing the candidates below the one you are determining the score for by a box.

For A:

	Number of voters (7)						
Rank	1	1	1	1	1	1	1
First	C	D	C	B	E	D	C
Second	A	A	E	D	D	E	A
Third	☐	☐	D	A	A	A	☐
Fourth	☐	☐	A	☐	☐	☐	☐
Fifth	☐	☐	☐	☐	☐	☐	☐

The Borda score for candidate A is 16 since there are 16 boxes.

Continued on next page

14. (b) continued

For *B*:

Rank	Number of voters (7)						
	1	1	1	1	1	1	1
First	C	D	C	B	E	D	C
Second	A	A	E	☐	D	E	A
Third	E	E	D	☐	A	A	E
Fourth	B	C	A	☐	C	B	B
Fifth	☐	B	B	☐	B	☐	☐

The Borda score for candidate *B* is 7 since there are 7 boxes.

For *C*:

Rank	Number of voters (7)						
	1	1	1	1	1	1	1
First	C	D	C	B	E	D	C
Second	☐	A	☐	D	D	E	☐
Third	☐	E	☐	A	A	A	☐
Fourth	☐	C	☐	E	C	B	☐
Fifth	☐	☐	☐	C	☐	C	☐

The Borda score for candidate *C* is 14 since there are 14 boxes.

For *D*:

Rank	Number of voters (7)						
	1	1	1	1	1	1	1
First	C	D	C	B	E	D	C
Second	A	☐	E	D	D	☐	A
Third	E	☐	D	☐	☐	☐	E
Fourth	B	☐	☐	☐	☐	☐	B
Fifth	D	☐	☐	☐	☐	☐	D

The Borda score for candidate *D* is 16 since there are 16 boxes.

For *E*:

Rank	Number of voters (7)						
	1	1	1	1	1	1	1
First	C	D	C	B	E	D	C
Second	A	A	E	D	☐	E	A
Third	E	E	☐	A	☐	☐	E
Fourth	☐	☐	☐	E	☐	☐	☐
Fifth	☐	☐	☐	☐	☐	☐	☐

The Borda score for candidate *E* is 17 since there are 17 boxes.

(c) In sequential pairwise voting with the agenda *A*, *B*, *C*, *D*, *E*, we first pit *A* against *B*. There are 6 voters who prefer *A* to *B* and 1 prefers *B* to *A*. Thus, *A* wins by a score of 6 to 1. *B* is therefore eliminated, and *A* moves on to confront *C*.

There are 4 voters who prefer *A* to *C* and 3 prefer *C* to *A*. Thus, *A* wins by a score of 4 to 3. *C* is therefore eliminated, and *A* moves on to confront *D*.

There are 2 voters who prefer *A* to *D* and 5 prefer *D* to *A*. Thus, *D* wins by a score of 5 to 2. *A* is therefore eliminated, and *D* moves on to confront *E*.

There are 3 voters who prefer *D* to *E* and 4 prefer *E* to *D*. Thus, *E* wins by a score of 4 to 3.

Thus, *E* is the winner by sequential pairwise voting with the agenda *A*, *B*, *C*, *D*, *E*.

Continued on next page

14. continued

(d) Since A has the least number of first-place votes (see Part a), A is eliminated.

Rank	Number of voters (7)						
	1	1	1	1	1	1	1
First	C	D	C	B	E	D	C
Second	E	E	E	D	D	E	E
Third	B	C	D	E	C	B	B
Fourth	D	B	B	C	B	C	D

B now has 1 first-place vote. C now has 3 first-place votes. D now has 2 first-place votes. E has 1 first-place vote. Since B and E have the least number of first-place votes, they are both eliminated.

Rank	Number of voters (7)						
	1	1	1	1	1	1	1
First	C	D	C	D	D	D	C
Second	D	C	D	C	C	C	D

C now has 3 first-place votes. D now has 4 first-place votes. Thus, D is the winner by the Hare system.

15.

Rank	Number of voters (7)						
	1	1	1	1	1	1	1
First	C	D	C	B	E	D	C
Second	A	A	E	D	D	E	A
Third	E	E	D	A	A	A	E
Fourth	B	C	A	E	C	B	B
Fifth	D	B	B	C	B	C	D

(a) A has 0 last-place votes. B has 3 last-place votes. C has 2 last-place votes. D has 2 last-place votes. E has 0 last-place votes. Since B has the most last-place votes, B is eliminated.

Rank	Number of voters (7)						
	1	1	1	1	1	1	1
First	C	D	C	D	E	D	C
Second	A	A	E	A	D	E	A
Third	E	E	D	E	A	A	E
Fourth	D	C	A	C	C	C	D

A has 1 last-place vote. C has 4 last-place votes. D has 2 last-place votes. E has 0 last-place votes. Since C has the most last-place votes, C is eliminated.

Rank	Number of voters (7)						
	1	1	1	1	1	1	1
First	A	D	E	D	E	D	A
Second	E	A	D	A	D	E	E
Third	D	E	A	E	A	A	D

A has 3 last-place votes. D has 2 last-place votes. E has 2 last-place votes. Since A has the most number of the last-place votes, A is eliminated.

Rank	Number of voters (7)						
	1	1	1	1	1	1	1
First	E	D	E	D	E	D	E
Second	D	E	D	E	D	E	D

D now has 4 last-place votes. E now has 3 last-place votes. Thus, E is the winner by the procedure of Clyde Coombs.

Continued on next page

15. continued

(b) To show that it is possible for two voters and three candidates to result in different outcomes using different methods (Coombs procedure and the Hare method), we need to find an example that illustrates such an occurrence.

One possible scenario is having candidates *A*, *B*, and *C* with the following preference lists.

Rank	Number of voters (2)	
	1	1
First	*A*	*C*
Second	*B*	*B*
Third	*C*	*A*

Using the Coombs procedure, both *C* and *A* have the same number of last-place votes. They are both therefore eliminated leaving only *B*. *B* therefore is the winner using the Coombs procedure.

Using the Hare method, *B* has the least number of first-place votes. *B* is therefore eliminated resulting in the following preference list.

Rank	Number of voters (2)	
	1	1
First	*A*	*C*
Second	*C*	*A*

Since *A* and *C* both have the same number of first-place votes, a tie is declared.

16. (a) Condorcet's method satisfies the Pareto condition because if a candidate, say *A*, is the winner by Condorcet's method, *A* would have beaten every other candidate in a one-on-one contest. Thus, none of the other candidates would be a winner.

(b) Condorcet's method satisfies the monotonicity because if a candidate, say *A*, is the winner by Condorcet's method, *A* would have beaten every other candidate in a one-on-one contest. To move *A* higher on the preference list would not alter this outcome. *A* would still beat every other candidate in a one-on-one contest and thus would still be the winner.

17. (a) Plurality voting satisfies the Pareto condition because if everyone prefers *B* to *D*, for example, then *D* has no-first place votes at all. Thus, *D* cannot be among the winners in plurality voting.

(b) Plurality voting satisfies the monotonicity because if a candidate wins on the basis of having the most first-place votes, then moving that candidate up one spot on some list (and making no other changes) neither decreases the number of first-place votes for the winning candidate nor increases the number of first-place votes for any other candidate. Hence, the original winner remains a winner in plurality voting.

18. (a) Borda count satisfies the Pareto condition because if everyone prefers *B* to *D*, for example, then *B* receives more points from each list than *D*. Thus, *B* receives a higher total than *D* and so *D* is certainly not among the winners.

(b) Borda count satisfies the monotonicity because suppose *X*'s position with the candidate above *X* on some list adds one point to the score of *X*, subtracts one point from the score of the candidate that had been above *X* on that list, and leaves the score of all other candidates the same.

19. (a) Sequential pairwise voting satisfies the Condorcet winner criterion because a Condorcet winner always wins the kind of one-on-one contest that is used to produce the winner in sequential pairwise voting.

(b) Sequential pairwise voting satisfies the monotonicity because moving a candidate up on some list only improves that candidate's chances in one-on-one contests.

20. The Hare system satisfies the Pareto condition because if everyone prefers B to D, for example, then D is not on top of any list. Thus, either we have immediate winners and D is not among them, or the procedure moves on and D is eliminated at the very next stage. Hence, D is not among the winners.

21. In the plurality runoff method, in order to have one candidate's ranking be consistently higher than another candidate's would imply that only one candidate would be considered. This candidate would have received all first-place votes and is therefore the winner. Thus, none of the other candidates are being considered and cannot be the winner. Pareto condition is therefore satisfied.

22.

	Number of voters (5)		
Rank	**2**	**2**	**1**
First	A	B	C
Second	C	C	B
Third	B	A	A

Since A and B have the most number of first-place votes, C is eliminated.

	Number of voters (5)		
Rank	**2**	**2**	**1**
First	A	B	B
Second	B	A	A

A now has 2 first-place votes. B has $2 + 1 = 3$ first-place votes. Since B has the majority of the first-place votes, B is the winner by the plurality runoff method.

Now using Condorcet's method, we must check the one-on-one scores of A versus B, A versus C, and B versus C.

A versus B: A is over B on 2 ballots, while the reverse is true on $2 + 1 = 3$ ballots. Thus, B defeats A, 3 to 2.

A versus C: A is over C on 2 ballots, while the reverse is true on $2 + 1 = 3$ ballots. Thus, C defeats A, 3 to 2.

B versus C: B is over C on 2 ballots, while the reverse is true on $2 + 1 = 3$ ballots. Thus, C defeats B, 3 to 2.

Thus, the winner by Condorcet's method is C. Thus, using this example we see that the plurality runoff method does not satisfy the CWC since there is a winner by Condorcet's method (C) and it is not the same as the winner by the plurality runoff method (B).

23.

	Number of voters (13)				
Rank	4	3	3	2	1
First	A	B	C	D	E
Second	B	A	A	B	D
Third	C	C	B	C	C
Fourth	D	D	D	A	B
Fifth	E	E	E	E	A

Since *A* has the highest number of first-place votes and *B* and *C* have the same number of second-place votes, *D* and *E* are eliminated.

	Number of voters (13)				
Rank	4	3	3	2	1
First	A	B	C	B	C
Second	B	A	A	C	B
Third	C	C	B	A	A

A now has 4 first-place votes. *B* has 3 + 2 = 5 first-place votes. *C* has 3 + 1 = 4 first-place votes. Since *B* has the most first-place votes, *B* is the winner by the plurality runoff method.

Now if the single voter on the far right in our original preference lists moved *B* to the top, we would have the following.

	Number of voters (13)				
Rank	4	3	3	2	1
First	A	B	C	D	B
Second	B	A	A	B	E
Third	C	C	B	C	D
Fourth	D	D	D	A	C
Fifth	E	E	E	E	A

Since *A* and *B* have the same number of first-place votes, *C*, *D* and *E* are eliminated.

	Number of voters (13)				
Rank	4	3	3	2	1
First	A	B	A	B	B
Second	B	A	B	A	A

A now has 4 + 3 = 7 first-place votes. *B* now has 3 + 2 + 1 = 6 first-place votes. Since *A* has the majority of the first-place votes, *A* is the winner by the plurality runoff method. This does not satisfy monotonicity since a ballot change favorable to *B* resulted in *B* losing.

24. (a) In the first election, if plurality voting is used; A wins with two first-place votes.

Rank	Number of voters (4)			
	1	**1**	**1**	**1**
First	A	A	B	C
Second	B	B	C	B
Third	C	C	A	A

If the second is calculated the same way, then A and B tie with two first-place votes.

Rank	Number of voters (4)			
	1	**1**	**1**	**1**
First	A	A	B	B
Second	B	B	C	C
Third	C	C	A	A

Thus, B has gone from non-winner status to winner status even though no voter reversed the order in which he or she had ranked B and the winning candidate from the previous election (i.e. A).

(b) Using the Hare system in the first election, we eliminate both B and C since they lave the least number of first-place votes. A is thus the winner of the first election.

If the second is calculated the same way, C is eliminated since C has the least number of first-place votes.

Rank	Number of voters (4)			
	1	**1**	**1**	**1**
First	A	A	B	B
Second	B	B	A	A

A and B now tie with two first-place votes.

Thus, B has gone from non-winner status to winner status even though no voter reversed the order in which he or she had ranked B and the winning candidate from the previous election (i.e. A).

25. One possible scenario is having candidates A, B, and C with the following preference lists.

Rank	Number of voters (5)	
	3	**2**
First	A	B
Second	B	C
Third	C	A

Preference	1st place votes $\times$ 2	2nd place votes $\times$ 1	3rd place votes $\times$ 0	Borda score
A	3×2	0×1	2×0	6
B	2×2	3×1	0×0	7
C	0×2	2×1	3×0	2

Thus, B has the highest Borda score and is declared the winner.

Continued on next page

25. continued

Note, the Borda score for each candidate could also have been determined firstly by individually replacing the candidates below the one you are determining the score for by a box.

For *A*:

Rank	Number of voters (5)	
	3	**2**
First	*A*	*B*
Second	☐	*C*
Third	☐	*A*

To show that the Borda score for candidate *A* is 6, it needs to be noted that each box below *A* counts 3 times in the first column. The Borda score for *A* is $3 \times 2 = 6$.

For *B*:

Rank	Number of voters (5)	
	3	**2**
First	*A*	*B*
Second	*B*	☐
Third	☐	☐

To show that the Borda score for candidate *B* is 7, it needs to be noted that each box below *B* counts 3 times in the first column and 2 times in the second column. The Borda score for *B* is $(1 \times 3) + (2 \times 2) = 3 + 4 = 7$.

For *C*:

Rank	Number of voters (5)	
	3	**2**
First	*A*	*B*
Second	*B*	*C*
Third	*C*	☐

To show that the Borda score for candidate *C* is 2, it needs to be noted that each box below *C* counts 2 times in the second columns. The Borda score for *C* is $1 \times 2 = 2$.

Now using Condorcet's method, we must check the one-on-one scores of *A* versus *B*, *A* versus *C*, and *B* versus *C*.

A versus *B*:   *A* is over *B* on 3 ballots, while the reverse is true on 2 ballots. Thus, *A* defeats *B*, 3 to 2.

A versus *C*:   *A* is over *C* on 3 ballots, while the reverse is true on 2 ballots. Thus, *A* defeats *C*, 3 to 2.

B versus *C*:   *B* is over *C* on all 5 ballots. Thus, *B* defeats *C*, 5 to 0.

The winner by Condorcet's method is *A*.

In this case the Borda count produces *B* as the winner while *A* is the Condorcet winner. Thus, this example shows that the Borda count does not satisfy the Condorcet winner criterion.

26.

	Number of voters (17)			
Rank	**7**	**5**	**4**	**1**
First	A	C	B	D
Second	D	A	C	B
Third	B	B	D	A
Fourth	C	D	A	C

Since D has the least number of first-place votes, D is eliminated.

	Number of voters (17)			
Rank	**7**	**5**	**4**	**1**
First	A	C	B	B
Second	B	A	C	A
Third	C	B	A	C

A now has 7 first-place votes. B now has $4 + 1 = 5$ first-place votes. C now has 5 first-place votes. Since B and C have the least number of first-place votes, they are both eliminated. Thus, A is the winner by the Hare system.

Now suppose the voter on the far right moves A up. Our new preference list would be as follows.

	Number of voters (17)			
Rank	**7**	**5**	**4**	**1**
First	A	C	B	D
Second	D	A	C	A
Third	B	B	D	B
Fourth	C	D	A	C

Using the Hare system again, D is eliminated since D has the least number of first-place votes.

	Number of voters (17)			
Rank	**7**	**5**	**4**	**1**
First	A	C	B	A
Second	B	A	C	B
Third	C	B	A	C

A now has $7 + 1 = 8$ first-place votes. B now has 4 first-place votes. C now has 5 first-place votes. Since B has the least number of first-place votes, B is eliminated.

	Number of voters (17)			
Rank	**7**	**5**	**4**	**1**
First	A	C	C	A
Second	C	A	A	C

A now has $7 + 1 = 8$ first-place votes. C now has $5 + 4 = 9$ first-place votes. Thus, C is now the winner by the Hare system.

This demonstrates nonmonotonicity since there was a change that was favorable to candidate A, but A was not the winner in the second calculation.

27.

Rank	Number of voters (21)			
	7	6	5	3
First	A	B	C	D
Second	B	A	B	C
Third	C	C	A	B
Fourth	D	D	D	A

(a) Since D has the least number of first-place votes, D is eliminated.

Rank	Number of voters (21)			
	7	6	5	3
First	A	B	C	C
Second	B	A	B	B
Third	C	C	A	A

A now has 7 first-place votes. B now has 6 first-place votes. C now has $5 + 3 = 8$ first-place votes. Since B has the least number of first-place votes, B is eliminated.

Rank	Number of voters (21)			
	7	6	5	3
First	A	A	C	C
Second	C	C	A	A

A now has $7 + 6 = 13$ first-place votes. C now has $5 + 3 = 8$ first-place votes. Thus, A is the unique winner by the Hare system.

(b)

Rank	Number of voters (21)			
	7	6	5	3
First	A	B	C	A
Second	B	A	B	D
Third	C	C	A	C
Fourth	D	D	D	B

Since D has the least number of first-place votes, D is eliminated.

Rank	Number of voters (21)			
	7	6	5	3
First	A	B	C	A
Second	B	A	B	C
Third	C	C	A	B

A now has $7 + 3 = 10$ first-place votes. B now has 6 first-place votes. C now has 5 first-place votes. Since C has the least number of first-place votes, C is eliminated.

Rank	Number of voters (21)			
	7	6	5	3
First	A	B	B	A
Second	B	A	A	B

A now has $7 + 3 = 10$ first-place votes. B now has $6 + 5 = 11$ first-place votes. Thus, B is the winner by the Hare system.

28. (a) In sequential pairwise voting, if there is an odd number of voters then each one-on-one competition will yield a unique candidate that has preference over the other because a majority of voters will have a preference. Since each of these one-on-one competitions yields a unique winner, ultimately there will be a unique winner at the end of the sequential one-on-one competitions.

(b) In the Hare system, if the final comparison is between two candidates they cannot both have the same number of votes if the number of voters is odd. Thus, we cannot have exactly two winners.

29. If a candidate, say B, is ranked last on a majority of votes (over 50% of the votes are for last-place) then this candidate may or may not be considered in the runoff. Obviously, if this candidate is not considered in the runoff, then this candidate cannot be among the winners.

Now suppose this candidate is considered in the runoff. Since we assume there are no ties for second-place, then candidate B is having a runoff against another candidate, say candidate A. Since candidate B has the majority of the last-place votes, candidate A must have the majority of the first place votes and is hence the winner.

30.

Rank	Number of voters (7)		
	3	2	2
First	C	A	B
Second	A	B	A
Third	B	C	C

C has the majority of the last-place votes (over 50%), but is the winner by the plurality voting since C has the highest number of first-place votes.

31. Consider the following set of preference lists.

Rank	Number of voters (3)		
First	A	B	A
Second	B	C	C
Third	C	A	B

Checking the one-on-one scores of A versus B and A versus C, we see that candidate A is a Condorcet winner.

A versus B: A is over B on 2 of the ballots, while the reverse is true on 1. Thus, A defeats B, 2 to 1.

A versus C: A is over C on 2 of the ballots, while the reverse is true on 1. Thus, A defeats C, 2 to 1.

Since candidate A is the Condorcet winner, it must be the unique winner under our hypothetical voting rule. Therefore, A is a winner and B is a nonwinner for these preference lists.

Because our hypothetical voting rule satisfies IIA, we know that candidate B will remain a non-winner as long as no voter reverses his or her ordering of B and A. But to arrive at the preference lists from the voting paradox, we can move C (the candidate that is irrelevant to A and B) up one slot on the third voter's list.

Rank	Number of voters (3)		
First	A	B	C
Second	B	C	A
Third	C	A	B

Thus, because of IIA, we know that candidate B is a nonwinner when our voting rule is confronted by the preference lists from the voting paradox of Condorcet.

Continued on next page

31. continued

Now consider the following set of preference lists.

Rank	Number of voters (3)		
First	B	B	C
Second	A	C	A
Third	C	A	B

Checking the one-on-one scores of *B* versus *A* and *B* versus *C*, we see that candidate *B* is a Condorcet winner.

B versus *A*:   *B* is over *A* on 2 of the ballots, while the reverse is true on 1. Thus, *B* defeats *A*, 2 to 1.

B versus *C*:   *B* is over *C* on 2 of the ballots, while the reverse is true on 1. Thus, *B* defeats *C*, 2 to 1.

Since candidate *B* is the Condorcet winner, it must be the unique winner under our hypothetical voting rule. Therefore, *B* is a winner and *C* is a nonwinner for these preference lists.

Because our hypothetical voting rule satisfies IIA, we know that alternative *C* will remain a nonwinner as long as no voter reverses his or her ordering of *C* and *B*. But to arrive at the preference lists from the voting paradox, we can move *A* (the candidate that is irrelevant to *B* and *C*) up one slot on the first voter's list.

Rank	Number of voters (3)		
First	A	B	C
Second	B	C	A
Third	C	A	B

Thus, because of IIA, we know that candidate *C* is a nonwinner when our voting rule is confronted by the preference lists from the voting paradox of Condorcet.

32.

Candidates	Voters									
	1	2	3	4	5	6	7	8	9	10
A		X	X	X			X	X	X		X
B			X	X	X	X	X	X	X	X	
C			X						X		
D		X	X	X	X	X		X	X	X	X
E		X		X		X		X		X	
F		X		X	X	X	X	X	X		X
G		X	X	X	X	X		X			
H			X		X		X		X		X

A has 7 approval votes, *B* has 8, *C* has 2, *D* has 9, *E* has 5, *F* has 8, *G* has 6, and *H* has 5. Ranking the candidates we have, *D* (9), *B* and *F* (8), *A* (7), *G* (6), *E* and *H* (5), and *C* (2).

(a)   Since *D* has the most votes, *D* is chosen for the board.

(b)   The top four are *A*, *B*, *D*, and *F*.

(c)   Candidates *B*, *D* and *F* have at least 80% (8 out of 10) approval.

(d)   Candidates *A*, *B*, *D*, *F* and *G* have at least 60% (6 out of 10) approval. But since at most four candidates can be elected, only *A*, *B*, *D*, and *F* are considered.

33.

Nominee	Number of voters (45)							
	7	8	9	9	6	3	1	2
A	X			X	X		X	
B		X		X		X	X	
C			X		X	X	X	

A has $7+9+6+1=23$ approval votes. B has $8+9+3+1=21$ approval votes.

C has $9+6+3+1=19$ approval votes.

(a) Since A has the most approval votes, A is selected for the award.

(b) Since B has the second highest number of approval votes, B is announced as the runner-up.

(c) Suppose A had a approval votes, B had b, and C had c, where $a \geq b \geq c$. If an additional voter abstains, then clearly there is no change in the arrangement since $a+0=a$, $b+0=b$, and $c+0=c$. If an additional voter approves all nominees, then A would have $a+1$ votes, B would have $b+1$ votes, and C would have $c+1$ votes. Since we assumed $a \geq b \geq c$, clearly $a+1 \geq b+1 \geq c+1$. Thus, there would be no difference in the arrangement of the nominees.

Word Search Solution

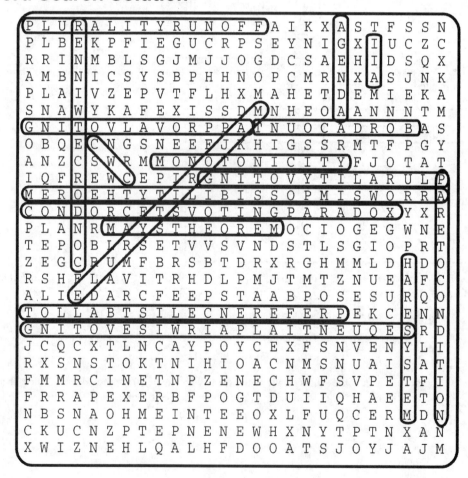

Chapter 10
The Manipulability of Voting Systems

Chapter Outline

Introduction
Section 10.1   Majority Rule and Condorcet's Method
Section 10.2   Other Voting Systems for Three of More Candidates
Section 10.3   Impossibility
Section 10.4   The Chair's Paradox

Chapter Summary

Manipulation of a voting system allows a voter or a group of voters to change the outcome of an election based on the knowledge of the other voters' preference list ballots. The different voting systems examined in Chapter 9 will again be considered in light of whether they can be manipulated or not. A voting system is said to be *manipulable* by a *unilateral* change if there exist two sequences of preference list ballots and a voter such that neither election results in a tie, the only ballot change is by voter casting the *disingenuous ballot,* and that voter prefers the outcome of the second election compared to the first.

Majority rule and Condorcet's Method will be shown to be non-manipulable given certain conditions, which includes an odd number of voters. Borda count will be manipulable under certain conditions and non-manipulable given others. The same will be shown for plurality voting in which group manipulation is the condition for manipulation. The runoff systems discussed in Chapter 9 are revisited. Both plurality runoff and the Hare system turn out to be manipulable. Finally, sequential pairwise voting will be examined in two ways. This voting system can be manipulated by a unilateral change and a fixed agenda. This voting system can also be manipulated not by altering a preference list ballot, but by altering the agenda.

May's theorem for manipulability establishes that given the initial conditions (odd number of voters and only two candidates) majority rule is the only voting method that satisfies three important properties. This theorem recognizes that majority rule is non-manipulable. Another important theorem discussed in this chapter is the *Gibbard-Satterthwaite Theorem* which says that with three or more candidates and any number of voters, there does not exist (and never will exist) a voting system that always has a winner, no ties, satisfies the Pareto condition, is non-manipulable, and is not a dictatorship.

Finally, this chapter will examine the *chair's paradox.* The interesting outcome involved in the chair's paradox is that although the chair has tie-breaking power, he or she would be in a better strategic advantage by handing this power off to another voter.

Skill Objectives

1. Explain what is meant by voting manipulation.

2. Determine if a voter, by a unilateral change, has manipulated the outcome of an election.

3. Determine a unilateral change by a voter that causes manipulation of an election with different in the Borda count voting method.

4. Explain the three conditions to determine if a voting system is manipulable.

5. Discuss why the majority method may not be appropriate for an election in which there are more than two candidates.

6. Explain four desirable properties of Condorcet's method.

7. Explain why Condorcet's method is non-manipulable by a unilateral change in vote.

8. Recognize when the Borda count method can be manipulated and when it can't.

9. Determine a unilateral change by a voter that causes a no-winner manipulation of an election in Condorcet's method.

10. Determine a unilateral change by a voter that causes manipulation of an election in the plurality runoff method.

11. Determine a unilateral change by a voter that causes manipulation of an election in the Borda count voting method.

12. Determine a unilateral change by a voter that causes manipulation of an election in the Hare method.

13. Determine a group change by a block of voters that causes manipulation of an election in the plurality method.

14. Determine an agenda change by a voter that causes manipulation of an election in the sequential pairwise voting method, with agenda.

15. Explain the Gibbard-Satterthwaite theorem (GS theorem) and its weak version.

16. Explain the chair's paradox and what is meant by *weakly dominates* as it relates to a voting strategy.

Teaching Tips

1. In trying to determine what unilateral change will cause a manipulation to an election, you may choose to point out to students that they must always first determine the outcome using the original preference list ballots. Given voters that will cast the disingenuous ballot and their true preferences, focus on the candidates above the winner of Election 1. If any of these can become the winner of Election 2, then voters have manipulated the outcome by choosing a more-preferred candidate. It is possible that candidate may not be their first choice.

2. Students may need a quick review of the voting method used in the discussion of each (non) manipulation. By briefly describing the method, you may find it easier to discuss whether the system is manipulable or not. Also, state the conditions such as whether or not only an odd number of voters is considered.

3. You should find the Excel spreadsheets for 3 and 4 candidates a tremendous help in either determining how to manipulate the outcome of an election or by showing that a particular voter cannot get a more-preferred outcome. They are particularly helpful in demonstrating manipulation in the Borda count voting system, sequential pairwise voting, as well as sequential pairwise voting, with agenda. Suppose you want to make a handout that has four candidates and five voters. To get a template for this, you can copy part of the spreadsheet and paste it into a word processor such as Word.

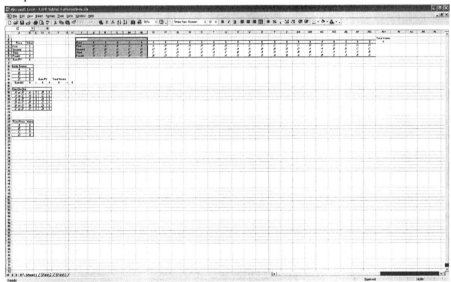

Rank	0	0	0	0	0
First	A	A	A	A	A
Second	B	B	C	C	D
Third	C	D	B	D	B
Fourth	D	C	D	B	C

You can then make you choices of preference list ballots in the spreadsheet. If you are using the Borda Count, the results are calculated given the place values you choose. The default is 0, 1, 2, and 3 for the four-candidate spreadsheet. You can copy and the paste the results in the document.

Continued on next page

3.   continued

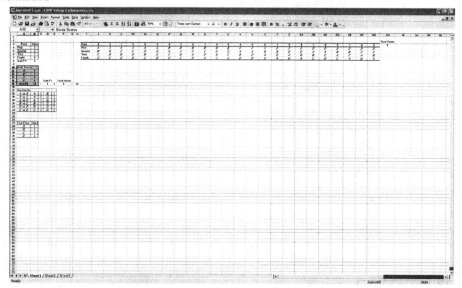

Borda Scores	
A	5
B	9
C	8
D	8
Sum BS	30

Similarly if you are using sequential pairwise voting and wish to manipulate the agenda, the one-on-one scores are very helpful.

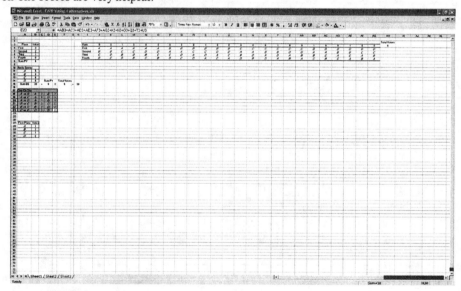

Continued on next page

3.   continued

One-On-One				
A vs B	A:	2	B:	3
A vs C	A:	2	C:	3
A vs D	A:	1	D:	4
B vs C	B:	3	C:	2
B vs D	B:	3	D:	2
C vs D	C:	3	D:	2

To complete the desired preference list ballots, you can individually copy and paste them into your template.

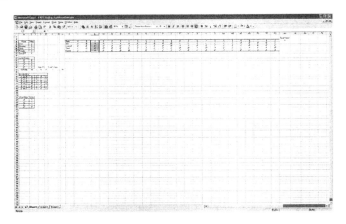

Rank	1	1	1	1	1
First	A	B	C	D	D
Second	C	C	B	A	B
Third	B	D	D	B	C
Fourth	D	A	A	C	A

4.   In discussing a system that is manipulable, don't be surprised if students question whether it really is manipulable by giving what they feel is a counter-example. In discussing manipulable systems, you may wish to make the point more than once that a system is manipulable if there is at least one scenario in which manipulation occurs. Because of the possibility of ties with an even number of voters, students may come to the conclusion that a system is not manipulable because they may not be able to manipulate certain examples.

5.   Students may view voting manipulation as kind of a "do over" so to speak. You may wish to convey to students that Election 2 is the election that prevails due to the casting of the disingenuous ballot.

Research Paper

Have students investigate the life and contributions of Ramon Llull (1235–1316), the Spanish mathematician and missionary. Llull proposed in the 13th century a voting system based on the principle of fairness. Other figures such as Nicholas of Cusa (1401–1464) had access to some works by Llull. However, a full description of Llull's voting system was not published until 2001! Some of Cusa's work centered on how to elect German kings while Llull's work had an impact 500 years later on the work of Condorcet.

Collaborative Learning

Rock Paper Scissors

Variations of the game Rock Paper Scissors (RPS) have been around for a very long time. Even as early as 50,000 B.C. hand games had been used to resolve issues such as mating and food issues. The first variation of Rock Paper Scissors was known as Janken. The earliest possible date for the actual name of Rock Paper Scissors would be around 500 A.D., when scissors were invented by a hair cutter (Isidore of Seville). This game has made headlines recently when two action houses (Sotheby's and Christie's) played RPS to settle who would receive the rights to sell four multimillion-dollar paintings.

Although there are different variations of RPS, in the case of three options, the principle is the same. The system is known as *non-transitive*. If a relation is transitive then if A is preferred to B and B is preferred to C, then it is necessary that A is preferred to C. In the case of a non-transitive relation then a loop of preference occurs. For example:

- A is preferred to B

- B is preferred to C

- C is preferred to A

A set-up like this is reminiscent of the Condorcet's voting paradox of Chapter 9 where three or more candidates in an election yield no winner using Condorcet's method.

Rank	Number of voters (3)		
	1	1	1
First	A	B	C
Second	B	C	A
Third	C	A	B

In the game, we have the following rules with the hand symbols.

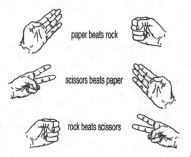

paper beats rock

scissors beats paper

rock beats scissors

Now this game is generally played with two players only. But let's assume be have three players and they rank their choices

Game 1

Round	Number of players (3)		
	YOU	Player X	Player Y
First	Rock	Rock	Paper
Second	Paper	Scissors	Scissors
Third	Scissors	Paper	Rock

In the first round, Player Y beats You and Player X. Player Y is declared the winner. Suppose you knew how Player X and Player Y were going to make their preferences. You could alter your choices.

Continued on next page

Game 2

	Number of players (3)		
Round	YOU	Player X	Player Y
First	*Paper*	*Rock*	*Paper*
Second	*Rock*	*Scissors*	*Scissors*
Third	*Scissors*	*Paper*	*Rock*

In the first round, You and Player Y beat Player X. You and Player Y go to the second round. Since rock beats scissors, you are declared the winner.

You were able to manipulate the outcome of the game by knowing the choices that would be made by Players X and Y.

In the following tables, determine what the outcome of the contest would be if your actual preference list is as follows.

YOU
Rock
Paper
Scissors

Then try to find a sequence of *Rock Paper Scissors* that would manipulate the outcome. If you were the winner, then no manipulation is necessary. Note that if *Rock Paper Scissors* all appear in the first round, then there is a three-way tie and all three players go forward to the second round. With three players in the second round, if there is a three-way tie, then the game would be tied.

	Number of players (3)		
Round	YOU	Player X	Player Y
First		*Rock*	*Paper*
Second		*Scissors*	*Rock*
Third		*Paper*	*Scissors*

	Number of players (3)		
Round	YOU	Player X	Player Y
First		*Rock*	*Rock*
Second		*Scissors*	*Scissors*
Third		*Paper*	*Paper*

	Number of players (3)		
Round	YOU	Player X	Player Y
First		*Rock*	*Rock*
Second		*Paper*	*Paper*
Third		*Scissors*	*Scissors*

	Number of players (3)		
Round	YOU	Player X	Player Y
First		*Paper*	*Scissors*
Second		*Scissors*	*Paper*
Third		*Rock*	*Rock*

Now, have two players (X and Y) actually play Rock Paper Scissors and record the results. In this case any of the three options can appear more than once.

Game 1

	Number of players (3)		
Round	Player Z	Player X	Player Y
First			
Second			
Third			

Game 2

	Number of players (3)		
Round	Player Z	Player X	Player Y
First			
Second			
Third			

Game 3

	Number of players (3)		
Round	Player Z	Player X	Player Y
First			
Second			
Third			

Game 4

	Number of players (3)		
Round	Player Z	Player X	Player Y
First			
Second			
Third			

Game 5

	Number of players (3)		
Round	Player Z	Player X	Player Y
First			
Second			
Third			

Game 6

	Number of players (3)		
Round	Player Z	Player X	Player Y
First			
Second			
Third			

Game 7

	Number of players (3)		
Round	Player Z	Player X	Player Y
First			
Second			
Third			

For each game involving Players X and Y, state who the winner is using the rule that 2 out of 3 or 3 out of 3 winning rounds win a game. It is possible to have a two-way tie of a game.

After completing all seven games, determine if the third player (Player Z) can manipulate the outcome if he or she must use all three choices of Rock, Paper, and Scissors. The manipulation would be done in the same way as it was shown at first, round by round.

Now consider a variation of the RPS where you add *Water* and *Dynamite*. Dynamite blows up rock and burns paper. Dynamite is put out by water and the fuse is cut by scissors. Water puts out dynamite and rusts scissors. Water is splashed by rock and absorbed by paper.

Have each player independently create their preference list ballot (no repeats) and put them in the table. Determine the outcome of the rounds.

Round	Number of players (3)		
	Player *A*	Player *B*	Player *C*
First			
Second			
Third			
Fourth			
Fifth			

Have each player see if they can manipulate the outcome by changing their preferences.

Now have all three players play games by using the symbol of pointing a finger for dynamite ☞

and a spread out hand for water ✋ .

For each round, discuss how a player could alter the results by making a different choice. Do this five times.

Game 1

Number of players (3)		
Player *A*	Player *B*	Player *C*

Game 2

Number of players (3)		
Player *A*	Player *B*	Player *C*

Game 3

Number of players (3)		
Player *A*	Player *B*	Player *C*

Game 4

Number of players (3)		
Player *A*	Player *B*	Player *C*

Game 5

Number of players (3)		
Player *A*	Player *B*	Player *C*

Solutions

Skills Check:

1. c   2. c   3. c   4. c   5. a   6. c   7. c   8. b   9. a   10. b

11. c   12. a   13. c   14. c   15. a   16. a   17. d   18. b   19. a   20. b

1. One example of two such elections is the following:

Election 1

Rank	Number of voters (3)		
First	A	A	B
Second	B	B	A

Election 2

Rank	Number of voters (3)		
First	B	A	B
Second	A	B	A

With the voting system in which the candidate with the fewest first-place votes wins, B is the winner in the first election. However, if the leftmost voter changes his or her ballot as shown in the second election, then A becomes the winner. Taking the ballots in the first election to be the sincere preferences of the voters, the leftmost voter (who prefers A to B) has secured a more favorable outcome by the submission of a disingenuous ballot.

2. One example of two such elections is the following:

Election 1

Rank	Number of voters (3)		
First	A	A	B
Second	B	B	A

Election 2

Rank	Number of voters (3)		
First	B	A	B
Second	A	B	A

With the voting system in which the candidate receiving an odd number of first-place votes wins, B is the winner in the first election. However, if the leftmost voter changes his or her ballot as shown in the second election, then A becomes the winner. Taking the ballots in the first election to be the sincere preferences of the voters, the leftmost voter (who prefers A to B) has secured a more favorable outcome by the submission of a disingenuous ballot.

3. One example of two such elections is the following:

Election 1

Rank	Number of voters (3)		
First	A	B	B
Second	B	A	A

Election 2

Rank	Number of voters (3)		
First	B	B	B
Second	A	A	A

With the voting system in which the candidate receiving an even number of first-place votes wins, B is the winner in the first election. However, if the leftmost voter changes his or her ballot as shown in the second election, then A becomes the winner. Taking the ballots in the first election to be the sincere preferences of the voters, the leftmost voter (who prefers A to B) has secured a more favorable outcome by the submission of a disingenuous ballot.

4. (a) The voting system does not treat both *candidates* the same.
    (b) Candidate A wins regardless of the ballots.
    (c) Candidate B wins regardless of the ballots.

5. (a) The voting system does not treat all *voters* the same.

    (b) A dictatorship in which Voter #1 is the dictator.

    (c) A dictatorship in which Voter #2 is the dictator and a dictatorship in which voter #3 is the dictator.

6.

22%	23%	15%	29%	7%	4%
D	D	H	H	J	J
H	J	D	J	H	D
J	H	J	D	D	H

We must check the one-on-one scores of *D* versus *H*, *D* versus *J*, and *H* versus *J*.

D versus *H*: *D* is over *H* on 22% + 23% + 4% = 49% of the ballots, while the reverse is true on 15% + 29% + 7% = 51%. Thus, *H* defeats *D*, 51% to 49%.

D versus *J*: *D* is over *J* on 22% + 23% + 15% = 60% of the ballots, while the reverse is true on 29% + 7% + 4% = 40%. Thus, *D* defeats *J*, 60% to 40%.

H versus *J*: *H* is over *J* on 22% + 15% + 29% = 66% of the ballots, while the reverse is true on 23% + 7% + 4% = 34%. Thus, *H* defeats *J*, 66% to 34%.

Since *H* can defeat both *D* and *J* in a one-to one competition, Elizabeth Holtzman (*H*) is the winner by Condorcet's method.

7.   Election 1

	Number of voters (2)	
Rank	**1**	**1**
First	B	A
Second	C	D
Third	A	C
Fourth	D	B

Preference	1st place votes × 3	2nd place votes × 2	3rd place votes × 1	4th place votes × 0	Borda score
A	1×3	0×2	1×1	0×0	4
B	1×3	0×2	0×1	1×0	3
C	0×3	1×2	1×1	0×0	3
D	0×3	1×2	0×1	1×0	2

With the given ballots, the winner using the Borda count is *A*. However, if the leftmost voter changes his or her preference ballot, we have the following.

Election 2

	Number of voters (2)	
Rank	**1**	**1**
First	C	A
Second	B	D
Third	D	C
Fourth	A	B

Preference	1st place votes × 3	2nd place votes × 2	3rd place votes × 1	4th place votes × 0	Borda score
A	1×3	0×2	0×1	1×0	3
B	0×3	1×2	0×1	1×0	2
C	1×3	0×2	1×1	0×0	4
D	0×3	1×2	1×1	0×0	3

With the new ballots, the winner using the Borda count is *C*.

8. One way to get an example of manipulation of the Borda count with seven candidates and eight voters is to alter the elections in Example 2 of the text by adding *F* and *G* to the bottom of each of the six ballots in both elections, and then adding the two rightmost columns as shown. The last two voters contribute exactly 6 to the Borda score of each candidate, and so, taken together have no effect on who is the winner of the election.

Election 1

	Number of voters (8)							
Rank	**1**	**1**	**1**	**1**	**1**	**1**	**1**	**1**
First	A	B	A	E	A	E	A	G
Second	B	C	B	D	B	D	B	F
Third	C	A	C	C	C	C	C	E
Fourth	D	D	D	B	D	B	D	D
Fifth	E	E	E	A	E	A	E	C
Sixth	F	F	F	F	F	F	F	B
Seventh	G	G	G	G	G	G	G	A

Preference	1st place votes × 6	2nd place votes × 5	3rd place votes × 4	4th place votes × 3	5th place votes × 2	6th place votes × 1	7th place votes × 0	Borda score
A	4×6	0×5	1×4	0×3	2×2	0×1	1×0	32
B	1×6	4×5	0×4	2×3	0×2	1×1	0×0	33
C	0×6	1×5	6×4	0×3	1×2	0×1	0×0	31
D	0×6	2×5	0×4	6×3	0×2	0×1	0×0	28
E	2×6	0×5	1×4	0×3	5×2	0×1	0×0	26
F	0×6	1×5	0×4	0×3	0×2	7×1	0×0	12
G	1×6	0×5	0×4	0×3	0×2	0×1	7×0	6

Thus, *B* has the highest Borda score and is declared the winner. This was the expected result.

The voter on the far left prefers *A* to *B*. By casting a disingenuous ballot (still preferring *A* to *B* though), the outcome of the election is altered.

Election 2

	Number of voters (8)							
Rank	**1**	**1**	**1**	**1**	**1**	**1**	**1**	**1**
First	A	B	A	E	A	E	A	G
Second	D	C	B	D	B	D	B	F
Third	C	A	C	C	C	C	C	E
Fourth	B	D	D	B	D	B	D	D
Fifth	E	E	E	A	E	A	E	C
Sixth	F	F	F	F	F	F	F	B
Seventh	G	G	G	G	G	G	G	A

Preference	1st place votes × 6	2nd place votes × 5	3rd place votes × 4	4th place votes × 3	5th place votes × 2	6th place votes × 1	7th place votes × 0	Borda score
A	4×6	0×5	1×4	0×3	2×2	0×1	1×0	32
B	1×6	3×5	0×4	3×3	0×2	1×1	0×0	31
C	0×6	1×5	6×4	0×3	1×2	0×1	0×0	31
D	0×6	3×5	0×4	5×3	0×2	0×1	0×0	30
E	2×6	0×5	1×4	0×3	5×2	0×1	0×0	26
F	0×6	1×5	0×4	0×3	0×2	7×1	0×0	12
G	1×6	0×5	0×4	0×3	0×2	0×1	7×0	6

Thus, *A* has the highest Borda score and is declared the winner.

Continued on next page

8. continued

One could also add two ballots canceling each other out first, and then add F and G to the bottom of all eight ballots in each election. By doing this, the last two voters contribute exactly 6 to the Borda score of each of the top five candidates, and so taken together have no effect on who is the winner of the election. Because F and G hold the sixth and seventh places, respectively, on all ballots, they have no effect on the candidates above them.

Election 1

Rank	Number of voters (8)							
	1	1	1	1	1	1	1	1
First	A	B	A	E	A	E	A	E
Second	B	C	B	D	B	D	B	D
Third	C	A	C	C	C	C	C	C
Fourth	D	D	D	B	D	B	D	B
Fifth	E	E	E	A	E	A	E	A
Sixth	F	F	F	F	F	F	F	F
Seventh	G	G	G	G	G	G	G	G

Preference	1st place votes × 6	2nd place votes × 5	3rd place votes × 4	4th place votes × 3	5th place votes × 2	6th place votes × 1	7th place votes × 0	Borda score
A	4×6	0×5	1×4	0×3	3×2	0×1	0×0	34
B	1×6	4×5	0×4	3×3	0×2	0×1	0×0	35
C	0×6	1×5	7×4	0×3	0×2	0×1	0×0	33
D	0×6	3×5	0×4	5×3	0×2	0×1	0×0	30
E	3×6	0×5	0×4	0×3	5×2	0×1	0×0	28
F	0×6	0×5	0×4	0×3	0×2	8×1	0×0	8
G	0×6	0×5	0×4	0×3	0×2	0×1	8×0	0

Thus, B has the highest Borda score and is declared the winner. This was the expected result.

The voter on the far left prefers A to B. By casting a disingenuous ballot (still preferring A to B though), the outcome of the election is altered.

Election 2

Rank	Number of voters (8)							
	1	1	1	1	1	1	1	1
First	A	B	A	E	A	E	A	E
Second	D	C	B	D	B	D	B	D
Third	C	A	C	C	C	C	C	C
Fourth	B	D	D	B	D	B	D	B
Fifth	E	E	E	A	E	A	E	A
Sixth	F	F	F	F	F	F	F	F
Seventh	G	G	G	G	G	G	G	G

Preference	1st place votes × 6	2nd place votes × 5	3rd place votes × 4	4th place votes × 3	5th place votes × 2	6th place votes × 1	7th place votes × 0	Borda score
A	4×6	0×5	1×4	0×3	3×2	0×1	0×0	34
B	1×6	3×5	0×4	4×3	0×2	0×1	0×0	33
C	0×6	1×5	7×4	0×3	0×2	0×1	0×0	33
D	0×6	4×5	0×4	4×3	0×2	0×1	0×0	32
E	3×6	0×5	0×4	0×3	5×2	0×1	0×0	28
F	0×6	0×5	0×4	0×3	0×2	8×1	0×0	8
G	0×6	0×5	0×4	0×3	0×2	0×1	8×0	0

Thus, A has the highest Borda score and is declared the winner.

9. Election 1

	Number of voters (3)		
Rank	**1**	**1**	**1**
First	A	B	B
Second	B	A	A
Third	C	C	C
Fourth	D	D	D

With the given ballots, the winner using the Borda count is B.

Preference	1st place votes × 3	2nd place votes × 2	3rd place votes × 1	4th place votes × 0	Borda score
A	1×3	2×2	0×1	0×0	7
B	2×3	1×2	0×1	0×0	8
C	0×3	0×2	3×1	0×0	3
D	0×3	0×2	0×1	3×0	0

The voter on the far left prefers A to B. By casting a disingenuous ballot (still preferring A to B though), the outcome of the election is altered.

Election 2

	Number of voters (3)		
Rank	**1**	**1**	**1**
First	A	B	B
Second	C	A	A
Third	D	C	C
Fourth	B	D	D

Preference	1st place votes × 3	2nd place votes × 2	3rd place votes × 1	4th place votes × 0	Borda score
A	1×3	2×2	0×1	0×0	7
B	2×3	0×2	0×1	1×0	6
C	0×3	1×2	2×1	0×0	4
D	0×3	0×2	1×1	2×0	1

Thus, A has the highest Borda score and is declared the winner.

10. The last two voters contribute exactly 3 to the Borda score of each candidate, and so taken together have no effect on who is the winner of the election. The desired ballots (obtained as suggested in the statement of the exercise) are as follows.

Election 1

	Number of voters (5)				
Rank	**1**	**1**	**1**	**1**	**1**
First	A	B	B	A	D
Second	B	A	A	B	C
Third	C	C	C	C	B
Fourth	D	D	D	D	A

Preference	1st place votes × 3	2nd place votes × 2	3rd place votes × 1	4th place votes × 0	Borda score
A	2×3	2×2	0×1	1×0	10
B	2×3	2×2	1×1	0×0	11
C	0×3	1×2	4×1	0×0	6
D	1×3	0×2	0×1	4×0	3

Thus, B has the highest Borda score and is declared the winner. This was the expected result.

Continued on next page

10. continued

The voter on the far left prefers A to B. By casting a disingenuous ballot (still preferring A to B though), the outcome of the election is altered.

Election 2

Rank	Number of voters (5)				
	1	1	1	1	1
First	A	B	B	A	D
Second	D	A	A	B	C
Third	C	C	C	C	B
Fourth	B	D	D	D	A

Preference	1st place votes × 3	2nd place votes × 2	3rd place votes × 1	4th place votes × 0	Borda score
A	2×3	2×2	0×1	1×0	10
B	2×3	1×2	1×1	1×0	9
C	0×3	1×2	4×1	0×0	6
D	1×3	1×2	0×1	3×0	5

Thus, A has the highest Borda score and is declared the winner.

11. The following is one such example:

Election 1

Rank	Number of voters (9)								
	1	1	1	1	1	1	1	1	1
First	A	B	B	A	D	A	F	A	F
Second	B	A	A	B	C	B	E	B	E
Third	C	C	C	C	B	C	D	C	D
Fourth	D	D	D	D	A	D	C	D	C
Fifth	E	E	E	E	E	E	B	E	B
Sixth	F	F	F	F	F	F	A	F	A

Preference	1st place votes × 5	2nd place votes × 4	3rd place votes × 3	4th place votes × 2	5th place votes × 1	6th place votes × 0	Borda score
A	4×5	2×4	0×3	1×2	0×1	2×0	30
B	2×5	4×4	1×3	0×2	2×1	0×0	31
C	0×5	1×4	6×3	2×2	0×1	0×0	26
D	1×5	0×4	2×3	6×2	0×1	0×0	23
E	0×5	2×4	0×3	0×2	7×1	0×0	15
F	2×5	0×4	0×3	0×2	0×1	7×0	10

Thus, B has the highest Borda score and is declared the winner. This was the expected result.

The voter on the far left prefers A to B. By casting a disingenuous ballot (still preferring A to B though), the outcome of the election is altered.

Election 2

Rank	Number of voters (9)								
	1	1	1	1	1	1	1	1	1
First	A	B	B	A	D	A	F	A	F
Second	D	A	A	B	C	B	E	B	E
Third	C	C	C	C	B	C	D	C	D
Fourth	B	D	D	D	A	D	C	D	C
Fifth	E	E	E	E	E	E	B	E	B
Sixth	F	F	F	F	F	F	A	F	A

Continued on next page

11. continued

Preference	1st place votes × 5	2nd place votes × 4	3rd place votes × 3	4th place votes × 2	5th place votes × 1	6th place votes × 0	Borda score
A	4×5	2×4	0×3	1×2	0×1	2×0	30
B	2×5	3×4	1×3	1×2	2×1	0×0	29
C	0×5	1×4	6×3	2×2	0×1	0×0	26
D	1×5	1×4	2×3	5×2	0×1	0×0	25
E	0×5	2×4	0×3	0×2	7×1	0×0	15
F	2×5	0×4	0×3	0×2	0×1	7×0	10

Thus, A has the highest Borda score and is declared the winner.

12. Election 1

	Number of voters (4)			
Rank	**1**	**1**	**1**	**1**
First	B	D	C	B
Second	C	C	A	A
Third	D	A	B	C
Fourth	A	B	D	D

Preference	1st place votes × 3	2nd place votes × 2	3rd place votes × 1	4th place votes × 0	Borda score
A	0×3	2×2	1×1	1×0	5
B	2×3	0×2	1×1	1×0	7
C	1×3	2×2	1×1	0×0	8
D	1×3	0×2	1×1	2×0	4

Thus, C has the highest Borda score and is declared the winner. But the winner becomes B if the leftmost voter changes his or her ballot as follows.

Election 2

	Number of voters (4)			
Rank	**1**	**1**	**1**	**1**
First	B	D	C	B
Second	D	C	A	A
Third	A	A	B	C
Fourth	C	B	D	D

Preference	1st place votes × 3	2nd place votes × 2	3rd place votes × 1	4th place votes × 0	Borda score
A	0×3	2×2	2×1	0×0	6
B	2×3	0×2	1×1	1×0	7
C	1×3	1×2	1×1	1×0	6
D	1×3	1×2	0×1	2×0	5

Thus, B has the highest Borda score and is declared the winner.

13. Election 1

	Number of voters (4)			
Rank	**1**	**1**	**1**	**1**
First	A	C	B	D
Second	B	A	D	C
Third	C	B	C	A
Fourth	D	D	A	B

Preference	1st place votes $\times$ 3	2nd place votes $\times$ 2	3rd place votes $\times$ 1	4th place votes $\times$ 0	Borda score
A	1×3	1×2	1×1	1×0	6
B	1×3	1×2	1×1	1×0	6
C	1×3	1×2	2×1	0×0	7
D	1×3	1×2	0×1	2×0	5

Thus, C has the highest Borda score and is declared the winner. But the winner becomes B if the leftmost voter changes his or her ballot as follows.

Election 2

	Number of voters (4)			
Rank	**1**	**1**	**1**	**1**
First	B	C	B	D
Second	A	A	D	C
Third	D	B	C	A
Fourth	C	D	A	B

Preference	1st place votes $\times$ 3	2nd place votes $\times$ 2	3rd place votes $\times$ 1	4th place votes $\times$ 0	Borda score
A	0×3	2×2	1×1	1×0	5
B	2×3	0×2	1×1	1×0	7
C	1×3	1×2	1×1	1×0	6
D	1×3	1×2	1×1	1×0	6

Thus, B has the highest Borda score and is declared the winner.

14. Election 1

	Number of voters (4)			
Rank	**1**	**1**	**1**	**1**
First	A	C	A	D
Second	B	E	E	B
Third	C	D	D	E
Fourth	D	B	C	C
Fifth	E	A	B	A

We need to determine the winner of 10 one-to-one preferences (ties are possible since we have an even number of voters).

There are 2 voters who prefer A to B and 2 prefer B to A. Thus, A and B tie by a score of 2 to 2. Award A and B each ½ point.

There are 2 voters who prefer A to C and 2 prefer C to A. Thus, A and C tie by a score of 2 to 2. Award A and C each ½ point.

There are 2 voters who prefer A to D and 2 prefer D to A. Thus, A and D tie by a score of 2 to 2. Award A and D each ½ point.

Continued on next page.

14. continued

There are 2 voters who prefer A to E and 2 prefer E to A. Thus, A and E tie by a score of 2 to 2. Award A and E each ½ point.

There are 2 voters who prefer B to C and 2 prefer C to B. Thus, B and C tie by a score of 2 to 2. Award B and C each ½ point.

There is 1 voter who prefers B to D and 3 prefer D to B. Thus, D wins by a score of 3 to 1. Award D 1 point.

There are 2 voters who prefer B to E and 2 prefer E to B. Thus, B and E tie by a score of 2 to 2. Award B and E each ½ point.

There are 2 voters who prefer C to D and 2 prefer D to C. Thus, C and D tie by a score of 2 to 2. Award D and C each ½ point.

There are 2 voters who prefer C to E and 2 prefer E to C. Thus, C and E tie by a score of 2 to 2. Award C and E each ½ point.

There are 2 voters who prefer D to E and 2 prefer E to D. Thus, D and E tie by a score of 2 to 2. Award E and D each ½ point.

	A	B	C	D	E
	$\frac{1}{2}$	$\frac{1}{2}$	$\frac{1}{2}$	$\frac{1}{2}$	$\frac{1}{2}$
	$\frac{1}{2}$	$\frac{1}{2}$	$\frac{1}{2}$	1	$\frac{1}{2}$
	$\frac{1}{2}$	0	$\frac{1}{2}$	$\frac{1}{2}$	$\frac{1}{2}$
	$\frac{1}{2}$	$\frac{1}{2}$	$\frac{1}{2}$	$\frac{1}{2}$	$\frac{1}{2}$
Total	2	$1\frac{1}{2}$	2	$2\frac{1}{2}$	2

With the given ballots, the winner using Copeland's rule is D. But the winner becomes C if the leftmost voter changes his or her ballot as the following shows.

Election 2

	Number of voters (4)			
Rank	**1**	**1**	**1**	**1**
First	C	C	A	D
Second	A	E	E	B
Third	B	D	D	E
Fourth	D	B	C	C
Fifth	E	A	B	A

There are 2 voters who prefer A to B and 2 prefer B to A. Thus, A and B tie by a score of 2 to 2. Award A and B each ½ point.

There is 1 voter who prefers A to C and 3 prefer C to A. Thus, C wins by a score of 3 to 1. Award C 1 point.

There are 2 voters who prefer A to D and 2 prefer D to A. Thus, A and D tie by a score of 2 to 2. Award A and D each ½ point.

There are 2 voters who prefer A to E and 2 prefer E to A. Thus, A and E tie by a score of 2 to 2. Award A and E each ½ point.

There is 1 voter who prefers B to C and 3 prefer C to B. Thus, C wins by a score of 3 to 1. Award C 1 point.

There is 1 voter who prefers B to D and 3 prefer D to B. Thus, D wins by a score of 3 to 1. Award D 1 point.

Continued on next page.

14. continued

There are 2 voters who prefer B to E and 2 prefer E to B. Thus, B and E tie by a score of 2 to 2. Award B and E each ½ point.

There are 2 voters who prefer C to D and 2 prefer D to C. Thus, C and D tie by a score of 2 to 2. Award D and C each ½ point.

There are 2 voters who prefer C to E and 2 prefer E to C. Thus, C and E tie by a score of 2 to 2. Award C and E each ½ point.

There are 2 voters who prefer D to E and 2 prefer E to D. Thus, D and E tie by a score of 2 to 2. Award E and D each ½ point.

	A	B	C	D	E
	$\frac{1}{2}$	$\frac{1}{2}$	1	$\frac{1}{2}$	$\frac{1}{2}$
	0	0	1	1	$\frac{1}{2}$
	$\frac{1}{2}$	0	$\frac{1}{2}$	$\frac{1}{2}$	$\frac{1}{2}$
	$\frac{1}{2}$	$\frac{1}{2}$	$\frac{1}{2}$	$\frac{1}{2}$	$\frac{1}{2}$
Total	$1\frac{1}{2}$	1	3	$2\frac{1}{2}$	2

15. Election 1

	Number of voters (5)				
Rank	**1**	**1**	**1**	**1**	**1**
First	A	B	B	A	A
Second	B	C	C	C	C
Third	C	A	A	B	B

Since Candidates A and B both have the same (high) number of last-place votes, they are both eliminated, leaving Candidate C as the winner using Coombs rule. But the winner becomes A if the leftmost voter changes his or her ballot as the following shows.

Election 2

	Number of voters (5)				
Rank	**1**	**1**	**1**	**1**	**1**
First	A	B	B	A	A
Second	C	C	C	C	C
Third	B	A	A	B	B

B has the most last-place votes, thus Candidate B is eliminated, and we have the following.

	Number of voters (5)				
Rank	**1**	**1**	**1**	**1**	**1**
First	A	C	C	A	A
Second	C	A	A	C	C

C now has the most last-place votes, thus Candidate C is eliminated, and A becomes the winner by the Coombs method.

16. Election 1

Rank	Number of voters (5)				
	1	1	1	1	1
First	A	B	C	C	D
Second	B	A	B	B	B
Third	C	C	A	A	C
Fourth	D	D	D	D	A

A, B, and D have the fewest first-place votes and are thus eliminated leaving C as the winner using the Hare system. But the winner becomes B if the leftmost voter changes his or her ballot as the following shows.

Election 2

Rank	Number of voters (5)				
	1	1	1	1	1
First	B	B	C	C	D
Second	A	A	B	B	B
Third	C	C	A	A	C
Fourth	D	D	D	D	A

A has the fewest first-place votes and is eliminated.

Rank	Number of voters (5)				
	1	1	1	1	1
First	B	B	C	C	D
Second	C	C	B	B	B
Third	D	D	D	D	C

D now has the fewest first-place votes and is eliminated

Rank	Number of voters (5)				
	1	1	1	1	1
First	B	B	C	C	B
Second	C	C	B	B	C

C now has the fewest first-place votes and is eliminated, leaving B as the winner.

17. Election 1

Rank	Number of voters (5)				
	1	1	1	1	1
First	A	A	C	C	B
Second	B	B	A	A	C
Third	C	C	B	B	A

Since A and C have the most number of first-place votes, B is eliminated.

Rank	Number of voters (5)				
	1	1	1	1	1
First	A	A	C	C	C
Second	C	C	A	A	A

Since C has the most number of first-place votes, the winner using the plurality runoff rule is C. But the winner becomes B if the leftmost voter changes his or her ballot as the following shows.

Continued on next page

17. continued

Election 2

	Number of voters (5)				
Rank	1	1	1	1	1
First	B	A	C	C	B
Second	A	B	A	A	C
Third	C	C	B	B	A

Since B and C have the most number of first-place votes, A is eliminated.

	Number of voters (5)				
Rank	1	1	1	1	1
First	B	B	C	C	B
Second	C	C	B	B	C

Since B has the most number of first-place votes, the winner using the plurality runoff rule is B.

18. Election 1

	Number of voters (3)		
Rank	1	1	1
First	A	B	C
Second	B	C	A
Third	C	A	B

In sequential pairwise voting with the agenda A, B, C, we first pit A against B. There are 2 voters who prefer A to B and 1 prefers B to A. Thus, A wins by a score of 2 to 1. B is therefore eliminated, and A moves on to confront C.

There is 1 voter who prefers A to C and 2 prefer C to A. Thus, C wins by a score of 2 to 1.

Thus, C is the winner by sequential pairwise voting with the agenda A, B, C. But the winner becomes B if the leftmost voter changes his or her ballot as the following shows.

Election 2

	Number of voters (3)		
Rank	1	1	1
First	B	B	C
Second	A	C	A
Third	C	A	B

In sequential pairwise voting with the agenda A, B, C, we first pit A against B. There is 1 voter who prefers A to B and 2 prefer B to A. Thus, B wins by a score of 2 to 1. A is therefore eliminated, and B moves on to confront C.

There are 2 voters who prefer B to C and 1 prefers C to B. Thus, B wins by a score of 2 to 1.

Thus, B is the winner by sequential pairwise voting with the agenda A, B, C.

19.

	Number of voters (3)		
Rank	**1**	**1**	**1**
First	A	C	B
Second	B	A	D
Third	D	B	C
Fourth	C	D	A

(a) For B to win, consider the agenda D, A, C, B.

In sequential pairwise voting with the agenda D, A, C, B, we first pit D against A. There is 1 voter that prefers D to A and 2 prefer A to D. Thus, A wins by a score of 2 to 1. D is therefore eliminated, and A moves on to confront C.

There is 1 voter who prefers A to C and 2 prefer C to A. Thus, C wins by a score of 2 to 1. A is therefore eliminated, and C moves on to confront B.

There is 1 voter who prefers C to B and 2 prefer B to C. Thus, B wins by a score of 2 to 1.

Thus, B is the winner by sequential pairwise voting with the agenda D, A, C, B.

(b) For C to win, consider the agenda B, D, A, C.

In sequential pairwise voting with the agenda B, D, A, C, we first pit B against D. There are 3 voters that prefer B to D and 0 prefer D to B. Thus, B wins by a score of 3 to 0. D is therefore eliminated, and B moves on to confront A.

There is 1 voter who prefers B to A and 2 prefer A to B. Thus, A wins by a score of 2 to 1. B is therefore eliminated, and A moves on to confront C.

There is 1 voter who prefers A to C and 2 prefer C to A. Thus, C wins by a score of 2 to 1.

Thus, C is the winner by sequential pairwise voting with the agenda B, D, A, C.

(c) For D to win, consider the agenda B, A, C, D.

In sequential pairwise voting with the agenda B, A, C, D, we first pit B against A. There is 1 voter that prefers B to A and 2 prefer A to B. Thus, A wins by a score of 2 to 1. B is therefore eliminated, and A moves on to confront C.

There is 1 voter who prefers A to C and 2 prefer C to A. Thus, C wins by a score of 2 to 1. A is therefore eliminated, and C moves on to confront D.

There is 1 voter who prefers C to D and 2 prefer D to C. Thus, D wins by a score of 2 to 1.

Thus, D is the winner by sequential pairwise voting with the agenda B, A, C, D.

Note: In any of the three parts, the first two candidates can be switched and the outcome will be the same.

20. If the system fails to satisfy the Pareto condition, then we can choose a sequence of ballots in which every voter prefers A to B, but B is the winner. But now if every voter changes his or her ballot by moving A to the top, then this group has achieved an election outcome - namely A, by unanimity -- that everyone in the group prefers.

21. Election 1

22%	23%	15%	29%	7%	4%
D	D	H	H	J	J
H	J	D	J	H	D
J	H	J	D	D	H

D has 22% + 23% = 45% of the first-place votes. H has 15% + 29% = 44% of the first-place votes. J has 7% + 4% = 11% of the first-place votes. Since D has the most first-place votes, Alfonse D'Amato (D) is the winner by plurality voting. The plurality rule is group manipulable as the following shows if the voters in the 7% group all change their ballots.

Election 2

22%	23%	15%	29%	7%	4%
D	D	H	H	H	J
H	J	D	J	J	D
J	H	J	D	D	H

D has 22% + 23% = 45% of the first-place votes. H has 15% + 29% + 7%= 51% of the first-place votes. J has 4% of the first-place votes. Since H has the most first-place votes, Elizabeth Holtzman (H) is the winner by plurality voting.

22. (a) Assume that the winner with the voting paradox ballots is A. Consider the following two elections:

Election 1

Rank	Number of voters (3)		
First	A	B	C
Second	B	C	A
Third	C	A	B

Election 2

Rank	Number of voters (3)		
First	A	C	C
Second	B	B	A
Third	C	A	B

In Election 1, the winner is A (our assumption in this case) and in Election 2, the winner is C (because we are assuming that our voting system agrees with Condorcet's method when there is a Condorcet winner, as C is here). Notice that the voter in the middle, by a unilateral change in ballot, has improved the election outcome from his or her third choice to being his or her second choice. This is what that voter set out to do and is the desired instance of manipulation.

(b) Assume that the winner with the voting paradox ballots is B. Consider the following two elections:

Election 1

Rank	Number of voters (3)		
First	A	B	C
Second	B	C	A
Third	C	A	B

Election 2

Rank	Number of voters (3)		
First	A	B	A
Second	B	C	C
Third	C	A	B

In Election 1, the winner is B (our assumption in this case) and in Election 2, the winner is A (because we are assuming that our voting system agrees with Condorcet's method when there is a Condorcet winner, as A is here). Notice that the voter on the right, by a unilateral change in ballot, has improved the election outcome from his or her third choice to being his or her second choice. This is what that voter set out to do and is the desired instance of manipulation.

23. Properties 1, 2, and 3.

24. Properties 1 and 4.

25. Properties 1, 2, and 4.

26. Consider the following scenario: The chair votes for *A* and I vote for *C*. If you vote for *B*, the winner is *A* (your least preferred outcome) while the winner is *C* if you vote for *C*. This shows that voting for *B* does not weakly dominate your strategy of voting for *C*.

27. Consider the following scenario: The chair votes for *A* and I vote for *B*. If you vote for *C*, the winner is *A* (your least preferred outcome) while the winner is *B* if you vote for *B*. This shows that voting for *C* does not weakly dominate your strategy of voting for *B*.

Word Search Solution

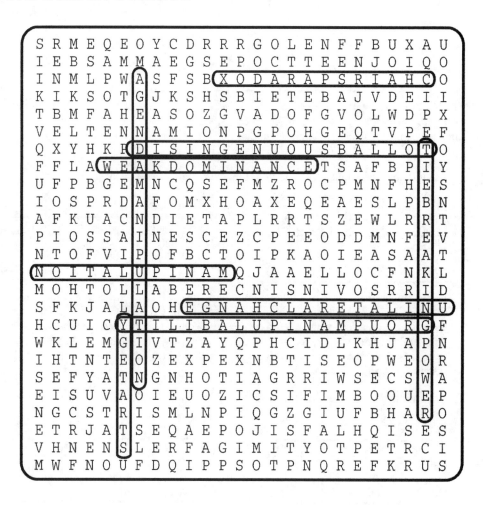

Chapter 11
Weighted Voting Systems

Chapter Outline

Introduction
Section 11.1   The Shapley-Shubik Power Index
Section 11.2   The Banzhaf Power Index
Section 11.3   Comparing Voting Systems

Chapter Summary

Weighted voting systems are decision-making procedures in which the participants (voters) have varying numbers of votes. Examples of such systems are shareholder elections in which each shareholder of a company votes with a number of votes equal to the number of shares of stock he or she owns. In analyzing such systems, we need some measure of the power of each participant. We will interpret power as the ability to influence decisions. Two common measures of power, the *Banzhaf power index* and the *Shapley-Shubik power index*, are introduced in this chapter.

To begin an analysis of a weighted voting system, we need three pieces of information.

- how many voters there are
- how many votes each voter has
- how many votes it takes to approve an issue (the system quota)

The usual notation for systems provides a list of numbers, the first being the quota and the rest being the number of votes held by the individual voters. An obvious requirement is that the quota be greater than one-half the total number of votes in the system.

A system may have a *dictator*, an individual voter having at least as many votes as the quota. By any measure of power, such a voter has all the power in the system, rendering all other voters powerless. Voters with no power to influence decisions are called *dummy* voters. The existence of a dictator or a dummy is a serious defect in a system.

Voters often group together in an attempt to amass enough votes to meet or exceed the quota. Such groups of voters are called *coalitions*, which can contain any number of voters in the system (from all to none). A coalition is *winning* if its vote total is at least as large as the quota, and it is *blocking* if it has enough votes to defeat a measure by opposing it. (Blocking coalitions are not necessarily winning ones.) Finally, a winning coalition is *minimal* if a defection by any one of its members turns it into a losing coalition. A voter is called *critical* if his or her defection from a coalition causes it to change from winning to losing, or from blocking to nonblocking. Finding the critical voters is simplified by determining extra votes. A voter in a coalition is critical if his weight exceeds the difference between the total weight of the coalition and the quota. In a *minimal winning coalition*, every member of the coalition is critical. A voter's Banzhaf index is equal to the total number of winning and blocking coalitions for which that voter is critical.

A voter's Banzhaf index is equal to the total number of winning coalitions and blocking coalitions for which that voter is a swinger. The same relative power structure can be obtained by taking the index to be the number of losing coalitions that a voter can change to winning coalitions. In the latter case, the index of each voter will be exactly half that obtained in the former.

The Shapley-Shubik index is computed somewhat differently. Coalitions are built one voter at a time from permutations of the voter set. For a given permutation, the voter whose votes change the coalition from losing to winning is called the pivot for that coalition. The Shapley-Shubik index for a voter is the fraction obtained by dividing the number of permutations for which the voter is a pivot by the total number of permutations.

Each index has its uses but there are situations too complicated to be modeled by either scheme. In any event, the indices give us some insight into weighted voting systems. In particular, they show us that the relative numbers of votes held by the voters is not a reliable indicator of their actual power in the system.

Finally, one can compare voting systems by determining if they are *equivalent*. Two voting systems are equivalent is there is a way to exchange all voters from the first system with voters of the second while maintaining the same winning coalitions. A *minimal winning coalition* is one in which each voter is critical to the passage of a measure. Examining minimal winning coalitions allows one to completely describe a voting system.

Skill Objectives

1. Interpret the symbolic notation for a weighted voting system by identifying the quota, number of voters, and the number of votes each voter controls.

2. Identify if a dictator exists in a given weighted voting system.

3. Identify if a dummy exists in a given weighted voting system.

4. Identify if a single voter has veto power in a given weighted voting system.

5. Calculate the number of permutations of voters in a given weighted voting system.

6. List the possible permutations for a three- or four-voter weighted voting system.

7. Given a permutation of voters, identify the pivotal voter.

8. Calculate the Shapley-Shubik index for a three- or four-voter weighted voting system.

9. Identify winning coalitions by analyzing a given weighted voting system.

10. Identify blocking coalitions by analyzing a given weighted voting system.

11. When given a specific winning or blocking coalition from a weighted voting system, determine the critical voters.

12. Determine the extra votes for a winning coalition.

13. Calculate the Banzhaf power index for a given weighted voting system.

14. Determine a specific value of C_k^n by using the combination formula as well as Pascal's triangle.

15. Determine if two voting systems are equivalent and when given a voting system, find an equivalent system.

16. Explain the difference between a winning coalition and a minimal winning coalition.

Teaching Tips

1. When indicating winning and losing voter coalitions, students have a tendency to list the voter's number of votes, rather than the voter's name or other identifying factor. The text lists voters by name (letter) which may help alleviate this problem. Nonetheless, it may be helpful to set up a correspondence at the beginning of a problem between the voter's identification factor and his or her number of votes.

2. Because a yes/no vote constitutes a binomial structure, listing all possible voting combinations (coalitions) for a weighted voting system is structurally similar to constructing a tree diagram or creating a table of values for the experiment of tossing a given number of coins. Students may find it interesting to see the same structure used in different applications.

3. In determining the Banzhaf power index, it helps to consider pairs of complementary coalitions. The index of a voter is the number of complementary pairs in which that voter's vote is critical.

4. Most people think of a coalition as meaning two or more, yet a single voter (a one-member subset) and even no voter (the null set) are both considered coalitions. It may be helpful to mention that to students.

5. After completing the time-consuming and tedious task of listing all combinations for how voters can vote yes or no on a given issue and then analyzing each voter in each situation to determine whether or not he is critical, students often tally the number of times a player is critical. They then report this number in the voter's position in the Banzhaf power index. In so doing, they forget that they have counted both the number of times that the voter changed a winning coalition to a losing one and a losing coalition to a winning one. Thus, the value of the number is double what it should be.

6. Point out that in computing the Banzhaf index, there are cases in which a winning coalition has a single critical voter, other cases with several critical voters, and still others with none at all. On the other hand, each permutation in the computation of the Shapley-Shubik index has *exactly* one pivot.

Research Paper

Have students investigate the U.S Electoral College (Spotlight 11.1) in which the number of votes allotted each state is based upon its population. Students can give a summary of how the process works today, how the Florida vote had an impact on the 2000 Presidental election, and when and why this system was originally proposed. Students may also investigate other systems that were proposed and what made them undesirable. There are many interesting occurrences in the electing of a U.S. President. Other points of interest are:

- In 1800 the Democratic-Republican Electors gave Thomas Jefferson and Aaron Burr an equal number of electoral votes. The House of Representatives settled in Jefferson's favor. The 12th Amendment came about to effectively prevent this from happening again.

- In 1824, with four viable candidates in the Democratic-Republican Party, the provisions of the 12th Amendment allowed the choice of president to be determined by the House of Representatives who selected John Quincy Adams even though Andrew Jackson had more electoral votes.

If you wish to assign a research paper with older historical references, you may choose to ask students to investigate the constitution of the Roman Republic. After 509 B.C., a series of documents were gradually created that together constitute the Roman constitution of today. The Struggles of the Orders was a struggle between the patrician and plebeian classes. Although plebeians gained the right to vote, the patricians could form a block against other groups due to ordering of the votes. Also, as changes occurred, certain groups gained absolute veto power.

Spreadsheet Project

To do this project, go to http://www.whfreeman.com/fapp7e.

This activity examines weighted voting systems with a variety of voters and weights.

Collaborative Learning

Power among Partners

Part I

Discuss the following problem in groups. The first two or three companies should be readily found. The fourth one, however, will lead to a better understanding of the need for a formal definition of power.

Consider the following partnerships, in which each of the partners holds a certain amount of stock. In each case, how is power distributed among the partners? (Here, power means the ability to influence decisions.)

Company 1:	Partner	Stock	Power
	A	51%	
	B	49%	

Company 2:	Partner	Stock	Power
	A	49%	
	B	49%	
	C	2%	

Company 3:	Partner	Stock	Power
	A	35%	
	B	30%	
	C	25%	
	D	10%	

Company 4:	Partner	Stock	Power
	A	40%	
	B	20%	
	C	20%	
	D	20%	

Part II

Analyze the following situation in groups.

A committee consists of a chairman and 3 ordinary members. Each member, including the chairman, has one vote, but in case of a tie the chairman has the power to break the tie.

    a.   Calling the chairman A, and the ordinary members B, C, and D, list all of the winning coalitions.

    b.   Convert this situation into one involving weighted voting.

HINT: Assign 1 vote each to B, C, and D. Then find a value of the quota and a weight for A that will produce the winning coalitions you found in part a.

Solutions

Skills Check:

1. b   2. c   3. c   4. b   5. b   6. b   7. a   8. a   9. b   10. b

11. c   12. a   13. b   14. c   15. c   16. a   17. a   18. c   19. c   20. b

Cooperative Learning:

Part I: Company 1: $A - 100\%$, $B - 0\%$

Company 2: A, B, and C share power equally.

These two examples show that power is *not* proportional to the amount of stock owned.

Company 3: A, B, and C share power equally while D is a dummy.

Company 4: A, B, C, and D are all equal, but the amount of power depends upon a appropriate definition of power. Hence, this example is an excellent introduction to the need for such a definition.

Part II: a. Winning coalitions are $\{A,B\}$, $\{A,C\}$, $\{A,D\}$, $\{A,B,C\}$, $\{A,B,D\}$, $\{A,C,D\}$, $\{B,C,D\}$, and $\{A,B,C,D\}$.

b. $\{3: 2, 1, 1, 1\}$

Exercises:

1. (a) A winning or blocking coalition would be 50 senators plus the vice president, or more than 50 senators.

   (b) The vice president will not be able to break a tie. A winning or blocking coalition requires 50 or more senators.

   (c) A winning coalition require at least 67 senators. A coalition of 34 or more senators can block.

2. No. Suppose the sum of the voting weights of all of voters is n, and the quota is q. Then a coalition with more than $n-q$ votes is needed to block a measure. Because $q > \frac{1}{2}n$, $n - q < \frac{1}{2}n$, and hence $q > n - q$. It follows that a coalition with q votes can block a measure.

3. (a) No. A dictator needs 9 votes.

   (b) The weight-5 and weight-4 voters have veto power, because the coalition of all the voters has only 3 extra votes, less than they have.

   (c) The weight-3 voter is a dummy, because the only winning coalition he or she he belongs to is the coalition with all the voters, and it has 3 extra votes.

4. (a) The weight-30 voter. If any voter with less weight had veto power, he or she would, too.

   (b) The sum of all the weights is 100. We know that the coalition of all the voters except the weight-30 voter is a losing coalition, so the quota is more than 70. However, the voter with weight 29 does not have veto power, so the coalition that consists of all voters except him or her is winning. That coalition has a total weight of 71. It follows that the quota is 71.

   (c) No. To form a winning coalition, it takes the weight-30 voter and two others – it doesn't matter which two. The three voters whose weights are less than 30 have equal voting power.

5. No. If a voter X is pivotal in a permutation, then that voter is a critical voter in the winning coalition consisting of X and every voter that precedes X in the permutation. A dummy voter is not a critical voter in any winning coalition.

6. The last juror in the permutation is the pivotal voter.

7. Let's call the voters A, B, C, and D. This weighted voting system can be written as $[q : w_A, w_B, w_C, w_D] = [51 : 30, 25, 24, 21]$. No voter has veto power; this means that the last voter in a permutation can never be the pivot. No voter is a dictator; thus the first voter in a permutation isn't a pivot either.

    (a) The weight-30 voter (Voter A) is pivotal in all permutations where he or she occupies position 2 because her weight, combined with any other voter's, is enough to win. A is also the pivot in all permutations where he or she occupies position 3, because the two voters ahead of him or her would have a combined weight of at most 49, less than the quota. There are 12 permutations to list:

Permutations
$B\,A\,C\,D$
$B\,A\,D\,C$
$B\,C\,A\,D$
$B\,D\,A\,C$
$C\,A\,B\,D$
$C\,A\,D\,B$
$C\,B\,A\,D$
$C\,D\,A\,B$
$D\,A\,B\,C$
$D\,A\,C\,B$
$D\,B\,A\,C$
$D\,C\,A\,B$

    (b) Voters other than A will be pivotal if and only if they are second in the permutation and A is first, or they are third in the permutation and A last. Thus, B is pivotal in the following four permutations:

Permutations
$A\,B\,C\,D$
$A\,B\,D\,C$
$C\,D\,B\,A$
$D\,C\,B\,A$

    (c) A is pivotal in 12 permutations, and B, C, and D are each pivotal in 4. There are $4! = 24$ permutations in all. The Shapley-Shubik power index of this weighted voting system is therefore $\left(\dfrac{12}{24}, \dfrac{4}{24}, \dfrac{4}{24}, \dfrac{4}{24} \right) = \left(\dfrac{1}{2}, \dfrac{1}{6}, \dfrac{1}{6}, \dfrac{1}{6} \right)$.

8. Let's call the voters A, B, C, D, and E. This weighted voting system can be written as $[q : w_A, w_B, w_C, w_D, w_E, w_F] = [7 : 3, 2, 2, 2, 2, 2]$.

    (a) Voter A is pivotal if he or she is in position 3, where he or she brings the weight to 7. Voter A is also pivotal if he or she is in position 4, where he or she brings the weight from 6 to 9.

    (b) There are 5 weight-2 voters, and the weight-3 voter (Voter A) doesn't care about their order. There are $2 \times 5! = 2 \times 120 = 240$ permutations in which the weight-3 voter is pivotal.

    (c) There are a total of $6! = 720$ permutations. There are $720 - 240 = 480$ permutations in which one of the 5 weight-2 voters is pivotal. That would imply each weight-2 voter is pivotal $480 \div 5 = 96$ times. Thus, the Shapley-Shubik index of the system is as follows.

    $$\left(\frac{240}{720}, \frac{96}{720}, \frac{96}{720}, \frac{96}{720}, \frac{96}{720}, \frac{96}{720} \right) = \left(\frac{1}{3}, \frac{2}{15}, \frac{2}{15}, \frac{2}{15}, \frac{2}{15}, \frac{2}{15} \right)$$

9. None of these voting systems have dictators, nor does anyone have veto power. Therefore the pivotal position in each permutation is in position 2 or 3. Let's call the voters A, B, C, and D. This weighted voting system can be written as $[q : w_A, w_B, w_C, w_D] = [q : 30, 25, 24, 21]$.

(a) $[q : w_A, w_B, w_C, w_D] = [52 : 30, 25, 24, 21]$

A is pivot in four permutations where he or she is in position 2, and in all six permutations where she is in position 3: that's 10 in all.

Permutations
$B\ A\ C\ D$
$B\ A\ D\ C$
$C\ A\ B\ D$
$C\ A\ D\ B$

Permutations
$B\ C\ A\ D$
$B\ D\ A\ C$
$C\ B\ A\ D$
$C\ D\ A\ B$
$D\ B\ A\ C$
$D\ C\ A\ B$

B is pivot in two positions where he or she is in position 2 and four permutations where he or she is in position 3. Thus, Voter B is a pivot in 6 permutations.

Permutations
$A\ B\ C\ D$
$A\ B\ D\ C$

Permutations
$A\ D\ B\ C$
$D\ A\ B\ C$
$C\ D\ B\ A$
$D\ C\ B\ A$

C has the same power as B, and D is a pivot in the remaining two permutations.

Permutations
$B\ C\ D\ A$
$C\ B\ D\ A$

The Shapley-Shubik power index of this weighted voting system is therefore the following.

$$\left(\tfrac{10}{24}, \tfrac{6}{24}, \tfrac{6}{24}, \tfrac{2}{24}\right) = \left(\tfrac{5}{12}, \tfrac{1}{4}, \tfrac{1}{4}, \tfrac{1}{12}\right)$$

(b) $[q : w_A, w_B, w_C, w_D] = [55 : 30, 25, 24, 21]$

Now A is pivotal in only two permutations where he or she is in position 2. Voter A is still pivotal in all permutations when in position 3. Thus, Voter A is a pivot in 8 permutations.

Permutations
$B\ A\ C\ D$
$B\ A\ D\ C$

Permutations
$B\ C\ A\ D$
$B\ D\ A\ C$
$C\ B\ A\ D$
$C\ D\ A\ B$
$D\ B\ A\ C$
$D\ C\ A\ B$

B now has the same voting power as A. C and D are also equally powerful. Each is pivot in four permutations in which he or she is in third position and not preceded by A and B. Thus, the Shapley-Shubik power index of this weighted voting system is the following.

$$\left(\tfrac{8}{24}, \tfrac{8}{24}, \tfrac{4}{24}, \tfrac{4}{24}\right) = \left(\tfrac{1}{3}, \tfrac{1}{3}, \tfrac{1}{6}, \tfrac{1}{6}\right)$$

(c) $[q : w_A, w_B, w_C, w_D] = [58 : 30, 25, 24, 21]$

Any three voters have enough votes to win, and no two can win. The voters have equal power and the Shapley-Shubik power index of this weighted voting system is therefore $\left(\tfrac{1}{4}, \tfrac{1}{4}, \tfrac{1}{4}, \tfrac{1}{4}\right)$.

10. Bush's margin in Nevada would be $\dfrac{414,939-1000}{393,372+1000}=1.0496$. This would move Nevada past Ohio in the permutations. Now Ohio's votes bring the total to 269 for Bush-Cheney, less than the quota. Nevada's 5 votes raises the total to 274, more than the quota. Therefore Nevada would be the pivot.

11. (a) We can represent a "yes" with 1, and a "no" with 0. Then the voting combinations are the 16 four-bit binary numbers: 0000, 0001, 0010, 0011, 0100, 0101, 0110, 0111, 1000, 1001, 1010, 1011, 1100, 1101, 1110, 1111.

   (b) $\{\ \}$, $\{D\}$, $\{C\}$, $\{C,D\}$, $\{B\}$, $\{B,D\}$, $\{B,C\}$, $\{B,C,D\}$, $\{A\}$, $\{A,D\}$, $\{A,C\}$, $\{A,C,D\}$, $\{A,B\}$, $\{A,B,D\}$, $\{A,B,C\}$, and $\{A,B,C,D\}$.

   (c) If the first bit of a given permutation is 1, then A votes "yes". If the second bit is 1, B votes "yes" in the corresponding coalition. The third bit tells us how C votes, and the fourth indicates the vote of D.

   (d) i.　1
       ii.　4
       iii.　6

12. Let's call the voters A, B, C, and D. This weighted voting system can be written as $[q:w_A,w_B,w_C,w_D]=[51:30,\ 25,\ 24,\ 21]$.

   The winning coalitions are those whose weights sum to 51 or more.

Winning coalition	Weight	Extra votes	Critical votes A	B	C	D
$\{A, B, C, D\}$	100	49	0	0	0	0
$\{A, B, C\}$	79	28	1	0	0	0
$\{A, B, D\}$	76	25	1	0	0	0
$\{A, C, D\}$	75	24	1	0	0	0
$\{B, C, D\}$	70	19	0	1	1	1
$\{A, B\}$	55	4	1	1	0	0
$\{A, C\}$	54	3	1	0	1	0
$\{A, D\}$	51	0	1	0	0	1
			6	2	2	2

   (a) Any voter that has a weight that exceeds the number of extra votes will be critical to that coalition. The critical voters in a coalition are indicated by a 1 in the table above.

   (b) A has a critical vote in 6 coalitions; B, C, and D each have critical votes in 2. Doubling to account for blocking coalitions, the Banzhaf power index is $(12,4,4,4)$.

   (c) If the combined weight of all voters is n voters, then a blocking coalition must have a weight at least $n-q+1$. For this weighted voting system, a blocking coalition must have a weight of at least $(30+25+24+21)-51+1=100-51+1=50$.

Blocking coalition	Weight	Dual winning coalition
$\{A, C, D\}$	75	$\{A, B\}$
$\{A, D\}$	51	$\{A, B, C\}$
$\{A, C\}$	54	$\{A, B, D\}$
$\{A, B, D\}$	76	$\{A, C\}$
$\{A, B\}$	55	$\{A, C, D\}$
$\{A, B, C\}$	79	$\{A, D\}$

13. Let's call the voters A, B, C, and D. This weighted voting system can be written as $[q : w_A, w_B, w_C, w_D] = [q : 30, 25, 24, 21]$.

(a) $[q : w_A, w_B, w_C, w_D] = [52 : 30, 25, 24, 21]$

We'll copy the table of coalitions we made for Exercise 12, reducing the extra votes of each by 1. The coalition $\{A, D\}$ becomes a losing coalition because its weight is only 51. It will be marked losing, and dropped when we increase the quota again.

Winning coalition	Weight	Extra votes	Critical votes			
			A	B	C	D
$\{A, B, C, D\}$	100	48	0	0	0	0
$\{A, B, C\}$	79	27	1	0	0	0
$\{A, B, D\}$	76	24	1	1	0	0
$\{A, C, D\}$	75	23	1	0	1	0
$\{B, C, D\}$	70	18	0	1	1	1
$\{A, B\}$	55	3	1	1	0	0
$\{A, C\}$	54	2	1	0	1	0
$\{A, D\}$	51	losing				
			5	3	3	1

Doubling to account for blocking coalitions, the Banzhaf power index is $(10, 6, 6, 2)$.

(b) $[q : w_A, w_B, w_C, w_D] = [55 : 30, 25, 24, 21]$

We copy the table from part (a), dropping the losing coalition and reducing quotas by 3. One more coalition will lose.

Winning coalition	Weight	Extra votes	Critical votes			
			A	B	C	D
$\{A, B, C, D\}$	100	45	0	0	0	0
$\{A, B, C\}$	79	24	1	1	0	0
$\{A, B, D\}$	76	21	1	1	0	0
$\{A, C, D\}$	75	20	1	0	1	1
$\{B, C, D\}$	70	15	0	1	1	1
$\{A, B\}$	55	0	1	1	0	0
$\{A, C\}$	54	losing				
			4	4	2	2

Doubling to account for blocking coalitions, the Banzhaf power index is $(8, 8, 4, 4)$.

(c) $[q : w_A, w_B, w_C, w_D] = [58 : 30, 25, 24, 21]$

We copy the table from part (b), dropping the losing coalition and reducing quotas by 3. One more coalition will lose.

Winning coalition	Weight	Extra votes	Critical votes			
			A	B	C	D
$\{A, B, C, D\}$	100	42	0	0	0	0
$\{A, B, C\}$	79	21	1	1	1	0
$\{A, B, D\}$	76	18	1	1	0	1
$\{A, C, D\}$	75	17	1	0	1	1
$\{B, C, D\}$	70	12	0	1	1	1
$\{A, B\}$	55	losing				
			3	3	3	3

Doubling to account for blocking coalitions, the Banzhaf power index is $(6, 6, 6, 6)$.

Continued on next page

13. continued

(d) $[q : w_A, w_B, w_C, w_D] = [73 : 30, 25, 24, 21]$

We copy the table from part (c), dropping the losing coalition and reducing quotas by 15. One more coalition will lose. A acquires veto power.

Winning coalition	Weight	Extra votes	Critical votes A	B	C	D
$\{A, B, C, D\}$	100	27	1	0	0	0
$\{A, B, C\}$	79	6	1	1	1	0
$\{A, B, D\}$	76	3	1	1	0	1
$\{A, C, D\}$	75	2	1	0	1	1
$\{B, C, D\}$	70	losing				
			4	2	2	2

Doubling to account for blocking coalitions, the Banzhaf power index is $(8, 4, 4, 4)$.

(e) $[q : w_A, w_B, w_C, w_D] = [76 : 30, 25, 24, 21]$

We copy the table from part (d), dropping the losing coalition and reducing quotas by 3. One more coalition will lose.

Winning coalition	Weight	Extra votes	Critical votes A	B	C	D
$\{A, B, C, D\}$	100	24	1	1	0	0
$\{A, B, C\}$	79	3	1	1	1	0
$\{A, B, D\}$	76	0	1	1	0	1
$\{A, C, D\}$	75	losing				
			3	3	1	1

Doubling to account for blocking coalitions, the Banzhaf power index is $(6, 6, 2, 2)$.

(f) $[q : w_A, w_B, w_C, w_D] = [79 : 30, 25, 24, 21]$

We copy the table from part (e), dropping the losing coalition and reducing quotas by 3. One more coalition will lose. In this system, D is a dummy.

Winning coalition	Weight	Extra votes	Critical votes A	B	C	D
$\{A, B, C, D\}$	100	21	1	1	1	0
$\{A, B, C\}$	79	0	1	1	1	0
$\{A, B, D\}$	76	losing				
			2	2	2	0

Doubling to account for blocking coalitions, the Banzhaf power index is $(4, 4, 4, 0)$.

(g) $[q : w_A, w_B, w_C, w_D] = [82 : 30, 25, 24, 21]$

Only one winning coalition is left, with 18 extra votes. This is less than the weight of each participant. All voters are critical. In this system, a unanimous vote is required to pass a motion.

Winning coalition	Weight	Extra votes	Critical votes A	B	C	D
$\{A, B, C, D\}$	100	18	1	1	1	1
			1	1	1	1

Doubling to account for blocking coalitions, the Banzhaf power index is $(2, 2, 2, 2)$.

14. In each system, the voters will be denoted A, B, ...

(a) $[q : w_A, w_B] = [51 : 52, 48]$

The winning coalitions are $\{A\}$ with 1 extra vote and $\{A, B\}$ with 49 extra votes. A is a dictator, the Banzhaf power index is $(4, 0)$.

(b) $[q : w_A, w_B, w_C] = [3 : 2, 2, 1]$

The winning coalitions are $\{A, B, C\}$, with 2 extra votes, $\{A, B\}$ with 1 extra vote, and $\{A, C\}$ and $\{B, C\}$ both with 0 extra votes. No one is critical in the coalition $\{A, B, C, D\}$ but all voters are critical in the other three, so each voter casts 2 critical votes in winning coalitions, and another 2 critical votes in blocking coalitions. The Banzhaf power index is $(4, 4, 4)$.

(c) $[q : w_A, w_B, w_C] = [8 : 5, 4, 3]$

In this system, A has veto power. The winning coalitions are $\{A, B, C\}$ with 4 extra votes, $\{A, B\}$ with 1 extra vote, and $\{A, C\}$ with 0 extra votes. Thus A casts 3 critical votes in winning coalitions, while B and C cast only 1. The Banzhaf power index is $(6, 2, 2)$.

(d) $[q : w_A, w_B, w_C, w_D] = [51 : 45, 43, 8, 4]$

Let's notice that any two of A, B, C have at least 51 votes, but D cannot join any other voter to make the quota. Therefore, D is a dummy. The winning coalitions are $\{A, B\}$, $\{A, C\}$, $\{B, C\}$, $\{A, B, D\}$, $\{A, C, D\}$, and $\{B, C, D\}$ in which all except D are critical voters; and the following coalitions that contain no critical voters at all: $\{A, B, C\}$ and $\{A, B, C, D\}$. Thus, A, B, and C each have 4 critical votes in winning coalitions, which we double to obtain the Banzhaf power index: $(8, 8, 8, 0)$.

(e) $[q : w_A, w_B, w_C, w_D] = [51 : 45, 43, 6, 6]$

The winning coalitions, with extra vote counts, are as follows.

Winning		Extra	Critical votes			
coalition	Weight	votes	A	B	C	D
$\{A, B, C, D\}$	100	49	0	0	0	0
$\{A, B, C\}$	94	43	1	0	0	0
$\{A, B, D\}$	94	43	1	0	0	0
$\{A, B\}$	88	37	1	1	0	0
$\{A, C, D\}$	57	6	1	0	0	0
$\{B, C, D\}$	55	4	0	1	1	1
$\{A, C\}$	51	0	1	0	1	0
$\{A, D\}$	51	0	1	0	0	1
			6	2	2	2

A casts a critical vote in 6 winning coalitions, while B, C, and D each cast one in 2. Doubling to count the critical votes in blocking coalitions, we find that the Banzhaf power index is $(12, 4, 4, 4)$.

15. Generating powers of 2 is often helpful in such conversions.

n	0	1	2	3	4	5	6	7
2^n	1	2	4	8	16	32	64	128

n	8	9	10	11	12	13	14
2^n	256	512	1024	2048	4096	8192	16,384

(a) Since 2^9 represents the largest power of 2 that doesn't exceed 585, we start there.

$$585 - 512 = 585 - 2^9 = 73$$
$$73 - 64 = 73 - 2^6 = 9$$
$$9 - 8 = 9 - 2^3 = 1$$
$$1 - 1 = 1 - 2^0 = 0$$

Thus, the nonzero bits are b_9, b_6, b_3 and b_0. The binary expression is 1001001001.

(b) Since 2^{10} represents the largest power of 2 that doesn't exceed 1365, we start there.

$$1365 - 1024 = 1365 - 2^{10} = 341$$
$$341 - 256 = 341 - 2^8 = 85$$
$$85 - 64 = 85 - 2^6 = 21$$
$$21 - 16 = 16 - 2^4 = 5$$
$$5 - 4 = 5 - 2^2 = 1$$
$$1 - 1 = 1 - 2^0 = 0$$

Thus, the nonzero bits are $b_{10}, b_8, b_6, b_4, b_2,$ and b_0. The binary form is 10101010101.

(c) Since 2^{10} represents the largest power of 2 that doesn't exceed 2005, we start there.

$$2005 - 1024 = 2005 - 2^{10} = 981$$
$$981 - 512 = 981 - 2^9 = 469$$
$$469 - 256 = 469 - 2^8 = 213$$
$$213 - 128 = 213 - 2^7 = 85$$
$$85 - 64 = 85 - 2^6 = 21$$
$$21 - 16 = 16 - 2^4 = 5$$
$$5 - 4 = 5 - 2^2 = 1$$
$$1 - 1 = 1 - 2^0 = 0$$

Thus, the nonzero bits are $b_{10}, b_9, b_8, b_7, b_6, b_4, b_2,$ and b_0. The binary form is 11111010101.

16. (a) $C_3^7 = \dfrac{7!}{3!(7-3)!} = \dfrac{7!}{3!4!} = \dfrac{7 \times 6 \times 5}{3 \times 2 \times 1} = 7 \times 5 = 35.$

(b) We can't use the formula that applied in part (a) because we'd get $\frac{50!}{100!(-50)!}$ and factorials of negative numbers are not defined. But really, the definition is all we need. If there are 50 voters, how many coalitions are there with 100 "yes" votes? NONE. The answer is $C_{100}^{50} = 0.$

(c) $C_2^{15} = \dfrac{15!}{2!(15-2)!} = \dfrac{15!}{2!13!} = \dfrac{15 \times 14}{2 \times 1} = 15 \times 7 = 105.$

(d) By the duality formula, $C_{13}^{15} = C_2^{15} = 105.$ by the result of part (c).

17. (a) $C_3^6 = \dfrac{6!}{3!(6-3)!} = \dfrac{6!}{3!3!} = \dfrac{6 \times 5 \times 4}{3 \times 2 \times 1} = 5 \times 4 = 20.$

(b) $C_2^{100} = \dfrac{100!}{2!(100-2)!} = \dfrac{100!}{2!98!} = \dfrac{100 \times 99}{2 \times 1} = 50 \times 99 = 4950.$

(c) By the duality formula, $C_{98}^{100} = C_2^{100} = 4950.$ by the result of part (b).

(d) $C_5^9 = \dfrac{9!}{5!(9-5)!} = \dfrac{9!}{5!4!} = \dfrac{9 \times 8 \times 7 \times 6}{4 \times 3 \times 2 \times 1} = 9 \times 2 \times 7 = 126.$

18. (a) The higher quota gives the smaller communities voting power. They would argue that since they pay taxes, they deserve some influence in county affairs. The larger communities would (and did) argue that the higher quotas (supermajorities) prevent representatives of a majority of the county's voters from getting their way.

(b) In 1958, B, G, and L were dummies. In 1964, N, G and L were dummies. There were no dummies in later years.

(c) In 1958 and 1964, Hempstead would dictate; all of the other supervisors would be dummies. In 1970 and 1976, the Hempstead supervisors need at least one other voter. Thus, there would still be no dummies. In 1982, G would be a dummy.

(d) In 1958 and 1964, Hempstead would dictate; all of the other supervisors would be dummies.

The Hempstead supervisors (think as one voter with weight 18 or 62, depending on the year) are critical voters in $C_0^4 + C_1^4 + C_2^4 + C_3^4 + C_4^4$ coalitions. Performing this calculation (or using Pascal's triangle), we have the following.

$$C_0^4 + C_1^4 + C_2^4 + C_3^4 + C_4^4 = 1 + 4 + 6 + 4 + 1 = 16$$

Thus, the Hempstead supervisors are critical voter in 16 coalitions; doubling this, we find that their Banzhaf power index is 32.

Year	Banzhaf index
1958	$(32,0,0,0,0)$
1964	$(32,0,0,0,0)$

In 1970 and 1976, the Hempstead supervisors need at least one other voter. Thus, there would still be no dummies. The Hempstead supervisors (think as one voter with weight 62 or 70, depending on the year) are critical voters in $C_1^4 + C_2^4 + C_3^4 + C_4^4$ coalitions. Performing this calculation (or using Pascal's triangle), we have the following.

$$C_1^4 + C_2^4 + C_3^4 + C_4^4 = 4 + 6 + 4 + 1 = 15$$

Thus, the Hempstead supervisors are critical voter in 15 coalitions; doubling this, we find that their Banzhaf power index is 30. Each of the remaining voters are only critical once. Thus, each of the other voters have a Banzhaf power index of 2.

Year	Banzhaf index
1970	$(30,2,2,2,2)$
1976	$(30,2,2,2,2)$

Continued on next page

18. **(d)**   continued

In 1982, the Hempstead supervisors need at least 1 of the three voters (N, B, or L) to have a motion to pass. G would be a dummy.   Since G can be there or not, the Hempstead supervisors (think as one voter with weight 58) are critical voters in twice $C_1^3 + C_2^3 + C_3^3$ coalitions. Performing this calculation (or using Pascal's triangle), we have the following.

$$C_1^3 + C_2^3 + C_3^3 = 3 + 3 + 1 = 7$$

Thus, the Hempstead supervisors are critical voters in 14 coalitions; doubling this, we find that their Banzhaf power index is 28.   Since G can be there or not, N, B, and L are each critical in $2 \times 1 = 2$ coalitions. Thus, N, B, and L each have a Banzhaf power index of 4.

Year	Banzhaf index
1982	$(28, 4, 4, 0, 4)$

(e) $[q : w_H, w_N, w_B, w_G, w_L] = [72 : 58, 15, 22, 6, 7]$

The G and L supervisors are dummy voters. N and B have the same power.   The Hempstead supervisors need at least 1 of the two voters, N or B to have a motion to pass.   The Hempstead supervisors would be critical in $\left(C_1^2 + C_2^2\right)\left(C_0^2 + C_1^2 + C_2^2\right)$ coalitions.

$C_1^2 + C_2^2$ for either having one or both of B or G in a winning coalition

$C_0^2 + C_1^2 + C_2^2$ for either having none, one, or both of G and L in a winning coalition

Since $\left(C_1^2 + C_2^2\right)\left(C_0^2 + C_1^2 + C_2^2\right) = (2+1)(1+2+1) = (3)(4) = 12$ the Hempstead supervisors are critical voters in 12 coalitions; doubling this, we find that their Banzhaf power index is 24.

N and B are critical in winning coalitions that contain just one of them, the Hempstead supervisors, and either none, one or both of G and L.   This occurs in $C_0^2 + C_1^2 + C_2^2 = 1 + 2 + 1 = 4$ ways. Thus, N and B each have a Banzhaf power index of 8.

Thus, we have a Banzhaf power index of $(24, 8, 8, 0, 0)$.

(f)   Let's convert Table 11.6 into a table of percentages.

Supervisor from	Population	Percent of votes	Banzhaf power index	
Quota			65	72
Hempstead (Presiding)	56%	28%	29%	28%
Hempstead		26%	25%	24%
North Hempstead	16%	14%	17%	20%
Oyster Bay	23%	20%	21%	20%
Glen Cove	2%	6%	2%	2%
Long Beach	3%	6%	6%	7%

It is apparent that the percentages of power closely match the population.   That is the argument that was used to justify this voting system.   However, Hempstead has a majority of the population.   If every citizen of Hempstead were for a measure, and the rest of the county were opposed, the measure would not pass.   Although the Hempstead supervisors have a majority of the votes, they have less than the quota.

19. (a) $\{A, C, D\}$ and $\{A, B\}$

(b) A belongs to each winning coalition, so if A opposes a motion it will not pass. There are no other minimal blocking coalitions that include A, but we may notice that every winning coalition contains either B or C and D. Thus, if B can combine forces with either C or D to defeat a motion, $\{B, C\}$ and $\{B, D\}$ are also minimal blocking coalitions.

(c) A has veto power and thus is a critical voter in all 5 of the winning coalitions. B is critical in 3 winning coalitions: $\{A, B, C\}$, $\{A, B, D\}$, and $\{A, B\}$. Finally, C and D are only critical in one coalition: $\{A, C, D\}$. The Banzhaf power index is $(10, 6, 2, 2)$.

(d) $[q : w_A, w_B, w_C, w_D] = [5 : 3, 2, 1, 1]$ is one set of weights that works, but there are many other solutions. One can reason that A, the only voter with veto power, must have the most votes, while B is more powerful than C or D (who are equally powerful).

(e) A will pivot in any permutation in which he or she comes after B or after C and D. He or she automatically pivots in the 6 permutations where he or she is in position 4, and also the 6 permutations where he or she is in position 3 because if B is not last in such a permutation, then he or she comes before A, and if Voter A is last, then C and D come before A. There are two permutations, $BACD$ and $BADC$ where A pivots in position 2. This adds up to $2 + 6 + 6 = 14$ pivots for A. D pivots in permutations where A and C appear before him or her, and B is last. There are 2 such permutations: $ACDB$ and $CADB$. C has the same number of pivots as D. We have accounted for $14 + 2 + 2 = 18$ permutations. The remaining 6 belong to B. The Shapley-Shubik index is $\left(\dfrac{14}{24}, \dfrac{6}{24}, \dfrac{2}{24}, \dfrac{2}{24}\right) = \left(\dfrac{7}{12}, \dfrac{1}{4}, \dfrac{1}{12}, \dfrac{1}{12}\right)$.

20. Let's call the chairperson A, and the other members B_1, B_2, B_3, and B_4. The minimal winning coalitions have the form $\{A, B_i\}$, for $i = 1, 2, 3, 4$, and $\{B_1, B_2, B_3, B_4\}$ is a winning coalition because the chairperson can't block a motion unless another member joins him or her. With the proposed weights, each of these coalitions has weight 4, and it follows that all winning coalitions have weight at least 4. Losing coalitions (the chair alone, or 3 or fewer of the other members) would have weight less than 4. Thus the voting system is equivalent to the one with the proposed weights.

21. Let's call the chairperson A, and the other members B_1, B_2, B_3, and B_4. A is a critical voter in all winning coalitions that include at least one other voter but not all of them. There are $2^4 - 2 = 16 - 2 = 14$ such coalitions. Each of the B_i is a critical voter in two coalitions: $\{A, B_i\}$ for $i = 1, 2, 3, 4$, and $\{B_1, B_2, B_3, B_4\}$. The Banzhaf power index is $(28, 4, 4, 4, 4)$.

22. (a) Give the dean 2 votes, and each faculty member 1 vote. The quota would have to be 4. We would have $\left[q : w_D, w_{F_1}, w_{F_2}, w_{F_3}\right] = [4 : 2, 1, 1, 1]$.

(b) Give the dean and the provost each 2 votes (they have equal power on the committee), and each faculty member 1 vote. The quota is 6. We would have the following.

$$\left[q : w_D, w_P, w_{F_1}, w_{F_2}, w_{F_3}\right] = [6 : 2, 2, 1, 1, 1]$$

23. Let's look at the minimal winning coalitions. We call the faculty members F_1, F_2, F_3, and F_4. We call the administrators A_1, A_2, and A_3. The following are two winning coalitions: $\{F_1, F_2, F_3, F_4, A_1, A_2\}$, in which the administrators are critical, but the faculty members aren't; and $\{F_1, F_2, F_3, A_1, A_2, A_3\}$ in which the faculty members are critical and the administrators are not. In any weighted voting system, the critical voters in a coalition must have more weight than those who are not critical. The first coalition that we cited indicates that the administrators should have more weight, while the second indicates that the faculty members have more weight. These contradictory requirements cannot be satisfied, so the system is not equivalent to a weighted voting system.

24. An administrator casts a critical vote in any coalition that includes one other administrator and three or four faculty members. There are 2 ways to choose the other administrator, and 5 ways to choose the group of faculty members: 10 winning coalitions in which the administrator is critical.

A faculty member is critical in any coalition that includes exactly 2 other faculty members, and 2 or 3 administrators. There are 3 ways to choose the other faculty members, and 4 ways to assemble 2 or 3 administrators: 12 winning coalitions in which the faculty member is critical. The Banzhaf power index is $(24, 24, 24, 24, 20, 20, 20)$. The administrators probably think they are more powerful, but actually they aren't.

25. There are $7! = 5040$ permutations, so let's not make a list. Consider F_4. He or she will be critical in a permutation when he or she is fifth, followed by another faculty member and an administrator (in either order), or sixth, followed by a faculty member. If F_4 is fifth, there are 3 ways to choose the faculty member, 3 ways to choose the administrator, and 2 ways to put those two in order, The remaining 4 participants, who come before F_4 in the permutation, can be ordered 4! ways. Thus, there are $3 \times 3 \times 2 \times 4! = 432$ permutations where F_4 is a pivot in position 5. If F_4 is in position 6 and another faculty member in position 7, there are 5! ways to order the voters coming before the two faculty members, and 3 ways to choose the last voter in this type of permutation: $5! \times 3 = 360$ permutations in all. The number of permutations in which F_4 is a pivot is thus $432 + 360 = 792$. The other three faculty members are each pivot in 792 permutations, so the faculty members are pivot in a total of $4 \times 792 = 3168$ permutations. That leaves $5040 - 3168 = 1872$ permutations for the administrators, 624 each. The Shapley-Shubik index of this voting system is (in lowest terms)

$$\left(\frac{11}{70}, \frac{11}{70}, \frac{11}{70}, \frac{11}{70}, \frac{13}{105}, \frac{13}{105}, \frac{13}{105} \right)$$

By this measure, each faculty member is more powerful than any administrator. A faculty member has about 15.7% of the power, and an administrator has about 12.4%.

26. A voter has veto power if and only if he or she belongs to every winning coalition. Because each winning coalition contains at least one minimal winning coalition (you can obtain a minimal winning coalition by removing non-critical voters, one at a time, until there are no more), a voter who belongs to all minimal winning coalitions has veto power. If there is only one minimal winning coalition, then every voter in that coalition has veto power, and every voter who does not belong is a dummy. If there are only two minimal winning coalitions, since they overlap, at least one voter belongs to both and thus has veto power.

27. All four-voter systems can be presented as weighted voting systems.

Minimal winning coalitions	Weighted voting systems
$\{A, B, C, D\}$	[4:1,1,1,1]
$\{A, B\}, \{A, C, D\}$	[5:3,2,1,1]
$\{A, B, C\}, \{A, B, D\}$	[5:2,2,1,1]
$\{A, B\}, \{A, C\}, \{A, D\}$	[4:3,1,1,1]
$\{A, B\}, \{A, C\}, \{B, C, D\}$	[5:3,2,2,1]
$\{A, B\}, \{A, C, D\}, \{B, C, D\}$	[4:2,2,1,1]
$\{A, B, C\}, \{A, B, D\}, \{A, C, D\}$	[4:2,1,1,1]
$\{A, B\}, \{A, C\}, \{A, D\}, \{B, C, D\}$	[4:3,2,1,1]
$\{A, B, C\}, \{A, B, D\}, \{A, C, D\}, \{B, C, D\}$	[3:1,1,1,1]

28. (a) Let's call the voters A, B, C, and D. This weighted voting system can be written as $[q : w_A, w_B, w_C, w_D] = [51 : 48, 23, 22, 7]$.

Winning coalition	Weight	Extra votes	Losing coalition	Weight	Votes needed
$\{A, B, C, D\}$	100	49	$\{A\}$	48	3
$\{A, B, C\}$	93	42	$\{B, C\}$	45	6
$\{A, B, D\}$	78	27	$\{B, D\}$	30	21
$\{A, C, D\}$	77	26	$\{C, D\}$	29	22
$\{A, B\}$	71	20	$\{B\}$	23	28
$\{A, C\}$	70	19	$\{C\}$	22	29
$\{A, D\}$	55	4	$\{D\}$	7	44
$\{B, C, D\}$	52	1	$\{\ \}$	0	51

(b) A cannot sell more than 4 shares to B, because that is all the extra votes of $\{A, D\}$. The right column of the table in part (a) indicates that all of the losing coalitions involving B need more than 4 votes, so no additional winning coalitions would be created.

(c) When selling to D, the extra votes of $\{A, D\}$ are unaffected. A can sell 19 shares to D. without changing any winning coalitions. The strongest losing coalition involving D needs 21 votes, and its status would not be affected by the sale.

(d) A is again limited to the extra votes of $\{A, D\}$, 4 shares. Before starting, 8 new winning coalitions should be created, by combining E and each of the winning coalitions, and 8 losing coalitions would be created, combining E with the previous losing coalitions. No vote counts would change, because E has 0 shares at the outset. The sale would not affect the losing coalition E; it would still need 3 shares to win. The first losing coalition that would gain shares is $\{B, C, E\}$, which would still need 2 more shares to win.

(e) D can either sell 4 shares to B or C (here the limitation is to the coalition $\{A, D\}$ because $\{B, C, D\}$ would not be affected); or D can sell 1 share to A or E: now the limitation is the extra votes of $\{B, C, D\}$.

(f) D can sell 2 shares to A: if she sells more than that, $\{A\}$ would become a winning coalition and the rest of the shareholders (D included) would be dummies. She can sell 5 shares to B or C, more than that would cause $\{A, D\}$ to lose and $\{B, C\}$ to win, leaving no critical votes for D. She could sell 5 shares to E: that would cause $\{B, C, D\}$ and $\{A, D\}$ to lose, but it would create new winning coalitions, including $\{B, C, D, E\}$, which would have 1 extra vote, and D, who still has 2 shares, would be a critical voter.

(g) The limiting coalitions are $\{A, B\}$, with 20 extra votes, and $\{C, D\}$, which is 22 shares short of winning. B can sell 20 shares to C.

29. The minimal winning coalitions are $\{A, B\}$ $\{A, C\}$, $\{A, D\}$, and $\{B, C, D\}$. Thus, A is more powerful than the others, and B, C, and D have equal power, even though their voting weights are different. Let's go through the list and see which gives the same minimal winning coalitions.

(a) Each minimal winning coalition has 3 voters. Eliminated.

(b) The minimal winning coalitions are A combined with another voter, or $\{B, C, D\}$. This matches our system.

(c) The minimal winning coalitions are A combined with 2 other voters. Eliminated.

(d) $\{A, C\}$ and $\{A, D\}$ are not winning coalitions. Eliminated.

The answer: (b).

30. To determine the Banzhaf index, refer to the table in answer 28(a). A, with 48 votes, is critical in 6 winning coalitions; B, C, and D are each critical in only 2 winning coalitions: when joined by A and no one else, or in a coalition without A. Doubling to include blocking coalitions, the Banzhaf power index is $(12, 4, 4, 4)$. To determine the Shapley-Shubik power index, consider the permutations in which D is pivot. These are $ADBC$, $ADCB$ (if A is before D, then B and C must be after D, or one of them would be the pivot), $BCDA$, and $CBDA$. Similarly, B and C pivot in 4 permutations. There are $4! = 24$ permutations in all and B, C, and D pivot in 12. In the remaining 12, A pivots. The Shapley-Shubik power index is the following.

$$\left(\frac{12}{24}, \frac{4}{24}, \frac{4}{24}, \frac{4}{24} \right) = \left(\frac{1}{2}, \frac{1}{6}, \frac{1}{6}, \frac{1}{6} \right)$$

31. (a) The ordinary members are equally powerful, so each gets 1 vote. The quota is 8, to make the coalition of all ordinary members winning, but 7 members losing. The chair gets 6 votes, enough to combine with 2 ordinary members and win. In our notation, the weighted voting system is $\left[q : w_C, w_{O_1}, w_{O_2}, w_{O_3}, w_{O_4}, w_{O_5}, w_{O_6}, w_{O_7}, w_{O_8} \right] = [8 : 6, 1, 1, 1, 1, 1, 1, 1, 1]$.

(b) The chairperson is critical in all winning coalition she belongs to, except the one in which the committee is unanimous. The number of these coalitions is $2^8 - C_0^8 - C_1^8 - C_8^8 = 256 - 1 - 8 - 1 = 246$, because there are 2^8 coalitions of ordinary members in all, of which we must eliminate $C_0^8 + C_1^8$ because they consist of 0 or 1 members, who cannot form a winning coalition with the chairperson, and C_8^8, because when all 8 ordinary members join the chairperson, the chairperson isn't critical. An ordinary member is critical in 8 winning coalitions: when joined by the rest of the ordinary members, and when joined by the chairperson and one of the other 7 ordinary members. Counting an equal number of blocking coalitions, the Banzhaf power index of this system is $(492, 16, 16, 16, 16, 16, 16, 16, 16)$.

(c) Divide the permutations into 9 groups, according to the location of the chairperson. She is pivot in groups 3, 4, 5, 6, 7, and 8. Therefore his or her Shapley-Shubik power index is $\frac{6}{9} = \frac{2}{3}$. Each ordinary member has $\frac{1}{8}$ of the remaining $1 - \frac{2}{3} = \frac{1}{3}$ of the power; hence the Shapley-Shubik power index of this system is as follows.

$$\left(\frac{2}{3}, \frac{1}{24}, \frac{1}{24}, \frac{1}{24}, \frac{1}{24}, \frac{1}{24}, \frac{1}{24}, \frac{1}{24}, \frac{1}{24} \right)$$

(d) In this system, the chairperson is 30.75 times as powerful as an ordinary member according to the Banzhaf index, but only 16 times as powerful by the Shapley-Shubik power index.

32. (a) A coalition with exactly 6 votes is a minimal winning coalition. If there are 7 or more votes, the coalition isn't minimal, because it must include a borough president, who, with 1 vote, would not be critical. Thus, the minimal winning coalitions would consist of one of the following:

   i.   3 city officials,

   ii. 2 city officials and 2 borough presidents, or

   iii. 1 city official and 4 borough presidents.

Continued on next page

32. continued

(b) The city officials are critical in all coalitions of the types listed in part (a). They are also critical in each coalition formed by one of these, and an additional borough president. The mayor (and the comptroller and the city council president) is therefore a critical voter in 6 winning coalitions of type (i). For type (ii) coalitions, the mayor could be joined by another city official in $C_1^2 = 2$ ways, and 2 borough presidents in $C_2^5 = 10$ ways – that's 20 coalitions. The mayor could also be joined by another city official and 3 borough presidents, another 20 winning coalitions in which the mayor is critical. Turning to type (iii) coalitions, the mayor would be critical in any winning coalition where he or she is joined by 4 or all 5 borough presidents: another 6 coalitions. This makes 52 coalitions in which the mayor is a critical voter. The mayor's Banzhaf power index (and that of the comptroller and the city council president) is therefore 104 (as usual, we have to double to account for the blocking coalitions).

There are $C_2^3 \times C_1^4 = 3 \times 4 = 12$ ways to choose the city officials and the other borough president to form a winning coalition of type (ii) in which the Manhattan Borough president is critical. There are $C_1^3 \times C_3^4 = 3 \times 4 = 12$ ways to assemble a winning coalition of type (iii) in which the Manhattan Borough president is critical. Taking the 24 critical votes of the Manhattan Borough president in winning coalitions, and another 24 critical votes in blocking coalitions, we find that his or her Banzhaf power index is 48. The other borough presidents have the same index.

33. Let's determine the minimal winning coalitions. They would be of the following types:

(a) 3 city officials

(b) 2 city officials and 1 borough president

(c) 1 city official and all of the borough presidents.

Thus, the city officials all have the same power, and the borough presidents, although weaker than the city officials, also have equal power. We will assign a voting weight of 1 to each borough president. Let C denote the voting weight of a city official and let q be the quota. To make the coalition of type (i) win, and 2 city officials lose, we have

$$2C < q \le 3C.$$

To make coalitions of type (ii) win, we require $2C + 1 \ge q$. Combining these inequalities, we see that (if C is an integer), $q = 2C + 1$. The 5 borough presidents plus one city official can win, but 4 borough presidents plus a city official is a losing coalition: therefore

$$C + 4 < q \le C + 5$$

and hence $q = C + 5$. We now have two expressions for q, $2C + 1$ and $C + 5$. Equating them, $2C + 1 = C + 5$, which we can solve for C to obtain $C = 4$, and hence $q = 9$. Finally, the 5 borough presidents form a losing coalition, but win if joined by a city official: this will hold provided

$$5 < q \le C + 5$$

This is also valid for $q = 9$ and $C = 4$.

The weighted voting system is $\left[q : w_M, w_C, w_{CCP}, w_{P_1}, w_{P_2}, w_{P_3}, w_{P_4}, w_{P_5} \right] = \left[9 : 4, 4, 4, 1, 1, 1, 1, 1 \right].$

34. (a) A minimal winning coalition consists of all 5 permanent members and 4 other members. If one permanent member joins the opposition, and the 6 other members join, a losing coalition results. Therefore each permanent member must have more weight than 6 ordinary members. We give each of the permanent members 7 votes and each ordinary member 1 vote. The minimal winning coalition then has $5 \times 7 + 4 = 39$ votes, so the quota is 39.

(b) Each permanent member has the following Banzhaf index.

$$2 \times \left(C_4^{10} + C_5^{10} + C_6^{10} + C_7^{10} + C_8^{10} + C_9^{10} + C_{10}^{10} \right)$$

$$
\begin{array}{ccccccccccc}
 & & & & & 1 & & & & & \\
 & & & & 1 & & 1 & & & & \\
 & & & 1 & & 2 & & 1 & & & \\
 & & 1 & & 3 & & 3 & & 1 & & \\
 & 1 & & 4 & & 6 & & 4 & & 1 & \\
1 & & 5 & & 10 & & 10 & & 5 & & 1 \\
\end{array}
$$

1 6 15 20 15 6 1

1 7 21 35 35 21 7 1

1 8 28 56 70 56 28 8 1

1 9 36 84 126 126 84 36 9 1

1 10 45 120 210 252 210 120 45 10 1

Using Pascal's triangle, we have $2 \times (210 + 252 + 210 + 120 + 45 + 10 + 1) = 2 \times 848 = 1696$.

An ordinary member has an index of $2 \times C_3^9 = 2 \times 84 = 168$. By this index, a permanent member is about 10 times as powerful as an ordinary member.

(c) A minimal winning coalition has 6 votes, including all 5 permanent members. If n is the number of votes assigned to each permanent member, then the quota will be $q = 5n + 1$ (for 5 permanent members and one non-permanent member).

The coalition that includes the entire Council except for one permanent member (who vetoes) has weight $4n + 6$ and is losing. Therefore, $4n + 6 < 5n + 1$. Subtract $4n + 1$ from each side of this inequality to obtain $5 < n$. Hence we can put $n = 6$ and $q = 31$. The weighted voting system is $[31: 6,6,6,6,6,1,1,1,1,1,1]$.

To determine the Banzhaf power index, note that all winning coalitions can be formed by combining the coalition of all the permanent members with any coalition of non-permanent members except the empty coalition, $\{\ \}$. There are $2^6 = 64$ coalitions of the 6 non-permanent members; excluding $\{\ \}$ we have 63 winning coalitions in all. Each permanent member, with veto power, is critical in all of them. Doubling to account for the blocking coalitions, we find that the Banzhaf power index of each permanent member is 126.

A non-permanent member casts a critical vote in only one winning coalition – when it is the only non-permanent member to join the permanent members in voting "yes." Doubling, to account for the blocking coalition consisting of all the non-permanent members, the Banzhaf power index of each non-permanent member is 2. The Banzhaf power index of this voting system is therefore $(126, 126, 126, 126, 126, 2, 2, 2, 2, 2, 2)$.

In this system, each permanent member is 63 times as powerful as each non-permanent member. We have seen that in the current system, the corresponding ratio of power is 10 to 1. Thus the permanent members did relinquish some power by including four more non-permanent members in the Security Council.

35. The three weight-3 voters, or 2 weight-3 voters and one weight-1 voter form minimal winning coalitions.

A weight-3 voter, A, is critical in any winning coalition with 7, 8, or 9 votes. There are 6 weight-7 coalitions that include A, because they are formed by assembling one of the other 2 weight-3 voters, and one of the 3 weight-1 voters. There are also 6 weight-8 coalitions with A: they also need one of the other 2 weight-3 voters and 2 of the 3 weight-1 voters (the number of ways to choose 2 weight-1 voters is $C_2^3 = 4$). Finally, there are 3 coalitions of weight 9 to which A belongs: all 3 weight-3 voters is one of them; the other 2 consist of A and one of the other 2 weight-3 voters, and all of the weight-1 voters. Thus A is critical in a total of 15 winning coalitions, and A's Banzhaf power index is 30.

A weight-1 voter, D, is critical in 3 winning coalitions, formed by assembling D with 2 of the 3 weight-3 voters. Doubling, we see that the Banzhaf power index of D is 6.

The Banzhaf power index of this system is $(30, 30, 30, 6, 6, 6)$.

36. The minimal winning coalitions found in the solution of Exercise 35 are still minimal winning coalitions. There is another type of weight-7 minimal winning coalition as well: one weight-3 voter and all of the weight-1 voters.

Banzhaf power index of a weight-3 voter (as usual, only winning coalitions are counted):

Weight 7 The voter is critical in $C_1^2 \times C_1^4 = 2 \times 4 = 8$ coalitions in which he or she is joined by one of the 2 other weight-3 voters and one of the 4 weight-1 voters. He or she is also critical in 1 coalition where she is joined by all of the weight-4 voters and no other weight-3 voters. **Total: 9 critical votes.**

Weight 8 The voter is critical in $C_1^2 \times C_2^4 = 2 \times 6 = 12$ coalitions where he or she is joined by 1 other weight-3 voter and 2 weight-1 voters. **Total: 12 critical votes.**

Weight 9 The voter is critical in $C_1^2 \times C_3^4 = 2 \times 4 = 8$ coalitions involving the voter, one other weight-3 voter, and 3 weight-1 voters. He or she is also critical in one winning coalition consisting of the 3 weight-3 voters. **Total: 9 critical votes.**

The weight-3 voter is thus critical in 30 winning coalitions, and her Banzhaf power index is 60.

The weight-1 voter has the opportunity to be a critical voter only in weight-7 coalitions. There are $C_2^3 = 3$ such coalitions in which he or she is joined by two weight-3 voters, and $C_1^3 = 3$ coalitions in which he or she is joined by 1 weight-3 voter, and the other 3 weight-1 voters. This is a total of 6 coalitions, so the weight-1 voter's Banzhaf power index is 12.

Each voter's Banzhaf power index has doubled as a result of including the additional voter, and the weight-1 voter still has $\frac{1}{5}$ of the power of the weight-3 voter. However, an individual weight-1 voter now has $\frac{1}{19}$ of the voting power $\left(\frac{12 \text{ critical votes}}{4 \times 12 + 3 \times 60} \right)$, and before the new voter joined, he or she had $\frac{1}{18}$. His or her share of the power has diminished slightly; so has that of each weight-3 voter.

37. Let's start with a weight-1 voter, A.

Case I: 3 weight-1 voters

A will be pivot in permutations where he or she is in position 3, and positions 1 and 2 are occupied by weight-3 voters. There are $C_2^3 = 3$ ways to choose the weight-3 voters who come first, 2 ways to put them in order, and 3! ways to put the voters following A in order. Thus the Shapley-Shubik power index of A is $\dfrac{3 \times 2 \times 3!}{6 \times 5 \times 4 \times 3!} = \dfrac{3 \times 2}{6 \times 5 \times 4} = \dfrac{1}{5 \times 4} = \dfrac{1}{20}$.

The other weight-1 voters have the same power, and the weight-3 voters share the remaining $1 - 3 \times \dfrac{1}{20} = 1 - \dfrac{3}{20} = \dfrac{17}{20}$ of the power.

Case II: 4 weight-1 voters

Now A will be pivot in permutations where he or she is in position 3, and positions 1 and 2 are occupied by weight-3 voters. There are still 3 ways to select the 2 weight-3 voters and 2 ways to put them in order, but now there are 4! ways to arrange the voters who follow A in the permutation. This gives $6 \times 4!$ permutations in which A is pivot.

A will also be pivot in any permutation where he or she is in position 5 and the final two positions are occupied by weight-3 voters. There are the same number of these permutations. The Shapley-Shubik power index for A is therefore $\dfrac{2 \times 6 \times 4!}{7 \times 6 \times 5 \times 4!} = \dfrac{2 \times 6}{7 \times 6 \times 5} = \dfrac{2}{7 \times 5} = \dfrac{2}{35}$. The

other 3 weight-1 voters have the same power, and the remaining $1 - 4 \times \dfrac{2}{35} = 1 - \dfrac{8}{35} = \dfrac{27}{35}$ of the

power belongs to the weight-3 voters.

Although each voter's share of power decreased proportionally in the Banzhaf model when a new voter joined the system, in this particular situation, each weight-1 voter's power, measured by the Shapley-Shubik model, increased when the new voter was included, because $\dfrac{2}{35} > \dfrac{1}{20}$.

38. We will try to assign weights to make this a weighted voting system. Give each recent graduate (RG) a weight of 1, and let X be the weight of each of the rich alumni (RA). The quota will be denoted Q.

Let's consider the minimal winning coalitions. There are 15 members of the committee, so a majority is 8. The minimal winning coalitions comprise either 3 rich alumni RA and 5 (RG), with $5 + 3X$ votes, or 2 RA and 6 RG, with $6 + 2X$. The weights of these coalitions are at least the quota. Therefore, the following two inequalities hold.

$$5 + 3X \ge Q$$
$$6 + 2X \ge Q$$

Because it is not a majority, 4 RG and 3 RA form a losing coalition; thus $4 + 3X < Q$. Comparing this with the second of the above inequalities, we have $4 + 3X < 6 + 2X$.

Subtract $4 + 2X$ from each side of this inequality to obtain $X < 2$. The weight of one RA has to be less than that of 2 RG.

A coalition comprising 1 RA and all 12 RG is a losing coalition, because the votes of at least 2 RA are needed to pass a motion. Therefore, $12 + X < Q$. Comparing this with the inequality $6 + 2X \ge Q$ yields $12 + X < 6 + 2X$. Subtract $6 + X$ from each side of this inequality to obtain $6 < X$. Each RA must have more voting weight than 6 RG.

It's impossible for each RA to have less weight than 2 RG, and at the same time to have more weight than 6 RG. Therefore, this voting system is not equivalent to a weighted voting system.

39. Consider Maine, which has 2 congressional districts. Ignoring the rest of the country, Maine would be a 3-voter system, in which the state has 2 votes, and each congressional district has 1. There are 3! permutations of voters, but only 2 are possible: 1M2 and 2M1, where the congressional districts are identified by numerals, and the state is M. The reason is as follows. Each entity (district or statewide) is given a score, which is the number of votes recorded for the Bush-Cheney ticket, divided by the number of votes cast in that entity for the Kerry-Edwards ticket. The entity's position in the permutation is determined by that ratio.

Let $r_1, r_2,$ and r_M denote the ratios for the two districts and the state as a whole, respectively, and let $y_1, y_2,$ and y_M be the number of votes cast for the Kerry-Edwards ticket in each entity. The reason that some electoral permutations are impossible is that $y_M = y_1 + y_2$. Each vote is actually counted twice: once for the elector representing the voter's congressional district, and once for the two statewide electors. The number of votes for the Bush-Cheney ticket in the three entities were $r_1 y_1$, $r_2 y_2$, and $r_M (y_1 + y_2)$. Because the number of statewide votes for the Bush-Cheney ticket can also be determined by adding the votes in the two districts,

$$r_M (y_1 + y_2) = r_1 y_1 + r_2 y_2.$$

Dividing by $(y_1 + y_2)$ we can obtain a formula for r_M:

$$r_M = \frac{r_1 y_1 + r_2 y_2}{y_1 + y_2}.$$

Suppose that $r_1 > r_2$. Then $r_1 y_2 > r_2 y_2$, and thus

$$r_1 = \frac{r_1 (y_1 + y_2)}{y_1 + y_2} = \frac{r_1 y_1 + r_1 y_2}{y_1 + y_2} > \frac{r_1 y_1 + r_2 y_2}{y_1 + y_2} = r_M$$

Also, $r_1 y_1 > r_2 y_1$, so

$$r_M = \frac{r_1 y_1 + r_2 y_2}{y_1 + y_2} > \frac{r_2 y_1 + r_2 y_2}{y_1 + y_2} = \frac{r_2 (y_1 + y_2)}{y_1 + y_2} = r_2.$$

These inequalities, taken together show that $r_1 > r_M > r_2$, if $r_1 > r_2$. Of course, if $r_1 > r_2$, the same argument would show $r_2 > r_M > r_1$.

Any permutation of the states in which the statewide electors for Maine do not fall between the electors for the two congressional districts is therefore impossible. The same is true for Nebraska: at least one district elector must come before the statewide electors, and one must come after them.

The Shapley-Shubik power index should be computed by using only the possible permutations. A given entity's Shapley-Shubik power index would be the number of possible permutations in which it is pivot, divided by the total number of possible permutations.

Word Search Solution

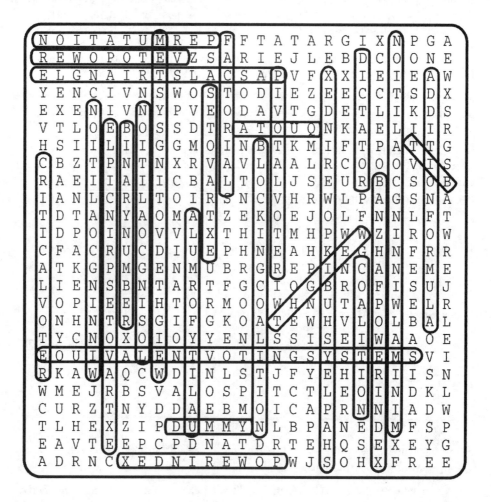

Chapter 12
Electing the President

Chapter Outline

Introduction

Chapter Summary

The procedure for electing the American president is unique among world democracies. No other country incorporates an institution similar to the Electoral College, a feature that plays a large role in both determining the outcome of our elections, as well as in the strategies of the candidates. The selection of the nominees who compete in a grueling series of primary elections is also unique to the American political process.

To try to make mathematical sense of these features, we make certain assumptions. We assume that the candidates are completely aware of the positions of the voters along the spectrum of political opinion. We also assume that the outcome of an election hinges on a single issue (and not on grounds of personality, ethnicity, and so forth), with each citizen choosing to vote for the candidate whose opinion lies closest to his own. Under these simplifying assumptions, the problem for the candidates is thus reduced to deciding where to situate themselves on the political spectrum in order to maximize their vote totals. In the case of just two candidates, the *optimal position* for each is at the median. This choice is in *equilibrium,* in the sense that if either candidate deviates from this position, then the opponent can exploit this movement to his own benefit.

Multi-candidate elections are both more interesting and more difficult to analyze. Such situations occur regularly in primaries, as well as in general elections with serious third-party candidates, such as Ross Perot in 1992 or Ralph Nader in 2000. While unable to win, such candidates may play the role of spoilers who can affect the outcome of the election. In particular, questions arise as to whether it pays for a third (or fourth) candidate to enter the race and where to position himself if he does. The answers to these questions depend upon the political stances of those who have preceded him. For example, if the first two candidates are centrists who have positioned themselves at the median (the optimal choice for two candidates), then a third entry can benefit by moving slightly to the right or left of the median. Of course, the entry of the third candidate may cause the first two to jockey for more attractive positions. The *1/3-separation obstacle* and the *2/3-separation opportunity* help us understand the dynamics of new candidates entering the race. Moreover, anticipation of the entry of additional candidates may affect the original positions adopted by the earlier candidates.

These dynamics are also affected by those who drop out of the race, either because of poor poll performance or because they lost some of the early primaries. In some situations, we can determine which of the remaining candidates benefit from the reduced field.

Following the 2000 election, many ideas arose for reform of the presidential election process, including the possibility of eliminating the Electoral College or eliminating its winner-take-all feature. Although not aired in the general public, *approval voting* has been discussed in the mathematical community, and it has several positive aspects which would affect multi-candidate elections. It is likely that Al Gore would have won the 2000 election under approval voting, since many of Ralph Nader's supporters would have cast approval votes for Gore as well. A voter is said to have *dichotomous preferences* if he divides the set of candidates into two subsets – a preferred subset and a nonpreferred one – and is indifferent among all candidates in each of these subsets. A *dominant strategy* for a dichotomous voter is to vote for all candidates in his preferred subset and no others. Under approval voting, if all voters have dichotomous preferences and chose their dominant strategy, then a Condorcet winner will always be elected.

A major decision confronting the nominees of the two main parties is the allocation of resources. We assume that the votes in a state for each candidate will be proportional to the amounts spent there. Clearly, the candidates will concentrate their spending in the toss-up states, but within this category it turns out that the lion's share will go to the largest states. The *3/2's rule*, under which parties allocate their resources to the toss-up states according to the $\frac{3}{2}$ power of their electoral votes, maximizes the expected electoral vote of a candidate, provided that his opponent adheres to the same rule. This rule is a *local maximum,* in that it is invulnerable to small deviations by the opponent. But this rule is vulnerable to large deviations, such as when a candidate spends little or nothing in certain states (thereby conceding those states) and uses the money saved there in other battleground states. However, this strategy is dangerous, since if his opponent becomes aware of it at an early stage, he can exploit this knowledge to his benefit. Hence, allocation decisions put us in the realm of game theory.

A robust choice of allocations is the *proportional rule* in which resources are divided according to the sizes of the toss-up states. This rule maximizes the expected total popular vote for a candidate, regardless of whether his opponent adheres to it or not, so that it yields a *global maximum.* However, since the presidential election is determined by winning a majority of the electoral votes, rather than the popular votes, adopting this strategy may lead to a situation similar to 2000, in which the winner of the popular vote lost the election.

Skill Objectives

1. To determine the equilibrium positions of the candidates.

2. To determine the optimal positions of the candidates.

3. To determine the effect that a new candidate who enters the field has on previous candidates.

4. To determine which candidates benefit when another drops out of the race.

5. To understand the 1/3-separation obstacle and 2/3-separation opportunity.

6. To apply the proportional rule for allocation of resources.

7. To apply the 3/2's rule for the allocation of resources.

Teaching Tips

1. This chapter has a very contemporaneous feel to it, motivated partially by the presidential election of 2000. As we move away from the events of that year, it might be a good idea to refresh the students' memories by reviewing the details of that election.

2. Point out to the students that this chapter incorporates just about all of the topics found in this part of the book: various voting methods, Condorcet winner, approval voting, weighted voting, sincere and insincere voting, and apportionment (which decides the distribution of votes in the Electoral College).

Research Paper

Have students to research one of the following questions. The suggested length for the first writing project is 1 to 2 pages and for the second is 2 to 3 pages.

1. What evidence is there that the median-voter theorem applies in presidential elections with only two serious contenders? In cases where the candidates do not approach the median, is this because they view their main supporters as more extreme and do not want to alienate them?

2. It is generally agreed that presidential nomination races today are "front-loaded" – candidates must devote most of their resources to the early primaries even to stay in contention, much less win. Does this fact tend to help moderates or extremists as the field is narrowed? Would this be true under approval voting? Is it desirable that momentum plays such a large role in presidential primaries?

Spreadsheet Project

To do this project, go to http://www.whfreeman.com/fapp7e.

This activity provides an examination of the popular vote and the Electoral College.

Collaborative Learning

Primary Battles

The following is a major group project to be done mainly out of class. Choose several presidential election years in which there were interesting primary contests, with several candidates initially in the field. Among others, these include Democratic primaries in 1960, 1972, 1976, and 1988, and Republican ones in 1976, 1996, and 2000.

Divide the class into groups and assign to each group one of these interesting primary battles. By consulting contemporary sources, have the students research the development of the nominating races, culminating in the selection of one of the candidates. The students should focus on the positions of the candidates, the order in which they entered the race, the effect that new candidates had, when candidates dropped out, and so forth, all in the light of the concepts developed in this chapter. Then have each group report back to the class.

Solutions

Skills Check:

1. b   2. b   3. c   4. a   5. c   6. c   7. a   8. c   9. c   10. b

11. b   12. b   13. a   14. a   15. b   16. b   17. c   18. a   19. b   20. a

Exercises:

1. Assume a distribution is skewed to the left. The heavier concentration of voters on the right means that fewer voters are farther from the median. Because there are fewer voters "pulling" the mean rightward, it will be to the left of the median. Likewise, a distribution skewed to the right will have a mean to the right of the median.

2. Assume the candidates take a common position at 0.6. Then there are 12 voters to the left and 11 voters to the right of this position. If one of the candidates moves left to 0.5, then the opponent will win by 13 to 12 votes. If one of the candidates moves right to 0.7, then the opponent will win by 14 to 11 votes. Hence, neither candidate has an incentive to depart from position 0.6, making it an equilibrium position.

3. While there is no median position such that half the voters lie to the left and half to the right, there is still a position where the middle voter (if the number of voters is odd) or the two middle voters (if the number of voters is even) are located, starting either from the left or right. In the absence of a median, less than half the voters lie to the left and less than half to the right of this middle voter's (voters') position (positions).

    Hence, any departure by a candidate from a position of a middle voter to the position of a non-middle voter on the left or right will result in that candidate's getting less than half the votes – and the opponent's getting more than half. Thus, the middle position (positions) is (are) in equilibrium, making it (them) the extended median.

4. No, because if a candidate moved to 0.5, he would get 8 votes and his opponent at 0.6 would get 11 votes, whereas if he stayed at 0.6 with his opponent, he would split the 18 votes, leading to a tie. Similarly, if one candidate moved to 0.7, she would get 8 votes, but her opponent at 0.6 would get 10 votes. Hence, 0.6 remains an equilibrium position if only the voter at 0.1 might not vote. On the other hand, if the three voters at 0.2 might not vote, then it would pay for one candidate to move to 0.7, getting 8 votes, because her opponent at 0.6 would get only 7 votes.

5. When the four voters on the left refuse to vote for a candidate at 0.6, his opponent can do better by moving to 0.7, which is worse for the dropouts.

6. The extended median would remain 0.6 if there were the two dropouts at 0, and similarly if there was also the dropout at 0.9. The extended median may change if there are more dropouts, however, when voters increasingly refuse to vote for candidates who are not close to them. In the extreme case, if voters do not vote for a candidate unless he or she takes exactly their position, then 0.8, where there are the most votes (6), would be the extended median.

7. The voters are spread from 0.1 to 0.9, so it is a position at 0.5 that minimizes the maximum distance (0.4) a candidate is from a voter. If the candidates are at the median of 0.6, the voter at 0.1 would be a distance of 0.5 from them. In this sense, the median is worse than the mean of 0.56, which would bring the candidates closer to the farthest-away voter and, arguably, be a better reflection of the views of the electorate.

8. If neither candidate has an incentive to depart from an equilibrium position, but in fact departs, he or she would want to return to that position. But this is to say that if one candidate is at that position, the other candidate cannot do better than also take that position.

9. The middle peak will be in equilibrium when it is the median or the extended median. Yes, it is possible that, say, the peak on the left is in equilibrium, as illustrated by the following discrete-distribution example, in which the median is 0.2:

Position i	1	2	3	4	5	6	7
Location (l_i) of position i	0.1	0.2	0.3	0.5	0.6	0.8	0.9
Number of voters (n_i) at position i	7	8	1	2	1	2	1

10. Assume B's position is to the right of the median. Clearly, A maximizes his vote total by being just to B's left and therefore closer to the median. Analogously, if B's position is to the left of the median, A does best being just to B's right. If B is at the median, then from the median-voter theorem, A can do no better than be at the median, too.

11. If the population is not uniformly distributed and, say, 80% live between $\frac{3}{8}$ and $\frac{5}{8}$ and only 10% live to the left of $\frac{3}{8}$ and 10% to right of $\frac{5}{8}$, then the bulk of the population will be well served by two stores at $\frac{1}{2}$. In fact, stores at $\frac{1}{4}$ and $\frac{3}{4}$ will be farther away for 80% of the population, so it can be argued that the two stores at $\frac{1}{2}$ provide a social optimum.

12. Probably most people would argue that members of the city council should represent people at different positions so, for example, a 20% minority would have one representative on the council. But if only one candidate is to be elected, he or she presumably, having to represent everybody, should be someone whose position is a centrist one.

13. Presumably, the cost of travel would have to be weighed against how much lower more competitive prices are.

14. Assume the first district comprises the seven voters at positions 1 – 3, the second district the seven voters at positions 4 – 6, and the third district the seven voters at positions 7 – 9:

Position i	1	2	3	4	5	6	7	8	9
Location (l_i) of position i	0.1	0.2	0.3	0.4	0.5	0.6	0.7	0.8	0.9
Number of voters (n_i) at position i	2	3	1	3	1	2	2	3	1

Their extended medians are 0.2, 0.4 or 0.5, and 0.8, respectively, whereas the extended median for the major is 0.4 or 0.5. If the candidate in the district at positions 4 – 6 chooses the extended median 0.4, and the mayor the extended median 0.5, then none of the district extended medians match the mayor's median. Whether such differences are the basis of mayor-council disagreements would have to be investigated.

15. Since the districts are of equal size, the mayor's median or extended median must be between the leftmost and rightmost medians or extended medians; otherwise, at least $\frac{2}{3}$ of the voters would be on one side of the mayor's position, which would preclude it from being the median or extended median. This is not true of the mean, however, if, say, the left-district positions are much farther away from the mayor's median or extended median than the right-district positions. In such a case, the mayor's mean would be in the interval of the left-district positions.

16. C should take a position just to the left or right of A/B, on the side closer to the median. Thereby C will receive a majority of the votes, and A and B will split the remainder.

17. If, say, A takes a position at M and B takes a position to the right of M, C should take a position just to the left of M that is closer to M than B's position, giving C essentially half the votes and enabling him or her to win the election. If neither A nor B takes a position at M, C should take a position next to the player closer to M; the position that C takes to maximize his or her vote may be either closer to M (if the candidates are far apart) or farther from M (if the players are closer together), but this position may not be winning. For example, assume the voters are uniformly distributed over $[0,1]$. If $\frac{3}{16}$ of the voters lie between A (to the left of M) and M, and $\frac{3}{16}$ of the voters lie between M and B (to the right of M), then C does best taking a position just to the left of A or just to the right of B, obtaining essentially $\frac{5}{16}$ of the vote. To be specific, assume C moves just to the left of A. Then A will obtain $\frac{3}{16}$ of the vote, but B will win with $\frac{1}{2}$ of the vote (that to the right of M), so C's maximizing position will not always be sufficient to win.

18. If the distribution is not symmetric but the areas separating A and B from M are the same, then there is still a 1/3-separation obstacle. If the areas are different − say, A is closer to M than B is − then C does better moving just to the left of A rather than just to the right of B. Now if A is very close to M, then C will get almost half the vote, whereas A and B will split the remainder, enabling C to win.

19. Following the hint, C will obtain $\frac{1}{3}$ of the vote by taking a position at M, as will A and B, so there will be a three-way tie among the candidates. Because a non-unimodal distribution can be bimodal, with the two modes close to M, C can win if he or she picks up most of the vote near the two modes, enabling C to win with more than $\frac{1}{3}$ of vote.

20. Following the hint, B will win when C enters to the left of A, A will win when C enters to the right of B, and A or B will win or at least tie when C enters in between. For example, if C enters at $\frac{1}{2}$, A and B will tie with $\frac{3}{8}$ of the vote each to C's $\frac{1}{4}$ of the vote.

21. B should enter just to the right of $\frac{3}{4}$, making it advantageous for C to enter just to the left of A, giving C essentially $\frac{1}{4}$ of the vote. With C and A almost splitting the vote to the left of M and a little beyond, B would win almost all the vote to the right of M. (If C entered at $\frac{1}{2}$, he or she would get slightly more than $\frac{1}{4}$ of the vote but lose to A, who would get $\frac{3}{8}$.)

22. Assume the distribution is triangular, so $y = 4x$ for $0 \le x \le \frac{1}{2}$ and $y = 4 - 4x$ for $\frac{1}{2} < x \le 1$. It is not difficult to show that $\frac{1}{2}$ the area lies between $x = 0.354$ and $x = 0.646$. If C takes a position at $\frac{1}{2}$, he or she will win the votes of all voters between $x = .427$ and $x = .573$ when A and B take positions at .354 and 0.646, respectively. In this case, C will obtain 27.1% of the vote, whereas A and B will tie with 36.5% each, so this distribution does not rise steeply enough in the middle to enable C to win. Clearly, a distribution that rises very sharply near $x = \frac{1}{2}$ is needed to give C more than 33.3% of the vote and, thereby, enough to beat A and B.

23. If the distribution is uniform, these positions are $\frac{1}{6}$, $\frac{5}{6}$, and $\frac{1}{2}$ for A, B, and C, respectively, making D indifferent between entering just to the left of A, just to the right of B, or in between A and C at $\frac{1}{3}$ or between C and B at $\frac{2}{3}$, which would give D $\frac{1}{6}$ of the vote in any case.

24. If all Buchanan supporters switched to Bush, that would give Bush a 49% to 48% lead over Gore in the popular vote, and so presumably the election. However, if only half of Buchanan supporters switched to Bush, then Bush would tie with Gore, 48% to 48%. But if Gore picks up a little of Buchanan's support, the tie would be broken in favor of Gore.

25. No, because Gore would get 49%, the same as Bush, so instead of winning Gore would tie with Bush.

26. There is no evidence that such deals were offered, much less made. The fear of discovery and serving jail time is certainly a major factor in deterring bribes or other shady deals. In addition, some politicians find such behavior inherently unethical and so steer clear of it for that reason.

27. It seems far too complicated a "solution" for avoiding effects caused by the Electoral College. Why not just abolish the Electoral College?

28. Because the votes for all other candidates, including the Condorcet winner, shift completely to the top two candidates identified by the poll, only one of these two candidates can win. If the poll identifies the top three candidates, and the Condorcet candidate is not among them, then the Condorcet winner will lose for the same reason − he or she will receive no votes, according to the Poll Assumption.

29. By definition, more voters prefer the Condorcet winner to any other candidate. Thus, if the poll identifies the Condorcet winner as one of the top two candidates, he or she will receive more votes when voters respond to the poll by voting for one or the other of these candidates. The possibility that the Condorcet winner might not be first in the poll, but win after the poll is announced, shows that the plurality winner may not be the Condorcet winner. Some argue that the Condorcet winner is always the "proper" winner, but others counter that a non-Condorcet winner who is, say, everybody's second-most-preferred candidate is a better social choice than a 51%-Condorcet winner who is ranked last by the other 49%.

30. *C* will defeat *A* by 7 votes to 5 votes. This is a desirable result if one believes that the Condorcet winner is always a desirable social choice. But because the 2 class IV voters rank *C* last, and *A* is not ranked last by any voters, *A* may be considered a more desirable "compromise" choice.

31. *D* is the Condorcet winner. It is strange in the sense that a poll that identifies either the top two or the top three candidates would not include *D*.

32. The poll will identify *A* and *B* as the top two candidates. Because the class III and class IV voters prefer *B* to *A*, *B* will defeat *A* by 6 votes to 4 votes.

33. *A* would win with 4 votes to 3 votes for *B* and 3 votes for *C*. It is strange that the number of top contenders identified by a poll can result in opposite outcomes (*A* in this exercise, whereas *B* defeats *A* when only two top contenders are identified by a poll, as in Exercise 32).

34. *A* defeats *B* by 6 votes to 3, *B* defeats *C* by 7 votes to 2, but *C* defeats *A* by 5 votes to 4, so there is Condorcet winner. *A* (4 votes) and *B* (3 votes) are distinguished by the poll; because the 2 class III voters prefer *A* to *B*, *A* will defeat *B* by 6 votes to 3 after the poll is announced. The fact that class II and III voters prefer *C* to *A* might suggest that the choice of *A* is unfair. On the other hand, *whichever* candidate is selected, there is a majority of voters who prefer another candidate because of the absence of a Condorcet winner. When majorities "cycle" in this manner, every outcome might be considered unfair—there is no candidate who is the indisputable majority choice.

35. Assume a voter votes for just a second choice. It is evident that voting for a first choice, too, can never result in a worse outcome and may sometimes result in a better outcome (if the voter's vote for a first choice causes that candidate to be elected).

36. Assume that the voting of all other voters creates a tie for first place between your two most-preferred candidates, with your least-preferred candidate "out of the running." Clearly, voting for your single most-preferred candidate is better than voting for your two most-preferred candidates, because your vote for your single most-preferred candidate would break the tie and elect him or her.

37. Following the hint, the voter's vote for a first and third choice would elect either *A* or *C*. If the voter also voted for *B*, then it is possible that if *A* and *B* are tied for first place, then *B* might be elected when the tie is broken, whereas voting for just *A* and *C* in this situation would elect *A*.

38. No. A vote for a worst choice may help in electing this candidate, which is never something one would want to do.

39. No. Voting for a first choice can never hurt this candidate and may help elect him or her.

40. Because a Condorcet winner is preferred by a majority to every other candidate, he or she must get more approval votes than any other candidate when voters choose their dominant strategies of voting for all candidates in their preferred subsets. Since the Condorcet candidate is in more preferred subsets, the approval-vote winner must be more preferred than any other candidate.

41. No. If class I and II voters vote for all candidates in their preferred subsets, they create a three-way tie among *A*, *B*, and *C*. To break this tie, it would be rational for the class III voter to vote for both *D* and *C* and so elect *C*, whom this voter prefers to both *A* and *B*. But now class I voters will be unhappy, because *C* is a worst choice. However, these voters cannot bring about a preferred outcome by voting for candidates different from *A* and B.

42. After the class III voter switches, the new poll will indicate *A* and *C* to be the top two candidates, with 3 approval votes each. But no voters will have any incentive to switch from voting for *A* or *C*, so this result will hold after all subsequent polls. In fact, neither of these candidates is preferred by a majority to the other, so both might be considered desirable social choices.

43. Without polling, *A* in case (i), *D* in case (ii), and *B* and *D* in case (iii); with polling, *B* in case (i), *D* in case (ii), and *D* in case (iii).

44. Approval voting seems more likely to find Condorcet winners without polling, but with polling it is difficult to say.

45. Exactly half the votes, or 9.5 votes each.

46. If the Democrat ignores the smallest state and makes proportional allocations to the two largest states, the allocations will be 43.75 units to the 7-voter state and 56.25 units to the 9-voter state. The Republican's optimal response will also be 0 units to the 3-voter state and proportional allocations to the other two states.

47. Substitute into the formula for r_i, in Exercise 46, $d_i = (n_i / N) D$ and $D = R$. The proportional rule is "strategy-proof" in the sense that if one player follows it, the other player can do no better than to follow it. Hence, knowing that an opponent is following the proportional rule does not help a player optimize against it by doing anything except also following it.

48. No, because the formula for r_i, given in Exercise 46, says that proportionality is still optimal when $R \neq D$. However, it is optimal to concentrate one's resources on the two smaller states, which have a majority, in order to maximize one's probability of winning a majority of votes in these two states. In particular, if the Democrat has only half the resources of the Republican, the Democrat can almost match the Republican's expenditures in these two states when the Republican allocates proportionally over all three states.

49. To win in states with more than half the votes, any two states will do. Thus, there is no state to which a candidate should not consider allocating resources. In the absence of information about what one's opponent is doing, all states that receive allocations should receive equal allocations since all states are equally valuable for winning.

50. In the absence of information about what one's opponent is doing, all states that receive allocations should receive equal allocations since all states are equally valuable for winning. But only two of the three states should be targeted for allocations; which two should be determined randomly. Then minimal-winning majorities of voters in each targeted state should be chosen randomly; the state allocations should be divided equally among all members of the minimal-winning majority selected.

51. The Democrat can win the election by winning in any two states or in all three. The first three expressions in the formula for PWE_D give the probabilities of winning in the three possible pairs of states, whereas the final expression gives the probability of winning in all three states.

52. For candidates who desire to win, PWE_D is better, but its maximization does not give a formula as simple as the 3/2's rule. To maximize PWE_D, it is best to choose states with a minimal-winning majority of electoral votes randomly and then allocate resources disproportionally to the larger states in this set, as in the case of the 3/2's rule. However, this strategy, if chosen by both candidates, yields only a local maximum.

53. Yes, but in a complicated way. Intuitively, the large states that are more pivotal, and whose citizens therefore have more voting power (as shown in Chapter 11), are more deserving of greater resources (as shown in this chapter).

Word Search Solution

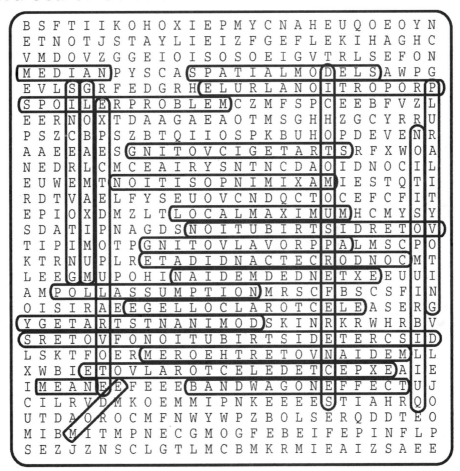

Chapter 13
Fair Division

Chapter Outline

Introduction

Chapter Summary

The *fair-division problem* is to divide a collection of goods among several players in such a way that each player perceives that he or she has received a fair and unbiased share of the goods. Such problems arise often, whether in dividing an estate among heirs or in cutting the cake at a child's birthday party. The fair-division problem is considered for two different cases: the continuous case, in which the goods are finely divisible, and the discrete case, in which the goods are essentially indivisible. The methods discussed involve only the players themselves.

Examples involving cake cutting are particularly apt in the continuous case. For two players, a good method is to have one player cut and the other choose. This method achieves a fair division, provided: (1) either player can cut the cake so that either piece is acceptable to that player; and (2) given any division, the player choosing will find at least one piece acceptable.

A similar method, *lone-divider*, extends "cut-and-choose" reasoning to the three-player case. One player cuts the cake into three pieces and the other two indicate which pieces they find acceptable. A problem arises only if the second and third players agree that just one of the pieces is acceptable. In this case, one of the unacceptable pieces is given to the cutter (who feels that they are *all* equal), the two remaining pieces are reassembled, and we are back to the case of a two-player division.

An alternative multiple player scheme is *last-diminisher*. One player cuts what he or she considers a fair piece. In turn, the other players can pass the piece on or diminish its size. The piece goes to the last player to diminish it. The remaining players repeat the process until all are served.

In 1949, Hugo Steinhaus proved that, for any size group of players, there is a fair-division scheme that is envy-free; that is, each player has a strategy that guarantees him a piece at least as large as any other player's (as each player perceives the allocations), no matter what the other players do. In 1992, Steven Brams and Alan Taylor actually devised such a method for three or more players.

The discrete case is treated in the context of divorce and estate settlement. In the *Adjusted Winner Procedure* each party starts with 100 points and bids on each item.

Initially, each item is allocated to the highest bidder. If each party has received the same total number of points, the process stops. If, however, they differ, then assets (or portions thereof) are transferred in order to equalize the number of points each receives.

For estate settlement, which may involve many heirs and unequal shares, an auction scheme has been devised by *Knaster*. Each heir fixes his estimate of the value of the estate by bidding on the items in it. The fair share of each heir is determined from the sum of his or her bids. Surplus value in the estate is divided among the heirs in accordance with the share to which each is entitled. An interesting feature of this scheme is that each heir receives value greater than the fair share expected, based on his or her valuation of the estate. Modifications of this scheme are discussed in the chapter exercises. Trimming (or diminishing) procedures can be introduced into this scheme if the estate has a large amount of cash or many small objects, thus providing a component of the estate that is essentially finely divisible.

Another method involves taking turns, in which the participants alternately choose items from the estate. While this method is easy to understand and implement, it leads to a considerable amount of strategic planning and insincere choices, based upon each participant's knowledge of the preferences of his opponent. For example, one of the players may initially pass over his first choice if he knows that his opponent does not care for that item and is unlikely to choose it.

Skill Objectives

1. Describe the goal of a fair-division problem.

2. Define the term "player".

3. Define the set-theoretic term "partition" and describe its application to a fair-division problem.

4. List three different categories of fair-division problems.

5. Explain what is meant by a continuous case, fair-division problem and give an example.

6. List two approaches to solving a continuous case, fair-division problem.

7. Explain what is meant by a discrete case, fair-division problem and give an example.

8. Describe a method for solving a discrete case, fair-division problem.

9. Calculate a discrete, fair division for a small number of players and objects when:

    a. each player has an equal share;

    b. the players all have different shares.

Teaching Tips

1. To explain fair division of discrete objects, start with the case of two people and one object using an appropriate chart. Add a second object to the problem and rework it. Finally, go to the case of three people and three objects. The students should be able to do any problem now.

2. As an extra-credit exercise, students can write an original narrative describing a fair allocation problem that has affected their personal relationships, describe how the allocation was determined at the time, and then apply the methods of this chapter to calculate a fair division.

Research Paper

Steven J. Brams and Alan D. Taylor are two of the authors of your text. Have students investigate their contributions to fair division and cake cutting via research on the Internet. Other mathematical figures, such as D. Marc Kilgour and Francis E. Su, have contributions in this area. An interesting website for students to investigate is http://www.math.hmc.edu/~su/fairdivision. There is a fair division calculator applet and other useful links.

Collaborative Learning

Fair Division—The Cake Problem

Two people wish to divide a cake in such a way that each of them feels that he or she has received at least one-half of the cake. An old method for doing this is for one of the people to cut the cake into what he or she perceives as two equal pieces, and the second person chooses the piece that he or she thinks is larger.

Now suppose that three people wish to divide a cake in such a way that each of them feels that he or she has received at least one-third of the cake. Devise a procedure to accomplish this.

Fair Division—The Inheritance Problem

Eccentric, but *very* rich Aunt Millie died recently, leaving a rather peculiar estate and will. Her liquid assets (approximately $20,000,000) go to a local hospital. Her mansion and surrounding 30 acres are to be turned into a home for animals, and her stretch limousine will be used for taking homeless people to shelters. Aside from clothing (bought in thrift shops) and some worthless costume jewelry, the following are the only remaining items of value:

• Babe Ruth's rookie card, with his signature

• A Ming vase

• The first printed edition of Euclid's *Elements*

• The original score of Beethoven's Ninth Symphony

• Ringo Starr's drums that he played in the first Beatles' concert

Bob, Ann, and Tom will inherit these items. However, there are some catches:

1. Under the terms of the will, *nothing* can be sold.

2. The three of you will inherit equal portions.

3. Since Aunt Millie accumulated her huge estate through frugality, she won't allow you to waste any money on appraisers. In other words, you'll have to devise a method for dividing these five items equally without professional help.

Now, the problem facing you is that you don't agree on the value of the items. These are the values that you attach to them:

	Bob	Ann	Tom
Ruth's card	$6,000	$3,000	$5,000
Ming vase	$5,000	$13,000	$10,000
Euclid	$7,000	$11,000	$13,000
Beethoven	$9,000	$15,000	$12,000
Ringo	$12,000	$6,000	$11,000

Can you devise a procedure that will satisfy everyone? That is, try to find a method of division under which everyone believes that he or she has obtained at least a fair share. (Note: Although nothing may be sold, money may change hands among the heirs.)

Fair Division—The Roommate Problem

Bob and Tom shared an apartment for their four college years, and accumulated a number of items that they want to keep. The problem is that both of them would like to have these items. They devise the following procedure for dividing the items fairly.

The roommates are each given 100 points, and they can place as many of these points as they wish on the individual items.

Item	Bob's points	Tom's points
Encyclopedia	20	25
Easy chair	15	10
Painting	30	25
Rug	20	15
Kitchen set	15	25

It is logical to give each item to the person who values it most. However, if we do that, then the roommates will end up with different point totals. Can you figure out a way to equalize the point totals?

Solutions

Skills Check:

1. a   2. b   3. a   4. b   5. d   6. c   7. b   8. c   9. b   10. c

11. b   12. c   13. a   14. a   15. b   16. c   17. a   18. b   19. b   20. a

Exercises:

1. Donald initially receives the Palm Beach mansion (40 points) and the Trump Tower triplex (38 points) for a total of 78 points. Ivana initially receives the Connecticut estate (38 points) and the Trump Plaza apartment (30 points) for a total of 68 points. Because Ivana has fewer points than Donald, she receives the cash and jewelry (on which they both placed 2 points) bringing her total to 70 points. As Donald still has more points (78 to 70), we begin transferring items from him to her. To determine the order of transfer, we must calculate the point ratios of the items that Donald now has.

    The point ratio of the Palm Beach mansion is $\frac{40}{20} = 2.0$.

    The point ratio of the Trump Tower triplex is $\frac{38}{10} = 3.8$.

    Because $2.0 < 3.8$, the first item to be transferred is the Palm Beach mansion. However, if all of it were given to Ivana, her point total would rise to $70 + 20 = 90$, and Donald's point total would fall to $78 - 40 = 38$. This means that only a fraction of the Palm Beach mansion will be transferred from Donald to Ivana.

    Let x be the fraction of the Palm Beach mansion that Donald retains, and let $1 - x$ be the fraction of it that is given to Ivana. To equalize point totals, x must satisfy $38 + 40x = 70 + 20(1 - x)$. Thus, using algebra to solve this equation yields the following.

    $$38 + 40x = 70 + 20 - 20x$$
    $$38 + 40x = 90 - 20x$$
    $$60x = 52$$
    $$x = \tfrac{52}{60}$$
    $$x = \tfrac{13}{15}$$

    Thus Donald receives the Trump Tower triplex and $\frac{13}{15}$ (about 87%) ownership of the Palm Beach mansion for a total of about 72.7 of his points, and Ivana gets the rest (for about 72.7 of her points).

2. Calvin initially receives the cannon (10), the sword (15), the cannon ball (5), the wooden leg (2), the flag (10) and the crow's nest (2) for a total of 44 points. Hobbes initially receives the anchor (20), the unopened chest (20), the doubloon (14), and the figurehead (30) for a total of 84 points. To determine the order of transfer, we must calculate the point ratios of the items that Hobbes has.

    The point ratio of the anchor is $\frac{20}{10} = 2.0$.

    The point ratio of the unopened chest is $\frac{20}{15} = 1.33$.

    The point ratio of the doubloon is $\frac{14}{11} = 1.27$.

    The point ratio of the figurehead is $\frac{30}{20} = 1.5$.

    Continued on next page

2. (continued)

The first item to be transferred is the doubloon because it has the lowest point ratio. Calvin's point total now becomes $44 + 11 = 55$, and Hobbes's point total now becomes $84 - 14 = 70$. Because the transfer of the unopened chest would result in Calvin having more points than Hobbes, this is the one item they will have to split or share. Let x be the fraction of the unopened chest that Hobbes retains, and let $1-x$ be the fraction of it that goes to Calvin. To equalize point totals, x must satisfy $50 + 20x = 55 + 15(1-x)$.

Thus, using algebra to solve this equation yields the following.
$$50 + 20x = 55 + 15 - 15x$$
$$50 + 20x = 70 - 15x$$
$$35x = 20$$
$$x = \tfrac{20}{35}$$
$$x = \tfrac{4}{7}$$

Thus Hobbes keeps $\tfrac{4}{7}$ (about 57%) of the unopened chest, and Calvin gets $\tfrac{3}{7}$ (about 43%) of it.

All in all, Calvin gets the cannon, the doubloon, the sword, the cannon ball, the wooden leg, the flag, the crow's nest, and 43% of the unopened chest for a total of 61.4 of his points. Hobbes gets the rest.

3. Mike initially gets his way on the room party policy (50), the cleanliness issue (6), and lights-out time (10) for a total of 66 points. Phil initially gets his way on the stereo level issue (22), smoking rights (20), phone time (8), and the visitor policy (5) for a total of 55 points. Because Phil has fewer points that Mike, he gets his way on the alcohol use issue, on which they both placed 15 points, bringing his total to 70. To determine the order of transfer (from Phil to Mike), we must calculate the point ratios of the issues on which Phil got his way.

Point ratio of the stereo level issue is $\tfrac{22}{4} = 5.5$.

Point ratio of the smoking rights issue is $\tfrac{20}{10} = 2.0$.

Point ratio of the alcohol issue is $\tfrac{15}{15} = 1.0$.

Point ratio of the phone time issue is $\tfrac{8}{1} = 8.0$.

Point ratio of the visitor policy issue is $\tfrac{5}{4} = 1.25$.

The first issue to be transferred is the alcohol issue, because it has the lowest point ratio. However, if all of it were given to Mike, his point total would rise to $66 + 15 = 81$, and Phil's point total would fall to $70 - 15 = 55$. This means that only a fraction of the alcohol issue will be transferred from Phil to Mike.

Let x be the fraction of the alcohol issues that Phil retains, and let $1-x$ be the fraction of it that is given to Mike. To equalize point totals, x must satisfy $55 + 15x = 66 + 15(1-x)$.

Thus, using algebra to solve this equation yields the following.
$$55 + 15x = 66 + 15 - 15x$$
$$55 + 15x = 81 - 15x$$
$$30x = 26$$
$$x = \tfrac{26}{30}$$
$$x = \tfrac{13}{15}$$

Thus, Phil gets his way on the stereo level issue, the smoking rights issue, the phone time issue, the visitor policy issue, and $\tfrac{13}{15}$ (about 87%) of his way on the alcohol issue for a total of 68 points. Mike gets his way on the rest.

4. Labor initially gets its way on the benefits issue (35) and the issue of vacation time (15) for a total of 50 points, while management gets its way on the base salary issue (50) and salaries (40) for a total of 90 points. To determine the order of transfer, we must calculate the point ratios of the issues on which management got its way.

The point ratio of the base salary issue is $\frac{50}{30} = 1.67$.

The point ratio of the salary increase issues is $\frac{40}{20} = 2.0$.

The first issue to be transferred is the base salary issue, because it has the lowest point ratio. But if all of it were transferred, labor would then have more points than management. Let x be the fraction of the base salary issue that management retains. To equalize point totals, x must satisfy $40 + 50x = 50 + 30(1 - x)$.

Thus, using algebra to solve this equation yields the following.

$$40 + 50x = 50 + 30 - 30x$$
$$40 + 50x = 80 - 30x$$
$$80x = 40$$
$$x = \frac{40}{80}$$
$$x = \frac{1}{2}$$

Thus management gets its way on the salary increase issue and 50% of its way on the base salary issue for a total of 65 points. Labor gets its way on the rest.

5. – 6. Answers will vary.

7. Allocation 1:
   (a) Not proportional: Bob gets 10% in his eyes.
   (b) Not envy-free: Bob, for example, envies Carol.
   (c) Not equitable: Bob thinks he got 10% and Carol thinks she got 40%.
   (d) Example: Give Bob X, Carol Y, and Ted Z.

Allocation 2:
   (a) Not proportional: Carol gets 30% in her eyes.
   (b) Not envy-free: Carol, for example, envies Bob.
   (c) Not equitable: Bob thinks he got 50% and Carol thinks she got 30%.
   (d) Example: Give Bob Y, Carol X, and Ted Z.

Allocation 3:
   (a) Not proportional: Carol and Ted get 0% in their eyes.
   (b) Not envy-free: Carol and Ted envy Bob.
   (c) Not equitable: Bob thinks he got 100% and Carol thinks she got 0%.
   (d) It is Pareto optimal – for Carol or Ted to get anything, Bob will have to get less.

Allocation 4:
   (a) Not proportional: Carol gets 30% in her eyes.
   (b) Not envy-free: Carol, for example, envies Bob.
   (c) Not equitable: Bob thinks he got 50% and Carol thinks she got 30%.

Allocation 5:
   (a) It is proportional.
   (b) Not envy-free: Bob, for example, envies Carol.
   (c) It is equitable.

8. Mary gets the car and places $\frac{32,100}{2} = 16,050$ in a kitty. John takes out $\frac{28,225}{2} = 14,112.50$. The remaining $16,050 - 14,112.50 = 1,937.50$ is split equally. The net effect of this is that Mary receives the car and pays John $15,081.25.

9. They handle the car first, as in Exercise #8. Then Mary gets the house and places $\frac{59,100}{2} = 29,550$ in a kitty. John takes out $\frac{55,900}{2} = 27,950$ and they split the remaining $29,550 - 27,950 = 1,600$ equally. Thus, for the house, Mary gets it and gives John $28,750. In total, Mary gets both the car and the house and pays John $15,081.25 + \$28,750 = \$43,831.25$.

10. Answers will vary.

11. First, C gets the house and places two-thirds of 165,000 (i.e., 110,000) in a kitty. A then withdraws one-third of 145,000 (i.e., 48,333) and B withdraws one-third of 149,999 (i.e., 50,000). They divide the remaining 11,667 equally among the three of them.

Second, A gets the farm and places two-thirds of 135,000 (i.e., 90,000) in a kitty. B then withdraws one-third of 130,001 (i.e., 43,334) and C withdraws one-third of 128,000 (i.e., 42,667). They divide the remaining 3,999 equally among the three of them.

Third, C gets the sculpture and deposits two-thirds of 127,000 (i.e., 84,667) in a kitty. A then withdraws one-third of 110,000 (i.e., 36,667) and B withdraws one-third of 80,000 (i.e., 26,667). They divide the remaining 21,333 equally among them.

Thus, A gets the farm and receives $52,222 + \$43,778$ and pays $44,667 + \$44,000$, so A, in total, receives the farm plus $7,333. Similarly, B receives $132,334 and C receives both the house and the sculpture, while paying $139,667.

12. First, E receives the Duesenberg and deposits $12,000, and then F and G each withdraw $5,000. They divide the remaining $2,000 equally among the three of them.

Second, F receives the Bentley and deposits $16,000, and then E withdraws $6,000 and G withdraws $6,667. They divide the remaining $3,333 equally among the three of them.

Third, G receives the Ferrari and deposits $11,000, and then E withdraws $5,333 and F withdraws $4,000. They divide the remaining $1,667 equally among the three of them.

Fourth, F receives the Pierce-Arrow and deposits $10,000, and then E withdraws $4,667 and G withdraws $4,500. They divide the remaining $833 equally among the three of them.

Fifth, E receives the Cord and deposits $16,000, and then F withdraws $6,000 and G withdraws $7,333. They divide the remaining $2,667 equally among the three of them.

For the final resolution, E receives the Duesenberg and Cord and pays $8,500, F receives the Bentley and Pierce-Arrow and pays $7,500, and G receives the Ferrari plus $16,000.

13. The bottom-up strategy fills in the blanks as follows:

Bob:	investments		car		CD player
Carol:		boat		television		washer-dryer

Thus, Bob first chooses the investments, and the final allocation has him also receiving the car and the CD player.

14. The bottom-up strategy fills in the blanks as follows:

Carol:	investments		boat		washer-dryer	
Bob:		car		television		CD player

Thus, Carol first chooses the investments, and the final allocation has her also receiving the boat and the washer-dryer.

15. The bottom-up strategy fills in the blanks as follows:

Mark:	tractor		truck		tools	
Fred:		boat		car		motorcycle

Thus, Mark first chooses the tractor, and the final allocation has him also receiving the truck and the tools.

16. The bottom-up strategy fills in the blanks as follows:

Fred:	boat		car		motorcycle	
Mark:		tractor		truck		tools

Thus, Fred first chooses the boat, and the final allocation has him also receiving the car and the motorcycle.

17. The bottom-up strategy fills in the blanks as follows (CT stands for Connecticut):

Donald:	mansion		triplex		cash and jewelry
Ivana:		CT estate		apartment	

Thus, Donald first chooses the Palm Beach mansion, and the final allocation has him also receiving the Trump Tower triplex and the cash and jewelry.

18. The bottom-up strategy fills in the blanks as follows (CT stands for Connecticut):

Ivana:	CT estate		apartment		cash and jewelry
Donald:		mansion		triplex	

Thus, Ivana first chooses the Connecticut estate, and the final allocation has her also receiving the Trump Plaza apartment and the cash and jewelry.

19. The chooser. As divider, I'd get exactly 50% (or risk getting less). As chooser, I have a guarantee of getting at least 50% and the possibility (depending on the division) of getting more than 50%.

20. One way is to have Bob divide the cake into four pieces and to let Carol choose any three. Another is to have Bob divide the cake into two pieces and then let Carol choose one. Then they can do divide-and-choose on the piece that Carol did not choose.

21. (a) Bob gets a piece whose value to him is 9 units (assuming that Bob is the divider), and Carol gets a piece whose value to her is 12 units.

    (b) Carol gets a piece whose value to her is 9 units (assuming that Carol is the divider), and Ted gets a piece whose value to him is 15 units.

22. (a) Bob should be the divider. That way, he can get 12 units of value instead of 9 units of value.

(b) Here, Bob knows the preferences of the other party. In Exercise 19, we assumed that the divider didn't know the preferences of the other party.

23. (a) See figures below.

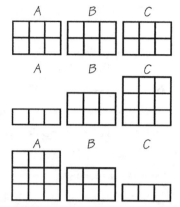

(b) Player 2 finds B acceptable (6 square units) and C acceptable (9 square units). Player 3 finds A acceptable (9 square units) and B acceptable (6 square units).

(c) Player 3 chooses A (9 square units). Player 2 chooses C (9 square units). Player 1 chooses B (6 square units). Yes, there is another order. Player 2 chooses C (9 square units). Player 3 chooses A (9 square units). Player 1 chooses B (6 square units).

24. (a) See figures below.

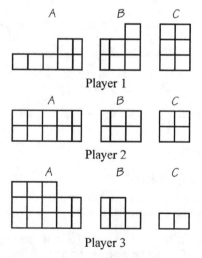

(b) Player 2 finds A acceptable (9 square units), but not B (5 square units) or C (4 square units). Player 3 finds A acceptable (12 square units), but not B (4 square units) or C (2 square units).

(c) Players 2 and 3 both find B and C unacceptable. (C is on the right.)

Continued on next page

24. (continued)

(d) (i) Assume C is given to Player 1. If Player 2 cuts the rest, he will make each piece 7 square units. Player 3 will choose the leftmost piece, which he thinks is 10 square units. Thus, Player 1 gets a piece he thinks is 6 square units. Player 2 gets a piece he thinks is 7 square units, and Player 3 gets a piece he thinks is 10 square units.

(ii) If Player 3 cuts the rest, she will make each piece 8 square units. (This requires a vertical cut two-thirds of the way across the third triple of squares.) Player 2 will choose the rightmost piece, which she thinks is $8\frac{2}{3}$ square units. Thus, Player 1 gets a piece she thinks is 6 square units, Player 2 gets a piece she thinks is $8\frac{2}{3}$ square units, and Player 3 gets a piece she thinks is 8 square units.

25. (a) See figure below.

(b) Player 2 will further trim the piece:

in Player 2's eyes.

(c) Player 3 will further trim the piece:

in Player 3's eyes.

(d) Player 3 receives it, and thinks it is 6 units of value. The one leaving with the first piece always thinks it is one-nth of the value with n players.

(e) Assume Player 1 is the divider. He sees it as 16 units of value, and he divides it as follows:

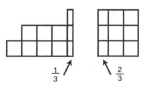

Player 2 chooses the piece on the left, which he sees as follows:

(f) Assume Player 2 is the divider. He sees it as 14 units of value, and he divides it as follows:

Player 1 chooses the piece on the right, which he sees as follows:

26. (a) Ted thinks he is getting at least one-third of the piece that Bob initially received and at least one-third of the piece that Carol initially received. Thus, Ted thinks he is getting at least one-third of part of the cake (Bob's piece) plus one-third of the rest of the cake (Carol's piece).

   (b) Bob gets to keep exactly two-thirds (in his own view) of the piece that he initially received and thought was at least of size one-half. Two-thirds times one-half equals one-third.

   (c) If, for example, Ted thinks the "half" Carol initially gets is worthless, then Ted may wind up thinking that he (Ted) has only slightly more than one-third of the cake, while Bob has (in Ted's view) almost two-thirds of the cake. In such a case, Ted will envy Bob.

27. Bob, Carol, and Ted each divide the piece he or she has in four parts (equal in his or her own estimation). Alice then chooses one of Bob's four pieces, one of Carol's four pieces, and one of Ted's four pieces.

28. (a) If a player follows the suggested strategy, then clearly he or she will receive a piece of size exactly one-fourth *if* he or she does, in fact, call cut at some point. How could a player (Bob, for example) fail to call cut when using this strategy? Only if each of the other three players "preempted" Bob by calling cut before he did each time the knife was set in motion. But this means that each of the other three is left with a piece that Bob considered to be of size less than one-fourth. Hence, when the other three players have left with their shares, there is, in Bob's view, over one-fourth of the cake left for him.

   (b) If you call cut first – and thus exit the game with a piece of size exactly one-fourth in your estimation – you will envy the next player to receive a piece *if* no one calls cut until the next piece is larger than one-fourth in your estimation.

   (c) If there are four players and the first player has exited with his or her piece, then you could wait to call cut until the knife reaches the point where one-half of the original cake is left. Alternatively, you could wait until the knife passed over one-third of what was left.

29. (a) See figures below.

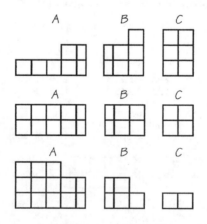

   (b) See figures below.

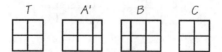

   (c) Player 3 will choose A (which he thinks is of size 6 square units). Player 2 will choose B (which he thinks is of size 5 square units). Player 1 will receive C (which he thinks is of size 6 square units). The proviso does not come into Play (since Player 3 took the trimmed piece).

30. (a) The knife on the left would be at the point where the other knife started. (Thus, the portion between the knives would be the complement of the piece *A*.)

(b) If, for example, Carol thinks the portion between the knives at the beginning (i.e., piece *A*) is of size less than one-half, then she definitely will think the portion between the two knives at the end (i.e., the complement of piece *A*) is of size greater than one-half. Because this portion of cake between the two knives goes from being of size less than one-half in her estimation to being of size greater than one-half in her estimation, there must be a point where it is of size exactly one-half in her estimation. An analogous argument applies if Carol thinks that *A* is of size greater than one-half.

Word Search Solution

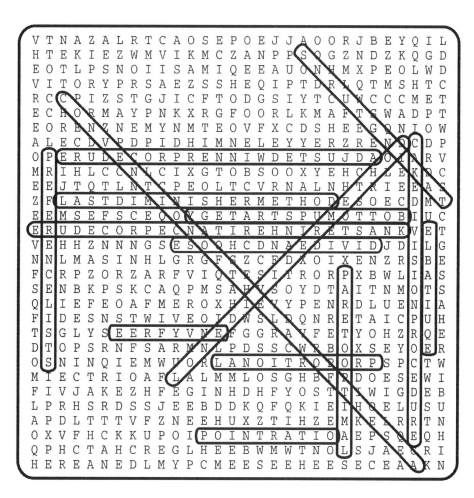

Chapter 14
Apportionment

Chapter Outline

Introduction
Section 14.1   The Apportionment Problem
Section 14.2   The Hamilton Method
Section 14.3   Divisor Methods
Section 14.4   Which Divisor Method is Best?

Chapter Summary

The apportionment problem is to round a set of fractions so that their sum is maintained at a constant value. This problem occurs in several contexts, among them the apportioning of representative bodies such as the United States House of Representatives. Following the ideal of proportional representation, the number of House seats (quota) to which a state is entitled is unlikely to be a whole number. This fact necessitates rounding these quotas to obtain apportionments whose sum is 435, the current number of seats in the House.

Methods of apportionment differ in how they compute quotas and then obtain apportionments. The Hamilton method determines the quota for a state by determining the fraction of the U.S. population that resides in that state and setting the quota equal to that fraction of 435. Apportionment takes place in two stages. First, each state is assigned a number of seats equal to the integer part of its quota. Second, seats unapportioned are assigned to states, one seat per state, based on the size of the fractional part of the state's quota. The state with the largest fractional part gets the first unassigned seat, the state with the next largest fraction the second seat, and so on until all seats are assigned. Note that some states will fail to get an extra seat in this second stage.

Three other procedures that have been used to apportion the House of Representatives are divisor methods. These methods, proposed by Jefferson, Webster, and Hill-Huntington, divide each state's population by a fixed number d to determine the state's modified quota. One may think of d as the average size of a congressional district. But a choice of d, which may not be unique, is determined by the House size and the manner in which the particular appointment method rounds its fractions.

A trial-and-error method for determining d starts with a value of d obtained by dividing the U.S. population by 435, the current House size. This value of d can then be raised or lowered depending on whether the resulting apportionment exceeds or falls short of 435. A systematic way of determining a decisive value of d is by calculating the critical divisors for each state.

The three methods round fractions in different ways. In the Jefferson method, all of the fractions are rounded down, and if the total number of seats apportioned totals 435, then d is a decisive divisor for this method, and the procedure terminates. In the Webster method, fractions are rounded up or down in the usual way. The Hill-Huntington method, which has been in use since 1940, is slightly more complicated; the cutoff point for rounding up is not

0.5 as in Webster, but depends on the state's modified quota. If the integer part of this quota is n, then the cutoff point is $\sqrt{n(n-1)}$, the geometric mean of n and $n-1$. For example, if the modified quota of a state is between 7 and 8, then it will receive eight seats if this quota exceeds $\sqrt{7 \times 8} \approx 7.4833$. Otherwise, it receives just seven seats.

There are several conditions that a good apportionment method should satisfy, three of which are pertinent to our discussion: (1) quota condition: requires that a state's apportionment be equal to the integer part of the state's quota, or to the integer part plus 1; (2) house monotone condition: an increase in House size cannot cause a state's apportionment to go down; (3) population monotone condition: if a state's population increases while all other populations remain constant, then the state's apportionment should not go down.

Hamilton's method satisfies (1) but not (2) (Alabama paradox). The work of Balinski and Young establishes that (2) and (3) are satisfied by divisor methods only. Unfortunately, every divisor method will violate (1) under certain circumstances (Webster's method is least likely to). Thus, there is no "perfect" apportionment method. However, each divisor method minimizes some measure of inequity in apportionment and so the choice of apportionment method becomes essentially a political decision.

Skill Objectives

1. State the apportionment problem.

2. Explain the difference between quota and apportionment.

3. State the quota condition and be able to tell which apportionment methods satisfy it and which do not.

4. Do the same for the house monotone and population monotone conditions.

5. Know that some methods have bias in favor of large or small states.

6. Recognize the difference in computing quotas between the Hamilton method and divisor methods.

7. Calculate the apportionment of seats in a representative body when the individual population sizes and number of seats are given, using the methods of Hamilton, Jefferson, Webster, and Hill-Huntington.

8. Be able to give at least three reasons to support the claim that Webster's method is the "best" apportionment method.

9. Calculate the critical divisor for each state.

Teaching Tips

1. The apportionment of the U.S. House of Representatives can be discussed and results given. One might not want to do the whole House in class, but a few states can be treated and the results given. Spreadsheet software can be used to compute apportionments using various methods and various divisors.

2. When using Hamilton's method, the number of seats unapportioned after the first stage is always less than the number of states. This is due to the fact that this number of seats is the sum of fifty fractional parts, each of which is less than one.

3. Emphasize how the value of the divisor d is changed based on how the apportionment turns out. If the apportionment is too large, the value of d should be increased (to decrease quotas). Similarly, if the apportionment is too small, the value of d should be decreased.

4. Students often find methods of rounding other than the standard one unnatural. It may take some time for them to become comfortable with these new rounding rules. Examples can help.

5. One can find support for rounding fractions as in the Jefferson method in the wording of Article 1 of the U.S. Constitution: ". . .The number of Representatives shall not exceed one for every thirty thousand."

6. Emphasize to the students that the meaning of the word "quota" in this chapter is very different from that in Chapter 11. Students have a tendency to confuse these two uses of the same term.

7. In the previous editions of the book, the search for a decisive divisor in the methods of Jefferson, Webster, and Hill-Huntington was carried out by trial-and-error. In the current edition, a systematic calculation is performed using critical divisors for each state. However, this computation is not trivial, and many students may prefer to use the trial-and-error approach.

Research Paper

Investigating the lives and contributions of Michel L. Balinsky and H. Peyton Young may be of interest to students. There is historical background to complement that given in the text. Interpreting an article such as, "The Apportionment of Representation" by M. L. Balinski and H. P. Young (pp. 1–29, *Fair Allocation, Proceedings of Symposia in Applied Mathematics,* Vol. 3, American Mathematical Society, Providence, RI, 1985) may be of additional interest.

Collaborative Learning

Section Allocation

1 You are chairman of the Mathematics Department of a small high school. Registrations for the coming year are as follows:

- Algebra   94 students
- Geometry   74 students
- Calculus   32 students

The chairman teaches four sections and the other member of the department teaches five sections. Hence there are a total of nine sections to be allocated among the three subjects. Ask the students to come up with a fair method of deciding how many sections of each subject should be scheduled.

2. After introducing the subject of apportionment and the Hamilton method, but before discussing the various paradoxes, have the students determine the allocation of sections in the previous problem according to Hamilton. After completing this exercise, announce that the chairman has decided to teach a fifth section, so that 10 sections in all are now available. Recompute the Hamilton allocation, and note that the Alabama paradox occurs.

Solutions

Skills Check:

1. c   2. a   3. b   4. a   5. a   6. b   7. c   8. a   9. a   10. b

11. a   12. b   13. c   14. c   15. a   16. b   17. c   18. a   19. c   20. c

Cooperative Learning:

No single answer to Exercise 1. In Exercise 2, with 9 sections the allocation is 4 for Algebra, 3 for Geometry, and 2 for Calculus. With 10 sections, Algebra has 5, Geometry has 4, and Calculus only 1, which is a manifestation of the Alabama paradox.

Exercises:

1. Jane's total expenses are $71. The calculation of the percentages is shown in the table.

	Percentage	rounded
Rent	$\frac{31}{71} \times 100\% = 43.66\%$	44%
Food	$\frac{16}{71} \times 100\% = 22.54\%$	23%
Transportation	$\frac{7}{71} \times 100\% = 9.86\%$	10%
Gym	$\frac{12}{71} \times 100\% = 16.90\%$	17%
Miscellaneous	$\frac{5}{71} \times 100\% = 7.04\%$	7%

The percentages add up to 101%.

2. There are 20 teaching assistants and 1125 students: That is $1125 \div 20 = 56.25$ students per teaching assistant. We obtain the quota for each level by dividing that level's enrollment by 56.25. The results are shown in the following table.

Calculus I	$500 \div 56.25 =$	8.89
Calculus II	$100 \div 56.25 =$	1.78
Calculus III	$350 \div 56.25 =$	6.22
Calculus IV	$175 \div 56.25 =$	3.11
Total		20

Round these quotas to obtain the numbers of teaching assistants assigned to each level of the course.

Calculus I	9
Calculus II	2
Calculus III	6
Calculus IV	3
Total	20

3. The new enrollments are obtained by subtracting from the enrollment of each level the number of students who are moving to a lower level, and add to each the number of students who are moving from a higher level. Here are the calculations.

Calculus I	$500 + 45 =$	545
Calculus II	$100 - 45 + 41 =$	96
Calculus III	$350 - 41 + 12 =$	321
Calculus IV	$175 - 12 =$	163

The total number of students enrolled remains 1125, and the average number of students per teaching assistant is still 56.25. Here are the new quotas.

Calculus I	$545 \div 56.25 =$	9.69
Calculus II	$96 \div 56.25 =$	1.71
Calculus III	$321 \div 56.25 =$	5.71
Calculus IV	$163 \div 56.25 =$	2.90

The new rounded quotas are as follows.

Calculus I	10
Calculus II	2
Calculus III	6
Calculus IV	3
Total	21

This calls for too many teaching assistants, so the numbers must be adjusted. The apportionment methods introduced in this chapter present a variety of approaches to solving this problem.

4. The fractional part of each number is less than 0.50, so all are rounded down as follows.

$$8 + 10 + 12 + 5 + 3 = 38$$

To preserve the sum of 40, we must either add 2 to one of the rounded numbers, or supplement two of the rounded numbers by 1. Apportionment methods provide ways of selecting the amounts to be increased in equitable ways, but each has a different answer to the question, "what is equitable?"

5. Rounding each of the summands down, the sum of the lower quotas is $0 + 1 + 0 + 2 + 2 + 2 = 7$. The three numbers with the greatest fractional parts, 0.99, 1.59, and 2.38, receive their upper quotas. The apportioned sum is $0 + 2 + 1 + 2 + 3 + 2 = 10$.

6. (a) The populations in this apportionment problem are the amounts invested, the seats are the numbers of pearls awarded, and the states are the three friends. The standard divisor is as follows.

$$\$14,900 \div 36 = \$413.89$$

(This is the average price paid for one of the pearls.) Here are the quotas.

Abe	$\$5,900 \div \$413.89 =$	14.255 pearls
Beth	$\$7,600 \div \$413.89 =$	18.363 pearls
Charles	$\$1,400 \div \$413.89 =$	3.383 pearls

The lower quotas, 14, 18, and 3 add up to 35, so one more pearl has to be apportioned. It goes to Charles because his quota has the greatest fractional part. The apportionment is as follows.

Abe	14 pearls
Beth	18 pearls
Charles	4 pearls

Continued on next page

6. continued

    (b) The standard divisor (average cost per pearl) has fallen to $14,900 ÷ 37 = $402.70. Here are the new quotas.

Abe	$5,900 ÷ $402.70 =	14.651 pearls
Beth	$7,600 ÷ $402.70 =	18.873 pearls
Charles	$1,400 ÷ $402.70 =	3.477 pearls

The lower quotas still sum to 35, so we have to give Abe and Beth, whose quotas have the largest fractional parts, their upper quotas. The new apportionment is as follows.

Abe	15 pearls
Beth	19 pearls
Charles	3 pearls

In effect, the newly found pearl goes to Abe, and Charles has to give one of his pearls to Beth.

    (c) This is an instance of the Alabama paradox!

7. The total population is 510,000, so the standard divisor is 510,000 ÷ 102 = 5,000. The quotas are obtained by dividing each state's population by this divisor, obtaining 50.8, 30.6, and 20.6, respectively. The lower quotas add up to 100, so we must increase the apportionment of two states to their upper quotas. The first state, whose quota of 50.8 has the largest fractional part, gets an increase. The fractional parts of the quotas of the remaining two states are both equal to 0.6: they are tied for priority in receiving the last seat. A coin toss is probably the fairest way to settle this dispute.

8. The total population is 97. The number of sections (these are the seats in this apportionment problem) is 5, so the average class size (the standard divisor) is 97 ÷ 5 = 19.4. The quotas are as follows.

Geometry	52 ÷ 19.4 =	2.68 sections
Algebra	33 ÷ 19.4 =	1.70 sections
Calculus	12 ÷ 19.4 =	0.62 sections

The sum of the lower quotas is 3, so we must give two subjects their upper quotas. The subjects with the greatest fractional parts are geometry and algebra. The final apportionment is as follows.

Geometry	3 sections
Algebra	2 sections
Calculus	Cancelled!

9. The total enrollment is 115, and the standard divisor is 23. The quotas are as follows.

Geometry	77 ÷ 23 =	3.35 sections
Algebra	18 ÷ 23 =	0.78 sections
Calculus	20 ÷ 23 =	0.87 sections

The lower quota for geometry is 3, and the other two subjects have 0 lower quotas. Because they have larger fractional parts than geometry, they both receive their upper quotas, 1 each. The apportionment is as follows.

Geometry	3 sections
Algebra	1 section
Calculus	1 section

10. The standard divisor according to the old census is 130,609.62, and with the new census it has increased a little, to 132,517.70. Dividing state populations by these we obtain the following quotas.

State	Old	New
A	42.305	42.693
B	26.569	26.468
C	29.586	29.322
D	1.540	1.517

In each case the lower quotas add up to 98, leaving two seats to be apportioned. In the old census, these go to B and C, but in the new census they go to A and D. The apportionments are given in the following table.

State	Old census	New census
A	42	43
B	27	26
C	30	29
D	1	2
Total	100	100

States B and C had population increases, and decreased apportionments. Although the population of state D decreased slightly, its apportionment increased. This is an example of the population paradox.

11. The states in this apportionment problem are the investors, the seats are the 100 coins, and the populations are the individual investments. Thus, the standard divisor is $10,000 ÷ 100 coins = $100 per coin. The quotas, which represent the number of coins each investor should receive if fractional coins were possible, are obtained by dividing each investment by this divisor.

	Quota	Lower quota
Abe	36.190	36
Beth	18.620	18
Charles	22.580	22
David	20.100	20
Esther	2.510	2
Total	100.00	98

Two investors will receive their upper quotas: Beth and Charles, who have the largest fractions. Here are the apportionments, *before the excise tax was paid.*

Abe	36
Beth	19
Charles	23
David	20
Esther	2
Total	100

When the excise tax is added, populations change, and the standard divisor changes as follows.

$$10,050 ÷ 100 = $100.50 \text{ per coin}$$

We have to recalculate the quotas. The revised investments are divided by the new standard divisor as follows.

	Investment	Quota	Lower quota
Abe	$3,635	36.169	36
Beth	$1,864	18.547	18
Charles	$2,259	22.478	22
David	$2,042	20.318	20
Esther	$250	2.488	2
Total	$10,050	100.000	98

Again, two investors will receive their upper quotas: Beth and Aunt Esther. The final apportionments are as follows.

	Before tax	After tax
Abe	36	36
Beth	19	19
Charles	23	22
David	20	20
Esther	2	3
Total	100	100

So, Aunt Esther not only got a dollar back, but Charles had to give her one of his rare coins! At least it's still in the family. The cause of this confusion is, of course, the **population paradox**.

12. The first census recorded a total population of 230,000, and the second census recorded 232,265. Therefore, the standard divisors (the average number of residents for each of the 100 seats in the legislature) are 2,300 and 2,322.65, respectively. To obtain the quotas, divide each state population by the standard divisor. The result is as follows.

Quotas for two censuses		
	Censuses	
	Last year	This year
Standard Divisor	2,300.00	2,322.65
Province		
Ash	40.570	41.095
Beech	15.590	15.468
Chestnut	17.620	17.468
Date	24.720	24.485
The desert	1.500	1.484

Here are the lower quotas, based on each of the two censuses.

Lower quotas for two censuses		
	Censuses	
Province	Last year	This year
Ash	40	41
Beech	15	15
Chestnut	17	17
Date	24	24
The desert	1	1
Total	97	98

For last year's census, the three provinces with the largest quotas get their upper quotas, because the lower quotas only fill 97 of the 100 seats. Thus, Date, Chestnut and Beech Provinces receive increased apportionments. In this year's census, only two provinces receive their upper quotas: Date and the desert. The resulting apportionments are as follows.

Apportionment according to two censuses		
Province	Last year	This year
Ash	40	41
Beech	16	15
Chestnut	18	17
Date	25	25
The desert	1	2
Total	100	100

There is a paradox: Chestnut province gained population and lost a seat, while the desert lost population and gained a seat. This is an instance of the population paradox.

13. In the following table, the critical divisors and quotas are displayed.

House size	82	83	84	89	90	91
Divisor	220,997	218,334	215,735	203,615	201,353	199,140
				Quotas		
A	25.233	25.540	25.848	27.387	27.694	28.002
B	6.278	6.354	6.431	6.814	6.890	6.967
C	15.087	15.271	15.455	16.375	16.559	16.743
D	33.995	34.410	34.824	36.897	37.312	37.7276
E	1.407	1.424	1.442	1.527	1.544	1.562

The next table displays the lower quotas and their sum for each of the house sizes under consideration.

State			Lower Quotas			
A	25	25	25	27	27	28
B	6	6	6	6	6	6
C	15	15	15	16	16	16
D	33	34	34	36	37	37
E	1	1	1	1	1	1
Total	80	81	81	86	87	88
Shortage	2	2	3	3	3	3

The last row of the above table records the number of seats that still must be apportioned. These seats go to the states whose quotas have the largest fractional parts. The final apportionments are as follows.

State	State Population			Apportionments			
A	5,576,330	25	26	26	27	28	28
B	1,387,342	6	6	6	7	7	7
C	3,334,241	15	15	16	16	17	17
D	7,512,860	34	34	35	37	37	38
E	310,968	2	2	1	2	1	1
Total	18,121,741	82	83	84	89	90	91

The Alabama paradox occurs when the apportionment for the smallest state decreases from 2 to 1 as the house size increases from 83 to 84, and it occurs again as the house size increases from 89 to 90.

14. The Webster method rounds all numbers x with fractional parts ≥ 0.5 up, and numbers x with fractional parts less than 0.5 down. We have to verify that the formula $\lfloor x+0.5 \rfloor$ does the same thing. Let $n = \lfloor x \rfloor$. Thus, x is a number at least n but less than $n+1$. If the fractional part of x is less than 0.5, then $x+0.5$ is still a number between n and $n+1$, and hence $\lfloor x+0.5 \rfloor = n$. If $x \geq n+0.5$, then $x+0.5 \geq n+1$ and hence $\lfloor x+0.5 \rfloor = n+1$. In both cases the formula $\lfloor x+0.5 \rfloor$ agrees with the Webster rounding of x.

15. As with the Hamilton method, we have the following quotas.

Geometry	3.35 sections
Algebra	0.78 sections
Calculus	0.87 sections

The tentative apportionments are geometry, 3; algebra and calculus, 0. The critical divisors are determined by adding 1 to the tentative apportionments and dividing the result into the population of the subject, and are as follows.

Geometry	$77 \div 4 =$	19.25 students
Algebra	$18 \div 1 =$	18 students
Calculus	$20 \div 1 =$	20 students

Calculus has the greatest critical divisor, and its tentative apportionment is now 1. It receives a new critical divisor, $20 \div 2 = 10$. Now the greatest critical divisor is that of geometry, so its apportionment is 4. The house is full, and the Jefferson apportionment is

Geometry	4 sections
Algebra	cancelled!
Calculus	1 section

16. Let's just round off the quotas (found in Exercise 8): 3, 2, and 1 sections for geometry, algebra, and calculus, respectively. These sum to 6, so we have to figure out critical divisors.

Geometry	$52 \div (3-0.5) =$	20.8 students
Algebra	$33 \div (2-0.5) =$	22 students
Calculus	$12 \div (1-0.5) =$	24 students

Geometry has the least critical divisor, so its apportionment is reduced to 2. The final Webster apportionment is as follows.

Geometry	2 sections
Algebra	2 sections
Calculus	1 section

17. All three divisor methods start with the quotas, which were computed in Exercise 6.

	36 pearls	37 pearls
Abe	14.25	14.65
Beth	18.36	18.87
Charles	3.38	3.48

Jefferson method: The tentative apportionments are, for 36 or 37 pearls, Abe, 14; Beth, 18; and Charles, 3. With 36 pearls, 1 is left to be apportioned; with 37 there are 2 left. Here are the critical divisors.

Abe	$\$5,900 \div 15 =$	$\$393.33$
Beth	$\$7,600 \div 19 =$	$\$400.00$
Charles	$\$1,400 \div\ 4 =$	$\$350.00$

The 36th pearl goes to Beth. When the 37th pearl is discovered, there is no need to repeat the calculations. Beth's critical divisor (only) has to be recomputed, because she has another pearl now. Now her critical divisor is $\$7,600 \div 20 = \$380.00$. The highest priority for the 37th pearl goes to Abe. Here are the final Jefferson apportionments.

	36 pearls	37 pearls
Abe	14	15
Beth	19	19
Charles	3	3

Webster method: The tentative apportionments are obtained by rounding the quotas. With 36 pearls, all the quotas are rounded down, so the tentative apportionments add up to 35. We will have to calculate critical divisors to allocate the 36th pearl.

Abe	$\$5,900 \div 14.5 =$	$\$406.90$
Beth	$\$7,600 \div 18.5 =$	$\$410.81$
Charles	$\$1,400 \div\ 3.5 =$	$\$400.00$

Beth, with the greatest critical divisor, gets the 36th pearl. With 37 pearls, Abe's and Beth's quotas are both rounded up, and Charles's is rounded down. These tentative apportionments, 15, 19, and 3, add up to 37. Abe receives the 37th pearl. Here are the final Webster apportionments.

	36 pearls	37 pearls
Abe	14	15
Beth	19	19
Charles	3	3

Hill-Huntington method: The rounding point for numbers between 3 and 4 is $\sqrt{3 \times 4} = 3.464$; for numbers between 14 and 15 it is $\sqrt{210} = 14.491$; and for numbers between 18 and 19 it is $\sqrt{342} = 18.493$. Rounding *a la* Hill-Huntington, we obtain the following tentative apportionments.

	36 pearls	37 pearls
Abe	14	15
Beth	18	19
Charles	3	4
Total	35	38

Continued on next page

17. continued

When the calculation is done with 36 pearls, only 35 are accounted for by the tentative apportionments, and with 37, the apportionments add up to 38. Let's calculate critical divisors to determine who gets the 36th and 37th pearls.

Abe	$\$5,900 \div \sqrt{14 \times 15} =$	$\$407.14$
Beth	$\$7,600 \div \sqrt{352} =$	$\$405.08$
Charles	$\$1,400 \div \sqrt{12} =$	$\$404.15$

Abe has priority for the 36th pearl, and once he receives it, his critical divisor is recomputed as $\$5,900 \div \sqrt{15 \times 16} = \$380.84$. The priority for the 37th pearl goes to Beth. Here are the final Webster apportionments.

	36 pearls	37 pearls
Abe	15	15
Beth	18	19
Charles	3	3

With 36 pearls, there is a difference between the Hill-Huntington apportionment and the others, but with 37, the three methods produce the same results. If there is a principle on which to choose a method, it would probably be to choose the method by which the cost per pearl is as close as possible to the same for each of the friends. The cost per pearl is the district size. The method that minimizes relative differences in the cost per pearl is Hill-Huntington method. If the friends would prefer to minimize absolute differences, they would have to use the Dean method, which was not covered in this chapter. Charles might want to study up on it, though, because it allocates the 36th pearl to Beth, and the 37th to him!

18. The average price per diamond is $\$1,000$, and that is the critical divisor. The quotas are Abe, 15.5; Beth, 10.5; and Charles, 10. With the Webster method, they would have to round Abe's and Beth's apportionments, and since their fractional parts are both equal to 0.5, that can't work out.

Here's a suggestion: If Abe gets 16 diamonds, his cost is $\$15,500 \div 16 = \$968.75$ per diamond. In this case, Beth would get 10 diamonds for $\$10,500 \div 10 = \$1,050$ per diamond. She is paying $\$81.25$ more per diamond (or 8.39% more) than Abe.

If we gave the 36th diamond to Beth instead of Abe, his cost per diamond would be $\$15,500 \div 15 = \$1,033.33$ and hers would be $\$10,500 \div 11 = \$954.55$. Now Abe is paying $\$78.78$ more per diamond (8.25% more). Thus, to make the cost per diamond as close to the same (on an absolute *or* relative basis) for each of the friends, the 36th diamond should be Beth's.

19. The percentages are the quotas.

Hamilton method: Start with the lower quotas, $87 + 10 \times 1$, whose sum is 97. The three percentages with the greatest fractional parts, 87.85, 1.26, and 1.25, are rounded up to get the upper quotas; the remaining percentages are rounded down. The final apportionment is

$$88 + 2 + 2 + 1 + 1 + 1 + 1 + 1 + 1 + 1 + 1 = 100\%.$$

The first three percentages are rounded to upper quotas, and the remaining percentages are rounded to lower quotas. The quota condition is satisfied.

Jefferson method: Tentatively apportion to each percentage its lower quota. The critical divisors are then the unrounded percentage divided by (1 + the tentative apportionment). Thus, the critical divisor belonging to 87.85% is $87.85 \div 88 = 0.9983$, while the critical divisors belonging to the smaller percentages range from $1.26 \div 2 = 0.63$ down to $1.17 \div 2 = 0.585$. The largest critical divisor belongs to 87.85%, so its tentative apportionment is increased to 88 and its new critical divisor is $87.85 \div 89 = 0.9871$. This is still the largest critical divisor, so the apportionment of 87.85% is increased to 89. The new critical divisor, $87.85 \div 90 = 0.9761$, is still the largest, so its apportionment is increased to 90. Now the house is full, and the Jefferson apportionment is

$$90 + 1 + 1 + 1 + 1 + 1 + 1 + 1 + 1 + 1 + 1 = 100\%.$$

This apportionment rounds 87.85% to 90%, more than the upper quota. The quota condition is violated.

Webster method: The rounded percentages add up to 98, so we need to calculate critical divisors. The critical divisor belonging to 87.85% is $87.85 \div 88.5 = 0.9927$. Among the smaller percentages, the largest critical divisor is that of 1.26%, which is $1.26 \div 1.5 = 0.84$. The point goes to 87.85%, whose apportionment increases to 89. This calls for a new critical divisor, $87.85 \div 89.5 = 0.9816$, which exceeds the critical divisors of the smaller percentages. The apportionment of 87.85% is therefore increased again to 90. The final apportionment is the same as the Jefferson apportionment, so it too violates the quota condition.

20. The percentages are the quotas.

Hamilton method: Start with the lower quotas, $92 + 5 \times 1$, whose sum is 97. The three percentages with the greatest fractional parts, 1.59, 1.58 and 1.57 are rounded up to get the upper quotas; the remaining percentages are rounded down. The final apportionment is

$$92 + 2 + 2 + 2 + 1 + 1 = 100\%.$$

Three percentages are rounded to upper quotas, and three are rounded to lower quotas. The quota condition is satisfied.

Jefferson method: Tentatively apportion to each percentage its lower quota. The critical divisors are then the unrounded percentages divided by (1 + the tentative apportionment). Thus, the critical divisor belonging to 92.15% is $92.15 \div 93 = 0.9909$, while the critical divisors belonging to the smaller percentages range from $1.59 \div 2 = 0.795$ down to $1.55 \div 2 = 0.775$. The largest critical divisor belongs to 92.15%, so its tentative apportionment is increased to 93 and its new critical divisor is $92.15 \div 94 = 0.9803$. This is still the largest critical divisor, so the apportionment of 92.15% is increased to 94. The new critical divisor, $92.15 \div 95 = 0.97$, is still the largest, so its apportionment is increased to 95. Now the house is full, and the Jefferson apportionment is

$$95 + 1 + 1 + 1 + 1 + 1 = 100\%.$$

This apportionment rounds 92.15% to 95%, more than the upper quota. The quota condition is violated.

Continued on next page

20. continued

Webster method: The rounded percentages add up to 102, so we need to calculate critical divisors. These are equal to the unrounded percentages, divided by (tentative apportionment − 0.5). The tentative apportionment of the percentage with the least critical divisor is reduced. The critical divisor belonging to 92.15% is $92.15 \div 91.5 = 1.0071$. Among the smaller percentages, the critical divisors range from $1.55 \div 1.5 = 1.0333$ to $1.59 \div 1.5 = 1.06$. These smaller percentages have the largest critical divisors; thus the apportionment of 92.15% is reduced to 91. The new critical divisor is $92.15 \div 90.5 = 1.0182$, still the smallest. Therefore the apportionment of 92.15% is reduced to 90, and the final apportionment is

$$90 + 2 + 2 + 2 + 2 + 2 = 100.$$

This apportionment gives 92.15% less than its lower quota, and violates the quota condition.

21. (a) $\sqrt{0 \times 1} = 0$

(b) $\sqrt{1 \times 2} = 1.4142$

(c) $\sqrt{2 \times 3} = 2.4495$

(d) $\sqrt{3 \times 4} = 3.4641$

22. The average section will have $(56 + 28 + 7) \div 5 = 18.2$ students; that is the standard divisor. The quotas are as follows.

Algebra	$56 \div 18.2 =$	3.077 sections
Geometry	$28 \div 18.2 =$	1.538 sections
Calculus	$7 \div 18.2 =$	0.385 sections

The Hill-Huntington method always rounds numbers between 0 and 1 up to 1. Numbers between 1 and 2 are rounded up if they are greater than $\sqrt{2} = 1.4142$, and numbers between 3 and 4 are rounded up if they are greater than $\sqrt{12} = 3.4641$. Thus, the rounded quotas are 3, 2, and 1, respectively. This makes 6 sections, so we have to change one of these apportionments. The critical divisors are given by the formula $d = p \div \sqrt{a(a-1)}$, where p is the population of the students enrolled for the subject, and a is the tentative number of sections apportioned to the subject. The section with the least critical divisor will have its tentative apportionment reduced. Here are the critical divisors.

Algebra	$56 \div \sqrt{6} =$	22.86 students
Geometry	$28 \div \sqrt{2} =$	19.7990 students
Calculus	$7 \div 0 =$	∞ students

Geometry has the least critical divisor, and its apportionment is reduced. The final apportionment is as follows.

Algebra	3 sections
Geometry	1 section
Calculus	1 section

23. The standard divisor is $(36+61+3) \div 5 = 20$ students. The quotas are as follows.

Algebra	$36 \div 20 =$	1.8 sections
Geometry	$61 \div 20 =$	3.05 sections
Calculus	$3 \div 20 =$	0.15 sections

Webster would round the quotas to 2, 3, and 0, respectively. These tentative apportionments add up to 5, the house size, and are the final Webster apportionments. Because Hill-Huntington rounds all numbers between 0 and 1 to 1, its tentative apportionment would be 2, 3, and 1. This would exceed the house size by 1, so we have to reduce one of the tentative apportionments. This requires critical divisors. They are as follows.

Algebra	$36 \div \sqrt{2 \times 1} =$	25.456 students
Geometry	$62 \div \sqrt{3 \times 2} =$	24.903 students
Calculus	$7 \div \sqrt{1 \times 0} =$	∞ students

The least critical divisor belongs to Geometry, so its apportionment is decreased to 2. In summary, here are the apportionments.

	Webster	Hill-Huntington
Algebra	2	2
Geometry	3	2
Calculus	cancelled!	1

It's likely that the principal would prefer the Webster method, because classes as small as the calculus class, with 3 students, should be cancelled. Notice that the Hill-Huntington apportionment gives Geometry less than its lower quota in order to accommodate Calculus.

24. (a) To see that the triangle is a right triangle, we use the converse of Pythagoras's theorem.

$$\left(\sqrt{AB}\right)^2 + \left(\frac{A-B}{2}\right)^2 = \frac{4AB}{4} + \frac{A^2 - 2AB + B^2}{4} = \frac{A^2 + 2AB + B^2}{4} = \left(\frac{A+B}{2}\right)^2$$

The hypotenuse of this right triangle is the arithmetic mean of A and B, and the base is the geometric mean. Because the hypotenuse is the longest side in any right triangle, the arithmetic mean of two numbers A and B is greater than the geometric mean, unless $A = B$ (when the altitude of the triangle is 0 and the two means are equal).

(b) Let $n = \lfloor q \rfloor$. Provided that q is not an integer, $\lceil q \rceil = n+1$. Let n^* be the geometric mean of n and $n+1$: $n^* = \sqrt{n(n+1)}$. The arithmetic mean of n and $n+1$ is as follows.

$$\frac{n + (n+1)}{2} = \frac{2n+1}{2} = n + \tfrac{1}{2}$$

By part (a), $n^* < n + \tfrac{1}{2}$. If $q < n^*$, then Webster and Hill-Huntington both round q down to n. If $q \geq n + \tfrac{1}{2}$, then both round q to $n + 1$. The methods differ when $n^* \leq q < n + \tfrac{1}{2}$ because then Hill-Huntington rounds q to $n + 1$ and Webster rounds q to n.

Continued on next page

24. continued

(c) The sum of the rounded quotas under the Webster method is less than or equal to the sum of the Hill-Huntington rounded quotas, because part (b) tells us that each individual quota, rounded *a la* Webster, is less than or equal to the same quota, rounded *a la* Hill-Huntington. Therefore, if the sum of the rounded quotas is greater than the house size under Webster, so that Webster must use a divisor larger than the standard divisor, Hill-Huntington will certainly have to do the same, and will use a divisor even larger than Webster's. This favors small states. If the Webster rounded quotas add up to the house size, so that Webster is neutral, Hill-Huntington rounded quotas may still add up to more than the house size, making an increased divisor necessary and thus also favoring small states. Finally, if Webster requires a decreased divisor, because the sum of the rounded quotas is less than the house size (this would favor large states), Hill-Huntington will use a larger divisor, which will give less benefit to the larger states.

25. Let's start by taking a seat from California, putting it in play. This leaves 52 seats for California, and California's priority for getting the extra seat is measured by its critical divisor,

$$\frac{\text{Population of California}}{\sqrt{52 \times 53}} = 646{,}330.227.$$

To secure the seat in play, Utah's population has to increase enough so that its critical divisor,

$$\frac{\text{Revised population of Utah}}{\sqrt{3 \times 4}},$$

surpasses California's. Thus, Utah needs a population of more than the following.

$$646{,}330.227 \times \sqrt{12} = 2{,}238{,}954$$

The 2000 census recorded Utah's population as 2,236,714, so an additional 2241 residents would be needed.

26. Yes, and here is an example involving just two states, with populations

$$p_1 = 1{,}000{,}000 \text{ and } p_2 = 6{,}000{,}000,$$

and with a house size $h = 10$. The standard divisor is $d = 700{,}000$, so the quotas are as follows.

$$q_1 = 1{,}000{,}000 \div 700{,}000 = 1.4286, \text{ and } q_2 = 6{,}000{,}000 \div 700{,}000 = 8.5714$$

With the Hill-Huntington method, a number q between 1 and 2 is rounded to 2 if $q \geq \sqrt{2} = 1.4142$. Therefore, the tentative apportionments are $n_1 = 2$, $n_2 = 9$, for a total of 11 seats. The critical divisors are as follows.

$$d_1 = \frac{1{,}000{,}000}{\sqrt{2 \times 1}} = \frac{1{,}000{,}000}{\sqrt{2}} = 500{,}000 \times \sqrt{2}$$

and

$$d_2 = \frac{6{,}000{,}000}{\sqrt{9 \times 8}} = \frac{6{,}000{,}000}{6\sqrt{2}} = 500{,}000 \times \sqrt{2}$$

Because their critical divisors are exactly equal, the states are tied when it comes to relinquishing a seat.

27. Before the excise tax was included, the quotas, calculated as in Exercise 11, are rounded to obtain a tentative apportionment.

	Quota	Rounded quota
Abe	36.19	36
Beth	18.62	19
Charles	22.58	23
David	20.10	20
Esther	2.51	3
Total	100.00	101

One quota must be reduced, so we calculate critical divisors as follows.

Abe	$\$3619 \div (36 - 0.5) =$	$\$101.94$
Beth	$\$1862 \div (19 - 0.5) =$	$\$100.65$
Charles	$\$2258 \div (23 - 0.5) =$	$\$100.36$
David	$\$2010 \div (20 - 0.5) =$	$\$103.08$
Esther	$\$251 \div (3 - 0.5) =$	$\$100.40$

The least critical divisor is Charles's, so his apportionment is 22. After the tax is added, new rounded quotas are calculated.

	Quota	Rounded quota
Abe	36.17	36
Beth	18.55	19
Charles	22.48	22
David	20.32	20
Esther	2.49	2
Total	100.01	99

Now one of the tentative apportionments must increase, so we must again compute critical divisors.

Abe	$\$3635 \div (36 + 0.5) =$	$\$99.589$
Beth	$\$1864 \div (19 + 0.5) =$	$\$95.590$
Charles	$\$2259 \div (22 + 0.5) =$	$\$100.400$
David	$\$2042 \div (20 + 0.5) =$	$\$99.610$
Esther	$\$250 \div (2 + 0.5) =$	$\$100.000$

Charles has the largest critical divisor, so his apportionment is increased to 23. The final apportionments are as follows.

	Before tax	After tax
Abe	36	36
Beth	19	19
Charles	22	23
David	20	20
Esther	3	2
Total	100	100

Esther must give one of her three rare coins to her nephew.

28. The quotas were determined in the solution of Exercise 12. They are shown in the columns labeled q in the table below. The columns q^* display $\sqrt{\lfloor q \rfloor \times \lceil q \rceil}$. If $q \geq q^*$, then the Hill-Huntington method assigns a tentative apportionment $a = \lceil q \rceil$; and if $q < q^*$ the tentative apportionment is $a = \lfloor q \rfloor$.

Tentative apportionment, Hill-Huntington Method

Apportionment according to two censuses

Province	Last year			This year		
	q	q^*	a	q	q^*	a
Ash	40.570	40.497	41	41.095	41.497	41
Beech	15.590	15.492	16	15.468	15.492	15
Chestnut	17.620	17.493	18	17.468	17.493	17
Date	24.720	24.495	25	24.485	24.495	24
The desert	1.500	1.414	2	1.484	1.414	2
Total	100.000	—	102	100.000	—	99

The sum of the tentative apportionments from this year's census must be increased by 1. The critical divisors are shown in the following table.

Province	Population	Tentative	Critical divisor
Ash	95,450	41	$95,450 \div \sqrt{41 \times 42} = 2300.17$
Beech	35,926	15	$35,926 \div \sqrt{15 \times 16} = 2319.01$
Chestnut	40,572	17	$40,572 \div \sqrt{17 \times 18} = 2319.35$
Date	56,870	24	$56,870 \div \sqrt{24 \times 25} = 2321.71$
The desert	3,447	2	$3,447 \div \sqrt{2 \times 3} = 1407.23$

The largest critical divisor belongs to Date, and its apportionment is therefore 25. The other provinces receive their original tentative apportionments. The sum of the tentative apportionments for last year must be reduced by 2. We calculate the critical divisors, as shown in the following table.

Province	Population	Tentative	Critical divisor
Ash	93,311	41	$93,311 \div \sqrt{41 \times 40} = 2304.15$
Beech	35,857	16	$35,857 \div \sqrt{16 \times 15} = 2314.56$
Chestnut	40,526	18	$40,526 \div \sqrt{18 \times 17} = 2316.72$
Date	56,856	25	$56,856 \div \sqrt{25 \times 24} = 2321.14$
The desert	3,450	2	$3,450 \div \sqrt{2 \times 1} = 2439.52$

Continued on next page

28. continued

Ash has the least critical divisor, and we apportion to it 40 seats. Its new critical divisor is $93,311 \div \sqrt{40 \times 39} = 2362.49$. Now the least critical divisor belongs to Beech, and its tentative apportionment is reduced to 15. The final apportionments are as follows.

Hill-Huntington Apportionment according to two censuses

Province	Last year	This year
Ash	40	41
Beech	15	15
Chestnut	18	17
Date	25	25
The desert	2	2
Total	100	100

Again, there is a loser (Chestnut), and a gainer (Ash). However, the population of Ash increased over the year, from 93,311 to 95,450. Chestnut's population increased less, from 40,526 to 40,572. This is not a paradox.

29. The quota for the Liberals is $99 \times 49\% = 48.51$, and the Tories' quota is 50.49. With the Hamilton method, the lower quotas add up to 98, and the additional seat goes to the party whose quota has the largest fractional part. This gives the Liberals 49 votes, and the Tories have 50. The Webster method yields the same result because it would round the Liberals' quota up, and the Tories' down.

The Jefferson starts by giving each party its lower quota, 48 for the Liberals and 50 for the Tories. The last seat is given to the party with the largest critical divisor. The formula for critical divisors is (percent of vote received) ÷ (1 + tentative apportionment). Thus the critical divisor for the Liberals is $49 \div (1 + 48) = 1$, and the critical divisor for the Tories is $51 \div (1 + 50) = 1$. There is a tie for the 99th seat.

30. (a) One quota will be rounded up, and the other down to obtain the Webster apportionment. The quota that is rounded up will have fractional part greater than 0.5, and will be greater than the fractional part of the quota that is rounded down. The Hamilton method will give the party whose quota has the larger fractional part an additional seat. Thus the apportionments will be identical.

(b) These paradoxes never occur with the Webster method, which gives the same apportionment in this case.

(c) The Hamilton method, which always satisfies the quota condition, gives the same apportionment.

(d) No. Assume that parliament has 100 seats. If one party gets only 0.6% of the vote, and the other party gets 99.4%, the Jefferson critical divisor for the former party will be $\frac{0.6}{1}$, and the latter party will have a critical divisor of $\frac{99.4}{100}$. Jefferson would therefore apportion all 100 seats to the second party, since its critical divisor is the larger. Hamilton would apportion one seat to the first party. On the other hand, Hill-Huntington will give at least one seat to any party that receives at least one vote. Thus, their apportionment would differ from Hamilton's if the vote were to split 0.4% − 99.6%.

31. The following table displays the quotas and tentative apportionment due to the Webster method.

State	Population	Quota	Tentative apportionment
Virginia	630,560	18.310	18
Massachusetts	475,327	13.803	14
Pennsylvania	432,879	12.570	13
North Carolina	353,523	10.266	10
New York	331,589	9.629	10
Maryland	278,514	8.088	8
Connecticut	236,841	6.877	7
South Carolina	206,236	5.989	6
New Jersey	179,570	5.214	5
New Hampshire	141,822	4.118	4
Vermont	85,533	2.484	2
Georgia	70,835	2.057	2
Kentucky	68,705	1.995	2
Rhode Island	68,446	1.988	2
Delaware	55,540	1.613	2
Totals	3,615,920	105	105

Because the tentative apportionment results in the assignment of 105 seats, there is no need for critical divisors: it is the final apportionment. In effect, a seat that had been assigned to Vermont moves to Pennsylvania.

32. The relative difference is the absolute difference, $7 - 5$, divided by the lesser of the two numbers, 5. The quotient is $0.4 = 40\%$.

33. Jim is 7 inches taller than Alice. The relative difference of their heights is 7 inches divided by Alice's height, 65 inches: $\frac{7}{65} = 10.77\%$.

34. (a) North Carolina, because its congressional districts are smaller in population.

   (b) The Montana district population is 284,726 larger than the North Carolina district population. That is 45.88% of the North Carolina district population.

35. (a) California, $33,930,798 \div 53 = 640,204$; Utah, $2,236,714 \div 3 = 745,571$.

   (b) Absolute difference, $745,571 - 640,204 = 105,367$,

   Relative difference, $105,367 \div 640,204 = 16.46\%$

   (c) The district size for California would be $33,930,798 \div 52 = 652,515$, and the district size for Utah would be $2,236,714 \div 4 = 559,178.5$. The absolute difference is $652,515 - 559,178 = 93,336.5$. The relative difference is $93,336.5 \div 559,178.5 = 16.69\%$

   (d) The absolute difference in district populations would be less if California had 52 seats, and Utah had 4. With that revised apportionment, the relative differences would be greater. Thus, the Hill-Huntington method, which was used in apportioning Congress after the 2000 census, did not minimize absolute differences in district population. It minimized relative differences.

36. The absolute difference in district populations is as follows.

$$\frac{P_A}{a_A} - \frac{P_B}{a_B} = \frac{a_B P_A}{a_B a_A} - \frac{a_A P_B}{a_A a_B} = \frac{a_B P_A - a_A P_B}{a_A a_B}$$

To obtain the relative difference, divide this absolute difference by the smaller district population, $\frac{P_B}{a_B}$, and express the resulting fraction as a percent.

$$\frac{a_B P_A - a_A P_B}{a_A a_B} \div \frac{P_B}{a_B} = \frac{a_B P_A - a_A P_B}{a_A a_B} \times \frac{a_B}{P_B} = \frac{a_B P_A - a_A P_B}{a_A P_B}$$

(a_B has been cancelled from the numerator and denominator.)

The relative difference in district population is $\dfrac{a_B P_A - a_A P_B}{a_A P_B} \times 100\%$.

The state with the smaller representative share is A, so the relative difference is as follows.

$$\left(\frac{a_B}{P_B} - \frac{a_A}{P_A} \right) \div \left(\frac{a_A}{P_A} \right) \times 100\%$$

$$\left(\frac{a_B P_A}{P_B P_A} - \frac{a_A P_B}{P_A P_B} \right) \times \left(\frac{P_A}{a_A} \right) \times 100\% = \left(\frac{a_B P_A - a_A P_B}{P_A P_B} \right) \times \left(\frac{P_A}{a_A} \right) \times 100\%$$

$$\frac{a_B P_A - a_A P_B}{a_A P_B} \times 100\%$$

Because this formula is identical to the formula for relative difference in district population, the two measures on inequity yield the same result.

37. With 10 seats for Massachusetts, and 6 for Oklahoma, the representative shares (per million population) for these states are $10 \div 6.029051 = 1.6586$ seats per million for Massachusetts, and $6 \div 3.145585 = 1.9074$ for Oklahoma. The inequity in representative share is in favor of Oklahoma, by 0.2488 seats per million population. If Massachusetts had 11 seats, and Oklahoma 5, the respective representative shares would be 1.8245 and 1.5895. The inequity, in favor of Massachusetts, is 0.235 seats per million population. Therefore, the Webster apportionment would give Massachusetts the seat.

38. (a) The sum of the quotas is h and unless each quota is a whole number, some state will receive more than its quota. Therefore the total number of seats apportioned will be more than h.

  (b) Let p be the total population and p_i be the population of state i. Then the standard divisor is

$$d = \frac{p}{h}, \text{ and } a_i = \left\lceil \frac{p_i}{d} \right\rceil \text{ is the apportionment for state } i. \text{ Also let } h' \text{ be the actual house size}$$

resulting from this apportionment. In part (a), we saw that $h' > h$. California is a populous state. If the apportionment had been done by the Hill-Huntington method, it is possible that California would have received its upper quota anyway. If not, it would have received at least its lower quota (it's very unlikely that the Hill-Huntington method will violate the quota condition). The amount that California has to gain is relatively small, but some other states will surely gain, and California's share of the house seats will be less than it would have been if the Hill-Huntington method had been used.

39. (a) Lowndes favors small states, because in computing the relative difference, the fractional part of the quota will be divided by the lower quota. If a large state had a quota of 20.9, the Lowndes relative difference works out to be 0.045. A state with a quota of 1.05 would have priority for the next seat.

(b) Yes, because like the Hamilton method, the Lowndes method presents a way to decide, for each state, if the lower or upper quota should be awarded.

(c) Yes. Since the method is not a divisor method, the population paradox is inevitable.

(d) Let r_i denote the relative difference between the quota and lower quota for state i. The following table displays the numbers r_i for each state. Because the lower quotas add up to 97, the 8 states with the largest values in the r_i column will receive their upper quotas.

State	p_i	q_i	$\lfloor q_i \rfloor$	r_i	rank	a_i
Virginia	630,560	18.310	18	1.7%	14	18
Massachusetts	475,327	13.803	13	6.2%	8	14
Pennsylvania	432,879	12.570	12	4.8%	9	12
North Carolina	353,523	10.266	10	2.7%	13	10
New York	331,589	9.629	9	7.0%	7	10
Maryland	278,514	8.088	8	1.1%	15	8
Connecticut	236,841	6.877	6	14.6%	6	7
South Carolina	206,236	5.989	5	19.8%	5	6
New Jersey	179,570	5.214	5	4.3%	10	5
New Hampshire	141,822	4.118	4	3.0%	11	4
Vermont	85,533	2.484	2	24.2%	4	3
Georgia	70,835	2.057	2	2.9%	12	2
Kentucky	68,705	1.995	1	99.5%	1	2
Rhode Island	68,446	1.988	1	98.8%	2	2
Delaware	55,540	1.613	1	61.3%	3	2
Totals	3,615,920	105	97	–	–	105

40. (a) No. Unless a state's quota is a whole number, its tentative apportionment will be more than its quota. Of course, in the unlikely event that a state's quota is a whole number, its tentative apportionment would equal its quota. The sum of all the quotas is equal to the house size, so the tentative apportionments will add up to more than the house size. Critical divisors will have to be used to decide which states should receive reduced tentative apportionments.

(b) Let state i have population p_i. Its critical divisor d_i will be the greatest divisor that will reduce its tentative apportionment n_i to $n_i - 1$. Thus, $n_i - 1 = \dfrac{p_i}{d_i}$ and hence $d_i = \dfrac{p_i}{n_i - 1}$.

The state with the least critical divisor receives the reduced tentative apportionment, and then its critical divisor is recomputed. The process is complete when the sum of the tentative apportionments has been reduced to the house size.

(c) The method favors small states, because it can never increase any state's tentative apportionment. The apportionments are calculated by multiplying each quota by an adjustment factor that is *less* than 1, and rounding up. A populous state's quota will be reduced more than a small state's. Also, a state will never receive more than its upper quota, but can receive less that its lower quota.

(d) If a state's tentative apportionment is 1, then its critical divisor is ∞. Its tentative apportionment will not be reduced. Of course, this method does not work if the number of states is more than the house size!

41. (a) Let $n = \lfloor q \rfloor$. If q is between n and $n + 0.4$, then the Condorcet rounding of q is equal to n. Since $q + 0.6 < n + 1$ in this case, it is also true that $\lfloor q + 0.6 \rfloor = n$. On the other hand, if $n + 0.4 \le q < n + 1$, then the Condorcet rounding of q is $n + 1$, and also $n + 1 \le q + 0.6 < n + 1.6$, so $\lfloor q + 0.6 \rfloor = n + 1$.

(b) The method favors small states, since numbers will be rounded up more often than down; and this makes it more likely that the quotas will be adjusted downward.

(c) If the sum of the tentative apportionments is less than the house size, the critical divisor for state i, with population p_i, is the greatest divisor d_i that would apportion another seat to the state. Thus, if the tentative apportionment is n_i, then $n_i + 0.4 = \dfrac{p_i}{d_i}$, and hence

$d_i = \dfrac{p_i}{n_i + 0.4}$. The state with the largest critical divisor gets the next seat, and then its critical divisor is recomputed. The process stops when the house is full.

If the total apportionment is more than the house size, then the critical divisor for state i is the least divisor that would cause the state's tentative apportionment to decrease. Thus

$n_i - 1 + 0.4 = \dfrac{p_i}{d_i}$, so $d_i = \dfrac{p_i}{n_i - 0.6}$. The state with the least critical divisor of all has its tentative apportionment decreased by 1. Its critical divisor is then recomputed. The process stops when enough seats have been removed so that the number of seats apportioned is equal to the house size.

42. (a) Hill-Huntington rounds all numbers between 0 and 1 to 1. Thus, no finite divisor would cause a tentative apportionment of 0. The critical divisor to reduce a tentative apportionment of 1 to 0 by the Hill-Huntington method is infinite.

The Hamilton, Jefferson, and Webster methods can all produce zero apportionments. For example, suppose that there are 10 seats to be apportioned, state 1 has a population of 97, and state 2 has a population of 3. The standard divisor is 10, and the quotas are 9.7 and 0.3, respectively. Hamilton would give both states their lower quota, 9 and 0, and then state 1, with the larger fraction, would get the 10th seat as well. Webster would round the quota for the states to 10 and 0, respectively. Jefferson would give 9 to state 1, 0 to state 2, and they would compete for the last seat on the basis of critical divisors: $97 \div 10 = 9.7$ for state 1, and $3 \div 1 = 3$ for state 2. State 1 would get the last seat, leaving state 1 with 0.

(b) Yes, for the reason noted in the solution of Exercise 40.

(c) Let n_i be the apportionment of state i and p_i be its population. If $n_i = 0$ then the district population for this state is infinite. When we compare this with the finite district population of any state with more than one seat, we see that a transfer of a seat to state i would create a situation in which both states have finite district populations. Thus, instead of an infinite difference in district populations, we have a finite difference. Thus a Dean apportionment cannot have two states, one with zero apportionment while the other has two or more seats.

43. Let $f_i = q_i - \lfloor q_i \rfloor$ denote the fractional part of the quota for state i. Since the Hamilton method assigns to each state either its lower or its upper quota, each absolute deviation is equal to either f_i (if state i received its lower quota) or $1 - f_i$ (if it received its upper quota). For convenience, let's assume that the states are ordered so that the fractions are decreasing, with f_1 the largest and f_n the smallest. If the lower quotas add up to $h - k$, where h is the house size, then states 1 through k will receive their upper quotas. The maximum absolute deviation will be the larger of $1 - f_k$ and f_{k+1}.

The maximum absolute deviation for the Hamilton method is less than 1, because each fractional part f_i and its complement, $1 - f_i$, is less than 1. If a particular apportionment fails to satisfy the quota condition, then for al least one state, the absolute deviation exceeds 1, and hence the maximum absolute deviation is greater than that of the Hamilton apportionment.

If an apportionment satisfies the quota condition then — as with the Hamilton method — k states receive their upper quotas and $n - k$ states receive their lower quotas.

If a state j, where $j \leq k$, receives its lower quota, then — to compensate — a state l, where $l > k$, must get its upper quota. The absolute deviations for these states would be f_j and $1 - f_l$, respectively. Because of the way the fractions have been ordered, we have $1 - f_l \geq 1 - f_k$. Therefore, the absolute deviation for one of states j and l will be equal to or exceed the maximum absolute deviation of the Hamilton apportionment. We conclude that no apportionment is better than Hamilton's, if what we mean by "better" is "smaller maximum absolute deviation."

44. (a) Use the Jefferson method. If d is the divisor used in that apportionment, subject i gets $\lfloor p_i \div d \rfloor$ sections (where p_i is the number of students enrolled to take the course in subject i). The minimum class size is d.

   (b) Use the method of John Quincy Adams described in Exercise 40. Now if d is the divisor, the apportionment to subject i is $\lceil p_i \div d \rceil$ sections. The maximum section size is d.

   (c) The Webster method minimizes differences in representative share.

   (d) The Hill-Huntington method minimizes relative differences in district population.

   (e) The Adams and Hill-Huntington methods will apportion one class to any course that has an enrollment of at least one, so they should be avoided.

Word Search Solution

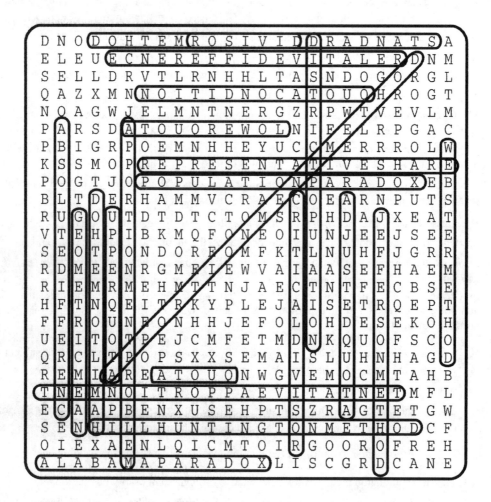

Chapter 15
Game Theory: The Mathematics of Competition

Chapter Outline

Chapter Summary

Game theory is the mathematical discipline that analyzes situations of conflict and cooperation. Modern game theory originated in 1944 with the publication of *The Theory of Games and Economic Behavior*, by John von Neumann and Oskar Morgenstern.

A mathematical game involves two or more players who can choose between various strategies that have payoffs for the players. It is assumed that the players will act in a rational manner.

In games of total conflict, a payoff representing a gain for one player represents a corresponding loss for the other(s). It is natural to assume that players will seek a strategy that will maximize their gain (or minimize their loss). A basic type of total-conflict game is the two-person, zero-sum game. These games are also called matrix games because they can be represented by a matrix.

In a two-person, matrix game, there is one row for each strategy of one player (row player) and one column for each strategy of the other (column player). The entries in the matrix represent the payoffs to the row player (the negatives of these are the payoffs to the column player). If the payoff matrix has a *saddlepoint*, an entry simultaneously the smallest in its row and largest in its column, then neither player can do better than to employ the strategy corresponding to the row (for row player) and column (for column player) containing the saddlepoint. In this case, we say that in the solution to the game (i.e., the specification of each player's optimal strategy), each player has a pure strategy. The value of the game is taken to be the payoff to the row player.

If the payoff matrix does not have a saddlepoint, then the best a player can do is adopt a mixed strategy. Such a strategy involves a player playing each of his or her strategies with a certain probability. The existence of *optimal mixed strategies* for each player is the content of the minimax theorem. In this situation, the value of the game is the expected payoff to the row player if the player plays his or her strategies with the probabilities specified by the optimal strategy.

Two-person games of partial conflict, such as chicken or *prisoner's dilemma*, produce payoff matrices whose entries are ordered pairs representing the respective payoffs to the row and column players. Games of this type are not usually zero-sum. Typically, each player will benefit if the pair cooperates. However, a player can usually obtain a higher payoff, at the expense of the other player, by being selfish. When neither player can benefit by departing unilaterally from his or her strategy associated with an outcome, the strategies of the players constitute a *Nash equilibrium*. Often, if both players are selfish, the result is detrimental to both. Thus, these games mirror a common social paradox. In the context of larger games, the *status-quo paradox* is an interesting example of this phenomenon. It leads to the notion of sophisticated voting, in which the voters anticipate the moves of their opponents, thereby adjusting their own votes.

In classical game theory, the players choose their options independently and then reveal their choices simultaneously. In a recent extension of the classical case, known as the *Theory of Moves* (*TOM*), a dynamic element is introduced, in which the players move sequentially. An example illustrating this theory is a truel, a three-person version of a duel, in which each player can choose to fire or not fire his gun at either of the other two players. Assuming each player has exactly one bullet, and each is a perfect shot, the question is how a player should proceed in order to maximize his chance of survival (his primary objective), preferably with as few survivors as possible (his secondary objective). In classical game theory, where the players must choose simultaneously, it pays for each player to fire at one of his opponents, thereby killing that person. The probability of any player surviving is just 0.25. Applying TOM, however, each player can look ahead at the consequences of this strategy and determine that it is in his best interest not to fire. Thus, all of the players will survive, which achieves the primary objective of each of them.

Skill Objectives

1. Apply the minimax technique to a game matrix to determine if a saddlepoint exists.

2. When a game matrix contains a saddlepoint, list the game's solution by indicating the pure strategies for both row and column players and the playoff.

3. Interpret the rules of a zero-sum game by listing its payoffs as entries in a game matrix.

4. From a zero-sum game matrix whose payoffs are listed for the row player, construct a corresponding game matrix whose payoffs are listed for the column player.

5. If a two-dimensional game matrix has no saddlepoint, write a set of linear probability equations to produce the row player's mixed strategy.

6. If a two-dimensional game matrix has no saddlepoint, write a set of linear probability equations to produce the column player's mixed strategy.

7. When given either the row player's or the column player's strategy probability, calculate the game's payoff.

8. State in your own words the minimax theorem.

9. Apply the principle of dominance to simplify the dimension of a game matrix.

10. Construct a model for an uncomplicated two-person game of partial conflict.

11. Determine when a pair of strategies is in equilibrium.

12. Be able to interpret and construct game trees.

Teaching Tips

1. In applying the minimax technique to a given matrix, students may become confused about the "column maxima" and the "row minima." For these students, a visual approach may be helpful. First, draw a circle around the minimum number in each row. Next, draw a square around the maximum number in each column. If a matrix entry has both a circle and a square drawn around it, that location represents a saddlepoint.

2. Students are sometimes unclear about the form of a game matrix solution. It may be helpful to reinforce the idea that each row of the matrix represents a different strategy option for the row player; and each column, a different strategy option for the column player. Because a saddlepoint exists at the intersection of a row and a column, those corresponding strategies are the pure strategies to be selected by each player. Each player will then fare best by choosing that one strategy all the time. The numerical value in the saddlepoint location is then the payoff to the player in question (i.e., the average value he or she can hope to achieve through repeated plays of the game).

3. Often students find the graphical approach to a mixed-strategy problem a compelling argument; however, the relationship between the probability equations taken from the matrix and the lines themselves is occasionally blurred. The following review work could prove helpful:

a. Construct a formula for expected value;

b. Derive the slope-intercept form for the equation of a line;

c. Develop the equation of each line from its two given points.

4. Using the principle of dominance to reduce the size of a game matrix by deleting rows or columns, whose numerical entries are overpowered by corresponding entries from other rows or columns of the matrix, will sometimes require practice by the student. This somewhat tedious work can be softened if the student understands that he or she is simplifying the matrix so that he or she can restrict the problem to two dimensions and thus produce a graph.

Research Paper

As stated in the opening paragraph of this chapter, conflict has been prevalent throughout human history. The Babylonian Talmud compiles ancient law and traditions for the first five centuries A.D. (0–500 A.D.). Have students research the "marriage contract problem." They can research how the Talmud makes recommendations of estate distribution, depending on the value. They are not proportional to the three wives, depending on the value of the estate. In 1995, this problem was recognized to have anticipated modern theory of cooperative games. Each recommendation for the distribution of the estate corresponds to an appropriately defined game.

Spreadsheet Project

To do this project, go to http://www.whfreeman.com/fapp7e.

The spreadsheet project, *Game Theory*, allows you to analyze mixed strategies for fastballs and curveballs for a pitcher and batter.

Collaborative Learning

The Coin Problem #1

This exercise is to be done in pairs. Designate one of the two members of the pair as Player 1 and the other as Player 2. The players each have two coins: a penny and a nickel. On each round of the game, the players simultaneously put out one of the coins. Note that the coins are not flipped; each of the players chooses which of the coins to put out.

1. The first game is played as follows: If the two coins match, Player 1 wins $1. If they do not match, Player 2 wins $1. Play this game 25 times, keep score of the outcomes, and see if you can develop a good strategy for playing this game. Does the game seem to be fair?

2. In the second game, change the payoffs. Once again, Player 1 wins when both coins match. This time, however, he wins $1 if both coins are pennies, but $5 if both are nickels. When the coins are different, Player 2 wins $3. Play this game 25 times and answer the same questions that you answered for Part 1.

The Coin Problem #2

This exercise is a follow-up to the previous problem. We agreed that the game

$$
\begin{array}{cc}
 & \begin{array}{cc} P & N \end{array} \\
\begin{array}{c} P \\ N \end{array} & \begin{pmatrix} 1 & -1 \\ -1 & 1 \end{pmatrix}
\end{array}
$$

was a fair one. Thus, the value of the game is 0. This means that each player, in the long run, can achieve the outcome 0 by optimal play.

Working with your partner, try to develop an optimal strategy that will guarantee you a long-term outcome of 0.

TOM

Ask the students to discuss a recent long-standing political conflict in the context of TOM. Good examples include the Middle East and Northern Ireland.

Solutions

Skills Check:

1. c   2. c   3. b   4. c   5. a   6. c   7. a   8. a   9. c   10. a

11. a   12. b   13. c   14. b   15. b   16. b   17. b   18. c   19. b   20. b

Cooperative Learning:
The Coin Problem #1:

1. The game is fair.
2. The game is not fair (it favors Player 2).

The Coin Problem #2:

Choose P and N randomly with probability $\frac{1}{2}$.

Exercises:

1.

$$\begin{bmatrix} 6 & 5 \\ 4 & 2 \end{bmatrix} \quad \begin{matrix} \text{Row Minima} \\ \boxed{5} \\ 2 \end{matrix}$$

Column Maxima   6 $\boxed{5}$

(a) - (b) Saddlepoint at row 1 (maximin strategy), column 2 (minimax strategy), giving value 5.

(c) Row 2 and column 1.

2.

$$\begin{bmatrix} 0 & 3 \\ -5 & 1 \\ 1 & 6 \end{bmatrix} \quad \begin{matrix} \text{Row Minima} \\ 0 \\ -5 \\ \boxed{1} \end{matrix}$$

Column Maxima $\boxed{1}$ 6

(a) - (b) Saddlepoint at row 3 (maximin strategy), column 1 (minimax strategy), giving value 1.

(c) Rows 1 and 2, column 2.

3.

$$\begin{bmatrix} -2 & 3 \\ 1 & -2 \end{bmatrix} \quad \begin{matrix} \text{Row Minima} \\ \boxed{-2} \\ \boxed{-2} \end{matrix}$$

Column Maxima $\boxed{1}$ 3

(a) No saddlepoint.

(b) Rows 1 and 2 are both maximin strategies; column 1 is the minimax strategy.

(c) None.

4.   Row Minima

$$\begin{bmatrix} 13 & 11 \\ 12 & 14 \\ 10 & 11 \end{bmatrix} \quad \begin{matrix} 11 \\ \boxed{12} \\ 10 \end{matrix}$$

Column Maxima $\boxed{13}$ 14

(a) No saddlepoint.

(b) Row 2 is the maximin strategy; column 1 is the minimax strategy.

(c) Row 3.

5.   Row Minima

$$\begin{bmatrix} -10 & -17 & -30 \\ -15 & -15 & -25 \\ -20 & -20 & -20 \end{bmatrix} \quad \begin{matrix} -30 \\ -25 \\ \boxed{-20} \end{matrix}$$

Column Maxima -10 -15 $\boxed{-20}$

(a) - (b)   Saddlepoint at row 3 (maximin strategy), column 3 (minimax strategy), giving value -20.

(c) Column 3 dominates columns 1 and 2, so column player should avoid strategies from columns 1 and 2.

6.

		Pitcher		Row Minima
		Fastball	Curve	
Batter	Fastball	0.300	0.200	$\boxed{0.200}$
	Curve	0.100	0.400	0.100
	Column Maxima	$\boxed{0.300}$	0.400	

There is no saddlepoint.

		Pitcher		
		Fastball	Curve	
Batter	Fastball	0.300	0.200	q
	Curve	0.100	0.400	$1-q$
		p	$1-p$	

Batter:

$$E_F = 0.3q + 0.1(1-q) = 0.3q + 0.1 - 0.1q = 0.1 + 0.2q$$

$$E_C = 0.2q + 0.4(1-q) = 0.2q + 0.4 - 0.4q = 0.4 - 0.2q$$

$$E_F = E_C$$

$$0.1 + 0.2q = 0.4 - 0.2q$$

$$0.4q = 0.3$$

$$q = \frac{0.3}{0.4} = \frac{3}{4}$$

$$1 - q = 1 - \frac{3}{4} = \frac{1}{4}$$

The batter's optimal mixed strategy is $(q, 1-q) = \left(\frac{3}{4}, \frac{1}{4}\right)$.

Continued on next page

6. continued

Pitcher:

$$E_F = 0.3p + 0.2(1-p) = 0.3p + 0.2 - 0.2p = 0.2 + 0.1p$$

$$E_C = 0.1p + 0.4(1-p) = 0.1p + 0.4 - 0.4p = 0.4 - 0.3p$$

$$E_F = E_C$$

$$0.2 + 0.1p = 0.4 - 0.3p$$

$$0.4p = 0.2$$

$$p = \tfrac{0.2}{0.4} = \tfrac{1}{2}$$

$$1 - p = 1 - \tfrac{1}{2} = \tfrac{1}{2}$$

The pitcher's optimal mixed strategy is $(p, 1-p) = \left(\tfrac{1}{2}, \tfrac{1}{2}\right)$, giving value as follows.

$$E_F = E_C = E = 0.2 + 0.1\left(\tfrac{1}{2}\right) = 0.2 + 0.05 = 0.250$$

7.

		Pitcher		Row Minima
		Fastball	Knuckleball	
Batter	Fastball	0.500	0.200	0.200
	Knuckleball	0.200	0.300	0.200
	Column Maxima	0.500	0.300	

There is no saddlepoint.

		Pitcher		
		Fastball	Knuckleball	
	Fastball	0.500	0.200	q
Batter	Knuckleball	0.200	0.300	$1-q$
		p	$1-p$	

Batter:

$$E_F = 0.5q + 0.2(1-q) = 0.5q + 0.2 - 0.2q = 0.2 + 0.3q$$

$$E_K = 0.2q + 0.3(1-q) = 0.2q + 0.3 - 0.3q = 0.3 - 0.1q$$

$$E_F = E_K$$

$$0.2 + 0.3q = 0.3 - 0.1q$$

$$0.4q = 0.1$$

$$q = \tfrac{0.1}{0.4} = \tfrac{1}{4}$$

$$1 - q = 1 - \tfrac{1}{4} = \tfrac{3}{4}$$

The batter's optimal mixed strategy is $(q, 1-q) = \left(\tfrac{1}{4}, \tfrac{3}{4}\right)$.

Continued on next page

7.   continued
Pitcher:

$$E_F = 0.5p + 0.2(1-p) = 0.5p + 0.2 - 0.2p = 0.2 + 0.3p$$

$$E_K = 0.2p + 0.3(1-p) = 0.2p + 0.3 - 0.3p = 0.3 - 0.1p$$

$$E_F = E_K$$

$$0.2 + 0.3p = 0.3 - 0.1p$$

$$0.4p = 0.1$$

$$p = \frac{0.1}{0.4} = \tfrac{1}{4}$$

$$1 - p = 1 - \tfrac{1}{4} = \tfrac{3}{4}$$

The pitcher's optimal mixed strategy is $(p, 1-p) = \left(\tfrac{1}{4}, \tfrac{3}{4}\right)$, giving value as follows.

$$E_F = E_K = E = 0.2 + 0.3\left(\tfrac{1}{4}\right) = 0.2 + 0.075 = 0.275$$

8.

		Pitcher		Row Minima
		Blooperball	Knuckleball	
Batter	Blooperball	0.400	0.200	0.200
	Knuckleball	0.250	0.250	0.250
	Column Maxima	0.400	0.250	

Saddlepoint at knuckleball for each player, giving value 0.250.

9.   The following table represents the gain or loss for the businessman.

		Tax Agency		Row Minima
		Not Audit	Audit	
Businessman	Not Cheating	$100	−$100	−$100
	Cheating	$1000	−$3000	−$3000
	Column Maxima	$1000	−$100	

Saddlepoint is "not cheat" and "audit," giving value −$100.

10.

		Defense		Row Minima
		Run	Pass	
Offense	Run	0.5	0.8	$\boxed{0.5}$
	Pass	0.7	0.2	0.2
	Column Maxima	$\boxed{0.7}$	0.8	

There is no saddlepoint.

		Defense		
		Run (R)	Pass (P)	
Offense	Run (R)	0.5	0.8	q
	Pass (P)	0.7	0.2	$1-q$
		p	$1-p$	

Offense:
$$E_R = 0.5q + 0.7(1-q) = 0.5q + 0.7 - 0.7q = 0.7 - 0.2q$$
$$E_P = 0.8q + 0.2(1-q) = 0.8q + 0.2 - 0.2q = 0.2 + 0.6q$$
$$E_R = E_P$$
$$0.7 - 0.2q = 0.2 + 0.6q$$
$$0.5 = 0.8q$$
$$q = \frac{0.5}{0.8} = \frac{5}{8}$$
$$1 - q = 1 - \frac{5}{8} = \frac{3}{8}$$

The offense's optimal mixed strategy is $(q, 1-q) = \left(\frac{5}{8}, \frac{3}{8}\right)$.

Defense:
$$E_R = 0.5p + 0.8(1-p) = 0.5p + 0.8 - 0.8p = 0.8 - 0.3p$$
$$E_P = 0.7p + 0.2(1-p) = 0.7p + 0.2 - 0.2p = 0.2 + 0.5p$$
$$E_R = E_P$$
$$0.8 - 0.3p = 0.2 + 0.5p$$
$$0.6 = 0.8p$$
$$p = \frac{0.6}{0.8} = \frac{3}{4}$$
$$1 - p = 1 - \frac{3}{4} = \frac{1}{4}$$

The defense optimal mixed strategy is $(p, 1-p) = \left(\frac{3}{4}, \frac{1}{4}\right)$, giving value as follows.

$$E_R = E_P = E = 0.2 + 0.5\left(\frac{3}{4}\right) = 0.2 + 0.375 = 0.575$$

11. (a)

	Officer does not patrol	Officer patrols
You park in street	0	−$40
You park in lot	−$32	−$16

(b)

	Officer does not patrol (*NP*)	Officer patrols (*P*)	
You park in street (*S*)	0	−$40	q
You park in lot (*L*)	−$32	−$16	$1-q$
	p	$1-p$	

You:
$$E_P = (0)q + (-32)(1-q) = 0 - 32 + 32q = -32 + 32q$$
$$E_{NP} = -40q + (-16)(1-q) = -40q - 16 + 16q = -16 - 24q$$
$$E_P = E_{NP}$$
$$-32 + 32q = -16 - 24q$$
$$56q = 16$$
$$q = \tfrac{16}{56} = \tfrac{2}{7}$$
$$1 - q = 1 - \tfrac{2}{7} = \tfrac{5}{7}$$

Your optimal mixed strategy is $(q, 1-q) = \left(\tfrac{2}{7}, \tfrac{5}{7}\right)$.

Officer:
$$E_S = (0)p + (-40)(1-p) = 0 - 40 + 40p = -40 + 40p$$
$$E_L = -32p + (-16)(1-p) = -32p - 16 + 16p = -16 - 16p$$
$$E_S = E_L$$
$$-40 + 40p = -16 - 16p$$
$$56p = 24$$
$$p = \tfrac{24}{56} = \tfrac{3}{7}$$
$$1 - p = 1 - \tfrac{3}{7} = \tfrac{4}{7}$$

The officer's optimal mixed strategy is $(p, 1-p) = \left(\tfrac{3}{7}, \tfrac{4}{7}\right)$, giving the following.

$$E_S = E_L = E = -16 - 16\left(\tfrac{3}{7}\right) \approx -16 - 6.86 = -22.86$$

The value is −$22.86.

(c) It is unlikely that the officer's payoffs are the opposite of yours—that she always benefits when you do not.

(d) Use some random device, such as a die with seven sides.

12. A pure strategy is one in which a player *always* chooses the same course of action, which is to say that he or she chooses it with probability 1 and all other possible courses of action with probability 0. Thus, a pure strategy is a mixed strategy in which all the probability is concentrated on one course of action.

13. (a) Move first to the center box; if your opponent moves next to a corner box or to a side box, move to a corner box in the same row or column. There are now six more boxes to fill, and you have up to three more moves (if you or your opponent does not win before this point), but the rest of your strategy becomes quite complicated, involving choices like "move to block the completion of a row/column/diagonal by your opponent."

   (b) Showing that your strategy is optimal involves showing that it guarantees at least a tie, no matter what choices your opponent makes.

14. Player I will choose H $\frac{3}{4}$ of the time and T $\frac{1}{4}$ of the time.

   For player II, $E_T = \frac{3}{4}(1) + \frac{1}{4}(-1) = \frac{3}{4} - \frac{1}{4} = \frac{2}{4} = \frac{1}{2}$ and $E_H = \frac{3}{4}(-1) + \frac{1}{4}(1) = -\frac{3}{4} + \frac{1}{4} = -\frac{2}{4} = -\frac{1}{2}$.

   Thus, player II should always play T, winning $\frac{1}{2}$ on average.

15. Player II will choose H $\frac{1}{2}$ of the time and T $\frac{1}{2}$ of the time.

   For player I, $E_H = 8\left(\frac{1}{2}\right) - 3 = 4 - 3 = 1$ and $E_T = -4\left(\frac{1}{2}\right) + 1 = -2 + 1 = -1$.

   Thus, player I should always play H, winning \$1 on average.

16.

		Economy		
		Poor (P)	Good (G)	
Quantity	Small	\$500,000	\$300,000	q
	Large	\$100,000	\$900,000	$1-q$
		p	$1-p$	

$E_P = 500{,}000q + 100{,}000(1-q) = 500{,}000q + 100{,}000 - 100{,}000q = 100{,}000 + 400{,}000q$

$E_G = 300{,}000q + 900{,}000(1-q) = 300{,}000q + 900{,}000 - 900{,}000q = 900{,}000 - 600{,}000q$

$$E_P = E_G$$
$$100{,}000 + 400{,}000q = 900{,}000 - 600{,}000q$$
$$1{,}000{,}000q = 800{,}000$$
$$q = \frac{800{,}000}{1{,}000{,}000} = \frac{4}{5}$$
$$1 - q = 1 - \frac{4}{5} = \frac{1}{5}$$

Your optimal mixed strategy is $(q, 1-q) = \left(\frac{4}{5}, \frac{1}{5}\right)$, giving the following.

$$E_P = E_G = E = 100{,}000 + 400{,}000\left(\tfrac{4}{5}\right) = 100{,}000 + 320{,}000 = 420{,}000$$

Thus, the value is value \$420,000.

The main alternative is that the economy will perform according to whatever forecast you believe to be most accurate. For example, if you believe the best forecast is that it will be poor with probability $\frac{1}{4}$ and good with probability $\frac{3}{4}$, then choosing "small" will give you an expected payoff of \$350,000, and choosing "large" will give you an expected payoff of \$700,000, so you would choose large. On the other hand, if you wish to maximize your minimum payoff (maximin), then you do better choosing "small," which guarantees you at least \$300,000, whatever the economy does.

17. Rewriting the matrix using abbreviations we have the following.

		Player II		
		F	C	R
Player I	F	−.25	0	.25
	BF	0	0	−.25
	BC	−.25	−.25	0

(a) Player I should avoid "Bet, then call" because it is dominated by "fold" (all entries in F row are bigger than corresponding entries in BC). Player II should avoid "call" because "fold" dominates it (all entries in F column are smaller than corresponding entries in C).

(b) Player I will never use "Bet, then call", and Player II will never use "Calls". Removing these, we are left with the following.

		Player II		
		F	R	
Player I	F	−.25	.25	q
	BF	0	−.25	$1-q$
		p	$1-p$	

$$E_F = -.25q + 0(1-q) = -.25q$$
$$E_R = .25q + (-.25)(1-q) = .50q - .25$$

$$E_F = E_R$$
$$-.25q = .50q - .25$$
$$-.75q = -.25$$
$$q = \tfrac{-.25}{-.75} = \tfrac{1}{3}$$
$$1-q = 1 - \tfrac{1}{3} = \tfrac{2}{3}$$

Player I's strategy for (F, BF, BC) is $\left(\tfrac{1}{3}, \tfrac{2}{3}, 0\right)$.

$$E_F = -.25p + .25(1-p) = -.25p + .25 - .25p = .25 - .50p$$
$$E_{BF} = (0)p + (-.25)(1-p) = -.25 + .25p$$

$$E_F = E_{BF}$$
$$.25 - .50p = -.25 + .25p$$
$$-.75p = -.50$$
$$p = \tfrac{-.50}{-.75} = \tfrac{2}{3}$$
$$1-p = 1 - \tfrac{2}{3} = \tfrac{1}{3}$$

Player II's strategy for (F, C, R) is $\left(\tfrac{2}{3}, 0, \tfrac{1}{3}\right)$.

$$E_F = E_{BF} = E = -.25 + .25\left(\tfrac{2}{3}\right) = -\tfrac{1}{4} + \tfrac{1}{4}\left(\tfrac{2}{3}\right) = -\tfrac{3}{12} + \tfrac{2}{12} = -\tfrac{1}{12}$$

The value is value $-\tfrac{1}{12}$.

(c) Player II. Since the value is negative, player II's average earnings are positive and player I's are negative.

(d) Yes. Player I bets first while holding L with probability $\tfrac{2}{3}$. Player II raises while holding L with probability $\tfrac{1}{3}$, so sometimes player II raises while holding L.

18. (a) Whatever box the first player chose, choose a box as close as possible to that box. If there are several equally close boxes (e.g., that are all adjacent to the box the first player chose), choose one of these closest boxes at random.

    (b) No.

19. (a) Leave umbrella at home if there is a 50% chance of rain; carry umbrella if there is a 75% chance of rain.

    (b) Carry umbrella in case it rains.

    (c) Saddlepoint at "carry umbrella" and "rain," giving value –2.

    (d) Leave umbrella at home.

20. The Nash equilibrium is $(4,4)$, but neither player has a dominant strategy. Notice that the players' second strategies guarantee each at least a payoff of 2, whereas their first strategies could result in either $(1,3)$ or $(3,1)$ —as well as $(4,4)$ —which means that a player could end up with a payoff of only 1 by choosing his or her first strategy. In this sense, the players' first strategies, although associated with the mutually best outcome and Nash equilibrium of $(4,4)$, are "riskier."

21. The Nash equilibrium outcomes are $(4,3)$ and $(3,4)$. [It would be better if the players could flip a coin to decide between $(4,3)$ and $(3,4)$.]

22. The Nash equilibrium is $(4,2)$, and Player I's first strategy is dominant. Notice that Player I ranks the outcomes as if he were playing Prisoners' Dilemma, in which his first strategy is cooperative ("disarm" in the text), whereas Player II ranks the outcomes as if she were playing Chicken, in which her second strategy is cooperative ("swerve" in the text). Like Prisoners' Dilemma and Chicken, the $(3,3)$ cooperative/compromise outcome is not a Nash equilibrium. In this game, it turns out, it is the Chicken player that does worse, at least in terms of comparative rankings, than the Prisoners' Dilemma player.

23. The Nash equilibrium outcome is $(2,4)$, which is the product of dominant strategies by both players.

24. Player II's first strategy is dominant; $(3,4)$ is a Nash equilibrium.

25. The players would have no incentive to lie about the value of their own weapons unless they were sure about the preferences of their opponents and could manipulate them to their advantage. But if they do not have such information, lying could cause them to lose more than 10% of their weapons, as they value them, in any year.

26. These choices give x as an outcome. X certainly would not want to depart from a strategy that yields a best outcome; furthermore, neither Y's departure to another outcome in the first column, nor Z's departure to another outcome in the second row, can improve on x for these players. It seems strange, however, that Z would choose x over z, since z is sincere and dominates x. Thus, there seem few if any circumstances in which this Nash equilibrium would be chosen.

27. The sophisticated outcome, x, is found as follows: Y's strategy of y is dominated; with this strategy of Y eliminated, X's strategy of x is dominated; with this strategy of X eliminated, Z's strategy of z is dominated, which is eliminated. This leaves X voting for xy (both x and y), Y voting for yz, and Z voting for zx, creating a three-way tie for x, y, and z, which X will break in favor of x.

28. Consider the 7-person voting game in which 3 voters have preference *xyz* (one of whom is chair), 2 voters have preference *zxy,* and 2 voters have preference for *zyx.* Then for the 3 *xyz* voters, voting for both *x* and *y* dominates voting for only *x*; and for the 2 *zyx* voters, voting for only *z* dominates voting for both *z* and *y*. With the dominated strategies of *x* and *zy* eliminated, in the second-reduction matrix *z* dominates *zy* for the 2 *zyx* voters, yielding the sophisticated outcome *z*, which is the chair's worst outcome.

29. The payoff matrix is as follows:

		Even		
		2	**4**	**6**
	1	$(2,1)$	$(2,1)$	$(2,1)$
Odd **2**		$(2,4)$	$(6,3)$	$(6,3)$
	3	$(2,4)$	$(4,8)$	$(10,5)$

Odd will eliminate strategy 1, and Even will eliminate strategy 6, because they are dominated. In the reduced 2×2 game, Odd will eliminate strategy 5. In the reduced 1×2 game, Even will eliminate strategy 4. The resulting outcome will be $(2,4)$, in which Odd chooses strategy 3 and Even chooses strategy 2. The outcome $(2,1)$, in which Odd chooses strategy 1 and Even chooses strategy 2, is also in equilibrium.

30. In the following 3×3 two-person zero-sum game, the saddlepoint—associated with the second strategies of each player—is 2:

$$\begin{vmatrix} 4 & 1 & 0 \\ 3 & 2 & 3 \\ 0 & 1 & 4 \end{vmatrix}$$

Because the three strategies of each player are undominated, however, none can be eliminated through the successive elimination of dominated strategies.

31. If the first player shoots in the air, he will be no threat to the two other players, who will then be in a duel and shoot each other. If a second player fires in the air, then the third player will shoot one of these two, so the two who fire in the air will each have a 50–50 chance of survival. Clearly, the third player, who will definitely survive and eliminate one of her opponents, is in the best position.

32. (a) If A hates B, B hates C, and C hates A, A does not shoot B, lest he be shot by C. B shoots C, putting her in the best position, because she shoots her antagonist, though A also survives.
    (b) If B hates A rather than C, A will shoot B, lest he be shot by B. C will then shoot A, so C is in the best position (she alone survives) and A the next-best position (he eliminates his antagonist). By comparison, if A did not shoot B in this case, B would shoot A and survive, because C would not shoot B—and this is worse for A than not shooting since his antagonist survives. These conclusions apply if the players all have only one turn, but if subsequent rounds occur, then in (a) A will shoot B on the second round. So B should not shoot C on the first round; C will not shoot A, because B will then shoot C. Hence, nobody will shoot, because the cycle will repeat itself, and shooting by any player will mean the shooter's death. In (b), subsequent rounds would not change incentives—C, the player nobody hates, would be the sole survivor, because nobody would shoot her on subsequent rounds.

33. In a duel, each player has incentive to fire – preferably first – because he or she does better whether the other player fires (leaving no survivors, which is better than being the sole victim) or does not fire (you are the sole survivor, which is better than surviving with the other player). In a truel, if you fire first, then the player not shot will kill you in turn, so nobody wants to fire first. In a four-person shoot-out, if you fire first, then you leave two survivors, who will not worry about you because you have no more bullets, leading them to duel. Thus, the incentive in a four-person shoot-out—to fire first—is the same as that in a duel.

34. B will shoot C, because it leads to $(3,3,1)$, which is better for B than $(2,2,2)$. Because $(3,3,1)$ is also better for A than either $(1,1,4)$ or $(1,4,1)$—the survivors of the other branches that A can choose—A will not shoot initially, and B will shoot C.

35. Nobody will shoot.

36. B will be indifferent between shooting or not shooting C, because whatever B does, he or she will be shot in the end by A.

37. The possibility of retaliation deters earlier shooting.

Word Search Solution

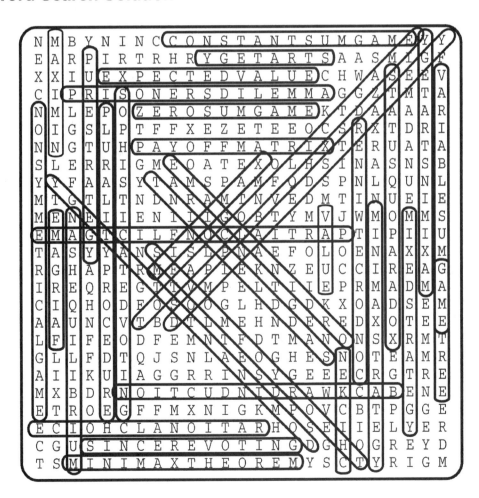

Chapter 16
Identification Numbers

Chapter Outline

Introduction
Section 16.1   Check Digits
Section 16.2   The ZIP Code
Section 16.3   Bar Codes
Section 16.4   Encoding Personal Data

Chapter Summary

Coding data facilitates the accurate and efficient transfer of information. Grocery stores use the *Universal Product Code* (*UPC*), and books use the *International Standard Book Number* (*ISBN*) method. In this chapter several different methods used in our daily lives of encoding information will be discussed.

To at least partially ensure accuracy, a coding scheme should have some means of *detecting errors*. Many codes use *check digits* for this purpose. Many places such as blood banks and libraries use *Codabar*. What types of errors can be detected and the rates of success for detecting them depend on the design of the code. Efficiency will be enhanced if it is easy to encode data and if the code represents data compactly. Good codes thus perform a delicate balancing act: sophisticated enough to detect high percentages of (perhaps) several kinds of errors, yet simple enough to provide for quick and compact coding of data. Not surprisingly, number theory, the mathematics of the integers, has proved useful in designing good codes. Our current "Information Age" would seem to ensure that codes will be a topic of interest for some time to come.

Identification numbers serve to unambiguously identify individuals (people, books, products, or whatever). Most schemes used to produce these numbers use check digit codes. The need to ensure accuracy is perhaps obvious if the identification number happens to be that of an individual's bank account. A situation that may not come so quickly to mind, except to the person in inventory control, is the parts identification numbers that help fill orders and keep track of available stock. Indeed, there are many numbers that enter our lives as identification numbers of one kind or another. Because of the availability of different examples of identification numbers, this chapter should be very accessible and interesting to its readers.

Skill Objectives

1. Understand the purpose of a check digit and be able to determine one for various schemes.

2. Given an identification number and the scheme used to determine it; be able to decide if the number is a valid number for that scheme.

3. Be able to convert a given ZIP code to its corresponding bar code, and vice versa.

4. Be able to convert a given UPC number to its corresponding bar code.

Teaching Tips

1. Have students analyze the UPC bar codes on products they have purchased recently.

2. Have students think of various numbers that are a regular part of their lives; then have them decide which of these numbers are identification numbers and which are not.

3. Joseph Gallian gave an informative and entertaining talk on identification numbers during the 75th anniversary celebration of Pi Mu Epsilon, the National Mathematics Honor Society. This tape may be borrowed from Robert Woodside, Department of Mathematics, East Carolina University, Greenville, NC. Professor Woodside is the National Secretary for Pi Mu Epsilon.

4. Some coding schemes fail to detect certain kinds of errors: either some substitutions of one digit for another, or some types of transpositions. Why this is the case can be illustrated very easily by a few examples. This is especially true in schemes that use remainders modulo some fixed integer. Gallian's College Math Journal article listed in the suggested readings is a good source for this.

Research Paper

Have students research the history of the United States Postal Service and the introduction of the ZIP code. Also delivery, in general, is rich in history. Around 500 B.C. the Greek philosopher Herodotus of Halicarnassus penned the phrase, "Neither snow nor rain nor heat or gloom of night stays these couriers from the swift completion of their appointed rounds." He was describing the Persian "postal" system. His quote is inscribed on the New York Post Office building.

Collaborative Learning

Bar Codes

To motivate learning about ZIP codes, have students bring in an article of mail for them to compare. Since most students should live in the same general area, they should see some common patterns in the first several groupings of bars. You could also ask the students to bring in envelopes after the lesson and ask them to decode each other's envelopes.

Solutions

Skills Check:

1. a   2. c   3. b   4. b   5. b   6. c   7. b   8. a   9. a   10. a

11. b   12. b   13. c   14. b   15. b   16. c   17. c   18. c   19. c   20. a

Exercises:

1. Since $3+9+5+3+8+1+6+4+0 = 48 = 9 \times 5 + 3$, the check digit is 3.

2. Since $7+2+3+4+5+4+1+7+8+0 = 41 = 9 \times 4 + 5$, the check digit is 5.

3. Since $873345672 = 7 \times 124763667 + 3$, the check digit is 3.

4. Since $2+7+7+5+0+4+2+1+1+6 = 35 = 9 \times 3 + 8$, the error is not detected.

5. Since $30860422052 = 7 \times 4408631721 + 5$, the check digit is 5.

6. Since $540047 = 7 \times 77149 + 4$, the check digit is 4.

7. Since $3 \cdot 3 + 8 + 3 \cdot 1 + 3 + 3 \cdot 7 + 0 + 3 \cdot 0 + 9 + 3 \cdot 2 + 1 + 3 \cdot 3 = 69$, the check digit is 1.

8. Since $3 \cdot 0 + 5 + 3 \cdot 0 + 7 + 3 \cdot 4 + 3 + 3 \cdot 1 + 1 + 3 \cdot 5 + 0 + 3 \cdot 2 = 52$, the check digit is 8.

9. Since $10 \cdot 0 + 9 \cdot 6 + 8 \cdot 6 + 7 \cdot 9 + 6 \cdot 1 + 5 \cdot 9 + 4 \cdot 4 + 3 \cdot 9 + 2 \cdot 3 = 265 = 11 \times 24 + 1$, the check digit is X.

10. Since $10 \cdot 0 + 9 \cdot 6 + 8 \cdot 6 + 7 \cdot 9 + 6 \cdot 3 + 5 \cdot 3 + 4 \cdot 9 + 3 \cdot 0 + 2 \cdot 7 = 248 = 11 \times 22 + 6$, the check digit is 5.

11. Since $7 \cdot 0 + 3 \cdot 9 + 9 \cdot 1 + 7 \cdot 9 + 3 \cdot 0 + 9 \cdot 2 + 7 \cdot 0 + 3 \cdot 4 = 129$, the check digit is 9.

12. Since $7 \cdot 0 + 3 \cdot 9 + 9 \cdot 1 + 7 \cdot 0 + 3 \cdot 0 + 9 \cdot 0 + 7 \cdot 0 + 3 \cdot 1 = 39$, the check digit is 9.

13. Since $4+6+1+2+1+2+0+2+3 = 21$, the check digit is 6.

14. Since $(3+4+0+3+0+3+2+7) \times 2 = 44$ and one of the summands exceeds 4, we have $44 + 1 + (5+1+2+2+0+3+2+0) = 60$. So, the number is valid.

15. Since $7 \cdot 3 + 8 + 7 \cdot 1 + 3 + 7 \cdot 7 + 0 + 7 \cdot 0 + 9 + 7 \cdot 2 + 1 + 7 \cdot 3 = 133$, the check digit is 7. This check-digit scheme will detect all single-digit errors.

16. The check digit is 7. The errors are not detected because the errors increase the sum by 10, and so the new weighted sum is still divisible by 10. In the odd numbered positions, if a digit a is replaced by the digit b where $a - b = \pm 5$ the error is not detected.

17. In the odd-numbered positions, if a digit a is replaced by the digit b where $a - b$ is even, the error is not detected.

18. The weight 9 will detect all errors in its position. The weights 4, 6, and 8 will not detect all errors.

19. We begin with $(3+0+2+6+0+9+4+1)\times 2 = 50$. Adding 2, we obtain 52 and have the following.

$$52+0+1+5+0+1+6+3 = 68$$

So, the check digit is 2.

20. First convert JM1GD222J1581570 to 1417422211581570. Then we have the following.

$$8\cdot 1+7\cdot 4+6\cdot 1+5\cdot 7+4\cdot 4+3\cdot 2+2\cdot 2+10\cdot 2+$$
$$9\cdot 1+8\cdot 1+7\cdot 5+6\cdot 8+5\cdot 1+4\cdot 5+3\cdot 7+2\cdot 0 = 269 = 11\times 24+5$$

Thus, the check digit is 5.

21. (a) Since $1\cdot 0+1\cdot 1+3\cdot 2+3\cdot 1+1\cdot 6+3\cdot 9+1\cdot 0 = 43$, the check digit is 7.

(b) Since $1\cdot 0+1\cdot 2+3\cdot 7+3\cdot 4+1\cdot 5+3\cdot 5+1\cdot 1 = 56$, the check digit is 4.

(c) Since $1\cdot 0+1\cdot 7+3\cdot 6+3\cdot 0+1\cdot 0+3\cdot 2+1\cdot 2 = 33$, the check digit is 7.

(d) Since $1\cdot 0+1\cdot 4+3\cdot 9+3\cdot 6+1\cdot 5+3\cdot 8+1\cdot 0 = 78$, the check digit is 2.

22. (a) Since $1\cdot 0+1\cdot 7+3\cdot 5+1\cdot 4+3\cdot 7+3\cdot 0 = 47$, the check digit is 3

(b) Since $1\cdot 0+1\cdot 7+3\cdot 7+1\cdot 4+3\cdot 7+3\cdot 1 = 56$, the check digit is 4

(c) Since $1\cdot 0+1\cdot 7+3\cdot 2+1\cdot 4+3\cdot 4+3\cdot 4 = 41$, the check digit is 9

23. First observe that the given number 0669039254 results in a weighted sum that has a remainder of 5 after division by 11. So all we need to do is check for successive pairs of digits of this number that results in a contribution to the weighted sum of 5 less or 6 more, since either of these will make the weighted sum divisible by 11. Checking each pair of consecutive digits, we see that 39 contributes $5\cdot 3+4\cdot 9 = 51$ whereas 93 contributes $5\cdot 9+4\cdot 3 = 57$. So, the correct number is 0669093254.

24. In the bank scheme 751 contributes $7\cdot 7+3\cdot 5+9\cdot 1 = 73$ to the sum, whereas 157 contributes $7\cdot 1+3\cdot 5+9\cdot 7 = 85$ to the sum. Since the last digit of 73 and the last digit of 85 do not match, the check digit for the correct number will not match the last digit of the sum obtained with 157. Thus, the error is detected. In the UPC scheme both 751 and 157 contribute the same amount to the relevant sum so that the sum for the incorrect number would still end in a zero. Thus, the error is not detected.

25. Notice that when we add the weighted sum used for the actual check digit:
$$7a_1 +3a_2 +9a_3 +7a_4 +3a_5 +9a_6 +7a_7 +3a_8$$
and the weighted sum
$$3a_1 +7a_2 +a_3 +3a_4 +7a_5 +a_6 +3a_7 +7a_8,$$
we obtain
$$10a_1 +10a_2 +10a_3 +10a_4 +10a_5 +10a_6 +10a_7 +10a_8,$$
which always ends with 0. So, the actual check digit and the check digit calculated with the weighted sum $3a_1 +7a_2 +a_3 +3a_4 +7a_5 +a_6 +3a_7 +7a_8$ are both 0 or their sum is 10.

26. Since the check digit is determined by the sum of the noncheck digits, transposing any two noncheck digits does not change the sum. This means that the remainder after division by 9 will remain the same. Transposing the check digit does change the sum if the transposed digits are distinct.

27. Replacing Z by 9 or vice versa is not detected.

28. Since the sum of the digits is not changed by rearranging the terms, the sum of the rearranged digits is divisible by 9.

29. Since the value of the weighted sum determines whether or not a number is valid, the position of the check digit is not relevant.

30. Replacing a 0 by a 9 or vice versa changes the sum by 9 or -9. In either case, the remainder after division by 9 is unchanged.

31. Since the remainder after dividing by 9 is between 0 and 8, 9 cannot be a check digit.

32. If the remainder after dividing the sum by 9 is k, then the check digit is $9-k$ unless $k=0$. When $k=0$, the check digit is 0. So, 9 can never be a check digit.

33. If the remainder of the sum of the noncheck digits after dividing by 7 is k, then the check digit is $7-k$ if $k \neq 0$ and 0 if $k=0$. So, 7,8, and 9 can never be a check digit.

34. All adjacent transposition are detectable except the transposition of the last two digits.

35. Yes. The ISBN scheme detects all transposition errors.

36. In the UPS scheme the substitution a for b is undetectable if and only if $a-b=\pm7$.

37. For the transposition to go undetected, it must be the case that the difference of the correct number and the incorrect number is evenly divisible by 11. That is,
$$(10a_1 + 9a_2 + 8a_3 + \cdots + a_{10}) - (10a_3 + 9a_2 + 8a_1 + \cdots + a_{10})$$
is divisible by 11. This reduces to $2a_1 - 2a_3 = 2(a_1 - a_3)$ is divisible by 11. But $2(a_1 - a_3)$ is divisible by 11 only when $a_1 - a_3$ is divisible by 11 and this only happens when $a_1 - a_3 = 0$. In this case, there is no error. The same argument works for the fourth and sixth digits.

38. The check digit is the same in both cases. To see this, note that because both
$$11a_1 + 11a_2 + \cdots + 11a_9 + 11a_{10}$$
and
$$10a_1 + 9a_2 + \cdots + 2a_9 + a_{10}$$
are divisible by 11, so is their difference $a_1 + 2a_2 + \cdots + 9a_9 + 10a_{10}$.

39. The combination 72 contributes $7 \cdot 1 + 2 \cdot 3 = 13$ or $7 \cdot 3 + 2 \cdot 1 = 23$ (depending on the location of the combination) towards the total sum, while the combination 27 contributes $2 \cdot 1 + 7 \cdot 3 = 23$ or $2 \cdot 3 + 7 \cdot 1 = 13$. So, the total sum resulting from the number with the transposition is still divisible by 10. Therefore, the error is not detected. When the combination 26 contributes $2 \cdot 1 + 6 \cdot 3 = 20$ towards the total sum, the combination 62 contributes $6 \cdot 1 + 2 \cdot 3 = 12$ toward the total sum; so the new sum will not be divisible by 10. Similarly, when the combination 26 contributes $2 \cdot 3 + 6 \cdot 1 = 12$ to the total, the combination 62 contributes $6 \cdot 3 + 2 \cdot 1 = 20$ to the total. So, the total for the number resulting from the transposition will not be divisible by 10 and the error is detected. In general, an error that occurs by transposing ab to ba is undetected if and only if $a-b=\pm5$

40. The 53 contributes $7 \cdot 5 + 3 \cdot 3 = 44$ towards the weighted sum, whereas 35 contributes $7 \cdot 3 + 3 \cdot 5 = 36$ towards the weighted sum. Thus the transposition changes the last digit and consequently the error is detected. In 237 the 2 and 7 contribute $7 \cdot 2 + 9 \cdot 7 = 77$ towards the weighted sum, whereas in 732 the 7 and 2 contribute $7 \cdot 7 + 9 \cdot 2 = 67$. Thus, the last digit of the weighted sum remains unchanged after the transposition. This means that the error is undetected.

41. The error $\cdots abc \cdots \rightarrow \cdots cba \cdots$ is undetectable if and only if $a - c = \pm 5$. To see this in the case that the weights for abc are 7, 3, 9, notice that a and c contribute $7a + 9c$ toward the weighted sum, whereas in the case of cba, the c and a contribute $7c + 9a$. Thus, the error is undetectable if and only if $7a + 9c$ and $7c + 9a$ contribute equal amounts to the last digit of the weighted sum. This means that they differ by a multiple of 10. That is, $-2a + 2c = 2(c - a)$ is a multiple of 10. This occurs when $c - a = 0$ or $c - a = \pm 5$. When $c - a = 0$, there is no error.

42. (a) Since $9 \cdot 1 + 8 \cdot 4 + 7 \cdot 9 + 6 \cdot 1 + 5 \cdot 0 + 4 \cdot 5 + 3 \cdot 7 + 2 \cdot 3 = 157$, the check digit is 3.

    (b) Since $9 \cdot 1 + 8 \cdot 4 + 7 \cdot 9 + 6 \cdot 1 + 5 \cdot 0 + 4 \cdot 5 + 3 \cdot 2 + 2 \cdot 6 + 7 = 155$ is not divisible by 10, the number is not valid. The correct number cannot be determined because the mistake could have occurred in several possible positions or there could have been more than one error. If you knew the error occurred in the seventh position, the error could be corrected since 7 is the only digit that results in a weighted sum divisible by 10.

    (c) Since the number 199105767 gives the weighted sum

$$9 \cdot 1 + 8 \cdot 9 + 7 \cdot 9 + 6 \cdot 1 + 5 \cdot 0 + 4 \cdot 5 + 3 \cdot 7 + 2 \cdot 6 + 7 = 210,$$

which is divisible by 10, the error is undetected.

    (d) Say the transposition is $\cdots ab \cdots \rightarrow \cdots ba \cdots$ with a weighted with $i + 1$ and b weighted with i. The transposition is undetected only if $a(i+1) + bi$ and $b(i+1) + ai$ end in the same digit. This simplifies to their difference, $a - b$, ending in 0. Since a and b are distinct and between 0 and 9, this can never happen.

43. Since any error in the position with weight 10 does not change the last digit of the weighted sum, no error in that position is detected. In the position with weight 5, replacing an even digit by any other even digit is not detected. In positions with weights 12, 8, 6, 4, or 2, replacing a by b is undetectable if $a - b = \pm 5$. In positions 11, 9, 7, 3, or 1, all errors are detected.

44. They predate computers.

45. Since both numbers are valid the difference of the weighted sums is divisible by 10. That is, $(7w + 3 + 2w + 1 + 5w + 6 + 7w + 4) - (7w + 3 + 2w + 1 + 5w + 6 + 6w + 1)$ is divisible by 10. The difference simplifies to $w + 3$. So, $w = 7$.

46. Suppose that x is a weighted sum of all the digits of the U.S. ISBN excluding the check digit and c is the check digit for the German ISBN. Since both $30 + x + c$, the weighted sum of the German ISBN, and $x + 1$, the weighted sum of the U.S. ISBN, are divisible by 11 so is their difference $29 + c$. Thus, the check digit is 4.

47. (a) The code is 51593-2067; since $5 + 1 + 5 + 9 + 3 + 2 + 0 + 6 + 7 = 38$, the check digit is 2.

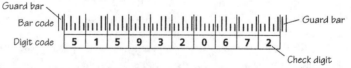

    (b) The code is 50347-0055; since $5 + 0 + 3 + 4 + 7 + 0 + 0 + 5 + 5 = 29$, the check digit is 1.

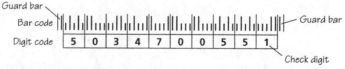

    (c) The code is 44138-9901; since $4 + 4 + 1 + 3 + 8 + 9 + 9 + 0 + 1 = 39$, the check digit is 1.

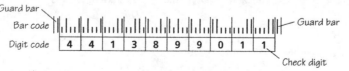

48. (a) The code is 19092-2760; since $1+9+0+9+2+2+7+6+0 = 36,$ the check digit is 4.

(b) The code is 60714-9960; since $6+0+7+1+4+9+9+6+0 = 42,$ the check digit is 8.

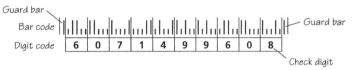

(c) The code is 32231-9871; since $3+2+2+3+1+9+8+7+1 = 36,$ the check digit is 4.

49. (a) Since the sixth block of five bars (ignoring the first bar) has one long bar and four short bars, that block is incorrect. Call the digit corresponding to that block x. Then the code is $20782x960$. Since the sum of the digits is $x+41, x=9$. Finally, we write 20782-9960.

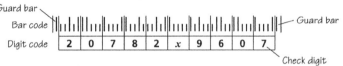

(b) Since the eighth block of five bars (ignoring the first bar) has three long bars and two short bars, that block is incorrect. Call the digit corresponding to that block x. Then the code is $5543599x2$. Since the sum of the digits is $x+42, x=8$. Finally, we write 55435-9982.

(c) Since the tenth block of five bars (ignoring the first bar) has one long bar and four short bars, that block is incorrect. Since this is the check digit, the nine-digit ZIP code is 52735-2101.

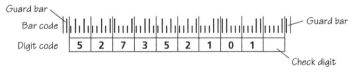

50. The ZIP+4 is 55811-2742. The last two digits of the street address are 22, and the check digit is 1.

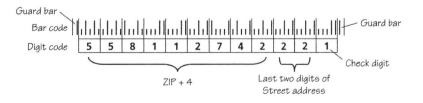

51. If a double error in a block results in a new block that does not contain exactly two long bars, we know this block has been misread. If a double error in a block of five results in a new block with exactly two long bars, the block now gives a different digit from the original one. If no other digit is in error, the check digit catches the error, since the sum of the 10 digits will not end in 0. So, in every case an error has been detected. Errors of the first type can be corrected just as in the case of a single error. When a double error results in a legitimate code number, there is no way to determine which digit is incorrect.

52. 000111000100110 where 0 represents a short bar and 1 a long bar.

53. The strings are *aaabb, aabab, aabba, abaab, ababa, abbaa, baaab, baaba, babaa,* and *bbaaa* (in alphabetical order). If you replace each short bar in the bar code table (page 603) by an *a* and replace each long bar in the bar code table by a *b*, the resulting strings are listed in alphabetical order.

54. The UPC number for books beginning with a 9 are followed by two blocks of six digits; whereas, on grocery items, the lead digit is followed by two blocks of five digits. Moreover, for books, the check digit is printed within the guard pattern; whereas, for grocery items it is not. The UPC number begins with 978 and is followed by the ISBN number with the ISBN check digit replaced by a UPC check digit. The check digit is chosen so that the number $a_1 a_2 \cdots a_{13}$, including the check digit, has the property that the following ends with a 0.

$$a_1 + 3a_2 + a_3 + 3a_4 + a_5 + 3a_6 + a_7 + 3a_8 + a_9 + 3a_{10} + a_{11} + 3a_{12} + a_{13}$$

55. Since there is an even number of 1's in 1000100, the scanner is reading from right to left.

56. The manufacturer's number and the product number are 6 digits long instead of 5. This bar code is the European UPC code.

57. Wyoming, Nevada, and Alaska.

58. States have lower numbers than those states to their west. States have lower numbers than those directly south of them.

59. The size of the population.

60. Nevada is the most likely to need a new allotment.

61. The Canadian scheme detects any transposition error involving adjacent characters. Also, there are $26^3 \times 10^3 = 17,576,000$ possible Canadian codes but only $10^5 = 100,000$ U.S. five-digit ZIP codes. Hence the Canadian scheme can target a location more precisely.

62. S-530 for each name.
    Smith → Smit → 2503 → 2503 → 503 → 53 → S-530
    Schmid → Scmid → 22503 → 2503 → 503 → 53 → S-530
    Smyth → Smyt → 2503 → 2503 → 503 → 53 → S-530
    Schmidt → Scmidt → 225033 → 2503 → 503 → 53 → S-530

63. Skow → Sko → 220 → 20 → 0 → all numbers gone → S-000
    Sachs → Sacs → 2022 → 202 → 02 → 2 → S-200
    Lennon → Lennon → 405505 → 0505 → 55 → L-550
    Lloyd → Lloyd → 44003 → 403 → 03 → 3 → L-300
    Ehrheart → Ereart → 060063 → 06063 → 6063 → 663 → E-663
    Ollenburger → Ollenburger → 04405106206 → 0405106206 → 405106206 → 451626 → O-451

64. 42 are the first two digits. The remaining three come from $40(7-1)+18+500=758$. Thus, the number is 42758

65. A person born in 1999 is too young for a driver's license.

66. Since the birthyear is 1942, 42 are the first two digits. For the months of January through May, we have $31(5)=155$. Add to this the 18 days of June we have $155+18=173$. Since the individual is male, the five digits are 42173.

67. For a woman born in November or December the formula $40(m-1)+b+600$ gives a number requiring four digits.

68. The first two digits indicate the birthyear of 1977. Since $61=31+30$, the birthday would have to be February 30.

69. The 58 indicates that the year of birth is 1958. Since 818 is larger than $12 \cdot 31=372$, we subtract 600 from 818 to obtain 218. Then $218=7 \cdot 31+1$ tells us that the person was born on the first day of the eighth month. So, the birth date is August 1, 1958.

70. 42218: Since 42 are the first two digits, the birthyear is 1942. Also, $218=40(6-1)+18$. Thus the birthday is June 18.

53953: Since 53 are the first two digits, the birthyear is 1953. Since 953 exceeds $40(12-1)+31=471$, the person is female and we subtract 500. Since $953-500=453$ and $453=40(12-1)+13$, the birthday is December 13.

71. Since $248=63(3)+58+1$, the number 248 corresponds to a female born on March 29; since $601=63(9)+34$ the number corresponds to a male born on September 17.

72. Since many people don't like to make their age public, this method is used to make it less likely that people would notice that the license number encodes year of birth.

73. Likely circumstances could be twins; sons named after their fathers (such as John L. Smith, Jr.); common names such as John Smith and Mary Johnson; and states that do not include year of birth in the code.

74. In many cases the code will be the same.

75. Because of the short names and large population there would be a significant percentage of people whose names would be coded the same.

Word Search Solution

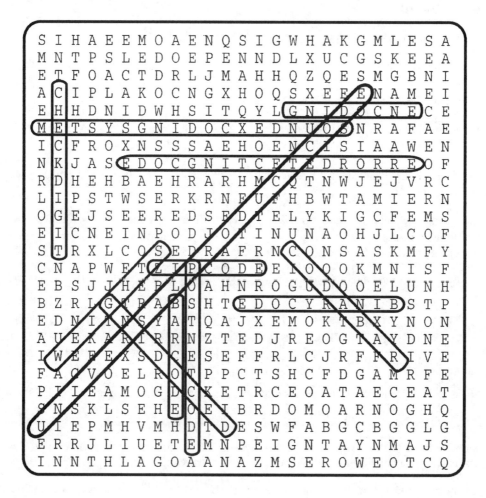

Chapter 17
Information Science

Chapter Outline

Introduction
Section 17.1   Binary Codes
Section 17.2   Encoding with Parity-Check Sums
Section 17.3   Cryptography
Section 17.4   Web Searches and Mathematical Logic

Chapter Summary

Data that are stored or transmitted can be corrupted in a variety of ways. Mathematics can be employed to detect and correct the resulting errors. Mathematical methods are also useful in data compression (which helps reduce transmission time and storage space) and *cryptography* (which ensures secure transmission of data by protecting it from "eavesdroppers").

The circuitry of digital computers makes the binary system the most convenient system to use for representing data. Mathematics (particularly abstract algebra) provides us with methods for systematically introducing redundancy into our data so that we can detect and in certain instances, correct errors that occur during storage or transmission. Ideally, a code will correct up to some fixed number of errors in a code word, regardless of where those errors occur.

Codes are constructed in different ways. The *binary linear codes* use code words consisting of strings of n 0's and 1's. Typically, the first k digits are the "message part" and encode a piece of our data (perhaps a single symbol). The remaining $n - k$ digits are *parity-check digits*. The value of each check digit is chosen so that the sum of certain components of the code word is even (a parity-check sum). The set of check digits in a code word is uniquely determined by the message part and represents the redundancy in the message. The check digits ensure that the number of code words ($2k$) is but a small fraction of the total number of n-tuples of 0's and 1's ($2n$). By carefully choosing the parity-check sums, we can further guarantee that the distance between any pair of code words (the number of components in which they disagree) is never less than a certain value t.

So constructed, our binary linear code can detect up to $t - 1$ errors and correct up to $\frac{t-1}{2}$ errors (if t is odd) or $\frac{t-2}{2}$ errors (if t is even), although it may not be able to do both simultaneously. The decoding of messages is done by the *nearest-neighbor rule*, as follows: if we receive word v, we decode it as the code word w lying closest to the word v. The word w will be unique if the number of errors that occurred during transmission does not exceed the correcting capability of the code. Otherwise, there may be several choices for w, or we may not be able to tell any errors occurred. If error correction is our goal, we should choose a code that will correct at least as many errors as are likely to occur. Error detection is clearly easier: if the word received is not a code word, then errors have occurred.

The binary linear codes are fixed length in that all code words have the same length. Some codes, such as the Morse code, use *variable-length code* words. The number of dots and dashes used for frequently occurring letters is small and is somewhat larger for less frequently occurring ones. On average, this allows more information to be transmitted with a given number of symbols than would be possible with a fixed-length code. Variable-length codes are therefore useful in *compressing data* for speedier transmission or more efficient storage.

A form of coding in 1951 was developed by David Huffman. *Huffman coding* assigns short code words to characters with higher probabilities of occurring. Even with this relatively recent development of coding, the need to transmit secure messages has a long history. One of the earliest codes (although hardly a secure one) is attributed to Julius Caesar. The *Caesar cipher* involves a substitution of letters based on a shift of the alphabet. The *Vignère cipher* involves choosing a key word and applying modular arithmetic. In the 1970s, a method known as public key cryptography was discovered by Rivest, Shamir, and Adelman. Utilizing modular arithmetic, the security of the system is due to the difficulty in factoring very large numbers. The method of digital signatures is an important application of public key cryptography.

Finally, in this age of Internet usage, this chapter addresses how *Boolean logic* is used to make search engines more efficient. Connectives and the construction of *truth tables* are examined.

Skill Objectives

1. Know what a binary code is.

2. Use the diagram method to determine or verify a code word, given the message.

3. Use the diagram method to decode a received message.

4. Be able to compute check digits for code words given the parity-check sums for the code.

3. Be able to determine the distance between two n-tuples of 0's and 1's.

4. Be able to determine the weight of a code word and the minimum weight of the nonzero code words in a code (for binary codes, the minimum weight is the same as the minimum distance between code words).

5. Know what nearest-neighbor decoding is and be able to use it for decoding messages received in the Hamming code of Table 17.2.

6. Be able to encode and decode messages that have symbols (such as letters of the alphabet) expressed in binary form.

7. Be able to make observations regarding frequently (or infrequently) occurring letters.

8. Be able to decode using a Huffman code and be able to create a Huffman code given a table of probabilities.

9. Be able to encode and decode messages using the Caesar and Vigenère ciphers.

10. Be able to add binary strings.

11. Be able to perform calculations using modular arithmetic.

12. Understand how the RSA public key encryption scheme works.

13. Be able to complete a truth table given 2 or 3 statements and the connectives NOT, OR, and AND.

14. Be able to determine if two statements are logically equivalent.

Teaching Tips

1. The Hamming code listed in Table 17.2 can correct one error and detect two, but it can't do both simultaneously. This is not a universal defect. There are linear codes that can do both at the same time (we need t to be 4 rather than 3; add a fourth check digit that is an overall parity check to the code of Table 17.2).

2. Nearest-neighbor decoding is another example of enlisting the aid of probability. We decode to the nearest code word because a smaller number of errors is more likely than a larger one. (This type of decoding is also known as maximum-likelihood decoding.)

3. Stress geometric thinking. It can be an important intuitive aid.

4. The main set of ideas is that error detection is impossible if every n-tuple is a code word, yet it gets easier if the fraction of n-tuples that are code words is small. Finally, the ability to correct is enhanced if code words are kept far apart.

5. The idea of secret codes (cryptography) can be fascinating to students. The security of the RSA public-key cryptosystem is based on the computational difficulty of finding prime factors of very large integers. This topic provides a good excuse for discussing primes and the fundamental theorem of arithmetic in a context that emphasizes a practical application of material students may have found esoteric or boring (or both).

6. Students may need to be reminded in various encoding/decoding methods that when the alphabet is correlated to a set of 26 positions, they can begin at 0 or 1, depending of the method.

Research Paper

Ask students to investigate the history of the Internet and search engines in general. Students may describe several different search engines and how they prepare the retrieved information. Also, students can investigate whether the results change (and by how much) if connectives are used or altered from one search to another (searching for the same type of information).

Collaborative Learning

Caesar Cipher

The Caesar cipher can serve as a good icebreaker for the subject of coding and decoding. Break the class up into pairs, and have each student construct a message of about 10 words, and then encode the message using the Caesar cipher, each choosing the size of the shift. Then have the students exchange coded messages and attempt to decode them.

Solutions

Skills Check:

1. b   2. b   3. b   4. c   5. a   6. b   7. a   8. c   9. b   10. b

11. a   12. b   13. c   14. a   15. c   16. b   17. c   18. c   19. a   20. a

Exercises:

1. For 0101:

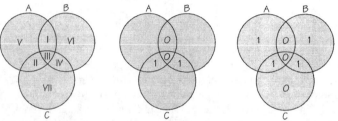

The code word given by regions I, II, III, IV, V, VI, VII is 0101110.

For 1011:

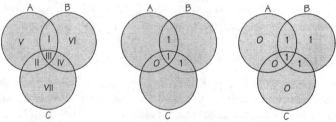

The code word given by regions I, II, III, IV, V, VI, VII is 1011010.

For 1111:

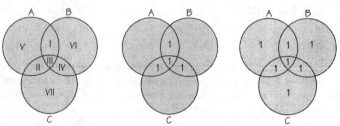

The code word given by regions I, II, III, IV, V, VI, VII is 1111111.

2. For 0111011:

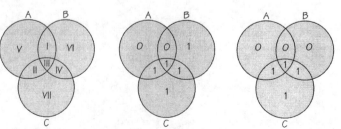

The decoded word given by regions I, II, III, IV, V, VI, VII is 0111001.

Continued on next page

2. continued

For 1000101:

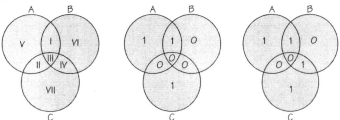

The decoded word given by regions I, II, III, IV, V, VI, VII is 1001101.

3. (a) When you compare **11011011** and **10100110**, they differ by 6 digits. Thus, the distance is 6.

   (b) When you compare **01110100** and **11101100**, they differ by 3 digits. Thus, the distance is 3.

4. For 0000110, 1000110 only differs by 1 digit. Thus, 0000110 is decoded as 1000110.
   For 1110110, 1110100 only differs by 1 digit. Thus, 1110110 is decoded as 1110100.

5. There would be no change to 1001101 since the total number of 1's in each circle is even.

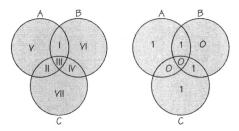

6. No errors were made in transmission or at least two errors were made in transmission.

7. Consider the following table.

	$a_2 + a_3$	c_1	$a_1 + a_3$	c_2	$a_1 + a_2$	c_3	Code word
000	0	**0**	0	**0**	0	**0**	**000000**
100	0	**0**	1	**1**	1	**1**	**100011**
010	1	**1**	0	**0**	1	**1**	**010101**
001	1	**1**	1	**1**	0	**0**	**001110**
110	1	**1**	1	**1**	2	**0**	**110110**
101	1	**1**	2	**0**	1	**1**	**101101**
011	2	**0**	1	**1**	1	**1**	**011011**
111	2	**0**	2	**0**	2	**0**	**111000**

Thus, the binary linear code is 000000, 100011, 010101, 001110, 110110, 101101, 011011, 111000.

8. Since the weight of the code is 4, it will correct any single error or detect any 3 errors.

9. Consider the following table.

	$a_2+a_3+a_4$	c_1	a_2+a_4	c_2	$a_1+a_2+a_3$	c_3	Code word
0000	0	0	0	0	0	0	0000000
1000	0	0	0	0	1	1	1000001
0100	1	1	1	1	1	1	0100111
0010	1	1	0	0	1	1	0010101
0001	1	1	1	1	0	0	0001110
1100	1	1	1	1	2	0	1100110
1010	1	1	0	0	2	0	1010100
1001	1	1	1	1	1	1	1001111
0110	2	0	1	1	2	0	0110010
0101	2	0	2	0	1	1	0101001
0011	2	0	1	1	1	1	0011011
1110	2	0	1	1	3	1	1110011
1101	2	0	2	0	2	0	1101000
1011	2	0	1	1	2	0	1011010
0111	3	1	2	0	2	0	0111100
1111	3	1	2	0	3	1	1111101

Thus, the binary linear code is 0000000, 1000001, 0100111, 0010101, 0001110, 1100110, 1010100, 1001111, 0110010, 0101001, 0011011, 1110011, 1101000, 1011010, 0111100, 1111101. No, since 1000001 has weight 2.

10. The nearest neighbors of 11101 are 11100 and 11001, so we do not decode; 01100 is decoded as 11100. The intended code word for the received word 11101 cannot be determined since there are two code words that have distance 1 from it.

11. Consider the following table.

	a_1+a_2	c_1	a_2+a_3	c_2	a_1+a_3	c_3	Code word
000	0	0	0	0	0	0	000000
100	1	1	0	0	1	1	100101
010	1	1	1	1	0	0	010110
001	0	0	1	1	1	1	001011
110	2	0	1	1	1	1	110011
101	1	1	1	1	2	0	101110
011	1	1	2	0	1	1	011101
111	2	0	2	0	2	0	111000

Thus, the binary linear code is 000000, 100101, 010110, 001011, 110011, 101110, 011101, 111000. 001001 is decoded as 001011; 011000 is decoded as 111000; 000110 is decoded as 010110; 100001 is decoded as 100101.

12. Consider the following table.

	Weight	Append	Code word
0000000	0	0	00000000
0001011	3	1	00010111
0010111	4	0	00101110
0100101	3	1	01001011
1000110	3	1	10001101
1100011	4	0	11000110
1010001	3	1	10100011
1001101	4	0	10011010
0110010	3	1	01100101
0101110	4	0	01011100
0011100	3	1	00111001
1110100	4	0	11101000
1101000	3	1	11010001
1011010	4	0	10110100
0111001	4	0	01110010
1111111	7	1	11111111

The extended code is 00000000, 00010111, 00101110, 01001011, 10001101, 11000110, 10100011, 10011010, 01100101, 01011100, 00111001, 11101000, 11010001, 10110100, 01110010, 11111111. The code will detect any three errors or correct any single error.

13. Consider the following table.

	Weight	Append	Code word
0000000	0	0	00000000
0001011	3	1	00010111
0010111	4	0	00101110
0100101	3	1	01001011
1000110	3	1	10001101
1100011	4	0	11000110
1010001	3	1	10100011
1001101	4	0	10011010
0110010	3	1	01100101
0101110	4	0	01011100
0011100	3	1	00111001
1110100	4	0	11101000
1101000	3	1	11010001
1011010	4	0	10110100
0111001	4	0	01110010
1111111	7	1	11111111

The extended code is 00000000, 00010111, 00101110, 01001011, 10001101, 11000110, 10100011, 10011010, 01100101, 01011100, 00111001, 11101000, 11010001, 10110100, 01110010, 11111111. The code will detect any three errors or correct any single error.

14. It will correct any two errors or detect any five errors.

15. There are $2^5 = 32$ possible messages of length 5. There are $2^8 = 256$ possible received words.

16. Such a binary linear code has 8 code words including 000000. For such a code to correct all double errors, the weight of the code would have to be 5. This means that each of the 7 nonzero code words must have at most one 0. Thus, the code would have to be as follows.

$$\{000000, 011111, 101111, 110111, 111011, 111101, 111110, 111111\}$$

One mistake in 111111 could not be detected.

17. Consider the following table.

	$a_1 + a_2$	$c_1 = (a_1 + a_2) \bmod 3$	$2a_1 + a_2$	$c_2 = (2a_1 + a_2) \bmod 3$	Code word
00	0	0	0	0	0000
10	1	1	2	2	1012
20	2	2	4	1	2021
01	1	1	1	1	0111
02	2	2	2	2	0222
11	2	2	3	0	1120
22	4	1	6	0	2210
21	3	0	5	2	2102
12	3	0	4	1	1201

Thus, the ternary code is 0000, 1012, 2021, 0111, 0222, 1120, 2210, 2102, 1201.

18. 1211 would be decoded as 1201.

Code word	1211 differs by
0000	4 digits
1012	2 digits
2021	3 digits
0111	2 digits
0222	3 digits
1120	3 digits
2210	2 digits
2102	4 digits
1201	**1 digit**

19. There are $3^4 = 81$ possible messages of length 5. There are $3^6 = 729$ possible received words.

20. 0, 10, 0, 0, 111, 110, 0, 0, 1, 0 would be written as 010001111100010.

21. 001100001111000 can be written as 0, 0, 110, 0, 0, 0, 111, 10, 0, 0. Thus we have, AATAAAGCAA.

22. 0, 1111, 0, 0, 1110, 10, 0, 0, 10, 110, 10 would be written as 011110011101000101010.
010001101000111111110 can be written as 0, 10, 0, 0, 110, 10, 0, 0, 1111, 1110. Thus we have, *ABAACBAAED*.

23. 1111, 0, 10, 0, 0, 1110, 0, 10, 10 would be written as 111101000111001010. 0010001100111110111010 can be written as 0, 0, 10, 0, 0, 110, 0, 1111, 0, 1110, 10. Thus we have *AABAACAEADB*.

24. $A \to 0$, $B \to 10$, $C \to 110$, $D \to 1110$, $E \to 11110$, $F \to 111111$.

25. *t*, *n*, and *r* would be the most frequently occurring consonants. *e* would be the most frequently occurring vowel.

26. Many of the occurrences of *H* are due to the word "the" which is typically omitted in telegrams.

27. In the Morse code, a space is needed to determine where each code word ends. In a fixed-length code of length k, a word ends after each k digits.

28. Any guess between 15% and 20% is an excellent guess. The approximate value is 18.6%.

29. Given the following:

2015	2015
$2057 - 2015$	42
$2079 - 2057$	22
$2060 - 2079$	-19
$2050 - 2060$	-10
$2053 - 2050$	3
$2065 - 2053$	12
$2030 - 2065$	-35
$2025 - 2030$	-5
$2002 - 2025$	-23

the compressed numbers are 2015 42 22 -19 -10 3 12 -35 -5 -23; We go from 49 characters to 34 characters, a reduction of $\dfrac{49-34}{49} = \dfrac{15}{49} \approx 30.6\%$.

30. Given the following:

1207	1207
$1207 + 373$	1580
$1580 - 57$	1523
$1523 - 97$	1426
$1426 - 234$	1192
$1192 - 105$	1087
$1087 + 178$	1265
$1265 - 73$	1192
$1192 + 275$	1467
$1467 + 79$	1546
$1546 - 183$	1363
$1363 - 146$	1217
$1217 - 94$	1123
$1123 + 129$	1252

the original numbers are:

1207 1580 1523 1426 1192 1087 1265
1192 1467 1546 1363 1217 1123 1252.

31. 1110010000100111011001101010 can be written as 1110, 01, 00, 00, 10, 01, 110, 110, 01, 10, 10. Thus, the message is decoded to be *BCEEFCDDCFF*.

32. Arranging these is order we have the following.

$$
\begin{array}{ll}
C & 0.015 \\
A & 0.025 \\
B & 0.150 \\
D & 0.170 \\
E & 0.200 \\
G & 0.215 \\
F & 0.225
\end{array}
$$

Since *C* can *A* are the least likely to occur, we begin the tree by merging them.

$$
\begin{array}{ll}
CA & 0.040 \\
B & 0.150 \\
D & 0.170 \\
E & 0.200 \\
G & 0.215 \\
F & 0.225
\end{array}
$$

Now *CA* and *B* are least likely, so we merge them.

$$
\begin{array}{ll}
D & 0.170 \\
CAB & 0.190 \\
E & 0.200 \\
G & 0.215 \\
F & 0.225
\end{array}
$$

Now *D* and *CAB* are least likely, so we merge them.

$$
\begin{array}{ll}
E & 0.200 \\
G & 0.215 \\
F & 0.225 \\
DCAB & 0.360
\end{array}
$$

Now *E* and *G* are least likely, so we merge them.

$$
\begin{array}{ll}
F & 0.225 \\
DCAB & 0.360 \\
EG & 0.415
\end{array}
$$

Now *F* and *DCAB* are least likely, so we merge them.

$$
\begin{array}{ll}
EG & 0.415 \\
FDCAB & 0.585
\end{array}
$$

And finally,

$$
\begin{array}{ll}
EGFDCAB & 1.000
\end{array}
$$

Continued on next page

32. continued

Working backwards we have the following diagram.

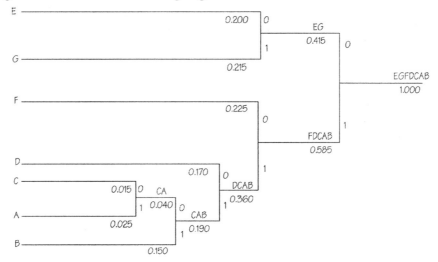

Thus, we have $A = 11101$, $B = 1111$, $C = 11100$, $D = 110$, $E = 00$, $F = 10$, $G = 01$.

33. B is the least likely letter, J is the second least likely, and G is the third least likely letter.

34. (a) 16 mod 7 = 2, so add 2 days onto Wednesday.

    (b) 37 mod 12 = 1, so add 1 hour to 4 o'clock.

    (c) 37 mod 24 = 13, so add 1300 to 0400.

    (d) July and August have 31 days and 65 mod 31 = 3, so add 3 days to 20.

    (e) An odometer uses mod 100000, so $(97000 + 12000)\,\text{mod}\,100000 = 9000$.

35. RETREAT would be encrypted as UHWUHDW.   DGYDQFH would be decoded as ADVANCE.

36. It would take 26 iterations.

37. One can take a position, such as 0 and determine that it takes 13 iterations to arrive at 0 again.

$$(0+8)\,\text{mod}\,26 = 8\,\text{mod}\,26 = 8$$
$$(8+8)\,\text{mod}\,26 = 16\,\text{mod}\,26 = 16$$
$$(16+8)\,\text{mod}\,26 = 24\,\text{mod}\,26 = 24$$
$$(24+8)\,\text{mod}\,26 = 32\,\text{mod}\,26 = 6$$
$$(6+8)\,\text{mod}\,26 = 14\,\text{mod}\,26 = 14$$
$$(14+8)\,\text{mod}\,26 = 22\,\text{mod}\,26 = 22$$
$$(22+8)\,\text{mod}\,26 = 30\,\text{mod}\,26 = 4$$
$$(4+8)\,\text{mod}\,26 = 12\,\text{mod}\,26 = 12$$
$$(12+8)\,\text{mod}\,26 = 20\,\text{mod}\,26 = 20$$
$$(20+8)\,\text{mod}\,26 = 28\,\text{mod}\,26 = 2$$
$$(2+8)\,\text{mod}\,26 = 10\,\text{mod}\,26 = 10$$
$$(10+8)\,\text{mod}\,26 = 18\,\text{mod}\,26 = 18$$
$$(18+8)\,\text{mod}\,26 = 26\,\text{mod}\,26 = 0$$

38. H is in the position 7; E is in position 4; L is in position 11; P is in position 15.

Original	Location			Encrypted
P	15	7	$(15+7) \bmod 26 = 22 \bmod 26 = 22$	W
H	7	4	$(7+4) \bmod 26 = 11 \bmod 26 = 11$	L
O	14	11	$(14+11) \bmod 26 = 25 \bmod 26 = 25$	Z
N	13	15	$(13+15) \bmod 26 = 28 \bmod 26 = 2$	C
E	4	7	$(4+7) \bmod 26 = 11 \bmod 26 = 11$	L
H	7	4	$(7+4) \bmod 26 = 11 \bmod 26 = 11$	L
O	14	11	$(14+11) \bmod 26 = 25 \bmod 26 = 25$	Z
M	12	15	$(12+15) \bmod 26 = 27 \bmod 26 = 1$	B
E	4	7	$(4+7) \bmod 26 = 11 \bmod 26 = 11$	L

The encrypted message would be WLZCL LZBL.

39. Given the key word BEATLES, we note that B is in the position 1; E is in position 4; A is in position 0; T is in position 19; L is in position 11; S is in position 18.

Encrypted	Location				Decrypted
S	18	1	$18 = 18 \bmod 26 = (17+1) \bmod 26$	17	R
S	18	4	$18 = 18 \bmod 26 = (14+4) \bmod 26$	14	O
L	11	0	$11 = 11 \bmod 26 = (11+0) \bmod 26$	11	L
E	4	19	$4 = 30 \bmod 26 = (11+19) \bmod 26$	11	L
T	19	11	$19 = 19 \bmod 26 = (8+11) \bmod 26$	8	I
R	17	4	$17 = 17 \bmod 26 = (13+4) \bmod 26$	13	N
Y	24	18	$24 = 24 \bmod 26 = (6+18) \bmod 26$	6	G
T	19	1	$19 = 19 \bmod 26 = (18+1) \bmod 26$	18	S
X	23	4	$23 = 23 \bmod 26 = (19+4) \bmod 26$	19	T
O	14	0	$14 = 14 \bmod 26 = (14+0) \bmod 26$	14	O
G	6	19	$6 = 32 \bmod 26 = (13+19) \bmod 26$	13	N
P	15	11	$15 = 15 \bmod 26 = (4+11) \bmod 26$	4	E
W	22	4	$22 = 22 \bmod 26 = (18+4) \bmod 26$	18	S

The original message was ROLLING STONES.

40. C is in the position 2; L is in position 11; U is in position 20; E is in position 4.

Original	Location			Encrypted
T	19	2	$(19+2) \bmod 26 = 21 \bmod 26 = 21$	V
H	7	11	$(7+11) \bmod 26 = 18 \bmod 26 = 18$	S
E	4	20	$(4+20) \bmod 26 = 24 \bmod 26 = 24$	Y
W	22	4	$(22+4) \bmod 26 = 26 \bmod 26 = 0$	A
A	0	2	$(0+2) \bmod 26 = 2 \bmod 26 = 2$	C
L	11	11	$(11+11) \bmod 26 = 22 \bmod 26 = 22$	W
R	17	20	$(17+20) \bmod 26 = 37 \bmod 26 = 11$	L
U	20	4	$(20+4) \bmod 26 = 24 \bmod 26 = 24$	Y
S	18	2	$(18+2) \bmod 26 = 20 \bmod 26 = 20$	U
W	22	11	$(22+11) \bmod 26 = 33 \bmod 26 = 7$	H
A	0	20	$(0+20) \bmod 26 = 20 \bmod 26 = 20$	U
S	18	4	$(18+4) \bmod 26 = 22 \bmod 26 = 22$	W
P	15	2	$(15+2) \bmod 26 = 17 \bmod 26 = 17$	R
A	0	11	$(0+11) \bmod 26 = 11 \bmod 26 = 11$	L
U	20	20	$(20+20) \bmod 26 = 40 \bmod 26 = 14$	O
L	11	4	$(11+4) \bmod 26 = 15 \bmod 26 = 15$	P

The encrypted message would be VSY ACWLYU HUW RLOP.

41. I'll.

42. that

43. To start, X would be an encrypted A or I. Similarly, G would be an encrypted A or I. The original statement is "I am a man."

44. The letter *e* never is used.

45. could've or would've.

46. your and you.

47. and

48. But, in a larger sense, we can not dedicate – we cannot consecrate – we can not hallow – this ground. The brave men, living and dead, who struggled here, have consecrated it, far above our poor power to add or detract. The world will little note, nor long remember what we say here, but it can never forget what they did here. It is for us the living, rather, to be dedicated here to the unfinished work which they who fought here have thus far so nobly advanced. It is rather for us to be here dedicated to the great task remaining before us – that from these honored dead we take increased devotion to that cause for which they gave the last full measure of devotion – that we here highly resolve that these dead shall not have died in vain – that this nation, under God, shall have a new birth of freedom – and that government of the people, by the people, for the people, shall not perish from the earth.

49. Oh, I love your magazine. Especially the "Enrich Your Word Power" section. I think it's really, really, really good.

50. No person shall be held to answer for a capital, or otherwise infamous crime, unless on a presentment or indictment of a grand jury, except in cases arising in the land or naval forces, or in the militia, when in actual service in time of war or public danger; nor shall any person be subject for the same offense to be twice put in jeopardy of life or limb; nor shall be compelled in any criminal case to be a witness against himself, nor be deprived of life, liberty, or property, without due process of law; nor shall private property be taken for public use, without just compensation. (Amendment V of the U. S. Constitution.)

51. (a)   10111011

        + 01111011

         11000000

(b)   11101000

        + 01110001

        10011001

52. (a) In order to show that a set cannot be a binary code one needs to find any instance where two words sum to be a non-word. In this case, $0011 + 0111 = 0100$ demonstrates that this is not a binary code. (There are other examples.)

(b) In order to show that a set cannot be a binary code one needs to find any instance where two words sum to be a non-word. In this case, $0010 + 0111 = 0101$ demonstrates that this is not a binary code. (There are other examples).

(c) In order to show that a set is a binary code, one needs to show that all sums of words are in turn words.

+	0000	0110	1011	1101
0000	0000	0110	1011	1101
0110	0110	0000	1101	1011
1011	1011	1101	0000	0110
1101	1101	1011	0110	0000

Thus, (a) and (b) cannot be binary codes.

53. 1.   VIP converts to 220916.

2.   We will send 22, 09, and 16 individually.

3.   Since $p = 5$ and $q = 17$, $n = pq = 5 \cdot 17 = 85$.

Since $\text{GCF}(22,85) = 1$, $\text{GCF}(9,85) = 1$, and $\text{GCF}(16,85) = 1$, we can proceed. (GCF stands for *greatest common factor*.) Thus, $M_1 = 22$, $M_2 = 09$, and $M_3 = 16$.

4.   Since $R_i = M_i^r \bmod n$ and $r = 3$, we have the following.

$$R_1 = 22^3 \bmod 85 = (2 \cdot 11)^3 \bmod 85 = \left[\left(2^3 \cdot 11 \right) \cdot 11^2 \right] \bmod 85$$

$$= \left[\left[\left(2^3 \cdot 11 \right) \bmod 85 \right] \left[11^2 \bmod 85 \right] \right] \bmod 85$$

$$= \left[(88 \bmod 85)(121 \bmod 85) \right] \bmod 85 = (3 \cdot 36) \bmod 85 = 108 \bmod 85 = 23$$

$$R_2 = 9^3 \bmod 85 = \left(3^2 \right)^3 \bmod 85 = 3^6 \bmod 85 = \left[\left(3^5 \bmod 85 \right) \left(3 \bmod 85 \right) \right] \bmod 85$$

$$= \left[(243 \bmod 85)(3 \bmod 85) \right] \bmod 85 = (73 \cdot 3) \bmod 85 = 219 \bmod 85 = 49$$

$$R_3 = 16^3 \bmod 85 = \left(2^4 \right)^3 \bmod 85 = 2^{12} \bmod 85 = \left[\left(2^7 \bmod 85 \right) \left(2^5 \bmod 85 \right) \right] \bmod 85$$

$$= \left[(128 \bmod 85)(32 \bmod 85) \right] \bmod 85 = (43 \cdot 32) \bmod 85 = (43 \cdot 2 \cdot 16) \bmod 85$$

$$= \left[(43 \cdot 2) \cdot 16 \right] \bmod 85 = \left[(86 \bmod 85)(16 \bmod 85) \right] \bmod 85$$

$$= \left[1 \cdot (16 \bmod 85) \right] \bmod 85 = (16 \bmod 85) = 16$$

Thus, the numbers sent are 23, 49, 16.

54. 1. Since $p = 5$ and $q = 17$, $n = pq = 5 \cdot 17 = 85$.

2. Since $p - 1 = 5 - 1 = 4$ and $q - 1 = 17 - 1 = 16$, m will be the least common multiple of 4 and 16, namely 16.

3. We need to choose r such that it has no common divisors with 16. Thus, r can be 3. This confirms that $r = 3$ is a valid choice.

4. We need to find s such that $rs = 1 \bmod m$.

$$r^2 \bmod m = 3^2 \bmod 16 = 9 \bmod 16 = 9$$

$$r^3 \bmod m = 3^3 \bmod 16 = 27 \bmod 16 = (1 \cdot 16 + 11) \bmod 16 = 11$$

$$r^4 \bmod m = 3^4 \bmod 16 = 81 \bmod 16 = (5 \cdot 16 + 1) \bmod 16 = 1$$

Thus $t = 4$.

Since $s = r^{t-1} \bmod m$, where $r = 3$, $m = 16$, and $t = 4$, we have the following.

$$s = 3^{4-1} \bmod 16 = 3^3 \bmod 16 = 27 \bmod 16 = 11$$

5. Since $52^{11} \bmod 85 = \left[\left(52^4 \right)^2 \cdot 52^3 \right] \bmod 85 = \left[\left(\left(52^4 \right) \bmod 85 \right)^2 \cdot 52^3 \bmod 85 \right] \bmod 85$

$$= \left(1^2 \cdot 18 \right) \bmod 85 = 18 \bmod 85 = 18, \ R_1 = 18.$$

Since $72^{11} \bmod 85 = \left[\left(72^4 \right)^2 \cdot 72^3 \right] \bmod 85 = \left[\left(\left(72^4 \right) \bmod 85 \right)^2 \cdot 72^3 \bmod 85 \right] \bmod 85$

$$= \left(1^2 \cdot 13 \right) \bmod 85 = 13 \bmod 85 = 13, \ R_2 = 13.$$

Thus, the letters received are R and M.

55. 1. Since $p = 5$ and $q = 17$, $n = pq = 5 \cdot 17 = 85$.

2. Since $p - 1 = 5 - 1 = 4$ and $q - 1 = 17 - 1 = 16$, m will be the least common multiple of 4 and 16, namely 16.

3. We need to choose r such that it has no common divisors with 16. Thus, r can be 5. This confirms that $r = 5$ is a valid choice.

4. We need to find s such that $rs = 1 \bmod m$.

$$r^2 \bmod m = 5^2 \bmod 16 = 25 \bmod 16 = 9$$

$$r^3 \bmod m = 5^3 \bmod 16 = 125 \bmod 16 = 13$$

$$r^4 \bmod m = 5^4 \bmod 16 = 625 \bmod 16 = 1$$

Thus $t = 4$.

Since $s = r^{t-1} \bmod m$, where $r = 5$ and $t = 4$, we have the following.

$$s = 5^{4-1} \bmod 16 = 5^3 \bmod 16 = 125 \bmod 16 = 13$$

56. Because 3 has a divisor other than 1 in common with the least common multiple of 6 and 10 (which is 30).

57. N converts to 14 and O converts to 15, but 14 and 77 have a greatest common divisor of 7. On the other hand, using blocks of length 4, NO converts to 1415 and the greatest common divisor of 77 and 1415 is 1.

58. $13^9 \bmod 77 = 6$, $13^6 \bmod 77 = 64$. Google yields $13^{15} \bmod 77 = 0$, so we can calculate $13^{15} \bmod 77$ by doing $\left(13^9 \right) \bmod 77 \times \left(13^6 \right) \bmod 77 = \left(6 \times 64 \right) \bmod 77 = 76$.

59. As the following shows, since the entries in the column for the variable P are exactly the same as the entries in the column for $P \vee (P \wedge Q)$, the two expressions are logically equivalent.

P	Q	$P \wedge Q$	$P \vee (P \wedge Q)$
T	T	T	T
T	F	F	T
F	T	F	F
F	F	F	F

60. First we construct the truth table for $\neg(P \vee Q)$.

P	Q	$P \vee Q$	$\neg(P \vee Q)$
T	T	T	F
T	F	T	F
F	T	T	F
F	F	F	T

Next we construct the truth table for $\neg P \wedge \neg Q$.

P	Q	$\neg P$	$\neg Q$	$\neg P \wedge \neg Q$
T	T	F	F	F
T	F	F	T	F
F	T	T	F	F
F	F	T	T	T

Since the last columns of the two truth tables are identical, the expression $\neg(P \vee Q)$ is logically equivalent to $\neg P \wedge \neg Q$.

61. First we construct the truth table for $\neg(P \wedge Q)$.

P	Q	$P \wedge Q$	$\neg(P \wedge Q)$
T	T	T	F
T	F	F	T
F	T	F	T
F	F	F	T

Next we construct the truth table for $\neg P \vee \neg Q$

P	Q	$\neg P$	$\neg Q$	$\neg P \vee \neg Q$
T	T	F	F	F
T	F	F	T	T
F	T	T	F	T
F	F	T	T	T

Since the last columns of the two truth tables are identical, we have shown that $\neg(P \wedge Q)$ is logically equivalent to $\neg P \vee \neg Q$.

62. First we construct the truth table for $P \vee (Q \wedge R)$.

P Q R	$Q \wedge R$	$P \vee (Q \wedge R)$
T T T	T	T
T T F	F	T
T F T	F	T
T F F	F	T
F T T	T	T
F T F	F	F
F F T	F	F
F F F	F	F

Next we construct the truth table for $(P \vee Q) \wedge (P \vee R)$.

P Q R	$P \vee Q$	$P \vee R$	$(P \vee Q) \wedge (P \vee R)$
T T T	T	T	T
T T F	T	T	T
T F T	T	T	T
T F F	T	T	T
F T T	T	T	T
F T F	T	F	F
F F T	F	T	F
F F F	F	F	F

Since the last columns of the two truth tables are identical, the expression $P \vee (Q \wedge R)$ is logically equivalent to $(P \vee Q) \wedge (P \vee R)$.

63. First we construct the truth table for $P \wedge (Q \vee R)$.

P Q R	$Q \vee R$	$P \wedge (Q \vee R)$
T T T	T	T
T T F	T	T
T F T	T	T
T F F	F	F
F T T	T	F
F T F	T	F
F F T	T	F
F F F	F	F

Continued on next page

63. continued

Next we construct the truth table for $(P \wedge Q) \vee (P \wedge R)$.

P Q R	$P \wedge Q$	$P \wedge R$	$(P \wedge Q) \vee (P \wedge R)$
T T T	T	T	T
T T F	T	F	T
T F T	F	T	T
T F F	F	F	F
F T T	F	F	F
F T F	F	F	F
F F T	F	F	F
F F F	F	F	F

Since the last columns of the two truth tables are identical, the expression $P \wedge (Q \vee R)$ is logically equivalent to $(P \wedge Q) \vee (P \wedge R)$.

64. Let P denote "lots of anchovies," let Q denote "spicy," and let R denote "large portion." Then the patron's order can be represented as the expression $(P \vee \neg Q) \wedge R$. The waiter's statement to the chef can be expressed as $(P \wedge R) \vee (Q \wedge R)$. A truth table for $(P \vee \neg Q) \wedge R$ is as follows.

P Q R	$\neg Q$	$P \vee \neg Q$	$(P \vee \neg Q) \wedge R$
T T T	F	T	T
T T F	F	T	F
T F T	T	T	T
T F F	T	T	F
F T T	F	F	F
F T F	F	F	F
F F T	T	T	T
F F F	T	T	F

A truth table for $(P \wedge R) \vee (Q \wedge R)$ is as follows.

P Q R	$P \wedge R$	$Q \wedge R$	$(P \wedge R) \vee (Q \wedge R)$
T T T	T	T	T
T T F	F	F	F
T F T	T	F	T
T F F	F	F	F
F T T	F	T	T
F T F	F	F	F
F F T	F	F	F
F F F	F	F	F

Because the last columns of these truth tables are not identical, we conclude that the two expressions are not logically equivalent. Thus, the waiter did not communicate the patron's wishes to the chef.

65. The truth table for $\neg P \vee Q$ is as follows.

P	Q	$\neg P$	$\neg P \vee Q$
T	T	F	T
T	F	F	F
F	T	T	T
F	F	T	T

Because the last column of this truth table is identical for the one for $P \rightarrow Q$, we conclude that the two expressions are logically equivalent.

66. Let P denote "the Vikings win," let Q denote "the Vikings make the playoffs". Then the coach's statement to the team is $P \rightarrow Q$ and the given conditions are P is F and Q is T. From the truth table, we have that $P \rightarrow Q$ is true.

67. Let P denote "it snows" and let Q denote "there is school." Then the statement "If it snows, there will be no school" can be expressed as $P \rightarrow \neg Q$. Similarly, the statement "it is not the case that it snows and there is school" can be expressed as $\neg(P \wedge Q)$. We now construct the truth tables for each of these expressions. A truth table for $P \rightarrow \neg Q$ is as follows.

P	Q	$\neg Q$	$P \rightarrow \neg Q$
T	T	F	F
T	F	T	T
F	T	F	T
F	F	T	T

A truth table for $\neg(P \wedge Q)$ is as follows.

P	Q	$P \wedge Q$	$\neg(P \wedge Q)$
T	T	T	F
T	F	F	T
F	T	F	T
F	F	F	T

Because the two tables have identical last columns, the two expressions are logically equivalent.

Word Search Solution

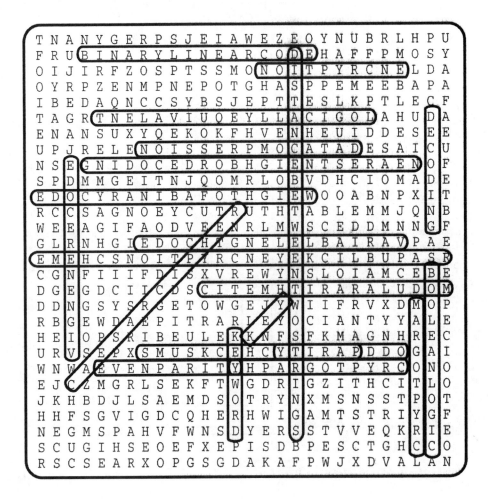

Chapter 18
Growth and Form

Chapter Outline

Chapter Summary

All living things encounter the problem of scale: how to adapt and survive as their size changes from the beginning of life to maturity. There are physical limits to size, and the force of gravity has a profound effect on the size and shape that objects and living creatures can assume.

We can gain insight into the effects of size change by examining simple geometric examples. Geometrically, objects are considered similar if they have the same shape. The *scaling factor* tells us the change in *dimension* if we enlarge (or shrink) an object. Changing dimension induces a corresponding change in *area* or *volume*. For example, doubling the sides of a square increases area by a factor of four. Similarly, doubling the edges of a cube increases volume by a factor of eight (and surface area by a factor of four). Generally speaking, volume changes proportionally with the cube of the scaling factor; and area, proportionally with its square.

A real object (living or not) is composed of matter. This matter has a *mass* determined by the volume of the object and the *density* of its matter. The force of gravity acting on this mass is what gives the body *weight*. Finally, the object must be able to support this weight, which exerts pressure on that portion of the object supporting the weight.   Now pressure increases proportionally with the scaling factor. Hence, when the scaling factor is made large enough, the object will crumble under its own weight. To solve this problem of scale, it may be necessary to change the material from which the object is made, change the object's shape, or both. In some cases (buildings, airplanes), we may be able to make the changes necessary for building larger and larger things. In other cases (mountains, trees, people), the demands are clearly beyond our capability.

The ability of an animal to survive falls, hold its breath under water, jump, and fly also depends on the size of the animal, and increases (or decreases) proportionally with the scaling factor. The need for animals to keep themselves warm (or to cool themselves off) produces an interesting interplay between their volume and surface area. The volume of the animal determines the amount of matter to be warmed or cooled, but the rate at which the warming or cooling takes place depends on its surface area. A few basic geometric and physical concepts have allowed us to show that none of the living beings and objects in our world could exist on vastly different scales, larger or smaller, without fundamental changes in shape or composition.

Skill Objectives

1. Determine the scaling factor when given the original dimensions of an object and its scaled dimensions.

2. Given the original dimensions of an object and its scaling factor, determine its scaled dimensions.

3. Calculate the change in area of a scaled object when its original area and the scaling factor are given.

4. Calculate the change in volume of a scaled object when its original volume and the scaling factor are given.

5. Determine whether two given geometric objects are similar.

6. Locate on a number line the new location of a scaled point.

7. When given the two-dimensional coordinates of a geometric object, its center, and the scaling factor, calculate its new coordinates after the scaling has taken place.

8. Calculate from given formulas the perimeter and area of a two-dimensional object.

9. Calculate from given formulas the surface area and volume of a three-dimensional object.

10. Describe the concept of area-volume tension.

11. Explain why objects in nature are restricted by a potential maximum size.

Teaching Tips

1. To explain why weight is proportional to volume, you might consider using the metric system example: 1 gram of water is defined to be the mass of 1 cubic centimeter of water.

2. The concept of geometric similarity may be introduced on an intuitive level by appealing to the student's visual sense. Using the overhead projector and prepared diagrams, many examples of similar and non-similar pairs of objects could be discussed. In particular, showing that any two squares are similar, but pointing out that two rectangles may or may not be similar, should help the student discriminate more clearly.

3. The concept of proportionality is important in many applications of mathematics. This chapter provides an opportunity to review the process of solving a proportion through cross-multiplication. Additional practice on the topic can be gained from finding the lengths of sides of a similar object when given the corresponding dimensions of the original object and the length of one side of its similar counterpart.

4. The Suggested Readings section of this chapter contains some interesting materials that, because of their visual nature, most students will be able to understand. You may wish to assign specific readings from these as extra-credit projects.

5. This chapter provides an unusually good opportunity for class discussion. You may find that students who rarely speak up in class will be motivated by the topic to participate.

6. Students who are amateur photographers can be encouraged to photograph examples of similar objects that exist in nature. If these are produced as slides, they can then be shown to the class.

Research Paper

Have students investigate the history of measurement. Although this is a broad topic, specific topics such as

- History of the cubit
- History of the Imperial system
- Origin of the inch, foot, and yard
- History of the metric system
- Units of type measurement
- Units of angular measurement

can be readily assigned. A website such as http://en.wikipedia.org/wiki/History_of_measurement can be very helpful to start research or assign topics. A more current topic of interest may be the "Metric Martyrs."

Spreadsheet Project

To do this project, go to http://www.whfreeman.com/fapp7e.

This spreadsheet project explores the impact of scale on the design of buildings.

Collaborative Learning

1. Photographic enlargement is an example of scaling that is familiar to almost everyone. Photocopy a photograph, preferably one that has a shape in it whose area can be easily calculated, such as a rectangle. Then enlarge the copy by a certain scaling factor, and ask the students to calculate the ratios of various linear measurements in the two photos, and then the ratios of the areas in the two photos. With some hints and prodding, the students will soon have a concrete example of how area scales as the square of the scaling factor.

   Note: A scaling factor of 2 or 3 will help students discover this principle more quickly. Many copy machines allow you to set the scaling factor, although only in a limited range, so you may have to enlarge the original several times to obtain an integral scaling factor.

2. **a)** Ask the students to bring in graphics or other diagrams that visually "lie," similar to the ones at the end of the chapter (after the problem set), as well as others that they believe tell the truth. Working in pairs, have them analyze each other's examples.

   b) Have the students construct their own diagrams or graphics that are examples of "How to Lie with Statistics." Again, have them work in pairs, criticizing each other's works.

Solutions

Skills Check:

1. c   2. c   3. a   4. c   5. b   6. c   7. c   8. b   9. c   10. b

11. a   12. a   13. c   14. c   15. a   16. a   17. b   18. c   19. a   20. a/b

Exercises:

1. (a) A contact print is the same size as the negative, so the scaling factor is 1.

    (b) The scaling factor is the ratio of the length of the enlargement to the original, hence 3; the area of the enlargement will be $3^2 = 9$ times as much.

    (c) Since we have $4 = 4 \times 1$ and $6 = 4 \times 1\frac{1}{2}$, the scaling factor is 4.

    (d) Yes. For the negative, the width is $\frac{1.5}{1} = 1.5$ times the height; for the print, the ratio (with the length and height converted to thirty-seconds of an inch) is $\frac{147}{98} = 1.5$.

    (e) The 5×7, 8×10, 11×14, and 16×20 are not geometrically similar to the negative, because their lengths are not exactly 1.5 times their heights; in printing one of those, the negative must be cropped.

    (f) Based just on paper used, the 8×12 would cost $2^2 = 4$ times as much as the 4×6.

    (g) The 5×7, with 35 in.^{2} $1.79/35 in.$^2 \approx \$0.0511$/in.^{2}; the 8×10, costs about $\$0.0499$/in.^{2}. So you could expect the 11×14, with an area of 154 in.^{2}, to cost about $154 \times \$0.05 = \$7.70$ (probably \$7.79 or \$7.99), based just on cost of the paper.

    (h) The 20×30 is 600 in.^{2}. Since $\left(600 \text{ in.}^2\right)\left(\$0.0499/\text{in.}^2\right) = \$29.94$, the price should probably be \$29.99, based just on cost of the paper.

2. (a) $\dfrac{16 \text{ in.}}{10 \text{ in.}} = 1.6$.

    (b) $(1.6)^2 = 2.56$ times as large.

    (c) $\dfrac{\frac{1}{4}\pi(10 \text{ in.})^2}{\$6.30} \approx 12.5 \text{ in.}^2/\$$; $15.4 \text{ in.}^2/\$$; $18.4 \text{ in.}^2/\$$; $21.3 \text{ in.}^2/\$$; we assume that the thickness of the topping isn't scaled up and hence is the same for all the pizzas.

    (d) No. the best deal, the extra large pizza, gives 12.0 in.2 per dollar.

    (e) The new prices have been scaled linearly from the old ones.

3. (a) The linear scaling factor is $\dfrac{4 \text{ cm}}{160 \text{ cm}} = \dfrac{1}{40} = 0.025$.

    (b) The volume of the real person goes up as the cube of the scaling factor and so is $40^3 = 64,000$ times as large as the volume of the Lego.

    (c) $40 \times 10 \text{ cm} = 400 \text{ cm} = 4.00 \text{m} = 400 \text{ cm} \times \dfrac{1 \text{ in}}{2.54 \text{ cm}} \approx 157.5 \text{ in.} \approx 13.1 \text{ ft.}$

4. (a) $\dfrac{1}{12}$.

(b) The dollhouse would weigh $\left(\dfrac{1}{12}\right)^3 = \dfrac{1}{1728} \approx 0.00058$ times as much.

5. The linear scaling factor for men compared to women (on average) is 1.08; if the brain scales as the cube of height, then men's brains (on average) would be $1.08^3 \approx 1.26$ times as large as women's, or 26% larger.

6. Geometrically similar: $\left(\dfrac{12}{10}\right)^3 = 1.73$ times as heavy. Geometrically similar except for thickness of metal: $\left(\dfrac{12}{10}\right)^2 = 1.44$ times as heavy.

7. (a) The new altar would have a volume 8 times as large – not "8 times greater than" or "8 times larger than", and definitely not twice as large, as the old altar.

(b) Since the volume scales as the cube of the side, the side scales as the cube root of the volume: $\sqrt[3]{2} \approx 1.26$.

8. (a) The resulting coin would have 8 times the weight of a quarter.

(b) $\dfrac{1}{16}$ in,

(c) Diameter $= \sqrt[3]{4} \times \dfrac{15}{16}$ in. ≈ 1.49 in., thickness $= \sqrt[3]{4} \times \dfrac{1}{16}$ in. ≈ 0.10 in.   These are almost exactly the dimensions of the older Eisenhower dollar coin.

9. The writer meant that the volume was 2.5 times as much before packaging. Since 2.5 bags have been compressed to 1 bag, the new volume is $\dfrac{1}{2.5} = 0.4$ "times as much as" before. We could also correctly say that the peat moss has been compressed "to 40% of its original volume" or "by 60%," or that the compressed volume is "60% less than" the original volume.

10. (a) Nothing can be reduced by more than 100%.

(b) If it had improved 100%, there would be *no* lost luggage (and no room for further improvement!).

(c) It is a 50% reduction (and a drop of 5 percentage points).

11. You don't have to be an expert in management to see that answers A, B, and E are totally irrelevant (despite the claims at Microedu.com) and that the given statement is about costs being less than in country Q, thus eliminating D (with any percentage). If the original statement read instead "a car costs 120% more in Country Y than in Country Q," then C is correct. We can cast this into algebra, using q for the price in country Q, y for the price in Country Y, T for the tariff, and t for the transportation cost. The statements say that $q + t + T < y = q + 1.2q = 2.2q$, from which we find $T < t + T < 1.2q$, which is what C says.

12. Expenditures cannot go down by more than 100%. Oklahoma spends $100\% \times \dfrac{\$6.06}{\$13.17} \approx 46\%$ as much as, or $100\% \times \dfrac{\$13.17 - \$6.06}{\$13.17} \approx 54\%$ than, the national average. The regional expenditures of $8.12 per capita is $100\% \times \dfrac{\$8.12 - \$6.06}{\$6.06} \approx 34\%$ more than in Oklahoma.

13. Answers will vary.

14. (a) The worth (according to the city) is $100\% \times \dfrac{\$259,000 - \$107,500}{\$259,000} \approx 58\%$ less.

    (b) The charge can't be more than 100% less.

    (c) The 7% in British Columbia is $100\% \times \dfrac{14.7\% - 7\%}{14.7\%} \approx 52\%$ less than Alberta's.

15. $\$0.80 = \$0.80 \times \dfrac{\text{€}1}{\$1.30} = \text{€}\dfrac{0.80}{\$1.30} \approx \text{€}0.62$. (This is only a little more than the cost of a domestic letter in Germany, € 0.55, which, however, is delivered overnight.)

16. $\text{US}\$0.60 \times \dfrac{\text{Cdn}\$1.23}{\text{US}\$1} \approx \text{Cdn}\$0.74$.

17. The car gets 100 km per 7.3 L, which is $\dfrac{100 \text{ km}}{7.3 \text{ L}} = \dfrac{100 \times 0.621 \text{ mi}}{7.3 \times 0.2642 \text{gal}} \approx 32.2$ or 32 mpg.

18. $60 \text{ mpg} = 60 \dfrac{\text{mi}}{\text{gal}} \approx 60 \dfrac{\text{mi}}{4 \text{qt}} \times \dfrac{1.61 \text{ km}}{1 \text{ mi}} \times \dfrac{1.057 \text{ qt}}{1 \text{ L}}$

    $\approx \dfrac{60 \times 1.61 \times 1.057}{4} \dfrac{\text{km}}{\text{L}} \approx 25.5 \text{ km/L} = \dfrac{1 \text{ km}}{\frac{1}{25.5} \text{L}} \approx \dfrac{100 \text{ km}}{\frac{100}{25.5} \text{L}} \approx \dfrac{100 \text{ km}}{3.9 \text{ L}}$.

    So it uses 3.9 L per 100 km. The car is (barely) what the Germans call a "three-liter car".

19. (a) $\left(\dfrac{1}{87}\right)^3 \times 88 \text{ tons} \approx 0.00013364 \text{ tons}$.

    (b) We assume that all parts of the scale model are made of the same materials as the real locomotive.

    (c) $0.00013364 \text{ tons} = 0.00013364 \times 2000 \text{ lb} \approx 0.267 \text{ lb}$.

    (d) $0.267 \text{ lb} = 0.267 \times 0.45359237 \text{ kg} \approx 0.121 \text{ kg}$.

    (e) $0.121 \text{ kg} = 0.121 \text{ kg} \times \dfrac{1 \text{ metric tonne}}{1000 \text{ kg}} = 0.000121 \text{ metric tonnes}$.

20. A hectare equals 0.003861 mi^2 or 2.471 acres.

21. $\dfrac{€1.169}{1\,L}\times\dfrac{\$1.30}{€1}\times\dfrac{1\,L}{1000\,\text{cm}^3}\times\dfrac{(2.54\,\text{cm})^3}{(1\,\text{in})^3}\times\dfrac{231\,\text{in}^3}{1\,\text{gal}}\approx\$5.75/\text{gal.}$ or

$\dfrac{€1.169}{1\,L}\times\dfrac{\$1.30}{€1}\times\dfrac{1\,L}{0.2642\,\text{gal}}\approx\$5.75/\text{gal.}$

22. $45{,}000{,}000\,\text{yen}\times\dfrac{\$1}{125\,\text{yen}}=\$360{,}000$

23. $607\,\text{ft}=607\times0.3048\,\text{m}=185\,\text{m.}$

24. Answers will vary with assumptions made. The top of the building is 1671 ft above ground level; that is an average of $\dfrac{1671\,\text{ft}}{101\,\text{floors}}\approx16.5$ ft/floor. Assume that the floor of the elevator starts at ground level, and we neglect any additional height due to the roof or peak. The floor of the elevator needs to make it to the floor level of the 101st floor, which is 16.5 ft below the top of the building, at height $1671\,\text{ft}-16.5\,\text{ft}=1654.5\,\text{ft.}$ At 55 ft/s, the trip will take $\dfrac{1654.5\,\text{ft}}{55\dfrac{\text{ft}}{\text{s}}}\approx30.1$ s, not counting additional time for acceleration and deceleration.

25. (a) $55\,\text{ft/s}=\dfrac{55\times1\,\text{ft}}{1\,\text{s}}=\dfrac{55\times\dfrac{1}{5280}\,\text{mi}}{\dfrac{1}{3600}\,\text{h}}=\dfrac{55\times3600\,\text{mi}}{5280\,\text{h}}=37.5\,\text{mph.}$

(b) $1\,\text{ft/s}=\dfrac{\dfrac{1}{5280}\,\text{mi}}{\dfrac{1}{3600}\,\text{h}}=\dfrac{3600}{5280}\,\text{mph}\approx0.68182\,\text{mph,}$ so $41\,\text{ft/s}\approx41\times0.68182\,\text{mph}\approx28.0\,\text{mph.}$

(c) $\dfrac{1\,\text{mi}}{0.5\,\text{min}}=\dfrac{1\,\text{mi}}{0.5\,\text{min}}\times\dfrac{60\,\text{min}}{1\,\text{h}}=120\,\text{mph.}$

26. The home currency is the Middie and the target currency is the dollar.
We have (new value of 1 Middie − old value of 1 Middie) = $\$1-\$2=-\$1.$

(a) We divide the −$1 by the new trading value, $1, and multiply by 100, arriving at −100%, or a loss of 100% (this answer should make you question Option A, since the Middie did not become completely worthless!).

(b) We divide the −$1 by the old trading value, $2, and multiply by 100, arriving at −50%, a loss of 50%.

27. (a) $\dfrac{1.00\,\text{Middie}-0.50\,\text{Middie}}{1.00\,\text{Middie}}\times100\%=50\%.$

(b) $\dfrac{1.00\,\text{Middie}-0.50\,\text{Middie}}{0.50\,\text{Middie}}\times100\%=100\%.$

28. The home currency is the dollar and the target currency is the euro.
We have (new value of $1 − old value of $1) = (€0.7435 − €1.160)= €−0.4165.

(a) We divide the €−0.4165 by the new trading value, €0.7435, and multiply by 100, arriving at −56%, or a loss of 56%.

(b) We divide the €−0.4165 by the old trading value, EUR 1.160, and multiply by 100, arriving at −36%, a loss of 36%.

29. (a) $\dfrac{\$1.345-\$0.862}{\$1.345} \times 100\% = 35.9\%.$

(b) $\dfrac{\$1.345-\$0.862}{\$0.862} \times 100\% = 56.0\%.$

30. (a) Answers will vary. An analogous situation: Suppose that you make $2000 per month and your friend makes $4000 per month; you are making 50% less than she is, but she is making 100% more than you are. The relationship between a loss L and a corresponding gain G, when both are measured as signed numbers, is not additive but multiplicative. For Option A, we have $(1-L)(1-G)=1$. (Check this for the Middie as home currency, where $L = -100\% = -1$ from Exercise 26a and $G = 50\% = 0.5$ from Exercise 27a.) For Option B, the relationship is $(1+L)(1+G)=1$. (Check this for the Middie as home currency, where $L=-50\%=-0.5$ from Exercise 26b and $G=100\%=1$ from Exercise 27b.) The connections between the two options (as can be shown easily using the notation in the solution for Exercise 31) are that $L_A = -G_B$ and $G_A = -A_B$, where L_A (respectively L_B) is the loss of currency 1 against currency 2 under Option A (respectively B) and G_A (respectively G_B) is the gain of currency 2 against currency 1 under option A (respectively B). (Check this for the results of Exercise 27.) For either Option, for a small change (under 5%, say), the size of the gain by the one currency is approximately the same as the size of the loss by the other. For example, under Option B, $1+G=\dfrac{1}{1+L}\approx 1-L,$ $G \approx -L,$ or $|G| \approx |L|.$

(b) In light of the unnnatural result of Exercise 26a for Option A, we prefer Option B.

31. (a) For Option A, yes; for Option B, no. Let the previous value of the currency be C and the new value be D. Then Option A gives $\dfrac{D-C}{D}\times100\% = \left(1-\dfrac{C}{D}\right)\times100\% < -100\%$ if $C > 2D$. Option B gives $\dfrac{D-C}{C}\times100\% = \left(\dfrac{D}{C}-1\right)\times100\% \geq -100\%$ for all nonzero C, D.

(b) If the new trading value is higher than the old one, the percentage in Option B is higher than that in A: With $D > C$, Option A $= \dfrac{D-C}{D}\times100\% < \dfrac{D-C}{C}\times100\% =$ Option B. If the new trading value is lower than the old one, then both options give negative numbers but the absolute value of the percentage in Option B is higher than that in A: With $D < C$, Option A $\dfrac{D-C}{D}\times100\% < \dfrac{D-C}{C}\times100\% =$ Option B. In both cases, the absolute value of the percentage is higher for Option B.

(c) Either way, use Option B.

32. (a) $\dfrac{500 \text{ lb}}{144 \text{ in.}} \approx 3.47 \text{ lb/in.}^2$

   (b) $3.47 \text{ lb/in.}^2 \times \dfrac{1 \text{ atm}}{14.7 \text{ lb/in.}^2} \approx 0.24 \text{ atm}$

33. (a) The layer of soil has volume $100 \text{ ft}^2 \times 0.5 \text{ ft} = 50 \text{ ft}^3$. The density is the weight divided by the volume, so $45{,}000 \text{ lb/50 ft}^3 = 900 \text{ lb/ft}^3$.

   (b) The density of steel is 500 lb/ft^3, so the claim is that the soil is $900/500 \approx 1.8 \approx 2$ times as dense as steel.

   (c) Since 230 lb of compost is supposed to add about 5%, the original should be about 230 lb divided by 0.05, or 4,600 lb. The revised quotation should say that the mineral soil weighs about 4,500 to 4,600 lb.

34. (a) $\left(\dfrac{1}{2}\right)^3 \times 400 \text{ lb} = 50 \text{ lb.}$

   (b) We assume that the gorilla undergoes geometric growth.

   (c) $\dfrac{400 \text{ lb}}{1 \text{ ft}^2} = \dfrac{400 \text{ lb}}{1 \text{ ft}^2} \times \dfrac{1 \text{ ft}^2}{144 \text{ in.}^2} \approx 2.8 \text{ lb/in.}^2$

35. (a) Weight scales as the cube of the linear scaling factor, so KK would have to weigh $400 \text{ lb} \times 10^3 = 400{,}000 \text{ lb.}$

   (b) The surface area of feet scales as the square of the linear scaling factor, so the area of KK's feet is $1 \text{ ft} \times 10^2 = 100 \text{ ft}^2$, and the pressure is $400{,}000 \text{ lb/100 ft}^2 = 4{,}000 \text{ lb/ft}^2 = 4{,}000 \text{ lb/144 in.}^2 \approx 28 \text{ lb/in.}^2$.

36. (a) Solutions will vary. One strategy is to convert the measurements to feet, multiply to find the volume in cubic feet, convert cubic feet to cubic meters, convert cubic meters to liters, and then find the weight in kg and convert that to lb. The volume is $80 \text{ in.} \times 60 \text{ in.} \times 12 \text{ in.} \approx$

   $6.6667 \text{ ft} \times 5 \text{ ft} \times 1 \text{ ft} \approx 33.333 \text{ ft}^3 = 33.333 \text{ ft}^3 \times \dfrac{1 \text{ m}^3}{35.31 \text{ ft}^3} \approx 0.944 \text{ m}^3 =$

   $0.944 \text{ m}^3 \times \dfrac{1000 \text{ L}}{1 \text{ m}^3} = 944 \text{ L}$, which weighs $944 \text{ kg} = 944 \text{ kg} \times \dfrac{2.205 \text{ lb}}{1 \text{ kg}} \approx 2080 \text{ lb.}$

   (b) $\dfrac{2080 \text{ lb}}{4 \times (2 \text{ in.} \times 2 \text{ in.})} = \dfrac{2080 \text{ lb}}{16 \text{ in.}^2} = 130 \text{ lb/in.}^2.$

   (c) The person exerts $\dfrac{130 \text{ lb}}{0.25 \text{ ft}^2} = 520 \text{ lb/ft}^2 = 520 \text{ lb/ft}^2 \times \dfrac{1 \text{ ft}^2}{144 \text{ in.}^2} \approx 3.6 \text{ lb/in.}^2.$

37. We have $r = 3 \text{ ft}$ and $h = 3.5 \text{ ft}$, so the tub has volume $\pi r^2 h \approx (3.14)(3^2)(3.5) \text{ ft}^3 \approx 99.0 \text{ ft}^3$. Per the text, 1 ft^3 of water weighs about 62 lb, so the water in the spa weighs $99.0 \text{ ft}^3 \times 62 \text{ lb/ft}^3 \approx 6100 \text{ lb} \approx 2800 \text{ kg.}$

38. The circumference at the base is $2\pi r = 40$ ft, so $r = \dfrac{40}{2\pi}$ ft ≈ 6.37 ft. So the volume is

$$\frac{1}{3}\pi r^2 h \approx \frac{3.14 \times \left(6.37 \text{ ft}\right)^2 \times 360 \text{ ft}}{3} \approx 15,289 \text{ ft}^3. \quad \text{Since wood weighs about } 31 \text{ lb/ ft}^3, \text{ the}$$

weight is—15,289 ft³ × 31 lb/ ft³ = 473,959 lb – over 230 tons.

39. The lights are strung around the outside of the tree branches, so in effect they cover the outside "area" of the tree (thought of as a cone). Hence, the number of strings needed grows in proportion to the square of the height: a 30-ft tree will need $5^2 = 25$ times as many strings as a 6-ft tree. However, you could also argue that a 30-ft tree is meant to be viewed from farther away, so that stringing the lights farther apart on the 30-ft tree would produce the same effect as with the shorter tree.

40. (a) Assuming pace is proportional to height (and vice versa), Hercules was 30% taller, hence $6\frac{1}{2}$ ft tall.

    (b) With the shorter Hercules and the shorter cubit:

$$4 \text{ cubits} = 4 \text{ cubits} \times \frac{17 \text{ in.}}{1 \text{ cubit}} = 68 \text{ in.} = 5 \text{ ft } 8 \text{ in.}$$

    With the taller Hercules and the longer cubit:

$$4 \text{ cubits} + 1 \text{ "foot"} = 4 \text{ cubits} \times \frac{22 \text{ in.}}{1 \text{ cubit}} + 12 \text{ in.} = 88 \text{ in.} + 12 \text{ in.} = 100 \text{ in.} = 8 \text{ ft } 4 \text{ in.},$$

    assuming that a Greek "foot" was equal in length to a modern ft.

41. The lower estimate of 17 in. for a cubit leads to a height of 6×17 in.+ 9 in. = 111 in. = 9 ft 3 in. = 111 in. × 2.54 cm/in. ≈ 282 cm. Similarly, the upper estimate of 22 in. for a cubit leads to a height of 11 ft 9 in ≈ 358 cm. In modern times, there have been men over 9 ft tall, but not over 11 ft tall.

42. $\text{BMI} = \dfrac{\text{weight (kg)}}{\left(\text{height (m)}\right)^2} = \dfrac{65 \text{ kg}}{\left(1.60 \text{ m}\right)^2} = \dfrac{65 \text{ kg}}{2.56 \text{ m}^2} \approx 25.4 \left(\text{kg/m}^2\right);$ she is just barely overweight.

43. The weight W must satisfy $\text{BMI} = \dfrac{W}{h^2} = \dfrac{W}{1.90^2} < 25$, so $W < \left(1.90\right)^2 \times 25 = 90.25$ kg.

44. $\dfrac{1 \text{ kg}}{\left(1 \text{ m}\right)^2} = \dfrac{2.205 \text{ lb}}{\left(39.37 \text{ in.}\right)^2} \approx \dfrac{2.205 \text{ lb}}{1550 \text{ in.}^2} \approx \dfrac{1 \text{ lb}}{703 \text{ in.}^2}.$ You must multiply the value calculated from pounds and inches by 703.

45. Answers will vary.

46. A Lilliputian would weigh $\left(\dfrac{1}{12}\right)^3 \approx 0.00058$ times as much as an adult human. A Lilliputian corresponding to a 140-lb adult human would weigh 0.08 lb, or about an ounce and a quarter. Human infants may be only a foot long at birth, barely twice Lilliputian size. Other mammals – either as infants (e.g., pandas) or as adults (e.g., mice) – are smaller than Lilliputians. So Lilliputians are not ruled out by area-volume considerations.

47. (a) If the species grew geometrically: Weight would scale as the cube of wingspan, so an individual with half the wingspan of an adult would have one-eighth the weight. However, the dimensions of this dinosaur probably did *not* grow geometrically; the wingspan probably grew not in proportion to the length of the dinosaur but more rapidly, so as to support the weight. Then an individual with half the wingspan would have one-fourth the wing area, so could support in flight only one-fourth the weight, or 25 lb.

  (b) If the species grew geometrically: Weight would scale as the cube of wingspan, so an individual weighing half as much as an adult would have a wingspan $\sqrt[3]{\dfrac{1}{2}} \approx 0.79$ times as great. If instead the wingspan grew to support the weight: An individual weighing half as much as an adult would need half the wing area; with both length and width of the wing growing in the same proportion, wing area (and hence weight) would scale as the square of wingspan. Hence wingspan would scale as the square root of weight. The half-weight dinosaur would need a wingspan $\sqrt{\dfrac{1}{2}}$ times as large, or 50 ft $\times \sqrt{0.5} \approx 35$ ft.

48. $\sqrt{12} \times 20$ mph ≈ 69 mph.

49. Answers will also vary with assumptions about the height of Icarus. A 5-ft tall Icarus would have been about 15 times as long as a sparrow and hence had to fly $\sqrt{15} \times 20$ mph ≈ 77 mph. We assume that Icarus was a scaled-up sparrow, so that his wing loading was proportional to his length; with disproportionately large wings, the wing loading – and hence the minimum speed – would have been lower.

50. It has disproportionately large wings compared to geometric scaling up of a bird, hence lower wing loading and lower minimum flying speed. Also, in part it glides rather than flies.

51. (a) (i) The giant ants are 8 m = 800 cm long, compared to the 1-cm length of a common ant. So the linear scaling factor is 800.
  (ii) Since area scales as the square of the linear scaling factor, the surface area of the giant ant is $800^2 = 640,000$ times as large.
  (iii) Since volume scales as the cube of the linear scaling factor, the volume of the giant ant is $800^3 = 512,000,000$ times as great.

  (b) The giant ant has 800 times as much volume per unit of surface area, so its skin could supply one eight-hundredth of what it would need.
  (c) There couldn't be any such giant ants.

52. $20\left(\dfrac{60}{30}\right)^{1/4} = 20 \cdot 2^{1/4} \approx 23.8$ m.

53. Because $h \propto t^{1/4}$, we have $t \propto h^4$. For a tree to grow to 40 m tall, compared to a tree growing to 20 m tall, it will take $\left(\dfrac{40}{20}\right)^2 = 2^4 = 16$ times as long. So if it takes 30 years to grow to 20 m, it would take $16 \times 30 = 480$ years to grow to 40 m.

54. Since $h \propto t^{1/4}$, we have $t \propto h^4$, or $t \propto kh^4$ for a constant k. So 2 times as high will take $2^4 = 16$ times as long. In detail: Since $h = 100$ m when $t = 1000$ yr, we have

$$k = \frac{t}{h^4} = \frac{1000 \text{ yr}}{(100 \text{ m})^4} = 10^{-5} \text{ yr/m}^4.$$

Thus, for $h = 200$ m, we have $t = 10^{-5}$ yr/m$^4 \times (200 \text{ m})^4 = 16,000$ yr.

55. $A \propto d^2$ and $A \propto M^{3/4} \propto (d^2 h)^{3/4} = d^{3/2} h^{3/4}$, so $d^2 \propto d^{3/2} h^{3/4}$, hence $d^{1/2} \propto h^{3/4}$, and $d \propto h^{3/2}$.

56. A major component of water loss is transpiration and evaporation through the skin. A taller person has a greater ratio of volume to surface area than a shorter person and hence loses less water per pound in a given time interval. On the other hand, the shorter person loses more heat per pound in a given time interval. (Note that deserts can be cold at night.)

57. A small warm-blooded animal has a large surface-area-to-volume ratio. Pound for pound, it loses heat more rapidly than a larger animal, hence must produce more heat per pound, resulting in a higher body temperature.

58. (a) On log-log paper:

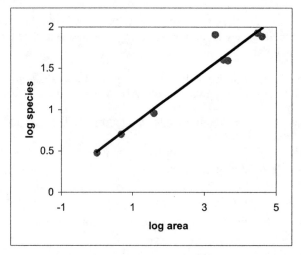

(b) The relationship is allometric, because on the log-log graph the points lie close to a straight line. Let A represent area and S represent species. The graph shows the line of best fit, whose equation is $\log_{10} S = 0.3423 \log_{10} A$, or $S = 10^{0.4931} A^{0.3423} \approx 3.11 A^{0.3423}$.

(c) For an area of 400 sq mi, we have $\log_{10} A = \log_{10} 400 \approx 2.60$; so from the graph or from the line of best fit, $\log_{10} S \approx 1.3$, from which we get (using the 10^x key) approximately 20 species.

(d) It approximately doubles, since $10^{0.3423} \approx 2.2$.

59. (a) On log-log paper:

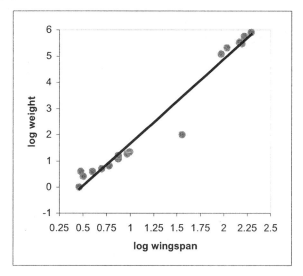

(b) Both relationships are allometric, since the results are good fits to straight lines whose slopes are not 1. For birds, the slope of the least-squares fit to the log-log graph is about 1.6; for planes, it is about 2.4. Because these slopes are not equal to 1, the relationships are not proportional. The data for birds and planes are graphed separately along with their corresponding lines on the same set of axes.

For Birds:

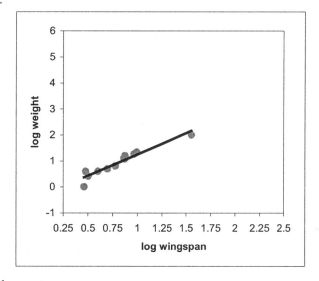

Continued on next page

59. (b) continued
        For Planes:

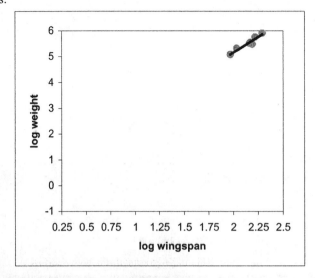

(c) The slope for birds (1.6) is less steep than for planes (2.4). The slope of the least-squares fit
     for both combined (a bad idea!) is about 3.4.

Word Search Solution

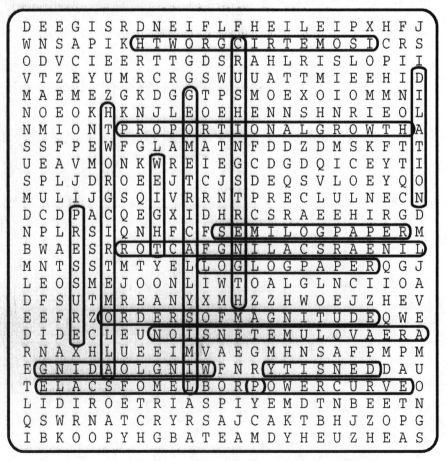

Chapter 19
Symmetry and Patterns

Chapter Outline

Introduction

Chapter Summary

Our sense of *symmetry* helps us appreciate patterns. Pleasing patterns exhibit elements of *balance*, *similarity*, and *repetition*. We find symmetry in crystals, the spiral patterns of sunflower seeds and pineapple scales, and the arrangement of petals on a flower. The *Fibonacci numbers* have a mysterious connection with the number of spirals in patterns such as those of sunflower seeds and pineapple scales.

Legend has it that the *golden ratio* $\left(\dfrac{1+\sqrt{5}}{2} \right)$ was the centerpiece of the Greek ideas of beauty and symmetry. Recent research discounts this theory. Nonetheless, the golden ratio is an interesting number. If we divide a line segment of length l into two pieces of lengths, s and w, so that $\dfrac{1}{s} = \dfrac{s}{w}$, then the common value of these fractions is the golden ratio. Further, the golden ratio is the ratio of a diagonal of a pentagon to one of its sides. Finally, the ratio of successive Fibonacci numbers provides ever better approximations to the golden ratio.

A pattern with repetition is classified by the types of *rigid motions* that preserve it, i.e., that move it in such a way that we cannot distinguish the displaced pattern from the original. A rigid motion is a transformation of a pattern such as a *rotation*, *reflection*, or *translation* that does not change the size or shape of the pattern.

This chapter discusses plane patterns. These can be divided into three categories having indefinitely many repetitions in no direction, exactly one direction, or more than one direction. The first type consists of the *rosette patterns*, which are basically patterns preserved by rotations. Essentially, a rosette pattern describes a petal arrangement for a flower. There are two classes of rosettes, *dihedral* and *cyclic*, depending on whether the petals have reflection symmetry or not. These are the only two possibilities (*Leonardo's theorem*).

Strip patterns repeat in one direction and can have *translation, reflection,* and *glide reflection* symmetries. They are classified by the combinations of these symmetries. An analysis of the possibilities demonstrates that there are only seven possible strip patterns, which serve as good examples of symmetry groups. The patterns in the final class are referred to as *wallpaper patterns*, and there are only seventeen possibilities.

Methods for classifying patterns, originated with crystallographers. Crystal structures are three-dimensional patterns and analysis has shown that there are exactly 230 possibilities. It should be emphasized that pattern analysis has nothing to do with the individual elements (or motifs) of the pattern design; rather, it concerns how the repetition of the motifs across the plane is structured.

Computers provide a modern way of producing symmetric patterns, obtained by iterating certain polynomial functions a large number of times, and coloring each pixel according to how many times it is visited.

Skill Objectives

1. List the first ten terms of the Fibonacci sequence.

2. Beginning with the number 3, form a ratio of each term in the Fibonacci sequence with its next consecutive term and simplify the ratio; then identify the number that these ratios approximate.

3. List the numerical ratio for the golden section.

4. Name and define the four transformations (rigid motions) in the plane.

5. Analyze a given rosette pattern and determine whether it is dihedral or cyclic.

6. Given a rosette pattern, determine which rotations preserve it.

7. Analyze a given strip pattern by determining which transformations produced it.

Teaching Tips

1. To help explain glide reflection you can point out that if a strip pattern has reflection along a horizontal axis, it will by necessity have glide reflection along that axis as well.

2. Islamic art is filled with designs that demonstrate both line symmetry and rotational symmetry. Much of this art and many other patterns are found in the Alhambra in Spain. The Metropolitan Museum of Art in New York has available Islamic art slides that your class may find interesting.

3. As mentioned in the chapter summary, it is important to emphasize that saying only so many patterns are possible is not saying only so many designs are possible. Pattern analysis concentrates on how the repetition of the motifs is structured.

4. An interesting approach, which presents a different method of classification as well as a computer tutorial, is found in an article by Russell J. Hendel, "A Symmetry Tutor for Introductory Liberal Arts Mathematics Courses," *Collegiate Microcomputer,* 11 (1993), 80 –88.

Research Paper

In Section 19.1, Wolfgang Amadeus Mozart (1756 – 1791) was mentioned as someone who was fascinated by mathematics. Students can research his life and involvement in mathematics and patterns via his compositions and method of composition. One interesting aspect of his times in composing music was the introduction of *dice music*. Students, particularly those that have an interest in music, may enjoy researching this topic and its connection to randomness (dice) and musical fragments (patterns) from an array of choices.

Spreadsheet Project

To do this project, go to http://www.whfreeman.com/fapp7e.

This project guides students to use spreadsheets to generate and investigate Fibonacci and Lucas sequences.

Collaborative Learning

Finding and Seeing Patterns

1. After the basic ideas of this chapter have been introduced, a good, out-of-class assignment is to have pairs of students walk around campus to look for strip patterns, sketch them, and return to class to report on their findings.

2. Although there are pictures in the book illustrating the existence of Fibonacci numbers in spirals, it is difficult to do the actual counting that verifies this fact. If you can get hold of a number of pine cones, you can ask the students to do the verification.

Solutions

Skills Check:

1. a   2. a   3. b   4. c   5. b   6. c   7. b   8. a   9. b   10. b

11. c   12. b   13. b   14. a   15. c   16. c   17. a   18. b   19. a   20. c

Exercises:

1. 5, 8 and 13

2. Answers will vary with species of pinecone but will be consecutive Fibonacci numbers.

3. Answers will vary but will be Fibonacci numbers.

4. (a) At end of each month, just before any births: 1, 2, 3, 5, 8, 13 pairs.
   (b) 1, 1, 2, 3, 4, 6 pairs.

5. (a) The digits after the decimal point do not change.
   (b) The digits after the decimal point do not change.
   (c) $\phi^2 = \phi + 1$
   (d) $\dfrac{1}{\phi} = \phi - 1$

6. $(1-\phi)^2 = 1 - 2\phi + \phi^2 = 1 - 2\phi + (\phi+1) = (1-\phi) + 1$

7. (a) $\sqrt{3 \times 27} = \sqrt{81} = 9$
   (b) The area of the rectangle is $4 \times 64 = 256$, so the square must have side $\sqrt{256} = 16$.

8. (a) $4 \times 9 = 6$
   (b) $2l + 2w = 6$ and $\dfrac{l}{w} = \phi$, so $l = \phi w$ and $2\phi w + 2w = 6$, hence $w(\phi + 1) = 3$. The rectangle must be $\dfrac{3}{1+\phi}$ by $\dfrac{3\phi}{1+\phi}$.

9. (a) 4, 7, 11, 18, 29, 47, 76, 123.
   (b) 3, 1.333, 1.75, 1.571, 1.636, 1.611, 1.621, 1.617, 1.618; The ratios approach ϕ.

10. (a) $n = 1$: $F_1 = \dfrac{1}{\sqrt{5}}\left(\dfrac{1+\sqrt{5}}{2}\right)^1 - \dfrac{1}{\sqrt{5}}\left(\dfrac{1-\sqrt{5}}{2}\right)^1 = \dfrac{1+\sqrt{5}}{2\sqrt{5}} - \dfrac{1-\sqrt{5}}{2\sqrt{5}} = \dfrac{1+\sqrt{5}-1+\sqrt{5}}{2\sqrt{5}} = \dfrac{2\sqrt{5}}{2\sqrt{5}} = 1$

   $n = 2$: $F_2 = \dfrac{1}{\sqrt{5}}\left(\dfrac{1+\sqrt{5}}{2}\right)^2 - \dfrac{1}{\sqrt{5}}\left(\dfrac{1-\sqrt{5}}{2}\right)^2 = \dfrac{1}{\sqrt{5}}\left(\dfrac{1+2\sqrt{5}+5}{4}\right) - \dfrac{1}{\sqrt{5}}\left(\dfrac{1-2\sqrt{5}+5}{2}\right)$

   $= \dfrac{1}{\sqrt{5}}\left(\dfrac{6+2\sqrt{5}}{4}\right) - \dfrac{1}{\sqrt{5}}\left(\dfrac{6-2\sqrt{5}}{4}\right) = \dfrac{3+\sqrt{5}}{2\sqrt{5}} - \dfrac{3-\sqrt{5}}{2\sqrt{5}} = \dfrac{3+\sqrt{5}-3+\sqrt{5}}{2\sqrt{5}} = \dfrac{2\sqrt{5}}{2\sqrt{5}} = 1$

   (b) $n = 5$: $F_5 = \dfrac{1}{\sqrt{5}}\left(\dfrac{1+\sqrt{5}}{2}\right)^5 - \dfrac{1}{\sqrt{5}}\left(\dfrac{1-\sqrt{5}}{2}\right)^5 = 5$

   (c) 233

11. Answers will vary

12. (a) In a single day, Joe can do $\frac{1}{3}$ of the ditch and Sam can do $\frac{1}{4}$, so together they can do $\left(\frac{1}{3}+\frac{1}{4}\right)$ in a day. To do the whole job (1 ditch), it will take $\dfrac{1}{\frac{1}{3}+\frac{1}{4}}=\dfrac{12}{7}\approx 1.7$ days

(b) Suppose that $\dfrac{2}{\frac{1}{x}+\frac{1}{y}}>\sqrt{xy}$, or $\dfrac{xy}{\frac{x+y}{2}}>(xy)^{1/2}$, or $(xy)^{1/2}>\frac{x+y}{2}$. But this is a contradiction to the result of Exercise 11, that the geometric mean is always less than or equal to the arithmetic mean. Hence our initial supposition must have been false, and we conclude that the harmonic mean is always less than or equal to the geometric mean.

(c) Using H, G, and A for the harmonic, geometric, and arithmetic means, we have

$$H_{x,y}=\frac{1}{A_{A,B}}\geq\frac{1}{G_{A,B}}=G_{x,y},$$

where the inequality comes from the fact that the geometric mean is always less than or equal to the arithmetic mean.

(d) $\sqrt[3]{xyz}$; $\sqrt[n]{x_1 x_2 \cdots x_n}$.

(e) $\dfrac{3}{\frac{1}{x}+\frac{1}{y}+\frac{1}{y}}$; $\dfrac{n}{\frac{1}{x_1}+\frac{1}{x_2}+\cdots+\frac{1}{x_n}}$.

13. $m+n+(m+n)+(m+2n)+(2m+3n)+(3m+5n)+(5m+8n)$
$\qquad + (8m+13n)+(13m+21n)+(21m+34n)=55m+88n,$

eleven times the seventh number $5m+8n$.

14. (a) To express a positive integer as a sum of Fibonacci numbers, repeatedly take out the largest Fibonacci number possible; if the integer is a Fibonacci number, it is represented by just itself. The winning strategy is to remove from the pile of counters the last (smallest) number in the Fibonacci representation of the number of counters. Piles with a Fibonacci number of counters are unsafe − no matter what you do, your opponent can win. The strategy works because the Fibonacci representation never uses two consecutive Fibonacci numbers, so that each Fibonacci number in a representation is about $\phi^2 \approx 2.6$ times as large as the next smallest one; the opponent may take at most twice as many counters as you remove, hence cannot reduce the pile to a Fibonacci number of counters. For example, $49 = 34 + 13 + 2$ (so that the intermediate Fibonacci numbers 21, 8, 5, and 3 are not used). To win, remove 2 counters; the opponent can then take at most 4. Say the opponent takes 4; then the number remaining is $43 = 34 + 8 + 1$, so on the next turn you take 1.

(b) For this game, the unsafe positions are piles with a number of counters that is a Fibonacci number plus 1. The winning strategy is to write (the number in the pile minus one) in a Fibonacci representation (as in part (a)) and remove the smallest Fibonacci number used in the representation.

15. (a) 1, 1, 3, 5, 11, 21, 43, 85, 171, 341, 683, 1,365

(b) $B_n = B_{n-1} + 2B_{n-2}$

(c) 1, 3, 1.667, 2.2, 1.909, 2.048, 1.977, 2.012, 1.994, 2.003, 1.999

(d) $x = 2, -1$; we discard the -1 root.

(e) $B_n = \dfrac{2^n - (-1)^n}{3}$

16. (a) 1, 1, 4, 7, 19, 40, 97, . . . ; $G_n = G_{n-1} + 3G_{n-2}$; 1, 4, 1.75, 2.714, 2.105, 2.425, . . . ; we solve

    $x^2 = x + 3$, whose positive solution is $x = \dfrac{1 + \sqrt{13}}{2} \approx 2.30277$.

    (b) 1, 1, $1+q$, $1+2q$, $1+3q+q^2$, $1+4q+3q^2$, . . . ; $Q_n = Q_{n-1} + qQ_{n-2}$; 1, 1 + q, − subsequent

    ratios are complicated; we solve $x^2 = x + q$, whose positive solution is $x = \dfrac{1 + \sqrt{1+4q}}{2}$,

    which is approximately $\sqrt{q}$ for large q.

17. Silver mean: $1 \pm \sqrt{2} \approx 2.414$; bronze mean: $\frac{1}{2}\left(3 \pm \sqrt{13}\right) \approx 3.303$;

    copper mean: $2 \pm \sqrt{5} \approx 4.236$; nickel mean: $\frac{1}{2}\left(5 \pm \sqrt{29}\right) \approx 5.193$.

    General expression: $\frac{1}{2}\left(m + \sqrt{m^2 + 4}\right)$.

18. (a) Answers will vary.

    (b) x solves $x = p + q\left(\dfrac{1}{x}\right)$, or $x^2 - px - q = 0$, so $x = \frac{1}{2}\left(p \pm \sqrt{p^2 + 4q}\right)$.

    (c) If p and q have opposite signs, then after the first few terms, the signs of the terms of the sequence may alternate between positive and negative. Other behaviors are possible; for instance, try $p = 1$ with $q = -1$.

19. All are true.

20. a, b, and d are true.

21. (a) B, C, D, E, H, I, K, O, X
    (b) A, H, I, M, O, T, U, V, W, X, Y
    (c) H, I, N, O, S, X, Z

22. (a) c, l (in some fonts), o, x
    (b) i, l (in some fonts), o, v, w, x
    (c) l (in some fonts), o, s, x, z

23. (a) MOM, WOW; MUd and bUM reflect into each other, as do MOM and WOW.
    (b) pod rotates into itself; MOM and WOW rotate into each other.
    (c) Here are some possibilities: NOW NO; SWIMS; ON MON; CHECK BOOK BOX; OX HIDE.

24. Answers will vary.

25. For all parts, translations.
    (a) Reflection in vertical lines through the centers of the A's or between them.
    (b) Reflection in the horizontal midline, glide reflections.
    (c) Reflection in the horizontal midline, reflections in vertical lines through the centers of the O's or between them, 180" rotation around the centers of the O's or the midpoints between them, glide reflections.
    (d) None other than translations.

26. For all parts, translations.

    (a) 180° rotations around the centers of the N's or the midpoints between them.

    (b) Reflection in vertical lines between b and d or between d and b.

    (c) Reflection in vertical lines between d and b or between p and q.

27. (a) *c5*

    (b) *c12*

    (c) *c22*

28. (d) *c2*

    (e) *d3*

    (f) *d16*

29. (a) *c6*

    (b) *d2* (CBS)

    (c) *d1* (Dodge Ram)

30. (d) *d3*

    (e) *c2*

    (f) *d3*

31. (a) *c4*

    (b) *d2*

32. (a) *c4*

    (b) *c4*

33. *p111, p1a1, p112, pm11, p1m1, pma2, pmm2*

34. (a) Reflection in the vertical line between them; translation; half-turn (rotation by 180°); glide reflection.

    (b)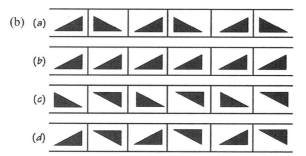

    (c) *pm11; p111; p112; p1a1*

35. (a) *pmm2*

  (b) *p1a1*

  (c) *pma2*

  (d) *p112*

  (e) *pmm2* (perhaps)

  (f) *p1m1*

  (g) *pma2*

  (h) *p111*

36. (a) *p111*

  (b) *p1m1*

  (c) *pm11*

  (d) *p112*

  (e) *p1a1*

  (f) *pma2*

  (g) *pmm2*

37. (a) Half-turns are preferred on MesaVerde pottery, while reflections predominate on Begho smoking pipes.

  (b) Neither culture completely excludes any strip type. Begho designs are heavily concentrated (almost 90%) in *p1m1*, *p112*, or *pmm2*, while Mesa Verde designs are more evenly distributed over the seven patterns.

  (c) (a) *pm11* or *pma2*: Mesa Verde. (b) *p112*: Mesa Verde. (c) *pmm2*: Begho. (d) *pm11*: Begho. (e) *p1m1*: Difficult to say. (f) *pmm2*: Begho. (g) *pmm2*: Begho. (h) *pma2*: Mesa Verde. (i) *p1a1*: Mesa Verde.

38. (a) *p1m1*

  (b) *p1mg*

39. (c) Smallest rotation is 90°, there are reflections, there are reflections in lines that intersect at 45°: *p4m*.

  (d) Smallest rotation is 90°, there are no reflections: *p4*.

40. (a) Reflection in a vertical line

  (b) Glide reflection

  (c) See figure below.

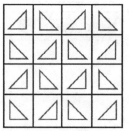

  (d) *c1g1*

41. Certainly none of the patterns with rotations at 60° or 120° can arise from this method, which eliminates the five patterns in the two bottom branches of the identification flowchart. For the vertical motion, four orientations are possible for the second triangle in the first column, corresponding to rotations clockwise by 0, 1, 2, or 3 times a rotation of 90° of the triangle in the upper left square around the center of its square. Similarly, for the horizontal motion, there are four choices, which we number in the same fashion. Then there are 16 combinations, which we can denote (with vertical motion first) as 00, 01, 02, 03, 04, 10, . . . , 44. However, some horizontal motions are not compatible with some vertical motions, and some of the patterns are reflections of others along the diagonal from upper left to lower right. In fact, the patterns *p4g* and *p4* cannot be realized because the original triangle has symmetry within itself, patterns *cm* and *cmm* cannot be realized because every square contains a triangle. The remaining eight can all be formed by the technique.

42. *p111*

43. There are no knights facing up or down (so no rotations of 90°), no knights who are upside down (so no rotations of 180°, and no knights at 60° or 120° angles. So the smallest rotation is 360°, there are no reflections, but there is a glide reflection that takes yellow knights into brown knights. So the pattern is *pg*, provided color is disregarded; if not, then *p1*.

44. *p111*, if different-colored camels are regarded as not the same; *p211* if, for example, we may rotate a white camel into a red one.

45. The block of three pentagons shaded in gray is repeated at rotations of 60° around the center of the "snowflake" outlined in red. There are no reflections, so the pattern is *p6*.

46. *p6mm*

47. The intersection of the dashed lines are 120° rotation centers, but there are no reflection lines, so the pattern is *p3*

48. - 49. Answers will vary.

50. (a) Ye.

   (b) No; 0 does not have an inverse.

51. (a) *d2*.

   (b) Any two of: R (180° rotation around the center), V (reflection in vertical line through its center), H (reflection in horizontal line through its center).

   (c) $\{I, R, V, H\}$

52. (a) *d4*

   (b) 90° rotation R, plus any one of reflection H in horizontal midline, reflection V in vertical midline, reflection D_1 in the diagonal from upper left to lower right, or reflection D_2 in the diagonal from upper right to lower left.

   (c) $\left\{I, R, R^2, R^3, H, V, D_1 = R \circ H, D_2 = R \circ H\right\}$

53. Let R denote rotation counterclockwise by 90°, V reflection in vertical line through its center and H reflection in horizontal line through its center. Then the group can be written as $\left\{I, R, R^2, R^3, H, V, RH = VR, RV = HR\right\}$, where the last two elements are reflections across the diagonals.

54. (a) *d3*

   (b) *d1*

   (c) *c1*

55. Answers will vary. Here is one: $0 = (3 - 2) - 1 \neq 3 - (2 - 1) = 2$.

56. (a) $\left\langle T, R \mid R^2 = I, R \circ T = T^{-1} \circ R \right\rangle = \left\{ \ldots, T^{-1}, I, T^1, \ldots ; \ldots, T^{-1} \circ R, R, T^1 \circ R, \ldots \right\}$.

   (b) $\left\langle T, R, H \mid R^2 = H^2 = I, T \circ H = H \circ T, R \circ H = H \circ R, (T \circ R)^2 = I \right\rangle = $
   $\left\{ \ldots, T^{-1}, I, T, \ldots ; \ldots, T^{-1} \circ R, R, T^1 \circ R, \ldots ; \ldots, T^{-1} \circ H, H, T^1 \circ H, \right.$
   $\left. \ldots ; \ldots, T^{-1} \circ H \circ R, H \circ R, T^1 \circ H \circ R, \ldots \right\}$

57. As in Example 5, number fixed positions, label with letters copies of the pattern elements in the positions, and pick a fixed position about which to make a half-turn *R*.

   (a) $\left\langle T, R \mid R^2 = I, T \circ R = R \circ T^{-1} \right\rangle = \left\{ \ldots, T^{-1}, I, T^1, \ldots ; \ldots, R \circ T^{-1}, R, R \circ T^1, \ldots \right\}$.

   (b) $\left\langle T, R, H \mid R^2 = H^2 = I, T \circ H = H \circ T, R \circ H = H \circ R, (R \circ T)^2 = I \right\rangle = $
   $\left\{ \ldots, T^{-1}, I, T, \ldots ; \ldots, R \circ T^{-1}, R, R \circ T, \ldots ; \ldots, H \circ T^{-1}, H, H \circ T, \right.$
   $\left. \ldots ; \ldots, R \circ H \circ T^{-1}, R \circ H, R \circ H \circ T, \ldots \right\}$

58. $\left\langle R, H \mid R^4 = I, H^2 = I, H \circ R = R^{-1} \circ H \right\rangle = \left\{ I, R, R^2, R^3, H, R \circ H, R^2 \circ H, R^3 \circ H \right\}$, where *R* is a rotation by 90° and *H* is a reflection across a line of symmetry.

59. $\left\langle R \mid R^8 = I \right\rangle = \left\{ I, R, R^2, R^3, R^4, R^5, R^6, R^7 \right\}$, where *R* is a rotation by 45°.

60. There are 24 elements in the group, including the identity, rotations around axes through centers of opposite faces, rotations around diagonals between opposite corners, and rotations around axes through centers of opposite edges, for a total of 24. See

http://nothung.math.uh.edu/mike/hti/handouts/handout4/node4.html and

http://www.maths.uwa.edu.au/schultz/3P5.2000/3P5.2,3SquareCube.html.

61. Get an empty cardboard box as a visual and tactile aid. The situation is analogous to the rectangle of Example 3. Place the solid at the origin of a three-dimensional coordinate system with the axes aligned through its center. The solid can be rotated by multiples of 180° about any of the three axes; denote these rotations as $R_x, R_y,$ and R_z, with $R_x^2 = R_y^2 = R_z^2 = I$ and $R_z = R_x R_y = R_y R_x,$ $R_y = R_x R_z = R_z R_x,$ and $R_x = R_y R_z = R_z R_y$. Similarly, there are reflection symmetries across planes in each axis direction; call them *H*, *V*, and *Z*, with $H^2 = V^2 = Z^2 = I$. Because the dimensions of the solid are all unequal, there are no symmetries across diagonals through it. However, the composition *HVZ* produces one final symmetry, an "inversion" of the solid through its center: Each point goes to a point the same distance and the opposite direction from the center.

62. Answers will vary.

63. The carved head is reproduced in the same shape at different scales.

64. – 68. Answers will vary.

Word Search Solution

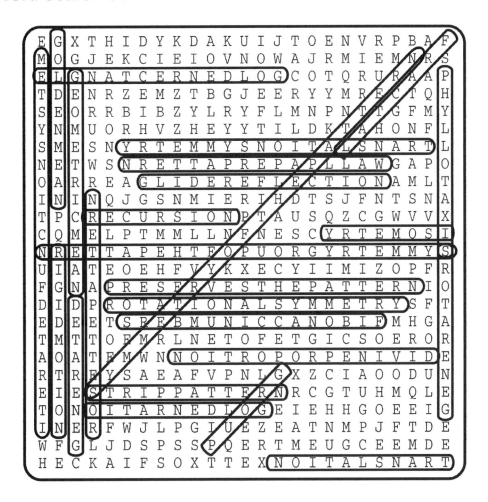

Chapter 20
Tilings

Chapter Outline

Introduction

Chapter Summary

A mosaic uses repeated shapes to cover a flat surface without overlap and, ideally, without gaps. If we call the shapes tiles, we have an example of a *tiling* (or *tessellation*). Tilings can be of practical interest: If we need to cut pieces of a certain shape and this shape can be used in a tiling, then we have a way to cut our pieces with little or no waste.

Monohedral tilings are the simplest type. They use tiles having the same size and shape. A tiling is called *regular* if it is monohedral and its tile is a regular polygon. For simplicity, only edge-to-edge tilings are considered. In such tilings, the edge of one tile coincides with the edge of a neighboring tile. The *vertex figure* for such a tiling is the tile configuration at points where the edges of different tiles meet. Examining this configuration, we can show that only three regular polygons can be used in a regular tiling of the plane: the equilateral triangle, the square, and the regular hexagon.

It is possible to mix shapes and obtain edge-to-edge tilings. A semiregular tiling uses different regular polygons arranged in such a way that all vertex figures are alike. There are only eight edge-to-edge tilings of this type. If the restriction on identical vertex figures is dropped, then there are infinitely many.

Natural extensions to consider are tilings with irregular polygons. Again, considering only monohedral edge-to-edge tilings, we can reach several conclusions: any triangle tiles; any quadrilateral, *convex* or not, tiles; exactly three classes of convex hexagons tile; and a convex polygon with at least seven sides cannot tile. What happens if convex pentagons are used is not completely understood.

Tiling by translation is accomplished by laying tiles edge-to-edge in rows. Of course, the tile must be able to fit exactly into each of its neighbors, including those above and below. A shape is suitable for such a tiling if it satisfies one of two conditions on its shape. If we are also allowed to turn our shape upside-down, we can consider tiling by translation and half-turns. Conway's criterion singles out those shapes that can be used in this way.

The Dutch artist *M. C. Escher* used tilings, some with two or more interlocking pieces, in his work. He also used tilings of the Poincare disk. Many of his tilings are *periodic*, the pattern repeating at regular intervals in one or more directions. Tilings whose patterns do not repeat by translation, or whose repetition is not completely regular, are called nonperiodic. In all known cases, if a shape can be used to make a *nonperiodic* tiling, then it can be used to make a periodic one. It had been conjectured that the same holds for any set of shapes. *Roger Penrose* discovered a counterexample in 1975 requiring a set of only two shapes.

Penrose tilings have arbitrarily large regions with 5-fold and 10-fold rotational symmetry. These tilings have been generalized to three dimensions and these space tilings are nonperiodic with 5-fold rotational symmetry. This feature has provided an unexpected connection with crystallography. Barlow's law shows that periodic tiling of the plane or of three-space cannot have 5-fold symmetry. However, Daniel Shectman discovered just such symmetry in examining crystals in a certain manganese-aluminum alloy. The apparent "forbidden symmetry" is due to the nonperiodic nature of the crystal array in the alloy. Since crystals have always been thought of as corresponding to periodic tilings, the new structures have been dubbed *quasicrystals*. Here is another instance of mathematical research "anticipating" scientific discovery.

Skill Objectives

1. Calculate the number of degrees in each angle of a given regular polygon.

2. Given the number of degrees in each angle of a regular polygon, determine its number of sides.

3. Define the term tiling (tessellation).

4. List the three regular polygons for which a monohedral tiling exists.

5. When given a mix of regular polygons, determine whether a tiling of these polygons could exist.

6. Explain the difference between a periodic and a nonperiodic tiling.

7. Discuss the importance of the Penrose tiles.

8. Explain why 5-fold symmetry in a crystal structure was thought to be impossible.

Teaching Tips

1. The tessellations of artist M. C. Escher are of great interest to many students. They often enjoy trying to create some of their own. The following instructions will produce the boundary of a rotational tessellation. After several attempts, students will find a boundary in which they visualize an object. They may add any markings inside the boundary to make their design more attractive or convincing, so long as they don't alter the boundary in any way. The important concepts used in this approach are rotational symmetry and preservation of area (when you add area onto the triangle by drawing a curve outside the triangle, and compensate for it by taking away the same amount on the inside of the triangle).

    a. Draw equilateral triangle ABC with a pencil.

    b. Beginning at vertex A, draw a curve that goes both inside and outside the triangle and ends at vertex B.

    c. Repeat this same curve identically along side CB, making sure that the point of the curve at vertex A is now at vertex C and B remains in the same place. (You are actually rotating the curve around point B.)

    d. Starting at vertex C, draw a curve inside the triangle that stops at the midpoint of side AC.

    e. Repeat this curve on the outside of the triangle by rotating it around the midpoint of side AC.

    f. Erase the lines of the triangle and focus only on the boundary you have created. You may turn it in any direction. Does this boundary suggest an object or a design to you? If so, add any marks you wish inside the boundary to enhance the image. Just be careful not to alter the boundary itself. If not, try the process again by starting with another equilateral triangle.

    g. When you have a design you like, make six copies of it on a copy machine. It's important to have all six identical.

    h. Arrange the six designs in a rotational pattern. (Hint: point C is critical; it is the point about which the rotation takes place. All six designs will have this point in the center of the overall pattern.)

2. Sets of tiles are now available commercially. They are typically used by elementary school teachers to explain the idea of tiling.

Research Paper

Have students research the life and contributions of Maurits Cornelis Escher (1898 – 1972). As the son of an engineer he had an early interest in carpentry and music. Escher's works are loved by millions, and many examples are available on the Internet.

Collaborative Learning

Creating Tilings

1. A good ice-breaker for this chapter is to cut out many copies of a quadrilateral (not a parallelogram) from sheets of paper. Distribute them to your class and ask your students to determine whether it is possible to tile the plane with copies of this quadrilateral.

2. Even though the author gives a detailed description of how to produce Escher-type tilings, it is unlikely that the students will attempt to make their own outside of class. It might be instructive to devote a few minutes of class time to the construction of such tilings. Try to keep things relatively simple, perhaps by starting with rectangles and having the students make minor modifications in just two sides, following the recipe in the book. After getting them started in class, you can ask the students to complete their "projects" at home.

Solutions

Skills Check:

1. b   2. b/c   3. c   4. b   5. a   6. c   7. b   8. c   9. a   10. a

11. c   12. b   13. c   14. b   15. b   16. c   17. b   18. b   19. c   20. a

Cooperative Learning:

The plane may be tiled with any shape quadrilateral.

Exercises:

1. Exterior: 45°. Interior: 135°.

2. Exterior: 36°. Interior: 144°.

3. $180° - \dfrac{360°}{n}$.

4. 3, 60°; 4, 90°; 5, 108°; 6, 120°; 7, $128\frac{4}{7}°$; 8, 135°; 9, 140°; 10, 144°; 11, $147\frac{3}{11}°$; and 12, 150°.

5. The usual notation for a vertex figure is to denote a regular n-gon by n, separate the sizes of polygons by periods, and list the polygons in clockwise order starting from the smallest number of sides, so that, e.g., 3.3.3.3.3.3 denotes six equilateral triangles meeting at a vertex. The possible vertex figures are 3.3.3.3.3.3, 3.3.3.3.6, 3.3.3.4.4, 3.3.4.3.4, 3.3.4.12, 3.4.3.12, 3.3.6.6, 3.6.3.6, 3.4.4.6, 3.4.6.4, 3.12.12, 4.4.4.4, 4.6.12, 4.8.8, 5.5.10, and 6.6.6.

6. 3.3.4.12, 3.4.3.12, 3.3.6.6, 3.4.4.6, and 5.5.10.

7. 3.7.42, 3.9.18, 3.8.24, 3.10.15, and 4.5.20.

8. 30°, 75°, 75°.

9. At each of the vertices except the center one, six triangles meet, with angles (in clockwise order) of 75°, 75°, 30°, 30°, 75°, and 75°.

10. A regular polygon with 12 sides has interior angles of 150°, and a regular polygon with 8 sides has interior angles of 135°. No integer combination of these numbers can add up to 360°.

11. Yes, because the half pentagon is a quadrilateral, and any quadrilateral can tile the plane.

12. See figures below.

(a)

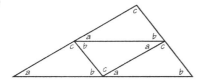

(b)

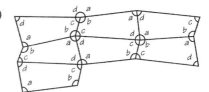

(c)

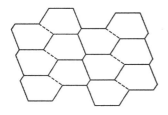

13. (a) No.

  (b) No.

  (c) No.

14. (d) Yes.

  (e) No.

  (f) No.

  (g) No.

15. Answers will vary.

16. Answers will vary.

17. No.; No.

18. The top of one L must go either under the left square of another (doing that leaves an unfillable square between them) or else under the right square (which works).

19. The only way to tile by translations is to fit the outer "elbow" of one tile into the inner "elbow" of another. Labeling the corners as follows works: the corners on the top A and B, those on the rightmost side C and D, the middle of the bottom E, and the middle of the leftmost side F.

20. Answers will vary.

21. Just label the four corners consecutively A, B, C, and D.

22. Solutions may vary. One solution: Label the four lower corners F, E, D, and C from left to right, and label the top corners of the middle square in the top row as A and B from left to right.

23. Place the skew-tetromino on a coordinate system with unit length for the side of a square and with the lower left corner at $(0,0)$. Then $A = (1,2)$, $B = (3,2)$, $C = (2,0)$, and $D = (0,0)$ works.

24. Solutions may vary. One solution: A is the upper leftmost corner, B is the upper left corner of the upper square, C is the upper right corner, D is the midpoint of the righthand side, E is one-third of the way along the bottom edge (from the left side), and F is the lower left corner.

25. Place the skew-tetromino on a coordinate system with unit length for the side of a square and with the lower left corner at $(0,0)$. Then $A = (0,1)$, $B = (1,2)$, $C = (3,2)$, $D = (3,1)$, $E = (2,0)$, and $F = (0,0)$ works.

26. If A and B coincide, so must D and E, and vice versa. Other such pairs: $B - C$ and $E - F$, and $C - D$ and $F - A$.

27. (a) Yes.

　(b) No.

　(c) No.

28. (d) Yes.

　(e) No.

　(f) Yes.

　(g) Yes.

29. See figure below.

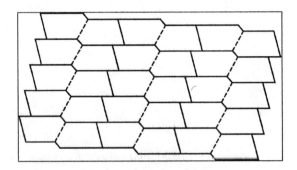

30. See figure below.

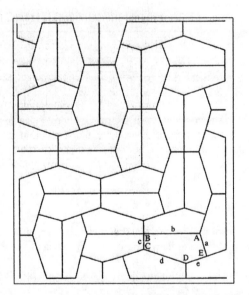

31. Answers will vary.

32. Answers will vary.

33. N, Z, W, P, y, I, L, V, X. See www.srcf.ucam.org/~jsm28/tiling/5-omino-trans.ps.gz.

34. Solutions may vary. One solution: Label the middle of the top side A, the upper right corner B, the far lower right corner D, the far left corner F, and C and E each one unit from D.

35. Place the U on a coordinate system with unit length for the side of a square and with the lower left corner at $(0,0)$. Then $A = (2,2)$, $B = (3,2)$, $C = (3,0)$, $D = (1,0)$, $E = (0,0)$, and $F = (0,1)$ works. See www.srcf.ucam.org/~jsm28/tiling/5-omino-rot.ps.gz .

36. Solutions may vary. One solution: Label the top left corner of the T *F* and the top right corner *A*. The corner below *A* is *B*, *C* and *D* are the corners at the foot of the T, and *E* is one unit up from *D*.

37. Answers will vary.

38. Solutions may vary. One solution: Label the top left corner *A*, the top right corner *B* = *C*, the bottom right corner *D*, and the bottom left corner *E* = *F*.

39. *ABAABABA*.

40. Two *B*'s in a row would indicate a baby pair that had a baby pair, which is impossible.

41. The two leftmost *A*'s would have had to come from two *B*'s in a row in the preceding month.

42. Verify that the sequence for the fourth month, *ABA*, follows the rule. Then, assuming that the rule holds for all previous months, consider last month and what happens as it transforms into the current month's sequence. Last month's sequence consists of a first part that is the sequence from two months ago; this first part, we know from our assumption, transforms into last month's sequence. The second part of last month's sequence is the sequence from three months ago, which we know from our assumption transforms into the sequence from two months ago. So the current month's sequence consists of last month's sequence followed by the sequence from two months ago, as claimed.

43. Let S_n, A_n, and B_n be the total number of symbols, the number of *A*'s, and the number of *B*'s at the nth stage. We note that the only *B*'s at the nth stage must have come from *A*'s in the previous stage, so $B_n = A_{n-1}$. Similarly, the *A*'s at the nth stage come from both *A*'s and *B*'s in the previous stage, so $A_n = A_{n-1} + B_{n-1}$. Using both of these facts together, we have $A_n = A_{n-1} + A_{n-2}$. We note that $A_1 = 0, A_2 = 1, A_3 = 1, A_4 = 2,\dots$. The A_n sequence obeys the same recurrence rule as the Fibonacci sequence and starts with the same values one step later; in fact, it is always just one step behind the Fibonacci sequence: $A_n = F_{n-1}$. Consequently, $B_n = A_{n-1} = F_{n-2}$, and $S_n = A_n + B_n = F_{n-1} + F_{n-2} = F_n$.

44. In an inflated sequence, the only way a *B* enters is as a *B* preceded by an *A*, so two *B*'s in a row cannot occur. If there were three *A*'s in a row, the first two cannot have been produced by the rule that replaces an *A* by *AB*, so they must have come from two *B*'s in a row, which we just showed is impossible.

45. If a sequence ends in *AA*, its deflation ends in *BB*, which is impossible for a musical sequence. Similarly, if a sequence ends in *ABAB*, its deflation ends in *AA*, which we just showed to be impossible.

46. Suppose that the kth musical sequence is the first not to be an initial subsequence of its inflation. Deflate the kth musical sequence once and its successor twice; these deflations must be the same (according to construction of musical sequences) but also must be different (two different musical sequences cannot deflate to the same sequence), which is a contradiction.

47. The first is, the second is not, part of a musical sequence: *ABAABABAAB* → *ABAABA* → *ABAB* → *AA* → (2nd special rule) *BA* → (1st special rule) *ABA* → *AB* → *A*.

ABAABABABA → *ABAAAB*, which has three *A*'s.

48. By Exercise 43, the numbers of *A*'s and *B*'s are consecutive Fibonacci numbers, whose ratio tends toward ϕ (Chapter 19, p. 711).

49. If the sequence were periodic, the limiting ratio of A's to B's would be the same as the ratio in the repeating part, which would be a rational number, contrary to the result of Exercise 48.

50. If the sequence were periodic, the limiting ratio of A's to B's would be the same as the ratio in the repeating part, which would be a fixed rational number. But by Exercise 48, the ratio tends toward ϕ, which is not rational.

Word Search Solution

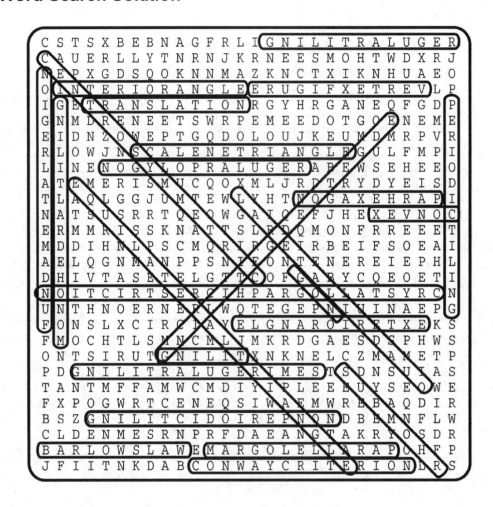

Chapter 21
Savings Models

Chapter Outline

Chapter Summary

Interest paid on money provides simple illustrations of both geometric and arithmetic growth. Suppose we deposit P dollars in a bank, with an interest rate of r% per year. With *simple interest*, only the principal earns interest and each year we get $.01Pr$ dollars in interest. In this case, the money in our account grows arithmetically. If, however, the interest is compounded annually, then over a number of years, we receive interest on our principal *and* on the accumulated interest. In this case, our money grows *geometrically*. Typically, banks compound more than once a year and the *effective annual yield* on our money is somewhat more than r%. However, there is a limit to the yield obtained through more and more frequent compounding, and this limit is determined by the number e. Mortgages, auto loans, and college loans require the repayment of the principal borrowed on a monthly basis over a period of years. The calculation of the monthly payment is made by summing a geometric series. The same technique can be used to find the final accumulation in systematic savings programs, in which equal payments are made periodically over the course of time.

Systematic savings programs are ones in which equal payments are made periodically over the course of time, with a constant interest rate. The final accumulation in such a program can be made by summing a geometric series.

During periods of inflation, prices increase in a geometric manner. As prices rise, the value of the dollar decreases, undergoing exponential decay, which is geometric growth with a negative rate of growth. The *Consumer Price Index* computes price increases over many years.

The price of a stock depends upon future potential dividends, and also takes into account the return possible from safer investments, such as government bonds, which carry no risk. Stocks that are predicted to have growing dividends will command higher prices than ones with stable dividend rates.

The importance of the pricing of options and other financial derivatives became known to the public when Robert Merton and Myron Scholes received the 1997 Nobel Prize in economics for work they had done in the 1970s with the late Fischer Black. Probabilistic notions, especially that of expected value, play a key role in these valuations.

Skill Objectives

1. Describe the difference between arithmetic and geometric growth.

2. List three applications of geometric growth.

3. Apply the formula for geometric growth to calculate compound interest.

4. Calculate the depreciation of an item by applying the formula for geometric growth.

5. Calculate the number of years necessary to double an investment value by applying the formula for geometric growth to given information.

6. Use the savings formula, $A = d \left[\dfrac{(1+i)^n - 1}{i} \right]$ to determine A or d.

7. Solve applications involving inflation and depreciation.

8. Solve applications using Consumer Price Index.

Teaching Tips

1. Many of the concepts in this chapter can be found in advertisements in newspapers. Among others, ads appear for certificates of deposit at banks, money market funds, 401k plans, and annuities for retirement. If you can get the students to look for such items regularly, the practical importance of this topic will be driven home.

2. During the course of the semester, ask the students to monitor the monthly announcements of the changes in the Consumer Price Index, which can be found on radio and TV, as well as in newspapers. Ask them to compare the actual CPI with the predicted value given in the text for 2006.

Research Paper

Have students research the origin of banking. It is believed that the very first banks were religious temples in the ancient world. There are records of loans, which date to the Babylonians around the 18th century BC. Ancient Greece and ancient Rome also has evidence of banking.

Another research paper could focus on more modern ways of banking. It may be of interest to compare and contrast the different types of banks such as central banks, investment banks, merchant banks, and universal banks.

Spreadsheet Project

To do this project, go to http://www.whfreeman.com/fapp7e.

This projects uses spreadsheets to compare prices using the Consumer Price Index as well as other financial and physical applications.

Collaborative Learning

Rate and Yield

1. Ask your students to bring in ads from banks for certificates of deposit. Such ads generally contain two numbers, one called the *rate,* the other the *yield.* Ask the students if they know what these numbers represent. This can be a good lead-in to the notion of compound interest. (The small print at the bottom of some of the ads may give partial explanations of how the yield is obtained from the rate. Also, some banks may use continuous compounding.)

2. If you had the students do the previous exercise, take one of the ads that they brought in (or bring in one of your own), which states a rate and a yield, but without explaining how they obtain the yield. Ask the students to try to discover the frequency of compounding. Since this involves solving a transcendental equation, the only method of solution available to the students is trial and error. Moreover, since the figures are usually given to just two decimal places, there will not be a unique answer to this question. For example, if the rate is 6% and the yield is stated to be 6.18%, then the compounding method could be continuous. However, daily compounding also results in a yield of 6.18%, rounded to two decimal places. So does weekly compounding (rarely used), but not monthly, whose yield is 6.17%. This exercise will help reinforce the fact that continuous compounding is not as powerful as one might expect.

Solutions

Skills Check:

1. c   2. a/c   3. b   4. c   5. b   6. c   7. c   8. a   9. b   10. c

11. b   12. c   13. b   14. a   15. a   16. b   17. b   18. c   19. b   20. b

Exercises:

1. (a) By the pattern shown, there is an increase by a factor if 2^n every $3n$ days. By doing some calculations, we can see that $2^{232} \approx 6.9 \times 10^{69}$ and $2^{233} \approx 1.4 \times 10^{70}$. So n is between 232 and 233. Thus, $3n$ is between 696 and 699. Calculating $2^{697/3}$ and $2^{698/3}$, we see that the better choice is 698 days.

    (b) We have $1000 = 10^3$. Since $\left(10^3\right)^{23} = 10^{69}$ and $\left(10^3\right)^{24} = 10^{72}$, an appropriate answer would be after 24 months.

2. There are $2^{64} - 1 \approx 1.845 \times 10^{19}$ kernels.

    Since a kernel is about $\left(\frac{1}{4} \text{in.}\right)\left(\frac{1}{16} \text{in.}\right)\left(\frac{1}{16} \text{in.}\right) = \frac{1}{1024} \text{in.}^3$, the kernels occupy about

    $\left(1.845 \times 10^{19}\right)\left(\frac{1}{1024} \text{in.}^3\right) \approx 1.801 \times 10^{16} \text{ in.}^3$.

    This occupies $1.801 \times 10^{16} \text{ in.}^3 \times \dfrac{1 \text{ mi}^3}{\left(12 \frac{\text{in}}{\text{ft}}\right)^3 \times \left(5280 \frac{\text{ft}}{\text{mi}}\right)^3} \approx 70.8 \text{ mi}^3$.

    (Answers in other units are possible).

3. (a) Since $A = P(1 + rt)$, we have $A = \$1000(1 + 0.03 \times 1) = \$1000(1.03) = \$1030.00$. The annual yield is 3% since we have simple interest.

    (b) Since $A = P(1 + i)^n$, $n = 1$, and $i = \frac{0.03}{1} = 0.03$, we have the following.

    $$A = \$1000(1 + 0.03) = \$1000(1.03) = \$1030.00$$

    The annual yield is 3% since we are dealing with simple interest because the money is compounded once during the period of one year.

    (c) Since $A = P(1 + i)^n$, $n = 4$, and $i = \frac{0.03}{4}$, we have the following.

    $$\$1000 \times \left(1 + \tfrac{0.03}{4}\right)^4 = \$1000(1.0075)^4 = \$1030.34$$

    Since $APY = \left(1 + \frac{r}{n}\right)^n - 1$, we have $APY = \left(1 + \frac{0.03}{4}\right)^4 - 1 \approx 3.034\%$.

    (d) $\$1000 \times \left(1 + \frac{0.03}{365}\right)^{365} = \$1000(1.000082192)^{365} = \$1030.45$, with the same result for a 360-day or 366-day year.

    Since $APY = \left(1 + \frac{r}{n}\right)^n - 1$, we have $APY = \left(1 + \frac{0.03}{365}\right)^{365} - 1 \approx 3.045\%$, with the same result for a 360-day or 366-day year.

4. (a) Since $A = P(1+rt)$, we have $A = \$1000(1+0.06\times1) = \$1000(1.06) = \$1060.00$. The annual yield is 6% since we have simple interest.

(b) Since $A = P(1+i)^n$, $n = 1$, and $i = \frac{0.06}{1} = 0.06$, we have the following.
$$A = \$1000(1+0.06) = \$1000(1.06) = \$1060.00$$
The annual yield is 6% since we are dealing with simple interest because the money is compounded once during the period of one year.

(c) Since $A = P(1+i)^n$, $n = 4$, and $i = \frac{0.06}{4}$, we have the following.
$$\$1000\times(1+\tfrac{0.06}{4})^4 = \$1000(1.025)^4 = \$1061.36$$
Since $APY = \left(1+\dfrac{r}{n}\right)^n - 1$, we have $APY = \left(1+\dfrac{0.06}{4}\right)^4 - 1 \approx 6.136\%$.

(d) $\$1000\times(1+\tfrac{0.06}{365})^{365} = \$1000(1.000164384)^{365} = \$1061.83$, with the same result for a 360-day or 366-day year.
Since $APY = \left(1+\dfrac{r}{n}\right)^n - 1$, we have $APY = \left(1+\dfrac{0.06}{365}\right)^{365} - 1 \approx 6.183\%$, with the same result for a 360-day or 366-day year.

5. Using 365-day years: The daily interest rate $i = \frac{0.03}{365}$ is in effect for $n = 8\times365 = 2920$ days. We have in the compound interest formula $A = \$10,000 = P(1+i)^n$, so we get $P = \frac{\$10,000}{1.2712366} = \$7866.36$. (Fine point: In fact, the 8 years must contain two Feb. 29 days. Calculating interest for $n = 6\times365 = 2190$ days at $i = \frac{0.03}{365}$ and for $n = 2\times366 = 732$ days at $i = \frac{0.03}{366}$ gives a result that differs by less than one one-hundredth of a cent.)

6. Using 365-day years: The daily interest rate $i = \frac{0.04}{365}$ is in effect for $n = 5\times365 = 1825$ days. We have in the compound interest formula $A = \$10,000 = P(1+i)^n$, so we get $P = \frac{\$10,000}{1.221389374} = \$8187.40$. (Fine point: In fact, the 5 years must contain one or two Feb. 29 days, but yields a negligible difference)

7. The interest is $26.14 on a principal of $7744.70, or $\frac{\$26.14}{\$7744.70}\times100\% = 0.3375211435\%$ over 34 days. The daily interest rate is $\left(1.003375211435^{1/34} - 1\right)\times100\% = 0.0099109\%$. The annual rate is then $\left(1.000099109^{365} - 1\right)\times100\% = 3.68\%$.

8. The interest is $22.16 on a principal of $7722.54, or $\frac{\$22.16}{\$7722.54}\times100\% = 0.2869522204\%$ over 27 days. The daily interest rate is $\left(1.002869522204^{1/27} - 1\right)\times100\% = 0.0106132038\%$. The annual rate is then $\left(1.000106132038^{365} - 1\right)\times100\% = 3.95\%$.

9. (a) 3%: Predicted doubling time is $\dfrac{72}{100\times0.03}=\dfrac{72}{3}=24.$

Since $A=P(1+i)^n$, $n=24$, and $i=\frac{0.03}{1}=0.03$, we have the following.

$$A=\$1000(1+0.03)^{24}=\$1000(1.03)^{24}=\$2032.79$$

4%: Predicted doubling time is $\dfrac{72}{100\times0.04}=\dfrac{72}{4}=18.$

Since $A=P(1+i)^n$, $n=18$, and $i=\frac{0.04}{1}=0.04$, we have the following.

$$A=\$1000(1+0.04)^{18}=\$1000(1.04)^{18}=\$2025.82$$

6%: Predicted doubling time is $\dfrac{72}{100\times0.06}=\dfrac{72}{6}=12.$

Since $A=P(1+i)^n$, $n=12$, and $i=\frac{0.06}{1}=0.06$, we have the following.

$$A=\$1000(1+0.06)^{12}=\$1000(1.06)^{12}=\$2012.20$$

(b) 8%: Predicted doubling time is $\dfrac{72}{100\times0.08}=\dfrac{72}{8}=9.$

Since $A=P(1+i)^n$, $n=9$, and $i=\frac{0.08}{1}=0.08$, we have the following.

$$A=\$1000(1+0.08)^9=\$1000(1.08)^9=\$1999.00$$

9%: Predicted doubling time is $\dfrac{72}{100\times0.09}=\dfrac{72}{9}=8.$

Since $A=P(1+i)^n$, $n=8$, and $i=\frac{0.09}{1}=0.09$, we have the following.

$$A=\$1000(1+0.09)^8=\$1000(1.09)^8=\$1992.56$$

(c) 12%: Predicted doubling time is $\dfrac{72}{100\times0.12}=\dfrac{72}{12}=6.$

Since $A=P(1+i)^n$, $n=6$, and $i=\frac{0.12}{1}=0.12$, we have the following.

$$A=\$1000(1+0.12)^6=\$1000(1.12)^6=\$1973.82$$

24%: Predicted doubling time is $\dfrac{72}{100\times0.24}=\dfrac{72}{24}=3.$

Since $A=P(1+i)^n$, $n=3$, and $i=\frac{0.24}{1}=0.24$, we have the following.

$$A=\$1000(1+0.24)^3=\$1000(1.24)^3=\$1906.62$$

36%: Predicted doubling time is $\dfrac{72}{100\times0.36}=\dfrac{72}{36}=2.$

Since $A=P(1+i)^n$, $n=2$, and $i=\frac{0.36}{1}=0.36$, we have the following.

$$A=\$1000(1+0.36)^2=\$1000(1.36)^2=\$1849.60$$

(d) For small and intermediate interest rates, the rule of 72 gives good approximations to the doubling time.

10. 23.1, 11.55, 7.7 yrs, all close to the predictions. The number 72 has the convenience of being evenly divisible by many small numbers.

It's a "rule of 110." Divide 110 by $100r$; for $r = 0.05$, you get 22 yrs.

11. (a) 2, 2.59, 2.705, 2.7169, 2.718280469

(b) 3, 6.19, 7.245, 7.3743, 7.389041321

(c) $e = 2.718281828 \ldots$; $e^2 = 7.389056098 \ldots$. Your calculator may give slightly different answers, because of its limited precision.

12. (a) 0, 0.35, 0.366, 0.3677, 0.367879257

(b) -1, 0.11, 0.133, 0.1351, 0.135335013

(c) $e^{-1} = \frac{1}{e} = 0.367879441 \ldots$; $e^{-2} = \frac{1}{e^2} = 0.135335283 \ldots$. Your calculator may give slightly different answers, because of its limited precision.

13. (a) Since $A = Pe^{rt}$ we have $A = \$1000e^{(0.03)(1)} = \$1000e^{0.03} = \$1030.45$. Thus, the interest is $\$1030.45 - \$1000.00 = \$30.45$.

(b) Since $A = P\left(e^{r/360}\right)^{360}$ we have $A = \$1000\left(e^{0.03/360}\right)^{360} = \$1030.45$. Thus, the interest is $\$1030.45 - \$1000.00 = \$30.45$.

(c) Since $A = P\left(e^{r/365}\right)^{365}$ we have $A = \$1000\left(e^{0.03/365}\right)^{365} = \$1030.45$. Thus, the interest is $\$1030.45 - \$1000.00 = \$30.45$.

In all cases, \$30.45, not taking into account any rounding to the nearest cent of the daily posted interest.

14. (a) $i = \$4632.10 - \$4532.10 = \$100.00$

Since effective rate would be $\dfrac{100}{4532.10} = 2.2065\%$.

(b) The bank is using the formula $A = P\left(e^{r/365}\right)^{365}$. Since $\$4532.10\left(e^{0.021825/365}\right)^{365} \approx \$4532.10$, 2.1825% will be the approximate nominal rate.

(c) In this case the difference is negligible, not taking into account any rounding in posting interest.

15. (a) $\left(e^{0.04} - 1\right) \times 100\% = 4.08108\%$.

(b) The approximation for effective rate is $r + \frac{1}{2}r^2 = 0.05 + \frac{1}{2} \times (0.05)^2 = 0.05 + 0.00125 = 0.05125$ or 5.125%, very slightly less than the true effective rate.

16. (a) Continuous compounding yields $\$1000e^{(0.04)(10)} = \$1491.82$.

True Difference: $D = \$1000\left[e^{(0.04)(10)} - \left(1 + \dfrac{0.04}{4}\right)^{(4)(10)} \right] \approx \$2.96$

Approximate Difference: $D \approx \$1000 \times \dfrac{(0.04)^2 \times 10 \times e^{(0.04)(10)}}{2 \times 4 + \dfrac{4 \times 0.04}{3} + \dfrac{(0.04)^2 \times 10}{2}} \approx \$2.96$

Continued on next page

16. continued

(b) Continuous compounding yields $\$1000e^{(0.18)(10)} = \$6049.65$.

True Difference: $D = \$1000\left[e^{(0.18)(10)} - \left(1+\dfrac{0.18}{365}\right)^{(365)(10)}\right] \approx \$2.68$

Approximate Difference: $D \approx \$1000 \times \dfrac{(0.18)^2 \times 10 \times e^{(0.18)(10)}}{2 \times 365 + \dfrac{4 \times 0.18}{3} + \dfrac{(0.18)^2 \times 10}{2}} \approx \$2.68$

17. Use the savings formula $A = d\left[\dfrac{(1+i)^n - 1}{i}\right]$, with $A = \$2000$, $i = \frac{0.05}{12}$, and $n = 24$.

$$\$2000 = d\left[\dfrac{\left(1+\frac{0.05}{12}\right)^{24} - 1}{\frac{0.05}{12}}\right] \approx 25.18592053d$$

$$d = \dfrac{\$2000}{25.18592053} = \$79.41$$

18. Use the savings formula $A = d\left[\dfrac{(1+i)^n - 1}{i}\right]$, with $A = \$2000$, $i = \frac{0.07}{12}$, and $n = 24$.

$$\$2000 = d\left[\dfrac{\left(1+\frac{0.07}{12}\right)^{24} - 1}{\frac{0.07}{12}}\right] \approx 25.68103157d$$

$$d = \dfrac{\$2000}{25.68103157} = \$77.88$$

19. Use the savings formula $A = d\left[\dfrac{(1+i)^n - 1}{i}\right]$, with $d = \$400$, $i = \frac{0.055}{12}$, and $n = 144$.

$$A = d\left[\dfrac{(1+i)^n - 1}{i}\right] = \$400\left[\dfrac{\left(1+\frac{0.055}{12}\right)^{144} - 1}{\frac{0.055}{12}}\right] = \$81,327.45$$

20. Use the savings formula, $A = d\left[\dfrac{(1+i)^n - 1}{i}\right]$ with $n = 35 \times 12 = 420$.

(a) With $d = \$100$ and $i = \frac{0.05}{12}$, we have the following.

$$A = d\left[\dfrac{(1+i)^{504} - 1}{i}\right] = \$100\left[\dfrac{\left(1+\frac{0.05}{12}\right)^{504} - 1}{\frac{0.05}{12}}\right] = \$171,134.87$$

(b) With $d = \$100$ and $i = \frac{0.075}{12}$, we have the following.

$$A = d\left[\dfrac{(1+i)^{504} - 1}{i}\right] = \$100\left[\dfrac{\left(1+\frac{0.075}{12}\right)^{504} - 1}{\frac{0.075}{12}}\right] = \$353,734.73$$

(c) With $d = \$100$ and $i = \frac{0.10}{12}$, we have the following.

$$A = d\left[\dfrac{(1+i)^{504} - 1}{i}\right] = \$100\left[\dfrac{\left(1+\frac{0.10}{12}\right)^{504} - 1}{\frac{0.10}{12}}\right] = \$774,429.65$$

21. Use the savings formula $A = d\left[\dfrac{(1+i)^n - 1}{i}\right]$, with $A = \$1,000,000$, $i = \frac{0.05}{12}$, and $n = 35 \times 12 = 420$.

$$\$1,000,000 = d\left[\dfrac{\left(1+\frac{0.05}{12}\right)^{420} - 1}{\frac{0.05}{12}}\right] \approx 1136.092425d$$

$$d = \dfrac{\$1,000,000}{1136.092425} = \$880.21$$

22. (a) Use the savings formula $A = d\left[\dfrac{(1+i)^n - 1}{i}\right]$, with $d = \$100$, $i = \frac{0.06}{12}$, and $n = 30 \times 12 = 360$.

$$A = d\left[\dfrac{(1+i)^n - 1}{i}\right] = \$100\left[\dfrac{\left(1+\frac{0.06}{12}\right)^{360} - 1}{\frac{0.06}{12}}\right] = \$100,451.50$$

(b) Use the savings formula $A = d\left[\dfrac{(1+i)^n - 1}{i}\right]$, with $A = \$250,000$, $i = \frac{0.075}{12}$, and $n = 20 \times 12 = 240$.

$$\$250,000 = d\left[\dfrac{\left(1+\frac{0.075}{12}\right)^{240} - 1}{\frac{0.075}{12}}\right] \approx 553.7307525d$$

$$d = \dfrac{\$250,000}{553.7307525} = \$451.48$$

23. (a) $\dfrac{\$100}{1-0.32} = \$147.06$

(b) Use the savings formula $A = d\left[\dfrac{(1+i)^n - 1}{i}\right]$, with $d = \$147.06$, $i = \frac{0.075}{12}$, and $n = 40 \times 12 = 480$ to calculate $A = \$147.06\left[\dfrac{\left(1+\frac{0.075}{12}\right)^{480} - 1}{\frac{0.075}{12}}\right] = \$444,683.29$.

(c) $0.68 \times \$444,683.29 = \$302,384.64$

24. (a) $\$302,382.22$. But when you take it out, you owe 32% tax on the part that is interest: $\$302,382.22 - 480 \times \$100 = \$254,382.22$. Your net is the $\$48,000$ contributed on which taxes were already paid plus $0.68 \times \$254,382.22 = \$172,979.91$, for a total of $\$220,979.91$.

(b) The entire $\$302,382.22$ is yours, with taxes already paid, at age 65. The answer in Exercise 23b is $\$9.68$ more because of rounding of $\$151.515152$ up to $\$151.52$.

25. (a) Write the series as $\frac{1}{2}\left(1 + \dfrac{1}{2^1} + \dfrac{1}{2^2} + \dfrac{1}{2^3} + \dfrac{1}{2^4}\right) = \frac{1}{2} \times \dfrac{\left(\frac{1}{2}\right)^5 - 1}{\frac{1}{2} - 1} = \dfrac{31}{32}$.

(b) $\dfrac{2^n - 1}{2^n}$

(c) 1

26. (a) $\dfrac{\left(-\frac{1}{3}\right)^5 - 1}{-\frac{1}{3} - 1} = \dfrac{-\frac{1}{243} - 1}{-\frac{1}{3} - 1} = \dfrac{-\frac{244}{243}}{-\frac{4}{3}} = \dfrac{61}{81}$

(b) $\dfrac{3\left[1 - \left(-\frac{1}{3}\right)^{n+1}\right]}{4}$, via the formula for sum of a geometric series.

(c) $\dfrac{3}{4}$

27. (a) $A = P(1.15)(1.07)(0.80) = 0.98440P$, so $r = (0.98440)^{1/3} - 1 = -0.00523 = -0.523\%$.

(b) It is the effective rate.

28. (a) – (c) Answers will vary.

(d) The ordinary IRA and the Roth IRA are equivalent provided the tax rate remains the same (however, they have different provisions regarding withdrawals and other considerations); the ordinary after-tax investment is worst.

(e) The Roth IRA is better in the first case (you pay the tax now at the lower rate), the ordinary IRA is better in the second case (you pay the lower tax rate later).

29. (a) $\$(1.04)^3 = \$1.12$

(b) $\$1/1.12 = \$0.89$

30. $\$10,000 \times (1 - 0.12)^3 = \$10,000 \times 0.68 = \$6800$

31. $\$10,000 \times (1 - 0.12)^6 \times \left(\dfrac{1}{1 + 0.03}\right)^6 \approx \$3900$

32. (a) Since $\dfrac{\text{cost in 2006}}{\$4.98} = \dfrac{\text{CPI for 2006}}{\text{CPI for 1965}} = \dfrac{200.5}{31.5} \approx 6.363079365$, we have the following.

$$\text{cost in 2006} = \$4.98(6.363079365) = \$31.70$$

Additional answers will vary.

(b) Since $\dfrac{\text{cost in 2006}}{\$40} = \dfrac{\text{CPI for 2006}}{\text{CPI for 1940}} = \dfrac{200.5}{14.0} \approx 14.32142857$, we have the following.

$$\text{cost in 2006} = \$40(14.32142857) = \$572.86$$

33. (a) Since $\dfrac{\text{cost in 2006}}{\$10.75} = \dfrac{\text{CPI for 2006}}{\text{CPI for 1962}} = \dfrac{200.5}{30.9} \approx 6.4898673139$, we have the following.

$$\text{cost in 2006} = \$10.75(6.4898673139) = \$69.75 \approx \$70$$

$$\$10.75 \times (6.4898673) = \$69.75 \approx \$70$$

Additional answers will vary.

(b) Since $\dfrac{\text{cost in 2006}}{\$0.25} = \dfrac{\text{CPI for 2006}}{\text{CPI for 1970}} = \dfrac{200.5}{38.8} \approx 5.167525773$, we have the following.

$$\text{cost in 2006} = \$0.25(5.167525773) = \$1.29$$

Since $\dfrac{\text{cost in 2006}}{\$0.25} = \dfrac{\text{CPI for 2006}}{\text{CPI for 1974}} = \dfrac{200.5}{49.3} \approx 4.06693712$, we have the following.

$$\text{cost in 2006} = \$0.70(4.06693712) = \$2.85$$

34. (a) $\dfrac{90.9-82.4}{82.4}=10.3\%$

(b) $184\times(1.03)^3\approx201.1$

35. Let the purchasing power of the original salary be P. Then the purchasing power of the new salary is $P\times1.10\times\dfrac{1}{1+0.20}\approx0.917P$, an 8.3% loss.

36. $\$2000\times\left[1+\left(\dfrac{1}{1.03}\right)^1+\ldots+\left(\dfrac{1}{1.03}\right)^{39}\right]=\$2000\times\dfrac{\left(\frac{1}{1.03}\right)^{40}-1}{\frac{1}{1.03}-1}\approx\$47,616.43$

37. Nowhere close

(a) As she ends her 35th year of service, her salary will be \$166,973.02, which we multiply by $\frac{1}{1.03^{35}}$ to get the equivalent in today's dollars: \$59,339.44. (We do not take into account that annual salaries are normally rounded to the nearest dollar or hundred dollars.) The result is easily obtained by use of a spreadsheet, proceeding through her salary year by year and then adjusting at the end for inflation. Here is the corresponding formula, using Fisher's effect with $r=0.04$ and $a=0.03$.

$$\left\{\left[\$42,000\left(1+\dfrac{0.01}{1.03}\right)^7+\$1500\left(\dfrac{1}{1.03}\right)^7\right]\left(1+\dfrac{0.01}{1.03}\right)^7+\$1500\left(\dfrac{1}{1.03}\right)^{14}\right\}$$
$$\times\left\{\left(1+\dfrac{0.01}{1.03}\right)^{20}\left(\dfrac{1}{1.03}\right)\right\}$$

The last factor is for inflation during her 35th year of service.

(b) \$57,394.20.

38. (a) Answers will vary with salary protocol that the student devises. Keeping the two promotion raises at \$1500 and varying only the initial salary requires an initial salary of \$64,737.85. Keeping the starting salary at \$42,000 but adjusting the raises for inflation to be \$1500 in 2005 dollars requires annual raises of 5.25%. (Answers can be derived by programming adaptations of the formula from the solution to Exercise 37 into a spreadsheet, calculator, or computer algebra system, and using either successive approximation or a Solve routine.)

(b) Answers will vary.

39. $\$2,000,000\times\left(1+x+\ldots+x^{19}\right)$, with $x=\frac{1}{1+a}=\frac{1}{1.03}$, giving \$29.8 million. If you can expect to earn interest rate r on funds once you receive them, through the last payment, then the present value of your stream of income of annual lottery payments P plus interest (with inflation rate a) is as follows.

$$P\left[\left(\dfrac{1+r}{1+a}\right)^{19}\cdot1+\left(\dfrac{1+r}{1+a}\right)^{18}\left(\dfrac{1}{1+a}\right)^1+\left(\dfrac{1+r}{1+a}\right)^{17}\left(\dfrac{1}{1+a}\right)^2+\ldots\right.$$
$$\left.\ldots+\left(\dfrac{1+r}{1+a}\right)^1\left(\dfrac{1}{1+a}\right)^{18}+1\cdot\left(\dfrac{1}{1+a}\right)^{19}\right]=P\dfrac{1}{(1+a)^{19}}\left[\dfrac{(1+r)^{20}-1}{r}\right]$$

For $P=\$2$ million, $r=4\%$, and $a=3\%$, we get \$33.4 million. If you can earn 4% forever but inflation stays at 3%, the present value is infinite!

40. Not taking into account interest earned on funds received, the present value is still $29.8 million. Using the formula from the solution to Exercise 39, if you can earn 6% through the last payment, the present value of the income stream through then is $42.0 million.

41. (a) Use the savings formula with $A = \$100,000$, $n = 35 \times 4 = 140$ quarters, and $i = \frac{0.072}{4}$ per quarter. You find $d = \$161.39$.

(b). $\dfrac{\$100,000}{(1.04)^{35}} = \$25,341.55$

(c) $\dfrac{\$100,000}{(1.04)^{65}} = \$7813.27$

42. (a) Since she wants income each year of $50,000 in 2005 dollars, the present value is $45 \times \$50,000 = \$2.25$ million.

(b) She needs $2.25 million in 2005 dollars, which at 4% inflation per year will be ($2.25 million)$\times 1.04^{35} \approx \$8.88$ million in 2040. We find the quarterly contribution d to this sinking fund by applying the savings formula, $A = d\left[\dfrac{(1+i)^n - 1}{i}\right]$, with fund $A = \$8,878,700.24$, quarterly interest $i = \frac{0.072}{4} = 0.018$, and $n = 140$ quarters.

$$\$8,878,700.24 = d\left[\dfrac{(1+0.018)^{140} - 1}{0.018}\right] \approx 619.6195407d$$

Perhaps your roommate should reassess her plans!

43. (a) $\frac{1.045^3}{1.031} - 1 = 0.01387 = 1.39\%$.

(b) $(1 - 0.30)\times 1.39\% = 0.97\%$ (however, some states and cities do not tax interest earned on U.S. government securities).

44. $\dfrac{r-i}{1+i}(1-t)$

45. The price before should have been about $\dfrac{D(1.03)}{0.15 - 0.03} = 8.583D$, the price after should have been

$\dfrac{D(1.03)}{0.1475 - 0.03} = 8.766D$, so the percentage change expected was $\dfrac{8.766D - 8.583D}{8.583D} = 2.13\%$,

which applied to the Dow Jones should have produced a rise of 188 pts. The answer does not depend on the value of D.

46. (a) $S\left[\dfrac{-\Delta r}{r + \Delta r - g}\right]$

(b) $0.0213S$

(c) $r = 3.25\%$

47. Programming the savings formula into the spreadsheet and varying the value of i until you find $A \geq \$5000$, using the Solver command in Excel, or otherwise: $i = 1.60\%$ per month, or an annual rate of $12 \times 1.60\% = 19.2\%$.

48. (a) $12,000

(b) The resulting equation is $\dfrac{100\left[(1+i)^{120}-1\right]}{i}=37{,}747$. Replacing i by $1+x$ and rearranging

gives $x^{120}-377.47x+376.47=0$. The solution is $x=1.016714122$, for an annual nominal rate of $12(0.016714122)=20.06\%$.

The effective annual yield (APY) is $(1.016714122)^{12}-1=22.01\%$.

49. 4.97%. It is the effective rate.

50. 0.00634% per month, or 7.61% annual rate.

Word Search Solution

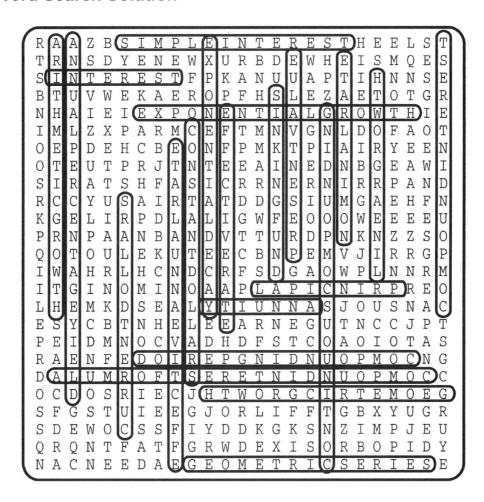

Chapter 22
Borrowing Models

Chapter Outline

Chapter Summary

The concepts of simple and compound interest, developed in Chapter 21 in the context of savings, play an equally important role in borrowing. Most loans, whether for buying a car, paying for college, or mortgages for buying a house, involve compound interest.

To better compare terms of different loans, specific terminology has been developed. The nominal rate is stated for any specific period of time, often monthly. The *effective annual rate* (*EAR*) is the actual percentage rate for a full year, taking compounding into account. The amortization formula, obtained by summing a geometric series, is used to compute the periodic payments (generally monthly) needed to repay a loan or mortgage.

While conventional mortgages have a fixed interest rate for the life of the loan, the interest rate in an *adjustable mortgage* is fixed for a much shorter period (often just one year), and then adjusts either up or down, depending upon interest rates in the economy. Since much of the risk of rising rates is on the borrower, such mortgages often come with a lower initial rate, which translates into lower initial payments. For some borrowers, these lower payments allow them to buy a more expensive house than they could afford with a conventional mortgage. However, because of the periodic adjustments, this type of mortgage may turn out to be more expensive in the long run than fixed-rate mortgages.

Skill Objectives

1. Become familiar with the various types of loans.

2. Become familiar with the terminology for loan rates.

3. Use the amortization formula to compute the monthly payment needed to repay a loan or mortgage.

Teaching Tips

1. As in the previous chapter, students will encounter numerous ads for loans, mortgages, and credit cards, which will contain much of the terminology used in this chapter. You can exploit these practical situations to supplement the problems in the text.

2. A significant proportion of the problems require the use of spreadsheets. Since many of the students in such a course will not be familiar with spreadsheets, be careful to avoid these exercises, unless you are prepared to devote class time to teaching this material.

Research Paper

Usury was originally defined as a fee charged for the use of money (Latin from *usus* or "used"). Have students investigate the origins of lending. Students may wish to include a comparison between biblical and Qur'anic injunctions against Usury.

Another research paper could involve having students investigate unfair lending practices such as "predatory lending" and legislation preventing such lending. Students may wish to discuss the Truth in Lending Act. There are many different tactics that could be considered predatory such as lending by making a secured loan when the borrower has no way to repay that loan.

Spreadsheet Project

To do this project, go to http://www.whfreeman.com/fapp7e.

This spreadsheet project allows students to model a mortgage and investigate the effects of extra payments.

Collaborative Learning

Actual Loan Cost

As an icebreaker, ask the students to estimate how much the total repayments will be on a variety of loans, such as:

3-, 4-, and 5-year car loans of $10,000 at 8% compounded monthly,

or

a 15-year mortgage of $100,000 at 6% compounded monthly,

or

a 30-year mortgage of $100,000 at 7% compounded monthly.

Their estimates may be far off the mark. Ask them to hold on to their results until they learn how to make these calculations, and then compare them. They may very well be shocked at the total cost, especially in the case of the 30-year mortgage.

Solutions

Skills Check:

1. b   2. c/a   3. a   4. b   5. b   6. a   7. b   8. a   9. a   10. c

11. a   12. b   13. c   14. b   15. c   16. c   17. c   18. c   19. c   20. b

Exercises:

1. (a) For the 11.25%, a cost of $15,529 has an annual yield of $\dfrac{0.0551(\$10,000)}{\$9802} = 5.62\%$.

   For the 5.51%, a cost of $9802 has an annual yield of $\dfrac{0.1125(\$10,000)}{\$15,529} = 7.24\%$.

   (b) Answers will vary but should remark that the first bond locks in the interest rate much farther into the future.

2. For the 5.75%, a cost of $10,318 has an annual yield of $\dfrac{0.0575(\$10,000)}{\$10,318} = 5.57\%$.

3. We add on interest of $4 \times 0.059 \times \$5000 = \$1180$.

   The monthly payment is $\dfrac{\$5000 + \$1180}{48} = \$128.75$.

4. We add on interest of $2 \times 0.085 \times \$3000 = \$510$.

   The monthly payment is $\dfrac{\$3000 + \$510}{24} = \$146.25$.

5. To realize the $3000 that you need, you need to borrow $\dfrac{\$3000}{1 - 0.09 \times 4} = \$4687.50$, for which the monthly payment is $\dfrac{\$4687.50}{48} = \$97.66$. If you do just the $3000 discounted loan, the lender gives you just $\$3000(1 - 0.09 \times 4) = \$1920$, on which the monthly payment is $\dfrac{\$1920}{48} = \$40.00$.

6. To realize the $3000 that you need, you need to borrow $\dfrac{\$3000}{1 - 0.085 \times 5} = \$5217.39$, for which the monthly payment is $\dfrac{\$5217.39}{60} = \$86.96$. If you do just the $3000 discounted loan, the lender gives you just $\$3000(1 - 0.085 \times 5) = \$1725$, on which the monthly payment is $\dfrac{\$3000}{60} = \$50.00$.

7. Answers will vary but should conclude that the add-on loan always has a lower payment.

8. Let the amount needed be P, with annual interest rate r and payment over t years (= $12t$ months). Then the monthly payment on the add-on loan is $\dfrac{P(1+rt)}{12t} = \dfrac{P}{12t}(1+rt)$. The monthly payment on the discounted loan is $\dfrac{\frac{P}{1-rt}}{12t} = \dfrac{P}{12t}\left(\dfrac{1}{1-rt}\right)$. For simplicity, let $a = rt$. For positive a, we have $1-a^2 = (1-a)(1+a) < 1$ and hence for $0 < a < 1$ we have (by dividing both sides of the inequality by $(1-a)$ also $1+a < \dfrac{1}{1-a}$. Thus, for an add-on loan and a discounted loan for which you receive the same amount from the lender, the monthly payment is always less on the add-on loan.

9. All but a tiny amount after 91 months

10. About $410

11. After 203 months (more than 16 years!), the balance is $500.16.

12. $3706.07

13. 294 months (= 24.5 years!), plus a few cents in the 295th month

14. 294 months (plus a few cents in the 295th month)

15. $\dfrac{\$24,995 - \$2000}{60} = \dfrac{\$22,995}{60} = \$383.25$

16. Use the amortization formula $d = \dfrac{Ai}{1-(1+i)^{-n}}$, with $A = \$7000$, $i = \frac{0.085}{12}$, and $n = 48$.

$$d = \frac{Ai}{1-(1+i)^{-n}} = \frac{\$7000 \times \frac{0.085}{12}}{1-\left(1+\frac{0.085}{12}\right)^{-48}} = \$172.54$$

17. The amortization formula gives $19.28 per month for each $1000 financed. Either I miscopied, or the difference is probably due to what is considered a month (30 days?) and what method is used to calculate the monthly interest rate.

18. (a) Use the amortization formula $d = \dfrac{Ai}{1-(1+i)^{-n}}$, with $A = \$1000$, $i = \frac{0.079}{12}$, and $n = 48$.

$$d = \frac{Ai}{1-(1+i)^{-n}} = \frac{\$1000 \times \frac{0.079}{12}}{1-\left(1+\frac{0.079}{12}\right)^{-48}} = \$24.37$$

(b) Use the amortization formula $d = \dfrac{Ai}{1-(1+i)^{-n}}$, with $A = \$1000$, $i = \frac{0.068}{12}$, and $n = 60$.

$$d = \frac{Ai}{1-(1+i)^{-n}} = \frac{\$1000 \times \frac{0.068}{12}}{1-\left(1+\frac{0.068}{12}\right)^{-60}} = \$19.71$$

Additional answers will vary.

19. Use the amortization formula $d = \dfrac{Ai}{1-(1+i)^{-n}}$, with $A = \$100,000$, $i = \frac{0.065}{12}$, and $n = 30 \times 12 = 360$.

$$d = \frac{Ai}{1-(1+i)^{-n}} = \frac{\$100,000 \times \frac{0.065}{12}}{1-\left(1+\frac{0.065}{12}\right)^{-360}} = \$632.07$$

20. Use the amortization formula $d = \dfrac{Ai}{1-(1+i)^{-n}}$, with $A = \$100,000$, $i = \frac{0.07125}{12}$, and $n = 30 \times 12 = 360$.

$$d = \frac{Ai}{1-(1+i)^{-n}} = \frac{\$100,000 \times \frac{0.07125}{12}}{1-\left(1+\frac{0.07125}{12}\right)^{-360}} = \$673.72$$

21. Use the amortization formula $d = \dfrac{Ai}{1-(1+i)^{-n}}$, with $A = \$100,000$, $i = \frac{0.06125}{12}$, and $n = 15 \times 12 = 180$.

$$d = \frac{Ai}{1-(1+i)^{-n}} = \frac{\$100,000 \times \frac{0.06125}{12}}{1-\left(1+\frac{0.06125}{12}\right)^{-180}} = \$850.62$$

22. Use the amortization formula $d = \dfrac{Ai}{1-(1+i)^{-n}}$, with $A = \$100,000$, $i = \frac{0.0675}{12}$, and $n = 15 \times 12 = 180$.

$$d = \frac{Ai}{1-(1+i)^{-n}} = \frac{\$100,000 \times \frac{0.0675}{12}}{1-\left(1+\frac{0.0675}{12}\right)^{-180}} = \$884.91$$

23. Use the amortization formula $A = d\left[\dfrac{1-(1+i)^{-n}}{i}\right]$, with $d = \$632.07$, $i = \frac{0.065}{12}$, and $n = 360 - 5 \times 12 = 360 - 60 = 300$.

$$A = d\left[\frac{1-(1+i)^{-n}}{i}\right] = \$632.07\left[\frac{1-\left(1+\frac{0.065}{12}\right)^{-300}}{\frac{0.065}{12}}\right] = \$93,611.27$$

Thus, the amount of equity is $\$100,000 - \$93,611.27 = \$6388.73$.

24. Use the amortization formula $A = d\left[\dfrac{1-(1+i)^{-n}}{i}\right]$, with $d = \$673.72$, $i = \frac{0.07125}{12}$, and $n = 360 - 5 \times 12 = 360 - 60 = 300$.

$$A = d\left[\frac{1-(1+i)^{-n}}{i}\right] = \$673.72\left[\frac{1-\left(1+\frac{0.07125}{12}\right)^{-300}}{\frac{0.07125}{12}}\right] = \$94,246.47$$

Thus, the amount of equity is $\$100,000 - \$94,246.47 = \$5743.53$.

25. Use the amortization formula $A = d\left[\dfrac{1-(1+i)^{-n}}{i}\right]$, with $d = \$850.62$, $i = \frac{0.06125}{12}$, and $n = 180 - 5 \times 12 = 180 - 60 = 120$.

$$A = d\left[\frac{1-(1+i)^{-n}}{i}\right] = \$850.62\left[\frac{1-\left(1+\frac{0.06125}{12}\right)^{-120}}{\frac{0.06125}{12}}\right] = \$76,186.80$$

Thus, the amount of equity is $\$100,000 - \$76,186.80 = \$23,813.20$.

26. Use the amortization formula $A = d\left[\dfrac{1-(1+i)^{-n}}{i}\right]$, with $d = \$884.91$, $i = \frac{0.0675}{12}$, and $n = 180 - 5 \times 12 = 180 - 60 = 120$.

$$A = d\left[\frac{1-(1+i)^{-n}}{i}\right] = \$884.91\left[\frac{1-\left(1+\frac{0.0675}{12}\right)^{-120}}{\frac{0.0675}{12}}\right] = \$77,066.56$$

Thus, the amount of equity is $\$100,000 - \$77,066.56 = \$22,933.44$.

27. Using Solver in Excel or otherwise, we get an annual rate of 3.68%.

28. Use the amortization formula $d = \dfrac{Ai}{1-(1+i)^{-n}}$, with $A = \$160,000$, $i = \frac{0.036}{12}$, and $n = 30 \times 12 = 360$.

The monthly payment would be $d = \dfrac{Ai}{1-(1+i)^{-n}} = \dfrac{\$160,000 \times \frac{0.036}{12}}{1-\left(1+\frac{0.036}{12}\right)^{-360}} = \$727.43$.

Regarding the difference, answers will vary.

29. Use the amortization formula $d = \dfrac{Ai}{1-(1+i)^{-n}}$, with $A = \$180,000$, $i = \frac{0.0675}{12}$, and $n = 30 \times 12 = 360$.

The monthly payment would be $d = \dfrac{Ai}{1-(1+i)^{-n}} = \dfrac{\$180,000 \times \frac{0.0675}{12}}{1-\left(1+\frac{0.0675}{12}\right)^{-360}} = \$1167.48$.

30. We must first solve $5000 = 128.75\left[\dfrac{1-(1+i)^{-48}}{i}\right]$. Using a spreadsheet or calculator, we have $i = 0.00900257$. Thus, APR is approximately $12 \times 0.00900257 = 10.80\%$. The EAR is $(1+0.00900257)^{12} - 1 = 11.35\%$.

31. We must first solve $3000 = 146.25\left[\dfrac{1-(1+i)^{-24}}{i}\right]$. Using a spreadsheet or calculator, we have $i = 0.01296119$. Thus, APR is approximately $12 \times 0.01296119 = 15.55\%$. The EAR is $(1+0.01296119)^{12} - 1 = 16.71\%$.

32. We must first solve $3000 = 97.66\left[\dfrac{1-(1+i)^{-48}}{i}\right]$. Using a spreadsheet or calculator, we have

$i = 0.01992686$. Thus, APR is approximately $12 \times 0.01992686 = 23.91\%$. The EAR is $(1+0.01992686)^{12} - 1 = 26.72\%$.

33. We must first solve $3000 = 86.96\left[\dfrac{1-(1+i)^{-60}}{i}\right]$. Using a spreadsheet or calculator, we have

$i = 0.02031339$. Thus, APR is approximately $12 \times 0.02031339 = 24.37\%$. The EAR is $(1+0.02031339)^{12} - 1 = 27.29\%$.

34. APR $= 365 \times 0.0004932 = 18.00\%$; EAR $= (1 + 0.0004932)^{365} - 1 = 19.72\%$. The company must disclose the APR.

35. The principal is $300 - \$54 = \$246$ and the (simple) interest over the two weeks is $54, so the interest rate is $100\% \times \frac{\$54}{\$246} = 21.95\%$ for 2 weeks, for an annual rate of $\frac{52}{2} \times 21.95\% = 571\%$. For a 365-day year, we get a daily rate of $\frac{21.95\%}{14} = 1.57\%$ per day and an annual percentage rate of $365 \times 1.57\% = 572\%$.

36. You pay back $d = \$354$ on amount $A = \$300$ after $n = 1$ compounding periods. From spreadsheet or otherwise, the solution i to the amortization formula for these amounts is $i = 0.18 = 18\%$ for the two-week period. The APR is thus $26 \times 18\% = 468\%$ (slightly more if done for 14 days on a 365-day/yr basis).

37. The principal is $1500 - \$88 = \$1412$ and the (simple) interest over the week is $88, so the interest rate is $100\% \times \frac{\$88}{\$1412} = 6.23\%$ for 1 week, for an annual rate of $52 \times 6.23\% = 324\%$. For a 365-day year, we get a daily rate of $\frac{6.23\%}{7} = 0.89\%$ per day and an annual percentage rate of $365 \times 0.89\% = 325\%$.

38. Because it is a discounted loan, you receive amount $A = \$1500 - \$88 = \$1412$ and pay $d = \$1500$ after $n = 1$ compounding periods. From spreadsheet or otherwise, the solution i to the amortization formula for these amounts is $i = 0.062323 = 6.2323\%$ for the 17-day period, or 0.3666% per day. The APR is thus $365 \times 0.3666\% \approx 134\%$.

39. (a) Use the amortization formula $d = \dfrac{Ai}{1-(1+i)^{-n}}$, with $A = \$100,000$, $i = \frac{0.08375}{12}$, and $n = 30 \times 12 = 360$.

$$d = \frac{Ai}{1-(1+i)^{-n}} = \frac{\$100,000 \times \frac{0.08375}{12}}{1-\left(1+\frac{0.08375}{12}\right)^{-360}} = \$760.07$$

(b) Use the amortization formula $A = d\left[\dfrac{1-(1+i)^{-n}}{i}\right]$, with $d = \$760.07$, $i = \frac{0.08375}{12}$, and $n = 360 - 5 \times 12 = 360 - 60 = 300$.

$$A = d\left[\frac{1-(1+i)^{-n}}{i}\right] = \$760.07\left[\frac{1-\left(1+\frac{0.08375}{12}\right)^{-300}}{\frac{0.08375}{12}}\right] = \$95,387.80$$

Thus, the amount of equity is $100,000 - \$95,387.80 = \$4612.20$.

Continued on next page

39. continued

(c) Use the amortization formula $d = \dfrac{Ai}{1-(1+i)^{-n}}$, with $A = \$95,387.80$, $i = \dfrac{0.070}{12}$, and $n = 30 \times 12 = 360$.

$$d = \frac{Ai}{1-(1+i)^{-n}} = \frac{\$95,387.80 \times \frac{0.070}{12}}{1-\left(1+\frac{0.070}{12}\right)^{-360}} = \$634.62$$

(d) Since the difference between the two payments is $\$760.07 - \$634.62 = \$125.45$, it would take $\dfrac{\$2000}{\$125.45} \approx 15.9426$ or 16 months.

40. (a) Use the amortization formula $d = \dfrac{Ai}{1-(1+i)^{-n}}$, with $A = \$180,000$, $i = \dfrac{0.08375}{12}$, and $n = 15 \times 12 = 180$.

$$d = \frac{Ai}{1-(1+i)^{-n}} = \frac{\$180,000 \times \frac{0.08375}{12}}{1-\left(1+\frac{0.08375}{12}\right)^{-180}} = \$1759.37$$

(b) Use the amortization formula $A = d\left[\dfrac{1-(1+i)^{-n}}{i}\right]$, with $A = \$160,000$, $d = \$1759.37$, $i = \dfrac{0.08375}{12}$.

$$A = d\left[\frac{1-(1+i)^{-n}}{i}\right]$$

$$\$160,000 = \$1759.37\left[\frac{1-\left(1+\frac{0.08375}{12}\right)^{-n}}{\frac{0.08375}{12}}\right]$$

$$n \approx 145$$

Thus, she has been paying for $180 - 145 = 35$ months.

(c) Use the amortization formula $d = \dfrac{Ai}{1-(1+i)^{-n}}$, with $A = \$174,000$, $i = \dfrac{0.0875}{12}$, and $n = 30 \times 12 = 360$.

$$d = \frac{Ai}{1-(1+i)^{-n}} = \frac{\$174,000 \times \frac{0.0875}{12}}{1-\left(1+\frac{0.0875}{12}\right)^{-360}} = \$1368.86$$

41. (a) $\$100,250$

(b) The payment is $\$648.60$.
The interest for one-twelfth of the year is $\$100,000 \times \frac{0.07}{12} = \$583.33$, so the payment on the principal is just $\$65.27$.

(c) $\$583.33 - 250.00 = \$333.33$.

(d) The inflation adjusted cost is $\dfrac{\$333.33}{1 + \frac{0.03}{12}} = \$332.50$; the interest rate for the month is $\frac{\$332.50}{\$100,000} = 0.0033250$, which is an annual rate of $12(0.0033250) = 3.99\%$. We have left out any costs (such as realtor's fee) involved in the sale.

42. (a) Consider the following balance sheet.

REVENUE		EXPENSES	
Equity in house	$5,869		
Sale of house	$125,000		
		Cost of house (including down payment)	$105,000
		Closing costs at purchase	$2,000
		Mortgage payments $(60 \times \$665.30)$	$39,918
		Insurance	$1,000
		Real estate taxes	$10,000
		Fee to realtor at sale	$9,000
		Closing costs at sale	$500
		Moving expense	$3,000
TOTALS	**$130,869**		**$170,418**

The calculation is in current dollars, so does not take into account inflation. We find the equity in the house by calculating how much of the remainder of the $100,000 mortgage would be paid off in the last 25 years. Use the amortization formula $A = d\left[\dfrac{1-(1+i)^{-n}}{i}\right]$,

with $d = \$665.30$, $i = \frac{0.07}{12}$, and $n = 25 \times 12 = 300$.

$$A = d\left[\frac{1-(1+i)^{-n}}{i}\right] = \$665.30\left[\frac{1-\left(1+\frac{0.07}{12}\right)^{-300}}{\frac{0.07}{12}}\right] = \$94,131.24$$

The payment is based off of financing $100,000. Thus, the amount of equity is as follows.

$$\$100,000 - \$94,131.24 = \$5,868.76 \ (\$5869, \text{ rounded})$$

During the five years, there was a loss.

$$\text{Revenue minus expenses} = \$130,869 - \$170,418 = -\$39,549$$

(b) This would be equivalent to making rent payments of $\dfrac{\$39,549}{60} = \$659.15.$

43. There would be $\dfrac{\$81.6 \text{ million}}{30} = \$2.72$ million paid annually (including immediately).

$$2.72 + 2.72\left(\frac{1}{1.07}\right) + 2.72\left(\frac{1}{1.07}\right)^2 + \ldots + 2.72\left(\frac{1}{1.07}\right)^{29}$$

This is a geometric series. From Chapter 21, the sum will be $2.72\dfrac{\left(\frac{1}{1.07}\right)^{30}-1}{\frac{1}{1.07}-1} \approx 36.1.$

Thus, the payoff is approximately $36.1 million.

44. We assume payments at the end of the month.

For men: The Excel command = PV(0.04/12,199,2000,0,0) yields $290,580.05.

For women: The Excel command = PV(0.04/12,235,2000,0,0) yields $325,514.35.

45. Because her payments increase each year exactly as much as inflation, she will receive $50,000 in 2005 dollars every year. So she needs to accumulate $45 \times \$50,000 = \$2.25$ million in 2005 dollars. Her effective yield on investment each year, taking into account inflation and using Fisher's formula, is $\dfrac{1+r}{1+a} - 1 = \dfrac{1.072}{1.04} - 1 = 3.076923077\%$. Use the savings formula with $A = 2{,}250{,}000$, $i = 0.03076923077$, and $n = 35 \times 4 = 140$ quarters.

$$A = d\left[\frac{(1+i)^n - 1}{i}\right] \Rightarrow 2{,}250{,}000 = d\left[\frac{\left(1 + \frac{0.03076923077}{4}\right)^{140} - 1}{\frac{0.03076923077}{4}}\right]$$

Thus, $d = \$8997.74$ per quarter.

46. The expected Social Security monthly income of $1628 in 2001 dollars is $\frac{\$1628 \times 195}{177.1} = \$1792.55$ in 2005 dollars, using the Consumer Price Index values from Table 21.5.

Her desired income in the first year of retirement is $50,000/year in 2005 dollars, or $4166.67/month, or $4166.67 - \$1792.55 = \$2374.12$ more than Social Security will provide. To determine how much she must accumulate to have this much monthly for 33 years, we apply the amortization formula, $A = d\left[\dfrac{1 - (1+i)^{-n}}{i}\right]$, with $d = \$2374.12$, $i = \frac{0.06}{12} = 0.005$, and $n = 33 \times 12 = 396$.

$$A = d\left[\frac{1 - (1+i)^{-n}}{i}\right] = \$2374.12\left[\frac{1 - (1 + 0.005)^{-396}}{0.005}\right] = \$408{,}941.18$$

This is how much her savings must be worth in 2005 dollars; in 2052 dollars, she must have $\$408{,}941.18 \times (1.03)^{47} = \$1{,}640{,}629.07$. We use the savings formula to save up this amount A over $n = 47 \times 12 = 564$ months with monthly interest rate $i = \frac{0.06}{12} = 0.005$.

$$A = d\left[\frac{(1+i)^n - 1}{i}\right] \Rightarrow \$1{,}640{,}629.07 = d\left[\frac{(1 + 0.005)^{564} - 1}{0.005}\right]$$

$$\$1{,}640{,}629.07 = d(3131.87597) \Rightarrow d = \frac{\$1{,}640{,}629.07}{3131.87597} = \$523.85$$

The monthly amount to save is $523.85.

If instead of the CPI from Ch. 21 we use 3% inflation per year, the expected Social Security monthly income of $1628 in 2001 dollars is $\$1628 \times (1.03)^4 = \$1832.33$ in 2005. Her desired income in the first year of retirement is $50,000/year in 2005 dollars, or $4166.67/month, or $4166.67 - \$1832.33 = \$2334.34$ more than Social Security will provide. To determine how much she must accumulate to have this much monthly for 33 years, we apply the amortization formula with payment $d = \$2334.34$, $n = 33 \times 12 = 396$ months with monthly interest rate $i = \frac{0.06}{12} = 0.005$.

$$A = d\left[\frac{1 - (1+i)^{-n}}{i}\right] = \$2334.34\left[\frac{1 - (1 + 0.005)^{-396}}{0.005}\right] = \$402{,}089.13$$

This is how much her savings must be worth in 2005 dollars; in 2052 dollars, she must have $\$402{,}089.13 \times (1.03)^{47} = \$1{,}613{,}139.39$.

Continued on next page

46. continued

We use the savings formula to save up this amount A over $n = 47 \times 12 = 564$ months with monthly interest rate $i = \frac{0.06}{12} = 0.005$.

$$A = d\left[\frac{(1+i)^n - 1}{i}\right] \Rightarrow \$1{,}613{,}139.39 = d\left[\frac{(1+0.005)^{564} - 1}{0.005}\right]$$

$$\$1{,}613{,}139.39 = d(3131.87597) \Rightarrow d = \frac{\$1{,}613{,}139.39}{3131.87597} = \$515.07$$

The monthly amount to save is \$515.07.

If the 6% APR is interpreted as 6% APY (a topic from Ch. 21), then the monthly interest rate is $1.06^{1/12} - 1 = 0.00486755$. The corresponding divisor is 2971.908212 (instead of 3131.87597), and she must put away \$552.05 (using CPI for inflation 2001–2005) or \$542.80 (using 3% annual inflation 2001–2005).

47. The expected Social Security monthly income of \$1628 in 2001 dollars is $\frac{\$1628 \times 195}{177.1} = \$1792.55$ in 2005 dollars, using the Consumer Price Index values from Table 21.5. Reduction of the benefit by 32.5% makes it $\$1792.55 \times (1 - 0.325) = \$1209.97$ per month. Her desired income in 2005 dollars is \$50,000/year = \$4166.67/month, or \$4166.67 − \$1209.97 = \$2956.70 more than Social Security will provide. To determine how much she must accumulate to have this much monthly for 32 years, we apply the amortization formula with payment $d = \$2956.70$, $n = 32 \times 12 = 384$ months, and $i = \frac{0.06}{12} = 0.005$.

$$A = d\left[\frac{1 - (1+i)^{-n}}{i}\right] = \$2956.70\left[\frac{1 - (1+0.005)^{-384}}{0.005}\right] = \$504{,}229.69$$

This is how much her savings must be worth in 2005 dollars; in 2053 dollars, she must have $\$504{,}229.69 \times (1.03)^{48} = \$2{,}083{,}604.08$. We use the savings formula to save up this amount A over $n = 48 \times 12 = 576$ months with monthly interest rate $i = \frac{0.06}{12} = 0.005$.

$$A = d\left[\frac{(1+i)^n - 1}{i}\right] \Rightarrow \$2{,}083{,}604.08 = d\left[\frac{(1+0.005)^{576} - 1}{0.005}\right]$$

$$\$2{,}083{,}604.08 = d(3337.37879) \Rightarrow d = \frac{\$2{,}083{,}604.08}{3337.37879} = \$624.32$$

The monthly amount to save is \$624.32.

If instead of the CPI from Ch. 21 we use 3% inflation per year (CPI is from Ch. 21), the expected Social Security monthly income of \$1628 in 2001 dollars is $\$1628 \times (1.03)^4 = \$1832.33$ in 2005 dollars. Reduction of the benefit by 32.5% makes it $\$1832.33 \times (1 - 0.325) = \$1236.82$. Her desired income is \$50,000/year = \$4166.67/month, or \$4166.67 − \$1236.82 = \$2929.85 more than Social Security will provide.

To determine how much she must accumulate to have this much monthly for 32 years, we apply the amortization formula with payment $d = \$2929.85$, $n = 32 \times 12 = 384$ months, and monthly interest rate $i = \frac{0.06}{12} = 0.005$.

$$A = d\left[\frac{1 - (1+i)^{-n}}{i}\right] = \$2929.85\left[\frac{1 - (1+0.005)^{-384}}{0.005}\right] = \$499{,}650.75$$

This is how much her savings must be worth in 2005 dollars; in 2053 dollars, she must have $\$499{,}650.75 \times (1.03)^{48} = \$2{,}064{,}682.75$.

Continued on next page

47. continued

We use the savings formula to save up this amount A over $n = 48 \times 12 = 576$ months with monthly interest rate $i = \frac{0.06}{12} = 0.005$.

$$A = d\left[\frac{(1+i)^n - 1}{i}\right] \Rightarrow \$2{,}064{,}682.75 = d\left[\frac{(1+0.005)^{576} - 1}{0.005}\right]$$

$$\$2{,}064{,}682.75 = d\,(3337.37879) \Rightarrow d = \frac{\$2{,}064{,}682.75}{3337.37879} = \$618.65$$

The monthly amount to save is $618.65.

If the 6% APR is interpreted as 6% APY (a topic from Ch. 21), then the monthly interest rate is $1.06^{1/12} - 1 = 0.00486755$. The corresponding divisor is 3162.54921 (instead of 3337.37879), and she must put away $658.84 (using CPI for inflation 2001–2005) or $652.85 (using 3% annual inflation 2001–2005).

Word Search Solution

Chapter 23
The Economics of Resources

Chapter Outline

Introduction

Chapter Summary

Geometric growth models for biological populations tend to use the *natural rate of increase* (the difference between the birth and death rates) to represent the growth rate of a population. Unfortunately, birth and death rates fail to remain constant over time. Nonetheless, such models can be used in short-term planning. Since human populations rely on resources to sustain them, it is important to be able to predict future amounts of both renewable and nonrenewable resources. The management of *renewable resources* poses a very interesting problem: determine how much of our resource we can harvest each year and still allow the resource to replenish itself. In other words, what is the maximum harvest our resource can sustain? Finding this value requires knowing the size of next year's population given this year's population. This information is usually provided by a reproduction curve for the resource. This problem is an important one in forest and fishery management. Not surprisingly, economic factors play a role in the management of resources. Harvesting will not take place if it is not profitable. Furthermore, the resource may be eliminated entirely if it is more profitable to invest the proceeds elsewhere than to sustain the resource over time. In dynamical systems the state of a system at any time depends upon its state at previous times. Certain *dynamical systems*, such as weather, are chaotic, in the sense that the evolution of the system is sensitive to initial conditions. That is, a small change in the initial conditions may result in large changes at some future time. Biological population growth can sometimes exhibit chaotic tendencies.

Skill Objectives

1. Determine a country's projected population in a given number of years when its current population and its projected growth rate are given.

2. Explain why a sustainable yield policy is needed for harvestable resources.

3. Given the current generation population size, use its reproduction curve to estimate the next generation's population.

4. Interpret the meaning of the line $y = x$ in relation to the reproduction curve.

5. Approximate from a reproduction curve the projected sustainable yield for a harvestable resource when the current generation population is given.

6. Estimate from the reproduction curve the maximum sustainable yield for a harvestable resource.

Teaching Tips

1. It's somewhat surprising to find that students with an algebra background often don't relate the value of a function to the height of its graph; consequently, the process of interpreting a reproduction curve may require some preparation in terms of discussing functions. Once that has been done, you might consider having students read the next generation population $(y - \text{value})$ for various current generation populations $(x - \text{values})$ before attempting to determine the sustainable yield.

2. When beginning to approach the concept of sustainable yield, some students need a review of the line $y = x$ in terms of identity function. Understanding that it represents an equality between the current population and the next-generation population sets the stage for finding the sustainable yield.

3. The notation $f(x) - x$ can sometimes be understood more clearly in terms of the physical subtraction of lengths of line segments If you use an overhead projector, drawing the vertical segments $f(x)$ and x in different colors on the graph of the reproduction curve may help emphasize this relationship. Drawing their difference in yet a third color and following this changing difference along the curve may help students visualize the maximization problem.

4. This chapter offers many possibilities for extra-credit projects. If your geographic area has a specific renewable resource industry such as lumber in the Pacific Northwest or fishing in the Northeast and the Gulf of Mexico, students can contact local agencies and companies to find out their policy on renewing the natural resources. It would then be interesting to report these finding back to the class.

Research Paper

Students should find researching the topic of fractals very interesting. They may wish to investigate the lives and contributions of mathematicians such as Benoit Mandelbrot (Polish) or Gaston Julia (French). Other students may wish to focus on the complex shapes generated by computers or fractals in nature. In all cases, students can find a wealth of information on the Internet

Spreadsheet Project

To do this project, go to http://www.whfreeman.com/fapp7e.

This spreadsheet project is designed to explore the unpredictable and chaotic aspects of the logistics model, including the effects of rounding.

Collaborative Learning

Industry Awareness

As an icebreaker, ask the students to form groups and determine if they are aware of industries that deal in renewable resources, and how they go about guaranteeing that the resource will not be eliminated. One obvious example is the paper industry, which plants new trees to replace those it cuts down, thereby replenishing its stock. The fishing industry is more difficult to manage, since individual fishermen have no control over the size of what their competitors catch. In this case, government intervention or agreement among the fishermen may be needed to maintain a stable population and regular harvests of fish.

Solutions

Skills Check:

1. b   2. a   3. c   4. b   5. a   6. a   7. c   8. b   9. c   10. c

11. b   12. a   13. c   14. a   15. c   16. b   17. b   18. a   19. a   20. c

Exercises:

1. In late summer 2023

2. population in mid-2025 is as follows.
    $$\left(\text{population in mid-2007}\right)\times\left(1+\text{growth rate}\right)^{18} = 4.056\left(1+0.018\right)^{18}\text{ billion} \approx 5.59\text{ billion}$$

3. population in mid-2025 is as follows.
    $$\left(\text{population in mid-2007}\right)\times\left(1+\text{growth rate}\right)^{18} = 4.056\left(1+0.017\right)^{18}\text{ billion} \approx 5.49\text{ billion}$$

4. 4.4 billion

5. The population of Africa would be $925\times\left(1.024\right)^{18} = 1418$ million, almost 100% greater than, or twice as large, as Europe's population.

6. (a) $\dfrac{70}{2.4} \approx 29$ years

    (b) $\dfrac{70}{0.8} \approx 88$ years

7. (a) $\dfrac{70}{0.6} \approx 117$ years

    (b) $\dfrac{70}{1.3} \approx 54$ years

8. (a) 2016

    (b) The demand will be not 2.0 but 2.12 times as much in 2016 as in 1991, of which business will account for almost two-thirds rather than half.

9. (a) population in mid-2025 is as follows.
    $$\left(\text{population in mid-2007}\right)\times\left(1+\text{growth rate}\right)^{18} = 6.593\left(1+0.013\right)^{18}\text{ billion} \approx 8.3\text{ billion}$$
    population in mid-2050 is as follows.
    $$\left(\text{population in mid-2007}\right)\times\left(1+\text{growth rate}\right)^{43} = 6.593\left(1+0.013\right)^{43}\text{ billion} \approx 11.5\text{ billion}$$

    (b) No change in growth rate, no change in death rates, no global catastrophes, etc.

10. (a) For 2025

More-developed countries	$1.216(1+0.001)^{18}$ billion $\approx$	1.238 billion
Less-developed countries (excluding China)	$4.056(1+0.018)^{18}$ billion $\approx$	5.592 billion
China	$1.321(1+0.006)^{18}$ billion $\approx$	1.471 billion
Sum		8.301 billion

For 2050

More-developed countries	$1.216(1+0.001)^{43}$ billion $\approx$	1.269 billion
Less-developed countries (excluding China)	$4.056(1+0.018)^{43}$ billion $\approx$	8.735 billion
China	$1.321(1+0.006)^{43}$ billion $\approx$	1.709 billion
Sum		11.713 billion

There is not much difference.

(b) Answers will vary.

11. (a) The static reserve will be $\dfrac{2934.8}{77.9} \approx 38$ years.

(b) The exponential reserve will be $\dfrac{\ln\left[1+\left(\frac{2934.8}{77.9}\right)(0.019)\right]}{\ln\left[1+0.019\right]} \approx 29$ years.

(c) Answers will vary.

12. (a) The static reserve will be $\dfrac{6076.5}{90} \approx 68$ years.

(b) The exponential reserve will be $\dfrac{\ln\left[1+\left(\frac{6075.5}{90}\right)(0.022)\right]}{\ln\left[1+0.022\right]} \approx 42$ years

(c) Answers will vary.

13. (a) The static reserve will be 100 years. We are seeking the exponential reserve. This will be
$\dfrac{\ln\left[1+100(0.025)\right]}{\ln\left[1+0.025\right]} \approx 51$ years.

(b) $\dfrac{\ln\left[1+1000(0.025)\right]}{\ln\left[1+0.025\right]} \approx 132$ years

(c) $\dfrac{\ln\left[1+10,000(0.025)\right]}{\ln\left[1+0.025\right]} \approx 224$ years

14. (a) The static reserve will be 100 years. We are seeking the exponential reserve. This will be
$\dfrac{\ln\left[1+100(0.0125)\right]}{\ln\left[1+0.0125\right]} \approx 65$ years.

(b) $\dfrac{\ln\left[1+1000(0.0125)\right]}{\ln\left[1+0.0125\right]} \approx 210$ years

(c) $\dfrac{\ln\left[1+10,000(0.0125)\right]}{\ln\left[1+0.0125\right]} \approx 389$ years

15. (a) $\dfrac{\ln\left[1-100(0.005)\right]}{\ln\left[1-0.005\right]}\approx 138$ years

(b) $\dfrac{\ln\left[1-100(0.01)\right]}{\ln\left[1-0.01\right]}=\dfrac{\ln(1-1)}{\ln(0.99)}=\dfrac{\ln 0}{\ln[0.99]}$

This theoretically would imply forever!

16. (a) The static reserve will be 10,000 years. We are seeking the exponential reserve. This will be $\dfrac{\ln\left[1+10,000(0.035)\right]}{\ln\left[1+0.035\right]}\approx 170$ years

(b) $\dfrac{\ln\left[1+5,000(0.035)\right]}{\ln\left[1+0.035\right]}\approx 150$ years

(c) Since $(1.035)^{150}\approx 174.2$ the static reserve will be $\dfrac{5000}{174.2}\approx 29$ years.

(d) Answers will vary.

17. $\dfrac{437\times 10^{9}\text{ tons}}{100\times 10^{6}\text{ plants}\times 800\text{ years}}\approx 5.5$ tons/plant/year ≈ 30 lb/plant/day, which is unreasonable.

18. $\dfrac{1}{7}\ln\left(\dfrac{7.211}{6.291}\right)\approx 1.95\%$

19. $\dfrac{1}{100}\ln\left(\dfrac{62.95}{3.93}\right)\approx 2.77\%$

20. $\dfrac{1}{117}\ln\left(\dfrac{301}{62.95}\right)\approx 1.34\%$

21. After the first year, the population stays at 15.

22. 10, 20, 0, 0, ...

23. 7, 18.2, 6.6, 17.6, 8.4, 19.5, 2.0, 7.3, 18.6, 5.3

24. 15

25. We must have $f(x_n)=x_n$, or $4x_n(1-0.05x_n)=x_n$. The only solutions are $x_n=0$ and $4(1-0.05x_n)=1$, or $x_n=15$.

26. Using $x_{n+1}=f(x_n)=3x_n(1-0.05x_n)$ with $x_1=5$ we have the following (rounded).

5, 11.3, 14.8, 11.6, 14.6, 11.8, 14.5, 11.9, 14.4, 12.1

27. Using $x_{n+1}=f(x_n)=3x_n(1-0.05x_n)$ with $x_1=10$ we have the following (rounded).

10, 15.0, 11.3, 14.8, 11.6, 14.6, 11.8, 14.5, 11.9, 14.4

The population is oscillating but slowly converging to $\frac{40}{3}\approx 13.3$.

28. Those are the only values.

29. We must have $f(x_n)=x_n$, or $3x_n(1-0.05x_n)=x_n$. The only solutions are $x_n=0$ and $3(1-0.05x_n)=1$, or $x_n=\frac{40}{3}\approx 13.3$.

30. Answers will vary.

31. The red dashed line indicates the same size population next year as this year; where it intersects the blue curve is the equilibrium population size.

32. The graph shows the function $x_{n+1} - x_n = 3x_n(1 - 0.05x_n) - x_n = 2x_n - 0.15x_n^2$, and we want to maximize this quantity. By graphing, symmetry of a parabola, or (for the instructor) by calculus, the maximum occurs at $x_n = \frac{20}{3} \approx 6.7$, for which the yield is $x_{n+1} - x_n \approx 2(6.7) - 0.15(6.7)^2 \approx 6.7$.

33. Using $x_{n+1} = f(x_n) = 1.5x_n(1 - 0.025x_n)$ with $x_1 = 11$ we have the following (rounded).
$$11, 12.0, 12.6, 12.9, 13.1, 13.2, 13.3, 13.3, 13.3, 13.3$$

34. Using $x_{n+1} = f(x_n) = 1.5x_n(1 - 0.025x_n)$ with $x_1 = 5$ we have the following (rounded).
$$5, 6.6, 8.2, 9.8, 11.1, 12.0, 12.6, 13.0, 13.1, 13.2$$

35. The population sizes are 11, 15.0, 13.7, 14.9, 14.9, 15.0, 14.8, 14.3, 13.0, 9.5 – and the following year the population is wiped out.

36. Using $x_{n+1} = f(x_n) = 1.5x_n(1 - 0.025x_n)$ with $x_1 = 1$ we have the following (rounded).
$$1.0, 1.5, 2.1, 3.0, 4.2, 5.6, 7.2, 8.9, 10.4, 11.5$$
Thus, after 10 years harvesting may resume.

37. About 15 million pounds. Maximum sustainable yield is about 35 million pounds for an initial population of 25 million pounds.

38. (a) About 6
    (b) MSY ≈ 7, for an initial population of approximately 12.

39. (a) The last entry shown for the first sequence is the fourth entry of the second sequence, so the first "joins" the second and they then both end up going through the same cycle (loop) of numbers over and over.
    (b) 39, 78, 56, and we have "joined" the second sequence. However, an initial 00 stays 00 forever; and any other initial number ending in 0 "joins" the loop sequence 20, 40, 80, 60, 20, ...
    (c) Regardless of the original number, after the second push of the key we have a number divisible by 4, and all subsequent numbers are divisible by 4. There are 25 such numbers between 00 and 99. You can verify that an initial number either joins the self-loop 00 (the only such numbers are 00, 50, and 25); joins the loop 20, 40, 80, 60, 20, . . . (the only such are the multiples of 5 other than 00, 50 and 25); or joins the big loop of the other 20 multiples of 4.

40. Answers will vary.

41. (a) 133, 19, 82, 68, 100, 1, 1, ... The sequence stabilizes at 1.
    (b) Answers will vary.
    (c) That would trivialize the exercise!
    (d) For simplicity, limit consideration to 3-digit numbers. Then the largest value of f for any 3-digit number is $9^2 + 9^2 + 9^2 = 243$. For numbers between 1 and 243, the largest value of f is $1^2 + 9^2 + 9^2 = 163$. Thus, if we iterate f over and over – say 164 times – starting with any number between 1 and 163, we must eventually repeat a number, since there are only 163 potentially different results. And once a number repeats, we have a cycle. Thus, applying f to any 3-digit number eventually produces a cycle. How many different cycles are there? That we leave you to work out.
    Hints: 1) There aren't very many cycles.
           2) There is symmetry in the problem, in that some pairs of numbers give the same result; for example, $f(68) = f(86)$.

42. (a) 1, 4, 2, 1, . .

  (b) 13, 40, 20, 10, 5, 16, 8, 4, 2, 1 . . . . .

  (c) 12, 6, 3, 10, 5, 16, 8, 4, 2, 1, . . .

43. (a) 0.0397, 0.15407173, 0.545072626, 1.288978, 0.171519142, 0.59782012, 1.31911379, 0.0562715776, 0.215586839, **0.722914301**, 1.32384194, 0.0376952973, 0.146518383, 0.521670621, 1.27026177, 0.240352173, 0.78810119, 1.2890943, 0.171084847, **0.596529312**

  (b) **0.723**, 1.323813, 0.0378094231, 0.146949035, 0.523014083, 1.27142514, 0.236134903, 0.777260536, 1.29664032, 0.142732915, **0.509813606**

  (c) **0.722**, 1.324148, 0.0364882223, 0.141958718, 0.507378039, 1.25721473, 0.287092278, 0.901103183, 1.16845189, **0.577968093**

44. (a) Unless $r = 0$ (which wouldn't be a very dynamic system), the only equilibrium points are $x = 0$ and $x = 1$.

  (b) For a logistic model with $\lambda \neq 0$, the only equilibrium points are $x = 0$ and $x = 1$ (carrying capacity).

45. Period 2 begins at $\lambda = 3$, period 4 at $1 + \sqrt{6} \approx 3.449$, period 8 at 3.544, period 3 at $1 + 2\sqrt{2} \approx 3.828$, and chaotic behavior onsets at about 3.57.

  See http://www.answers.com/topic/logistic-map .

Word Search Solution

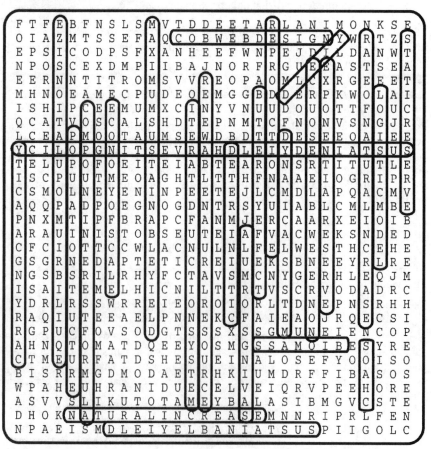